Australian Books and Authors in the American Marketplace 1840s–1940s

SYDNEY STUDIES IN AUSTRALIAN LITERATURE

Robert Dixon, Series Editor

The **Sydney Studies in Australian Literature** series publishes original, peer-reviewed research in the field of Australian literary studies. It offers engagingly written evaluations of the nature and importance of Australian literature, and aims to reinvigorate its study both locally and internationally. It will be of interest to those researching, studying and teaching in the diverse fields of Australian literary studies.

Alex Miller: The Ruin of Time
Robert Dixon

Australian Books and Authors in the American Marketplace 1840s–1940s
David Carter and Roger Osborne

Colonial Australian Fiction: Character Types, Social Formations and the Colonial Economy
Ken Gelder and Rachael Weaver

Contemporary Australian Literature: A World Not Yet Dead
Nicholas Birns

Elizabeth Harrower: Critical Essays
Ed. Elizabeth McMahon and Brigitta Olubas

The Fiction of Tim Winton: Earthed and Sacred
Lyn McCredden

Shirley Hazzard: New Critical Essays
Ed. Brigitta Olubas

Australian Books and Authors in the American Marketplace 1840s–1940s

David Carter and Roger Osborne

SYDNEY UNIVERSITY PRESS

First published by Sydney University Press
© David Carter and Roger Osborne 2018
© Sydney University Press 2018

Reproduction and communication for other purposes
Except as permitted under the Act, no part of this edition may be reproduced, stored in a retrieval system, or communicated in any form or by any means without prior written permission. All requests for reproduction or communication should be made to Sydney University Press at the address below:
Sydney University Press
Fisher Library F03
University of Sydney NSW 2006
AUSTRALIA
sup.info@sydney.edu.au
sydney.edu.au/sup

A catalogue record for this book is available from the National Library of Australia.

ISBN 9781743325797 paperback
ISBN 9781743325803 epub
ISBN 9781743325810 pdf

Cover image: *Morning on the River*, 1918, mezzotint by Martin Lewis (born 1881 in Castlemaine, Victoria; died 1962 in New York, New York). Reproduced by permission of the Old Print Shop, Inc., on behalf of the artist's estate.
Cover design by Miguel Yamin.

Contents

List of figures	vii
List of plates	ix
Acknowledgements	xi
Introduction: The Two-Sided Triangle	1
1 Antipodean Romance: Australian Fiction and the American Book Trade in the Nineteenth Century	15
2 International Reputations and Transatlantic Rights: Rosa Praed and Louis Becke	51
3 Crime, Sensation and the Modern Genre System: Australian Authors in the Popular Fiction Marketplace, 1890s–1920s	83
4 Renegotiating the American Connection: Australian Fiction 1900–1930s	111
5 Mystery and Romance: The Market for Light Fiction Between the Wars	161
6 Becoming Articulate: Henry Handel Richardson and Katharine Susannah Prichard	195
7 "Australia is very American": Australian Historical Fiction in America 1920s–1940s	231
8 "Australian moderns": Christina Stead and Patrick White in New York	271
9 Bestsellers, Modest Sellers and Commercial Failures: The Postwar Years	313
Epilogue: Completing the Triangle?	341
Works Cited	345
Index	359

List of figures

Figure 1.1 Charles Rowcroft, *The Australian Crusoes; or, The Adventures of an English Settler and his Family in the Wilds of Australia* (Philadelphia: Davis, Porter & Co., 1865). — 17

Figure 1.2 Tasma, *A Sydney Sovereign and Other Tales*, Aldine edition (New York: Frank F. Lovell & Co., 1890). — 40

Figure 1.3 Rolf Boldrewood, *The Crooked Stick or Pollie's Probation* (New York: Macmillan & Co., 1895). — 42

Figure 2.1 Advertisement for Rosa Praed, *Nùlma: An Anglo-Australian Romance* (New York: D. Appleton & Co., 1897). *New York Times*, 3 July 1897. — 56

Figure 2.2 "Mrs. Praed. The Novelist Whose 'Mrs. Tregaskiss' Has Made a Stir." *Louisiana Populist* (Natchitoches, LA), 21 February 1896. — 58

Figure 2.3 Louis Becke and Walter Jeffery, *The Mutineer: A Romance of Pitcairn Island* (Philadelphia: J. B. Lippincott Co., 1898). — 78

Figure 3.1 Fergus Hume, *The Steel Crown* (New York: G.W. Dillingham Co., 1911). — 95

Figure 3.2 Guy Boothby, *Dr. Nikola's Experiment* (New York: D. Appleton & Co., 1899) — 101

Figure 3.3 Advertisement for Guy Boothby's *The Race of Life* (New York: F.M. Buckles & Co., 1906). *New York Sun*, 19 May 1906. — 104

Figure 4.1 James Frances Dwyer, "The White Waterfall", announced for the *Cavalier*. *Washington Times*, 11 April 1912. — 123

Figure 4.2 Ethel Turner, *Seven Little Australians*, Girls' Own Library (Philadelphia: David McKay, 1909?). — 131

Figure 4.3 Advertisement for *All for Love* by Jean Devanny (New York: Macaulay Publishing Co., 1932). *New York Times*, 29 January 1933. — 136

Figure 4.4 Advertisement for Norman Lindsay's *Mr. Gresham and Olympus* (New York: Farrar & Rinehart, 1932). *New York Times*, 28 February 1932. — 144

Figure 5.1 Advertisement for A.E. Martin's *The Outsiders* (New York: Simon & Schuster, 1945). *New York Times*, 8 April 1945. — 172

Figure 5.2 Arthur Upfield in the Doubleday Crime Club. *New York Times*, 22 August 1948.   176

Figure 5.3 "America's best loved novelist". Advertisement for Alice Grant Rosman's *The Sleeping Child* (New York: Minton, Balch, 1935). *New York Times*, 23 June 1935.   179

Figure 6.1 Advertisement for Henry Handel Richardson's *Ultima Thule* (New York: W.W. Norton & Co., 1929). *New York Times*, 8 September 1929.   206

Figure 6.2 Advertisement for Henry Handel Richardson's *The Fortunes of Richard Mahony* trilogy. *Saturday Review of Literature*, 12 April 1930.   214

Figure 6.3 Advertisement for Katharine Susannah Prichard's *Coonardoo* (New York: W.W. Norton & Co., 1930). *New York Times*, 16 March 1930.   223

Figure 7.1 C. Hartley Grattan's review of Brian Penton's *Landtakers* (New York: Farrar & Rinehart, 1935). *New York Times*, 16 June 1935.   256

Figure 7.2 Advertisement for Xavier Herbert's *Capricornia* (New York: Appleton-Century, 1943). *New York Times*, 9 May 1943.   259

Figure 7.3 Eleanor Dark's *The Timeless Land* (New York: Macmillan, 1941). *Book-of-the-Month Club News*, September 1941.   268

Figure 8.1 Advertisement for Christina Stead's *Seven Poor Men of Sydney* (New York: D. Appleton-Century Co., 1935). *New York Times*, 24 March 1935.   274

Figure 8.2 Advertisement for *The Man Who Loved Children* (New York: Simon & Schuster, 1940). *New York Times*, 21 October 1940.   289

Figure 8.3 Advertisement for Patrick White's *The Tree of Man* (New York: The Viking Press, 1955). *New York Times*, 31 August 1955.   309

Figure 9.1 Advertisement for Jon Cleary's *You Can't See Around Corners* (New York: Charles Scribner's Sons, 1947). *New York Times*, 5 October 1947.   318

Figure 9.2 Advertisement for Kylie Tennant's *The Battlers* (New York: Macmillan, 1941). *New York Times*, 31 August 1941.   326

List of plates

Plate 1 Tasma *A Sydney Sovereign* (New York: George Munro, 1890).   151

Plate 2 Rosa Praed, *Fugitive Anne* (New York: R.F. Fenno & Co., 1904).   152

Plate 3 Louis Becke, *By Reef and Palm and His Native Wife* (Philadelphia: J.B. Lippincott Co., 1900).   153

Plate 4 The original *japoniste* cover of Carlton Dawe's *Rose and Chrysanthemum* (Boston: Knight & Millet, 1900).   154

Plate 5 Ambrose Pratt, *The Living Mummy* (New York: Frederick A. Stokes Co., 1910). Illustration by Louis D. Fancher.   155

Plate 6 Dale Collins, *Idolaters* (Boston: Little, Brown & Co., 1932).   156

Plate 7 Maysie Greig, "Kid Sisters Don't Count", *American Weekly*, 17 September 1933.   157

Plate 8 First edition dust-jacket of Christina Stead's *For Love Alone* (New York: Harcourt, Brace, 1944).   158

Plate 9 Kylie Tennant, *The Battlers* (New York: Macmillan, 1941).   159

Plate 10 Tom Collins [Joseph Furphy], *Such is Life* (Chicago: University of Chicago Press, 1948).   160

Acknowledgements

The research for this book was supported by an Australian Research Council Discovery Project grant (DP0771376: America Publishes Australia). Much of the research and writing was conducted within the School of English, Media Studies and Art History, then the School of Communication and Arts, at the University of Queensland, and with the support of Kerry Kilner and the staff of AustLit, located in the school, and the university's Fryer Library. Research was also conducted during David Carter's Harold White Fellowship at the National Library of Australia. Parts of the book were written in the Center for Pacific and American Studies at Tokyo University.

The authors would like to thank Susan Ballyn, Nicholas Birns, Barbara Brooks, Stephen Crofts, Maryanne Dever, Robert Dixon, Clay Djubal, Paul Eggert, Jason Ensor, Anna Gerber, Per Heningsgaard, Carol Hetherington, Lise Jaillant, Joan Keating, Marilyn Lake, Jenny Rundle, Lucy Sussex, Trysh Travis, Naomi Wakayama and Gillian Whitlock for their support and contributions to the book through discussions, research assistance or conference invitations. Sections of the research have been presented at conferences organised by the Association for the Study of Australian Literature (ASAL), the American Association of Australasian Literary Studies (AAALS), the Modern Languages Association (MLA), the Society for the History of Authorship, Reading and Publishing (SHARP), the Australian literature program of the Department of English at the University of Sydney, the Australian Centre, University of Melbourne, and the Australian Studies Centre (CEA), Universitat de Barcelona.

Extensive research was conducted in libraries and archives in Australia, the United States, and Britain. The authors would like to acknowledge the assistance of staff at the following institutions: Manuscripts, National Library of Australia; Mitchell Library, State Library of New South Wales; Baillieu Library, University of Melbourne; Fisher Library, University of Sydney; New York Public Library and the Berg Collection, New York Public Library; Library of Congress; Rare Books and Manuscript Library, Ohio State University; Lilly Library, University of Indiana; Rare Books and Manuscripts Library, Columbia University; Fales Library and Special Collections, New York University; Houghton Library, Harvard University; Harry Ransom Collection, University of Texas, Austin; Rare Books and Special Collections, Princeton University; University of North Carolina Library; Special Collections, University of Reading; London Metropolitan Archives; the British Library.

As editor of the Sydney Studies in Australian Literature series, Robert Dixon gave strong support to the project and its publication, backed by Susan Murray, Manager, Scholarly Publishing, and the editorial expertise and enthusiasm of Agata Mrva-Montoya and Denise O'Dea at Sydney University Press.

Research projects such as this do not stop at the gates of our institutions, and so additional time and support is regularly provided by those closest to us. Roger would like to acknowledge the ongoing support and encouragement of Sonya Osborne, a gift that extends far beyond the boundaries of this project. David would like to acknowledge Rebecca Chorfadi for all her support and patience, before, during and also far beyond.

The image of the dust-jacket for Christina Stead's *For Love Alone* was kindly provided by Cathy Lilburne, Antipodean Books, Maps & Pictures, Garrison, New York. The cover image from *Morning on the River* (1918) by Australian-born, New York-based artist Martin Lewis (1881–1962) is reproduced by kind permission of Robert K. Newman, The Old Print Shop, New York, on behalf of the Martin Lewis Estate.

Introduction: The Two-Sided Triangle

The story of Australian books and authors in the American marketplace has received little attention in Australian literary or publishing studies. If considered at all, an Australian presence in the US book market is probably understood as a recent phenomenon, beginning perhaps with the success of Peter Carey, Elizabeth Jolley and others in the 1970s, or in a different register with Colleen McCullough's international bestseller *The Thorn Birds* (1977) or Thomas Keneally's *Schindler's List* (1982). This "memory" might itself be the effect of framing Australian literature in predominantly national terms, as developing progressively or dialectically through colonial, national and modern phases, so that a serious international presence could only exist in the latest stage. The present study reveals a much longer history stretching back to the mid-nineteenth century, with a significant concentration of Australian novels published in the United States in the 1880s and 1890s, another period of marked impact between the wars, and significant instances of success in popular fiction across the twentieth century. It is also a much denser, more diverse history in terms of the sheer number and kinds of books and authors published. One of the earliest scholars to indicate that this might be the case was Laurie Hergenhan, in his 1995 study of the influential American Australianist C. Hartley Grattan:

> American editions of Australian works … [are] more extensive than has been realised, for they have been typically overshadowed by interest in … the English aspects of Australian publishing history. Few realise, for instance, that Patrick White's first popular success was the American edition of *The Tree of Man* (the first edition of that novel), that Martin Boyd's *Lucinda Brayford* was a Book Society's choice and bestseller in America or that Eleanor Dark's *The Timeless Land* was also popular as a Book of the Month choice.[1]

Some of the gaps in knowledge have been filled in recent years by major biographies of individual authors such as G.B. Lancaster, Christina Stead and Patrick White, and by scholarly editions of selected canonical works. To varying degrees, these publications offer specific histories of their subjects' American editions and critical reception, and we have drawn on them accordingly.

---

1 Laurie Hergenhan, *No Casual Traveller: Hartley Grattan and Australia–US Connections* (St Lucia: University of Queensland Press, 1995), 47.

Even so, the history of Australian books and authors in the United States remains very largely an untold story, not just in terms of numbers or the often surprising critical or sales success of individual titles and careers, but also in terms of the cultural and commercial dynamics and the personal, professional and institutional networks linking Australian authors with American publishers or putting obstacles in their way. To tell this story is not just to add a new layer to Australian literary history but to unsettle and reconfigure some of the foundational assumptions of that history. Once we add America into the picture things start to move, to shift beyond the framework of the national culture and the singular relationship between imperial centre and colonial outpost. Australia's place in the world republic of letters needs a new trigonometry.

What follows is a study of the relations between Australian authors, editors and publishers on one side and American publishers, editors, agents and reviewers on the other; or rather it is in part, for historically these relations were rarely simple or direct. The vast majority of Australian works that made their way to the United States did so via London, and hence via the intervention of *British* publishers, editors, agents and reviewers or the London-based representatives of American firms. The story thus, unavoidably, also involves the shifting relations each side had with the British book trade and how these relations in turn affected their understanding of each other as nation, industry or market. The history that needs telling is that of the triangulation of the Australian, British and American publishing industries and markets, a story of transnational structures and dynamics involving a complex mix of culture, copyright and commerce. It is to these relationships that our introduction's subtitle, "The Two-Sided Triangle", refers, for while there are clearly three nodes constituting this publishing triangle, for the most part only two "sides" were activated or rendered dynamic in the relationship: the imperial connection between Australia and London, and the transatlantic connection between the British and American book trades and book cultures. A number of recent studies have testified to the defining significance of the transatlantic book trade for the United States, but it was a major consideration for British publishers as well.[2] By the mid-twentieth century it was estimated that a British edition of a book would sell domestically at best only 10 per cent of what it would in the United States.[3] Publication in one market was often the start of a two- or three-step process that led to publication in the other, with the aim of increasing profits for publisher, author, or both. Our study shows that works of fiction by Australian authors should be recognised as a persistent, occasionally prominent element in this transatlantic trade.

---

[2] See Jessica Despain, *Nineteenth-Century Transatlantic Reprinting and the Embodied Book* (Farnham, UK: Ashgate, 2014); Nancy Glazener, *Literature in the Making: A History of US Literary Culture in the Long Nineteenth Century* (New York: Oxford University Press, 2016); Meredith McGill, *American Literature and the Culture of Reprinting 1834-1853* (Philadelphia: University of Pennsylvania Press, 2007); Michael Winship, "Anglo-American Literary Culture and the Transatlantic Book Trade in the Nineteenth Century", in *Reciprocal Influences: Literary Production, Distribution, and Consumption in America*, ed. Steven Fink and Susan Williams (Columbus: Ohio State University Press, 1999), 98–122. Also David Carter, "Transpacific or Transatlantic Traffic? Australian Books and American Publishers", in *Reading Across the Pacific: Australia–United States Intellectual Histories*, ed. Robert Dixon and Nicholas Birns (Sydney: Sydney University Press, 2010), 339-59.

[3] Mary Nell Bryant, "English Language Publication and the British Traditional Market Agreement", *Library Quarterly*, 49 (October 1979): 374.

Introduction: The Two-Sided Triangle

Australian publishing history has, with good reason, focused on the British or imperial connection, often framed through the themes of the British book trade's dominance over Australian publishing and its domestic book market or local publishing's emergence out from under the British yoke. The dominance of the British book trade is undeniably fundamental to any account of Australian literary or book history, a fact confirmed by the present study. As Richard Nile and David Walker have put it, London was the "production centre for Australian literature" and the "commercial centre of the literary world".[4] As a result, Australian publishing was a "tale of three cities", with Sydney and Melbourne subordinate to the great London publishing machine. But while this perspective expresses a central truth of Australian book history, it also renders invisible the other great commercial centre of the Anglophone literary world – New York (and Boston, Chicago, Philadelphia, the other main centres of American publishing). In so doing it ignores an important dimension of the histories of authors, books, and the book trade itself.

Recent studies of books and reading in colonial and early twentieth-century Australia have presented a complex picture of readers, writers and publishers engaging actively with both local and international, conventional and modernising print cultures.[5] This complication of what occurred within domestic boundaries is matched by the complications produced by extending the outward horizon as well, not just beyond the nation but also beyond the imperial connection. The new imperial history has foregrounded the dynamic interconnections between the imperial centre and its colonies and dominions, and more specifically the presence of a "mobile imperial commons" of print across the empire.[6] As such, the imperial connection can be understood not merely as a constraining factor but also a productive force, a critical vector of literary meaning and cultural modernity. If Australian novels were more or less compelled to travel first to London or to originate there to achieve book publication, London could also act as a relay station, giving books the power to travel further, and what we might call the power to be modern. But the emphasis on empire can also blind us to other networks and vectors of mobility. These might be complementary, as in the larger idea of an Anglo-Saxon world that embraced the United States; or they might need to be understood in quite other

---

4 Richard Nile and David Walker, "The 'Paternoster Row Machine' and the Australian Book Trade, 1890–1945", in *A History of the Book in Australia 1891–1945: A National Culture in a Colonised Market*, ed. Martyn Lyons and John Arnold (St Lucia: University of Queensland Press, 2001), 3 and 7; and "Marketing the Literary Imagination: Production of Australian Literature, 1915-1965", in *The Penguin New Literary History of Australia*, ed. Laurie Hergenhan (Ringwood, Vic.: Penguin, 1988), 286.

5 See, for example, Katherine Bode, *Reading by Numbers: Recalibrating the Literary Field* (London: Anthem Press, 2012); David Carter, *Always Almost Modern: Australian Print Cultures and Modernity* (North Melbourne, Vic.: Australian Scholarly Publishing, 2013); Ken Gelder and Rachael Weaver, *The Colonial Journals and the Emergence of Australian Literary Culture* (Crawley, WA: UWA Publishing, 2014); Susan Martin and Kylie Mirmohamadi, *Sensational Melbourne: Reading, Sensation Fiction and 'Lady Audley's Secret' in the Victorian Metropolis* (North Melbourne, Vic.: Australian Scholarly Publishing, 2011).

6 For an extended discussion of the concept of an imperial print commons that brings together perspectives from book history and the new imperial history, see Antoinette Burton and Isabel Hofmeyr, "The Spine of Empire? Books and the Making of an Imperial Commons", in *Ten Books That Shaped the British Empire: Creating an Imperial Commons*, ed. Antoinette Burton and Isabel Hofmeyr (Durham, NC: Duke University Press, 2014), 3–7. See also Robert Dixon, *Photography, Early Cinema and Colonial Modernity: Frank Hurley's Synchronized Lecture Entertainments* (London: Anthem Press, 2012), xxiv–xxix.

terms, the terms of trade for example, as when we understand the mobility of books primarily in their capacity as saleable commodities rather than bearers of ideology. The transatlantic book trade, crucial to the present study, was a complex mixture of both across two relatively autonomous industry structures, conscious equally of their complementarity and their distinctiveness. In many ways, New York was itself subordinate to London as a publishing centre for much of the period under discussion. Imports of British books remained high even as local publishing expanded in the United States from the 1920s. But the New York book trade was also powerful enough in its own right to attract writers and writing from across the globe.

Our focus is primarily on book publication rather than serialisation in newspapers and magazines, although we emphasise the major role that periodical publication could play in building authors' reputations and earnings. Among these published books, our focus is primarily on the novel and related forms, as fiction is far and away the largest and most visible category of Australian works published in the United States. It is impossible to fix absolutely reliable numbers of American editions of Australian works due to the patchiness of bibliographical and archival records and the widely varied practices of authorised and unauthorised reprinting. But research indicates that around one thousand editions of novels with a significant Australian connection were published in book form in the United States to 1950. This total comprises more than 760 different works, many in multiple editions, and almost certainly underestimates the number of reissues of individual titles. Almost 250 different authors appear from around 200 American publishing houses or major imprints. Doubleday in its various manifestations is by far the largest contributor, with more than one hundred titles between 1902 and 1950 and many more through its paperback subsidiaries; by the 1940s, it was America's largest publisher. Other mainstream American houses also published substantial numbers, including established firms such as Appleton, Scribner, Dodd, Mead, Dutton, Harper, Lippincott and Macmillan, hardback reprinters such as Grosset & Dunlap, and newer enterprises such as The Dial Press and the Macaulay Company. From the 1920s, the most important emerging publishers such as Farrar & Rinehart, Random House, Simon & Schuster, William Morrow, the Viking Press and W.W. Norton also become involved.

The chapters that follow examine the pathways and processes that determined how Australian novels came to American publishers and how American publishers came to Australian novels. Such a study demands close attention to the "undergrowth" as well as the tallest trees, to the many lesser-known writers who achieved American publication - and the extent and diversity of such publication is one of the findings of our research - as well as to the now canonical authors who succeeded or failed in the American marketplace. Taking its primary bearings from book history, on one level our approach means treating all books equally, as more or less tradeable and marketable commodities. Our focus is on fiction and books in the book trade, not on "literature", and from this perspective literary fiction and light fiction are merely different market sectors. At the same time, however, this very focus on the industry and the fiction marketplace demands heightened attention to the difference literature or literary value can make. For on another level, within the book trade itself, literary fiction and light fiction were not treated equally, even if as commodities they were subject to similar processes. Publishers, editors, agents and reviewers were acutely aware of the different kinds and levels of fiction, the different kinds of investment that might be risked (for example, in good books that were unlikely to return a profit), and the different kinds of reception books might receive. To borrow a notion from

Introduction: The Two-Sided Triangle

Ross Chambers, the "interpretability" of texts making claims to literary significance often produced a difference in both the quantity and quality of critical and editorial attention they received.[7] Of course, the contemporary evaluations of publishers and reviewers would not always be those of later criticism, but judgements as to quality and kind were the everyday business of the book trade.

In tracing publishing histories, then, we have paid close attention to these processes of evaluation, to the circulation of different notions of genre and literary value, and hence to the kinds of attention – in the industry and the marketplace – that a major work such as Henry Handel Richardson's *Fortunes of Richard Mahony* trilogy could receive. In line with a number of recent studies of publishing and modernity in early to mid-twentieth-century America, what has emerged clearly from our own work with publishers' and agents' records and the book pages of newspapers and magazines is that these mainstream institutions ranged widely and, for the most part, without anxiety across the field of fiction, accommodating both modernism and modern genre fiction (within certain limits).[8] Even as they register the twin forces of modernism and the popular fiction market, there is little evidence of the kind of dramatic polarisation of the field into antagonistic high/modernist and low/commercial categories that later criticism would project, although "excesses" and "fads" on either side were exposed and resisted. In publishers' lists and book review pages, crime and romance existed alongside realist family dramas, "modern novels", ambitious historical sagas, comic tales and the rest, not as the same kind of thing or as of equal value, but as belonging in the same field nevertheless. Literature and "good books" were valued, and Australian works could share in that prestige, but the ordinary business of books was broad in scope and generous in its sense of different kinds of books and readers.

Thus the books and authors we follow extend from the lightest of light fiction to the most literary of literary novels, from the most ephemeral of literary works to the most enduring of popular stories, as they variously reveal critical dimensions of our key questions: how Australian books and authors found their way into the American marketplace and how they flourished or floundered once they got there. Our focus is not simply on books as commodities, but on the relationships between the commodity, its creator and the various agents involved in its production as a book. The study thus works in two dimensions: on one side, tracing the careers or trajectories of individual writers and books in the American marketplace and American book culture; on the other, tracing the economic, legal and institutional forces shaping the American publishing industry and the transatlantic book trade, and shifts in taste and the language of literary appreciation that affected the publishing opportunities for Australian authors. We have not focused in as much detail on bookselling or distribution, except to describe the impact of the three major developments or disruptions in standard practice in the period covered: the rapid growth of cheap fiction libraries in the 1870s and 1880s; the launch of the

---

7   Ross Chambers, *Story and Situation: Narrative Seduction and the Power of Fiction* (Minneapolis: University of Minnesota Press, 1984), 12–13.
8   Gordon Hutner, *What America Read: Taste, Class, and the Novel, 1920–1960* (Chapel Hill: University of North Carolina Press, 2009); Lise Jaillant, *Modernism, Middlebrow and the Literary Canon: The Modern Library Series, 1917–1955* (London: Pickering & Chatto, 2014); Karen Leick, "Popular Modernism: Little Magazines and the American Daily Press", *PMLA* 123 (January 2008): 125–39; Joan Shelley Rubin, *The Making of Middlebrow Culture* (Chapel Hill: University of North Carolina Press, 1992); Catherine Turner, *Marketing Modernism Between the Two Wars* (Amherst: University of Massachusetts Press, 2003).

Book-of-the-Month Club and other book clubs between the wars; and the rise of the new paperback publishers in the 1940s and 1950s.

A group of major figures – Rosa Praed and Louis Becke, Henry Handel Richardson and Katharine Susannah Prichard, Christina Stead and Patrick White – have been selected for extended case studies, while the American careers of other writers with marked impact in the United States such as Rolf Boldrewood, Fergus Hume, Arthur Upfield, Dale Collins and Alice Grant Rosman receive extended treatment in chapters covering specific periods or market sectors. These case studies are embedded in discussions of the changing copyright regimes for foreign books in the United States, the structures of the American (and British and Australian) book trade, its patterns of growth or decline, the role of literary agents, and significant cultural transitions such as the emergence of the modern genre system, the shifting meanings of romance, realism and modernity, and the rise and fall of the historical saga as a prominent form between the wars. Alongside such industrial and commercial factors as changes in the composition of US publishing and the "business" of investing in new titles, *genre* emerges as a key driver in determining which books travelled and just how they arrived in the American marketplace. Modernity, too, emerges as an important measure for both literary and popular fiction. It could be difficult for Australian writers to be comprehended within modernity in quite the same way as their British or American contemporaries, although for certain books at certain times it provided the key framework for their reception.

An informal understanding between British and American publishers – sometimes contested but largely respected – divided the Anglophone publishing world into two spheres. Britain guarded its "traditional markets" – "Great Britain, its Colonies and Dominions" as contracts declared – while the United States had uncontested access to the Americas and the Philippines.[9] Canada was often disputed, and having access to the Canadian market could prove the difference between acceptance and rejection by a US publisher for a book on offer from London. With the global marketplace divided in this manner, and Australia locked firmly into the British sphere, there are relatively few instances of works travelling directly from Australia to the United States or of US publishers seeking new titles directly from publishers or authors in Australia, although we have noted examples of both. Angus & Robertson, for example, actively sought American publication for some of its successful titles in the 1930s and 1940s, bypassing London through direct negotiations with US publishers and its own literary agent in New York. But its success was limited.

Despite these constraints, and of course in response to them, many Australian writers were highly conscious of the American market and the opportunities it could provide for further publication, reputation and profits. The very dominance of London publishing's "Paternoster Row machine" made America an attractive proposition for Australian writers whether based in Australia, travelling, or expatriated overseas. From Rolf Boldrewood and Ada Cambridge, through Rosa Praed and Ethel Turner, to Maysie Greig, Xavier Herbert and Patrick White, Australian writers were keenly interested (in the full sense of that word) in being published, publicised and reviewed in America and in maximising their earnings from the publications that did occur. Many took matters into their own hands, arguing with their British publisher about their efforts in the American market, signing with a London-based literary agent in order to get better deals in the United States, engaging

---

9   Bryant, "English Language Publication", 374-78.

Introduction: The Two-Sided Triangle

an American agent directly, establishing personal relations with American publishers, travelling to the United States or writing expressly for that market, and badgering publishers and agents in both countries about the opportunities and obstacles presented by international copyright law and subsidiary rights. The separation of the British and American markets even as the transatlantic book trade was expanding led to a growing awareness among authors of the value of their works as literary property and of the management of rights and royalties, which led, in turn, to the increasing role of the literary agent in dealing across national borders. This was especially the case following the passing of the United States International Copyright or Chace Act of 1891, just as professional literary agents were coming into their own. In many ways, agents were especially critical for Australian authors seeking a wider market from a distance, and they emerge alongside in-house editors as among the most important gatekeepers and facilitators for those finding their way into the US market. Many of the case studies covered below indicate the importance of close working relations, professional but also often personal, between authors, agents and editors in enabling authors to establish their presence in the marketplace and the book talk that helped define it.

Within these structures, Australian novels made their way to American publishers along a wide variety of routes. Some authors, like Norman Lindsay and Patrick White, arrived in New York with books or manuscripts stowed in their luggage; some were noticed by American publishers or their agents in London; others built a reputation through the booming transatlantic magazine market; a few sent novels directly to American publishers in hope. Many others relied on their British publisher to cut a deal, whether simply out of commercial consideration or because of the publisher's faith in the book or its author, not an uncommon thing even where commercial prospects were uncertain. Increasingly, as suggested, authors relied on agents in London or New York to negotiate profitable deals in different territories. In many cases no direct evidence has survived as to why or how a particular book made its way to the United States despite the wealth of correspondence, contracts and production sheets in the archives, but we can often surmise through examination of the publisher's lists, its publicity, and the state of the market at the time of publication.

Australian authors could rarely escape the consequences of being located in or bearing the traces of belonging to a province within "international literary space".[10] But at the same time they could be conscious of also belonging to an expanding global marketplace for fiction, not merely a restricted colonial market. A sense of distance or belatedness was almost always in tension with an awareness of the potential, at least, of inhabiting parallel or proximate worlds, a sense of contemporaneity with American as well as British or imperial book cultures. Ethel Turner's *Seven Little Australians* (1894) is a good example of this double equation, the book's title announcing its local address to the nation then coming into being but also explicitly referencing the two most influential children's books of recent decades, both from America: Louisa May Alcott's *Little Women* from 1868 and Frances Hodgson Burnett's *Little Lord Fauntleroy* from 1886. As we detail in Chapter 4, Turner aggressively sought US publication for several decades, changing publishers and literary agents and even writing an "American novel" in her quest for American success. More broadly, the rise of a self-consciously modern national literature in Australia as

---

10 Pascale Casanova, *The World Republic of Letters*, trans. M.B. DeBevoise (Cambridge, MA: Harvard University Press, 2005), xii, 1-15.

manifested in the historical sagas and social realist fiction of the 1920s to 1940s was echoed in America's own search for a national story in the years culminating in *Gone with the Wind* (1936) and *The Grapes of Wrath* (1939).[11]

America, in short, was a significant part of the world a significant number of Australian authors imagined for their books – something acknowledged, for example, in the 1946 *Australian Writers and Artists' Market,* which printed advice from US literary agents about how to get published in America.[12] Australia could in turn impress itself upon *American* publishers, readers and reviewers, and with something of the same tension between a sense of distance or difference and a sudden realisation of proximity or similarity. Although the present book does not aspire to be a history of American attitudes to Australia, it does pursue the critical reception of Australian works in the American marketplace. A major revelation from our study is just how widely Australian books were noted and discussed in the American press, if not necessarily *as* Australian books: in most cases more widely in the United States than in Australia, and in many cases more widely than in Britain too. Books were extensively reviewed, not only in the increasingly influential New York papers, but in city, regional and small-town newspapers across the nation, often accompanied by columns or paragraphs of gossip from the book world. The reviews were mostly original, but others could be syndicated across a dozen or more different papers. Alongside the newspaper book pages were the prestigious weekly and monthly magazines, older titles such as *Harper's Magazine, Scribner's,* the *Bookman* or *Nation,* and newer publications such as the *New Republic* (1914), *American Mercury* (1924), the *Saturday Review of Literature* (1924) and the *New Yorker* (1925). The newer magazines added more weight to New York's influence over the literary field.

This distinctive context of reviewing in newspapers, literary supplements and magazines, and in assessments in-house by editors and publishers' readers, cannot be generalised as representing the American understanding of Australia. It has its own temporality in the weekly or monthly cycles of reviewing, its own genres and institutional protocols, its own communities of interest. But within these productive limitations, the reception of Australian fiction in the United States shows something very like the dialectic between proximity and distance that Paul Giles emphasises in his re-reading of American writing through its antipodean consciousness.[13] Australian books were often seen simply as British books, which – considered as tradeable property or commodities – the majority were. But the recognition of Australian distinctiveness or of unexpected parallels between Australia and the United States was also recurrent. In the late nineteenth century, Australian or Anglo-Australian novels might be considered as local variants of the broader themes of "Anglo-Saxon" fiction, a framing that could potentially bring them closer to American readers, closer even than their British contemporaries. A stronger sense of Australian difference (in relation to Britain) and of an unanticipated, even disconcerting sense of familiarity, might also be expressed – in the recognition of a distinctive form of "antipodean romance" in novels of the 1880s and 1890s for example, or, even more

---

11 Hutner, *What America Read*, Ch. 2, "The 1930s".
12 *Australian Writers and Artists' Market (Including New Zealand): A Practical Selling Guide for the Freelance* (Melbourne: Australian School of Journalism Pty Ltd and Art Training Institute Pty Ltd, 1946).
13 Paul Giles, *Antipodean America: Australasia and the Constitution of US Literature* (New York: Oxford University Press, 2013).

forcefully, in the sudden acknowledgement of parallel histories in the pioneering or intergenerational sagas of the interwar years as represented by the marked success in America of Richardson's *The Fortunes of Richard Mahony* trilogy and Eleanor Dark's *The Timeless Land*.

But even when such recognition was at its strongest it co-existed with a sense of Australia's *mere* otherness, its banal rather than exotic remoteness, the sense that American readers were unlikely to be interested in an "ordinary" novel about Australia. Over successive decades, Australia and its literature were repeatedly discovered – as if for the first time – and then forgotten or ignored again until the next moment of surprise discovery. More than once, what appears to be a consolidation of knowledge about Australian books over a number of years suddenly dissolves, with little apparent "institutional memory" in American book culture of earlier Australian titles or authors.

The history we recount is thus as discontinuous as it is continuous; certainly, no evolutionary pattern of steadily increasing awareness of Australian authors or Australian literature emerges over the decades. Instead, we find periods of relatively high visibility in certain sectors of the market which are relatively quickly forgotten, high-profile individual careers which cannot be transferred in any substantial way to a literary reputation or an appreciation of Australian literature more generally, or sustained careers that owe everything to genre, say, and little or nothing to any national framing. One of the ways in which the present study challenges assumptions based on nationalist models is the sheer absence of that national framework accompanying Australian works as they make their way into the American marketplace. We discover familiar texts in unfamiliar contexts, stripped of the defining logic of their place in the developing national story. And we discover many more books and authors that have fallen out of that story but re-emerge in the foreground of the American marketplace or enter the American scene as very different kinds of books than they were taken to be in Australia or Britain. Norman Lindsay's reception as a modern novelist in New York is just one example.

The triangulation of Australia, Britain and the United States thus achieves exactly the kind of "elliptical refraction" that David Damrosch sees as characteristic of a world literature perspective or, better, a transnational perspective: "instead of seeing London as the center of a circle … we can present the literary culture of London as one focus of an ellipse, or more precisely as one focus for many different, partially overlapping ellipses, each with a second focus elsewhere" (in our case London and Sydney, London and New York).[14] To follow Australian works into the American market is indeed to discover an elliptical refraction of Australian literature as a national literature and of Australian books as *Australian* books. In a material sense, these "Australian" (or British) books become American books, often bearing traces of their cultural origins of course, but manufactured, distributed, sold and read as commodities within the domestic US marketplace. Only a small number of the Australian novels appearing in America were published or received as instances of Australian literature per se; only a handful of publishers, critics or reviewers were interested in the question, although again, at certain points, the degree to which the question does arise is surprising. Instead, Australian novels appeared in America among the new books of the season, as English fiction or "modern novels", as romances, detective

---

14 David Damrosch, "Literary Study in an Elliptical Age", in *Comparative Literature in the Age of Multiculturalism*, ed. Charles Bernheimer (Baltimore, MD: Johns Hopkins University Press, 1995), 129-30.

tales or family sagas, as "light fiction" or serious literature. The national context was secondary – in publishers' decisions and reviewers' assessments – although certain books and authors could force it into view.

The absence of any sustained sense of Australian literature and the associated difficulty for Australian novelists of maintaining a reputation in American book culture between books or once new titles stopped appearing should not be surprising given Australia's peripheral status in the Anglophone literary world, the ease with which its books and authors "disappeared" into the larger sphere of British or English fiction, the relatively small number of Australian books appearing among the hundreds landing on reviewers' desks each week, and the lack of any established institutional support such as dedicated publishers' lists, college courses or critical studies. Indeed, for most of the period examined here, such institutional resources were underdeveloped in Australia itself despite the busy, crowded print culture that existed in its cities and towns. In Pascale Casanova's terms, Australia was poor in literary resources and literary capital, in literary institutions and prestige.[15] What's surprising, indeed, is not the ignorance or apathy towards Australian literature that we can note periodically among American publishers and reviewers but the recurrent examples of critical or sales success, of publishers willing to invest in new titles by relatively unknown authors from a relatively unknown place, and of reviewers' interest in the Australian scene, however occasional these might be.

We have used the terms "Australian author" and "Australian book" without restrictive definition to this point, and we might claim to do so as a matter of principle not just convenience. The point is less about inclusiveness than adequacy to the wide range of historical trajectories – into and out of Australian time and space – that both books and authors have taken. One of the key insights of the transnational turn in book history and literary studies is an increased appreciation of the sheer mobility of books and authors across local and national boundaries.[16] National literary space is an inadequate frame for containing or explaining the "careers" of either books or authors, especially in a study such as this which is explicitly located beyond those borders. Rather than a single national frame, we are working with a series of shifting frames – or "scales" in Robert Dixon's terms – and a diverse range of trajectories across local, national and international sites.[17] As suggested below in Chapter 1, the "Australian" in this study is a shifting field or network that writers and writing entered or passed through in various capacities and for varying periods of time, leaving different kinds of historical traces. Its framing must be flexible enough to encompass immigration and emigration, expatriation – a major strategy for participating in international markets – imperial commuting, transpacific "adventurism", and many other forms of transnational mobility. The point applies as much to those who stayed at home – while their books moved across the globe – as to those who left to make careers elsewhere.

Nor do we dwell on the strict bibliographical definition of an "edition" (that is, a wholly new setting) or focus in detail on textual variations between editions, although we

---

15 Pascale Casanova, "Literature as a World", *New Left Review* 31 (January-February 2005): 83.
16 See, for example, Sydney Shep, "Books in Global Perspectives" and Alistair McCleery, "The Book in the Long Twentieth Century", in *The Cambridge Companion to the History of the Book*, ed. Leslie Howsam (Cambridge: Cambridge University Press, 2014), 53-67, 162-80.
17 Robert Dixon, "Australian Literature, Scale, and the Problem of the World", in *Text, Translation, Transnationalism: World Literature in 21st Century Australia*, ed. Peter Morgan (North Melbourne, Vic.: Australian Scholarly Publishing, 2016), 173-95.

discuss revealing instances of changes made to texts and titles for American publication. More importantly, we register throughout the differences in how books appeared in the American marketplace, whether as new copyrighted American editions, new editions printed from English sheets, reprints from earlier American, British or Australian editions, or in other forms of reissue and distribution, for these have a significant bearing on the position of a book in that marketplace. We can talk about an Australian novel and an American book and mean the same thing, because of strict national regulations such as the Chace Act's "manufacturing clause", which demanded that literary property be printed and bound within the United States in order to be eligible for copyright protection.[18] For the vast majority of cases in this study, the Australian novel under discussion is an American book because it was made (if not born) in the USA.

As these arguments all indicate, the present study is framed necessarily as a contribution to transnational literary or print culture studies. It breaks down the model of an organically evolving entity – "Australian literature" – gradually filling the space of the nation, as it were, until it is adequate to itself, at once modern and mature as criticism has so often demanded.[19] Instead, as we put it below, we discover a literature that was international (and not merely imperial) long before it was national, and long after as well. From this enlarged perspective, instead of a parochial, backward period across the first two or three decades of the twentieth century, for example, we find Australian authors published widely alongside their international contemporaries in the two main Anglophone book markets. Instead of a local, provincial tradition of historical sagas we find Australian novels taking their place in the 1930s and 1940s alongside American and other international examples of the genre. None of this is to ignore the relatively weak, marginalised position of Australian books and authors in the world of letters or the legal, economic and other obstacles that so often defeated Australian writers' aspirations to a wider market. Nor is it to dismiss the serious, principled commitments of nationalist intellectuals and writers seeking to build a national literature in Australia. But it does suggest the significance of the United States to the long transnational history of Australian literature.

In addition to its larger conceptual moves beyond the logics of national cultural evolution, transnationalism in literary studies has been productively identified as an energising or confounding force in literary texts themselves, an imaginative capacity (and capaciousness), often manifest in complex forms of citation and multiple perspectives.[20] As a textual quality – or reading practice – transnationalism often comes to have an ethical as well as an intellectual force. At this point, however, more materialist approaches might

---

18   See Paul Eggert, *Securing the Past: Conservation in Art, Architecture, and Literature* (Cambridge: Cambridge University Press, 2009), 214-40, where he outlines the notion of the literary work as a regulating concept that allows us to talk about each edition under the same name (e.g. *Robbery Under Arms* or *Coonardoo*), but, at the same time, to separate one material book from another by acknowledging the mechanical, temporal and spatial properties that each book exhibits.
19   Carter, *Always Almost Modern*, 15-33.
20   See, for example, Dixon, "Australian Literature, Scale, and the Problem of the World"; "Scenes of Reading: Is Australian Literature a World Literature?", in *Republics of Letters: Literary Communities in Australia*, ed. Robert Dixon and Peter Kirkpatrick (Sydney: Sydney University Press, 2012), 71-83. Also Paul Giles, *Transatlantic Insurrections: British Culture and the Formation of American Literature, 1730-1860* (Philadelphia: University of Pennsylvania Press, 2001); *Transnationalism in Practice: Essays on American Studies, Literature and Religion* (Edinburgh: Edinburgh University Press, 2010).

sound a cautionary note, for as an ethical or aesthetic category the transnational all too easily becomes a mode of transcendence, its metaphors of border-crossing merely the latest in a long line of such euphemisms for literariness or liberation. From the perspective of publishing or book history, by contrast, certainly in the history examined here, we are confronted at every turn by the unequal distribution of power in the literary world system, the material and legal obstacles to border-crossing, and the insistent presence of national legislative or domestic market regimes, protecting local production and administering cultural flows. Transnationalism in this perspective is less a higher form of literary being than a mundane, if often conflicted cluster of institutional arrangements, formal agreements and habitual practices involving publishers, agents, copyright laws, distribution networks and so on, and operating variously on local, national and international scales. As Paul Eggert reminds us, "only some works 'travel'", and decisions are made "that permit the process to occur. Those decisions are made mainly by the book trade: the transnationalising phenomenon has a material basis".[21]

In some ways the present history might be described as "transnodal" rather than transnational given the dominance of London, New York and Sydney/Melbourne over their respective domestic markets, markets which were segmented and diversified internally and thus never identical with the nation. At the same time the continued significance of the national plane might be indicated by the centrality of copyright, an eminently international set of arrangements across most of the period examined here but one organised precisely through the recognition of distinct national territories. We can certainly speak of an international market for books, but one which is configured differently in each national and local situation. Domestic, national and international forces operate through each of the nodes relevant to the history of Australian books and authors in the American marketplace.

Chapter 1 examines the presence of Australian fiction and earlier travellers' tales in the United States in the second half of the nineteenth century. By the late 1880s and 1890s, Australian novels became identifiable as a distinct variation upon familiar, transatlantic romance conventions. Their visibility in the American marketplace depended in part on the booming fiction reprint industry and fiction libraries, largely driven by "pirate" publishers before the passing of the US International Copyright Act in 1891.[22] Chapter 2 focuses on the American and transatlantic careers of Rosa Praed and Louis Becke, both of whom received extensive critical praise in America over successive titles but who struggled to maintain their careers, due in different parts to the nature of their own output, the complexities of the copyright situation, and the changing values accorded to romance and realism in the literary field. Chapter 3 follows a group of writers whose careers overlap with those of Praed and Becke either side of the century's turn, but which depend rather on the emergence of the "new" genres of detective fiction, mysteries, spy stories and thrillers. The genre system itself multiplied the potential mobility of fiction across national borders and limited markets, and Australian authors were significant players in the new game.

Chapter 4 turns to the first three decades of the twentieth century, beginning with the relative decline in numbers of Australian novels published in the United States as a

---

21　Paul Eggert, *Biography of a Book: Henry Lawson's "While the Billy Boils"* (Sydney: Sydney University Press, 2013), 22.

22　As is explained in Chapter 1, "pirate" is a disputed term as the reprinters were not acting illegally in the absence of international copyright legislation protecting foreign editions.

consequence, in part, of the restrictive clauses of the new US international copyright law. Even so, the number of works published – many one-off titles but also successive books from authors with sustained careers – provides a much richer sense of Australian writing in these years. Australian works were able to participate in a range of different market sectors – "geographical romances", women's travel writing, the "modern girl" story, and, not least, the modern sex novel. Chapter 5 returns to the question of genre fiction, here from the 1920s to the 1940s (and beyond for the most successful authors). Again Australian authors emerge as major players in the game, most notably Arthur Upfield in crime and Maysie Greig in romance, managing transatlantic and, in their case, transpacific careers – although it was another romance author, Alice Grant Rosman, who was promoted as "America's best loved novelist".

Chapters 6 and 7 cover the period in the present study in which Australian literature had its greatest impact as "literature", and as "Australian" literature, from the late 1920s to the mid-1940s. Over these years a series of important novels appeared in America, and were received into a culture receptive to their generic ambitions as pioneering epics, family sagas and regional novels. Critics and reviewers commented repeatedly – with surprise – on the achievement of these novels and the parallels they saw with America's own story. Henry Handel Richardson's *Ultima Thule*, published by Norton in 1929, had extraordinary success critically and commercially; Norton followed with Richardson's other titles and two works by Katharine Susannah Prichard, enabling reviewers to begin connecting different Australian works, from M. Barnard Eldershaw's *A House is Built* to Frank Dalby Davison's *Red Heifer* to Xavier Herbert's *Capricornia*.[23] Dark's *The Timeless Land*, like *Ultima Thule* an American Book-of-the-Month Club selection, frames the period.

The careers of the two authors many would regard as the most important Australian novelists of the twentieth century – Christina Stead and Patrick White – are centrally stories of New York publishing and book reviewing. Their careers through to the early 1950s are the focus of Chapter 8. America was a publishing home for both but also a complex sign of their literary "homelessness" and their relation to an emerging modern tradition of the novel in these formative years. Chapter 9 gathers together many of the threads from previous chapters and brings them to bear on the final years of the period under study, the 1940s and especially the postwar years, when many believed or hoped that the presence of Australian literature in America could be consolidated or at least that a new period of growth was likely. While the Pacific war did prompt increased interest in Australian books, this interest appears to have been very short-lived and had little impact on publishers' attitudes or decisions. While certain writers, such as Kylie Tennant, found modest success in America, there was little continuity from the achievements of the interwar years. For new writers such as Jon Cleary it was a matter of starting from scratch and negotiating again the (often two-sided) triangle of American, British and Australian publishing markets.

---

23 *Red Heifer: A Story of Men and Cattle* was the US title of Davison's *Man-Shy*.

1
Antipodean Romance: Australian Fiction and the American Book Trade in the Nineteenth Century

> "Australia is beginning to claim something like its fair share of attention in the cosmopolitan world of fiction."
> —*Chicago Daily Tribune*, 16 February 1897

By the end of the nineteenth century, around one hundred Australian novels and travellers' tales had been published in American editions, with the bulk of these, over three-quarters, appearing in the final two decades of the century. While this represents only a small fraction of the imported novels published in America in this period, as a proportion of all Australian novels to 1900 the numbers are significant. Indeed, a more generous count would raise the total above 150. Any accounting of course depends on prior decisions about what qualifies as an Australian book and who qualifies as an Australian author, an unavoidable issue for every phase of the history examined here but present in a particularly acute form for the nineteenth and early twentieth centuries where patterns of immigration, expatriation, and "imperial commuting" were the norm. Only a handful of the books that might be considered from this period are by Australian-born authors and only a handful more by long-term residents. Of the Australian-born, many became permanent or serial expatriates, while some of the most influential novels were written by visitors.

Henry Kingsley's *The Recollections of Geoffry Hamlyn* (1859), for example, had become a canonical Australian novel by century's end despite the fact that Kingsley spent less than five years in the colonies, between December 1853 and February 1858.[1] It appeared in multiple editions in the United States throughout the nineteenth century. While Australian material figured in a number of subsequent works, Kingsley's career was as an English writer and his books travelled to the United States as English books. The same might be said of Australian-born Rosa Praed. Although Praed spent her first twenty-four years in the colonies and Australia provided settings and stories for much of her work, her career as a novelist was established after her departure for England and pursued in the context of the British book world. Ada Cambridge, by contrast, managed her career in the British book world and the United States from Australia. Born in England in 1844, she migrated to Victoria in 1870 and lived in Australia until 1909, then again from 1917 until her death

---

1   Paul Eggert, "Australian Classics and the Price of Books: The Puzzle of the 1890s", *Journal of the Association for the Study of Australian Literature (JASAL)* (2008): 135–36, 148–50.

in 1926. Twelve of her eighteen novels published as books in London also appeared in America between 1879 and 1907, in at least twenty-five different editions.

To comprehend the nineteenth and early twentieth century period – to understand the systems of writing and publication in which authors and stories participated and the routes along which both authors and texts travelled – we need definitions or working models elastic enough to include all these cases and others significantly more marginal. Australian books and writing need to be understood as constituting a broad and diverse field that authors and texts entered or passed through in various capacities, leaving different kinds of historical traces. Its boundaries must be provisional, with the limit cases as important as those well within its borders in representing Australia's position within what was an imperial and transnational trade in cultural commodities and careers. The point is less about the politics of inclusion than the pragmatics of charting historically the wide range of trajectories that books or authors followed in making their way into and out of Australia and then, in some instances, to the United States. As this chapter will show, Australian literature was international, not merely imperial, long before it was national.

In the Wilds of Australia

The earliest tales of the Australian colonies to reach the American marketplace were in the popular genres of the traveller's or emigrant's tale. Stories of shipwrecks, convicts, bush life and bushrangers began circulating from mid-century.[2] Charles Rowcroft's *The Bush Ranger of Van Diemen's Land* was the earliest novel, published by Harper & Brothers in New York in 1846, the same year as its London release, but with the three-volume English edition reduced to a mere 144 pages in double columns for Harper's twenty-five cent paper-covered Library of Select Novels.[3] We have no information about how Rowcroft's books found their way across the Atlantic, but as Michael Winship argues "the trade in texts was much more important and regular than many scholars recognize".[4] Harper would most likely have paid a flat fee to Rowcroft's English publisher, and other American publishers, following the accepted practices of the trade, would have recognised Harper's exclusive right as the book's first American publisher. As explained more fully below, while foreign books were freely available to American publishers without the barrier of copyright protection, according to the conventions of "trade courtesy" the first publisher to release or to announce its intention to release a book in the US market was generally acknowledged as having exclusive rights to that work. Rowcroft is described on the title page as the "Author of 'Tales of the Colonies' &c, &c", suggesting that his English reputation had preceded him. Harper reissued the novel

---

[2] The story of Eliza Fraser's shipwreck and life among Aborigines appeared in 1837 in *Narrative of the Capture, Sufferings, and Miraculous Escape of Mrs. Eliza Fraser* (New York: C.S. Webb). Authorship is uncertain. See Kay Schaffer, *In the Wake of First Contact: The Eliza Fraser Stories* (Cambridge: Cambridge University Press, 1998), 43-49.

[3] The English Smith, Elder edition of Rowcroft's book used the vernacular form "bushranger" as a single word in its title.

[4] Michael Winship, "The International Trade in Books", in *A History of the Book in America Volume 3: The Industrial Book, 1840–1880*, ed. Scott E. Casper et al. (Chapel Hill: University of North Carolina Press, 2007), 156.

1 Australian Fiction and the American Book Trade in the Nineteenth Century

Figure 1.1 Charles Rowcroft, *The Australian Crusoes; or, The Adventures of an English Settler and His Family in the Wilds of Australia* (Philadelphia: Davis, Porter & Co., 1865).

in 1855 and 1874.[5] Its popularity in America might be explained in part by its borrowing of crucial plot elements from James Fenimore Cooper's *The Last of the Mohicans* (1826).[6]

Rowcroft had spent around four years in Van Diemen's Land between 1821 and 1825 before returning to England where he began his career, first as a magazine editor, then, from 1843, as a novelist, with *Tales of the Colonies; or, the Adventures of an Emigrant*, first published in three volumes by Saunders & Otley of London in 1845, then republished as a single volume by Smith, Elder the same year. The burgeoning market for tales from the colonies saw two new English editions and ten reprintings through to 1887, Australian abridgements in the 1890s from J. Walch in Hobart, and at least nine American editions from 1853 to 1884. Retitled *The Australian Crusoes; or, The Adventures of an English Settler and his Family in the Wilds of Australia*, the book was first published in America by stationer and newsagent Willis P. Hazard of Philadelphia in 1853 and reprinted in 1856. The American title subtly shifts the generic frame from that of the Anglo-colonial emigrant story to the broader field of "settler-in the-wilderness" narratives. Under its new title, the book was published, again

---

5   Later English editions used the alternative title *Mark Brandon, the Convict*.
6   Elizabeth Webby, "The Novel Newspaper and Its Role in the Transmission of American Fiction to Australia", in *Reading Across the Pacific: Australia–United States Intellectual Histories*, ed. Robert Dixon and Nicholas Birns (Sydney: Sydney University Press, 2010), 175.

in Philadelphia, by J.W. Bradley in 1859 and 1860 and by Davis, Porter & Co. in 1865 (Fig. 1.1); in New York by Allen Brothers in 1869 and the World Publishing House in 1875; and in Boston by the established firm of Lee & Shephard in 1884. All were printed from the same Smith, Elder edition, although each publisher inserted its own illustrations. What encouraged so many different editions was not merely the popularity of the genre but the fact that as a foreign book *The Australian Crusoes* could not be copyrighted in the United States and so was freely available to any publisher. The illustrations, however, could be protected; even where copyright was not sought they made each edition unique. This pattern of multiple editions from different publishers becomes increasingly common from the 1870s to the 1890s and is significant in the publishing lives of many Australian authors.

Other travellers' tales of the Australian colonies to appear in the United States before the 1880s include books by American authors Louis A. Baker, who published *Harry Martingale: or, Adventures of a Whaleman in the Pacific Ocean* and *Lucy Marline; or, The Bush-Rangers: A Tale of New South Wales*, both in 1848, and William H. Thomes, who published at least four novels with an Australian tag, including *The Gold Hunters' Adventures, or Life in Australia* (1864) and *The Bushrangers. A Yankee's Adventures During his Second Visit to Australia* (1865). The latter were reissued in several editions in 1890-91 in the cheap Library of Choice Fiction published in Chicago by Laird & Lee. They also travelled back to the colonies, the two novels combined in one volume as *Life on the Goldfields of Australia* or *A Gold Hunter's Adventures*, published in Sydney, Melbourne and Hobart in 1891. German writer Friedrich Gerstaecker visited Australia for a year in 1851-52, and *The Two Convicts* (London, 1857) was released in 1871 by the New York dime novel publishers Beadle & Co., reconfigured as two separate titles for children: *The Bushranger; or, The Half-Breed Brigade: A Romance of the Bush* and *The Outlaw Hunter; or, Red John, the Bush-Ranger*. Perhaps most significant in terms of the author's later position in Australian literary history is Louisa Anne Meredith's non-fictional *My Home in Tasmania; or, Nine Years in Australia*, published in New York in 1853 by Bunce & Brother.

The titles of these publications indicate Australia's niche in the American marketplace in so far as it had one - sailors' and whalers' tales, convicts, settlers in the wild, station life, bushrangers, and gold-digging. If the goldrushes motivated the movement of people and goods across the globe at mid-century, they also motivated the movement of narratives and books for the rest of the century. After two years on the Victorian goldfields, William Howitt had two colonial tales published by the respected firm of Ticknor & Fields in Boston in 1855, *A Boy's Adventure in the Wilds of Australia* and *Land, Labor and Gold; or, Two Years in Victoria*. English traveller Charles Beach wrote the first fictional account of the Eureka uprising in *Lost Lenore; or, The Adventures of a Rolling Stone* (London, 1864; New York: Robert M. De Witt, 1866). From Boston, Irish-born John Boyle O'Reilly, who was transported to Western Australia in 1868 but escaped to America the following year, published his immensely popular convict, bushranger and goldmining novel *Moondyne: A Story from the Underworld* in 1879. Multiple editions appeared in the United States and Australia before its first appearance in England a decade later.[7]

A new phase began in the 1870s and continued through to the early years of the new century. It was driven by the rapid expansion in fiction publishing in the British and American

---

7   Editions include: Boston: Pilot Publishing Co., 1879; Boston: Roberts Bros, 1879; *Moondyne: A Story of Life in West Australia*, Melbourne: George Robertson, 1880; *Moondyne Joe*, Philadephia: H.L. Kilner, 188?; *Moondyne: A Tale of the Australian Bush*, Melbourne: E.W. Cole, 1880. The first English edition, *Moondyne: A Story of Convict Life* in Australia, was from Routledge in 1889.

domestic markets and the emergence of a transatlantic market for domestic, pastoral and frontier romance fiction; by the particular circumstances of the American fiction industry, above all the growth of cheap fiction libraries among both regular and "pirate" publishers; and by the increasing professionalisation of writing careers and contractual relations between publishers, authors and literary agents. The earlier travellers' or emigrants' tales were progressively absorbed within the conventions of romance and frontier adventure fiction, and those having novels published in American as well as English editions were increasingly likely to be professional authors with long-term careers *primarily* as novelists. English-born Benjamin Farjeon, immigrant, traveller, and expatriate, spent seven years in Victoria from 1854 before leaving for New Zealand where his first novels were published in the 1860s. He then settled in England where he built a successful literary career. A prolific novelist, Farjeon wrote in genres well suited to the transatlantic trade: sentimental tales, Dickensian Christmas stories, foggy mysteries, and, not least, colonial adventure and romance in a series of novels covering gold-digging, bushranging, convicts and pioneering. Farjeon's American career was remarkable: over forty individual titles published in seventy different editions in the final three decades of the century, with around twenty-five editions or reprintings in the 1870s, thirty in the 1880s, and another fifteen through to 1904. The majority were in cheap paperback series, but from 1871 to 1889 Harper alone published more than twenty of his books, some in cloth as well as paper, at prices ranging from twenty-five cents to $1.50. Paperback reprinters George Munro and John W. Lovell published more than twenty further books between them, often the same titles as Harper. Farjeon was hot property in a competitive marketplace, not least for his Australian tales including *Grif: A Story of Australian Life* (Harper, 1872; Robert M. De Witt, 1880; Munro, 1882; Lovell, 1892), *At the Sign of the Silver Flagon* (Harper, 1875; Munro, 1877), *Shadows in the Snow* (Harper, 1877; Munro, 1878) and *The Sacred Nugget* (Munro, 1884; Harper, 1885; Lovell, 1889).

Perhaps the most famous literary visitor to Australia was Anthony Trollope, who travelled around the colonies for a year in 1871-72 and again in 1875. Unsurprisingly, given his established reputation and popularity, Trollope's two Australian novels were published in America by Harper: *Harry Heathcote of Gangoil: A Tale of Australian Bush Life* in 1874, the same year as its London release, and *John Caldigate: A Novel*, "Trollope's most substantive Antipodean novel", in 1879.[8] In 1883, Harper published Trollope's *An Autobiography*, which revisits his Australian experience. George Munro followed suit, with a cheap edition of the *Autobiography* in the same year and a reprint of *John Caldigate* in 1885.

That Vast Web of Romance

Trollope not only put the Australian colonies before American readers, he did so through the idea of a greater "Anglo-Saxon" world that included the United States.[9] As Paul Giles argues, "there was an enormous amount of discussion about ways in which the United States might form part of a racial spectrum of English-speaking peoples that would achieve a beneficent

---

[8] Nicholas Birns, "Trollope and the Antipodes", in *The Cambridge Companion to Anthony Trollope*, ed. Carolyn Dever and Lisa Niles (Cambridge: Cambridge University Press, 2010), 182.

[9] Trollope published *The West Indies and the Spanish Main* (1860), *North America* (1862), *South Africa* (1872) and *Australia and New Zealand* (1873); the last appears not to have been published separately in the United States but it is likely the Chapman & Hall edition was distributed in America.

Anglo-Saxon world hegemony ... [A]t this time Australasia, America and Britain were often thought to operate within triangular rather than antithetical relationships".[10] This discussion was as common in New York as in London. The *New York Times* celebrated Queen Victoria's jubilee, for the achievements of her reign were the "achievements of men of the blood and race which most of us inherit, of the speech that all of us speak". Americans were a "great part of that Greater Britain which seems plainly destined to dominate this planet".[11] Even Mark Twain believed in the greater British family. As he put it in a speech in Melbourne in late 1895, "the Americans, and the English, and the great outflow in Canada and Australia are all one".[12] The triangulation might be imagined differently from each of its points, but it helps explain how from the American perspective Australia could appear both utterly remote and antipodean but also, at times, unexpectedly close and familiar, closer and more familiar than Britain itself, increasingly so in the 1890s. Indeed, rather than any single evolution towards (or away from) closer cultural connections between Australia and the United States, this dialectic between proximity and remoteness, resemblance and strangeness, continues well into the twentieth century.

If the flood of British books in the American marketplace was driven largely by commercial interests, it was also implicated in the idea of a shared Anglo-Saxon world, defined by race and destined through racial superiority to assume moral leadership across the globe. But this belief was itself rooted in fears of imperial decay and the hope of regeneration in the new colonial settlements or on the frontier.[13] It was at its strongest in the two decades either side of century's end, when many predicted a "coming race war" between the white and coloured races.[14] This was the height of the new imperialism movement as European powers competed for possessions in Africa and the Pacific, and the idea of a greater Anglo-Saxon empire could underwrite what can otherwise be seen as a "willed re-assertion of an imperial ideal on the wane".[15] Trollope's own works are interrogative, juxtaposing British, American and Australasian futures "within complex lines of triangulation".[16] But it is also likely his Australian novels were read in the 1880s within the dominant genres of popular romance that played a key role in reaffirming for readers across the Anglosphere the sense of an Anglo-Saxon world that was at once virile and domesticated, settled and adventurous. Jessica Despain has suggested that the passing of the US International Copyright Act in 1891 not only stabilised the transatlantic publishing industry; it also underwrote the political idea of an Anglo-American alliance, even a future Anglo-American empire.[17]

---

10   Paul Giles, *Antipodean America: Australasia and the Constitution of US Literature* (New York: Oxford University Press, 2013), 211. See also James Belich, *Replenishing the Earth: The Settler Revolution and the Rise of the Anglo-World, 1783–1939* (Oxford: Oxford University Press, 2009); Marilyn Lake and Henry Reynolds, *Drawing the Global Colour Line: White Men's Countries and the International Challenge of Racial Equality* (Carlton, Vic.: Melbourne University Press, 2008); Srdjan Vucetic, *The Anglosphere: A Genealogy of a Racialized Identity in International Relations* (Stanford: Stanford University Press, 2011), 22–53.
11   "America at the Jubilee", *New York Times*, 24 June 1897.
12   Cited in Giles, *Antipodean America*, 245.
13   Robert Dixon, *Writing the Colonial Adventure: Race, Gender, and Nation in Anglo-Australian Popular Fiction, 1875–1914* (Cambridge: Cambridge University Press, 1995), 1–8, 62–81.
14   Lake and Reynolds, *Drawing the Global Colour Line*, 91–94, 196; David Walker, *Anxious Nation: Australia and the Rise of Asia 1850–1939* (St Lucia: University of Queensland Press, 1999), 168–75.
15   Dixon, *Writing the Colonial Adventure*, 3.
16   Giles, *Antipodean America*, 219.
17   Jessica Despain, *Nineteenth-Century Transatlantic Reprinting and the Embodied Book* (Farnham, UK: Ashgate, 2014), 178–79.

1 Australian Fiction and the American Book Trade in the Nineteenth Century

The book pages of American newspapers and magazines were full of British books and book talk from London and the colonies, with little sense that these were foreign to American readers. Towards the end of the period under discussion, an article appeared in the *Salt Lake Tribune*, a special cable from a London correspondent, its headline announcing: "Oversea Writers Capture England ... Yankee Product Liked. All the Colonies Are Producing Vibrant Literature for Entertainment of John Bull".[18] After a paragraph outlining the success within "Anglo-Saxondom" of Australian authors including Rosa Praed, Rolf Boldrewood, Marcus Clarke and Ada Cambridge, the writer concludes: "Naturally, every part of Britain's colonial possessions contributes to the many hued colors of that vast web of romance being woven by British novelists and poets".

As this evocative image suggests, the Australian novels that travelled to the United States from the 1870s to the 1900s did so less as individual books than as members of a class, more or less interchangeable examples of the romance genre however much individual authors might build a reputation. If London was the originating centre of the romance boom, romance fiction also flourished in the American market, drawing in British and Australian works with a voracious appetite: "the romance became almost synonymous with the novel in the public mind and was the most popular form of reading".[19] The broad categories of romance and adventure covered a very large part of fiction publishing and absorbed most other generic divisions. Romance was especially capacious, including almost every kind of fiction, whether stories of imperial adventure in Africa or the South Seas, tales of the goldfields or pastoral Australia, or variations upon the marriage and inheritance plot.

The dominance of romance also goes a long way to explaining the absence in the American market of Henry Lawson and Joseph Furphy, the two authors who would become canonical in national literary histories of the 1890s and early twentieth century. Neither wrote according to romance conventions, indeed both wrote explicitly against them; and their realism evoked an overtly local address and topicality, even as they engaged with literary currents from England, America and Europe. Their publishing histories also made them invisible to the transatlantic book trade. In the period, only one of Lawson's short story collections was published in London, while Furphy's novels only appeared locally.[20]

Far from being residual, the meanings and forms of romance multiplied in the 1880s and 1890s, partly in opposition to the "new realism" of the period and partly through alignment with the new imperialism – the new Anglo-Saxonism – and its stories of national and racial adventure.[21] Through novelists such as Robert Louis Stevenson, H. Rider Haggard and William Clark Russell, or Australians with international standing such as Cambridge, Praed or Boldrewood, romance was not only newly popular but also newly respectable. For America, in the words of publishing historian John Tebbel, "The major trend of the late nineteenth century ... was the great outflow of what were known as novels

---

18 "Oversea Writers Capture England", *Salt Lake Tribune*, 16 July 1911.
19 James D. Hart, *The Popular Book: A History of America's Literary Taste* (New York: Oxford University Press, 1950), 183.
20 Lawson's *While the Billy Boils* was published by Simpkin, Marshall, Hamilton, Kent & Co. in 1897; Furphy's *Such is Life* was published in 1948 by the University of Chicago Press; see Chapter 9.
21 Peter Keating, *The Haunted Study: A Social History of the English Novel, 1875–1914* (London: Fontana, 1991), 344-5. For a discussion of the essential interconnections between romance fiction, New Imperialism and the newspapers of the period, see Andrew Griffiths, *The New Journalism, the New Imperialism, and the Fiction of Empire, 1870–1900* (Basingstoke, UK: Palgrave Macmillan, 2015).

of 'high romance,' mostly historical, which began in 1894 and went on for nearly ten years".[22]

Henry Kingsley's Remarkable Renaissance

The effect of these changes can be seen clearly in Henry Kingsley's career. *The Recollections of Geoffry Hamlyn* was Kingsley's first novel and so found its way to the United States without the benefit of an established English literary reputation. The book was first published in three volumes by Macmillan in London in April 1859, at the standard price of 31s. 6d. Only a month later, Ticknor & Fields, one of the most active American firms in the transatlantic book trade, published a one-volume edition at $1.25, a new setting based on advance sheets which had been sent to the American firm by Macmillan.[23] While the manuscript was still in the final stages of editing and redrafting, Kingsley, through the agency of London-based American journalist W.H. Hurlbert, had received an offer from Ticknor & Fields of a one-off payment of £50 for the novel on the condition they be given proofs before the book was published in England. Being able to print from proofs would allow the US firm to be "first in the field" and thus to establish its exclusive rights to the title according to the practices of trade courtesy.

Trade courtesy was not an enforceable copyright protection but a set of conventions by which the established publishing houses conducted business:

> The conventions of trade courtesy allowed American forms to acquire the right – if not a de jure copyright at least a trade-sanctioned de facto right – to an English publication. These conventions required that the firm be the first American firm to announce its intention to publish a work. Furthermore, a claim to a work was considered stronger if the American firm had made a direct payment to the London publisher or author. Since British copyright law required first publication in the United Kingdom, American publishers usually strove for simultaneous or nearly simultaneous publication in order to discourage competition. This frequently resulted in a payment to the British publisher or author for early sheets, proofs, or even a copy of the manuscript, sent from London.[24]

Those like Harper and Ticknor & Fields with branches or agents in London thus held an advantage. Further, it was generally recognised that the publisher who first reprinted the work of a foreign author "could exercise a claim on all of that author's subsequent works, thus associating that author with the house".[25] This practice was especially important in the

---

22 John Tebbel, *A History of Book Publishing in the United States. Volume II: The Expansion of an Industry, 1865–1919* (New York: Bowker, 1975), 650.

23 Publishing details for the American edition from J.S.D. Mellick, Patrick Morgan and Paul Eggert, introduction to *The Recollections of Geoffry Hamlyn*, by Henry Kingsley (St Lucia: University of Queensland Press, 1996), l-li. For Ticknor & Fields, see Michael Winship, "The International Trade in Books", 150-57. It printed 1500 copies initially, then reprinted seven times.

24 Michael Winship, "Anglo-American Literary Culture and the Transatlantic Book Trade in the Nineteenth Century", in *Reciprocal Influences: Literary Production, Distribution, and Consumption in America*, ed. Steven Fink and Susan Williams (Columbus: Ohio State University Press, 1999), 101, 105-6.

25 Jeffrey D. Groves, "Courtesy of the Trade", in *A History of the Book in America Volume 3*, ed. Scott E. Casper et al., 140-1.

case of canonical titles or authors with multiple works, for it established the firm as that author's authorised publisher. As the decision to publish an authorised edition of a foreign work demanded substantial investment in plates, publicity, and payments to the foreign author or publisher, mainstream firms were therefore ready to recognise the rights of other firms in order to have their own acknowledged in turn. Nonetheless, these rights were difficult to maintain for popular authors such as Scott or Dickens or the latest bestsellers.

In the absence of copyright protection for foreign books and hence the real possibility of "literary piracy" through unauthorised reprintings, trade courtesy was "a practical method of reducing competition and maintaining prices, but ... even more an effort by the American publisher to show the British publisher that he could behave in a gentlemanly fashion".[26] The main firms to participate were Charles Scribner's Sons, J.B. Lippincott Co., J.R. Osgood & Co., D. Appleton & Co., Roberts Brothers, G.P. Putnam's Sons, Harper, Macmillan, Houghton Mifflin, E.P. Dutton & Co., Henry Holt & Co. and Ticknor & Fields – all important publishers of Australian books. The most common practice was to purchase "advance sheets of the foreign edition for use as a setting copy or to enter an agreement with the author for permission to reprint" (merely importing books for distribution did not invoke trade courtesy).[27] In other cases, authors would be paid a fee retrospectively if their books had been profitable, while later in the century publishers began offering royalties on copies sold.

Frederick Macmillan advised Kingsley and Hulbert to hold out for £75, for he believed *Geoffry Hamlyn* would have large sales. He also thought that US publishers on the whole were "rascals" who "have the power over English authors as they can reprint without leave".[28] But Ticknor & Fields did remunerate foreign authors, and were ready to defend their own respectability. James Thomas Fields wrote to Macmillan in December 1859 explaining that his firm supported international copyright against "unprincipled publishers" at home who reprinted from the firm's list of British authors without permission. Probably on the advice of his more experienced brother, novelist Charles Kingsley, Henry accepted the offer of £50, meaning that despite the novel's American success he received no further income from its multiple editions.

Subsequent English editions of *Geoffry Hamlyn* appeared through to the turn of the century, in particular a revised one-volume edition from Macmillan in 1860 which was the basis of almost continuous reprints from different publishers through to the 1920s. The novel had a largely independent life in the American market. Ticknor & Fields reprinted their edition seven times through to 1869, almost four thousand copies in total over the decade alongside five later Kingsley novels, including two with an Australian interest, *Ravenshoe* (1862) and *The Hillyars and the Burtons* (1865, 1866). That the publishers took on the subsequent novels suggests that the first had enjoyed some critical or sales success. More significantly, the regular sequence of titles would have established Kingsley in the American market as a reliable, respectable English novelist. Harper also published two Kingsley titles in 1869, *Stretton* and the novella *Hetty*, and three further titles in the 1870s. Like Rowcroft before him, Kingsley, by this

---

26 James L.W. West III, *American Authors and the Literary Marketplace since 1900* (Philadelphia: University of Pennsylvania Press, 1988), 35. See also Robert Spoo, *Without Copyrights: Piracy, Publishing, and the Public Domain* (Oxford and New York: Oxford University Press, 2013), 18, 32–61.
27 Spoo, *Without Copyrights*, 37.
28 Macmillan quoted in Mellick, Morgan and Eggert, introduction, xxxvi.

time, had a tradeable reputation and could be presented to American readers in Harper's usual fashion as the "Author of 'Stretton,' 'Geoffry Hamlyn,' 'Ravenshoe,' &c, &c".

However, like Rowcroft again, it was not until the 1880s, after his death, that multiple editions of Kingsley's novels began to appear in the United States. Ticknor & Fields released four separate editions of *Geoffry Hamlyn* in the 1880s and 1890s, and there were further multiple releases from various New York publishers: Dodd, Mead in 1883; J.W. Lovell in 1886; Scribner in 1894, 1895 and 1899; and Longmans, Green in 1899. Lovell had picked up *The Hillyars and the Burtons* in 1877 before releasing four Kingsley titles in 1886, including *Geoffry Hamlyn* and *The Hillyars* once more. Dodd, Mead published *The Hillyars* in 1883, possibly also the date of their edition of *Ravenshoe*, and in the same year George Munro published *Leighton Court* in his Seaside Library. Then, in 1894-95, the London firm of Ward, Lock & Bowden, which had opened a New York branch, published a twelve-volume edition of Kingsley's fiction in the United States, even as George P. Brett of Macmillan in New York declined the opportunity to publish him: "there are only three or four of Henry Kingsley's books that any great number of people still care to read; most of them are quite unknown and will, I fear, remain so here".[29] Reading the market differently, Scribner published a six-volume uniform edition in 1895, including *Geoffry Hamlyn* and *Ravenshoe*, while Longmans, Green republished the Ward, Lock & Bowden series between 1899 and 1908.

This late interest in Kingsley's work, two decades after his death, was doubtless driven by the boom in romance fiction – historical, domestic, and frontier adventure – then sweeping across the Anglophone world. American readers could find Kingsley's novels "most readable and entertaining",[30] even if the sense of a trans-imperial British family dramatised in his novels' family romances largely excluded Americans. But his revival must also be understood in the context of the intense competition that had arisen in the 1870s and 1880s in the fiction market, driven by publishers such as Lovell and Munro, who issued cheap editions of foreign authors in extensive paperback libraries. In Lovell's case, the interest in *Geoffry Hamlyn* may have been nothing more than the availability of a saleable non-copyrighted story to add to his series, the novel perhaps having been brought to his attention by Dodd, Mead's edition. However, by the time Scribner entered the market with *Geoffry Hamlyn* in 1894, the pirate publishers had largely disappeared with the passage of the Chace Act of 1891.[31] Scribner could thus reposition Kingsley's works in the mainstream, as a writer of popular, respectable historical romance. Longmans, Green repeated the gesture with its collection at the end of the decade.

In September 1899, the *New York Times* noted a "really remarkable renaissance" for Kingsley's novels, although just a few months earlier it had claimed he was "hardly known among American readers of fiction". Of course, that itself was a market opportunity for an author deserving "no mean place in the republic of letters".[32] In announcing *Ravenshoe* as the first in its series, Scribner claimed that the moment was opportune "as Mr. Kingsley's novels have of late been receiving more of the attention their merit entitles them to".[33] No

---

29 Brett to Frederick Macmillan, 5 March 1894, Macmillan Archive, British Library, BL 54802.
30 "What Readers Think", *New York Times*, 29 July 1899.
31 The Act was passed in March and came into law in July 1891. See Catherine Seville, *The Internationalisation of Copyright Law: Books, Buccaneers and the Black Flag in the Nineteenth Century* (Cambridge: Cambridge University Press, 2006), 240-46.
32 "Henry Kingsley's Novels", *New York Times*, 30 September 1899; "Topics of the Week", *New York Times*, 22 July 1899.
33 Advertisement, *New York Times*, 22 September 1894.

1 Australian Fiction and the American Book Trade in the Nineteenth Century

doubt part of Kingsley's appeal was nostalgic; or rather it was a contemporary response to the new realism and its social modernity, and to the conflicting claims of realism and romance that framed so much of late nineteenth-century book culture. For one loyal American reader, Kingsley's novels were "dear to the belated remnant of readers who from time to time seek a refuge from the introspective and analytical apostles of modern realism, in the obsolete romances of that Golden Age when the merit of a story was rated more or less in accordance with the amount of pleasure to be derived from its perusal!"[34] If *Geoffry Hamlyn* was "really a series of Australian sketches strung on a slight connecting thread of romance", it was nonetheless "as full of local color and of individuality as is Lindsay Gordon's Australian verse: one feels the dazzling sunshine, hears the swift ripple of the shallow rivers, and smells the yellow wattle flowers". The colonies' most popular poet at the time, Adam Lindsay Gordon, was also known in America.

Marcus Clarke described *The Recollections of Geoffry Hamlyn* as "the best Australian novel that has been, and probably will be written".[35] Clarke was the first author permanently resident in the Australian colonies to have a novel published in America, although he had little say in the matter. After serialisation in the *Australian Journal* (1870-72) and first book publication in Melbourne (1874), Clarke's *His Natural Life*, a novel of the convict period that Twain thought a "great work of art", appeared in three volumes from Richard Bentley & Sons in London in 1875.[36] Then in early 1876, Harper published a one-volume, 178-page paperbound edition, no. 458 in its Library of Select Novels at seventy-five cents, where it joined multiple titles by Farjeon, Trollope and Kingsley.[37] It followed Bentley's edition, which had seen the Australian version heavily revised and bowdlerised in-house, but with the imposition of American spelling and punctuation. Although the two firms had business connections, Clarke knew nothing of Harper's edition until he received payment from them of £15: "Why this curious sum I don't know. I suppose it represents something in dollars – Harper's conscience, perhaps!"[38] But as Lurline Stuart points out, Harper, like Ticknor & Fields with Kingsley, were acting honourably, as well as protecting their edition, forwarding payment to Clarke in a situation where they were under no legal obligation to do so. The book was reviewed favourably in *Harper's Magazine* and the *Boston Review*, the former noting its resemblance to Victor Hugo and concluding that "the skill with which it is wrought out goes far to redeem its repulsive features … While it describes scenes of the most terrible vice and crime, its moral tone is pure".[39]

Like many of his Australian contemporaries, Clarke had a strong interest in American literature, especially Twain, Poe, Hawthorne, Melville and Bret Harte.[40] He sent a copy of the Australian edition of *His Natural Life* to Oliver Wendell Holmes, who replied that "the

---

34 "What Readers Think", *New York Times*, 29 July 1899.
35 Lurline Stuart, introduction to *His Natural Life* by Marcus Clarke (St Lucia: University of Queensland Press, 2001), xxii.
36 Twain quoted in Giles, *Antipodean America*, 256.
37 Stuart, introduction, xlviii–xlix; advertisement, *New York Times*, 26 February 1876. Stuart gives April 1876 as the publication date but the advertisement suggests the book was ready earlier, as part of Harper's winter list. Publishers would, however, advertise books before publication in order to announce their claims to a text as first in the field.
38 Clarke quoted in Stuart, introduction, xlix.
39 "Editor's Literary Record", *Harper's Magazine*, April 1876, 777.
40 Michael Ackland, "Marcus Clarke (1846–1881)", in *Australian Literature, 1788–1914*, ed. Selina Samuels, Dictionary of Literary Biography, Vol. 230 (Detroit, MI: Gale Research, 2001), 91.

colonists and thousands at home in the mother country would find it full of attraction in spite of all its painful revelations".[41] While this response suggests that to an American reader the book's interest appeared primarily English and colonial, *His Natural Life*, following the common pattern, had five more American editions in the 1880s and 1890s, and another in 1911, all based on the earlier Harper edition. Two cheap papercover reprints appeared in 1881, the year of Clarke's death, one in the Lakeside Library of Donnelly, Lloyd & Co. in Chicago, a "double issue" at twenty cents, and the other in Munro's Seaside Library. Further cheap editions followed: in the *New York Tribune's* monthly "Library of Tribune Extras" (1889), and from the Chicago publishers Donohue & Henneberry (c. 1890), E.A. Weeks (1893), no. 8 in its Marguerite Series alongside the ubiquitous Bertha Clay, and dime novel publishers Laird & Lee (1911). Neither Clarke's heirs nor his original publishers would have benefited financially from these editions, although possibly some payment was negotiated in 1896 when Lippincott published Clarke's earlier novel *Long Odds* (1869) with the new title *Heavy Odds*, and again when Harper reissued *His Natural Life* in 1913.

Other minor works with Australian settings or by authors with Australian experience appeared before the end of the century. Edward Maitland, a visitor to Australia in the 1850s, had two novels with Australian settings published in America by Putnam: *By and By: An Historical Romance of the Future* (1873), which envisages a powerful rising Australian nation, and the mystical *The Pilgrim and the Shrine* (1874). English traveller Arthur Louis [Keyser] published *An Exile's Romance or Realities of Australian Life* (Dillingham, 1887), a novel of horses, station life and bushrangers; and an even more obscure visitor, Gilbert Rock, published *The Crime of the Golden Gully: An Australian Romance* (Pollard & Moss, 1889). In 1884, the year of his return to London, editor and literary entrepreneur Douglas Sladen published an Australian novel, *A Summer Christmas*, released in New York by E.P. Dutton, and in 1890 his mammoth anthology, *Australian Poets 1788–1888*, was issued by Cassell's New York branch.[42] Titles released in the 1890s included, among the Australian-born authors, H.C.M. Watson's futuristic vision of *The Decline and Fall of the British Empire* (Minerva, 1890) and Mary Gaunt's *Deadman's* (New Amsterdam Publishing Co., 1899).

Among travellers and immigrants, Hume Nisbet, who spent seven years in the colonies in the 1860s and 1870s, had at least one of his more than forty works of fiction published in New York, a novel with a Pacific setting, *The Divers: A Romance of Oceania* (Macmillan, 1895). Scottish-born "Owen Hall" (Hugh Lusk), who spent several years in Australia before moving to the United States and later New Zealand, had a convict novel, *The Track of a Storm*, published by Lippincott in 1896. Two novels with Australian themes by "Iota" (Kathleen M. Caffyn), Irish-born but resident in Australia from 1880 to 1892, appeared in New York: *A Yellow Aster* (Appleton, 1894), a "new woman" novel set in Australia, and *A Comedy in Spasms* (Frederick A. Stokes, 1895), a novel of emigration. A.J. Dawson spent several years in Australia in the late 1880s and early 1890s before establishing a career as a journalist and novelist in London. The bush plays an inspirational and healing role in a number of his works published in the United States: *Middle Greyness* (John Lane, 1897), *The Story of*

---

41   Holmes quoted in Stuart, introduction, xlix.
42   Full titles: *A Summer Christmas and a Sonnet upon the S.S. "Ballaarat"* (London: Griffith, Farran, Okeden & Welsh; New York: E.P. Dutton, 1884); *Australian Poets 1788–1888: Being a Selection of Poems upon All Subjects Written in Australia and New Zealand during the First Century of the British Colonization* (London: Griffith, Farran, Okeden & Welsh, 1888; New York: Cassell, 1890).

1 Australian Fiction and the American Book Trade in the Nineteenth Century

Ronald Kestrel (Appleton, 1899) and *Daniel Whyte: An Unfinished Biography* (Brentano's, 1900). Further works that appeared in the United States before 1900 by Praed, Louis Becke, Fergus Hume, Guy Boothby and E.W. Hornung will be discussed in later chapters.

Convicts, bushrangers, goldmining and bush life dominated in a range of romance and adventure novels, including M.C. Walsh's story of convicts, gold and bushrangers, *The Golden Idol: A Tale of Adventure in Australia and New Zealand* (Donohue & Henneberry, 1891), John Mackie's *They That Sit in Darkness: A Story of the Australian Never-Never* (Frederick A. Stokes, 1897), Simpson Newland's *Paving the Way: A Romance of the Australian Bush* (Drexel Biddle, 1899), George Cossins' *The Wings of Silence: An Australian Tale* (Drexel Biddle, 1900), Evelyn Dickinson's *Hearts Importunate* (Dodd, Mead, 1900) and Lady Annie Wilson's *Two Summers* (Harper, 1900). All these authors had significant Australian connections, through birth, residency or migration. Popular British authors such as W. Clark Russell, David Christie Murray and Morley Roberts who had visited Australia, often during early travels before their writing careers were established, also published stories of Australian life on sea and in the bush that appeared on both sides of the Atlantic.

The Great Fiction Boom

Although these are scattered and, in some instances, marginal cases, they reveal a pattern of publication in the United States critical to the fortunes of Australian books making their way to America in the late nineteenth century. The volume of traffic to the United States for Australian books doubled each decade from 1870 to 1900. In addition to new titles being picked up, earlier books were recycled, often in multiple editions, as the publishing histories of Kingsley and Clarke indicate. Most, if not all, of these books arrived in America via London, after book publication or serialisation in England. Where agreements between publishers could be made, titles were released more or less simultaneously in the United States and Britain in order to discourage competition in the former and to secure copyright in the latter. The commerce in Australian books was almost entirely a transatlantic rather than a transpacific trade in literary property. Even where authors were Australian-born or long-term residents, their books travelled first and foremost as British books. Certainly they did so as commodities; as *stories*, they might be perceived as Anglo-Australian or antipodean variations within the more familiar British or Anglo-Saxon forms of the novel. Nonetheless, the presence of Australian authors and stories in the American market, especially in the last quarter of the nineteenth century, is clearly more significant than has previously been appreciated.

The growth in the number of Australian titles released in America was part of the general expansion in fiction publishing and sales on both sides of the Atlantic from the 1870s to the 1910s and the frenzied competition for British books in the US market. More specifically, it was a product of the rapid growth of cheap book publishing in the United States in the 1870s and 1880s, "the most flourishing, dynamic, and controversial era of paperbound publishing" in American history.[43] The annual number of new titles and editions in America grew sixfold from 1880 to 1910; as a percentage, fiction peaked

---

43   Tebbel, *History Vol. II*, 482, citing Kurt Enoch. The subtitle for this section comes from John Tebbel, *Between Covers: The Rise and Transformation of Book Publishing in America* (New York: Oxford University Press, 1987), 178.

in the 1890s.[44] A cluster of technological, legal and economic factors came together from the mid-1870s, enabling a boom in cheap editions and paperback series, dominated by imported fiction titles. In the absence of international copyright legislation before 1891, fiction by British (and Australian) authors was available for reprinting in the United States without any legal constraint or obligation to remunerate the authors or original publishers. Nor was this absence a matter of oversight but rather of explicit intent: "the American public domain was nothing less than an aggressively legislated commons, an invitation to piracy that served the interests of domestic publishers, typesetters, printers, binders, and the book-buying public".[45] Established houses such as Ticknor & Fields and Harper, as we have seen, did offer a flat fee, and for the most part had their investments protected in so far as other publishers respected the conventions of trade courtesy. Despite their reputation as profiteering pirates, the main houses usually enjoyed close business and personal relations with British publishers and authors.[46] And Harper's initial opposition to international copyright was at least partly principled: on the one hand, as printers, they sought to protect their business from foreign competition; on the other, they argued the case for the right of the "democratic" American readership to have access to cheap editions of the best British and European books.[47]

Nonetheless, the absence of copyright protection for foreign books meant that the market was always open to less principled operators and could be exploited once other factors such as developments in printing, new distribution arrangements and an expanding market made cheap publishing a profitable enterprise. While the availability of non-copyrighted material underwrote the explosion of new publishers in the 1870s and 1880s, its immediate catalysts were changes in the economies of publishing due to improved printing technologies and distribution that allowed a new business model based on "pirated titles, cheap materials, long press runs, low prices, and nontraditional outlets".[48] The new publishers could also take advantage of postal regulations, distributing their magazine-like publications as second-class mail at a cheaper rate than hardcover books. These "books in disguise"[49] were printed in magazine format, with two or three columns per page and paper covers, the format of the American editions of Clarke's and Farjeon's novels. Indeed, the reprint publishers sought to reproduce the features that had already made newspapers and magazines successful on a mass scale in the American market: regular issues, uniform appearance, numbered series, large print runs, cheap cover price, convenient size, annual subscription and sales at newsstands. By exploiting these methods, reprinting non-copyrighted material without payment, undercutting the

---

44 Michael Winship, "The Rise of a National Book Trade System in the United States", in *A History of the Book in America. Volume 4. Print in Motion: The Expansion of Publishing and Reading in the United States, 1880–1940*, ed. Carl F. Kaestle and Janice A. Radway (Chapel Hill: University of North Carolina Press, 2009), 57, 60-61.
45 Spoo, *Without Copyrights*, 3.
46 West, *American Authors*, 35.
47 Howard C. Horsford, "Harper and Brothers", in *American Literary Publishing Houses, 1638–1899*, ed. Peter Dzwonkoski, Dictionary of Literary Biography, Vol. 49 (Detroit, MI: Gale Research, 1986), 194.
48 West, *American Authors*, 41. See also Tebbel, *History Vol. II*, 482-507; Tebbel, *Between Covers*, 161-66; Sarah Wadsworth, *In the Company of Books: Literature and Its "Classes" in Nineteenth-Century America* (Amherst: University of Massachusetts Press, 2006), 112-33.
49 Robert A. Gross, "Building a National Literature: The United States 1800–1890", in *A Companion to the History of the Book*, ed. Simon Eliot and Jonathan Rose (Malden, MA: Blackwell, 2007), 326.

established trade publishers and ignoring trade courtesy, they could generate large sales and quick profits, not least by reissuing books for which the mainstream publishers had already created a market.

With no copyright protection for foreign books before July 1891, the pirate publishers were not in fact acting illegally; and they could attack trade courtesy "with an evangelical and egalitarian fervor" as undemocratic and anti-competitive.[50] Further, the line between the older established firms and the new cheap reprinters was not always clear-cut, for "reprinting was an enabling condition of much legitimate publishing in the United States", not least for firms such as Harper: "Americans were permitted, even encouraged, to import, reprint, publish, or sell foreign works without the permission of their authors or publishers".[51] Still, for Horace Scudder of Houghton Mifflin, the pirate publishers were guilty: they "steal the work of English authors; they hurt the sale of American authors; they hurt the responsible publisher who pays royalties to English authors; they ruin the reader's eyes with the poor-faced, fine type set in unleaded columns".[52] Typically for Australian writers, an authorised edition issued in London or America was followed by an unauthorised edition and often multiple editions from competing publishers.

The new wave of cheap paperback publishing was epitomised by the launch of George Munro's Seaside Library in May 1877, with a guaranteed seller in Mrs Henry Wood's *East Lynne* as its first number.[53] Seaside Library editions were paper cover quartos, printed in columns, and selling at ten cents a volume. The scale of production by Munro and other reprinters was massive. In its first two years, the Seaside Library distributed five and a half million copies, with many individual titles selling more than 50,000 and average sales of around 10,000 per volume. Almost all were reprints of popular British fiction titles, pirated either directly from British editions or from previous American editions. In the 1880s, a Pocket Edition of the Seaside Library was introduced, with around four thousand titles issued across the two series.[54] Other "libraries" followed. J.W. Lovell launched Lovell's Library in 1882, thereby beginning "an ambitious and unabashed trade as a book pirate, defying the publishing Establishment".[55] The series issued one, then three titles a week, and at times a new title daily, with sales of over seven million volumes a year; by 1890, the firm had published nearly 1500 different titles, literary "classics" as well as popular contemporary fiction, at prices ranging from ten to thirty cents, a little more for those issued in cloth as well.[56] In 1888, Lovell sent a young American, Wolcott Balestier, to London as his agent, offering "substantial payments to English authors for the use of advance sheets of their forthcoming books".[57] By 1890, "there were, perhaps, at any one time, a couple of dozen English novels in process of transmission to New York, sheet by

---

50 Spoo, *Without Copyrights*, 55.
51 Spoo, *Without Copyrights*, 26, 21.
52 Quoted in Charles A. Madison, *Book Publishing in America* (New York: McGraw-Hill, 1966), 53.
53 Tebbel, *History Vol. II*, 489.
54 Wadsworth, *In the Company of Books*, 114.
55 Tebbel, *Between Covers*, 148; *History Vol. II*, 346.
56 David Dzwonkoski, "John W. Lovell Company", in *American Literary Publishing Houses, 1638–1899*, ed. Dzwonkoski, 283.
57 Arthur Waugh, *One Man's Road: Being a Picture of Life in a Passing Generation* (London: Chapman & Hall, 1935), 177-8. Waugh writes that Lovell contracted "to pay sums of £100, or even £150, to £20 or even £10, according to the supposed value of the author in the American market" but payments, due upon publication, were often not delivered (194). The operation folded with Lovell's bankruptcy in early 1893 (210).

sheet", thus enabling more or less simultaneous publication in New York and London. Lovell's brother Frank controlled another publishing company, while George Munro's brother, Norman L. Munro, established his own series – Munro's Library, the Riverside Library, and then the Munro Library – between 1876 and 1884. Other libraries included Donnelly, Lloyd & Co.'s Lakeside Library, Beadle & Adams' Fireside Library and Frank Leslie's Home Library. By 1886, there were twenty-six such libraries.[58]

The result, in Brander Matthews' view, was that "the cheapest books to be bought to-day in the United States are mostly inferior stories by contemporary English novelists":

> The so-called libraries – the Seaside Library, for instance, the Franklin Square Library, and their fellows – contain nearly all the books which are cheap because they are not paid for. I do not mean to suggest that all the books reprinted in all these libraries are pirated; but piracy is the primary cause of their low prices. These libraries are devoted almost wholly to fiction ... nine volumes out of ten are novels [and] fully forty of the fifty-two annual numbers of any one of these libraries must be English novels. Now, there are not forty novels published in Great Britain in any one year which are worth reprinting in the United States ... Yet in one of the cheap libraries, issued three times a week, more than a hundred English novels are now published every year.[59]

But if the cheap libraries released popular sensational fiction, they also published respectable works like the novels of George Eliot, Walter Scott or Victor Hugo, the same works indeed as the mainstream publishers. The difference was in *how* they published and sold them, and the sense of moral and aesthetic "cheapening" their cheapness attracted. Their claims to be bringing the best authors to a broader public were countered by the charge that their indiscriminate practices were degrading literary tastes.[60]

Most established houses chose not to compete, convinced the cheap reprinters would destroy themselves through cost cutting and overproduction, and with the assistance of the Chace Act this is largely what happened. However, Harper and Appleton did launch their own cheap fiction libraries. As the wealthiest of the legitimate publishers and with its own modern printing press, Harper was best positioned to meet the pirate publishers on their own ground.[61] It reduced the price of its popular Library of Select Novels, already full of reprinted English novels, and in 1878 launched the Franklin Square Library in a similar format to Munro's Seaside Library, putting into paperback novels from its own backlist, even at a considerable loss, partly as a response to the fact that they were being reprinted by the pirate publishers in such large numbers it was hurting hardcover sales. Nonetheless, they continued to observe trade courtesy and pay royalties. Harper had been at an advantage in obtaining English books because of its capacity to pay high fees for advance sheets (£600 for a title by Scottish novelist William Black, rather dwarfing Clark's £15). As one newspaper article put it, Harper paid writers

---

58   Tebbel, *History Vol. II*, 486; Wadsworth, *In the Company of Books*, 114. The other quite distinct sector of the cheap paperback publishing industry, the dime novel, published mainly original American texts, especially westerns and thrillers.
59   Brander Matthews, "Cheap Books and Good Books", in *American Literary Publishing Houses, 1638–1899*, ed. Dzwonkoski, 580-81.
60   Wadsworth, *In the Company of Books*, 115-17, 128-30.
61   Madison, *Book Publishing in America*, 54, 64-66.

1 Australian Fiction and the American Book Trade in the Nineteenth Century

"with the promptness and liberality for which their name is a synonym".[62] It could also offer serialisation in its periodicals. As a result, it was often the first house to announce its intention to publish an imported title, and thus it benefited more than most from trade courtesy.

Harper's name gave a certain dignity to the Franklin Square Library and distinguished it from the less reputable reprinters. Among Australian authors, Tasma, Praed and Catherine Martin appeared in the series. Appleton was the second largest American publishing house, and its reputation, similarly, made respectable its Town and Country Library, launched in 1888 with new titles issued twice monthly at the slightly upmarket price of fifty cents in paper and a dollar in hardcover.[63] It could call on the "timeless" character of its editions as compared to the disposability of its rivals' productions (even as the mainstream publishers began "raiding the lists of the cheap libraries for new titles").[64] Both Harper's and Appleton's series survived into the 1890s, outliving most of the cheaper libraries.

By the late 1880s, the pirate industry was already in decline. The store of non-copyrighted materials had virtually been exhausted, the profit from cheap books was declining, and the number of publishers was increasing. Although cheap series continued into the early years of the new century, the passing of the International Copyright Act was the final nail in the coffin. In 1893, there were fifty publishers issuing paperback fiction and ninety-four series, but by 1910 there were only three publishers and nine series. Competing in the field of copyrighted American authors and, after 1891, copyrighted foreign authors, the paperback publishers had no advantage over the mainstream firms. By 1888, Munro himself was demanding a copyright bill, and Harper swung around to support legislation as a means of protecting its investment in foreign titles. Towards the end of the century, other mainstream publishers such as Ticknor & Fields, Scribner and Houghton Mifflin began to produce better quality paperbacks and cheaper clothbound books themselves. In the 1900s, reprints were largely in the hands of two newer, legitimate operators, A.L. Burt and Grosset & Dunlap, specialising in hardcover reissues made under licence from the mainstream houses.[65]

For the period 1875 to 1900, the main US publishers of Australian fiction were, in order, Appleton, Harper, Macmillan, Munro, Lippincott and Lovell. While they were active, the fiction libraries gathered in a significant number of Australian titles such that more than half of the Australian novels published in the United States in the 1880s and 1890s were issued by Munro, Lovell and similar houses or in the Harper and Appleton libraries. Despite the high numbers of new fiction titles and their often cheap formats, such books could help build a serious reputation. They were reviewed in both metropolitan and regional papers and the "news" they created was further circulated in literary columns that kept authors' names before the reading public. As Sarah Wadsworth argues, newspaper reviews were crucial in producing the sense of a nationwide audience for fiction in the United States.[66] As a result, they were also critical in creating among American readers and reviewers the sense of a distinctive antipodean literature.

---

62 "Two London Literary Women", *Daily Yellowstone Journal* (Montana), 17 March 1889. The article, reprinted from the *Pittsburgh Chronicle*, discusses Rosa Praed and Mrs Cashel Hoey.
63 George E. Tylutki, "D. Appleton and Company", in *American Literary Publishing Houses, 1638–1899*, ed. Dzwonkoski, 26. Henry Holt & Co. also launched the Leisure Moment Library, a cheaper companion to its Leisure Hour Library: Wadsworth, *In the Company of Books*, 125.
64 Wadsworth, *In the Company of Books*, 131.
65 Tebbel, *History Vol.II*, 487-88, 506-10.
66 Wadsworth, *In the Company of Books*, 132.

Ada Cambridge in America

Ada Cambridge is one of the most significant cases from the nineteenth century of a transnational literary career conducted largely from an Australian base, and her publishing history reveals a characteristic pattern for those writing from the colonies. The bulk of her novels were first serialised in the Australian press, then published in two or three volumes in London for the circulating libraries. Those that proved popular would then be released in a cheaper one-volume format and/or a special colonial edition.[67] Her American publishing history also followed characteristic patterns, with the appearance of multiple cheap editions of her most popular novels in the 1880s and 1890s. Less common was her sustained relationship with a single publisher, the house of Appleton, from 1881.

Cambridge's first novel to be published in the United States was *My Guardian*, issued by Appleton in 1879 in its Library of Choice Novels.[68] No doubt that brought it to the attention of George Munro, who published it in both the Seaside Library and Seaside Library Pocket Editions in the same year. It was reissued by Appleton in 1892, this time, more significantly, in a sequence of ten novels published between 1891 and 1901 in its Town and Country Library: *The Three Miss Kings: An Australian Story* (no. 75, 1891, the subtitle added for the American edition), *Not All in Vain* (no. 87, 1892), *My Guardian* (no. 89, 1892), *A Little Minx: A Sketch* (no. 114, 1893), *A Marriage Ceremony* (no. 133, 1894), *Fidelis* (no. 167, 1895), *A Humble Enterprise* (no. 196, 1896), *Materfamilias* (no. 242, 1898), *Path and Goal* (no. 293, 1900) and *The Devastators* (no. 304, 1901).[69] The Town and County Library was the most prestigious of all the fiction series, known for "the discrimination used in selecting tales that are clean, pure, and withal of interest to the average reader's intelligence".[70] A notice in the *Los Angeles Herald* on the appearance of *A Humble Enterprise* remarked that the novel was "sure to be welcomed as one of the ever welcome monthly visitors to so many households".[71] On the occasion of the three hundredth number in the series, announced in August 1901, Cambridge was mentioned among the important authors introduced to American readers by "the best library of fiction ever undertaken in America".[72]

The pirate publishers were no less active. Munro issued *The Three Miss Kings* in 1891, 1895 and 1898, plus two novels Appleton did not publish: *A Mere Chance* in 1882 and *A Marked Man* in 1890. *The Three Miss Kings* also appeared in two other New York fiction libraries in 1892, from F.M. Lupton Publishing Co. and M.J. Ivers & Co., in its American Series at twenty-five cents. Lovell released *A Marked Man: Some Episodes in His Life* in 1890 as no. 113 in his International Series of Modern Novels, an authorised edition

---

67 Elaine Zinkhan, "Ada Cambridge: *A Marked Man*, the *Manchester Weekly Times Supplement*, and Late-Nineteenth Century Fiction Publication", *Bibliographical Society of Australia and New Zealand Bulletin* 17, no. 4 (1993): 165–66; Elizabeth Morrison, introduction to *A Black Sheep: Some Episodes in His Life*, by Ada Cambridge, Colonial Texts Series (Canberra: Australian Scholarly Editions Centre, 2004), xxvi–xxxix.
68 First published in London by Cassell, Petter, Galpin & Co. in 1878 (but with New York also listed under the firm's name).
69 Elaine Zinkhan, "Ada Cambridge, 'A.C.' Later Mrs George Frederick Cross 1844–1926", in *The Cambridge Bibliography of English Literature: Volume 4, 1800–1900*, ed. Joanne Shattock (Cambridge: Cambridge University Press, 2000), 1481–83.
70 Quotation from the *New York Mail and Express* printed at the back of Appleton's edition of Rosa Praed's *Nùlma* (1897).
71 *Los Angeles Herald*, 19 July 1896.
72 *San Francisco Call*, 18 August 1901.

reset from advance proofs obtained from Heinemann through Balestier, Lovell's agent in London. The novel was reissued in 1890 by Lovell, Coryell & Co., and later advertised by the United States Book Co.[73] Most likely through agreements with Appleton, A.L. Burt released editions of *My Guardian*, *The Three Miss Kings* and *A Humble Enterprise* between 1905 and 1907 in its Cornell and Ivy series of hardcover reprints.

Most publishing of Australian books was opportunistic, feeding the appetite of the cheap paperback market for regular new titles. But Appleton's commitment to Cambridge represents something rarer, an ongoing investment in the author, even if this was in their cheaper series and at the cost of only modest advances. No doubt it was assisted by Appleton having a London-based representative who could negotiate directly with English publishers. From 1891, its editions were published simultaneously with or in some instances prior to the English editions; and being "electrotyped and printed at the Appleton Press, USA", they could be copyrighted in America.[74]

Cambridge's largest advance from Appleton was the earliest on record, £100 in March 1893 for *A Little Minx*, which had not yet been published in London and could therefore be copyrighted. Appleton reckoned the £100 advance equivalent to US$488.89.[75] The contract gave the firm "sole and exclusive rights to publish in the United States of America and the Dominion of Canada". Later, in October of the same year, it offered a £50 advance for *A Marriage Ceremony* and two years later £75 for *Fidelis*, for the same rights. The lower royalties were perhaps because *A Little Minx* had not earned out its advance despite selling more than 8000 copies from an initial printing of 9000. *A Marriage Ceremony* also sold around 8000 copies, and by October 1894, with its lower advance, Cambridge was $156.11 in credit.[76] Appleton printed 12,000 copies of *Fidelis* the following year, indicating a certain confidence in Cambridge's earning capacity even while their advances settled at £50 for *Materfamilias* in 1898, and for *Path and Glory* and *The Devastators*, both contracted in 1901 for United States book rights only. The contract specified that Appleton "shall take all necessary steps properly to secure the American copyright".[77] If these advances were much less than Harper's payments for the most prized English novelists, they were standard amounts for the period and in the same range as those paid by Cambridge's English publishers. Hutchinson, for example, offered £60 for *A Marriage Ceremony* and *Fidelis* for the right to publish in Great Britain, its colonies and dependencies, except Canada.[78] The royalty terms offered were also comparable: from Appleton, 10 per cent on copies sold at the standard price of $1.00 or $1.25, and from Hutchinson 10 per cent on the full-priced and cheap editions, threepence per copy on colonial editions.[79]

---

73 Zinkhan, "Ada Cambridge", 178. Morrison, introduction, xxxvii.
74 Statement printed in Appleton's edition of *The Little Minx*. The one-volume London edition of *Not All in Vain* was printed from Appleton's plates: Zinkhan, "Ada Cambridge", *Cambridge Bibliography*, 1482.
75 Appleton Statement of Earnings, 1 October 1894, A.P. Watt Records, 1888-1982, University of North Carolina, Collection 11036, Series 1: Private Account Files, 1880-1985 (Box 7).
76 Watt Records: Memorandum of Agreement, *A Marriage Ceremony*, 10 October 1893 and Statement of Earnings, 1 October 1894 (Box 8); Agreement, *Fidelis*, 10 January 1895 and Statement, 1 February 1896 (Box 13). Contract information also from Margaret Bradstock and Louise Wakeling, *Rattling the Orthodoxies: A Life of Ada Cambridge* (Ringwood, Vic.: Penguin, 1991), 251-62.
77 Agreement for *The Devastators*, 8 February 1901, Watt Records (Box 36); *Path and Goal*, 7 February 1901 (Box 32).
78 Canada remained a source of contention well into the twentieth century, with British publishers claiming it as one of their traditional markets and Americans claiming they were best positioned to make sales into Canada.
79 Bradstock and Wakeling, *Rattling the Orthodoxies*, 251-53.

The key factor in Cambridge's American success was almost certainly her relationship with London-based literary agent A.P. Watt, and in this her career signals another feature shared by many Australian authors seeking publication in the United States: the critical role played by agents in negotiating the passage of works across different markets and copyright territories. Watt began advertising as a literary agent in 1881 and is generally credited as the first to undertake such services systematically and professionally. By the 1890s, he was conducting business widely for authors, publishers and periodicals across the Anglophone world, selling fiction, for example, to McClure's Associated Literary Press Syndicate in America and to Australian periodicals such as the *Australasian*, a frequent place of first publication for Cambridge.[80] By the turn of the century, his list included the Australasian authors Louis Becke, Guy Boothby, Rolf Boldrewood, Mary Gaunt, Fergus Hume, G.B. Lancaster and Ethel Turner alongside the most esteemed and popular English writers of the day. All those named achieved multiple American editions.

Watt was joined in London by J.B Pinker and Curtis Brown (himself an American). Critical in the rise of the literary agent was the increased understanding among authors and publishers of "literary property" and the associated understanding that the sale or licensing of rights was as significant a source of income as direct book sales. The practice of authors selling their rights for a one-off payment rapidly diminished from the 1890s in favour of remuneration via royalties on copies sold: the author in effect leasing rather than selling his or her copyright to the publisher outright. Agents became crucial figures in negotiating royalty rates and advances against royalties, and in negotiating the sale of foreign rights, especially American after the passing of the Chace Act. Cambridge saw herself as "almost the first author to benefit" from the new US copyright regime.[81] Authors and agents increasingly sought to separate American from British and colonial rights, for example, and to retain dramatisation, serialisation and translation rights, as Cambridge did on most contracts, making the agent an essential intermediary between author and publisher.

In 1924, Cambridge wrote of her relation to Watt, "I had nothing to bother about – only to send home MSS. as fast as I could write them, sign agreements & bank the money – & had a faithful friend in A.P.W. for many years".[82] She formally appointed Watt her agent in October 1892, more than likely because of the new possibilities in the American market created by the Chace Act. Although discouraged from signing with Watt by her publisher, William Heinemann, among the most hostile of publishers towards the new "parasites", Cambridge clearly benefited from the arrangement.[83] This is indicated by the exclusion of US and Canadian book rights from her English contracts, the regular pattern of her agreements with Appleton, and the simultaneous publication of her novels in Britain and the United States. This logistically challenging practice was demanded by the Chace Act, which specified that in order to receive copyright protection in the United States a foreign

---

80 Elaine Zinkhan, "Early British Publication of *While the Billy Boils*: The A.P. Watt Connection", *Bibliographical Society of Australia and New Zealand Bulletin* 21, no. 3 (1997): 165–66.
81 Cambridge quoted in Morrison, introduction, xli. See also Mary Ann Gillies, "A.P. Watt, Literary Agent", *Publishing Research Quarterly* 9, no. 1 (Spring 1993): 21, and Linda Marie Fritschner, "Literary Agents and Literary Traditions: The Role of the Philistine", in *Paying the Piper: Causes and Consequences of Art Patronage*, ed. Judith Huggins Balfe (Urbana: University of Illinois Press, 1993), 54–72.
82 Quoted in Zinkhan, "Early British Publication", 167.
83 On Heinemann, see Gillies, "A.P. Watt", 25, citing Heinemann's "The Middleman as Viewed by a Publisher", *Athenaeum*, 11 November 1893.

book had to be published in America on or before the date of its publication overseas and manufactured in the United States.[84]

Watt also negotiated serialisation and the placement and copyrighting of stories in American magazines. In October 1900, an associate in New York wrote to Watt that he had sold Cambridge's story "The Third Officer and a Girl" to the *New York Press* at $7.50 per thousand words, adding, "As this writer is not very well known, I thought it best to accept this figure".[85] If Cambridge was not well known as a magazine writer, she had already built a reputation as a novelist. Only two months earlier, the *New York Times* had remarked that she stood "near the head of Australian popular writers", while Appleton's publicity from the same period claimed that with the publication of *The Three Miss Kings* a decade earlier, "Ada Cambridge gained at once a place in the affection of American readers, which she has maintained".[86]

The Three Miss Kings, in particular, appears to have "achieved considerable success", as the *New York Times* commented.[87] Its earlier review had found it "a good, honest story, and by changing localities it might be all true as the history of three Kansas or Montana girls".[88] The *Boston Times* went further, proclaiming it an "exceedingly strong novel … an Australian story, teeming with a certain calmness of emotional power that finds expression in a continual outflow of living thought and feeling".[89] When *Path and Goal* appeared in late 1900, the *Times* (Richmond, VA) could write simply that "the author's name is a sufficient guarantee of excellence".[90]

Much later in her career, Cambridge wrote that the London publication of *A Marked Man* in 1890 had "at once established me as a British author, so that I was no longer an Australian one in the press sense".[91] But as her American publishing history reveals, being taken up in London also meant access to "a network of domestic and international outlets, [to] plural publication and wide geographical distribution". If Cambridge became "a British author writing for international consumption", this development also enabled her to build an American reputation.[92] Her Australian settings and "local color" were noted in American reviews, but more in passing than as of primary interest. Her literary merit, however, was frequently acknowledged, even as she was appreciated as a writer of "charming", "delightful"

---

84 More specifically, the Act's "manufacturing clause" required an edition printed from type set or plates made in the United States to be deposited in Washington "on or before the day of publication in this or any foreign country". Simon Nowell-Smith, *International Copyright Law and the Publisher in the Reign of Queen Victoria* (Oxford: Clarendon Press, 1968), 65.

85 Vallentine to Watt, 19 October 1900. Watt Records (Box 38). The story appeared in the *New York Press*, 25 November 1900.

86 "Notes and News", *New York Times*, 18 August 1900. Advertisement for *Path and Goal*, *New York Times*, 27 October 1900. From 1909 to 1922 Cambridge also published essays in the *Atlantic Monthly* and the *North American Review*. Zinkhan, "Ada Cambridge", *Cambridge Bibliography*, 1484–85.

87 "Notes and News". Appleton's publicity claimed the novel had received "the unsolicited approval of numerous critics", *New York Tribune*, 4 February 1892. AustLit (www.austlit.edu.au) and WorldCat (www.worldcat.org) suggest multiple reissues of *The Three Miss Kings* by Appleton between 1893 and 1900.

88 *New York Times*, 30 August 1891.

89 Quoted in Appleton's edition of *Path and Goal*.

90 *Times* (Richmond, VA), 2 December 1900.

91 Cambridge quoted in Morrison, introduction, xl.

92 Morrison, introduction, xl, xlvii.

and "entertaining" stories. Whether this was high or faint praise depended on the reviewer's disposition, especially towards romance.

On its reissue in 1892, the *Chicago Evening Journal* found *My Guardian* "all that the most ardent romance-reader could desire".[93] Others praised more substantial qualities. Appreciation of Cambridge's method was perhaps strongest in a review of *Fidelis* in the influential weekly *Nation* in October 1895:

> Here is no fine, old-fashioned writing, no plodding or tarrying. Though full of detail, it speeds along without haste, without rest, till the tale is told ... It is the humor of Thackeray and of Du Maurier, and their prodigious, unsentimental sentiment ... The original flavour of Ada Cambridge is not lost but enriched by being engrafted on a sturdy stock. Her pictures of Australia and of rural England are as attractive as ever, her story better than ever. In "Fidelis" she has not only advanced beyond herself, but has written one of the best little novels of the year.[94]

Praise enough to sustain a reputation, although the use of "little" in the final sentence suggests a scaling down from full literary recognition. The hierarchies of critical evaluation remained very fluid, especially in the press, where reviewing seldom carried the full weight of criticism; words such as "entertaining" or "charming" did not have the negative sense they would have for many twentieth-century critics. Still, Cambridge's reputation would be circumscribed as much as bolstered by such praise as the *Saint Paul Daily Globe* offered: "In 'Fidelis' Ada Cambridge tells a very entertaining story of American and English life, in which she fully sustains her reputation as a charming story teller".[95] For the *New York Tribune*, announcing the appearance of *Materfamilias* in 1898, Cambridge was the author of "several clever minor novels".[96]

No new titles appeared after 1901, although five were published in London between 1904 and 1914. In the new century, as the claims of realism progressed, Cambridge was in danger of being seen only as a writer of "light novels".[97] After *The Three Miss Kings*, *Materfamilias* attracted most attention, although assessments were mixed. For the *Los Angeles Herald*, it was "purely entertaining" without demanding "higher recognition", while the *New York Times* praised the author precisely for turning her back on the contemporary fashion for "repellent" realism.[98] For the *Saint Paul Daily Globe*, *Materfamilias* was "quite above [Cambridge's] usual level ... and that is saying something considerable, for this abundant writer has done some quite good things now and then"; and yet, it was "not exceptional in any way". "The story is laid in Australia, but is essentially English in character, and is unquestionably written for a British public and has in view as probably [sic] readers all the wholesome young English girls of the wholesome middle-class families".[99]

---

93 Reproduced in a list of Cambridge's novels accompanied by quotations from reviews in Appleton's edition of her *Materfamilias*.
94 "Recent Novels", *Nation*, 3 October 1895, 243.
95 *Saint Paul Daily Globe*, 1 July 1895.
96 *New York Tribune*, 25 March 1898.
97 Review of *The Devastators*, *Houston Daily Post*, 13 October 1901.
98 *Los Angeles Herald*, 3 July 1898.
99 *Saint Paul Daily Globe*, 14 August 1898.

Cambridge is unusual among nineteenth-century Australian authors in America in that little is made of her Australian settings and characters, not much more than Appleton's claim for *Materfamilias* that her "intimate acquaintance with antipodean scenes and happenings is shown in her adroit use of local color".[100] Her romance plots were more generally taken as "essentially English". Perhaps most telling is that the *Daily Globe* reviewer is left wanting more – something more Australian.

The Australian *Mise en Couleur*: Catherine Martin and Tasma

The American careers of Catherine Martin, "Tasma" (Jessie Couvreur) and Rolf Boldrewood underscore the dynamics of transatlantic publication for Australian authors revealed in the case of Ada Cambridge. Only one of Catherine Martin's four novels was published in America. In 1892, *The Silent Sea* joined Tasma's *In Her Earliest Youth* and Praed's *The Rebel Rose* in Harper's Franklin Square Library, no. 728 in this enormously successful series. The novel first appeared in September 1892 in London, published by Richard Bentley & Son in the traditional three volumes at the same time as it was being serialised in Australia. Around this time Bentley also purchased from Martin, for £10, her half-share in the American rights to the novel, which she had originally retained.[101] Harper then purchased the rights from Bentley for £20 and published their edition a month after Bentley's, reset with American spelling and punctuation styles and other minor editorial changes. Rand McNally of Chicago also expressed interest in publishing the novel but apparently declined Bentley's request for $50 as a nominal payment for "the author's rights". Expressing the common view of English publishers, George Bentley replied to Rand McNally that "of course if you feel free to disregard the moral rights of people you can remit the book without any acknowledgement whatsoever, owing to the action of the United States Government in standing aloof from the Convention of Berne, (by which protection is accorded to literary property irrespective of Nationality)".[102]

Less than 450 copies of Bentley's edition were sold, although many more Australian readers would have been familiar with the novel through its serialisations. It is very likely, therefore, that with the imprimatur of the Franklin Square Library, *The Silent Sea* enjoyed its highest sales in the American market, but with no profit to Martin herself beyond the one-off sale of her rights. There is no evidence as to why Harper selected this particular novel from the season's offerings. While it has a love triangle and is in part "a thriller of considerable psychological plausibility", the novel is also markedly local, set in middle-class Adelaide, South Australian pastoral districts, and an outback goldmine. On the one hand, as suggested earlier, stories set in colonial, frontier or antipodean locales were already familiar within the broad genre of contemporary romance. Colonial romance was not a "local" genre, but one that travelled across Anglophone fiction markets. The

---

100 Advertisement, *San Francisco Call*, 9 June 1898.
101 Publishing information in this paragraph derived from Rosemary Foxton's introduction to the Colonial Texts Series edition of *The Silent Sea* (Sydney: UNSW Press, 1995), xv–xli. Both editions were published pseudonymously as by "Mrs. Alick Macleod" (Foxton, xxvi). See also Rosemary Foxton, "'Another Fresh Australian Tale': The American Publication of Catherine Martin's *The Silent Sea*", *Australian Literary Studies* 15, no. 4 (October 1992): 351–54.
102 Bentley, quoted in Foxton, introduction, xxvi. Bentley's letter to Rand McNally, 23 December 1892: British Library, Bentley Publishers archive, BL Add MSS 46646, f.72 (vol. 87).

novel was reviewed in Boston's *Literary World*, the reviewer noting that the "scene is laid in the Australian gold region, and the author has well availed herself of the opportunities for local color and romance".[103] On the other hand, it remains unclear whether setting or subject matter played any part in Harper's choice. Bentley had published Martin's *The Australian Girl* in 1890 with moderate success, and publication by Bentley would have been a recommendation in itself for *The Silent Sea*.[104] But there is a fascinating clue, perhaps, for Martin and other Australian authors, in a brief notice in the publisher's own periodical, *Harper's New Monthly Magazine*. The reviewer, Laurence Hutton, praised *The Silent Sea* as "another of the fresh, bright Australian tales which come like the breath of a west wind into the somewhat unaired spaces of English fiction".[105] Whether or not he had read the novel – Martin's scholarly editor doubts it – this comment, while clichéd, does suggest a space within the transatlantic fiction market where Australian stories might be identified as more or less distinctive and perhaps as more congenial to American readers than some of their English contemporaries.

In contrast to Martin's limited American exposure, all seven of Tasma's books were published in the United States, six novels and a collection of stories. Perhaps this is not surprising, for in the last two decades of the nineteenth century Tasma was "a famous woman", as her biographer puts it, not only in Britain but in France, in Belgium, where she spent most of her time after 1880, and to some extent at least in the United States. *Uncle Piper of Piper's Hill* was "the book of the season" when it was published in London for Christmas 1888, and it was reported to have been "a great success" in New York.[106] Reviews support this assessment, whether in Sacramento – "an admirably constructed romance, one, indeed, of exceedingly strong and well-sustained interest" – or for jaded reviewers in New York: "it has a fine and dainty literary quality that endears its unknown author to the much-enduring professional 'taster'".[107]

Tasma's publishing career in America was another product of the paperback revolution and its striking effects on mainstream publishing. After serialisation in the *Australasian* from January to May 1888, *Uncle Piper of Piper's Hill: An Australian Novel* was published by Trübner & Co. in London later that year.[108] Seven hundred and fifty copies were printed, quickly followed by a second edition of 500; these small numbers were typical of print runs in the British trade at this time.[109] The spectacular effects of the American marketplace, by comparison, can be seen in the fact that four separate US editions of the novel appeared in 1889 alone: in Lovell's International series (no. 33), Munro's Seaside Library (no. 1217), Harper's Franklin Square Library (no. 652) and Frank F. Lovell's cloth-covered Aldine series. Although Munro and the Lovells are most frequently identified as pirate publishers, the books reprinted in Lovell's International series, mainly British novels, were announced as authorised editions, "published by special arrangements of the company with the authors".[110]

---

103 *Literary World*, 28 January 1893, 26. Cited in Foxton, "'Another Fresh Australian Tale'", 353.
104 *The Australian Girl* sold 518 copies in three volumes, enough to justify a one-volume edition in 1891 which sold 1483 copies and an "Australian edition" which sold 869 copies. Rosemary Campbell, "Catherine Martin (ca. 1847–1937)", in *Australian Literature, 1788–1914*, ed. Samuels, 258.
105 *Harper's New Monthly Magazine*, February 1893, Supplement, 4. Foxton, introduction, xxix.
106 Patricia Clarke, *Tasma: The Life of Jessie Couvreur* (St Leonards, NSW: Allen & Unwin, 1994), xi.
107 *Sacramento Daily Record-Union*, 17 August 1897; *Harper's New Monthly Magazine*, November 1889, 4.
108 Published late 1888 although dated 1889: Clarke, *Tasma*, 114.
109 Clarke, *Tasma*, 117.
110 *San Francisco Call*, 26 October 1890.

1 Australian Fiction and the American Book Trade in the Nineteenth Century

As Tebbel remarks, "Unlike most of the other pirates, Lovell offered the British authors good money for the use of their plates, but his purpose was not a moral one; it was simply a way by which he could anticipate his fellow pirates".[111] It appears Tasma herself did not profit from Lovell's edition. While accepting praise from an American reader, she remarked: "But how little *material* benefit I have reaped from my work despite the fact that the Americans have issued four different editions of it".[112]

Tasma's later American publications show the infectious spread of Lovell's influence across the whole fiction industry. More or less simultaneously with their English editions, *A Sydney Sovereign and Other Tales* appeared in the International series, probably in 1889, and as an Aldine hardcover in 1890; *In Her Earliest Youth* was released in the International series in 1890, as well as by Harper in the Franklin Square Library in the same year; and in 1891, *The Penance of Portia James* appeared both in the International series and with a cloth cover under the new imprint of the United States Book Co.[113] Unlike the earlier books, this last carried a copyright message.[114] In "one of the most amazing and significant events in the annals of American publishing", Lovell had launched the United States Book Co. in 1890 with the aim of bringing all the cheap reprint publishers into a single organisation to control the problem of price-cutting. Lovell began by purchasing or leasing the plates owned by his competitors until he controlled more than three-quarters of the paperback field, and then flooded the market "with the widest range of 'series' the publishing industry had ever seen".[115] New subsidiaries were formed, including Lovell, Coryell & Co., which published Tasma's next novel *The White Feather* in 1891 (its first edition). The United States Book Co. folded in 1893, as competing series continued to multiply despite Lovell's strategies.

The books themselves suggest how they circulated beyond the city bookstores, as commodities among other general merchandise on newsstands, railway kiosks and in drygoods stores.[116] The Aldine editions carry advertisements for Singer sewing machines (Fig. 1.2), while the National Library of Australia copy of *A Sydney Sovereign* is stamped: "Chas E. Hughes / General Merchandise / Boschee's German Syrup / Green's August Flower / Warren, VA". Munro's Seaside Library Pocket edition of *A Sydney Sovereign* (Plate 1), also released in 1890, carries advertisements for Beecham's Pills, Athlophoros Extract and the Hospital Remedy Co.

After this remarkable initial burst of publishing activity – five novels in ten separate editions between 1889 and 1891 – two later works appeared, after the passage of the Chace Act. They followed the same, more mainstream course as Cambridge's novels, with London editions from Bentley and near-simultaneous New York editions in Appleton's Town and Country Library: *Not Counting the Cost* in 1895 (no. 175) and *A Fiery Ordeal*, posthumously, in 1898 (no. 233). For both, the author received a £30 advance against royalties of 15 per cent on the nominal selling price of one dollar. Tasma was also with A.P. Watt, and American rights were specifically excluded from her agreements with Bentley.[117]

In the decade from late 1889, seven of Tasma's books had been issued in America in twelve separate editions. In addition, she had a story reprinted in the *Living Age*, and

---

111 Tebbel, *History Vol. II*, 347.
112 Clarke, *Tasma*, 121. The sentence is from Couvreur's diary, 1 January 1890.
113 Nos 55 and 66 respectively in the International series.
114 "Copyright 1891 by United States Book Company. All Rights Reserved."
115 Tebbel, *History Vol. II*, 348–50.
116 Wadsworth, *In the Company of Books*, 112.
117 Agreement, *Not Counting the Cost*, 22 March 1895, Watt Records (Box 13); *A Fiery Ordeal*, 8 September 1897, Watt Records (Box 22).

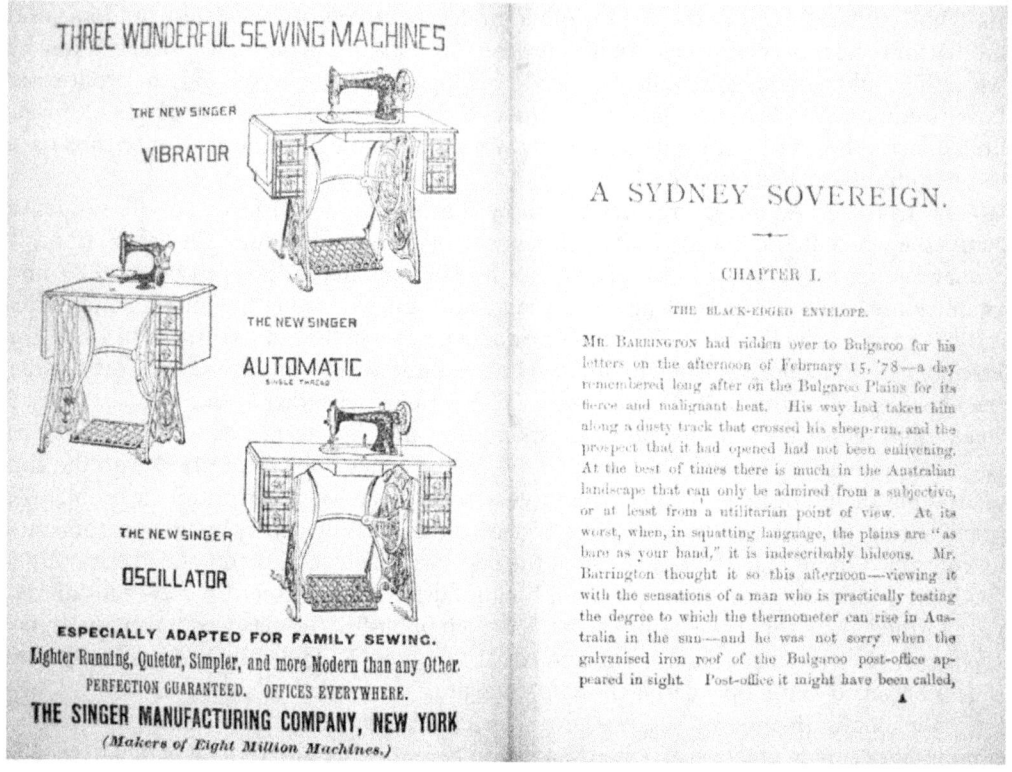

Figure 1.2 Tasma, *A Sydney Sovereign and Other Tales*, Aldine edition (New York: Frank F. Lovell & Co., 1890).

had contributed to a multi-authored novel, *The Fate of Fenella*, published in 1892 in New York by Cassell, in the company of Arthur Conan Doyle, Frances Trollope and Bram Stoker.[118] While she was unable to profit directly from the cheap fiction libraries, the flurry of activity in the early 1890s had established her not only as a popular novelist but as a writer of some literary standing. By 1895, Appleton could claim that the "literary value of her work has been abundantly recognized", and in the conventional manner for drawing attention to popular and literary success, it described her on its title pages as the "Author of *Not Counting the Cost, A Knight of the White Feather, Uncle Piper of Piper's Hill*, ETC".[119] Reviewing *Not Counting the Cost*, the *New York Times* noted that "the ability of Tasma is unquestioned", although in this case it was "a power without co-ordination".[120] After her early death in October 1897, she was remembered - in Nebraska - as having been "the best living delineator of life at the antipodes".[121]

---

118 "Iftar in a Harem", *Living Age*, 29 August 1891, 570; reprinted from *Temple Bar*. Advertisement, *Scribner's Magazine* 12, no. 6 (December 1892): 17.
119 Advertisement for *Not Counting the Cost*, *New York Times*, 17 August 1895. *A Knight of the White Feather* was the English title of *The White Feather*, suggesting that Tasma's relationship with Appleton was through London.
120 "An Exuberant Writer Wanting System", *New York Times*, 1 September 1895.
121 *Valentine Democrat* (Valentine, NE), 17 February 1898.

1 Australian Fiction and the American Book Trade in the Nineteenth Century

The Australian settings and themes of much of Tasma's work were a point of interest for reviewers and publicists. An early review of *Uncle Piper* from Harper's own magazine begins, "No doubt there is a profound significance in the fact that one of the best novels of the year comes to us from Australia".[122] Frustratingly, this is just a journalistic tease, for the point is that readers need not trouble themselves with such things but can simply enjoy the novel's "fine and dainty literary quality". Still, Australian novels were in the news, and the Australian cliché was already to hand, even for this largely urban novel: "The book is fresh and bright as the Australian spring". Appleton's publicity drew attention to the way *A Fiery Ordeal* "utilized certain dramatic possibilities of the life of the antipodes", while the *New York Times* reviewer concluded that the story "has the Australian *mise en couleur*."[123] The definite article again indicates a recognisable Australian "coloration" in the fiction marketplace.

Rolf Boldrewood and Transatlantic Publishing

Unusually, Rolf Boldrewood's American career owed nothing to the paperback revolution and the cheap libraries, although doubtless it owed something to "the literary mania which swept America at the turn of the nineteenth century".[124] Boldrewood's appearance in the American market was due rather to his publishing arrangements with Macmillan in London and the fact that the firm had a New York agency, established in 1869 and operating as a separate American company from 1896. As there was no market for triple-deckers in America, a common practice was for the later single-volume edition of Macmillan novels to be distributed in the United States by the New York branch. This was probably what occurred for Boldrewood's books until his last three-volume novel in 1894, although in the case of his most famous work, *Robbery Under Arms*, where the three-volume edition had originally been issued by another publisher, it was the revised Macmillan edition of 1889, in one volume, that found its way to America – just in time to catch the rising tide of romance. By this time the American branch was increasingly interested in becoming a publisher in its own right, not simply a distributor for the firm's London products. In 1891, the New York agency became an independent operation, and in 1896 it was incorporated as The Macmillan Company; the London firm became Macmillan and Company Limited.[125]

These shifting arrangements make it difficult to say which of Boldrewood's books should be identified as American editions in the strictest sense of the term, a difficulty compounded by the fact that both places of publication appeared on the title pages of Macmillan's books, all of which until 1896 bore the colophon: "London / Macmillan and Co. / and New York".[126] *Robbery Under Arms: A Story of Life and Adventure in the Bush and in the Goldfields of Australia* was certainly distributed in America, being noted in *Nation*'s "Books of the Week" in June 1889, soon after its London release, and reviewed the

---

122 "Literary Notes", *Harper's New Monthly Magazine*, November 1889, 4.
123 "An Australian Story", *New York Times*, 12 March 1898.
124 Elizabeth James, "Letters from America: The Bretts and the Macmillan Company of New York", in *Macmillan: A Publishing Tradition*, ed. Elizabeth James (Basingstoke, UK: Palgrave, 2002), 177.
125 James, "Letters", 176.
126 From 1896, Macmillan's colophon recognises the two separate companies: London / Macmillan and Co. Ltd / New York: The Macmillan Co.

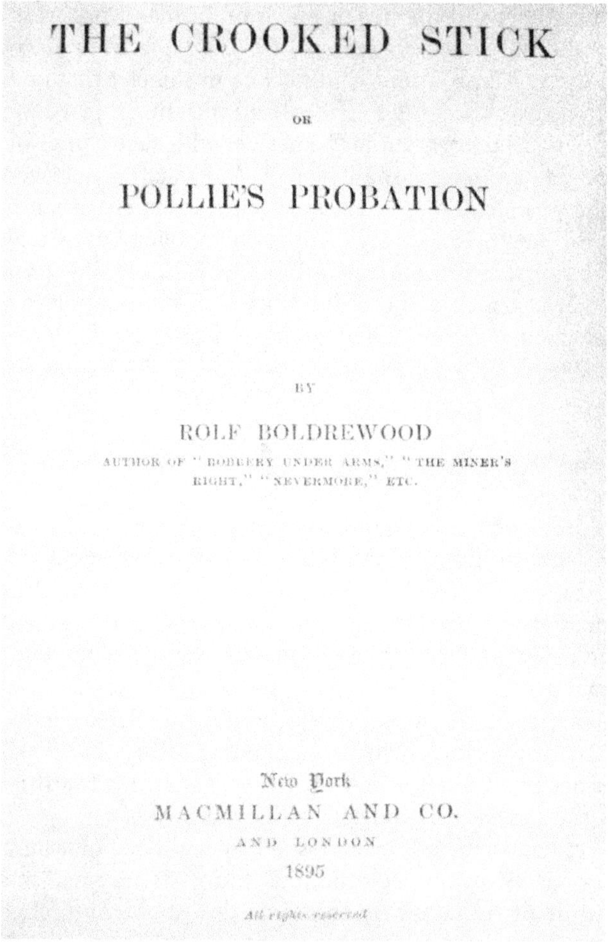

THE CROOKED STICK

OR

POLLIE'S PROBATION

BY

ROLF BOLDREWOOD

AUTHOR OF "ROBBERY UNDER ARMS," "THE MINER'S RIGHT," "NEVERMORE," ETC.

New York

MACMILLAN AND CO.

AND LONDON

1895

All rights reserved

Figure 1.3 Rolf Boldrewood, *The Crooked Stick or Pollie's Probation* (New York: Macmillan & Co., 1895).

following month in the *New York Times*, where the book's publishing details were recorded as "New York: Macmillan & Co".[127] It was also held by the Boston Library Society.[128] The majority of Boldrewood's titles were probably handled in a similar manner: distributed by Macmillan New York as their own books, even when materially and contractually they were products of the London firm. Remarkably, none appear to have been pirated, perhaps because of Macmillan's standing in the American marketplace; most appeared after the Chace Act was legislated.

Following the success of *Robbery Under Arms*, Macmillan in London began publishing earlier works of Boldrewood's that had been serialised in Australian newspapers and periodicals, some more than a decade old. From 1890 to 1896 - that is,

127 "Books of the Week", *Nation*, 27 June 1889, 534; "New Books", *New York Times*, 8 July 1889.
128 Stamped copy held in the Houghton Library, Harvard University.

to the American firm's incorporation – the London house published ten Boldrewood titles in editions for the home and colonial markets: *The Squatter's Dream* (1890), *The Miner's Right* (1890), *A Colonial Reformer* (1890), *A Sydney-Side Saxon* (1891), *Nevermore* (1892), *A Modern Buccaneer* (1894), *The Sphinx of Eaglehawk* (1895), *The Crooked Stick; or Pollie's Probation* (1895), *Old Melbourne Memories* (1896) and *The Sealskin Cloak* (1896). Notices or reviews have been located in the American press for seven of these: *A Sydney-Side Saxon*, *The Squatter's Dream*, *A Colonial Reformer*, *A Modern Buccaneer*, *The Crooked Stick*, *Old Melbourne Memories* and *The Sealskin Cloak*. More intriguingly, the American edition of *The Crooked Stick* bears a colophon that reverses the more familiar format, so that New York appears *above* the publisher's name and London below it (Fig. 1.3). The book is clearly printed in the United States and from a different setting to the London edition.[129] It carries advertisements for *Robbery Under Arms*, *The Miner's Right* and *The Squatter's Dream*, indicating they were distributed and promoted by the American firm as their own even though they were set and printed in Britain.[130] Correspondence between the New York and London offices indicates plans for simultaneous publication of *A Modern Buccaneer* in both markets, and as with *The Crooked Stick*, a separate edition was produced, in 1894, bearing the reversed colophon, the name of the book's American printer, and a catalogue of Boldrewood titles available from the New York office (those listed above plus *A Colonial Reformer*).[131] After 1896, notices or advertisements appeared in the US press for *My Run Home* (1897), *Babes in the Bush* (1900), *In Bad Company* (1901) and *The Ghost Camp or The Avengers* (1902); and curiously, *The Last Chance* (1905), while evidently printed in Britain, bears a United States copyright notice. New York is listed in the notices when place of publication is included. To all intents and purposes, then, we can say that these books circulated as American editions, even when printed abroad.

We do know that Boldrewood, like Cambridge, was keenly interested in the possibilities of American publication and earnings. On 20 July 1891, he wrote to Frederick Macmillan in London about the new copyright situation created by the Chace Act, which had become law only a few weeks earlier: "I shall be interested in knowing whether the apparently favourable American Copyright Bill will increase the receipts of English and Australian authors. I take it for granted that your firm will make all necessary arrangements for our mutual benefit".[132] Macmillan replied pointing out that the bill would not produce any benefits for Boldrewood's books to date, as they had all been published "in some form or other" before it had been passed. But he added: "Should you write an entirely new book we shall be able to get copyright for it in the United States". The first new book was *A Modern Buccaneer* and Boldrewood was immediately on the case: "Does the American new Copyright Act offer any advantage to simultaneous publication there? Would it be advisable to try that method of increasing the sale? They pay very little it seems at present & no doubt pirate a good deal".[133] This time Macmillan could respond positively:

---

129 New York / Macmillan and Co. / And London. Copy sighted in the Houghton Library, Harvard University.
130 US library copies examined bear the colophon with London on top and usually carry the London firm's catalogue and the name of its Edinburgh printer. The exception is *A Modern Buccaneer*.
131 Correspondence between Brett and Macmillan, 27 and 30 March 1894, Macmillan Archive, British Library, BL 54802 Vol. xvii.
132 Boldrewood to Frederick Macmillan, 20 July 1891; Macmillan to Boldrewood, 10 December 1891, BL 55434; Macmillan to Boldrewood, 5 May 1892, BL 55435.
133 Boldrewood to Macmillan, 3 January 1894, BL 55442; reply, 12 February 1894, BL 55443.

"We propose to take advantage of the American copyright law and to publish an edition in America simultaneously with the appearance of the book here". The royalties offered were the same as for a colonial edition, sixpence per copy, less than a separate American royalties agreement was likely to produce.

Boldrewood, who had lived in Australia since childhood, used businessman Robert Jeffray to handle his publications in London, but when the latter returned to Australia Boldrewood announced to Macmillan, in March 1892, that he had appointed Watt as his literary agent. Macmillan, like Heinemann, was unpersuaded of the need for the new middlemen, writing to Boldrewood, "it is far pleasanter for a publisher to feel that he is in direct relation with any client for whom he is acting ... [I]n the case of a successful author like yourself who has a firm of publishers willing to bring out his books on satisfactory terms, we fail to see what is the use of an Agent".[134] Boldrewood dropped the idea and worked again through Jeffray once the latter returned to England. In July 1895, however, he once again informed Macmillan that he intended to ask Watt to act on his behalf, and from this point on - whether because of Watt's intervention or because of new arrangements with Macmillan in New York - Boldrewood's contracts included specific clauses relating to publication in America.[135] The first such contract, dated 24 September 1895, is for *The Crooked Stick*. In the agreement, the author assigned exclusive rights to Macmillan to publish the work in "Great Britain, its Colonies and Dependencies and in the United States of America". More explicitly, it specified that the publisher "shall issue an edition of the said book in the United States of America", pay a 10 per cent royalty on all copies sold, and "take all precautions and steps which may be necessary under the US Copyright Act to secure their own rights and those of [the author] in the said new book".[136] This last clause disappears from later contracts, but that obliging the publisher to issue an American edition remains in place for all Boldrewood's subsequent books, ten titles in all.

There is evidence, then, to suggest more than a dozen American editions of Boldrewood's works, and that many of the titles published in London were in effect distributed as "American books". At the same time, there is evidence that George Brett in New York was increasingly conscious of differences between the American and British markets. These were partly about format and price, as American consumers were book buyers rather than borrowers and were habituated to cheaper books than their British contemporaries. But Brett was also conscious of a divergence in *taste* between American and British readers. While organising the simultaneous publication of *A Modern Buccaneer*, he drew attention to the distinctiveness of the American audience. The book, he wrote, "can hardly ... be said to be milk for babes and the American public which swallowed eagerly half a million copies of *Ben Hur* will, I am afraid, rather shy at it".[137] More common are remarks about American readers' disinclination towards certain kinds of English fiction. In February 1894, Brett wrote to Macmillan indicating his reluctance to take a new novel by Mrs Steel if it were no better than her last: "I mean no better as far as

---

134 Boldrewood to Macmillan, 20 March 1892, BL 55436; Macmillan to Boldrewood, 5 May 1892, BL 55843/355.
135 Boldrewood to Macmillan, 22 July 1895, BL 54939.
136 Contract, 24 September 1895, BL 54939. The contract for *Old Melbourne Memories* gives the same date and exactly the same terms. Further contracts are held in BL Add MS 54939 and the Watt Records.
137 Brett to Macmillan, 30 March 1894, BL 54802.

1 Australian Fiction and the American Book Trade in the Nineteenth Century

this country is concerned because I can see, I think, that it would do fairly well with you and very well indeed, I should imagine, in the Colonial Library".[138] And in January 1896:

> We seem to be most unfortunate in the sales of a certain class of novel on this side, the kind of novel which is usually described by our literary critics as the "conventional English novel" and I think that it will be best not to copyright such books in the future if it can be avoided …
>
> Some English novels, it is true, do find considerable sale in this country and I should be most sorry to miss one of these but it really seems lately as if we had been publishing more than our fair share of those that do not sell.[139]

But perhaps to an American reader, Boldrewood's works, with their vigorous outdoor style, were *unlike* the "conventional English novel" with their vigorous outdoor style. In 1902, Brett wrote to London with a query about a new book of poems by the author of *The Man from Snowy River* (A.B. "Banjo" Paterson). He was interested in publishing both his earlier and later volumes, indicating his sense of a wider market for colonial romance and adventure.[140] Almost all of Boldrewood's books appear to have been present in the American marketplace.

They were reviewed respectfully, for the most part, in the American press, their Australian or colonial elements highlighted within a frame defined by the romance–realism binary. The *Boston Advertiser* praised *Robbery Under Arms* for the "abundance and truth of its local color, its realistic treatment of characters and incidents which easily lend themselves to repellent romantic sentimentalism".[141] The *New York Times*, by contrast, thought the novel's influence decidedly bad, suggesting, perhaps not altogether seriously, that "cowboy ethics" had originated in Australia:

> People in the cattle business in Arizona, Montana, or Kansas may look leniently on the road agent, but stealing cattle … is generally discouraged, and by "discouraged" is meant punishment without giving the culprit any chance to reform; so although cowboy ethics may have been first formulated in Australia, there has been evolution in the United States … The influence of "Robbery Under Arms" is decidedly a bad one, but there is cleverness in the descriptions, of Australian bush life, and Rolf Boldrewood comes out remarkably strong when he writes about horses.[142]

Macmillan released three further books in 1890, then on average one new title a year until 1902.[143] *The Squatter's Dream* was praised for its "directness and force", and as a story that

---

138 Brett to Macmillan, 20 February 1894, BL 54802. The novel they had published was *Miss Stuart's Legacy*, by Mrs F.A. Steel (1893). As mentioned above, Brett also declined to handle Henry Kingsley's novels.
139 Brett to Macmillan, 14 January 1896, BL54802.
140 Brett to Macmillan, 24 October 1902, BL 54812. In October–November 1903, Brett sought to engage Macmillan in discussion of the Australian market, opening it to the American firm's books. Macmillan resisted (BL54812).
141 Review pasted into the copy of the novel held in the Houghton Library, Harvard University.
142 "New Books", *New York Times*, 8 July 1899.
143 The three books released in 1890 were *The Squatter's Dream*, *A Colonial Romancer* and *The Miner's Right*.

"might be told as literally true of hundreds of restless and ambitious young Australians".[144] There was little sense of its nostalgia for pastoral Australia, perhaps because it was read in the local context of American pioneering. The *New York Critic*, however, in reviewing *The Miner's Right*, was unable to resist the geographical metaphor. Boldrewood was "a characteristic product of his continent":

> He requires plenty of space to canter about in, an unlimited indulgence in the reader for his constant tendency to diverge from the main path of the narrative, or to proceed, like one of his high mettled charges, sideways or backwards. Anything will do to start a digression; he shys, so to speak, at every new thought that turns up. But when once he is off on an exciting series of adventures he makes excellent time: there is no pause until he gets to the end ... When he lays down the book, [the reader] is aware that he has become possessed of new ideas, impressions, views of life, and that he has acquired a keen appetite for more of the same sort.[145]

A Colonial Reformer was similarly criticised for its verbosity by the *New York Sun* ("we are borne frequently on the wings of quotation vast distances away from the Australian bush"), but praised elsewhere as "a stirring tale of Australian life ... told with simplicity and in an admirable literary style".[146] For the *Times*, the book's descriptions of "one of those terrific periodical droughts which are the terror of the great pastoral colony" have "a graphic force sufficient to carry home, even to one who has never been in Australia, the tremendous meaning of the simple words, 'no rain'".[147] Even more telling, the reviewer compared Boldrewood with his "two great predecessors": "While lacking the fierce dramatic energy of Charles Reade, he is equally free from the latter's coarse violence of expression, and if he falls short of Henry Kingsley's fine descriptive power, he has not a trace of that unpleasant affectation of half-slangy colloquialism which was the besetting sin of the author of 'Ravenshoe.'"[148] Something of a tradition or field for the colonial romance is present to the reviewer, no doubt underwritten by the presence of *other* Australian novelists on the American book scene at the same time.

Although in June 1896 the *New York Times* reviewer of *Old Melbourne Memories* could refer to Boldrewood as "a writer recently new to us", other evidence suggests that by the mid-1890s he had become well known as the author of "some undeniably clever and dramatic novels of Australian life".[149] We do know that *Robbery Under Arms*, *The Squatter's Dream* and *The Miner's Right* entered the St Paul Public Library soon after publication.[150] *A Modern Buccaneer*, a story largely "borrowed" from Louis Becke, was received as "a

---

144 Cited in Macmillan's edition of *The Crooked Stick*.
145 Review quoted in the *Australasian Critic* 1, no. 4 (January 1891): 85.
146 *New York Sun*, 31 January 1891; *Boston Traveller*, cited in Macmillan publicity, *New York Tribune*, 30 May 1891.
147 "New Publications", *New York Times*, 16 February 1891.
148 Reade never visited Australia but his play *Gold* (1853) was partially set there and the story was reworked for his novel *It is Never Too Late to Mend: A Matter-of-Fact Romance* (1856). The novel was published by Ticknor & Fields in the United States with multiple editions from different publishers through to the early twentieth century.
149 Review of *In Bad Company*, *New York Tribune*, 26 May 1901.
150 "For Book Lovers: New Volumes Added to the Public Library", *Saint Paul Daily Globe*, 20 October 1890.

work of uncommon force", perhaps without the same "note of reality'"as *Robbery Under Arms* but with a gain in "literary effectiveness".[151] *My Run Home* showed "the author's exuberant delight in all the details of vigorous outdoor life.[152] Even negatively, he was known for writing "of Australia with such passion for local color that in the long run the characters in the book become not human but – Australian".[153] Boldrewood was also before American magazine readers through the practice of reprinting articles from the British periodical press: his own "Australian Rough-Riders", for example, reprinted from *Macmillan's Magazine*, or articles by others on topics such as "Station Life in Australia" or "Anglo-Saxon Unity" that cited his works.[154] He even appeared in a comic sketch about impossible clients in public libraries.[155] Boldrewood became a reference point on both sides of the Atlantic for understanding aspects of Australian colonial life – pastoral settlement, gold, and of course bushranging, of which one essayist wrote, "almost the only thing that can be said in its favor is that it has furnished the scenery and characters for such stirring romances as those of 'Boldrewood' and other Australian novels".[156] Boldrewood's death in 1915 was noted in the New York papers.[157]

No Longer Rarities

By the turn of the century, Ada Cambridge, Tasma and Rolf Boldrewood had all had multiple editions of their works published in the United States. All had acquired at least modest reputations as popular and worthy authors. Although not in the ranks of the most famous of transatlantic novelists, they could be referred to in the book pages of the American press as if readers should recognise their names and have some knowledge of their works. Their American careers show the impress of the modern Anglophone publishing world then coming into being, with the centrality of literary agents, the royalty system and separation of subsidiary rights, the growth of cheaper fiction and a new popular readership, and closer relations between English and American publishers all settling into place in the decades around the turn of the century. Following the extraordinary boom in cheap fiction libraries in the 1880s, they were able to achieve regular publishing relations with established American houses.

Together with the other authors mentioned, they created a surprisingly strong presence for Australian fiction in the American marketplace, especially in the 1890s. The American publication of Australian novels depended on the sheer appetite of the domestic market for new titles and the "vast web of romance" that connected Anglophone

---

151 *Record-Union* (Sacramento, CA), 7 December 1894; *New York Tribune*, 30 May 1894. For Boldrewood's borrowing from Becke, see Paul de Serville, *Rolf Boldrewood: A Life* (Carlton, Vic.: Miegunyah, 2000), 249–58.
152 *New York Tribune*, 31 July 1897.
153 "Literary Notes", *New York Tribune*, 27 December 1896; the contrast was with E.W. Hornung, discussed in Chapter 3.
154 Boldrewood, "Australian Rough-Riders", *Living Age*, 19 May 1894, 429–33; Sidney Dickinson, "Station Life in Australia", *Scribner's Magazine*, 11, no. 2 (February 1892): 135–54; the Earl of Meath, "Anglo-Saxon Unity", *Living Age*, 16 May 1891, 400–5.
155 "Library Types", *New York Daily Tribune*, 12 February 1911.
156 "Australia and New Zealand", *New York Times*, 22 June 1901.
157 *New York Evening World*, 12 March 1915; *New York Times*, 12 March 1915.

readers across the globe rather than on the qualities of individual novels and authors or any particular interest in Australian literature as such. And yet readers and reviewers were compelled to note a distinctive form of " antipodean romance". The phrase comes from Appleton's publicity for Praed's *Nùlma: An Anglo-Australian Romance* published in 1897: "In this story ... the author returns to the field of antipodean romance which she has cultivated with such marked success".[158] Even at the beginning of the decade, a commentator in the *San Francisco Morning Call* could remark: "The Australian bush seems to be a land of treasure trove to the novelist. 'Tasma,' the writer of 'Uncle Piper of Piper's Hill,' Mrs. Campbell Praed, Ada Cambridge in 'A Marked Man,' and many others have recently used the bush-scenery as a background for their romances".[159] And again in 1896: "Novels of Australian life have ceased to be curiosities. The people of that far land have won their way into the field of literature and are so diligently cultivating it that Australian books are no longer rarities".[160] As the *Chicago Daily Tribune* had it, in 1897, "Australia is beginning to claim something like its fair share of attention in the cosmopolitan world of fiction".[161] When a reader contacted the *New York Times* in August 1899 seeking "a list of good novels dealing with Australian life", the paper could assemble more than eighty, including works by Boldrewood, Clarke, Farjeon, Praed, Tasma, Martin, Hume, Gaunt, Nisbet and Newland.[162] By 1901, Appleton's Town and Country Library boasted nineteen novels by Tasma, Praed and Cambridge, and an impressive thirty in total by Australian authors among its first 300 titles. Cambridge's *The Devastators* appeared later that same year at no. 304. In 1904, novels by Boldrewood, Cambridge, Clarke, Farjeon, Hornung, Kingsley and Tasma appeared in *A Thousand of the Best Novels*, published by the Newark Free Public Library. The standing of Australian writers in the American market might also be suggested by an odd piece of evidence from 1895, the presence of novels by Cambridge, Praed, Tasma, Farjeon and Hume in a list of free books available to subscribers of the *Omaha Daily Bee*.[163]

Reviewers at times felt so familiar with the formulas of antipodean romance they could joke about them. Boldrewood's "Australian romance", *The Crooked Stick*, was described as an "'opera of the wilderness' ... pitched in a key of lyrical exaggeration which is audible in the first page, when the 'blood red sun' sinks 'all too slowly, yet angrily, into a crimson ocean'".[164] His *The Sealskin Cloak* was described in the *New York Sun* as "a novel of the good old-fashioned sort" wherein the heroine "meets with a family of wealthy Australians, who are as kind of heart and as vulgar of speech as all good Australians are expected to be, in contemporary fiction, and with that she goes to live in the antipodes".[165]

---

158 Advertisement, *New York Times*, 3 July 1897.
159 "Literature", *San Francisco Morning Call*, 1 February 1891.
160 "Books and Bookmakers", review of *Mrs. Tregaskiss*, by Rosa Praed, *San Francisco Call*, 12 January 1896.
161 *Chicago Daily Tribune*, 16 February 1897.
162 "Questions and Answers", *New York Times*, 12 August 1899. See also "Australian Literary Notes", *New York Times*, 7 July 1900.
163 *A Thousand of the Best Novels* (Newark, NJ: Newark Free Public Library, 1904); for the third edition in 1908 they were joined by G.B. Lancaster. *Omaha Daily Bee*, 31 March 1895.
164 "New Novels: Love in the Antipodes and Elsewhere", review of *The Crooked Stick*, by Rolf Boldrewood, *New York Daily Tribune*, 5 April 1896.
165 "New Books", review of *The Sealskin Coat*, by Rolf Boldrewood, *New York Sun*, 21 November 1896.

1 Australian Fiction and the American Book Trade in the Nineteenth Century

The reviews suggest that the Australian stories appealed both for their sameness and their difference, readily accommodated within Anglo-American romance and adventure conventions and yet different enough to have American publishers, reviewers and readers take note and to draw Australian books or authors together *as* Australian. As Rosemary Foxton has suggested, Australian novels could be appreciated "not only for their novelty in terms of 'local color and romance,' but for a vitality and energy which in itself made them noteworthy among the host of foreign novels that had flooded the American literary marketplace".[166] Australian authors at home and abroad were able to benefit from the transatlantic book trade in terms of reputation and in some cases financially as well. But in a rapidly expanding market of old and new books, that recognition was difficult to sustain. If the presence of Australian authors in the nineteenth-century US book market was more significant than has generally been recognised, even more striking perhaps is that they appear to have left virtually no trace in American book culture once the genre networks through which they travelled began to fray. When in the 1930s Australian literature again began to be noticed in the United States, through a series of Australian historical novels and pioneering sagas, it was as if for the first time.

---

166 Foxton, "'Another Fresh Australian Tale'", 353.

2
International Reputations and Transatlantic Rights: Rosa Praed and Louis Becke

By the end of the nineteenth century, both Rosa Praed and Louis Becke had established international literary careers, in Australia, Britain and the United States. Praed has been claimed as "the first Australian-born novelist to achieve a significant international reputation".[1] Almost certainly she can lay claim to being the first Australian-born novelist to be published in the United States, although she had been resident in England for several years before her novel *Nadine* appeared in New York in Munro's Seaside Library in 1883. Of Praed's forty-seven published works, twenty-five appeared in American editions in the three decades from 1885 to 1915, including twenty-four of her thirty-eight novels in more than forty separate editions. Over the same period, Louis Becke achieved an even greater international reputation, if with a more spectacular rise and fall, primarily as a writer of tales of the South Seas. Across the fifteen years from 1895 to 1914, twenty-six of Becke's thirty-four books appeared in the American market.[2]

Across the first decade of the twentieth century, Praed and Becke were – with Rolf Boldrewood – the best-known and most highly regarded of Australian writers in America. In neither case were their American careers accidental. Praed worked hard at making sure her books found their way to America and maximising her chances of profiting should they be successful. Becke, too, kept a close watch on possibilities for his stories in the United States where their Pacific settings gave them a kind of market advantage. Yet despite their successes, their reputations were not sustained once new titles stopped appearing. Both came to seem old-fashioned, caught within nineteenth-century conventions of story-telling and on the wrong side of realism and the modern novel, however challenging to turn-of-the-century expectations they had once appeared to be.

---

1 Elizabeth Webby, cited in Patricia Clarke, "Rosa Praed (Mrs Campbell Praed) (1851–1935)", in *Australian Literature, 1788–1914*, ed. Selina Samuels, Dictionary of Literary Biography, Vol. 230 (Detroit, MI: Gale Research, 2001), 312.

2 There is some bibliographical uncertainty. AustLit includes a title, *New York's Chinatown* (1898), but with no further publishing details and it has not been traced; Becke provided an introduction for *Old Convict Days* (1899), sometimes counted among Becke's books, but he was not the author of the main text; and while it is possible that a simultaneous US edition of *Notes from My South Sea Log* (1905) was published, only a 1926 US edition has been traced.

Praed and the Fiction Libraries

Praed was born in 1851 in New South Wales, but in an area that became part of Queensland in 1859. In 1876 she left for England, where her first novel was published in 1880. In America, Praed suffered from piracy in the early stages of her career but it is also likely she benefited in one respect at least, gaining recognition even while she was losing potential earnings. Like Ada Cambridge, what did most to establish her reputation – and her US earnings – was a long-term relationship with D. Appleton & Co. across the 1890s. But although Praed continued to publish new novels in the new century, once her relationship with Appleton ceased she struggled to secure ongoing support from any individual publisher and to profit from the new international copyright regime. Praed's American career had almost begun in 1881 when G.P. Putnam's Sons, which had a long-established London office, expressed its interest in publishing an American edition of *Policy and Passion*, but nothing came of it.[3] Otherwise, as with her contemporaries, her early American career was almost exclusively a product of the cheap libraries that flourished before the introduction of the Chace Act. Between 1883 and 1891, seven of her books were published by George Munro, four by the Lovells, two by Harper, and one each by Lippincott and Rand McNally. The level of activity in these years was frenetic, eight different titles in eighteen different editions, although again it is unlikely that Praed profited in any significant way without copyright protection or formal agreements.

The first of Praed's novels available in the United States appeared in Munro's Seaside Library: *Nadine: The Story of a Woman* in 1883, Chapman & Hall's two-volume English edition having been reduced to only twenty-six pages, followed by *Zéro: A Story of Monte Carlo* in 1884, at forty pages.[4] The following year Munro reissued *Zéro* in two book formats, each a respectable 147 pages, in its Victor Series of Paperbacks and in the Seaside Library Pocket Editions (no. 428). *Affinities: A Romance of To-Day*, published in London by Richard Bentley in 1885, appeared as no. 477 in the Seaside Library in the same year, and *The Head Station: A Novel of Australian Life* as no. 811 in 1886. The difference in the numbers suggests just how quickly Munro was producing new titles. In 1890, Munro reissued *Zéro* and published Praed's earlier novel *An Australian Heroine*, first published in London a decade earlier but reissued by Ward & Downey in 1890, no doubt the edition that brought the title to Munro's attention.[5] In the following year, the year the Chace Act was passed, he published *The Ladies' Gallery* (co-authored with Justin McCarthy) and *The Soul of Countess Adrian* – and then stopped.

Munro was not alone of course. J.W. Lovell also published *The Head Station*, in Lovell's Library (no. 1340) in 1889, and it is likely that both the Lovell and Munro releases were pirated from an edition published by Harper in 1886, in one of Harper's own cheap libraries, the twenty-five cent Harper Handy Series. In 1890, Lovell published *The Rival Princess: A London Romance of To-Day* in hardcover in his International Series of Select Novels.[6] *The Rival Princess* was the new title for *The Rebel Rose*, which Harper had

---

3   George Bentley to Rosa Praed, 11 July 1881, Rosa Caroline Praed Papers, John Oxley Library, State Library of Queensland (9/4/24).
4   *Nadine*, Munro's Seaside Library, Vol. 76, no. 1542; *Zero*, Vol. 93, no. 1873. Both references from Chris Tiffin, *Rosa Praed (Mrs Campbell Praed) 1851–1935: A Bibliography*, Victorian Fiction Research Guides XV (St Lucia: Department of English, The University of Queensland, 1989).
5   Tiffin lists the Munro edition of *An Australian Heroine* but notes that the book has not been sighted.
6   Advertisement, *New York Times*, 11 May 1890.

2 International Reputations and Transatlantic Rights: Rosa Praed and Louis Becke

published in its Franklin Square Library in 1888. Perhaps in response to Lovell's new edition, Harper reissued the novel in 1890 using the new title. Lovell's United States Book Co. also published *The Soul of Countess Adrian* in its International series in 1891, the same year as Munro's edition. In a typical sequence, following an authorised edition in Appleton's Town and Country Library (no. 26), *The Ladies' Gallery* appeared in Frank Lovell's Household Library and Rand McNally's Globe Library in 1889, in 1891 from Munro, and in 1892 from the Continental Publishing Co. of Chicago.

From this point on, "Mrs. Campbell-Praed", like Cambridge before her, developed a regular publishing relationship with Appleton. The New York firm first published her in 1887 as co-author of *The Right Honourable: A Romance of Society and Politics*, written with her close friend Justin McCarthy, novelist, essayist and Irish Nationalist member of the British Parliament.[7] The novel was one of the earliest, no. 8, in the Town and Country Library. McCarthy had already published several books with Harper together with periodical essays on American and Irish affairs, and his established American reputation was no doubt a factor in Appleton's decision to publish *The Right Honourable*. Although Praed was already a celebrated author and society figure in London and had published seven novels, only four had previously appeared in America and all in cheap reprint libraries except for Lippincott's edition of *Moloch: A Story of Sacrifice*, also published in 1887. Praed and her husband accompanied McCarthy to the United States in September–November 1886, visiting New York, Boston, and other sites in New England. McCarthy was a high-profile figure with a strong constituency among Irish-Americans and Home Rule supporters, but Praed, "the Australian spiritualist and novelist", was also treated as a celebrity on her arrival.[8] In Boston, she met John Boyle O'Reilly, the escaped convict who had become an important figure in Boston's Irish community as an author and editor. O'Reilly's novel *Moondyne: A Story from the Underworld* - a tale of convicts, Aborigines, hidden goldmines and a hero who manages to drown during a bushfire - had been published several times in America and Australia by the time of Praed's visit.[9] O'Reilly would later be the model for the politician-bushranger hero of Praed's *Outlaw and Lawmaker*, first published by Chatto & Windus in London in 1893 and released by Appleton the following year.

Appleton next published *The Ladies' Gallery*, a further collaboration with McCarthy, in 1889. Both novels appear to have been steady sellers in the United States, for Appleton continued to issue them through 1898 and 1912 respectively.[10] However, Appleton did not publish Praed and McCarthy's other co-authored novel, *The Rebel Rose*. Whether this was because of the radical "Jacobite" theme embedded in its historical plot or simply because of trade courtesy is unclear.[11] This novel was originally written under the title "The Ladies' Gallery", and Praed and McCarthy had worked on it during their crossing to New York in 1886. In London, George Bentley agreed to publish it, but as it was "something of a

---

7   S.L. Gwynn, "Justin McCarthy", *Oxford Dictionary of National Biography*, rev. Alan O'Day, 2004. Online edition 2009. http://www.oxforddnb.com/index/101034681/Justin-McCarthy.
8   Patricia Clarke, *Rosa! Rosa!: A Life of Rosa Praed, Novelist and Spiritualist* (Melbourne: Melbourne University Press, 1999), 97–99.
9   First published in America by Pilot Publishing Co., then Roberts Bros, in Boston, 1879.
10 *The Right Honorable*: 1887, 1888, 1896, 1898; *The Ladies' Gallery*: 1889, 1895, 1898, 1912.
11 Clarke, "Rosa Praed", 307. Having been published earlier by Harper, albeit under a different title, Appleton would have been respecting trade courtesy in not publishing the book if it was offered to them.

political *roman à clef*" and McCarthy was such a well-known figure, he recommended it be published anonymously.[12] Perhaps there was also an element of commercial calculation in his advice, for he wrote to Praed that with anonymous publication "its chance of a huge success would be enhanced. There would be a mystery about it".[13] The novel's American history reveals the potential complications of transatlantic publishing. The change in title to *The Rebel Rose* occurred because Praed and McCarthy had earlier sold serial rights in the United States using the former title, and there was little point in publishing the book anonymously if prior serialisation would make its authorship well known. It was thus agreed they would write a *new* novel under the title *The Ladies' Gallery*. As it turned out, Bentley's manoeuvres were largely ineffectual. *The Rebel Rose* was less successful than the two authors' other collaborations in sales terms. Further, Praed and McCarthy had sold the US book rights to Harper before the novel's British release, and Harper's edition appeared – with the authors' names – in 1888, the same year as Bentley's. The second British edition, under the new title *The Rival Princess* and no longer anonymous, was published in London by F.V. White in 1890, and the later Harper and Lovell editions followed suit.

The first of Praed's sole-authored novels published by Appleton was *December Roses* in 1892 (no. 96 in the Town and Country Library), followed by *Christina Chard* (no. 130) in 1893 and 1894, *Outlaw and Lawmaker* (no. 146) in 1894 and 1899, *Mrs. Tregaskiss: A Novel of Anglo-Australian Life* (no. 181) in 1895, *Nùlma: An Anglo-Australian Romance* (no. 220) in 1897 (Fig. 2.1) – the subtitles are telling in generic terms – and finally *Madame Izàn: A Tourist Story* (no. 264) in 1899. Three of these were first editions, appearing in advance of their English release.[14] As published in the Town and Country Library, all were copyrighted editions, while *Christina Chard* and *Mrs. Tregaskiss* were also published outside the series. *Outlaw and Lawmaker* and *Mrs. Tregaskiss* were republished in 1912, along with *The Ladies' Gallery*.

The only other major book publications for Praed before the turn of the century were from Lippincott, which followed its earlier edition of *Moloch* with *The Romance of a Châlet* in 1892, chosen as the first title "by an English author" to appear in the publisher's Copyright Foreign Novels series, and reissued in 1897 in its Select Novels Library.[15] Lippincott's English connections did engage Praed in two collaborative books published in New York: *Over the Seas: Stories of Two Worlds*, a collection of children's stories including a number of bush tales, by Praed, Hume Nisbet and Tasma, in 1890; and *Seven Christmas Eves: Being the Romance of a Social Evolution* in 1894. Praed also published essays and stories in American magazines, including an article on "Literary Women in London Society" for the *North American Review* in September 1890 and a short story in *Lippincott's Magazine* in November 1899. Another story, "Mrs. Robinson: A Steamboat Episode", had been sold to the fiction and news syndicator Tillotsons, appearing in the *Pittsburgh Dispatch* in July 1892.[16]

---

12   Chris Tiffin, "'Our Literary Connexion': Rosa Praed and George Bentley", *Australian Literary Studies* 27, nos 3–4 (October–November 2012): 120–21.
13   George Bentley to Rosa Praed, 13 February 1888, Praed Papers (9/4/60).
14   *December Roses* (Appleton 1892; Simpkin 1893); *Christina Chard* (Appleton 1893; Chatto & Windus 1894); *Mrs. Tresgaskiss* (Appleton 1895; Chatto & Windus 1896).
15   Rosemary Foxton, "'Another Fresh Australian Tale': The American Publication of Catherine Martin's *The Silent Sea*", *Australian Literary Studies* 15, no. 4 (October 1992): 351–52.
16   Chris Tiffin, "'By Mrs Campbell Praed': Author and Text", *Bibliographical Society of Australia and New Zealand Bulletin* 22, no. 2 (1998): 77–79. In July 1894, Tillotson & Co., the syndicating agency,

2 International Reputations and Transatlantic Rights: Rosa Praed and Louis Becke

"A peacock's plume among a pile of geese feathers"

The Australian settings and characters of Praed's Anglo-Australian romances appear not to have been a drawback for Appleton; indeed, it played up these elements in its advertising. For *Outlaw and Lawmaker*: "In this romance of Australian life Mrs. Campbell Praed returns to the field in which she gained her first success. [It] will be ranked among the strongest of the novels which have had their scenes in the antipodes".[17] And for *Mrs. Tregaskiss*: "Mrs. Campbell Praed returns to Australia for the scene of this strong and absorbing story, which will be found to present a drama of singular force and interest".[18] In such terms, the (antipodean) romance was lifted above the level of popular melodrama. It was precisely as a well-known and respected writer of romances that Praed became a key figure in the increased presence of Australian fiction in the American marketplace in the 1890s, giving a more contemporary spin to the antipodean romance conventions established by Cambridge, Tasma and Boldrewood.

It was in the course of reviewing *Mrs. Tregaskiss*, in 1896, that the *San Francisco Call*'s reviewer made the remark quoted at the end of the previous chapter: that "novels of Australian life [had] ceased to be curiosities. The people of that far land have won their way into the field of literature and are so diligently cultivating it that Australian books are no longer rarities".[19] And within that field, Praed was outstanding not only for her representations of Australian life but also her popularity among American readers: "Among the authors who have given us pictures of bush life on the big ranges of that country none have made them more vivid or interesting than Mrs. Campbell-Praed, and her new novel, 'Mrs. Tregaskiss,' will be welcomed by a wide circle of readers, to whom she is already well and favourably known". While less than convinced by the novel's conventional love story, in a common pattern the reviewer praised its "descriptions of Australian scenery and the narration of incidents peculiar to Australian life", novelistic incidents with which she or he appeared quite familiar despite their peculiarity:

> The incidents of the story include a description of a drought in the cattle country, a strike of the shepherds, a forest fire, a camping-out picnic and the usual scenes of life remote from civilization. The picture given of Australian life is not wholly attractive, and yet it has its charms for those who like freedom and adventure.

Less familiar were the passages of "black fellows" dialect. Here the reviewer was well satisfied by the novel's resolution in which Mrs Tregaskiss receives a legacy of £20,000 and retires to England with her husband "thoroughly reformed". The *Saint Paul Daily Globe*, by contrast, thought that "material healing for wounds of the soul seems a little sordid, and the sense of ethical uplift is hardly perceptible". Nonetheless, again, "Australian life is vividly depicted".[20]

---

wrote to Praed stating that their best offer for a story "would be £50 for serial, translation and American rights": Praed Papers (9/1/29).
17 *New York Times*, 30 June 1894.
18 *New York Times*, 8 November 1895. Also the phrase quoted in Chapter 1 above regarding *Nùlma*: "In this story, which is written with great care and force, the author returns to the field of antipodean romance which she has cultivated with such marked success", *New York Times*, 3 July 1897. See Fig. 2.1.
19 *San Francisco Morning Call*, 12 January 1896.
20 *Saint Paul Daily Globe*, 26 January 1896.

NEW PUBLICATIONS.

D. APPLETON AND COMPANY'S NEW BOOKS.

Insect Life.

By JOHN HENRY COMSTOCK, Professor of Entomology in Cornell University. With Illustrations by ANNA BOTSFORD COMSTOCK, member of the Society of American Wood Engravers. 12mo. Cloth, $2.50.

A popular book of general value and interest which will meet a want felt by teachers and be indispensable for classes, and will also prove of constant service to those who have felt the need of a guide to the identification and study of insects. It is a book for amateurs and Summer tourists as well as for students, and is magnificently illustrated by Mrs. Comstock's accurate and beautiful wood engravings.

Nulma.

By Mrs. CAMPBELL-PRAED, author of "Mrs. Tregaskiss," "Outlaw and Lawmaker," "Christina Chard," etc. No. 220, Town and Country Library. 12mo. Cloth, $1.00; paper, 50 cents.

In this story, which is written with great care and force, the author returns to the field of antipodean romance which she has cultivated with such marked success. Her novel pictures social and official life, with its picturesque colonial environment, and as a story it will be found singularly sympathetic and interesting.

The Story of the Earth's Atmosphere.

By DOUGLAS ARCHIBALD, M. A., Fellow and sometime Vice President of the Royal Meteorological Society, London. A new volume in the Library of Useful Stories. Illustrated. 16mo. Cloth, 40 cents.

This little work puts forward the main features of our knowledge of the conditions which prevail in our atmosphere as they are interpreted through the science of to-day.

Appleton's Hand-Book of Summer Resorts.

New edition, revised to date. With maps, illustrations, and table of railroad fares, etc. Large 12mo. Paper, 50 cents.

For sale by all booksellers; or will be sent by mail o eccipt of price by the publishers,

D. APPLETON AND COMPANY,
72 Fifth Avenue, New York.

Figure 2.1 Rosa Praed, *Nùlma: An Anglo-Australian Romance* (New York: D. Appleton & Co., 1897). *New York Times*, 3 July 1897.

2 International Reputations and Transatlantic Rights: Rosa Praed and Louis Becke

Favourable or unfavourable, what is striking is just how widely Praed's novels were noticed and how familiar reviewers were with the author and her reputation. The nationwide spread of newspapers and weekly magazines meant that her novels were regularly reviewed across the country, especially with Appleton's consecutive releases in the 1890s. If an early reviewer wondered whether Praed's collaboration with McCarthy had "somehow fettered the masculine writer", a decade later, in 1896, another could remark that "the books which are entirely her own are much cleverer than those which she wrote in collaboration".[21] Appleton reprinted a selection of reviews inside each new book as it was published, and while obviously chosen for their positive spin they do indicate how extensively and generously her novels were discussed in this period. Reviews of *December Roses* were quoted from the *Cleveland Leader*, the *Boston Literary World*, the *Churchman* and the *Baltimore American*: "For nobility of conception, delicacy of touch, and sustained action, [the novel] excels any of the author's earlier efforts."[22] Reviews of *Christina Chard* were from the *Boston Saturday Evening Gazette* and *Boston Advertiser*: "The novel is one to be studied as well as read". For *Outlaw and Lawmaker*, the publishers quoted the *New York Tribune* and the *Detroit Free Press*, and for *Mrs. Tregaskiss*, the *Elmira Telegram* (New York) and the *San Francisco Morning Call*.

Outlaw and Lawmaker and *Mrs. Tregaskiss* in particular attracted favourable attention, leading to illustrated paragraphs as well as reviews, and recycled snippets from the London press (Fig. 2.2). In the process, Praed became a person of note, appearing in the social pages and book chat columns.[23] "Two London Literary Women", an article on Praed and Mrs Cashel Hoey, offered American readers a fascinating introduction to Praed as an author, revealing just why she divided reviewers, and why there was a kind of volatility in her deployment of the romance conventions despite her capacity to be "charming":

> Her novels are widely read, but in England are kept away from young readers exactly as those of Ouida. They are in a certain sense brilliant, but they are restricted to the delineation of scenes and manners of a fast and loose class of people … Her literary style violates all canons of art, as understood and studied by more serious writers; nevertheless, there is a glamour in her periods, a fascination in her study of character which causes a reader to pursue her fiction breathlessly to the end, and then tossing it away, vowing that the time spent in reading it might and should be more profitably employed.[24]

The article appeared in newspapers in Montana, Pittsburgh, and no doubt beyond. In 1901 and again in 1904, American papers repeated a joke that was doing the rounds in London: "Why did Anthony Hope? – Because Mrs. Campbell Praed".[25] Praed was certainly newsworthy, if never quite in the league of Ouida or Marie Corelli.

---

21 *New York Daily Tribune*, 13 November 1887; *Omaha Daily Bee*, 19 April 1896.
22 Quotations in this paragraph from the front matter of Appleton's 1897 edition of *Nùlma*.
23 For example, in the *Louisiana Populist*, the *Globe-Republican* (Dodge City, KS), the *Eddy Current* (New Mexico) and the *Stark County Democrat* (Ohio), February 1896.
24 "Two London Literary Women", *Daily Yellowstone Journal* (Montana), 17 March 1889; the article sources the *Pittsburgh Chronicle*.
25 *Minneapolis Journal*, 27 February 1901. In 1900, reporting "News of Australia", the *Hawaiian Gazette* noted that Australians would be concerned for Praed's delicate health: *Hawaiian Gazette*, 28 September 1900. Anthony Hope was the author of the bestselling *The Prisoner of Zenda*.

MRS. PRAED.

The Novelist Whose "Mrs. Tregaskiss" Has Made a Stir.

Mrs. Praed, whose last novel, "Mrs. Tregaskiss," has created a favorable impression, was born in Queensland. Her father, Murray Prior, was active in public affairs there. A nephew of Praed, the poet, was her husband. Her first novel was published in 1880 and called "An Australian Heroine." "Moloch," "The Head Station," "Outlaw and Lawmaker" are some of her books;

MRS. CAMPBELL PRAED, while, in collaboration with Justin McCarthy, she wrote "The Right Honorable" and "The Ladies' Gallery."

Grateful to the Stowaway.

Stowaways usually receive scant courtesy from the indignant officers of the ships on which they steal passage, and usually, too, scant rations and plenty of work, with a prospect of jail at the end of the trip. A stowaway on one of the Pacific steamers, however, on a recent trip from Yokohama to Tacoma, received not only the best of treatment, but a substantial present of money when he left the ship. The vessel encountered a heavy storm on the voyage, and the stowaway, who was working about the deck, distinguished himself by great bravery at one of the most perilous moments during the gale. The officers made up a purse of $20 for him to help him on his journey after he left the ship.

Figure 2.2 "Mrs. Praed. The Novelist Whose 'Mrs. Tregaskiss' Has Made a Stir." *Louisiana Populist* (Natchitoches, LA), 21 February 1896.

2 International Reputations and Transatlantic Rights: Rosa Praed and Louis Becke

In the book pages, reviewers juggled their responses to the novels' conventional and unconventional, charming, melodramatic or "graphic" elements but always within the frame of romance. Given the wide embrace of romance as a mode of literary understanding, that did not mean the works could not be considered as of literary significance but it did constrain the kinds of significance they might be accorded. There is little evidence that reviewers noted the "anti-romantic" elements that would interest critics a century later, in particular Praed's "analysis of the debilitating choices women are called upon to make in the course of their courtship and marriage".[26] The earliest American review discovered is of the United States Book Co.'s edition of *The Soul of Countess Adrian*, one of Praed's early forays into the occult. The *San Francisco Morning Call* thought it "a very charming novel that commends itself to all classes of readers", just the kind of notice a good conventional romance would attract.[27] The *New York Tribune* reviewer saw something more original in *Outlaw and Lawmaker*. While noting that the plot could not manage without "a certain melodrama", the drama nevertheless had "an air of truth … set forth with almost masculine vigor and humor": "To picture a girl whose breeding is deficient, whose flirtations are in extremely bad taste, and whose heart is rather hard, and yet make the reader like and pity her, is surely a triumph".[28] Turning this judgement around, the New York illustrated magazine *Outlook* thought Praed's "romance" offered a "graphic idea of Australian life in the early days of civilization there" but added a warning: "let no one expect too great literary merit as a characteristic of this merely melodramatic book".[29] Still, Praed's popularity among readers is evident, not least in the fact that in late 1897 she figured second only to Bret Harte among titles borrowed by adults from the Butte Public Library, Anaconda, Montana.[30]

Madame Izàn: A Tourist Story and *The Insane Root: A Romance of a Strange Country* were potentially more challenging than the Anglo-Australian romances, the former, with its Japanese hero and inter-racial love story, a more complex engagement with the East than most of the orientalist romances by Praed's male contemporaries;[31] the latter because of its apparently serious interest in the occult powers of the mandrake root. Surprisingly perhaps, *The Insane Root* from 1902 was taken more seriously as a literary work and produced some lively debate, not least because it provoked comparison with Robert Louis Stevenson's celebrated *Dr Jekyll and Mr Hyde*. As such, it could become something of a register for how romance was being reconfigured under the pressure of modernity. The comparison was sometimes to Praed's advantage: "when we find a novel which is superior to the foundation work of Stevenson's fame and is of the same character, we must perforce praise it or shame our modernity, since if this kind of work is melodramatic (as is charged

---

26 Tiffin, *Rosa Praed*, 10.
27 The first review of Praed's sole-authored novels. *San Francisco Morning Call*, 14 June 1891. See also reviews of *December Roses*, *New York Times*, 17 July 1892 and *Christina Chard*, *New York Times*, 21 January 1894.
28 *New York Daily Tribune*, 22 July 1894.
29 *Outlook*, September 1894, 439.
30 *Anaconda Standard* (Anaconda, MT), 20 December 1897. The list is of books borrowed by adults on a single day, 24 November 1897. Praed is one of a group of four authors with four books borrowed (against five by Harte), although the accompanying list includes only three, *Christina Chard*, *December Roses* and *Nùlma*.
31 Megumi Kato, *Narrating the Other: Australian Literary Perceptions of Japan* (Clayton, Vic.: Monash University Press, 2008), 29-31. See *New York Tribune Illustrated Supplement*, 11 June 1899.

by other reviewers) instead of psychological, then is the celebrity of RLS dependent upon a quality which his admirers would indignantly deny as possible to their idol".[32]

With a different sense of where modernity might be found, the *New York Times*, in the longest review any of her books received, reversed the assessment but still with serious praise: "Mrs. Praed does not reach, of course, the height which Stevenson attained in 'Dr. Jekyll and Mr. Hyde,' but she has certainly succeeded in lifting her story out of the region of the merely grotesque into the higher plane marked by that masterpiece, and that is no small achievement in dealing with materials so little in harmony with modern ideas".[33] For all the novel's "superstitious absurdities", the reviewer acknowledged the power of Praed's writing: "while one is eagerly turning the pages of this weird tale, he practically believes in all the mystical magical properties she ascribes to the plant which gives the book its name, and accepts as perfectly plausible and possible the supernatural mechanism by means of which she works out her plot to an impressive and powerful conclusion". Less justified perhaps was the notion that Praed's Australian birth made it "natural that her romances should partake somewhat of the strangeness of her native land".

An impassioned reader wrote to the *Times* the following week to bring the novel again to its readers' attention as "one of the most absorbingly interesting, most fantastically imaginative, and most weirdly beautiful of any book recently issued":

> I think this stands out like a peacock's plume among a pile of geese feathers. Among the insipid, prosy-prosy, spineless, commonplace rubbish that gluts our market, this book is an exception. It should by all means be a best-selling book. To every one who wants to read a good, a thorough story, a thrilling, exciting, yet comfortable piece of romance, rivalling in a way the "Arabian Nights," I emphatically want to recommend "The Insane Root," by Mrs. Campbell Praed, published a short time since by Funk & Wagnalls.[34]

Clearly, there was still a demand for thrilling yet comfortable romance, but there is no evidence to suggest that the book became the bestseller the reader thought it should or that it ever made the kind of impact reviewers entertained. As the *Times* suggested, it was perhaps "too little in harmony with modern ideas".

Testing Rights

Praed's record in the United States to 1900 was substantial enough to make her keenly interested in maximising her earnings in the American market. Her correspondence from the period reveals another Anglo-Australian author determined to succeed in the United States but uncertain how best to secure her interests, both before and after the passing of the Chace Act, but especially in the decade following her last new title with Appleton – *Madame Izàn* in 1899 – at a time when her popularity as an author on both sides of the Atlantic began to falter.[35] Appleton went into receivership in March 1900 and

---

32 "Compared with Stevenson", *Houston Daily Post*, 22 February 1903. See also *Outlook*, 8 November 1902, 612.
33 "Mrs. Praed's New Story", *New York Times*, 22 November 1902.
34 T. Everett Harry, "'The Insane Root'", *New York Times*, 29 November 1902.
35 Clarke, "Rosa Praed", 301-11.

2 International Reputations and Transatlantic Rights: Rosa Praed and Louis Becke

although the firm continued publishing, the Town and Country Library came to an end in 1903.[36] Whether Praed suffered from the firm's reversals or whether they were simply not interested in her later occult novels is unknown. It is slightly odd perhaps that it did not pick up her memoir, *My Australian Girlhood: Sketches and Impressions of Bush Life* (1902), given their earlier boosting of her Australian themes, but the timing was not propitious for the company and it might have been unwilling to take on something other than a novel (Unwin held the American rights). That Praed was writing the memoir of her early years in Queensland was noted in American papers, for example the *New York Tribune* and *New York Times*, but the book remained unpublished in the United States.[37] Apart from a later relationship with Cassell, Praed's subsequent novels all went to different American presses in a series of one-off publishing relations.

In May 1886, by which time Munro had already released a number of her titles, Praed's English publisher George Bentley wrote in response to her enquiries to advise her of just where she stood in relation to American publishers in the absence of copyright protection. In the process, he offered a contemporary British view of how piracy and trade courtesy operated across the Atlantic:

> I am afraid nothing can be done of any service to you in regard to America …
>
> Your only plan is to take whatever offer the American publisher of your last work makes you.
>
> [American publishers] stand shoulder to shoulder in robbing us, and if A has taken a book, B respects A's theft – in other words there is honour between thieves there. Holt is honest, but he dare not buy, because he would be what they call "printed upon" if he did.
>
> Whoever printed your last work is the best to apply to.[38]

Whether Praed was able to exert any influence at all over her American publications before Appleton became involved is not clear. In June 1889, the London-based Art in Advertising Association, which Praed had recently engaged to act as literary agents on her behalf, wrote to update her regarding opportunities in the American market, again in response to queries she had made. The agency's Mrs Smith wrote of having met "Mr Groves of the New York *World*", the controversial newspaper owned by Joseph Pulitzer, who was reported as saying that "Australia has no interest to the Americans". That was the bad news. The good news was that he had paid as much as £3000 for the American rights to a book – but also as low as £100. Smith thought that if Praed could complete a new book by the following year she "may have a chance of a big sum".[39]

After the passing of the Chace Act, with Appleton as her publisher and with an agent in London, a more regular set of agreements could be set in place. Praed reserved the US rights to *Christina Chard* and *Mrs. Tregaskiss* in her contracts with Chatto & Windus, and possibly for all the novels published by Appleton. Statements from the Authors Syndicate, which by August 1894 was acting as Praed's London agent, reveal that she received £55 for the US copyright on *Mrs. Tregaskiss* (whether this is a full or part payment is not clear) and

---

36   John Tebbel, *Between Covers: The Rise and Transformation of Book Publishing in America* (New York: Oxford University Press, 1987), 104–5.
37   *New York Tribune*, 2 March 1902; *New York Times*, 20 September 1902.
38   Bentley to Praed, 22 May 1886, Praed Papers (9/4/51).
39   Smith to Praed, 1 June 1889, Praed Papers (9/2/6).

an advance against royalties of £50 for the American edition of *Christina Chard*. She was still earning modest American royalties for *December Roses* two years after its release.[40]

At the same time, correspondence with William Morris Colles of the Authors Syndicate reveals the complications the Chace Act produced despite its potential benefits to foreign authors. In December 1898, Colles wrote to Praed that the Syndicate had copyrighted her novel *The Scourge-Stick* in America just before the Spanish–American war (April–August 1898) and had subsequently offered it to several American publishers in London.[41] This suggests either that Praed was looking for a better deal than she currently had with Appleton or that the American firm had already rejected this novel, which had been published in England that year. However, none of the American publishers Colles approached had taken the book, "mainly on account of timidity in consequence of the state of the book trade in America". Nonetheless, it remained in the hands of an American agent, and he was hopeful of being able to "make arrangements". Bibliographical records do indicate one American edition, published by J.W. Chartres, but Chris Tiffin has suggested this is "probably a phantom edition", printed and deposited in the Library of Congress in March 1898 in order to secure copyright, as the letter from Colles suggests.[42] It consists only of Book One of the Heinemann edition. Otherwise, the novel never appeared in the United States, although it was known there. It features in a *New York Times* essay from September 1900 on the unsatisfactory nature of heroines in fiction, reminding us again that English editions were widely distributed in the United States and remained central to the culture of American men of letters. The essay's author thought *The Scourge-Stick* a powerful novel despite its unhealthy heroine: "Clever Mrs. Campbell Praed, do not scourge us with such sharp sticks".[43]

In the early years of the new century, Praed also corresponded with G. Herbert Thring, a solicitor for the Society of Authors, regarding serial rights in England and the United States. Did securing copyright by serial publication prejudice book rights in America? More particularly, she sought advice regarding the strategy of copyrighting by publishing *portions* of a book in the United States. In December 1903, Thring replied:

> If you set up and bring out, only portions of the book in the United States you will only succeed in copyrighting those portions which are thus produced there. This proceeding has been taken frequently. It is best therefore, if you adopt this course, to take out the most prominent chapters and have them set up in the States, so that the book would be practically valueless without the insertion of these chapters.
>
> No case has been tried in the United States Courts, dealing with this subject, and I do not know how far the proceeding would be sanctioned. There is no harm however in your trying it if you have not the time to set up the whole book or if you do not care to run to so large an expense.[44]

---

40   Chatto & Windus contract for *Christina Chard*, 25 January 1896 (Praed Papers, 10/1/4); Author's Syndicate statements 23 August 1894 (Praed Papers, 10/1/11) and 13 January 1896 (Praed Papers, 10/1/5).
41   Colles to Praed, 14 December 1898, Praed Papers (9/2/32).
42   Tiffin, *Rosa Praed*, 28.
43   M.E.W. Sherwood, "Heroines", *New York Times*, 15 September 1900.
44   Thring to Praed, 18 December 1903 (Praed Papers, 9A/11/6); earlier letter re serial rights, 2 January 1903 (Praed Papers, 9A/11/4).

2 International Reputations and Transatlantic Rights: Rosa Praed and Louis Becke

No doubt Praed's mixed fortunes in the American market, both her success with Appleton and her subsequent difficulties, made her particularly concerned about her American rights in these years. After having had more than one title a year released in the United States for fifteen years – although it is extremely unlikely she was aware of all these releases – no new books appeared between 1899 and 1902 when *The Insane Root* was published by Funk & Wagnalls.[45] T. Fisher Unwin, who published the book in London in the same year, most likely sold printed sheets to the American firm.[46] Her next American title, *Fugitive Anne: A Romance of the Unexplored Bush*, was published in London by John Long at the end of 1902 and more than a year later, in 1904, by the New Amsterdam Book Co./R.F. Fenno in New York, the American edition using the English pages but with new illustrations added (Plate 2).[47] Then the American editions dried up, despite or because of the fact that in these years Praed produced "an avalanche of books, many written hurriedly to make money".[48]

Following *Fugitive Anne* and two further novels published in London, Praed worked particularly hard to copyright her new book, *Nyria*, in the United States. She had manually crossed out the clause granting American book rights to the publisher in her contract with Unwin, unlike in their earlier agreements for *The Insane Root* and *My Australian Girlhood* – "I don't feel prepared to give up control of American rights," she told Unwin.[49] Unwin had first contacted Praed in October 1900 with a view to publishing her, and Praed had forwarded the manuscript of *The Insane Root*.[50] Unwin asked, in turn, for a brief scenario of the book so he could show it "to American friends". Apparently he was unsuccessful in arousing American interest, writing to Praed that if he had been able to make arrangements "with America either for serial rights or volume publication" he would have been able to revise his offer to Praed, which stood at 250 guineas outright for "all rights whatsoever in the said work throughout the World". (The deal with Funk & Wagnalls must have come late in the piece.) *Nyria*, by contrast, was negotiated on a royalty basis, indeed a generous 25 per cent flat royalty, but without an advance. Unwin tried because of the work's length to reduce the royalty to 15 per cent, but finally relented. In December 1903, he too advised Praed on the strategy of securing American copyright by publishing part of a book in the United States, recommending, like Thring, that the most prominent chapters be published so that the book would be valueless without them. Praed also forwarded *Nyria* direct to Appleton.[51]

---

45 Established in 1877, it had developed a "Standard Series" for fiction comprising "cheap books of a 'better' class". John Tebbel, *A History of Book Publishing in the United States. Volume II: The Expansion of an Industry, 1865–1919* (New York: Bowker, 1975), 373.

46 The American edition has the same pagination as the English edition.

47 Illustrations by Clare Angell. Two editions are listed in the Library of Congress and New York Public Library: New Amsterdam 1903 and R.F. Fenno 1904 respectively. The book was copyrighted by the former in 1903 but published by the latter in 1904. A letter in Praed's papers from *Publishers' Weekly* to an American correspondent talks of the book having been transferred from the former to the latter when the former "gave up business", 16 January 1905, Praed Papers (8/5/13).

48 Clarke, "Rosa Praed", 310. The period was also marked by tragedies in Praed's personal life, including the death of her son Humphrey in a motor car accident in Los Angeles.

49 *Insane Root* contract dated 29 July 1901; *My Australian Girlhood* contract dated 30 May 1902; *Nyria* contract dated 27 March 1903. Praed to Unwin, 12 March 1903, Praed Papers (9A/1/16, 9A/3/6).

50 Correspondence between Unwin and Praed, 30 October 1900 to 8 October 1904, Praed Papers (9A/1/1-9A/3/46).

51 Appleton to Praed, 19-20 November 1903, Praed Papers (9/3/25-26).

The next phase in the unfortunate saga of *Nyria* was early in 1904 when Praed's friend and fellow theosophist Alfred Sinnett enquired of London publisher John Lane, founder of The Bodley Head, whether the latter could copyright a novel in the United States.[52] Lane had a New York office, established in 1896.[53] Following Sinnett's intelligence, Praed wrote to Lane who replied that for £10 he could indeed do as Praed wished, "have a portion of your new novel set up in America, and placed in the proper quarter demanded by the Copyright Law", in other words, registered at the Library of Congress.[54] But he could not guarantee that this would ensure copyright for the whole work. Lane also took the opportunity to state his interest in publishing one of Praed's books in England and America. While the length of her new novel meant prohibitive production costs, Lane looked forward to being offered "a book for both countries" in the future.

Praed forwarded her £10 and correspondence proceeded apace regarding the copyright situation and the simultaneous publication necessary to protect the work in the United States. Lane wrote in February of 1904 that "it is necessary to copyright in America not later than the day of publication in England, but my usual rule is simultaneous publication either formally or otherwise".[55] In April he asked for a fortnight's notice of the English publication date as he had heard from New York that "it is not absolutely safe to publish a book in America before it is issued in England, that is to say, that the copyright is not secure". Their careful planning for simultaneous publication, however, was thrown into disarray when Unwin delayed its publication date by nine days. On 10 May, Praed wrote to Lane: "I greatly fear from what you tell me that this jeopardises the copyright in the States, in so far as I was able to secure it, but I assume regretfully that nothing can now be done"; and to Unwin: "If, as I am told, this delay jeopardises the copyright in the States, it will be extremely vexatious & disappointing for me".[56] *Nyria* - or rather a portion - had been copyrighted in America by Lane's office in Praed's name on 9 May 1904.[57] But while this may have protected the book from unauthorised editions, probably a very slight risk in any case, it was an added complication for any publisher wanting full rights. Whether for this reason, or because of its length and occult theme, *Nyria* never did find an American publisher, despite being sent to Putnam and Appleton.[58] Praed wrote resignedly to Unwin in early April: "I should be glad if the announcement as to the United States copyright might be inserted though I believe this is not a legal essential".[59] Unwin agreed and thus the English edition unusually, and rather poignantly, carries a notice to the effect that the book had been copyrighted in the United States in 1904 by R.M. Praed.

Australian authors, like their British contemporaries, typically felt their London publishers or agents were not making as much effort as they could to secure American

---

52 Sinnett to Praed, 22 January 1904, Praed Papers (9/3/8).
53 Tebbel, *History Vol. II*, 357-58.
54 Lane to Praed, 26 January 1904, Praed Papers (9/3/9).
55 Lane to Praed, 29 February 1904, Praed Papers (9/3/10).
56 Lane to Praed, 25 April 1904, Praed Papers (9/3/11); Praed to Lane, 10 May 1904, Praed Papers (9/3/13); Praed to Unwin, 10 May 1904, Praed Papers (9A/3/36).
57 Lane to Praed, 11 May 1904, Praed Papers (9/3/14).
58 Tiffin's *Rosa Praed* bibliography records one edition of "Nyria: A Drama of the Days of Domitian", listed in the catalogue of Brown University (Rhode Island) but no longer traceable. He suggests it may be "an outline or section printed for copyright purposes, although it is not held by the Library of Congress" (30).
59 Praed to Unwin, 3 April 1904, Praed Papers (9A/3/33).

2 International Reputations and Transatlantic Rights: Rosa Praed and Louis Becke

publication. For those based in Australia, distance multiplied these anxieties. One response, as we have seen, was for the author to retain American book rights rather than assign them to the English publisher, in the hope of achieving a separate agreement with an American firm. Many of Praed's contracts with British houses thus exclude American book rights. Ideally, this meant an author or agent negotiating a separate copyrighted US edition with royalties for the author against an advance, rather than a "half-profits" arrangement with the English publisher where the costs of production, advertising and a percentage for the publisher's overheads had to be "worked off" before the author received any of their half-share of earnings. The risk of retaining rights was that it meant forgoing the income – possibly more modest but also more secure – that might be produced by the publisher selling the rights or at least selling plates or sheets to an American firm. James L.W. West argues that selling plates was relatively rare, as American publishers saw British plates as of inferior quality.[60] Selling sheets, however, was very common. In such cases, the published book would not be protected in the US market, although copyright notices would still sometimes appear in such editions. Stanley Unwin, writing in 1926, argued that authors were mostly better off leaving such rights with the publisher: "Every English publisher worth his salt tries to ensure American copyright for his authors' books by securing an offer from an American publisher to print their work in the States; if he fails, he sells sheets, which is usually less profitable to the author, though sometimes more".[61] In arguing this case, he was repeating the lesson his uncle had given Praed in 1904 in relation to *Nyria*: "I fear it is too late now to be successful in publishing the book in America. If the American market had been part of our contract no doubt we should have arranged affairs months ago when the book might have been published simultaneously in London and New York but I feel confident any arrangements I might make at this juncture would not be satisfactory to you".[62]

Even if her output was falling, Praed could still be newsworthy, her transatlantic reputation as a novelist and public figure sustained by all kinds of book talk circulating in the US papers. It is also likely that the English editions of her novels were distributed in the American marketplace. *Nyria* in particular was in the American news, not least when Praed's more famous contemporary, H. Rider Haggard, claimed to have been contacted telepathically by his dog as it lay dying. This news was joined by reports from London of Praed's claims to have received the story of *Nyria* from Nyria herself, "a young unmarried woman who remembers her previous existence, near 2000 years ago, as a martyr under Domitian".[63] As a headline in the *San Francisco Call* put it, "Rider Haggard's Strange Dream in Connection with his Dog, and Mrs. Praed's Communications with an Ancient Roman Girl, Interest Britons. Reincarnated Maiden Helps a Woman Write Novel".[64] Given such publicity, it is surprising that *Nyria* was not picked up in the United States, despite its unusual theme and messy copyright situation.

Praed's presence in the American market was only resumed with three titles published by Cassell & Co. in London and New York, following the opening of its New York office

---

60 James L.W. West III, "The Chase Act and Anglo-American Literary Relations", *Studies in Bibliography* 45 (1992): 305–6.
61 Stanley Unwin, *The Truth About Publishing* (London: George Allen & Unwin, 1926), 69–70.
62 Unwin to Praed, 8 October 1904, Praed Papers (9A/3/46).
63 *San Francisco Call*, 7 August 1904. See also 12 August 1904.
64 *San Francisco Call*, 13 September 1904.

in 1898: *By Their Fruits* in 1908, *Opal Fire* in 1910 and *The Body of His Desire: A Romance of the Soul* in 1912.[65] Only the middle title had an Australian setting. *By Their Fruits* was announced in September 1908 as "the first novel that has come from the pen of Mrs. Praed for some time past", true only in the American market.[66] By October, Cassell claimed the novel was in its third printing. Its publicity was a paragraph from Justin McCarthy via the New York *Independent* in which he sought to draw the novel to "the attention of American readers": *By Their Fruits* was "entirely out of the common, alike in conception, character drawing and in its curious blending of the real and the ideal".[67] *Opal Fire* was announced in October 1910 alongside John Foster Fraser's *Australia: The Making of a Nation*, also from Cassell. *The Body of Desire* was advertised in May 1912 with intriguing enticements: "The theme is the psychic conflict in the soul of a popular preacher, who materializes out of his own vital essence the spirit of one whom he has loved and forsaken in an earlier incarnation".[68] No American reviews of these works have been traced. A later novel, *The Mystery Woman* (Cassell, 1913), was on sale in the United States, but no evidence of an American edition has been located.[69]

Praed was also busy arranging publication for a collection of letters between herself and McCarthy, who had died in April 1912. Chatto & Windus published *Our Memories: Letters of Justin McCarthy to Mrs Campbell Praed* that year, but Harper, Appleton, Doran and Putnam all declined either to set up and copyright the book themselves or to print from the English sheets. Percy Spalding of Chatto & Windus offered the copyright to Harper for £200. He offered Doran three alternatives: copyright for £150, copyright for an advance on account of a 12½ per cent royalty for the author, or the purchase of sheets (500 at 2s 9d per copy).[70] As a final strategy, he suggested placing the book with the celebrated New York literary agent, America's first, Paul Revere Reynolds.[71] Eventually an edition of 250 copies was sold in sheets to Small, Maynard & Co. of Boston, who issued the book in 1913.[72] The *Boston Herald* felt the book would "surely appeal to a large class of American readers" but perhaps that was an especially Bostonian viewpoint.[73]

In 1912, as noted, Appleton republished *The Ladies' Gallery*, *Outlaw and Lawmaker* and *Mrs. Tregaskiss*. Otherwise, Praed's final appearance in the American market was an edition of *Lady Bridget in the Never-Never Land: A Story of Australian Life*, which was published in New York by Brentano's around October 1915.[74] It was reviewed in the *New*

---

65   Elizabeth Scott Pryor, "Cassell Publishing Company", in *American Literary Publishing Houses, 1638–1899*, ed. Peter Dzwonkoski, Dictionary of Literary Biography, Vol. 49 (Detroit, MI: Gale Research, 1986), 88. Unlike her earlier contracts, Cassell retained rights for publishing Praed's novels "in all forms and in all countries". Agreement for *By Their Fruits*, 18 June 1907, Praed Papers (10/4/6).
66   "Announcement of New York Books", *New York Times*, 12 September 1908.
67   *New York Times*, 12 September 1908; advertisement, *New York Sun*, 10 October 1908.
68   *New York Times*, 4 May 1912.
69   Statement from Cassell, 30 June 1913, Praed Papers (10/4/1).
70   Correspondence between Spalding and Praed, and Spalding and Doran, Praed Papers (9/6/14-45).
71   Reynolds established his agency in New York in 1893, and in the mid-1920s he was joined by his son Paul Reynolds Jnr, who features in later chapters of the present book.
72   *New York Times*, 16 February 1913. This edition is usually listed as 1912 but this 1913 article has the book as among Small, Maynard & Co.'s forthcoming spring releases.
73   *New York Times*, 6 April 1913. The book sold for a relatively expensive four dollars.
74   Advertised *New York Times*, 9 October 1915. Pagination is the same as the English edition, suggesting it was printed from sheets.

2 International Reputations and Transatlantic Rights: Rosa Praed and Louis Becke

York Times, and its assessment, perhaps like the novel itself, returned to the themes of a much earlier stage in Praed's career:

> The characters and plot of the story are of a familiar type – the misunderstandings between husband and wife, the appearance of the other man, the threatened tragedy and happy ending, with joy and prosperity galore – all these follow well-beaten paths. So far as these factors are concerned the book is an average novel, fairly well done and fairly interesting. But the locale of the tale is one which is still comparatively unusual and possessed of considerable freshness. The account of Lady Bridget's experiences in the bush is thus somewhat out of the ordinary, and therefore interesting.[75]

Praed, in short, could still interest American readers. But despite achieving a level of celebrity and more than a decade of favourable reviews, she left little trace in American book culture after *Lady Bridget*'s brief moment in the limelight. This was a result partly of her own faltering output and of her difficulties in securing simultaneous publication of her works for US release; in larger terms, it was a result of generational change in the American publishing industry as the houses that had supported her career closed or declined, and of shifting tastes as romance progressively lost its literary credibility. As such, it was also a "generic" effect. The sheer portability of romance conventions counted against the lasting impact of any particular novel, however unorthodox its subject, however unusual its local colouring.

The Bret Harte of the Pacific

Louis Becke's presence in the American book market began a decade after Praed's, but the 1890s were equally critical in terms of establishing his readership and reputation. Becke's literary standing would exceed Praed's in terms both of impact and longevity, but like her he found it difficult to profit in any significant way from his American sales. Although he was also in England during the most productive period of his writing career, he was less an expatriate than an inveterate traveller. As a teenager he had travelled to San Francisco before working as a sailor and trader in the South Pacific for much of the period from 1870 to 1892. He began publishing in the Sydney *Bulletin* in 1893. In 1896, after the success of his first book, he left for London where he was celebrated by major figures such as Rudyard Kipling, Joseph Conrad and Arthur Conan Doyle. He spent five years in England and two in Ireland, travelled to the Caribbean, the United States and Canada, and lived for a number of years in France before returning to Australia in 1909 and more Pacific travel.[76]

In Britain for a decade and a half from 1895, Becke was well known and critically esteemed as a major writer of South Seas stories and a forceful realist in this age of romance. In the words of the *Westminster Gazette*:

> The appearance of a new book by Mr Becke has become an event of note – and very justly. No living author, if we except Mr Kipling, has so amazing a command of that unhackneyed vitality of phrase that most people call by the name of realism. Whether it

---

75 *New York Times*, 16 April 1916.
76 A. Grove Day, *Louis Becke* (New York: Twayne, 1966), 19-57.

is scenery or character or incident that he wishes to depict, the touch is ever so dramatic and vivid that the reader is conscious of a picture and impression that has no parallel save in the records of actual sight and memory.[77]

In an article reprinted in America, the London *Times* described him as "that remarkable Ulysses of Pacific waters", and Becke soon became the best-known Australian author in the United States, "the Bret Harte of the Pacific".[78] As with Appleton's support for Praed, Becke had the advantage of regular publication by an established, reputable house. Twenty separate titles and numerous reissues appeared from J.B. Lippincott in these years.

The perception of a distinct genre of Pacific or South Sea tales was a relatively short-lived phenomenon, more or less coinciding with Becke's own publishing career from the mid-1890s to the Great War and dwindling just as the newer genres of detective, mystery and thriller fiction were consolidated. Nonetheless, it was acknowledged over this period as a field distinct from the broader categories of nautical tales or sea stories, one hovering between realism and romance, literary fiction and popular adventure, as Joseph Conrad came to understand.[79] Literary or popular, its significance grew in the late nineteenth century as the Pacific became a site, not just for curiosity, tourism or trade, but more dramatically for defining the nature of " white civilisation" at this critical moment in the empire's history, and in American history, too, as America's Pacific empire was established.[80] If Robert Louis Stevenson was the genre's founding father, Becke soon developed a reputation as its most knowledgeable practitioner and Stevenson's legitimate heir. Stevenson died in 1894, the year Becke's first book appeared. In the words of one American reviewer, "The literary mantle of the lamented Robert Louis Stevenson would fit this newer and as gifted an author of South Sea fables".[81] Becke was also linked to Conrad in American reviews as "a writer of the same school".[82] Their first books had appeared in London in the same year and from the same publisher, T. Fisher Unwin, and Conrad envied Becke's achievements.[83]

As the term "fable" suggests, the South Sea story could be linked to the nautical tales of an author such as W. Clark Russell, then at the height of his popularity, or to adventure-romance fiction. More particularly, given its recurrent focus on Europeans seeking fortune in either savage or exotic outposts of empire, it could be read alongside the imperial frontier romance. Yet, as Robert Dixon argues, Becke's stories often reveal the collapse of the adventure-romance from within, the disintegration of the "heroic attitude to adventure, and with it the ideology of imperialism", something they share with

---

77 Review of *Pacific Tales* (1897) printed in Unwin publicity in its edition of *The Mutineer* (1898).
78 "The Caroline Islands", *Record-Union* (Sacramento CA), 5 December 1898; James MacArthur, "A Bundle of Strange Tales", *Bookman*, September 1897, 69.
79 Peter D. McDonald, *British Literary Culture and Publishing Practice, 1880–1914* (Cambridge: Cambridge University Press, 1997), 22-7.
80 Robert Dixon, *Writing the Colonial Adventure: Race, Gender, and Nation in Anglo-Australian Popular Fiction, 1875–1914* (Cambridge: Cambridge University Press, 1995), 118-33; Roslyn Jolly, "Piracy, Slavery, and the Imagination of Empire in Stevenson's Pacific Fiction", *Victorian Literature and Culture* 35 (2007): 157-73; Marilyn Lake and Henry Reynolds, *Drawing the Global Colour Line: White Men's Countries and the International Challenge of Racial Equality* (Carlton, Vic.: Melbourne University Press, 2008), 95-113.
81 *Saint Paul Globe*, 26 August 1900.
82 *Washington Times*, 19 June 1898.
83 Grove Day, *Louis Becke*, 146.

2 International Reputations and Transatlantic Rights: Rosa Praed and Louis Becke

Stevenson's late work and with Conrad's mature fiction. If the repudiation of romance is never complete in Becke's tales, they often work to "strip the discourse of adventure of any semblance of moral justification, exposing its sordid economy of 'trade' and its connection with masculine violence".[84] They bring a new realism to the South Sea fable as the *Westminster Gazette* recognised, a realism drawing on Becke's own extensive Pacific experience but also influenced by J.F. Archibald's promotion of the contemporary realist sketch in his role as editor of the Sydney *Bulletin*. Thus "Becke's stories stand at the cross-roads of adventure/romance and realism ... Although the Pacific is still the space of adventure of a kind, adventure itself has been redefined, implying moral decadence, physical decay, and the greed and corruption of white men".[85] As Conrad's career indicates, this realism ultimately demanded a different and more sustained literary engagement than was within Becke's capacities or those of the journalistic sketch. The South Sea tale could not survive its own historical moment. Nonetheless, for a decade or more Becke enjoyed a serious transatlantic reputation.

Becke's first collection of stories, *By Reef and Palm*, was published by Unwin in 1894 and reprinted eight times to 1917; the 1895 edition in Unwin's Autonym Library claims copyright in Great Britain and the United States. The book was praised by Mark Twain, as standing "the sharp test of a third reading".[86] It was followed closely by *The Ebbing of the Tide* in 1895, and four more titles in 1896: *Pacific Tales*, the novella *His Native Wife*, and *A First Fleet Family* and *The Mystery of the Laughlin Islands*, two novels co-authored with Walter James Jeffery, editor of Sydney's *Town and Country Journal*.[87] All but the last were released in America. Lippincott published *By Reef and Palm* in 1895, *The Ebbing of the Tide* in 1896 and *His Native Wife* in 1897. In 1897, it also reissued *By Reef and Palm* in a new fiction series.[88] *A First Fleet Family* was published by Macmillan in New York in 1896 and *Pacific Tales* by the New Amsterdam Book Co. in 1897.[89]

By the end of 1900, eleven separate Becke titles, including three collaborations with Jeffery, had appeared in the United States. In addition to those listed above, Lippincott published the co-authored novel, *The Mutineer: A Romance of Pitcairn Island*, in 1898 and two collections of tales, *Rídan the Devil and Other Stories* and *Rodman the Boatsteerer*, in 1899. In 1900, they reissued *The Ebbing of the Tide* and a one-volume edition of *By Reef and Palm* and *His Native Wife* bound together (Plate 3).[90] New Amsterdam published the non-fiction sketches *Wild Life in Southern Seas* in 1898; and in 1899 they published *Old Convict Days*, a text written by William Derricourt but edited and introduced by Becke and commonly associated with his name. In the same year, Longmans, Green published Becke and Jeffery's *Admiral Phillip: The Founding of New South Wales*, originally commissioned by Unwin as part of its Builders of Great Britain series. In 1900, L.C. Page & Co. of Boston

---

84 Dixon, *Writing the Colonial Adventure*, 179–80.
85 Dixon, *Writing the Colonial Adventure*, 184.
86 Twain quoted in Giles, *Antipodean America*, 259.
87 The full subtitle of *A First Fleet Family* was *A Hitherto Unpublished Narrative of Certain Remarkable Adventures Compiled From the Papers of Sergeant William Dew of the Marines*.
88 *By Reef and Palm* is reviewed in the *Washington Times*, 21 March 1897, as a new book, released in Lippincott's "enjoyable Lotus series" following *The Ebbing of the Tide*.
89 As with Boldrewood's *A Crooked Stick*, the colophon printed in *A First Fleet Family* has New York first; the book is clearly set in the United States and was copyrighted there.
90 It carries a notice stating the book was printed by Lippincott, so perhaps from plates supplied by Unwin.

published the well-received novel *Edward Barry: South Sea Pearler*. With two exceptions, every book from that point on dealt with the Pacific or the closely related theme of Australia's early convict period. The exceptions were the "stories of Australian bush life" collected as *The Settlers of Karossa Creek* and a book of humorous tales from Becke's period in France, *Sketches from Normandy*, both published by Lippincott in 1907.

Between 1901 and 1909, when Becke's last new book appeared in America, fifteen new titles were released in the United States, never less than one a year. From Lippincott, in addition to those just mentioned, were *The Tapu of Banderah* (with Jeffery) and *Yorke the Adventurer and Other Stories* both in 1901, *Breachley, Black Sheep* in 1902, *The Strange Adventure of James Shervinton and Other Stories* and *Helen Adair* in 1903, *Chinkie's Flat and Other Stories* in 1904, *Under Tropic Skies* and *Tom Gerrard* in 1905, *The Adventures of a Supercargo* in 1906, *The Call of the South* in 1908, and in 1909 *The Adventures of Louis Blake* and *'Neath Austral Skies*.[91] The only other publisher to figure in this period was New Amsterdam, which released *By Rock and Pool on an Austral Shore and Other Stories* in 1901 and re-released *Old Convict Days* in 1909.

As a writer of stories and novelettes, Becke also benefited from the growth of fiction magazines and newspaper syndication on both sides of the Atlantic in these years. Among what are likely many more magazine and newspaper appearances, a sketch, "Sharks on Wooden Hooks", appeared in the *New York Times* as early as September 1896, another was announced for November the following year, and a story, "For We Were Friends Always", from *Pacific Tales*, was printed in March 1898. A later sketch appeared in the *Times* in August 1904, provoking some bright discussion about catching sharks using the limbs of deceased sailors as bait.[92] A story from *Cassell's Magazine* was reprinted in the *Saint Paul Globe* in 1899 and another from the *Pall Mall Gazette* appeared in the *New York Tribune* in 1900.[93] In May 1896, Paul Reynolds, probably representing Unwin, was attempting to place *The Mystery of Laughlin's Island* with Dodd, Mead, who agreed at one point in the negotiations to take the book, pay $50 for copyright in the United States, and in the process gain first refusal on Becke's next book. This slight romance never appeared in book form in America, but Reynolds did succeed "after considerable difficulty" in selling it to the Bacheller newspaper syndicate for five dollars per thousand words.[94] In 1903, Becke wrote a 3000-word story expressly for *Munsey's Magazine*, following an enquiry from its editor.[95] In 1905, he participated in an adventure series in the *Salt Lake Tribune* called "The Tightest Place I Was Ever In", and from January 1906 his novel *The Adventures of a Supercargo*

---

91   WorldCat lists a Lippincott edition of *Louis Blake* from 1908 but most records give T. Werner Laurie's edition as 1909 (it is not dated). The Lippincott edition carries both publishers' names. A notice in the *New York Tribune* of 17 January 1909 mentions the title as Becke's new novel without making clear whether the information is from England or New York.

92   *New York Times*, 27 September 1896; 5 November 1897; 6 March 1898; "Muriel Pithkethley, of the 'Peruvian'", 7 August 1904.

93   "Tale of the South Seas", *Saint Paul Globe*, 6 August 1899; "'Reo: A Napoleon of Samoan Finance", *New York Tribune*, 23 December 1900.

94   Reynolds to Dodd, Mead, 6 May and 11 May 1896. Dodd, Mead MSS, Lilly Library, Indiana University, Box 2.

95   Becke to William Morris Colles, 11 November 1903. Letters from Louis Becke, State Library of NSW, MLDOC 1404.

was serialised in the *Salt Lake Herald*.[96] Finally, in 1912, the year before his death, he contributed to the New York magazine *Adventure* following an invitation from its editor.[97]

An Eye Toward the American Market

In the words of A. Grove Day, Becke "had an eye always toward the American market".[98] His American editions, though, were almost wholly dependent upon his relations with his British agents and publishers, especially Unwin, and upon their links in turn with American publishers. In October 1893, Archibald sent Becke's earliest stories to H.W. Massingham, editor of the London *Daily Chronicle*, noting that although they were "at variance with the current fashion" - that is, the fashion for romance - not least in their focus on "the unconventional relations of the white man and the brown woman", their "freshness and novelty should pull them through".[99] Massingham forwarded the stories to Unwin, who then wrote to Becke offering him two plans for this and future publications: one for outright purchase of the first volume plus options on his next two books; the other for publishing all three books on royalty terms. As mentioned in Chapter 1, the royalty system, like the use of agents, was still very much in contention at this period.[100] Unwin advised Becke and Conrad at much the same time that if they chose royalties they would in effect share the risk of publication. Conrad was offered £20 outright for *Almayer's Folly*, while Becke was offered £30 for *By Reef and Palm*. Becke replied that while he was flattered he could not agree to terms "which amount to £30 for the copyright of the eleven tales now submitted and 10 per cent as computed by you of the profit in future books". He reluctantly accepted the sum for the copyright but "not future deals".[101] It appears that with the receipt of some additional tales for the collection, Unwin increased the offer to £65.[102] From then on Unwin published almost all of Becke's books through to 1905, twenty-three in total. Fifteen were shared with Lippincott, published more or less simultaneously in the two markets, in what appears to have been a settled agreement between the two houses.

It is not known whether Becke left Unwin or whether Unwin began rejecting Becke's submissions. Possibly the latter, for as early as 1897 Edward Garnett in a reader's report commented: "We think it is quite time Mr Becke called a halt in his own interests - as well as those of his publisher. His fecundity in the way of stories is alarming".[103] But even if the quantity of Becke's writing was overwhelming its quality, he was apparently still a good commercial proposition. His agreements with Unwin show a mix of outright sale in the early years and then royalty agreements once agents become involved. In July 1894, he

---

96 "The Tightest Place I Was Ever In. IV - My Race for Life", *Salt Lake Tribune*, 24 September 1905; "The Adventures of a Supercargo", *Salt Lake Herald*, 21 January 1906.
97 Arthur S. Hoffman to Becke, 19 January 1912, Louis Becke Papers, 1880-1913, MLMSS 248, State Library of NSW.
98 Grove Day, *Louis Becke*, 149.
99 Archibald to Massingham, 13 October 1893, A.P. Watt and Son Records 1861-1971, Berg Collection, New York Public Library.
100 Peter Keating, *The Haunted Study: A Social History of the English Novel, 1875-1914* (London: Fontana, 1991), 15-20.
101 Unwin to Becke, 14 December 1893; Becke to Unwin, 29 January 1894. A.P. Watt Records, New York Public Library.
102 Grove Day, *Louis Becke*, 40.
103 Report. n.d. (c. August 1897), A.P. Watt Records, New York Public Library.

accepted £60 in exchange for "all bookrights both English and American" in what became *Wild Life in Southern Seas*.[104] In June 1896, in contrast, royalty payments appear in the agreement for *The Mutineer* signed between Unwin and publishers Angus & Robertson in Sydney.[105] The contract granted exclusive serial and book rights in Great Britain and the United States to Unwin, who agreed in turn "to have the work published simultaneously in London and Australia by a reputable publishing house" and "to secure the American copyright of the work in the manner provided by the existing Copyright Law". Becke and Jeffery would receive an advance of £250 against royalties at a flat 15 per cent.[106]

Despite Lippincott's commitment to Becke, selling *The Mutineer* in America proved difficult, in part because of the clause pertaining to American copyright. In February 1898, Unwin wrote to A.P. Watt, acting for Angus & Robertson, that the firm was having "considerable difficulty in selling this book to America" because it was obliged to inform prospective clients that the story had already appeared in the English weekly *Lloyd's* and therefore the book could not be copyrighted. He thus sought authorisation "to sell a considerable quantity of sheets, say 1000 copies at a low rate" with a royalty of 10 per cent of the net receipts. Watt gave the authorisation, informing his clients: "As Mr Unwin is quite correct in saying that there is no copyright to be had on 'The Mutineer' in the United States, and as any pirate publisher can re-print the story there, any profit that may be derived from the sale of sheets or plates in that quarter is of course found money".[107] No doubt these were the terms under which Lippincott published the book. Across the first half of the twentieth century, many Australian novels would appear in the United States without copyright protection for the risk of pirating was low, although Becke's popularity would have meant some risk.

In May 1896, not long before he left for London, Becke wrote to Watt accepting his terms as literary agent, and in July Becke and Jeffery formally appointed Watt as their agent for works published individually or together.[108] Watt's influence can be seen in Becke's contracts over the next few years, which all specify royalties and include clauses relating to American rights, although the formulas vary considerably. The contract for *His Native Wife*, signed in August 1896, gave Unwin "exclusive right of printing and publishing in book form in Great Britain, its Colonies and Dependencies", and, in an interesting qualification, "as far as is possible in the United States of America".[109] In December, Watt wrote to Unwin that on Becke's instructions, Unwin was "at liberty to make the best arrangement you can for the publication of 'His Native Wife' in America, dividing any profits on the transaction equally between yourself and him".[110] This was one of the few Becke titles Lippincott copyrighted.

---

104 Agreement, 2 July 1894, A.P. Watt Records, New York Public Library.
105 Grove Day, *Louis Becke*, 86.
106 Agreement, 6 June 1896, A.P. Watt Records, New York Public Library.
107 Correspondence between Watt, Unwin, and Angus & Robertson, 23-25 February 1898, A.P. Watt Records, 1888-1892, University of North Carolina, Box 18.
108 Becke to Watt, 25 May 1896, A.P. Watt Records, New York Public Library, and 30 July 1896, A.P. Watt Records, University of North Carolina.
109 It specified a flat royalty of 2d a copy and an advance of £100 on account, equivalent to just over and just under 10 per cent for the paper and cloth editions respectively. Agreement 19 August 1896, A.P. Watt Records, University of North Carolina.
110 Watt to Unwin, 15 December 1896, A.P. Watt Records, University of North Carolina.

2 International Reputations and Transatlantic Rights: Rosa Praed and Louis Becke

Becke had earlier sold all "copyrights and interests" in his first four books to Unwin for only £50, and in 1896 he signed an extraordinary agreement granting Unwin all serial and book rights in all countries "to all works which said Becke may write within the next five years".[111] Advances would be calculated at one pound per thousand words and royalties at 20 per cent, or 10 per cent of the published price of any American edition. Despite the agreement, Watt was able to negotiate separate contracts for subsequent books. An agreement for a volume of stories (*Pacific Tales*) signed in March 1897 specified an advance of £100 on account of royalties of 25 per cent on the nominal selling price of a six-shilling edition and 10 per cent on the selling price for an American edition. United States book rights were granted to Unwin, who agreed to "use every endeavour to dispose of the said United States book rights".[112] A later agreement, from April 1898, for a collection of stories then called "Ned Prince and the Supercargo", specified payments of 25 per cent on all copies sold above half the published price covering Great Britain, its colonies and dependencies *and* the United States, again with an advance of £100. Quires or bound copies sold to America would come under the same royalty terms – the former almost certainly the arrangement made with Lippincott – while the publisher retained the power to sell the American rights, paying two-thirds of any profits to the author.[113] The agreement with Unwin for a one-volume edition of *By Reef and Palm* and *His Native Wife* together – published by Lippincott in 1900 – specified a royalty of 10 per cent "on the published price and net receipts of sales".[114]

Thus, although Watt was able to negotiate better terms for his author, Unwin still retained the rights to most of Becke's works, not least the right to sell them in the American market or otherwise sell plates or sheets. In 1901, the *New York Times* published an announcement from Unwin listing books for which "the United States rights are for sale" including Becke's *Tessa and The Trader's Wife* (which was not sold).[115] As we have seen, Unwin most likely sold unbound sheets to Lippincott and other publishers more often than he sold book rights as such. This common practice meant a small but guaranteed income for the English publisher and a relatively cheap investment for the American firm, but usually only modest returns for the author with either a percentage split between author and publisher on a one-off payment or a reduced royalty rate.

Lippincott's editions, however, were not cheaply produced. While the early titles were released in Lippincott's "handy little Lotus books series", by 1900 they had an attractive, uniform cloth binding with a striking red floral design on the cover and were sold at the standard price for hardback fiction of $1.50.[116] While some at least of the early titles were printed in the United States by Lippincott itself, from at least *Ridan the Devil* in 1899 the books showed both publishers' names on the title page, and Lippincott's editions retained Unwin's stylish use of red ink for the book title and author's name. New Amsterdam did the same for *Pacific Tales*, a "handsome volume", and again all their books show both New Amsterdam and Unwin as publishers.[117] L.C. Page's edition of *Edward Barry* was

---

111 Becke to Watt, 25 May 1896; agreements between Becke and Unwin, A.P. Watt Records, New York Public Library. This agreement must date from just before Becke had signed with Watt and perhaps was the reason for him wanting an agent.
112 Agreement, 12 March 1897, A.P. Watt Records, University of North Carolina, Box 20.
113 Agreement, 14 April 1898, A.P. Watt Records, New York Public Library, Folder 1.
114 Agreement, 7 March 1898, A.P. Watt Records, University of North Carolina, Box 18.
115 "Books and Authors", *New York Times*, 18 May 1901.
116 Lotus books: *Washington Times*, 21 March and 6 June 1897.
117 *Los Angeles Herald*, 3 October 1897.

also praised for its illustrations and "typographical excellence".[118] By contrast, one reviewer found the illustrations in Lippincott's edition of *The Strange Adventure of James Shervinton* "calculated to cause pain and to inspire in the discriminating a wish that the artist might himself take to piracy – or some other less heinous form of art".[119] Only Lippincott's edition of *His Native Wife*, Page's *Edward Barry* and Macmillan's *A First Fleet Family* were copyrighted, but all the volumes were well-produced hardcover books designed for "discriminating readers".

By late 1900, Becke had left Watt and like Praed was using William Morris Colles to place stories and novels. By 1910, he appears to have signed with the other major literary agent in London, J.B. Pinker. These agency shifts were perhaps a sign that Becke's bargaining power had weakened following his break with Unwin. In his first contract with T. Werner Laurie, for *Notes from my South Sea Log* in February 1905, a 12 per cent royalty was indicated and arrangements for American publication specified in terms similar to those offered by Unwin: a royalty of 10 per cent on net receipts should quires or bound copies be sold and if rights were sold a half-share in net profits. In September of the same year, Becke signed a new agreement for the same title, ceding to the publisher "all books rights whatsoever … throughout the world" for only £35. All later agreements were of this kind: £50 for a second series of stories (September 1905); then £35 for the same (October 1905); £35 again for a third volume (July 1906); and £80, in March 1908, for what became *The Adventures of Louis Blake*.[120] Like Unwin before it, Werner Laurie arranged with Lippincott for (non-copyrighted) American editions of *The Adventures of Louis Blake* and *Sketches from Normandy*, and the American firm also released *Call of the South* and *'Neath Austral Skies* jointly with London publisher John Milne.

Louis Becke's Genius

Becke's reputation in America was quickly established, widely broadcast, and sustained for over a decade. Among the earliest notices was the *New York Times* review of *By Reef and Palm* in January 1895, under the heading "Stories from Stevenson's Land". It was a lengthy review, remarkable for its considered assessment of Becke's literary "genius". Stevenson's recent death provided the starting point:

> It is by a most strange chance that, just after Stevenson's untimely death … should appear this little book; – most strange, because the book is written by a man whose life has been passed among the scenes upon which this half-century's deftest artificer in words looked last and most lovingly … by a man who is, as certainly as was he who lies cold, a genius …
>
> [To] assert of a man as yet entirely unknown, at least in this hemisphere, a man of one book, and it a book of short tales, that he is a man of genius and therefore a great man, involves too much danger … to permit of any delay in seeking whatever protection there may be in instant confession that the author of "By Reef and Palm" gives no proof of ability, developed or latent, to write anything so magnificent as "David Balfour." Or "Kidnapped."

---

118 *Saint Paul Globe*, 26 August 1900.
119 *New York Sun*, 14 March 1903.
120 Louis Becke Papers, 1881-1912, CY 4684, State Library of NSW.

2 International Reputations and Transatlantic Rights: Rosa Praed and Louis Becke

Or "Treasure Island." None the less is Louis Becke a great man. This book of his is a little book, in more ways than one, yet from its pages there shines, clear, though faint, the light of genius, and to possess even a gleam of that light is enough for greatness ...

It may be of course that the author of "By Reef and Palm" is only a man of talent; it may be that his South Sea stories owe as much to the absolute freshness of the material which his peculiar life has enabled him to gather as to his method of using that material. The same thing was said of Kipling and many another now undoubted genius. As a matter of fact, however, it takes a genius to discover that the new is new ...

Not a trace of what appears in "books of travel" is to be found in "By Reef and Palm." Neither the islands nor their people, white or brown, are treated as objects of curiosity and interest because they happen to be different from other countries and peoples. That is the standpoint of the explorer or the tourist. Mr. Becke is neither one nor the other ...

Exactly here lies the difference between this book and all the others – they are innumerable – that tell about Polynesia, and it is the apparently effortless maintenance of this attitude, or rather of this point of view, that proves the author's originality of mind and his genius. He is not an islander, nor is he writing for islanders, and therefore there is something of artifice underlying his work, but it never, for even a moment, comes to the surface, and justification of his method lies in its success, in the spontaneous and irresistible grip that his stories take on a reader's heart, and in the self-confirmed verity of their minutest detail. If this is not genius, talent is a marvellously good substitute for it and a lesser thing equals a greater.[121]

The review closes with a brief biographical introduction to Becke for the paper's readers. Although at the positive extreme of responses, it does indicate the impact that Becke's "little book" appears to have had for many. Looking back from 1898, another critic remarked, "As a new man, [Becke] made a wonderful start, for he at once met with general acceptance".[122] By 1899, his reputation was established: "It is enough to announce a new book by Mr. Louis Becke; it is superfluous to review it. He has gained the ear of a large public, who are attracted by his tales of the South Seas, and find them quite to their taste".[123] Becke was familiar enough to American readers for *The Strange Adventure of James Shervinton* to be described, when it appeared in 1903, as in his "accustomed manner": "a series of rattling good and interesting yarns, with much of actuality blended with their fiction".[124]

In June 1896, Becke's portrait appeared in Scribner's *Book Buyer* magazine, and from his earliest publications his authority in South Sea literature was accepted: "In the geography of contemporary fiction, Mr. Becke has pre-empted to himself the broad expanse of the Southern Pacific"; "Louis Becke has an undisputed sway in the South Sea Islands of the Pacific, in the sense of literary regency"; he "has taken that region for his own in the matter of fiction".[125] As a *New York Times* reviewer put it in 1899: "With our fresh interests in the South Seas the popularity of Louis Becke ought to grow in America ... The

---

121 "New Publications: Stories from Stevenson's Land", *New York Times*, 6 January 1895.
122 Joel Benton, "150 Books for Summer Reading", *New York Times*, 25 June 1898.
123 "Novel Notes", *Bookman*, August 1899, 34.
124 *New York Sun*, 14 March 1903.
125 *Washington Times*, 21 March 1897; *Washington Times*, 6 June 1897; *New York Tribune*, 6 January 1901.

Samoans, the Malays, the Maoris he knows as no other writer of his present distinction knows".[126] Becke's name was also kept before the American reading public through the *New York Times*' regular "London Literary Letter" by William L. Alden, a keen follower of Becke's career. Becke was especially prominent through late 1898 during the high-profile "Louis de Rougemont" hoax. In *The Adventures of Louis de Rougemont as Told by Himself*, also published by Lippincott, the author claimed to have travelled widely in Australia and the Pacific and to have lived among Aborigines and Pacific natives. Becke was a key witness for the sceptics.[127]

In August 1896, the *New York Times* reprinted a lengthy conversation with Becke from London's *Daily Chronicle* on the Pacific, missionaries, and Australian literature. Its introduction summarises the American response to Becke's early titles:

> When Louis Becke's first book, "By Reef and Palm," made its appearance, all the critics decided that the stories about the South Sea islands which it contained were good ones, while a few, more enthusiastic, declared that the tales were altogether out of the common, and with difficulty refrained from linking at once the name of their author with that of Stevenson. These impulsive persons were rather disappointed as time went on, to see that the reading public did not become at all excited over Mr. Becke's work, but they were in a measure reconciled by the fact that the book had a real though quiet success. Since then the antipodean writer has published "A First Fleet Family" and "The Ebbing of the Tide," and he is now recognised everywhere as a man of unusual talent, possessed of unusual and intensely interesting information, and destined to make for himself a permanent place in literature.[128]

The *Boston Transcript* review of *By Reef and Palm* suggests that this mixed early reception may have been linked to the way Becke's stories were located on the contemporary fault line between romance and realism: "A really queer little book of languorously [sic] picturesque yarns ... These little stories are indeed romance in an entirely new form."[129] The "romance of the South Seas" was an almost irresistible notion. In America as in Britain, it enabled readers to assimilate Becke to the adventure-romance or nautical tale – sometimes as a writer of adventure stories for boys – but also, for some, to praise him for his more demanding or satisfying realism. Becke's works themselves shifted uneasily across the romance/realism fault line, especially when he tried his hand at full-length novels which tended to be much more conventional romances.

The *Times* reviewer of *The Ebbing of the Tide*, for example, was offended by the book's brutality: "Dramatic fiction, or the compression of the dreadful, has its limits, and Mr. Becke has not the least comprehension when to come to a full stop with what is appalling. Around these disgusting islands it is not the blue tide which ebbs, but it is a crimson flood of gore".[130] *Pacific Tales* was praised in the *Bookman* for something very similar:

---

126 *New York Times*, 15 July 1899.
127 "Louis de Rougemont" was Swiss-born Henri Louis Grin. *The Adventures of Louis de Rougemont As Told by Himself* was published by Heinemann in London in 1899 and by Lippincott in 1900.
128 "A Talk with Louis Becke", *New York Times*, 23 August 1896.
129 Review printed in Lippincott's 1896 edition of *The Ebbing of the Tide*.
130 "Gore Galore", *New York Times*, 22 April 1896.

life throbs behind the pages; and as onlookers, the artist in the author has the power to make us quicken with sympathy or sicken with disgust, as he unveils the wickedness, the weakness, the crime existing alongside of the loveliness, the pathos, the strange, wild beauty of life in the islands afar off in the South Seas. A weird spell falls upon the reader when he comes under Mr. Becke's sway … There is a grim tenacity about the way in which his work fastens upon the imagination and haunts the memory … Mr. Becke has this power to vitalise the raw material which he has come by so richly, and with it he has also the power to enthral, to fascinate, but as frequently with repulsion as with attraction.[131]

Edward Barry asked to be read more simply as an adventure-romance and was praised accordingly: it showed "all the force of a master of fairy tales"; it would hold "the attention of mature years from beginning to end, and certainly will prove one of the most popular sea tales of the year for juvenile reading". Another reviewer praised "its thread of romance – a tender story of woman's devotion running through it". "Though there are some blood curdling and tragic occurrences, the story has a happy ending and Mr Becke deserves hearty congratulation upon the success of his first novel." Even for the *New York Times*, Becke, in this instance, was "to be congratulated for turning out so clean and wholesome a romance": it was "a boy's book … too hackneyed and bloody for 'grown-ups' … as exciting as a dime novel and as well put up as a 'one-fifty' … full of action and sensations [but] superior to the cheap tales of adventure so much in vogue in that it is more neatly written".[132]

A First Fleet Family was praised for its realism, although one reviewer felt the authors had sacrificed the possibilities of a "more thrilling tale" with their focus on historical veracity. While the *Bookman* admired its "actuality" and historical value, "admirably balanced by its romantic interest", the *Atlantic Monthly* regretted "that the realism of the tale should have been weakened at its close by the story-book marriages of the heroine and the Sergeant".[133] *The Mutineer*, by contrast, was described in advance notices as "Mr. Becke's first sustained effort at romance writing". Indeed, the *Times* praised it as a "patiently elaborated romance" despite its focus on the "cruel beginnings" of Pitcairn Island's European settlement (Fig. 2.3).[134]

Realism could still be challenging. Becke wrote to his collaborator Jeffery in May 1897 that Lippincott had declined to publish *The Mutineer*. Becke's view was that *His Native Wife* had been so unfavourably received that Lippincott were not prepared to take any more risks: "I quite expected a storm to ensue as *His Native Wife* is so antagonistic to American missionaries that another book by the same author would get a chill reception."[135] But while there may have been a delay, Lippincott did publish and copyright the book, and republished it in 1900. Reviews were also generally favourable, although *Outlook*'s notice described it as "overwrought and lacking literary restraint".[136] Certainly the theme of relations between white men and islander women had been noted as early as *The Ebbing of the Tide* as one

---

131 MacArthur, "A Bundle of Strange Tales", *Bookman*, September 1897, 69.
132 *Saint Paul Globe*, 26 August 1900; *San Francisco Call*, 7 October 1900; *New York Times*, 29 December 1900.
133 *Saint Paul Globe*, 2 August 1896; *Bookman*, August 1896, 554-55; "Comment on New Books", *Atlantic Monthly* 79 (January 1897): 135.
134 *Los Angeles Herald*, 24 April 1898; "The Mutiny on the Bounty", *New York Times*, 30 July 1898.
135 Becke quoted in Grove Day, *Louis Becke*, 149.
136 "Books of the Week", *Outlook*, 19 June 1897, 460.

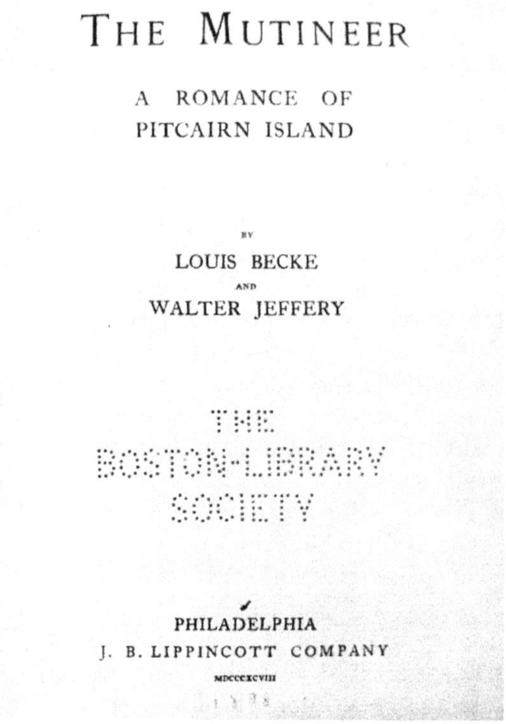
THE MUTINEER

A ROMANCE OF
PITCAIRN ISLAND

BY

LOUIS BECKE

AND

WALTER JEFFERY

PHILADELPHIA
J. B. LIPPINCOTT COMPANY
MDCCCXCVIII

Figure 2.3 Louis Becke and Walter Jeffery, *The Mutineer: A Romance of Pitcairn Island* (Philadelphia: J.B. Lippincott Co., 1898).

of Becke's trademarks. In an otherwise positive review, the brutality of his treatment of the theme was disturbing:

> At times Mr. Becke rises to the level of his opportunities. In the nature of things, his stories cannot be pleasant ones, as the brown characters are unfailingly devoid of that natural sweetness of disposition which Charles Warren Stoddard first taught us to associate with the natives of the South Seas, and the white characters consist of the scum of the earth. These are not the materials out of which pretty stories are made, but there are some ways of telling ugly stories which are more acceptable than other ways. In "Lupton's Guest" the author treats his material with imagination and restraint, and the results are as satisfactory as may be …The book is over-weighted, however, by the many brutal tales dealing with white men and native women, and loses greatly thereby. The stories are all alike, and all hideous … It is always wise for an author to consider the reader's comfort.[137]

His Native Wife was praised, even for its brutality: "The extreme favour with which the public received 'By Reef and Palm' will be extended in this volume also, which is a much more ambitious venture … It is a wild story, almost brutal in its simplicity of recital, yet

137 *Saint Paul Daily Globe*, 26 April 1896.

2 International Reputations and Transatlantic Rights: Rosa Praed and Louis Becke

curiously fascinating. In many ways it is very slight and lacking in finish, but it is powerful in its swift and striking ending".[138]

In 1901, at the height of his fame, Becke was invited by Putnam's in London to write the introduction to a new edition of Melville's *Moby-Dick*.[139] But while favourable reviews continued well into the new century, qualifications or "disappointment" became increasingly common. On *Rídan the Devil*: "His literary style is not to be commended as a model, but he expresses himself coherently and often with irresistible power. His book is full of humanity, the work of a whole-souled, sound-minded man who understands his fellows and likes them".[140] And again: "We find his material excellent within the limits of his rather narrow observation, and we always plunge into his books with an eager hope of being excited and invigorated. But nearly always we are repelled by the dullness of his manner. He is quite careless of effect, altogether monotonous in tone".[141] Becke's attempts at longer fiction – as he no doubt worked both to extend his literary career and make it more profitable – were seen as disappointingly conventional in comparison with the originality of his tales and sketches:

> In the vast army of present day novel writers there are very few whose names are a guarantee of something original, interesting, out of the common, and one comes into possession of a book by any one of them with a delightful assurance, the result of numerous confirmations in the past, that the time spent in reading it will be repaid. Mr. Louis Becke has, without doubt, been one of this select few, and his tales of the South Pacific islands have long been gratefully received by those weary of an endless diet of historical novels, problem novels, and novels with nothing in particular to recommend them. Hitherto his work has been, with one or two exceptions, in the form of short stories, or rather sketches, of the island life of the South Seas; but in "Helen Adair" he not only makes the departure of indulging in a regulation novel of 276 pages, but exchanges his island folk for much less interesting people – some Irish prisoners who have been transported for sedition to the Australian convict colony.
>
> The result will be as distinctly disappointing to Mr. Becke's admirers as was "James Shervinton," a previous attempt at long short story writing.[142]

Tom Gerrard, similarly, was just "one of those stories, quite without literary flavour, which are affected by a certain class of British periodical".[143]

Australian bush stories had themselves become conventional and ripe for taking down: "Mr. Becke tells you with enthusiasm of suppers of game out under the stars, of tea and damper from saddle bags, of gold miners and their reckless ways … of an affair with a cattle whip in a tavern, and a midnight assault away out upon the plains … In short, the story contains the usual Australian elements of interest".[144] *The Settlers of Karossa Creek*, "a

---

138 *Los Angeles Herald*, 6 June 1897.
139 London: G.P. Putnam's Sons, 1901; reprinted in *Moby-Dick* by Herman Melville, ed. Hershel Parker and Harrison Hayford, Norton Critical Edition (New York: Norton, 2002), 636-37. See "Philippine Folks", *New York Times*, 27 April 1901.
140 "Becke's South Sea Tales", *New York Times*, 15 July 1899.
141 "Novel Notes", *Bookman*, August 1899, 561.
142 "A Novel by Louis Becke", *New York Times*, 5 December 1903.
143 "Job of Australia", *New York Times*, 17 June 1905.
144 "Job of Australia", *New York Times*, 17 June 1905.

collection of Australian tales which shows an intimate acquaintance with 'bush' life and the types of characters which abound there", was more striking for its anti-romantic elements. The stories were "'plain, unvarnished tales,' with little glamour of romance ... calculated to disillusionize [sic] any one who has any idea of finding picturesqueness or beauty in the 'bush.' The climate is bad, moral standards are shaky and it's a hard time and a lonely one that awaits the Australian pioneer".[145]

Increasingly, Becke also suffered from comparison with Conrad, whose writing showed "a sustained power and an insight into the inner causes ... that the author of 'By Reef and Palm' has not shown".[146] *The Adventures of a Supercargo* in 1906 showed him "further than ever from the interpretative power with which a Conrad would have transformed such knowledge as this author must possess of a region practically his own for literary purposes".[147] As he continued to rework the Pacific theme, Becke could even suffer from comparison with his own achievements. As the *New York Sun* reviewer wrote of *The Adventures of a Supercargo*:

> A great opportunity has been wasted by Mr. Louis Becke. At a time when Stevenson had aroused a new craving for South Sea stories he showed that he had the knowledge and in his first short stories indicated that he had the ability to supply the demand. He has contented himself, however, with providing copy instead of developing his talent, and has fathered some pretty trashy stuff ... [T]here is an excess of irritatingly perfunctory work and of barefaced padding. A page and a half on the Samoan dialect and various long quotations from books must make the reader wonder what fiction is coming to.[148]

By the end of the decade, the stories and style that had once seemed original, breaking from the dominant adventure-romance conventions, could themselves be seen as conventional or simply old-fashioned. When *'Neath Austral Skies* was reviewed in 1909, Becke had slipped below Kipling and Stevenson as originators of the modern short story; indeed, he been pushed out of the modern line altogether. His stories, instead, had "the familiar schoolboyish tone which was found in all plain tales of the sea till the refinements of modern art in the hands of Stevenson and Kipling laid hold upon a homely and simple-minded school of fiction". Becke's narratives, by contrast, reminded the reviewer of the edifying Sunday School books of a previous generation, an extraordinary shift in perception given the emphasis on brutality and frankness in reviews from a decade earlier: "He is merely following the old model rather than the new".[149]

The Shifting Tide

The taste for South Sea Island or Pacific stories never completely disappeared, and Becke retained a small band of supporters (including James A. Michener).[150] But like the

---

145 "Bush Life Described", *New York Sun*, 21 December 1907.
146 Review of *An Outcast of the Islands*, by Joseph Conrad, *New York Sun*, 14 August 1897.
147 "The South Seas", *New York Times*, 12 May 1906.
148 *New York Sun*, 24 February 1906.
149 "Stories by Louis Becke", *New York Times*, 24 July 1909.
150 Grove Day, *Louis Becke*, 151.

romance conventions that supported Praed's career into the early years of the twentieth century, the genre's literary standing was greatly reduced from the 1920s, partly as a consequence of Conrad's critical success and the increasing divisions generally between serious and light fiction (and in this case, "fiction for boys"). But despite these shifts in critical taste, Becke remained profitable enough for Lippincott to stay engaged across the first decades of the twentieth century. Most strikingly, between 1924 and 1926, they collaborated with Unwin and Thomas Allen of Toronto in producing a uniform edition of Becke's work. At least nine titles were reissued in the series, including some, such as *Pacific Tales*, it had not previously published. No doubt the series was cheap to produce, but its duration over three years and the attractive presentation of the books themselves suggest that the three publishers believed there remained a considerable market for Becke's works.

Unfortunately, the critics did not agree. The *Times* reviewer of *James Shervinton* in its new edition thought the stories, with one exception, "written in the manner of a gracefully aging Victorian who after a lively youth has corrected his ways to decorum and is now confident of being more holy than thou".[151] The exception, Becke's portrait of Bully Hayes, "is a happy relief from these stories of such unabated lofty romance". Again, as he falls on the wrong side of modern taste, the reversal in understanding Becke's relation to romance or conventional Victorian fiction is striking.

This judgement was clear, too, in one of the new publications of the 1920s, the *Saturday Review of Literature*, when it surveyed five of the new editions. The South Sea genre was pronounced dead: "These five volumes of the promised Collected Edition of Louis Becke are inexplicable except as belated jetsam cast up in the wake of the recent South Sea wave". Realism had replaced romance as the literary benchmark:

> [Becke] was a man of extraordinary endurance and a quenchless *flair* for adventure and life in the raw; but he was also a man of thoroughly commonplace intellect and to the end unshaken in his adherence to the devout prejudices of Victorian Christendom … In his better stories, the surf, the coral, the palms become mere stage background for snappy tales, generally realistic, always ugly when interesting, full of sudden brutal murders, gin-drinking and cruelty, and only suggestively atmospheric when oppressively sentimental and machine-made. The brutality has evidently been felt, the rest as evidently manufactured … At his worst, as in "Helen Adaire," [sic] he belongs to the school of Ouida, The Duchess, and Mrs. E.D.E.N. Southworth.[152]

The fact that the next Australian author to make a significant impact among American critics was Henry Handel Richardson suggests the shifting tide that washed over the transatlantic reputations of Louis Becke and Rosa Praed.

---

151 "Rough Life", *New York Times*, 11 July 1926.
152 "Books of Special Interest: Louis Becke", *Saturday Review of Literature*, 29 May 1926, 824.

3

Crime, Sensation and the Modern Genre System: Australian Authors in the Popular Fiction Marketplace, 1890s–1920s

The American careers of Ada Cambridge, Rolf Boldrewood and Rosa Praed all extended into the first decade of the twentieth century, with new titles appearing alongside reprints of earlier works. Other authors whose careers in the US market began before the turn of the century but extended well beyond it include Fergus Hume, Guy Boothby and Carlton Dawe. Although forty years separate the birthdates of the oldest and youngest of these six authors, they were largely contemporaries in terms of their American publishing careers, with the majority of all their US titles appearing between 1890 and 1910. Yet to shift focus from the first to the second group is to find oneself in a changed literary space, marked by the emergence of the modern genre system on both sides of the Atlantic and hence in the Australian literary marketplace as well. As writers and readers, colonial Australians were subjects not only of the British Empire but also of a transnational Anglophone market for popular entertainment, not least for popular fiction. They participated in an expanding mass market, and not merely a contained and containing colonial system.

The Emergence of the Modern Genre System

Cambridge, Boldrewood and Praed wrote into a market where genre categories were abundant but relatively fluid and weakly defined. The contemporary forms of the novel were divided into numerous subgenres, from the bushranging tale to the nautical adventure to the sentimental Christmas story; and while certain forms such as the gothic or sensation novel had achieved more substantial definition over the course of the nineteenth century, the category of romance absorbed almost all other generic divisions, from imperial adventure to domestic marriage plots. Newer genre categories such as wild west adventure or the detective story operated more overtly in the cheaper forms of popular fiction, as penny and sixpenny paperbacks in Britain and dime novels in the United States, but these constituted a largely separate domain of mass-market production and distribution.[1] Thus, while savagely

---

1 James D. Hart, *The Popular Book: A History of America's Literary Taste* (New York: Oxford University Press, 1950), 153-56; J. Randolph Cox, *The Dime Novel Companion: A Source Book* (Westport, CT: Greenwood, 2000), xiii-xx; Erin A. Smith, "Pulp Sensations", in *The Cambridge Companion to Popular Fiction*, ed. David Glover and Scott McCracken (Cambridge: Cambridge University Press, 2012), 141-45.

witty or heavily moralised judgements against cheap and sensational fiction were frequent in the literary papers, generic divisions as such played a lesser role in determining literary hierarchies or the position of a work or author in the literary field than they would by the 1920s. Romances could be accorded the highest praise.

By contrast, the careers of Hume and Boothby, the most prominent among an emerging group of popular Australian authors, depended upon the newly determining presence of distinctive genres and subgenres understood together as constituting a relatively discrete field within mainstream publishing. The twin pressures of expansion and specialisation in the book trade, above all in the fiction market, produced a "relentless fragmentation and categorisation of fiction".[2] As Clive Bloom has argued, from the 1880s to the First World War, mass literacy in Britain produced, not a single "mass" readership as is often asserted, but new markets "divided and subdivided" into specialised groups, and hence new publishing categories: "These markets demanded fictions both diverse and plentiful with consequences that were far reaching for both authorship and subject matter".[3] There was a corresponding fiction boom in the United States over the same period, with new titles and editions growing rapidly after 1880 and peaking in the decade from 1900 to 1910 as the book trade stabilised after the decline of the pirate publishers and new firms arose, some, like Doubleday and the G.W. Dillingham Co., especially attuned to the newer forms of popular fiction.[4] In John Tebbel's words, "between 1890 and the First World War the reading of fiction in America became something of a mania".[5] And for the publishing industry itself, "one of the most conspicuous developments in the nineteenth-century … was its ability to target specific classes of readers with individual titles, series, or clusters of books tailored, packaged, and advertised to appeal to their particular interests".[6]

In both markets, the terms "mystery", "thriller", "adventure" and "romance" were still used "freely and interchangeably", such that Hume's detective novels could sometimes be called romances and sometimes mysteries, while writers such as Boothby and E.W. Hornung shuttled between the emerging genres and older romance modes. Adventure and romance tales continued to multiply, with historical, occult and oriental romances all enjoying bestselling moments in the first three decades of the new century; but despite such success they occupied a much diminished space in the broader literary field. By contrast, detective fiction, crime, thrillers, spy stories and science fiction "began to establish their own traditions and inspirational texts [and] were able to exist within a frame of reference created by their own conventions".[7] Hume and Boothby played significant roles internationally in this process

---

2   Peter Keating, *The Haunted Study: A Social History of the English Novel, 1875–1914* (London: Fontana, 1991), 340. See also David Glover, "Publishing, History, Genre", in *The Cambridge Companion to Popular Fiction*, ed. Glover and McCracken, 15-19.
3   Clive Bloom, *Bestsellers: Popular Fiction Since 1900* (Basingstoke, UK: Palgrave Macmillan: 2002), 10.
4   Michael Winship, "The Rise of a National Book Trade System in the United States", in *A History of the Book in America, Volume 4. Print in Motion: The Expansion of Publishing and Reading in the United States, 1880–1940*, ed. Carl F. Kaestle and Janice A. Radway (Chapel Hill: University of North Carolina Press, 2009), 60-61; John Tebbel, *A History of Book Publishing in the United States, Volume II: The Expansion of an Industry, 1865–1919* (New York: Bowker, 1975), 681-701.
5   John Tebbel, *Between Covers: The Rise and Transformation of Book Publishing in America* (New York: Oxford University Press, 1987), 178.
6   Sarah Wadsworth, *In the Company of Books: Literature and Its "Classes" in Nineteenth-Century America* (Amherst: University of Massachusetts Press, 2006), 5.
7   David Glover, "The Thriller", in *The Cambridge Companion to Crime Fiction*, ed. Martin Priestman (Cambridge: Cambridge University Press, 2003), 139; Keating, *The Haunted Study*, 342.

of consolidation and expansion of the genre system, led as it was by the detective, mystery and thriller genres. By the 1920s, these had assumed relatively fixed forms and nomenclature, while romance began to settle into its narrower modern meaning as one specialist sector of the popular fiction market, manifested in Mills & Boon's shift from general publishing to specialisation in women's romance.[8]

Although it is possible to trace antecedents for all these genres, they were experienced at the time as both new and characteristic of the age. Their co-presence (*as* a system) in the contemporary fiction market was indeed a sign of fundamental structural changes across publishing, authorship and reading. The ongoing expansion of the periodical and newspaper press meant an increased demand not only for the established modes of serialised fiction but also for new, shorter forms which were well suited to the emerging genres. The rise in demand for the "magazine story" encouraged literary specialisation as well as new stories in recognisable styles.[9] The effect was to promote both *repetition* and *innovation*, exactly what would consolidate the new genres both as literary forms and distinct market sectors. The relatively sudden disappearance in Britain of the standard three-volume novel in the mid-1890s also enabled the modern forms of popular genre fiction to flourish in the shorter one-volume format, which seemed to be the natural span for most "light" fiction. The result of the "unprecedented rise in mass literacy" was "an unprecedented form: truly *popular* literature, marketed on a mass-commercial and modern basis".[10]

There was enormous expansion in the magazine market on both sides of the Atlantic. In the United States, the 1890s saw the unprecedented growth of modern mass-circulation magazines aimed at the "vast middle-to-lowbrow American readership that hitherto had not been addressed successfully". Attractive, illustrated monthly magazines publishing large quantities of fiction could now be produced cheaply, with huge print runs, sustained by the contemporary boom in national retailing and brand advertising, and sold for ten or fifteen cents, "well within the reach of these new audiences".[11] Magazine publishing expanded much more rapidly than book publishing, with total circulation of the monthlies rising from about eighteen million in 1890 to sixty-four million in 1905, "far outpacing weeklies, newspapers, or books".[12] Between 1885 and 1905, 7500 new periodicals were established in the United States.[13] Magazines such as the *Saturday Evening Post*, *McClure's*, the *Ladies' Home Journal*, *Munsey's*, *Collier's*, *Woman's Home Companion* or *Cosmopolitan* opened up new, competitive, and potentially lucrative markets for fiction writers, especially writers of popular fiction, in the process making literary agents critical for

---

8   Joseph McAleer, *Passion's Fortune: The Story of Mills & Boon* (Oxford: Oxford University Press, 1999), 31–52.
9   Bloom, *Bestsellers*, 13. See also Mike Ashley, *The Age of the Storytellers: British Popular Fiction Magazines 1880–1950* (London & New Castle, DE: British Library & Oak Knoll Press, 2006); Glover, "Publishing", 25–26.
10 Bloom, *Bestsellers*, 12.
11 James L.W. West III, *American Authors and the Literary Marketplace since 1900* (Philadelphia: University of Pennsylvania Press, 1988), 103. See also Richard Ohmann, *Selling Culture: Magazines, Markets, and Class at the Turn of the Century* (London: Verso, 1996).
12 Richard Ohmann, "Diverging Paths: Books and Magazines in the Transition to Corporate Capitalism", *A History of the Book in America*, Vol. 4, ed. Kaestle and Radway, 102–3.
13 Ann Ardis and Patrick Collier, introduction to *Transatlantic Print Culture, 1880–1940: Emerging Media, Emerging Modernisms*, ed. Ann Ardis and Patrick Collier (Basingstoke, UK: Palgrave Macmillan, 2008), 1, citing Frank Luther Mott, *A History of American Magazines, Volume IV: 1885–1905* (Cambridge, MA: Belknap, 1957).

placing stories and negotiating subsidiary rights. A presence in such magazines would become an important way for Australian writers to establish their names and turn their writing to profit in the American marketplace. All-fiction magazines such as *The Argosy* also flourished, increasingly identified by genre, such as Street & Smith's *Detective Story Magazine* launched in 1915.

The expanding fiction market meant new opportunities for authors attempting to sustain professional careers, through contributions to newspapers and magazines even where book publication was difficult or unprofitable. The decades either side of the turn of the century represent a critical moment in the professionalisation of writing careers which saw the formation of the Society of Authors in Britain, and in the United States the American Booksellers and Publishers associations; the rise of literary agents and the royalty system; the wide syndication of fiction; and the institution of international copyright in America. These developments were themselves often the product of the transatlantic book trade: the royalty system, for example, like the term "bestseller", travelled from America to Britain at this time while the transatlantic trade was the key factor in American publishers' support for the Chace Act.[14] There was also mutual influence and competition in the magazine world. *Harper's Monthly*, *Century Illustrated*, *Scribner's Monthly* and *Lippincott's Magazine* established British editions between 1880 and 1890, while other American magazines such as *Cosmopolitan* circulated widely in Britain.[15] Their appearance encouraged new British magazines: the *Strand*, from 1891, and its competitors such as the *Pall Mall Magazine* (1893), the *Windsor Magazine* (1895), *Pearson's* (1896) and *Nash's* (1909), modestly priced "general-interest family magazines", printed on high-quality glossy paper, full of photographs and illustrations and, above all, short fiction. This new print ecology produced what's been called the great "age of the storytellers".[16] The *Strand*, in turn, was distributed in America in a separate US edition and influenced the new generation of American magazines. *Cassell's Magazine* and *Pearson's* also launched American editions, while American newspaper magnate William Randolph Hearst acquired *Nash's* in 1911 (and *Pall Mall* in 1914), enabling two-way traffic between the British magazine and the American *Cosmopolitan*.

Expatriation, Emigration and Imperial Commuting

It was in this "fiercely competitive, early twentieth-century Grub Street environment" that authors from Australia had to make their way, a world "of competing editors, competing magazines (both within and between England and the United States), competing English and American literary agents, and hundreds of competing authors".[17] Although stories of hardship and failure remained common, there are enough cases of remarkable success, including those of Hume and Boothby, to establish the fact of expanding opportunities for fiction writers; and many more instances of modest but sustained careers for others, such as Carlton Dawe or Ambrose Pratt. And success in this market almost always meant

---

14 On "bestseller": Keating, *The Haunted Study*, 15.
15 Ashley, *The Age of the Storytellers*, 10.
16 Ashley, *The Age of the Storytellers*, 1.
17 Terry Sturm, *An Unsettled Spirit: The Life and Frontier Fiction of Edith Lyttleton (G.B. Lancaster)* (Auckland: Auckland University Press, 2003), 118.

3 Crime, Sensation and the Modern Genre System: The Popular Fiction Marketplace

international success, in British, American and Australian markets simultaneously. The work of at least four major figures in the establishment of the new genre system – Hume, Boothby, E.W. Hornung and Nat Gould – bear the imprint of Australian experience and thus sent Australian stories and settings into wide circulation. This was truly an international industry in the business of creating a truly international marketplace.

Unsurprisingly, the careers of Hume, Boothby and their contemporaries show the strong impress of imperial networks. London mattered, not only as "the heart of the empire", but also as "the place where creative or professional success was defined, where the powerful arbiters were, [and where] the most important publishers, critics, audiences, [and] organizational headquarters" were to be found.[18] Hume, Boothby and Dawe moved to England permanently in the early stages of their careers as novelists, while Pratt, like Louis Becke and many others, spent an extended time in London in search of literary success. Their careers largely depended on the "Paternoster Row Machine" of London publishing, and all were influenced by the imperial market for frontier or antipodean adventure even as they worked the new veins of popular fiction.[19] But it would be misleading to see them simply as constrained within imperial or colonial frameworks, for what is most striking about the popular genres in which they wrote – alongside their power to reproduce themselves – is their capacity for crossing borders, their sheer mobility. While texts were more or less compelled to travel to London or originate there if they were to achieve book publication, in many cases they kept on travelling. London was not simply a consuming destination but also a clearing house, a relay station, giving texts the power to travel further. If this was potentially the case for all kinds of fiction, it was doubly so for the emerging popular genres. Their very reproducibility, their clear generic patterns and expectations, and in many cases their clear modernity in stories and physical format, made them ideally suited as international products, travelling beyond British and colonial networks into the American market, even where their settings and social habits were acutely localised.

Texts travelled – from Australia to London to American publishers and booksellers, from Australia to London and then back to Australia in colonial editions, or from America to Australia via London. Mobility was also a generic feature of much crime and mystery writing, with many plots turning on the speed of coach, rail, ship or air travel, and on the accelerated communication of telegrams or telephones. And it was a recurrent characteristic of the writers' own careers, especially for those on the empire's fringes. The imperial network itself encouraged the mobility of writers, not just between Australia and Britain, but "laterally" across imperial space and beyond it to the Pacific and the United States. Hume was born in England in 1859 but grew up and was educated in New Zealand, training as a barrister there before moving to Australia in 1885. He moved to London in 1888 following the bestselling success of *The Mystery of a Hansom Cab*, first published in Melbourne in 1886, in London the following year, and New York the year after that. Boothby was born in South Australia in 1867, but was educated in England before returning to Australia as a teenager. In the late 1880s, he began to publish stories in English magazines, and then, like Hume, relocated to London, in 1894, the year his first novel *In Strange Company: A Story of Chili and the South*

---

18 Angela Woollacott, "'All This is the Empire, I Told Myself': Australian Women's Voyages 'Home' and the Articulation of Colonial Whiteness", *American Historical Review* 102, no. 4 (October 1997): 1003.
19 Richard Nile and David Walker, "The 'Paternoster Row Machine' and the Australian Book Trade, 1890-1945", in *A History of the Book in Australia 1891–1945: A National Culture in a Colonised Market*, ed. Martyn Lyons and John Arnold (St Lucia: University of Queensland Press, 2001), 7.

Seas was published there. An American edition appeared in the same year. Dawe was born in Adelaide and grew up in Melbourne. He published two novels before relocating to England in 1892 in his late twenties, and travelled extensively both before and after his move. Pratt travelled the Pacific and outback Queensland before moving to London, where he stayed from 1898 to 1905 and where his literary career took off.

The same patterns of expatriation and emigration, of imperial commuting and literary tourism, also occurred in the other direction. Among the most popular literary travellers besides Robert Louis Stevenson was E.W. Hornung, creator of both Raffles, the gentleman thief or "Amateur Cracksman", and Stingaree, the gentleman bushranger, "the only bushranger who practices his art in jodhpurs and monocle".[20] Hornung spent just on two years in Australia as a young man from early 1884, but he drew on his Australian experience for many of his novels and stories including *A Bride from the Bush* (1890), *Tiny Luttrell* (1893), *The Boss of Taroomba* (1894), *Irralie's Bushranger* (1896), *The Rogue's March* (1896), *The Belle of Toorak* (1900) and *Stingaree* (1905). The genres that travelled for Hornung were both old and new, both Australian and international. On one side were his Australian bush romances and adventures, such as *The Rogue's March: A Romance* and *Irralie's Bushranger: A Story of Australian Adventure* (its opening line was the signature Australianese, "'Coooooooo-eeeee!'"). These novels drew on older colonial romance-adventure models but were consciously written for the new popular fiction market. They often included a mystery element, aligning them with the genre Stephen Knight has called the "squatter thriller" or "squatter mystery romance".[21] On the other side were Hornung's stories in the modern crime genre, initiated with those centred on Raffles and first published together as *The Amateur Cracksman* in 1899 (four more Raffles collections appeared through to 1914). A recent editor of the Raffles stories has linked the two genres, the bush romances and crime fiction, in arguing that "it is in [Hornung's] stories with Australian themes that the precursors of Raffles are to be found, in particular those which involve gentlemen-bushrangers".[22] The connection, in part, seems to be Hornung's own, for Raffles' first step in crime occurs in Australia when opportunity presents itself in an up-country bank ("Le Premier Pas").

Certainly *both* generic types travelled successfully into the American market, the Australian stories no less than the crime novels. Scribner alone published twenty Hornung titles between 1896 and 1913 including all the Australian bush and bushranger romances and all the Raffles (and other crime) volumes. Hornung's stories were bought by the McClure Syndicate, and many were serialised in *Collier's*, *Scribner's Magazine* and *Lippincott's Magazine*.[23] In this period Hornung was known not simply as the creator of Raffles but also, as the *Chicago Tribune* put it, as "one of the most successful delineators of Bush life".[24] As early as 1896, the *New York Tribune* remarked that he had "done much to make Australia more tangible in fiction than it has often been before".[25] Although now largely forgotten, the

---

20   Stephen Knight, *Continent of Mystery: A Thematic History of Australian Crime Fiction* (Melbourne: Melbourne University Press, 1997), 51.
21   Knight, *Continent of Mystery*, 118.
22   Richard Lancelyn Green, introduction to *Raffles: The Amateur Cracksman*, by E.W. Hornung (Camberwell, Vic.: Penguin, 2010), xx.
23   American magazine publications included in the Chronology printed in the 2010 Penguin edition cited above, ix-xiii.
24   Quotation from the *Chicago Tribune* cited in Scribner's edition of *The Amateur Cracksman*.
25   "Literary Notes", *New York Daily Tribune*, 27 December 1896 (on the occasion of the appearance of *The Rogue's March*).

3 Crime, Sensation and the Modern Genre System: The Popular Fiction Marketplace

bushranger Stingaree was in these years as popular as Raffles, with a play and two films to 1917. By contrast, the power of the emerging genre system is proved in the ongoing life of Raffles with dramatisations, movie adaptations and reprints on both sides of the Atlantic through to the present day. Although Raffles is an "amateur cracksman", a thief, rather than an amateur detective, the stories mirror and depend formally upon the crime-detection genre, for the principal narrative interest is in how the crime is performed and how the criminals will, in this case, *escape* detection or capture. Raffles is a "criminal version of the hero-detective", an amateur in the true, gentlemanly nineteenth-century sense of the term.[26] That he shares something of a family resemblance to Sherlock Homes is more than a coincidence, as Conan Doyle was Hornung's brother-in-law and had suggested to him that he write a series of stories with just such a "public-school villain" as hero.[27] The *New York Tribune* recognised a strong generic effect even in this original case, remarking that "Raffles is amazing; his resource is perfect; he talks like a gentleman and acts like one, except when occupied with pressing business in another man's house, at midnight, and naturally he has a 'cool nerve,' a nerve positively arctic. They all have nerves like that, these Raffleses".[28]

Horning's bestselling stories thus transported both antipodean romance and international/English crime into the American market and indeed across the Anglophone world. The "best-selling of all best-sellers", however, was Nat Gould, another traveller or rather immigrant to Australia.[29] What is most striking in Gould's case, by contrast, is the bestselling author's absence from the American market. Gould spent a substantial eleven years in the colonies, where his career as a novelist began. After some experience as a journalist in England, he arrived in Sydney in 1884, working on the *Brisbane Telegraph* and the Sydney *Referee*. His first novel began as a serial in the latter before it was noticed by Walter Home, a traveller for George Routledge & Sons, who offered a three-figure sum for it and also bought two further planned serials.[30] Published in 1891 as a cheap "yellowback", *The Double Event: A Tale of the Melbourne Cup* became an immediate bestseller in Australia and Britain and launched the formula that Gould repeated throughout the rest of his career, a story of horse-racing mixed with a mystery or crime plot. As an American reviewer wrote of a later novel: "there are horses, splendid horses [and] a world of quite simple virtues and quite simple wickednesses".[31] As with Hornung's tales, the story was also mobile across platforms with a dramatisation in Melbourne in 1893 and a silent film in 1911.[32]

Gould wrote a further seven novels before returning to England in 1895. From then on he produced more than 120 titles, usually four or more a year, with Routledge until 1900 and then John Long from 1905. Of these, more than half have significant Australian content. Indeed, in many of his stories Australia had significance beyond dramatic convenience or local colour. Describing a typical plot, from the novel *A Race for a Wife* (1918), in which the Australia-born heroine chooses the down-to-earth Jim rather than the wealthy

---

26 Stephen Knight, *Crime Fiction, 1800–2000: Detection, Death, Diversity* (Basingstoke, UK: Palgrave Macmillan, 2004), 71.
27 Green, introduction, xxi.
28 Quotation from the *New York Tribune*, cited in Scribner's edition of *The Amateur Cracksman*. It advertised the print run as the "30th Thousand".
29 Philip Waller, *Writers, Readers, and Reputations: Literary Life in Britain 1870–1918* (Oxford: Oxford University Press, 2008), 833.
30 Waller, *Writers, Readers and Reputations*, 835.
31 "Latest Works of Fiction", *New York Times*, 6 October 1918.
32 Katharine Brisbane, ed., *Entertaining Australia: An Illustrated History* (Sydney: Currency, 1991), 161.

Clifton Charlemont, Philip Waller writes that "Gould repeatedly deploys the Australian experience as a democratic calling card". Polly, the heroine, "is an independent creature, and this independence was bred in Australia".[33] Estimates of Gould's sales vary, but all agree on the high volume – six million sales across seventy titles by 1909, seven million copies for John Long alone by 1913, eleven million by 1918, twenty-four million by 1927.[34] In 1925, the *New York Times* reported that "in England his endless list of titles, produced one every three months as regularly as the leaves on a calendar, is estimated by sympathetic authorities to have run up a total sale of 100,000,000 copies".[35] Gould "exemplified the new phenomenon of the best-selling author"; so much so he became a byword for low reading tastes.[36] He was enormously popular with soldiers during the First World War and continued to sell through the interwar years.[37]

All of which makes it remarkable that Gould was largely invisible in America. As an exemplary product of the genre system, one would expect him to have been a bestseller in the United States no less than in Britain. But as the 1925 *New York Times* article put it, "America has never discovered him".[38] Routledge had a New York office until 1903, while John Long was well known as "a prolific publisher of popular fiction" associated with names such as "Guy Boothby, Dick Donovan, Fergus Hume, William Le Queux, Ouida, Morley Roberts and Nat Gould".[39] But it was not until 1918 that one of Gould's novels appeared in an American edition – *The Rider in Khaki* from the respectable New York publisher Frederick A. Stokes – and its appearance seems largely due to the war. The firm announced that "with this novel of sport and daring adventure in the Great War, Nat Gould is introduced to the American public", adding that 2000 copies of his work had been ordered for the American Army.[40] Stokes published a second title, *Fast as the Wind*, in the same year.[41] Otherwise, apart from some Routledge titles distributed through their New York office, there is no evidence of any further American editions.[42] Perhaps the explanation lies in Gould's belief that literary agents were unnecessary, for without an agent negotiating US rights on his behalf he was reliant on his publisher's efforts.[43] While it would seem unlikely, given their extraordinary sales, that no attempt was made to push Gould's books into the American

---

33 Waller, *Writers, Readers and Reputations*, 840.
34 Figures in order from Waller, *Writers, Readers and Reputations*, 836; Bloom, *Bestsellers*, 58; *New York Sun*, 26 May 1918; Waller, *Writers, Readers and Reputations*, 833.
35 "James Baldwin, a Best Seller", *New York Times*, 1 November 1925.
36 Bloom, *Bestsellers*, 122; Waller, *Writers, Readers and Reputations*, 841; Martin Lyons and Lucy Taksa, *Australian Readers Remember: An Oral History of Reading 1890-1930* (Melbourne: Oxford University Press, 1992), 55.
37 An article in the *Tacoma Times* (Washington), 20 March 1918, compared British and American soldiers' reading: Jack London topped the American list, Nat Gould the British list (with London second).
38 "James Baldwin, A Best Seller".
39 "John Long Dies at 71; Publisher in London", *New York Times*, 17 September 1935: "When the friendly association of Long and Gould had lasted eight or nine years, sales of Mr. Gould's sporting books exceeded 5,000,000 copies".
40 A list of books received in the *New York Times*, 31 March 1918, states of *The Rider in Khaki*: "the first of this popular English author's novels to be published in this country". See also advertisement, *New York Tribune*, 6 April 1918: "First Appearance in America of Nat Gould".
41 It was reprinted by A.L. Burt in 1919.
42 *Only a Commoner* was reviewed in the *New York Times*, 24 August 1895. Its publication details are listed as "New York: George Routledge & Sons". The story is partly set in Tasmania. The reviewer concluded: "there is a great deal about horses and horse racing in a rather commonplace story".
43 Waller, *Writers, Readers and Reputations*, 837.

market, perhaps the large and effortless British and dominion sales were sufficient for them. He also seldom published stories in the fiction magazines. But perhaps there was also a question of taste. The *New York Sun* reviewer of *The Rider in Khaki* remarked: "Nat Gould – judging him solely by his first American offering – lacks that touch wherewith the artist transmutes purely local characters into universal types. His characters, for the American reader, are pretty remote".[44] Similarly, the *Times* reviewer of *Fast as the Wind* seemed to find it rather distantly English: "Why grudge the Tommy his momentary delight in an ideal world where men, nearly as heroic as himself, sit easily on the sunny decks of trim yachts, dine with quiet splendour at the Savoy, and sit of evenings lost in the quiet lulling beauty of his own England?"[45] Or perhaps it was just that westerns crowded out the popular market for horse stories in the United States.

From Sensation to Detection: Fergus Hume

Fergus Hume has a weaker claim biographically than Gould to be considered an Australian author, having spent barely two years in Victoria and later insisting he belonged to New Zealand.[46] Bibliographically, though, the claim can be seen as much stronger. *The Mystery of a Hansom Cab* was the first locally published bestseller, an "overnight sensation" when first released in Melbourne in October 1886: "Australia would make him famous".[47] In Hume's own account, the manuscript was at first refused on all sides "on the ground that no Colonial could write anything worth reading".[48] Being thus "boycotted", Hume was encouraged by budding publisher Frederick Trischler in Melbourne. Although numbers are impossible to verify, Hume claims an initial edition of 5000 from Melbourne printers Kemp & Boyce which sold out in three weeks, and then a second printing which also sold out, at a time when local print runs were more likely to be in the 500 to 1000 range.[49] According to Simon Caterson, by the end of the year, 20,000 copies had been printed at a time when the city's population was less than half a million: "Virtually every literate adult in Melbourne must have read the book".[50] The cover announced "A Sensational Melbourne Novel".[51] Hume was then persuaded that it should be published in London, and sold his copyright for a mere £50 to a group of "speculators", in Hume's word, trading as The Hansom Cab Publishing Co. under Trischler's management. The novel was a massive seller in the British market, with an 1888 Hansom Cab edition listing 225,000 copies printed. Sales figures of 340,000

---

44 "The Rider in Khaki", *New York Sun*, 26 May 1918.
45 "Latest Works of Fiction", *New York Times*, 6 October 1918. A more enthusiastic review appeared in the *New York Tribune*, 5 October 1918: "After reading it nobody will wonder at the immense popularity which Mr. Gould's writings have attained".
46 Preface to the revised edition published by Jarrolds & Sons in London, 1896; the final paragraph that contains this claim disappears from later editions.
47 Simon Caterson, "Fergus Hume's Startling Story", introduction to *The Mystery of a Hansom Cab*, by Fergus Hume (Melbourne: Text Publishing, 1999), v; Lucy Sussex, *Blockbuster! Fergus Hume and the Mystery of a Hansom Cab* (Melbourne: Text Publishing, 2015), 57.
48 Fergus Hume, preface to *The Mystery of a Hansom Cab* (London: Jarrold & Sons, 1896), viii.
49 Sussex, *Blockbuster!*, 118-19.
50 Caterson, "Fergus Hume", vii.
51 Image: Rachel Franks, "Catching a Cab", www.sl.nsw.gov.au/stories/catching-cab.

by August 1888 seem reliable.[52] Caterson estimates that as many as 750,000 copies were sold during Hume's lifetime. In 1888, the *Illustrated London News* reported: "Persons were found everywhere eagerly devouring the realistic sensational tale of Melbourne social life. Whether travelling by road, rail, or river the unpretending little volume was ever present in some companion's or stranger's hands".[53]

The novel's other claim on Australian literary history is its creation of Melbourne as a complex modern metropolis, a place of mingled wealth and poverty, fashion and crime, respectability and scandal; a city where the modern figures of detective, journalist, lawyer and showgirl and the modern technologies of rail and hansom cab, newspaper, telegram and telephone, all play vital roles. As Mary Hammond has argued, sensation fiction and more particularly the emergence of detective fiction – "the emergence of novelistic suspense, of plots turning on delays, mistiming, missed opportunities and rescues in the nick of time" – can be linked to the new, accelerated rhythms of rail travel, and we might extend this point to include the even greater mobility of the hansom cab.[54] No doubt this modernity was also critical in the novel's ability to travel across different metropolitan markets. As critics have noted, the crucial revelation in the novel is less the identity of who murdered Oliver Whyte in the hansom cab than the scandalous secret at the heart of the wealthy Frettlby family, a secret paralleled by the slums and crime at the very heart of Melbourne's prosperity. Thus the "real mystery of the hansom cab is its ability to cross social and geographical boundaries", with a mobility that both creates the modern city and threatens to disrupt the social distinctions upon which it depends.[55]

For the present argument, the novel's prime significance lies in its contribution to a modern, international genre, that of detective fiction. It was, Caterson argues, the "best-selling crime novel of the nineteenth century", appearing a year before Sherlock Holmes "made what was, by comparison, a rather unspectacular debut in *A Study in Scarlet*".[56] For Stephen Knight, it was "the first best-selling crime fiction mystery novel in English" and "one of those remarkable books which set a trend [and] focus a genre".[57] Hutchinson, Hume's last publisher during his lifetime, described the novel as "a book destined not only to sell nearly three-quarters of a million copies, but to be one of the forerunners of a craze which to-day, nearly half a century later, shows no signs of diminishing":

---

52 Sussex, *Blockbuster!*, 159-60. An 1893 edition from A.P. Marsden listed 375,000 copies printed, and a 1916 Jarrolds reissue gives 550,000.
53 *Illustrated London News*, 6 October 1888, quoted in Christopher Pittard, "From Sensation to the *Strand*", in *A Companion to Crime Fiction*, ed. Charles J. Rzepka and Lee Horsley (Chichester, UK; Malden, MA: Wiley-Blackwell, 2010), 108.
54 Mary Hammond, *Reading, Publishing and the Formation of Literary Taste in England, 1880-1914* (Aldershot, UK: Ashgate, 2006), 56, discussing Nicholas Daly, "Railway Novels: Sensation Fiction and the Modernisation of the Senses", *English Literary History* 66 (Summer 1999): 461-87, and Laura Marcus, "Oedipus Express: Trains, Trauma and Detective Fiction", *New Formations* 41 (Autumn 2000): 173-88.
55 Pittard, "From Sensation", 3; Robert Dixon, *Writing the Colonial Adventure: Race, Gender, and Nation in Anglo-Australian Popular Fiction, 1875-1914* (Cambridge: Cambridge University Press, 1995), 159-60.
56 Caterson, "Fergus Hume", vii; also Sussex, *Blockbuster!*, 160-61.
57 Knight, *Crime Fiction*, 52; Knight, *Continent of Mystery*, 69.

3 Crime, Sensation and the Modern Genre System: The Popular Fiction Marketplace

> Here were thrills galore; here was crime to be enjoyed in security; furtive scoundrels; gallant heroes; lovely ladies; mystery and detection gloriously involved and astonishingly new! To-day, as thriller succeeds thriller, much of the old glamour has gone and a languid interest has replaced it.[58]

Most pointedly in terms of the novel's critical place in the emerging genre system, Christopher Pittard describes *The Mystery of a Hansom Cab* as the "most spectacular reimagining of the sensation novel, and a crucial point in the genre's transformation into detective fiction".[59] Even if the novel were written partly by accident, as Hume claimed, one of the striking things about it is its high degree of generic reflexivity. The "accidental" story Hume relates in his preface is that, having failed to interest anyone in his plays and having decided to write a novel instead, he "enquired of a leading Melbourne bookseller what style of book he sold most of".[60] The answer was the detective stories of Émile Gaboriau, creator of the fictional police detective Monsieur Lecoq. "As, at this time, I had never even heard of this author, I bought all his works – eleven or thereabouts – and read them carefully. The style of these stories attracted me, and I determined to write a book of the same class; containing a mystery, a murder, and a description of low life in Melbourne".

The novel itself is scattered with references to detective fiction and fictional detectives. It creates the sense of already belonging to a *series* of crime and detection novels (or "cases"), a generic series which it is in fact helping to create and define. The first line of the novel's opening newspaper report is richly conventional in this vein: "Truth is said to be stranger than fiction". Later in the same report the frame of reference is explicit: "it would seem as though the case itself had been taken bodily out of one of Gaboriau's novels, and that his famous detective Lecoq only would be able to unravel it". The opening chapter ends with a reference to "one of Du Boisgobey's stories" and a remark that both draws on and anticipates the public standing of celebrated fictional detectives: "Here is a great chance for some of our detectives to render themselves famous". There are other references too: to *The Leavenworth Case* by Anna Katherine Green, first published in 1878, and one of the earliest American detective novels, and to De Quincy's essays on murder. In this sense, as well as in its borrowings from Dickens and Wilkie Collins and references to the classics, *The Mystery of a Hansom Cab* is an intensely literary work – like many later detective novels.[61]

The novel's crucial position in pointing the crime genre towards detection emerges in the way the crime itself is set up as a "puzzle" or "riddle", not at all as a moral issue; in the amount of realistic detail, not least the "real life" fragments of newspaper and court reports, through which the facts are established; and in the nature of the detectives, who, as characters, are almost wholly detectives and nothing else. Having two rival detectives of very different personalities only underscores the point. While the detectives themselves do not ultimately solve the crime, detection drives the narrative forward, ultimately in pursuit of the larger mystery that indirectly led to the murder. The pattern of crime, mystery, clues and investigation, false suspects, explanations and resolution is strongly established, and

---

58 From the preliminary matter of *The Last Straw*, by Fergus Hume (London: Hutchinson, 1932), published posthumously in the year of Hume's death.
59 Pittard, "From Sensation", 108.
60 Hume, preface, viii.
61 See also Robert Dixon, introduction to *The Mystery of a Hansom Cab*, by Fergus Hume (Sydney: Sydney University Press, 2010), ix.

established here in a novel rather than in the short story. As Knight suggests, "Hume, via Gaboriau, made the crime novel a major force in the market".[62] *The Mystery of a Hansom Cab* can be claimed as one of the few Australian novels to have had imitators (including parodies) on the world literary stage.

The success of *The Mystery of a Hansom Cab* has overshadowed accounts of Hume's career, just as it haunted Hume during his lifetime. "That poor book!" he was recorded as saying. "It was the very first book I ever wrote. It made a tremendous sensation, and I have been judged by it ever since … The 'Hansom Cab' is a regular Frankenstein's monster to me, and I am pursued through life by this monster, which, after all, is but the creation of an immature boy."[63] Critics have noted the relative success of *Madame Midas: A Realistic and Sensational Story of Australian Mining Life*, but very few of Hume's other titles have been noticed, although there were at least 135 of them over a career that continued until 1932. Set in the goldfields of Ballarat and the Melbourne of *The Mystery of a Hansom Cab*, *Madame Midas* was also a crime mystery. Although less singularly driven by the puzzle-detection structure, it did feature the detective Kilsip again, if in a minor role. The novel was published in London by the Hansom Cab Publishing Co. and by Ward, Lock in 1888, selling in excess of 100,000 copies.[64] In the same year it had as many as five separate editions in the American market from the cheap paperback publishers George Munro, J.S. Ogilvie, M.J. Ivers, the American Publishers Corporation and Arthur Westbrook (no. 52 in the firm's Great American Detective series), several using the same plates.[65]

Hume's American Fortunes

The Mystery of a Hansom Cab enjoyed a similar American career soon after its first publication, with at least ten editions appearing in the United States between 1888 and the early 1890s. Publishers again included Munro, Ogilvie and Westbrook (American Detective Series no 36), plus the Worthington Co., J.W. Lovell and Lovell's International Book Co., all from New York; Rand McNally, Belford, Clark & Co., Donohue & Henneberry and W.B. Conkey from Chicago; and C.I. Hood & Co., from Lowell, Massachusetts. Further editions followed in the first decade of the twentieth century. The book was popular enough for Street & Smith to publish an edition in New York in German, *Der mord in der droschke*, in 1900. In 1888, a stage adaptation was performed at the Academy of Music in New York, "the matter … taken from an Australian novel by Fergus W. Hume": "The quality of this melodrama was rough and crude, and yet it appealed strongly to that taste which makes the great demand for cheap detective fiction".[66]

We have no evidence of Hume's earnings from either his English or American editions, or from the many titles that travelled back to Australia as colonial editions. He probably earned little before the turn of the century in the American market. Nonetheless, his

---

62 Knight, *Crime Fiction*, 52.
63 *Maitland Mercury & Hunter General Advertiser*, 19 January 1893.
64 Simon Caterson, "The Gilded Cage", introduction to *Madame Midas*, by Fergus Hume (Melbourne: Text Publishing, 1999), xiii.
65 Not all of these editions are dated. Westbrook purchased M.J. Ivers's stock and plates in the early 1900s (Tebbel, *History Vol. II*, 496). The Munro, Ivers and Westbrook editions all share the same pagination; the Ogilvie and American Publishers editions share another setting.
66 *New York Sun*, 8 May 1888.

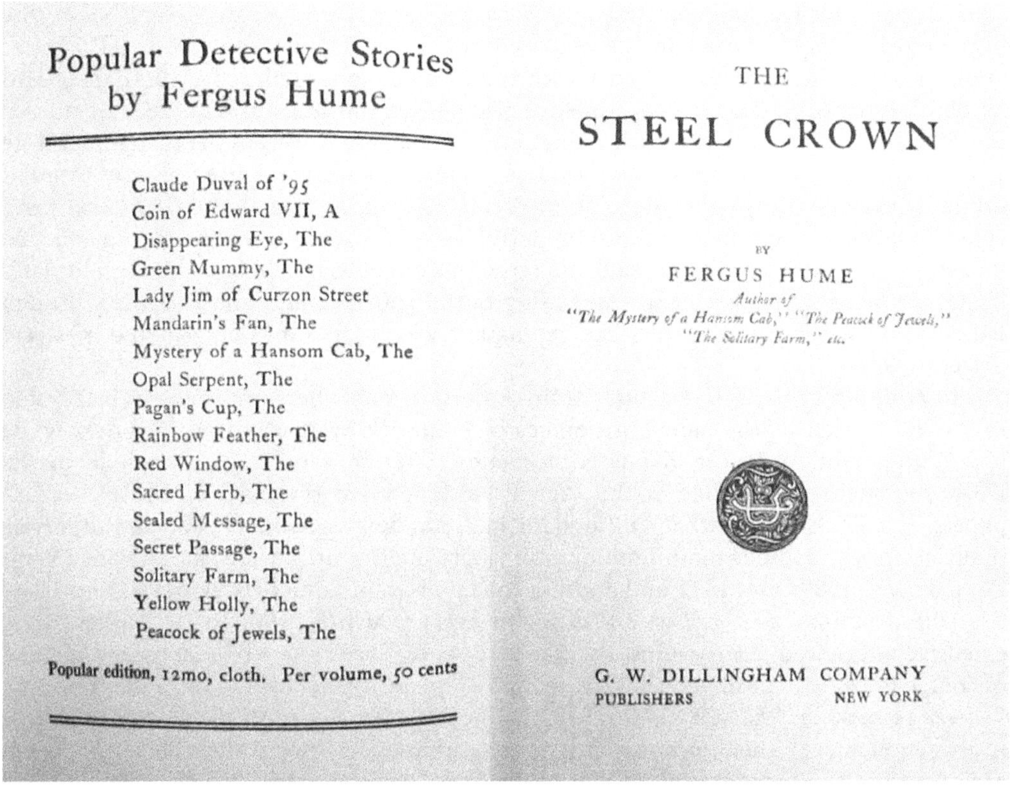

3 Crime, Sensation and the Modern Genre System: The Popular Fiction Marketplace

Figure 3.1 Fergus Hume, *The Steel Crown* (New York: G.W. Dillingham Co., 1911), with a list of other works by the author.

publishing record indicates his longevity as a popular novelist; on both sides of the Atlantic he was much more than a one-hit wonder. Many of his 135 or so titles had second, third and later editions in the British market through popular fiction publishers such as F.V. White, T. Werner Laurie and Ward, Lock, and he was at least a steady seller across three decades, if never again the spectacular bestseller he had been with his early novels.

Hume's American career was also sustained throughout his lifetime, with fifty-six American titles between 1888 and 1925. Not surprisingly, many of his early books were picked up by Lovell, Munro and the other reprinters, but in fact the bulk of his American editions appeared after the passing of the Chace Act. These ranged from respectable hardbacks to Street & Smith's cheap newsprint Columbia Library comprising "Tales of Adventure and of the Marvelous", which included *Madame Midas, A Creature of the Night: An Italian Enigma* and *The Year of Miracle: A Marvelous Tale of a Strange Plague*. Other publishers included the respectable firms of Houghton Mifflin (*Aladdin in London: A Romance*, 1892), Cassell (*The Lone Inn: A Mystery* and *The Third Volume*, 1895), Lippincott (*Chronicles of Fairyland*, 1911) and Small, Maynard & Co. (*The Whispering Lane*, 1925).

Hume's most important US publisher, however, was the G.W. Dillingham Co., publisher of the famous Pinkerton detective tales. Dillingham published twenty-one of Hume's novels, from *The Mystery of a Hansom Cab* and *Claude Duval of Ninety-Five* in

1897 through to *The Lost Parchment: A Detective Story* in 1914, two years before the firm went bankrupt.[67] Dillingham specialised in popular fiction, but it presented Hume's books in handsome hardback formats, with embossed designs on the cover, at the standard hardback price of $1.25. Internal evidence also suggests reissues of a number of titles.[68] By 1908, Dillingham was advertising thirteen of "The Best Novels of Fergus Hume".[69] By 1912, there were twenty titles, now listed as "Popular Detective Stories". These "Popular Editions" (12mo, cloth) were priced at fifty cents per volume (Fig. 3.1).[70] The lower price could be taken as a sign that Hume's popularity was waning, but given that it was attached to a series of regular new titles it suggests rather his ongoing saleability. Although his later novels ventured into other genres including occult romance and ghost stories, through Dillingham's series Hume's American reputation was located explicitly in the mystery/detective genre.

In addition to the fifty-six titles from American publishers, more were distributed in the US market by the New York offices of Frederick Warne and Ward, Lock, while F.V. White's edition of *The Yellow Hunchback* (1907) contains a "Copyrighted in the USA" statement. A number of the Warne editions were reviewed in the New York papers.[71] It is also likely that Dillingham had standing agreements for simultaneous publication with Hume's main London publishers. Eleven titles were shared with Digby, Long between 1897 and 1911 and another four with John Long between 1905 and 1908.

Dillingham released at least one new title every year from 1902 to 1912. These were extensively reviewed, often against the standard set by *The Mystery of a Hansom Cab*, and of course not always positively. Reviewing *Lady Jim of Curzon Street* (1906), the *New York Tribune* remarked: "The story is sordid in its motive, offensive in its details and repulsive in its denouement". The *Sun* was a little more enthusiastic: "Not a plausible story … but a story dramatic enough and sufficiently horrible".[72] Earlier, the *Atlantic Monthly* had described *The Man Who Vanished* (1892) as "manufactured ghastliness of a cheap sort".[73] *The Red Window* (1904) for the *New York Sun* was "a machine made story, no worse than many others of the sort, but a long way behind the 'Hansom Cab'".[74]

But Hume found his market and kept his name before the American mystery reading public. The *Tribune* noted in 1901 how Hume "has been known as a deft composer of

---

67 Susan K. Ahern, "The G.W. Dillingham Company", in *American Literary Publishing Houses, 1638–1899*, ed. Peter Dzwonkoski, Dictionary of Literary Biography, Vol. 49 (Detroit, MI: Gale Research, 1986), 124-25. See "Dillingham Book Co. Sued in Bankruptcy", *New York Times*, 31 August 1916.

68 An edition of *A Coin of Edward VII*, for example, is copyrighted 1903 and contains the statement "Issued February 1903" but the list of Hume novels printed includes titles first published in 1907 and 1908.

69 Listing in editions of *A Coin of Edward VII* (also subtitled *A Detective Story*) and *The Sacred Herb* (1908). By 1909, there were fifteen titles listed, all at seventy-five cents except *The Solitary Farm* (1909) at $1.25: listing printed in an edition of *Lady Jim of Curzon Street*, first released in 1906. The latest novel listed is *The Solitary Farm*, again indicating a reissue of *Lady Jim*.

70 Again: in an edition of *The Yellow Holly*, first published in 1903; the latest novels listed are from 1912, *The Mystery Queen* and *Red Money*.

71 Reviews from the *New York Sun*: *The Carbuncle Clue*, reviewed 21 March 1896; *Tracked by a Tattoo*, 24 April 1897; *The Clock Struck One*, 3 December 1898.

72 *New York Tribune*, 1 April 1906; *New York Sun*, 14 April 1906.

73 "Comment on New Books", *Atlantic Monthly* (October 1892): 563.

74 *New York Sun*, 14 September 1904.

3 Crime, Sensation and the Modern Genre System: The Popular Fiction Marketplace

exciting trifles ever since he published 'The Mystery of a Hansom Cab'".[75] He was also prominent in the periodical press. Between August 1903 and June 1908 he had a series of novels serialised in Joseph Pulitzer's one-cent sport and sensation paper, the New York *Evening World*, including "The New Mystery of a Hansom Cab" (the revised version) and "The Female Sherlock Holmes" (*Hagar of the Pawnshop*).[76] Hume also appeared in the illustrated ten-cent story magazine *Storiettes*, "the Cheapest and Best Magazine of Short Tales", and in the Christmas number of the *Commercial Advertiser* (alongside Guy Boothby).[77] Reviewing *The Steel Crown* in 1911, the *Sun* remarked that "there is a large and thoroughly justified circle of readers to welcome every new book from the pen of Mr. Fergus Hume".[78]

What is clear is that Hume's success depended not merely on his understanding of the pleasures of "ghastliness" but also his instinct for the serial nature of genre fiction, its appeal through variations upon recognisable and reproducible elements. Although he also worked the romance vein, his oeuvre is massively concentrated in detection and mystery. Seriality is evident in his titles, from *The Black Carnation* in 1892 to *The Black Image* in 1918 and including *The Blue Talisman*, *The Red Window*, *The Green Mummy*, *The Grey Doctor*, *The Scarlet Bat*, *The Yellow Holly* and *The Yellow Hunchback* along the way. His chapter headings explicitly announce the crime-investigation-revelation structure, with a romantic resolution to draw everything together. *The Steel Crown*, for example, proceeds from "Chapter I: Enter Romance" to "Chapter II: An Adventure", then through a sequence including "A Suspicious Character", "A New Clue", "A Fresh Discovery", "An Interesting Confession", and, finally, "All's Well That Ends Well", a chapter title Hume used at least half a dozen times. Elsewhere the final chapter is simply "The Truth". Hume used a similar device in each of his crime and mystery novels. His American success also suggests he understood the transnational appeal of the genre. Many titles take characters from a squire-ish England through metropolitan London, then into exotic locations before returning home. Australia, too, remained a useful plot device for moving characters around. Some novels seem explicitly to have an American audience in mind. *The Pagan's Cup* begins, "Certain portions of England yet remain undiscovered by Americans and uncivilized by railways". There is also evidence that Hume planned to visit the United States, although no evidence that he actually made the trip.[79]

---

75 *New York Tribune*, March 10 1901.
76 "The Pagan's Cup" ran in September 1903; "The Rainbow Feather", September–October 1903; "The New Mystery of a Hansom Cab", February–April 1905; "The Scarlet Bat", April–June 1905; "The Female Sherlock Holmes", July–August 1906; and "The Mystery of the Devil's Ace or The Manor Mystery", May–June 1908.
77 "The Red Star" was the featured story: advertisement, *Evening World*, 2 June 1894; advertisement for the *Commercial Advertiser*, *New York Sun*, 6 December 1902.
78 "Stories and Tales", *New York Sun*, 14 October 1911.
79 On 1 January 1905 he wrote to an American correspondent ("Benners" - possibly William J. Benners, 1863-1940, a writer and publisher of dime novels, http://dlib.nyu.edu/findingaids/html/fales/benners/): "It is not impossible that I may take a trip to the USA within a reasonable time, God willing … I am anxious to see your country". National Library of Australia, NLA MS 847.

Sublime Audacity: Guy Boothby

Guy Boothby's career, like Hume's, illustrates "just how transnational colonial Australian literary production" was around the turn of the century.[80] Like Hume, Boothby enjoyed an international writing career, both transatlantic and trans-imperial, managed through the principal London-based publishers of popular fiction: Ward, Lock (27 titles), F.V. White (17) and John Long (4). Both writers tried their hands unsuccessfully at serious drama, suggesting the high status the form held in the period, before turning to popular fiction and relocating to London. Both continued to send characters to Australia or find them there, Boothby even more than Hume. Each was present at the birth of a major genre, the thriller rather than detective fiction in Boothby's case. Like Hume again, Boothby was a prolific writer, producing around fifty-five books before his early death, aged thirty-seven, in February 1905, and the combined effect of the speed of composition and the pace of the narratives themselves meant his name became a byword on both sides of the Atlantic for a particular kind of sensational writing, "extraordinary adventures following one another at breathless speed".[81] In the decade around the turn of the century, he was among the best selling of all authors in the British Isles, alongside Robert Louis Stevenson, Conan Doyle, Rudyard Kipling, Marie Corelli and Hall Caine.[82] He also became famous for his mode of composition – dictating his stories at 6000 words a day into a wax-cylinder phonograph for transcription and typing by his two secretaries.[83] Finally, like Hume and many other popular authors, one major early success shaped Boothby's entire subsequent career.

Boothby had five books published in 1894, his first year in London. *On the Wallaby* recounted Boothby's experiences travelling through Australia, while early novels used the Torres Strait and the pearl industry as settings for adventure and intrigue. But it was with *A Bid for Fortune; or, Dr Nikola's Vendetta* in 1895 that Boothby became an international bestseller. It appeared as the very first serial in the *Windsor Magazine*, launched by Ward, Lock & Bowden in January of that year with a print run of 150,000, and its success helped shape the *Windsor*'s subsequent history.[84] Ward, Lock & Bowden then published the book version of *A Bid for Fortune* in late November. The novel appeared in the American market the same year, in Appleton's Town and Country Library, in which Boothby's *The Marriage of Esther: A Torres Strait Sketch* (1895) had already appeared.[85] The latter foreshadowed many elements that would become Boothby trademarks, with a plot that turned on "coincidences, inherited titles, hidden identities, significant dreams [and] a consummate villain".[86] The previous year, *In Strange Company: A Story of Chili and the*

---

80 Ken Gelder, "Guy Boothby, Fergus Hume and Arthur Upfield: Colonial Popular Fiction Acquisitions in the Special Collections", *University of Melbourne Library Journal* 10, no. 2 (December 2005): 4.
81 From a *New York Sun* review of *The Beautiful White Devil*, included in Appleton's publicity for Boothby's novels printed in its edition of *Dr. Nikola's Experiment*.
82 Troy J. Bassett and Christina M. Walter, "Booksellers and Best Sellers: British Book Sales as Documented by *The Bookman*, 1891–1906", *Book History* 4 (2001): 211, 224, 233.
83 "Boothby, Guy Newell (1867–1905)", *Australian Dictionary of Biography*, accessed 21 February 2016, http://adb.anu.edu.au/biography/boothby-guy-newell-5293/text8931.
84 Ashley, *The Age of the Storytellers*, 224.
85 Appleton's Town and Country Library, no. 166; *A Bid for Fortune: A Novel* was no. 179. Appleton did not use the subtitle "Dr Nikola's Vendetta".
86 Paul Depasquale, *Guy Boothby: His Life and Work* (Seacombe Gardens, SA: Pioneer Books, 1982), 32.

3 Crime, Sensation and the Modern Genre System: The Popular Fiction Marketplace

Southern Seas had appeared in Neely's International Library featuring an albino dwarf as its villain, and England, South America, the South Seas and Australia as its settings.

Boothby's early novels were already stories of intrigue and adventure mixed with romance, but it was with the creation of master criminal Dr Nikola, "the first international criminal mastermind in fiction", that he made a decisive intervention in the genre stakes.[87] Boothby thereafter became "the creator of the famous Nikola".[88] As John Sutherland has pointed out, Dr Nikola's first appearance is contemporaneous with Sherlock Holmes' arch enemy, Professor Moriarty, George Du Maurier's Svengali and Marie Corelli's Prince Lucio.[89] Like his evil contemporaries, Nikola is a mesmerist, a quality allied "with a Machiavellian skill in orchestration of villainy behind the scenes".[90] Like them, too, he is sexually and racially ambiguous: "He may be partly Jewish ... partly Russian, and partly oriental".[91] He is a scientist of the diabolical kind, and a student of occult and oriental wisdom, but also somewhat gentlemanly; he shares something with Holmes as well as with Moriarty. He is also geographically unstable, moving with uncanny speed and unpredictability across the globe, from England to Egypt to Australia and the South Seas, at home in the most exotic locations but also at the very heart of the empire.

Nikola, in short, is "un-English" in every aspect, in contrast to the hero of *A Bid for Fortune*, Richard Hatteras, "commonly called Dick, of Thursday Island, North Queensland, pearler, copra merchant, *bèche-de-mer* and tortoise-shell dealer, and South Sea trader generally"; but also, of course, by the end of the novel, Sir Richard Hatteras, for he inherits a title and an estate. Yet, as Robert Dixon argues, in a world of such "spectacular mobility", English or imperial identities are themselves unstable: "The speed of travel from one location to another is a synecdoche of identity in crisis".[92] The very reach of the empire means that racial and cultural boundaries are threatened, at home and abroad. Hatteras is himself a product of the empire's outer reaches, an adventurer and traveller, while his English family and ancestral estate are in decline. His task is to restore vitality – indeed Englishness – to the heart of empire, and to expel or contain the threat that Nikola represents. And yet it leaves the threat still lurking, larger than its immediate resolution. *A Bid for Fortune* invokes and justifies its readers' paranoia – Nikola is neither killed nor captured – even as it reassures them that the means for stability or renewal were already at hand.[93]

While these were in certain ways peculiarly English and imperial concerns, there were strong parallels across the Atlantic, for example in fears of looming confrontation between the Anglo-Saxon or white races and the coloured races in the Pacific. But no less important for understanding the trajectory and mobilities of the genre, although often ignored in critical interpretation, is that the ideological elements shaping narrative themselves become generic in a relatively short space of time; that is, they become "merely"

---

87 Ian Irvine, introduction to *A Bid for Fortune; or, Dr Nikola's Vendetta*, by Guy Boothby (Mt Waverley, Vic.: Chimaera, 2010), iii.
88 Review of *The Beautiful White Devil* quoted in Ward, Lock's edition of *Across the World for a Wife* (1898).
89 John Sutherland, introduction to *A Bid for Fortune; or, Dr Nikola's Vendetta*, by Guy Boothby (Oxford: Oxford University Press, 1996), ix.
90 Sutherland, introduction, x.
91 Gelder, "Guy Boothby", 4.
92 Dixon, *Writing the Colonial Adventure*, 162–63.
93 Dixon, *Writing the Colonial Adventure*, 178.

conventional, part of what the genre means, whether or not tied closely to any particular social context or cultural anxiety that may have been present at the genre's founding moment. As such, as conventional, they also become mobile and marketable.

The combination of master criminal, chase or flight across the globe, and mystery and intrigue, also often on a global scale, links Boothby to the two main variations on the tale of detection that emerged around the turn of the century: spy fiction and the thriller. He belongs with William Le Queux and E. Phillips Oppenheim as one of the founders of the thriller, especially, and as a precursor of Edgar Wallace, John Buchan and Sax Rohmer, whose Fu Manchu shows the influence of Dr Nikola. Boothby continued to use crime, detection and romance plots, but increasingly his novels manifest the characteristics through which the spy and thriller genres came to be distinguished from the classic detective tale. They are typically based less on a single, discrete crime and its explanation than on "a covert action which … transgresses conventional, moral, or legal boundaries".[94] The model is closer to a contagion than a discrete puzzle to be solved; or as Boothby himself dramatised it in *Pharos the Egyptian: A Romance* (1899): "I know that it was I, through you, who introduced the plague and carried it from Constantinople to London. Inhuman monster!"[95]

The stage is typically international, involving pursuit, flight, rivalry and confrontation across the globe, often in exotic locations, as the plot is revealed as progressively larger and more convoluted. The villains are likely to be foreign. The heroes, in this early period, are more likely gentleman amateurs than professionals, although secret agents become more common in the twentieth century. Boothby covers the range, with amateur detectives (an Australian bushman in *The Childerbridge Mystery*, 1902), police detectives, though usually in a secondary role (*A Millionaire's Love Story*, 1910), professional secret agents (*A Desperate Conspiracy*, 1904), even a gentleman thief who doubles as a private detective (*A Prince of Swindlers*, 1900).[96] What remains constant is the rapid movement of characters from location to location, with the effect of doubling the narrative pace:

> The life of a secret agent, Government spy, or whatever you may please to term him, makes for surprises, and one never knows from day to day what one may next be called upon to do. I remember once being sent to Constantinople on a mission that taxed all my energies and astuteness to the uttermost, and of being ordered off to St Petersburg on the very day that I brought it to a successful conclusion.[97]

Dr Nikola appeared in only five of Boothby's more than fifty novels, but the other elements described recur in the vast majority. The stress on sensational and "breathless" action in particular comes to define the thriller, as the word "sensation" itself shifts in meaning about this time from the moral ambiguities of the earlier sensation novel to the action of the thriller-adventure. Boothby's novels were described as "sensational-adventurous", indeed as "frank sensationalism carried to its furthest limits".[98] While it incorporates devices from

---

94 David Seed, "Spy Fiction", in Priestman, ed., *The Cambridge Companion to Crime Fiction*, ed. Priestman, 115.
95 Appleton, 1899, no. 261 in the Town and Country Library. Quotation: Ward, Lock edition, 355.
96 Seed, "Spy Fiction", 116.
97 *A Desperate Conspiracy* (London: F.V. White, 1904), 3.
98 Review of *In Strange Company* from the *World*, reproduced in Ward, Lock publicity in Boothby's books; Obituary, *Times* (London), 28 February 1905.

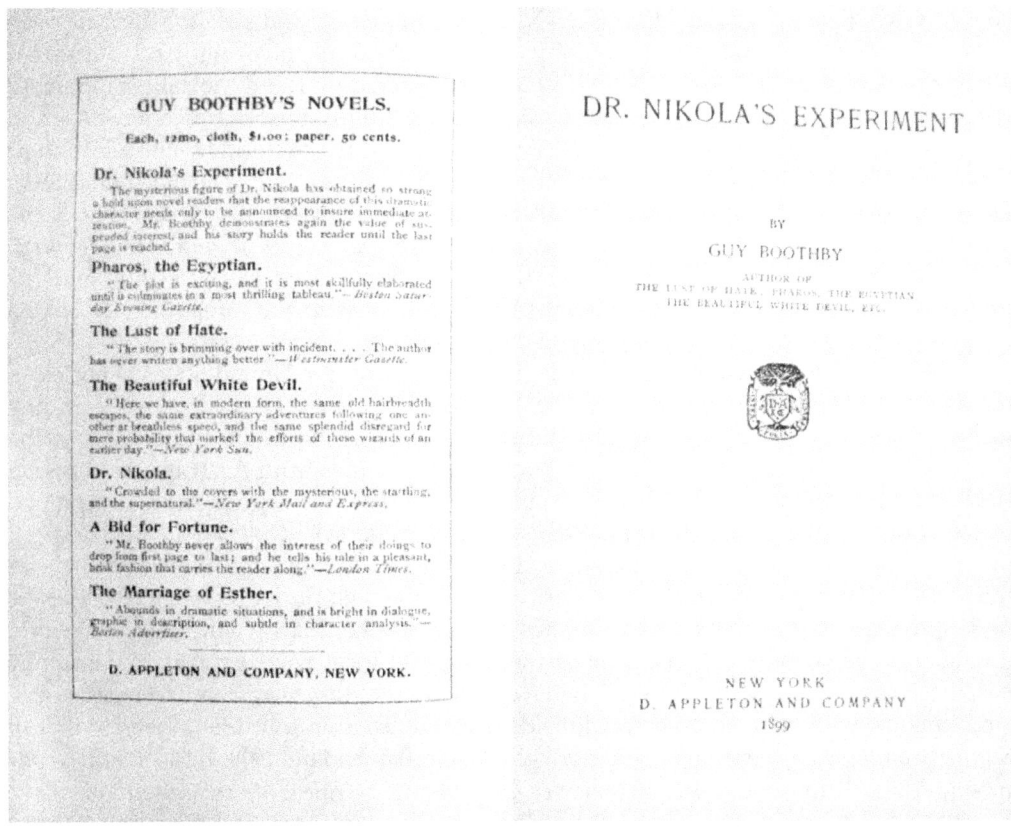

Figure 3.2 Guy Boothby, *Dr. Nikola's Experiment*, with a list of other works by the author (New York: D. Appleton & Co., 1899).

the detective story, "the thriller was and still is to a large extent marked out by the way in which it persistently seeks to raise the stakes of the narrative, heightening or transforming them into a rising curve of danger, violence or shock".[99] Or in the words of Boothby's American reviewers: "One hair-breadth escape succeeds another with a rapidity that scarce leaves the reader breathing space"; and, "Mr. Boothby can crowd more adventures into a square foot of canvas than any other novelist".[100]

No doubt these were the qualities that took Boothby's novels to the American market. From *In Strange Company* in 1894 through to *The Race of Life*, published posthumously in 1906, twenty-five different titles, or about half of Boothby's output, appeared from American publishers more or less simultaneously with their London release. In addition, there were later reprints of a number of titles from Street & Smith and Arthur Westbrook, and possible distribution of Ward, Lock titles through their New York office. Given Boothby's prodigious output and his short life, his market presence was unusually

---

99 Glover, "The Thriller", 137.
100 Quotations from reviews of *Sheilah McLeod* (*New York Times*) and *Dr Nikola* (*Scotsman*) reproduced in Ward, Lock editions of Boothby's books.

concentrated. Five American editions appeared in 1900 alone, and six the following year. But despite his sensational appeal, Boothby was not in the dime novel market. He attracted a range of publishers, mostly well-established firms, including Rand McNally, Lippincott, F.M. Buckles and Herbert S. Stone, each with two titles. But his most significant connection was with Appleton. Between 1895 and 1901, they included ten of Boothby's novels in their Town and Country Library, including four Dr Nikola novels – *A Bid for Fortune* (1895), *Dr. Nikola* (1896), *The Lust of Hate* (1898) and *Dr. Nikola's Experiment* (1899) (Fig. 3.2) – plus *The Marriage of Esther* (1895), *The Beautiful White Devil* (1897), *Pharos the Egyptian* (1899), *A Maker of Nations* (1900), *The Mystery of the Clasped Hands* (1901) and *My Indian Queen* (1901). Outside the library, they also published the remaining Dr Nikola title, *Farewell, Nikola*, in 1901, following their edition of *A Cabinet Secret* in 1900.

The exact order in which Boothby's fiction appeared in the United States is not clear, but as early as April 1895 a review of *The Marriage of Esther* suggests he was beginning to be known although still in need of introduction: "Guy Boothby, author of 'On the Wallaby,' has written a new novel … Mr. Boothby, who comes from Australia, has entered the first rank of antipodean writers of romance, and the dramatic situations and sustained interest of this new romance will enlarge his circle of readers".[101] *On the Wallaby* had been published the previous year by Longmans, Green in London, but this reference suggests the book had been released into the American market as well through the company's New York office.[102] A slightly later review implies even greater familiarity with Boothby's work, noting that the story had "very little of the delightful local coloring that Mr. Boothby usually gives to his books".[103] Boothby had had at least one story syndicated to newspapers, a sentimental wild west Australian goldfields tale, published in July 1894, the year that *In Strange Company* appeared in New York, while Macmillan had published *A Lost Endeavour* in mid-1895.[104] In June 1897, a reviewer in St Paul, Minnesota, remarked that "Mr. Boothby's name leads us to expect a decided treat in adventurous fiction"; unfortunately, in *The Beautiful White Devil*, the novel under review, "his accomplishment … [was] ordinary and stupid".[105] The *New York Sun* introduced Boothby as "a young Australian novelist", and found *The Beautiful White Devil*, by contrast, a successful *modern* romance, the adjective registering the effect of the emerging genre system on the romance form: "Here we have, in modern form, the same old hairbreadth escapes, the same extraordinary adventures following one another at breathless speed, and the same splendid disregard for mere probability that marked the efforts of those wizards of an earlier day".[106]

A Bid for Fortune does not appear to have been widely reviewed, but nonetheless it became the touchstone for Boothby's later novels. In Appleton's early publicity, it was promoted as an antidote to other forms of modern fiction, to be "welcomed as a relief from the novel of analysis and the discussion of marital infelicity".[107] Reviewers, though,

---

101 "Literary Notes", *Saint Paul Daily Globe*, 22 April 1895.
102 London and New York both listed on the title page as places of publication.
103 *Saint Paul Daily Globe*, 8 July 1895.
104 It appeared in the Virginian *Roanoke Times*, 5 July 1894, and the *Los Angeles Herald*, 22 July 1894. In 1902, the *Nebraska Advertiser* advertised a serialisation of the novel *My Strangest Case*, 13 June 1902, front page.
105 *Saint Paul Daily Globe*, 6 June 1897. A review of *Sheilah McLeod* later that same year could still introduce him as "a comparatively new name in fiction [who] shows considerable promise", *Kansas City Journal*, 6 December 1897.
106 "New Books", *New York Sun*, 8 May 1897.
107 Advertisement, *New York Sun*, 12 October 1895.

3 Crime, Sensation and the Modern Genre System: The Popular Fiction Marketplace

recognised the novel's own modernity, in one case explicitly linking the speed of the narrative with that of the railroad:

> Where are the railroad trains and the novelists going to stop in their endeavours to satisfy the demand of the public for rapidity of movement? When we are rushed past a landscape at the rate of 100 miles an hour it is quite certain that we shall not be able to enjoy the view; and it is equally probable that if the speed of the modern novel is increased beyond its present pace the impression it leaves upon our minds will be merely a featureless blur. These reflections arise in connection with "A Bid for Fortune," by Guy Boothby, a new Australian writer. It is a capital story, in which the action, though not yet too rapid, has reached the highest speed it can efficiently attain. Mystery and adventure, plot and counter-plot are unrolled before us with a swiftness to make the most hardened novel-reader catch his breath. The story is one which will be thoroughly enjoyed by the right readers.[108]

These are the qualities – including the qualification about the kind of reader one should be – that recur in most subsequent reviews, together with reference to the character of Dr Nikola, "a sort of Mephistopheles".[109] By 1901, Boothby's style could be summoned in a phrase or two: "Audacity, we need hardly say, is one of Mr. Boothby's characteristics as a novelist"; "written in the usual vein affected by Mr. Boothby, plenty of complications and adventure"; and "just such another fantastical tale of travel and adventure as this popular novelist has written again and again".[110]

Given such a reputation it is perhaps surprising that it was the Australianness of Boothby's last new book to be published in the United States that was promoted by its publishers – though less surprising once we are aware of the contemporary popularity of local Australian colour. Within a rather distorted outline of the Australian mainland, F.M. Buckles, the New York publisher, proclaimed: "Tipping his romance with the picturesque, throwing the glamour of the Australian Bush around the reader, Guy Boothby's last book *The Race of Life* is his best – never slow or stiff. The Bush is here, pulsating with mystery and tragedy" (Fig. 3.3).[111] That was certainly how it appeared in Omaha, where Australian bush stories (and to a surprising degree Australian slang) again seem to have been thoroughly familiar:

> "The Race of Life" by Guy Boothby is a stirring tale of love and adventure in the antipodes. Like Australian bush stories in general, it is rich in local colour and strong in the vernacular, but unlike most of them, it was written by a man whose personal knowledge of the scenes described was exact and intimate.
>
> Conjured up by his facile pen we may almost see the wide ranges of sun-baked planes and the dreamy, rainless wilderness of Northern Queensland in which the main

---

108 *Saint Paul Daily Globe*, 3 November 1895.
109 Review of *The Lust of Hate*, *Washington Times*, 25 September 1898.
110 Reviews of *The Mystery of the Clasped Hands* and *A Cabinet Secret*, *New York Daily Tribune*, 11 May 1901; *A Millionaire's Love Story*, *San Francisco Call*, 15 June 1902; *My Indian Queen*, *New York Daily Tribune*, 19 January 1902; also *Farewell, Nikola*, *New York Daily Tribune*, 20 October 1901: "In his crude, somewhat trashy way [Nikola] is still beguiling, and this book, though as mediocre as its predecessor, considered as literature, is worth reading, as they were, in a listless half hour".
111 Advertisement, *New York Sun*, 19 May 1906.

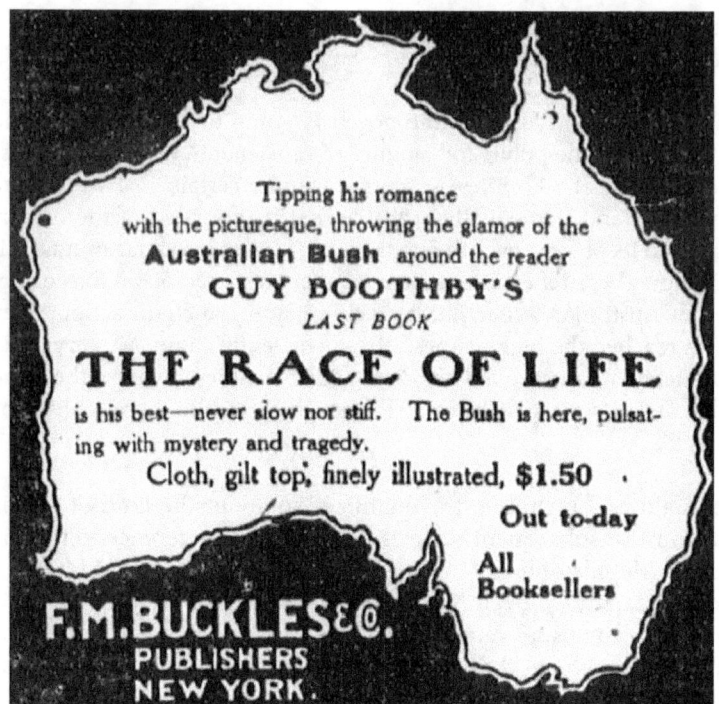

Figure 3.3 Advertisement for Guy Boothby's *The Race of Life* (New York: F.M. Buckles & Co., 1906), from the *New York Sun*, 19 May 1906.

incidents of the story occur. This region forms a fitting stage for the actions of the stockmen, bushrangers, gamblers and sundowners whose plots and counter-plots to win the mysterious "Moira," the beautiful heroine of the book, make a story of absorbing and thrilling interest.[112]

"Like Australian bush stories in general": the review helps to remind us that the bush romance survived into the twentieth century, though it did so here through the modern frame of adventure and thrills, through "plots and counter-plots", rather than the imperial drama of pioneering.

Fearfully Entertaining: Carlton Dawe and Ambrose Pratt

Two other Australian-born authors warrant consideration here as their careers bear the impress of the emerging genre system and both enjoyed a period of success in America on the back of success in the British market. Carlton Dawe is virtually forgotten today but was a prolific author, if not quite in Boothby's league, with at least seventy-seven novels and short story collections published in England by the major popular fiction publishers, Eveleigh Nash, John Long and Ward, Lock. Ambrose Pratt is remembered as a journeyman

---

112 *Omaha Daily Bee*, 11 July 1906.

3 Crime, Sensation and the Modern Genre System: The Popular Fiction Marketplace

author of popular Australiana mostly published through the NSW Bookstall Co. and more substantial non-fiction works on Australian topics.[113] But from 1900 to 1916 he had an international career as an author of popular fiction, with fourteen titles published in London, eight of these by Ward, Lock. Both Dawe and Pratt were travellers over imperial routes into the Pacific and to London, and in Dawe's case to Asia – Japan and China figure significantly in a number of his works. Both wrote explicitly for the popular fiction market and ranged across the generic possibilities old and new: adventure-romance, Australian bush stories including convict and bushranging tales, international mystery and intrigue, and, not least, crime and thrillers. Dawe had eight titles published in the United States between 1895 and 1916, Pratt five between 1901 and 1917.

Dawe began his career in Australia and then, from 1892, in England with Australian stories of convicts, exploration, bushrangers, gold and the "Lemurian" theme of a lost civilisation in the Australian interior.[114] His American career, however, begins with a very different theme, the adventures – and romance – of white men in the East, in the short story collection *Yellow and White* published in Boston by Roberts Brothers in 1895. This was followed by other titles in the same vein: *Kakemonos: Tales of the Far East* (John Lane, 1897), *A Bride of Japan* (Herbert S. Stone, 1898) and *Rose and Chrysanthemum* (Knight & Millet, 1900). That there was a profitable market for such exotic, orientalist tales is also reflected in the books' production qualities. For *Rose and Chrysanthemum* (Plate 4), Knight & Millet invested in a striking, original *japoniste* cover even though the edition could not be copyrighted (internal evidence shows the book was produced using sheets purchased from its English publisher Sands & Co.).[115] Another novel on a different but related theme, *The Voyage of the "Pulo Way": A Record of Some Strange Doings at Sea*, an adventure-romance involving piracy in the seas around China and the Philippines, was published by R.F. Fenno in 1899. Dawe also featured in the fiction magazines and newspapers: "Rose and Chrysanthemum" appeared in the *New Illustrated Magazine* in 1899; he contributed one of the "clever stories" to the May 1900 issue of the upmarket *Smart Set*; and in 1901 a story of the Chinese Boxer Rebellion, "The Yellow Man", was advertised as a serial in several papers. The publicity highlighted its generic appeal: "abounds in incidents the narration of which holds the reader enchanted. No lover of exciting fiction should miss reading The Yellow Man".[116]

The American reviews also suggest how Dawe's early stories were accommodated within a recognisable genre, tales of adventure and romance in the Far East, a genre overlapping with South Seas tales. This sometimes worked to the author's advantage, sometimes not. The *New York Tribune* thought *Yellow and White* an "excellent collection of short stories" excepting "a few vulgarities of expression and of thought", and it was happy to accept their generic predictability:

---

113 Carol Mills, *The New South Wales Bookstall Company as a Publisher* (Cook, ACT: Mulini Press, 1991).
114 *The Golden Lake; or, The Marvellous History of a Journey through the Great Lone Land of Australia* (1890), *Mount Desolation: A Romance* (1892), *The Emu's Head: A Chronicle of Dead Man's Flat* (1893). For *The Golden Lake* as a Lemurian novel, see John Docker, *The Nervous Nineties: Australian Cultural Life in the 1890s* (Melbourne: Oxford University Press, 1991), 172-76, 211-12.
115 The Scottish printing firm's name still appears on pages in the US edition.
116 *Saint Paul Globe*, 26 February 1899; *St Louis Republic*, 12 May 1900; *Leader* (Guthrie, OK), 3 January 1901.

The tales have at least one conspicuous merit: they are well written and put together. Mr. Dawe knows his business, and when he learns to avoid the outré, and to eschew certain affectations of style which are modish in the present day among our new writers, he may look forward to composing a book which every one will be delighted to read and to keep. There are nine brief tales in the present collection, the scenes being about evenly divided between China, Japan and Siam. An Englishman is invariably the hero, and the stories depict his adventures. These partake of the nature of pure adventure, either of courage or love.[117]

The *Times* was less accepting in noting the very same elements (wanting, perhaps, either more or less realism in the story-telling):

Mr. W. Carlton Dawe's themes in his stories are for the greater part the adventures of certain fascinating Englishmen, who, seeking "la bonne adventure" [sic] in the East, invariably bring about murder. The men live to tell the tale, but the women are invariably slaughtered. It is the same story, with various surroundings, in China or Singapore, or in Japan. Fortunately it is not always the same Briton, with the "blue eyes and the golden hair," who brings about the tragedy, but the conclusions are identical … Mr. Dawe's "Yellow and White" has a distinct and predominating tinge of crimson in it.[118]

Reviewers of popular fiction often enjoyed themselves playing up the pleasures of generic implausibility. *The Voyage of the "Pulo Way"* inspired one reviewer to reflect that while "the eccentricity of Fate" had often been remarked upon, it "is as nothing to the eccentricity of the untrammelled writer of romance", not least when Fate is "assisted by a novelist of such peculiar abilities as Mr. Carlton Dawe": "When the golden-haired girl is rescued from the reef, inherits a fortune and marries the second mate, we feel that fate and the novelist have arranged things as they should be".[119]

Kakemonos and *A Bride of Japan* deal with the more controversial theme of "the relationship between the yellow woman and the white man in the everyday life of the Japanese treaty ports".[120] Here, as with Louis Becke's tales of the Pacific, the conventions of adventure-romance could not carry or contain the story, as realism fractures the romance plot. *A Bride of Japan* was deemed "unpleasantly realistic throughout"; this at the end of a long, considered review of the novel in the *Washington Times* that described it as "one of those international romances which are becoming in some sort a literary fashion": "With the freer intermingling of races and nationalities in commerce and industry, there has come up the question of race intermixture, and it is one of those problems that the book treats … It inculcates the idea that the white race, being distinctly the superior race of the earth, degrades itself by alliance with any other".[121] The reviewer in fact takes Dawe to task for loading the story against any possible successful outcome for the European-Japanese marriage at its centre. The *Saint Paul Globe* was blunter, though with a comparison that Dawe may have valued: "A more drearily unrelieved tale of horror than this is hardly to

---

117 *New York Daily Tribune*, 26 July 1896.
118 *New York Times*, 15 September 1895.
119 *New York Sun*, 2 September 1899.
120 Review of *Kakemonos*, *New York Sun*, 22 May 1897.
121 *Washington Times*, 17 April 1898.

be found outside of Mr. Conrad's unholy stories of degeneration in Africa and alien lands to the southward. It is difficult to see why 'Carlton Dawe' – the name is new in fiction – thought the book worth while to write … [As] literature, in spite of the writer's many gifts of construction and expression, it is absolutely useless".[122]

Unlike Becke, Dawe ranged widely across both old and new genres, as is clear from the three further novels published in America. *The Woman, the Man and the Monster* (Stuyvesant Press, 1909) is a modern and "wholly unconventional" retelling of the Perseus and Andromeda story.[123] *The Super-Barbarians*, released by John Lane in early 1916, is a wartime submarine adventure whose unusual generic innovation was noted by the *New York Times*: "an absolutely new field of fiction … a novel of adventure with its scenes laid in the bowels of a fighting submarine".[124] For *The Redemption of Grace Milroy*, from October 1916, John Lane's publicity offered a neat generic summary: "What a young woman is bound to go through after the prison doors have closed behind her, and what through strength of character she can overcome and accomplish is aptly shown in this interesting tale in which Scotland Yard and the White Slave traffickers play a part".[125]

As this description suggests, Dawe's later works reveal the adventure-romance being shaped more explicitly into crime, thriller and espionage genres, with titles such as *The London Plot* (1903) and *The Knightsbridge Affair* (1927) among his English releases. In 1931, he launched the adventures of Leathermouth, *aka* "Colonel Gantian … that especially secret 'secret service' man", who by 1934 in the British sphere was "fast becoming one of the most popular personalities in sensational fiction".[126] Ward, Lock published eleven Leathermouth novels between 1931 and 1937. What is surprising, given Dawe's regular output in a saleable genre, his impact in the British market, and his successive US titles previously from John Lane, is that none of these later books had separate American editions. Ward, Lock may have distributed them in the United States, although no reviews have been discovered. Whatever the cause and despite his invention of a marketable protagonist, Dawe failed to achieve that serial investment by an American publisher in either his own name or that of his hero which proved so often to be the crucial element for sustaining a career. Perhaps he slipped from view when John Lane's American operations were purchased by Dodd, Mead in 1922; perhaps the market was simply too crowded for another "sensational" secret service series; or perhaps, alternatively, Dawe's British adventures did not meet the contemporary American taste for mysteries or thrillers. Despite the ongoing strength of the transatlantic book trade in the 1920s and 1930s, the two domestic markets were quite distinct.

Already a contributor to Australian magazines and newspapers, Ambrose Pratt left for England in 1898 to pursue a career in fiction writing and journalism. Again, like Dawe, he ranged widely and opportunistically across the genres. His first novel, *King of the Rocks*, published in London by Hutchinson in 1900, combined a crime adventure plot with local details of Sydney larrikin gangs. His second, *Franks, Duellist*, by contrast, was a historical romance and adventure intrigue set in Napoleonic times. As an American reviewer

---

122 "Literature of Today", *Saint Paul Globe*, 12 June 1898.
123 Review of *The Woman, the Man and the Monster*, *Salt Lake Tribune*, 20 June 1909 (novel released as *The New Andromeda* in London: Nash, 1909).
124 Review of *The Super-Barbarians*, *New York Times*, 26 March 1916.
125 Advertisement, *New York Times*, 21 October 1916.
126 Quotation from cover flap of *The Law of the Knife* (London: Ward, Lock, 1934).

commented, it "crowds within the covers a remarkable succession of daring adventures by a daring London man about town, as an expert duellist, gambler, and fascinator of women".[127] Published in 1901, again by Hutchinson, it was the first of three novels issued by R.F. Fenno in New York. The second, *The Counterstroke* (1907), shifted generic ground again, as a modern thriller about the defeat of Nihilism, here representing an international terrorist organisation. In the words of its publisher: "Plot and counterplot abound in this powerfully written and enthralling story, which deals with Nihilism and its fiendish machinations, happily varied by the 'Counterstrokes' throughout aimed at it in the novel".[128] For the *New York Sun*'s reviewer, though, it showed only the "romance of adventure without sense".[129] The book must have had some success commercially, as Fenno next picked up an earlier Pratt title, *Vigorous Daunt: Billionaire* (1908). For the *San Francisco Call*, this was a novel of "highly sensational" adventures, one that should not be taken seriously but could still be enjoyed "without drawing materially on one's intellectual powers".[130]

Pratt also appeared in the fiction magazines and newspapers. *Franks, Duellist* and *The Counterstroke* were serialised, while stories appeared in the *Pilgrim* magazine, the *Sunday Magazine* (alongside E. Phillips Oppenheim), *Lippincott's Magazine* and the *Washington Times*.[131] Pratt's surviving correspondence with J.B. Pinker reveals his interest in the sale of stories in the American market and of American serial rights in his novels. In 1902 he wrote, thanking but also perhaps reminding his agent, "I am glad you are selling the series to America – and that you'll obtain a good price".[132] He was keen to recoup money owing to him from Hutchinson as a result of their sale of the plates of *Franks, Duellist* to America. In this context he wrote to Pinker again in August 1903: "I am just completing a series of stories (highly sensational) which should do excellently well for magazine or other serial publication. They are more ingenious and much more exciting than Vigorous Daunt and they treat of an engaging rascal – and are *detective* – from the criminal's point of view". Raffles' influence was widely felt.

Pratt's most successful novel in the United States was certainly highly sensational and strikingly "generic" in its effects. This was *The Living Mummy*, published by Ward, Lock in London and Frederick A. Stokes in New York in 1910, the latter a handsomely produced edition with four neo-Egyptian art deco colour illustrations (Plate 5). As one reviewer commented, "Novels on Egypt are said to be the fad of the day, the land of the Pharaohs, with its Nile, its lotus flowers and its ruined temples having obsessed the popular imagination".[133] The novel was all its title promised – mystery and horror, international intrigue, a fiendish plot, hair-breadth escapes, a love interest, and, of course, a "thoroughly

---

127 *Minneapolis Journal*, 11 January 1902.
128 *New York Sun*, 10 August 1907.
129 *New York Sun*, 31 August 1907. Pratt's *Three Years with Thunderbolt* (Cassell 1907) was noted in the *New York Tribune*, 7 September 1907, as in press, but no further evidence of its US release has been located.
130 *San Francisco Call*, 9 August 1908. The review also noted that the book was "profusely illustrated with the worst pictures seen in a book for many a long day". See also *Washington Times*, 4 July 1908.
131 "A Sword Mislaid" appeared in the *Seattle Star* in 1905, "The Counterstroke" in the *Los Angeles Herald*, 1906; references to other publications include *Pilgrim* magazine in the *Minneapolis Journal*, 31 March 1903; *Sunday Magazine*: *Tribune*, 30 September 1906. The *Sunday Magazine* appeared as a supplement to numerous papers, including the *Tribune*; the story itself appeared on 30 September; *Washington Times*, 14 July 1907. *Lippincott's Magazine*: *Marion Daily Mirror* (Ohio), 25 February 1908.
132 Pratt to Pinker, 5 October 1902, James B. Pinker & Son Collection of Papers 1893–1940, New York Public Library, Berg Collection.
133 "The Living Mummy", *Times-Dispatch* (Richmond, VA), 28 February 1910.

dried-out and overworked" mummy that does "shocking deeds" when released in London. The novel was "full of highly exciting interest" that "will fearfully entertain the reader".[134] Stokes published two editions of the book in 1910. In his own modest way, perhaps Pratt, too, helped establish a genre, the orientalist adventure-horror tale of Egyptian mummies returning from the dead to wreak havoc in modern, European times.

Indeed, we might almost claim that Australians had the mummy market wrapped up. Hume's *The Green Mummy* was published by Dillingham in 1908, the same year as its London release, while Mary Gaunt's *The Mummy Moves* appeared in London in 1910 alongside Pratt's mummy thriller. Described as Gaunt's "most atypical and successful novel", it involved a "difficult detective, a bloodstained and mobile Egyptian mummy, a secret marriage, and an obscure African cult".[135] In the United States, it was revived (perhaps the appropriate term) with serialisation in the *Chicago Daily News* in 1919, for which the paper paid an extremely generous £1000, and then with book publication by Edward J. Clode in 1925.[136] Clode advertised it under the heading "Detective Stories", alongside the latest Fergus Hume.

Books in a Million

The popular fiction titles of the authors discussed in this chapter were books in a million, a handful of books in the thousand or more new fiction titles released each season in the American marketplace. They were books *for* the season, designed to sell quickly, and to be distinguished only as "one of a kind", more or less interchangeable with others of their kind, but dependent therefore on the name of the author, the generic signposting of the book's title, its hero or villain, the identity of a publisher's series or other paratextual devices in order to be noticed. They belong to the world of commercial popular entertainment, as their reviewers largely recognised, and as such they could be celebrated or criticised as more or less competent, pleasurable or thrilling examples of the type. "Sensation" almost by definition did not make the claims on permanence that might be associated with literature. Its effects did not bear re-reading; but they did encourage "re-writing", serially, in new novels and stories, new variations on the increasingly familiar conventions of adventure, detection, mystery and intrigue. Some, nevertheless, just like literary classics, withstood the test of time, not only being bestsellers when they first appeared but continuing to attract readers and publishers in different markets through to the present day.

Both Hume and Boothby helped define one of the dominant popular modern genres. Hume continued to write in various modes but it was the detective novel that defined his

---

134 "Old, but Mighty Lively", *New York Sun*, 26 February 1910. See also *Washington Times*, 19 February 1910.
135 Margaret Bradstock, "Mary Gaunt (1861–1942)", in *Australian Literature, 1788-1914*, ed. Selina Samuels, Dictionary of Literary Biography, Vol. 230 (Detroit, MI: Gale Research, 2001), 148.
136 It was reprinted in the same year by Grosset & Dunlap, the hardback reprinters, indicating strong sales on its initial release. One further book by Pratt appeared in the United States, *The Judgment of the Orient: Some Reflections on the Great War made by the Chinese Student and Traveller K'ung Yuan Ku'suh, Edited and Rendered into Colloquial English by Ambrose Pratt* (Dutton, 1917) to give it its full title. Its claim is that the "psychological genesis of the war between Germany and Europe is sexual" (61).

career. Boothby continued to draw on his Australian past, but it was thrillers that became the reference point. Dawe ranged widely across the field of popular fiction genres until concentrating his efforts in the secret service thriller, although it was his stories of the Far East that seemed to attract American publishers; how far this was a question of taste and how far one of mere opportunity or commercial calculation is unclear. Pratt also worked the generic changes, although after his success with *The Living Mummy*, the last of a series of crime-mystery adventures, he turned to popular Australian stories, to bushrangers, convicts and gold, for the rest of his fiction career.

These examples also make clear that in this formative period for modern fiction publishing between the 1890s and the 1920s, one way to American publication for Anglo-Australian writers was a strong "generic identity", a clear identification of the author's name with a particular genre or group of closely allied genres. The growth and consolidation of popular genres in the mainstream fiction market added a new dynamic to the international mobility of Australian books and authors, not least to their capacity to make a mark in the US book trade. In the strongest cases, this generic identity was reinforced through identification with a single publisher and sequential publication such as Hume found with Dillingham and Boothby with Appleton. Expatriation also remained a good career move for Australian authors, but for the writers discussed in this chapter we might recast it less as a mode of escape from colonial culture than a means of *participating in* the international circuits mobilised by genre fiction.

4
Renegotiating the American Connection: Australian Fiction 1900–1930s

The first three decades of the twentieth century present no clear pattern for the publication of Australian novels in the United States outside the serial relationships with publishers that certain genre writers were able to achieve. Otherwise, in all but a few cases, we see one-off or occasional publishing, with few signs of sustained investment in individual authors and even less in Australian books per se. Towards the end of the period, however, the situation changes quite suddenly with the enormous critical and sales success of Henry Handel Richardson's *Ultima Thule* in 1929, followed the year after by Katharine Susannah Prichard's *Coonardoo*, and these two authors will be the subject of Chapter 6. The present chapter surveys the presence in the American marketplace of Australian writers working in the broad field of commercial fiction but outside the popular genres of crime, mystery and women's romance. It examines the obstacles and opportunities for Australian authors and stories in America in these decades after the passing of international copyright legislation in the United States and as the structures of the modern, twentieth-century US publishing industry were set in place.

Beginning with an account of the copyright situation for British and Australian books in the United States, the chapter offers a brief overview of the changing fortunes of Australian books in the American marketplace for each of the first three decades of the century followed by a series of more detailed case studies. While there are many scattered and one-off titles there are also some surprising successes, not least the remarkable story of J.F. Dwyer, the sustained careers of women writer/travellers such as Mary Gaunt and G.B. Lancaster, and the participation of Australian authors in the vogue for "modern girl" stories and, in the later twenties, for "modern sex novels". Children's author Ethel Turner offers a study of the trials and tribulations faced by an Australian writer determined to achieve American publication but determined no less to manage her own career – her rights and earnings – as a professional author.

Copyrights Constraints

The most common pathway to American publication in the early twentieth century was still via London, but as indicated in Chapter 2, the introduction of the International Copyright Act of 1891 could prove a mixed blessing for authors published first in Britain or Australia. Although it enabled copyright protection in America for books first published overseas and hence lessened the chance of unauthorised editions, it did so under the strict conditions defined by the Act's manufacturing clause and the provisions requiring prior or simultaneous publication in the United States. The latter provisions were relaxed in 1909 with the introduction of *ad interim* copyright, extending the period for both registration and publication of a book first published overseas. For an English-language work, the *ad interim* terms allowed thirty days from first publication for the book to be registered in Washington and a further thirty days for the publisher to manufacture an American edition. However, at the same time, the manufacturing clause was tightened, as printing and binding had also to be done in the United States.[1] The *ad interim* terms were further relaxed in 1919, allowing sixty days for deposit and four months beyond that for publication, giving greater flexibility to American publishers deciding whether to take on a foreign title for a copyrighted edition.[2] A copyright notice had to be printed at the front of each book to secure copyright.

Even with these amendments, the practical effect was that American publishers had to make carefully calculated decisions about whether to issue a British book in a copyrighted edition and hence invest in typesetting, plate-making, printing and binding. Books by foreign authors sold in the United States now cost the same or more than those written by American authors.[3]:

> If a British book were apt to do well on the American market, it was necessary to protect it by copyright; this meant the American publisher had to invest his own capital and have the book manufactured by domestic typesetters and printers. If a British book were expected to sell only moderately well in America, copies could still be imported from the British publisher … but the book, when issued, would be in the public domain. This made both British and American publishers hesitate over marginal titles.[4]

The impact of these measures in the broader context of the American publishing industry is difficult to estimate. The total number of *ad interim* copyright registrations fell after the 1909 amendments to the Chace Act but rose sharply after 1919, especially from 1922; a high level was maintained until the war years.[5] James L.W. West argues that for many British (and hence Australian) authors the likelihood of being published in America was diminished. Least affected were established writers and popular, proven

---

1   Simon Nowell-Smith, *International Copyright Law and the Publisher in the Reign of Queen Victoria* (Oxford: Clarendon Press, 1968), 65–9; J. Hayden Boyd and William S. Lofquist, "New Interests in Old Issues: Antiprotection and the End of the Manufacturing Clause of the US Copyright Law", *Publishing Research Quarterly* (Winter 1991–1992): 23.
2   Robert Spoo, *Without Copyrights: Piracy, Publishing, and the Public Domain* (Oxford & New York: Oxford University Press, 2013), 68–9; also "The Manufacturing Clause: Copyright Protection to the Foreign Author", *Columbia Law Review* 50, no. 5 (May 1950): 689. *Ad interim* copyright was extended to five years (covering 1500 copies) in 1949 and the manufacturing clause was dropped for English-language books by foreign authors in 1954.
3   Jesicca Despain, *Nineteenth-Century Transatlantic Reprinting and the Embodied Book* (Farnham, UK: Ashgate, 2014), 178.
4   James L.W. West III, "The Chace Act and Anglo-American Literary Relations", *Studies in Bibliography* 45 (1992): 305.
5   Figures provided by Zvi S. Rosen, Abraham L. Kaminstein Scholar in Residence, United States Copyright Office.

sellers, authors whose new works were considered good investments and were thus likely to be manufactured and copyrighted in the United States as a matter of course. More vulnerable were those without an established reputation, the young and the unknown, for "American publishers ideally had to decide before publication to have the texts set and printed in the States. For unknown authors ... this was impractical and financially risky".[6] Australian authors, of course, were largely unknown authors.

In one view, then, the manufacturing clause "rewarded the proven, the safe, and the popular".[7] In contrast, publisher George Haven Putnam argued strongly at the time against the view that the copyright law would damage the transatlantic book trade. International copyright was advantageous to legitimate publishers of English books,

> for the simple reason that larger profits could be secured by controlling the market for authorized editions (even when these were sold at the lowest popular prices) than by dividing the market with a number of unauthorized editions. This being the case, it was of course to the interest of the publishers *to secure the protection of American copyright for as many foreign works as possible*, and the throwing over of any books to the unauthorized reprinters would entail loss upon publishers as well as upon authors.[8]

While the number of British titles published in the United States declined from the heady days of the 1880s, they remained a major presence. The expanding fiction market on both sides of the Atlantic created increased demand for British novels in the American market even as the demand for local fiction grew, offsetting the difficulties created by the Copyright Act. British titles comprised around 23 per cent of bestsellers in the American market between 1910 and 1919, rising to 28 per cent in the following decade.[9] The British and American publishing industries remained closely connected, with most American houses having representatives in London, such as Scribner's Lemuel Bangs. Doubleday, Page & Co. acquired Heinemann in 1920, although the latter continued to function independently; 40 per cent of the new books on Holt's list were British; and Hodder & Stoughton acquired a one-third financial stake in Doran.[10] The transatlantic magazine market also remained a critical source of earnings for writers in both countries. While British publisher Stanley Unwin claimed in 1926 that less than 5 per cent of non-fiction titles published in Great Britain were printed and copyrighted in a separate American edition, the numbers for fiction were significantly higher.[11] Still, in 1931, Michael Joseph estimated that "not more than twenty per cent of new novels by relatively unknown English authors find publication in America".[12]

---

6   West, "The Chace Act", 308–9.
7   Spoo, *Without Copyrights*, 72.
8   George Haven Putnam, "Analysis of the Provisions of the Copyright Law of 1891" (1891), in *American Literary Publishing Houses, 1638–1899*, ed. Peter Dzwonkoski, Dictionary of Literary Biography, Vol. 49 (Detroit, MI: Gale Research, 1986), 570–71.
9   John Sutherland, *Bestsellers: A Very Short Introduction* (Oxford: Oxford University Press, 2007), 11-12.
10 Catherine Turner, *Marketing Modernism Between the Two Wars* (Amherst: University of Massachusetts Press, 2003), 112; John Feather, *A History of British Publishing*, 2nd ed. (London: Routledge, 2006), 169; John Attenborough, *A Living Memory: Hodder and Stoughton, Publishers, 1868–1975* (London: Hodder & Stoughton, 1975), 57.
11 Stanley Unwin, *The Truth About Publishing* (London: George Allen & Unwin, 1926), 69.
12 Michael Joseph, *This Writing Business* (London: Faber & Faber, 1931), 23.

The effects for Australian books and authors were mixed. The total number of American editions of Australian books fell after the boom years of the 1890s, and yet a significant number of authors - including a number of significant authors - *were* able to achieve American publication. We estimate that for Australian novels, whatever their place of first publication, around 11 per cent achieved American editions in the two decades from 1900 to 1920, and around 13 per cent over the following decade. Less than half of these editions were copyrighted in America, although again American publishers did go to the expense of copyrighting more titles than we might expect. The advantage of doing so, even with a relatively unknown author, was that by holding copyright the publisher could then sell or license paperback, reprint, book club, serial and other subsidiary rights, which were typically more lucrative than bookstore sales of the original hardcover edition. Otherwise a range of strategies evolved to meet or circumnavigate the Chace Act's requirements, enabling wider publication of imported books than the strict application of the law would indicate. American publishers could purchase plates or unbound sheets from the British publisher, insert their own title page and other front matter before binding, and thereby produce their own edition without copyright protection. This was especially the case where the risk of unauthorised editions was slight, and Australian authors might in fact have benefited from being largely unknown in that the risk of piracy was minimal and a relatively cheap non-copyrighted edition might be published to test the market. The strategy was not without its own problems - duties had to be paid on imported sheets and there were the differences in British and American spelling and punctuation and different standards as to paper quality and page size. Nonetheless, it remained the most common practice for mid-list books and lesser-known authors.

In some cases, as we have seen, a portion of a book was printed and the title registered in Washington, which did not secure copyright for the whole book but might be enough to dissuade competitors. Alternatively, a new introduction or new illustrations could be inserted and copyrighted, creating the impression that the full text was protected.[13] In other cases, registering *ad interim* copyright or printing a copyright notice on the verso of the title page were used as a kind of bluff where copyright could not in fact be established in any complete form.[14] Most importantly, as Robert Spoo has argued, a modified form of trade courtesy continued after the passing of the Chace Act: the manufacturing clause in effect restricted access to full copyright protection meaning that "legalised piracy" had not been eliminated, "it had merely been limited in scope". In such circumstances, it was in the interest of the newer publishers no less than the established houses to maintain a version of trade courtesy, "more quietly and less systematically than in the previous century but with perhaps a keener sensitivity for foreign authors' rights".[15]

It is clear nonetheless that the transfer of titles from London to America remained a difficult proposition for the majority of Australian authors. A few established direct communications with American publishers, in-house editors or literary agents, and the London representatives of the major American houses actively sought out new titles, but many more were reliant on the will of their British publishers. Authors with agents in London could hope for representation of their interests in the United States, but the

---

13 Spoo, *Without Copyrights*, 94-105.
14 More rarely, British titles with potential in the two markets could be manufactured and copyrighted first in the United States; printed sheets would then be sent to Britain to be bound and copyrighted there.
15 Spoo, *Without Copyrights*, 63, 108.

4 Renegotiating the American Connection: Australian Fiction 1900–1930s

story was often one of frustration and disappointment. Despite the difficulties, it is clear that many Australian authors maintained a keen interest in being published in America, not only because of the greater sales and larger earnings the US market promised and the possibility of wider recognition, but also the prospect of a different kind of editorial attention, more professional and market savvy, and free from the colonial frameworks that still governed dealings with British houses, as reflected in the reduced royalties on colonial editions.[16]

Despite financial crises at Harper and Appleton, the established publishers such as Putnam's, Scribner, Lippincott, Macmillan and Dodd, Mead remained dominant in the early twentieth century. Publishers of popular fiction such as Dillingham, Rand McNally and Street & Smith also survived the turbulent years of cheap paperback publishing. At the same time, a new generation of publishers emerged, including Doubleday, Page & Co. from 1900, "really the first of a new era in publishing", followed by B.W. Huebsch (1902), George Doran (1908), Alfred Knopf (1915), Boni & Liveright (1917) and Harcourt, Brace (1919).[17] In James West's terms, the newer publishers "brought many ideas over from newspaper and magazine publishing, and they had the advantage of the 1891 international copyright agreement".[18] They were more active in seeking out authors, marketing books, and trying to meet the new, larger audiences demanding new fiction above all. A mix of new and established houses were important for Australian authors, especially Appleton, Lippincott, Scribner, Dillingham, Doubleday, Dutton, Frederick A. Stokes and Doran.

The Fall and Rise of Australian Fiction

We see the uneven effects of these constraints and of the collapse of an unconstrained paperback and reprint industry in the relative decline in American editions of Australian fiction in the early decades of the twentieth century. This decline is especially striking given the pattern of growth across the 1880s and 1890s. From 1900 to 1910, around seventy fiction titles with Australian provenance were released in the United States, but more than half of these appeared in the first three years, 1900 to 1902, and mainly from the pens of Guy Boothby, E.W. Hornung and Louis Becke. After this period, in most years only three or four new titles appeared. Important writers who did figure for the first time in the American market in this period include G.B. Lancaster from 1905 and Henry Handel Richardson from 1908, while Mary Gaunt's American career had a second, more substantial beginning in 1910.[19] Lilian Turner and Louise Mack each had a single novel

---

16 Carol Hetherington, "Authors, Editors, Publishers: Katharine Susannah Prichard and W.W. Norton", *Australian Literary Studies* 22, no. 4 (October 2006): 418-19.
17 Doubleday, Page & Co., 1900-1927, Doubleday, Doran & Co. 1927-1946, Doubleday & Co. 1946-1986; Harcourt, Brace & Howe 1919-1921, Harcourt, Brace & Co from 1921-1960. Quotation: Christopher Morley cited in John Tebbel, *Between Covers: The Rise and Transformation of Book Publishing in America* (New York: Oxford University Press, 1987), 134.
18 James L.W. West III, *American Authors and the Literary Marketplace since 1900* (Philadelphia: University of Pennsylvania Press, 1988), 43.
19 An earlier novel by Gaunt, *Deadman's*, had appeared from the New Amsterdam Book Co. in 1899, before Gaunt left Australia, but a new sequence began in 1910 after her expatriation. The earlier book was a success in the United States, passing through two editions in a few weeks: *New York Times*, 11 March 1899.

published in America, while Ethel Turner had six novels released between 1909 and 1910. E.J. Banfield's *The Confessions of a Beachcomber* was published by Appleton in 1909 and later reissued alongside *My Tropic Isle* in 1924.

The low average continued in the following decade with around forty-five new titles appearing between 1911 and 1920, and even these numbers depend upon the doubtful inclusion of Irish-born Beatrice Grimshaw, resident in New Guinea from 1907,[20] and Elinor Mordaunt, whose American career began in 1911 following her departure from Australia in 1909 after seven or eight years' residence. Mordaunt had nineteen books published in the United States to 1930, including five with Australian characters or settings.[21] A.J. Dawson had a number of books without Australian reference published in the United States after 1900, but returned to Australian settings for the semi-autobiographical novel *The Record of Nicholas Freydon* (Doran, 1914).[22] One-off authors for the period include "Mrs Æneas Gunn", whose *We of the Never-Never* was published by Macmillan in New York in 1911, among a very diverse group of familiar and unfamiliar names: William Gosse Hay, Alfred Buchanan, Dulcie Deamer, Ethel Gertrude Hart, Tarella Quin, David Hennessey, Dorota Flatau, Winifred James, Sumner Locke and Marie Bjelke-Petersen. South Australian Doris Egerton Jones managed to have three novels published by George W. Jacobs of Philadelphia between 1915 and 1919.

Surprisingly, given their exaggerated Australian vernacular, C.J. Dennis' popular verse narratives also appeared in America, and their history illustrates something of the demands the copyright law placed on publishers. John Lane's New York operation published *Doreen and the Sentimental Bloke* in one volume in 1916, then *Doreen* and *The Moods of Ginger Mick* separately in 1918. Lane's publicity declared *Doreen and the Sentimental Bloke* "a decided novelty in verse": "In thirteen poems, written in the slang peculiar to Australia, are set forth in most convincing and touching fashion, some experiences in the life of Bill".[23] In a familiar tactic, in order to copyright *The Moods of Ginger Mick*, Angus & Robertson in late 1916 cabled one line of every verse to John Lane at the high cost of "about £80" so that a volume could be set and printed in the United States. Only a small number of this edition, as few as twelve, was printed, but copyright was thus secured; or rather the publication made "the pirating of the balance set not worth anyone's while".[24] Lane published the complete volume only in 1918, with a print run of 2000 for Canada and the United States. Ian McLaren's research indicates that there were also two printings of *Doreen* in 1918, one for copyright and a second for general issue, suggesting there had been some success before that. Angus & Robertson tried periodically to interest American publishers in its better selling Australian titles, and in April 1922 the firm wrote to Dodd, Mead, which had recently taken over the American operations of John Lane, to

---

20 An earlier work by Grimshaw, *Broken Away* (John Lane, 1897), had also appeared in New York while the author was still in Ireland, but similarly a new sequence began in 1908 after the author's departure for the Pacific and New Guinea.
21 *A Ship of Solace* (Sturgis & Walton, 1911); *Lu of the Ranges* (Sturgis & Walton, 1913); *The Rose of Youth*, (John Lane, 1915); *The Dark Fire* (Century, 1927).
22 See Peter Morton, *Lusting for London: Australian Expatriate Writers at the Hub of Empire, 1870-1950* (New York: Palgrave Macmillan, 2011), 116-21.
23 *Doreen and the Sentimental Bloke* advertised in the *New York Times*, 24 September 1916.
24 Ian McLaren, *C.J. Dennis: A Comprehensive Bibliography* (Adelaide: Libraries Board of SA, 1979), 14, 102-3, 115-17, 122. A limited edition of 250 copies of *The Sentimental Bloke* was published by The Press of the Woolly Whale, New York, in 1932.

express its hope that the firm would continue the interest shown in Dennis' two books. Dodd, Mead replied that the books were indeed still on their list, but added "we … only wish that their success in America had been a fraction as large [as in Australia]. However, we will do the best we can to keep the books before the American public and, perhaps, some time they may 'break through'".[25] No further editions appeared.

The Moods of Ginger Mick, which takes Mick off to "the flamin' war", can be linked to a mini-boom in publishing about the Great War which drew Australian books into the American market. While the war produced a rise in printing costs and "shortages of everything needed to make a book", it also produced a high demand for books about the war: "For the publishers, it was a windfall".[26] Volumes of soldiers' verse, such as Tom Skeyhill's *A Singing Soldier*, and soldiers' testimonies such as R. Hugh Knyvett's *'Over There' with the Australians*, appeared in 1918-19. Among the best-known writers on the war in America was "Boyd Cable" (Ernest Andrew Ewart), who had spent his formative years in Australia before moving to London. Between 1915 and 1919, Dutton published copyrighted editions of five novels, two story collections, and several other books about the war, describing Cable as "the most vivid writer on trench warfare which the war has produced".[27] His book of war stories, *Between the Lines*, went into five editions between 1915 and 1917. In 1920, Dutton also published Sir John Monash's *The Australian Victories in France in 1918*.[28] Frederic Manning's important war novel, *Her Privates We*, was published by Putnam in 1930 in the expurgated version released that same year by Peter Davies in London. Dorota Flatau's only American title, *Yellow Souls*, was also a war story, written after her departure for England. Published by Doran in 1918, it was the story of a treacherous German resident in England, one of those who "pretended to become English citizens, though they were in truth nothing more than German spies".[29]

Over the next decade, 1921 to 1930, the number of Australian fiction titles published in America doubled to more than ninety titles, although it was only towards the end of the decade that there was a significant increase in annual output. Helen Simpson, Jean Devanny and Dale Collins all had more or less regular American releases from this time. Two of Roy Bridges' thirty-seven novels appeared from Appleton, in 1922 and 1924. Jack McLaren's *My Crowded Solitude* appeared in 1926 from R.M. McBride in New York, and in 1927 his novel *The Chain* was published by the Curtiss Press. These American editions followed McLaren's move to London in 1925 and remained there for the next thirty years writing journalism, fiction and non-fiction.[30] In 1925, the remarkable publishing career of Australian-born author, adventurer and mariner Alan Villiers began in the United States with *Whaling in the Frozen South*, from Bobbs-Merrill. A dozen other whaling and sailing titles would appear to 1940, from Holt, Doubleday, Scribner and Morrow, and new titles continued to appear into the 1970s.

---

25 F.S. Shenstone (Angus & Robertson) to Dodd, Mead & Co., 20 April 1922 and reply, 7 June 1922. Angus & Robertson Archives, State Library of NSW, MLMSS 314.
26 Tebbel, *Between Covers*, 196.
27 Titles included: *Between the Lines* (1915), *Action Front* (1916), *Doing Their Bit: War Work at Home* (1916), *Grapes of Wrath* (1917), *The Attack Was Broken* (1918), *A Good Day* (1918), *Front Lines* (1919), *Air Men o' War* (1919). Quotation from Dutton's 1917 fifth edition of *Between the Lines*.
28 Dutton advertisement, *New York Times* 17 October 1920. Monash's book was a pricey eight dollars.
29 Review of *Yellow Souls*, *New York Times*, 22 December 1918.
30 Morton, *Lusting for London*, 95.

At the more literary end of the market, a scattering of Australian works appeared from major US publishers. Chester Cobb's stream of consciousness novel, *Mr. Moffat*, was published by Doran in 1926, to mixed reviews.[31] Prichard's *Working Bullocks* appeared from Viking in 1927 and Martin Boyd's *The Aristocrat* and *The Madeleine Heritage* from Bobbs-Merrill in 1927 and 1928. D.H. Lawrence's two Australian novels had appeared earlier, *Kangaroo* in 1923 and *The Boy in the Bush*, co-authored with the Australian M.L. (Mollie) Skinner, in 1924. While Lawrence's "magic evocation of the glamorous Australian atmosphere" was noted and *The Boy in the Bush* highly praised in some quarters, they do not appear to have created any anticipatory or interpretive frame for the new Australian novels that began to appear more frequently at the end of the decade.[32] In 1929, a bumper year, M. Barnard Eldershaw's *A House is Built* was published by Harcourt, Brace, Dorothy Cottrell's *Singing Gold* by Houghton Mifflin, and Richardson's *Ultima Thule* by Norton. With these examples, Australian fiction began to register in the field of the "modern novel". The choice of *Ultima Thule* by the Book-of-the-Month Club as its main selection for August 1929, the first such selection for an Australian author, made Richardson for a time the most widely sold, widely read and most identifiably "Australian" Australian author in America.[33]

A second generation of genre fiction authors also emerged in these years. Among Australian authors in the American market, crime and mystery writers dominate – Arthur J. Rees, J.M. Walsh, Arthur Gask, Gavin Holt and Arthur Upfield – but the period also saw the beginning of the prolific career of modern romance authors Maysie Greig, from 1924, her novels mostly from Doubleday Doran, and Alice Grant Rosman from 1928, with novels published by Mills & Boon in England and Minton, Balch & Co. in America. These authors will be discussed in the next chapter.

Scattered Success

In the first two decades of the new century there was still a place for stories of convicts, gold and settlers, and for the Australian bush romance or frontier adventure. Herbert MacIlwaine's *Fate, the Fiddler* (Lippincott, 1901) is a story of cattle and gold in western and northern Queensland; Randolph Bedford's *The Snare of Strength* (Herbert B. Turner, 1906) a "semi-political and mining romance";[34] Hay's *Captain Quadring* (Dana Estes, 1912) a convict tale of estranged brothers; Hennessey's *The Outlaw* (Doran, 1913) a convict and bushranger story. *The Outlaw* was advertised in October 1913 alongside Lancaster's *The Law-Bringers*, a novel of the Canadian frontier, as one of the month's important "Novels of Action and Thrill".[35] At the same time, Roy Bridges' brief American presence in the early twenties shows that the romance or adventure that eschewed Australian settings, in his

---

31 "The Bookman's Guide to Fiction", *Bookman*, August 1926, 702; *Saturday Review*, 12 December 1925; *New York Times*, 20 June 1926; *Saturday Review of Literature*, 17 July 1926, 939.
32 Lillian C. Ford, "Australian Novel", *Los Angeles Times*, 29 June 1924. The novel received an extraordinarily celebratory review in the *New York Times*: Lloyd Morris, "Mr. Lawrence on the Frontiers of Civilization", *New York Times*, 26 October 1924.
33 See Chapter 6 below.
34 E. Morris Miller, *Australian Literature from its Beginnings to 1935 Volume II* (1940; Sydney: Sydney University Press, 1973), 494.
35 *New York Sun*, 18 October 1913.

4 Renegotiating the American Connection: Australian Fiction 1900–1930s

case for a generic old England, could also find its place in the networks of exchange that moved romance fiction across national borders.

The nineteenth-century novels had left a legacy among American readers that lingered as long as romance fiction remained a reputable and reviewable mode. Bedford's only American title, copyrighted by its Boston publisher, was described as "Australian and naught else; Australian in its glorification of the light and color and scent of the Australian land; its merciless description of the Australian rustic, ignorant to the core, speaking the speech of East London, incapable of thinking, the terror and danger of Australian politics".[36] Tarella Quin's *A Desert Rose* (Dutton, 1913) was noted for its "atmosphere", which the publisher described as "a bit of the Bush life as women know it".[37] A similar angle was present in June 1913 when the novel was recommended as one of the "One Hundred Books for Summer Reading" by the *New York Times*: "Mrs. Daskein [Quin], the author of this Australian novel, sets her story in the atmosphere of the bush. The woman's side of life on the edge of the Never-Never land is shown by the author in this old-fashioned love story, beyond which lies the feared and unknown desert".[38] Perhaps the idea of the Never-Never ("the more remote part of the northern Australia country") had been introduced by the earlier publication of *We of the Never-Never* in 1911. *Outlook*'s reviewer wished Gunn had explained "to the uninitiated reader some of the Australian terms used, and [told] a little more in detail just what was done on this enormous stock-farm".[39] *We of the Never-Never* was to have appeared with a preface by Jack London written expressly for the American edition, but this was omitted from the version that did appear.[40]

It is not clear whether any of these writers actively sought American publication or had it thrust upon them through arrangements made between publishers. We do know that Hodder & Stoughton offered to send proofs of Roy Bridges' biblical melodrama *The Vats of Tyre* to A.P. Watt, believing it to be "very suitable for American publication", but nothing eventuated. And in 1929, William Hurst, editor of the Melbourne *Australasian*, wrote to Bridges about opportunities for American publication: "I have a great notion of the possibility of America with regard to your writing … Watt ought to be able to work up something there, and I do not see why you should not get into the 'best sellers' list,' or in the *Bookman*'s list of 'Most in Demand', or be selected by the 'Book of the Month' Club".[41] In the early twenties, Bridges was also in contact with Charles Rodda, a former fellow-journalist on the Melbourne *Age* now resident in New York, working as a critic for *Musical America* and planning a literary career. Rodda wrote of seeing Bridges' *Rogue's Haven* displayed in a Fifth Avenue window: "Appleton's are advertising it big".[42] Writing for the American market was among both men's plans for the future; both knew J.F. Dwyer and

---

36 "Boston Notes", *New York Times*, 10 March 1906. First published by Heinemann in 1905, the novel was copyrighted in the United States in 1905 and published in March 1906. Under the copyright notice on the verso of the title page is printed "Entered at Stationers' Hall, London".
37 Advertisement, *New York Tribune*, 24 May 1913.
38 *New York Times*, 15 June 1913.
39 *Outlook*, 18 February 1911, 376. Macmillan's edition, released in 1911 and comprising sheets printed in England with a new title page inserted, carries the tag "Fifteenth Edition" (from the English sheets) despite being the only US release.
40 C. Hartley Grattan, "Australian Literature", *Bookman*, August 1928, 630.
41 Hurst to Bridges, 18 November 1929, Roy Bridges Papers, State Library of NSW, MLMSS 319.
42 Rodda to Bridges, 8 September 1922, Roy Bridges Papers.

his remarkable fortune in America. Rodda would later be reborn as the crime and mystery writer Gavin Holt.[43]

Despite these portents, Bridges was another Australian writer successful in the British sphere but unable to translate that success into the American market. As noted, only two of Bridges' thirty-seven novels appeared from Appleton, *Rogue's Haven* in 1922 and *Rat's Castle* in 1924. Between 1914 and 1923 he published nine titles with Hodder & Stoughton, by then one of the great English publishers of popular fiction. *Rogue's Haven* almost sold out its 2800 print run, about half in colonial editions, but did not go into a cheap edition. Novels that did, such as *The Fugitive* (1914) or *Dead Men's Gold* (1915), had print runs of ten to twenty thousand.[44] With *Rat's Castle*, Bridges moved to Hutchinson, where he stayed for another eighteen books. The vast majority of his novels were set in colonial Tasmania or Port Phillip (Victoria), although in the late 1930s Hutchinson contracted him to write "modern thrillers".[45] But neither of his American titles was among his Australian convict or pioneering novels. They were costume dramas, stories of pirates, intrigue and smuggling, set, like many historical romances of the period, in eighteenth-century England.[46]

In America, *Rat's Castle* was explicitly advertised as fiction "For Men & Boys", suggesting how the male adventure-romance had begun to contract from the general adult market.[47] *Rogue's Haven*, a pirate tale, had been received similarly, as a story that a "grown man" could read "with the sheer delight, the complete absorption, the blissful unconsciousness of literary methods, that are the natural possession of the boy of 15".[48] Bridges' scrapbooks contain clippings of fourteen reviews of *Rogue's Haven* from papers across the United States, all extremely favourable regarding the author's narrative skills, as the genre demanded: "A briskly galloping tale of old England is this, on the time-honored model of eighteenth-century lawlessness, smuggling and piratical wealth".[49] Bridges was compared to Robert Louis Stevenson and Jeffrey Farnol, the bestselling author of historical romances. But there is a note of defensiveness in some reviews, a sense of the passing of a genre, of holding out for "romantic adventure" against the modern world and modern fiction: "Stories of bygone days in England still find readers in our age of material progress … But this species of novel is bound to pass, for it has nothing in common with our age save that little-changing entity, human nature".[50] Even more telling was the *New York Times*' conclusion: "It is a story quite in the manner much despised and discredited by the cubistic authors of up-to-date fiction".[51]

Danish-born Tasmanian author Marie Bjelke-Petersen also wrote in the manner despised by "cubistic authors", but this did not prevent her from becoming a popular and respected novelist between the wars. Her first novel published overseas, *The Captive Singer*,

---

43 Rodda left for the United States in 1919 and then relocated to London in 1926. His first Gavin Holt novel, *Eyes in the Night*, was published by Hutchinson in 1927 and his first in the United States, *The Praying Monkey*, by the Dial Press in 1930.
44 Hodder & Stoughton Ltd Papers, London Metropolitan Archives, CLC/B/119, MS16312, vol. 7.
45 Telegram, Watt to Bridges, 28 September 1939, Roy Bridges Papers.
46 Christopher Baldick, *The Oxford English Literary History Volume 10. 1910–1940: The Modern Movement* (Oxford: Oxford University Press, 2004), 290.
47 Appleton advertisements, *New York Times*, 13 August 1922; 28 September 1924; 9 November 1924.
48 All quotations (here and below) from reviews in Bridges' scrapbooks: *Worcester Evening Gazette* (Worcester, MA), 28 August 1922; Samuel Churgel [?], "Rogue's Haven", *Brooklyn Daily Eagle* [?].
49 "Latest Works of Fiction", *New York Times*, 30 July 1922.
50 *Post Express* (Rochester, NY), n.d.
51 "Latest Works of Fiction", *New York Times*, 30 July 1922.

appeared in 1917 from Hodder & Stoughton and brought her to the attention of Harper, who began to solicit her for future work. She sent her second novel directly to them, upsetting Hodder & Stoughton in the process.[52] Harper published and copyrighted *The Immortal Flame* in October 1919.[53] Like *The Captive Singer*, it was a "landscape romance", praised for its description of Australian mountain and bush settings, if not for its romantic resolutions. The *New York Times* enjoyed itself at the expense of *The Immortal Flame* as it often did when presented with a ripe romance:

> [Lord Berriedale] was a remarkable person, whose "jet-black orbs, almost feminine in their liquid softness, gazing languidly beneath golden drooping lashes, could at times light up with volcanic fires and produce a very disquieting effect" – which is a not unusual result of volcanic fires … There are a large number of "stormy kisses" interspersed with "agitated rapture," and in short the author has tried very hard indeed to be hectic. After a while several of the characters, the villain included, get religion, one of them expires in the odor of sanctity, and to the great relief of the long-suffering reader, the book comes to an end.[54]

Like Bridges, Bjelke-Petersen later moved from Hodder & Stoughton to Hutchinson, and her new publishers reissued *The Immortal Flame* in 1926. A 1928 impression claimed it was the "13th Thousand", indicating her "saleability". Already in 1922, reporting the English release of *Dusk*, a Tasmanian story that the London reviews had rated "one of the leading novels of the season", the *New York Times* reckoned that "in point of sales [Bjelke-Petersen] bids fair to become the Marie Corelli of Australia".[55] But even this promise failed to produce any further American editions. Her next novel, *Jewelled Nights* (1923), had no separate American edition, but good American sales were reported.[56]

Getting Americanized in a Hurry: James Francis Dwyer and Sumner Locke

Other writers sought publication, profits and reputation in the United States in a more deliberate, determined fashion. After publishing stories in Australian periodicals, James Francis Dwyer left for England in 1906 to try his luck in the magazine market. He had some success but not enough to make a living, and his experience of being frozen out, as he saw it, by English editors led him to move to New York the following year. Dwyer represents perhaps the earliest example of an Australian-born writer transforming him or herself into an "American writer": that is, one whose primary orientation is to the American marketplace. While still in Australia, Dwyer had seen a copy of *Collier's Magazine* in the hands of fellow-writer Albert Dorrington and learnt that they paid five cents a word; then and there he determined to write for them.[57]

After a period working as a streetcar conductor in order "to get Americanized in a hurry", Dwyer began selling stories for $30 to $50 each to cheap magazines such as the *Red*

---

52 Alison Alexander, *A Mortal Flame: Marie Bjelke-Petersen, Australian Romance Writer 1874–1969* (Hobart: Blubber Head Press, 1994), 88.
53 Copyrighted 8 October 1919; copies deposited 11 October 1919.
54 "Latest Works of Fiction", *New York Times*, 18 January 1920.
55 "Books and Authors", *New York Times*, 16 April 1922.
56 Alexander, *Mortal Flame*, 128.
57 James Francis Dwyer, *Leg-Irons on Wings* (Melbourne: Georgian House, 1949), 125, 106–7.

Book, the *Blue Book*, the *Black Cat* and *Munsey's Magazine*. He claimed to have sold fifty-six stories to *Black Cat* within five months in 1908 and to have written all the stories in one issue under different names.[58] As Dwyer himself put it, the cheap magazines "bought at low prices … but they bought promptly and paid immediately", and through them he could earn five or six thousand dollars a year. He became a newsworthy character, too, because of his knockabout past and rapid success. As one headline put it: "Author Once a Street Car Conductor Here. James Francis Dwyer Tells of a Struggle Against Starvation in New York … Bought a Typewriter and Began Making Money Writing the Adventures He'd Lived".[59] Over time his prices rose − $800 to $1000 a story − and demand for his work grew among the "better" magazines, including *Collier's*: "stickily sentimental stories in the O. Henry vein seemed to go down best".[60] By 1913, Dwyer estimated earnings of around $20,000 annually from his stories, and his personalised stationery listed magazines in which he'd appeared: "*Collier's, Ladies Home Journal, Woman's Home Companion, Delineator, American, McCall's, Redbook, Liberty, Country Gentleman, The American Weekly, This Week, Vanity Fair, Popular, Blue Book, Adventure, Short Stories, Argosy*, ETC."[61] As a measure of his fame, in 1916 he was one of a group of celebrity authors including Zane Grey, Louis Vance and Mrs Woodrow Wilson chosen to write one episode each of a widely syndicated novel of political corruption called *Graft*, with each episode filmed by the Universal Film Manufacturing Co.[62]

Magazine fame could be turned to book publication. Dwyer's first novel, *The White Waterfall*, was serialised in Frank Munsey's *All-Story Cavalier Weekly* around the time of its publication in 1912 by Doubleday, Page & Co., among the most active publishers of new popular fiction (Fig. 4.1).[63] Published the following year in London by Cassell, it was a South Sea adventure with an American hero, a story "that out-thrills any story told since the days of Captain Cook … a big story of love and life".[64] Doubleday's publicity declared it "adventurous and romantic enough for any lover of wholesome and exciting tales of out-door life".[65] Reviews were generous, comparing it to Rider Haggard's fiction, even where the flaws of the genre were noted: "The grotesqueness of the incidents is almost ludicrous at times, but the author carries his readers along with him in the rush of his narrative".[66] Back in Sydney, the *Lone Hand* was less impressed, offering readers a sample of the "picturesque American in which the story is written".[67]

Doubleday next published *The Bust of Lincoln* in December 1912, as a short gift book. Described as a "love tale in which a youth in hard luck takes as his talisman an old bust of Abraham Lincoln", this sentimental story had been a spectacular success when first published

---

58   Dwyer, *Leg-Irons on Wings*, 154, 165.
59   "Literary Notes", *New York Sun*, 25 May 1912.
60   Dwyer, *Leg-Irons on Wings*, 193; Morton, *Lusting for London*, 92.
61   Dwyer, *Leg-Irons on Wings*, 177. Undated letter from Dwyer to Bridges, Roy Bridges Papers.
62   Series publicised in the *Logan Republican* (Utah), 30 December 1915; the first episode appeared on 11 January 1916. Dwyer's contribution appeared in the *Monroe City Democrat* (among other papers) on 27 July 1916.
63   Advertisement for the *Cavalier, Washington Times* 11 April 1912; advertisement for the novel, *New York Tribune*, 2 July 1912. Doubleday's contract specified a flat royalty of 15 per cent with an option on Dwyer's next two books. Harry Peyton Steger (Doubleday) to Dwyer, 27 October 1911, James Francis Dwyer correspondence, State Library of NSW MLMSS 1714.
64   Advertisement for the *Cavalier, Washington Times*, 11 April 1912.
65   Advertisement, *New York Tribune*, 2 July 1912.
66   "Some New Fiction", *New York Sun*, 29 June 1912.
67   "Recent Fiction", *Lone Hand*, January 1913, xxxii.

4 Renegotiating the American Connection: Australian Fiction 1900–1930s

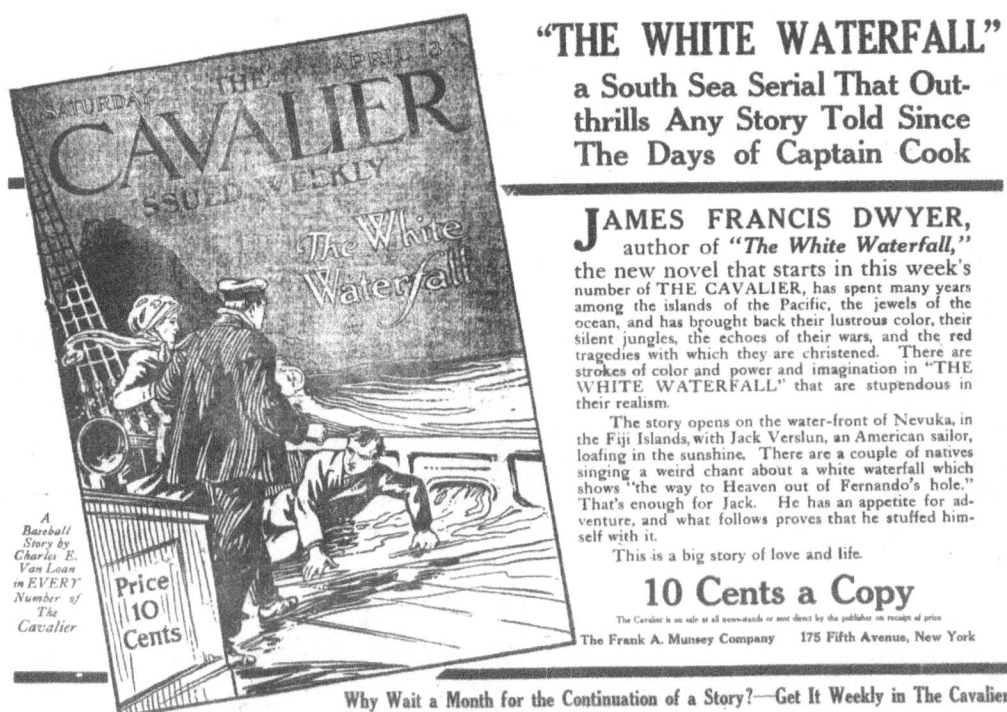

Figure 4.1 James Frances Dwyer, "The White Waterfall", announced for the *Cavalier*. *Washington Times*, 11 April 1912.

in the *American Magazine* and featured on its cover, generating invitations from a range of other publications.[68] In 1913, Doubleday followed up with another adventure, *The Spotted Panther*, this time set "in the wilds of Borneo", the "kind of tale in which the author must be followed blindly or not at all".[69] Both *The White Waterfall* and *The Spotted Panther* were reprinted by W.R. Caldwell of New York in the year of their original release, and *The Spotted Panther* was also serialised in the *Cavalier*. Indicating something of his contemporary standing in the American market, the *Cavalier*'s editor Robert H. Davis wrote to Dwyer: "I am going to have a very fine cover made for 'The Spotted Panther', and if you leave it to me, Jimmy, I will establish your fame in these United States and make you a permanent institution".[70] In 1912, the magazine had predicted that *The Bust of Lincoln* would become a classic.[71]

---

68 *Washington Herald*, 1 December 1912; "New Books this Fall Promise Big Season", *New York Sun*, 31 August 1912. The story appeared in the *American Magazine*, 4 February 1912. Invitations followed from the publisher of the *Red Book*, *Blue Book* and *Green Book Magazine* and of the *Housekeeper*: Dwyer correspondence.
69 "Literary Notes", *Washington Herald*, 14 September 1913; *New York Sun*, 20 September 1913.
70 Davis to Dwyer, 13 February 1913, Robert H. Davis Papers, New York Public Library, MssCol 739. *The Spotted Panther* includes a double copyright notice, for the magazine publisher Frank A. Munsey Co. and for Doubleday, Page & Co., both 1913.
71 Advertisement for *Cavalier* featuring Dwyer's "The Pearl of Bad Luck", *Washington Times*, 22 August 1912. It mentions that his income from writing is $10,000 a year, and that he "puts two volumes per annum on the market through his publishers".

Dwyer went further than most successful authors and married his American literary agent, Galbraith Welch, in late 1919.[72] Three more titles appeared before the couple left for Europe and Africa in 1921: *For Love of a Woman* in 1914, published in New York by Minden-Burkert, followed in 1915 by two books from A.C. McClurg of Chicago, the publisher at this time of Edgar Rice Burroughs' Tarzan novels. *Breath of the Jungle* was a collection of "breathlessly thrilling, weird, dramatic" stories of the Orient, *The Green Half-Moon* an international thriller with an American hero.[73] Dwyer's ability to earn a living by writing professionally to the demands of the market, and above all the American market, shared much with the crime and romance writers who were his contemporaries; and it foreshadowed the careers of later, successful authors of commercial fiction such as Jon Cleary and Morris West.

Helena Sumner Locke might have pursued a similar career in America if not for her early death. As Sumner Locke, she achieved early success in Australia with three bestselling rural comedies written for the NSW Bookstall Co. Then in England from 1912 to 1915, she began writing a novel, *Samaritan Mary*, expressly for the American market.[74] She sent the manuscript direct to Holt in New York in mid-1915 and they responded positively: "We think the public may like your *Samaritan Mary* as much as we do. Mary's cheeriness and good sense should prove a welcome contrast to the temper of the times".[75] Holt offered a royalty of 10 per cent of the published price to 10,000 copies sold and 15 per cent beyond that and sought first refusal on Locke's next two books. They foresaw "considerable success" in sales over the holiday season and asked only for some tempering of Mary's dialect. Working through an aunt then resident in Massachusetts, Locke accepted the terms and made the changes, and Holt copyrighted and published the book in February 1916.[76]

As an Australian commentator put it in 1922, "*Samaritan Mary* is one of the most remarkable literary feats essayed by an Australian – to write and publish in America a successful American novel".[77] A "really entertaining story of a triple romance that followed an automobile accident in an American village", it was not only set in rural America but written in an American vernacular, and both setting and speech were mostly convincing to the book's American reviewers.[78] For the *New York Times* reviewer, Mary's language, "a quaint mixture of uncouth country speech with modern slang and humorous flippant statement", was the novel's *raison d'être*.[79] Assumed to be male and American, Sumner Locke was "credited with giving ample measure in his first novel".[80] *Samaritan Mary* was often compared to the local bestseller, Alice Hegan Rice's *Mrs. Wiggs of the Cabbage*

---

72 Dwyer, *Leg-Irons on Wings*, 176-77, 197.
73 Advertisement, *New York Tribune*, 3 April 1915; advertisement, *New York Tribune*, 20 October 1915. Two later novels written in Europe appeared from the Vanguard Press: *Evelyn: Something More than a Story* (1929) and *O Splendid Sorcery* (1930).
74 Sharon Clarke, *Sumner Locke Elliott: Writing Life* (St Leonards, NSW: Allen & Unwin, 1996), 15-17.
75 Holt to Locke, 8 September 1915, Archives of Henry Holt & Co., Princeton University, Series 2, Box 70.
76 Clarke, *Sumner Locke Elliott*, 42-44. Her letters are addressed to Alfred Harcourt, then at Holt.
77 Mrs Vernon Williams, "Australian Women Novelists", *Corroboree* 1, no. 10 (July 1922): 8.
78 Holt advertisement, *New York Times*, 19 February 1916. See also *New York Sun*, 4 March 1916; *Nation*, 6 July 1916, 13.
79 "Samaritan Mary", *New York Times*, 16 April 1916. Rosa Praed's *Lady Bridget of the Never-Never* was reviewed in the same column.
80 Florence Finch Kelly, "Firstlings in Fiction", *Bookman*, May 1916, 325. A list of eleven reviews from US papers is given in Clarke, *Sumner Locke Elliott*, 265, to which the *Nation*, the *Sun*, and the *Bookman* can be added.

Patch.⁸¹ It also sold well initially, more than 3000 copies in the New York area alone in its first five weeks from a print run of just over 4000.⁸²

Writing to Holt in May 1916, Locke described her second novel as "American and written purely for H Holt and coy … the type of thing Gene Stratton Porter puts out".⁸³ But in October, Holt wrote rejecting "The Blue Sky Gentleman" on the basis of unfavourable readers' reports. Despite this rejection, Locke embarked on an ambitious journey to the United States. Her plan was to cross the continent, gathering material for a future novel, and then to meet with Holt in New York. After a difficult three-month journey, she arrived to find that Holt's interest and her own earnings were less than anticipated. Back in Australia, her career was tragically cut short by her death in October 1917 soon after giving birth to a son. As Sumner Locke Elliott, he would have a significant American literary career in his own right from the 1960s to the 1980s.⁸⁴

Geographical Romance: Mary Gaunt, Beatrice Grimshaw and G.B. Lancaster

Although atypical in many respects, Dwyer's success reveals that expatriation was still critical at this period for most Australian writers seeking international publication. Richardson, Cable, Simpson, Boyd, Manning, Flatau, Mack, Rosman, McLaren, Prichard and Sumner Locke all travelled to London, and in some cases further afield, initiating permanent or long-term expatriation. The conditions that prompted expatriation remained largely unchanged from the nineteenth century: the small scale of book and periodical publishing in Australia; the power of the British publishers over book rights and distribution; the much greater possibilities of earning a living from writing through newspapers and magazines in England; and, for some, the greater possibilities of establishing a foothold in America from an English base. Regardless of sentimental ties to the mother country, London "was the modern world's earliest and biggest metropolis", Australians were "free-born citizens" of this great city, and at its heart was an extraordinary industry in print and paper: "By 1900 the reader had a choice of well over 2000 monthly and weekly titles on the news-stands, and the capital supported more than a dozen daily newspapers".⁸⁵ London was also the capital of the English-language fiction industry. The output of novels increased steadily from 1900 to 1914, and then again in the 1920s.⁸⁶

Most striking from this period are the careers of women writers who were not just expatriates but global or imperial travellers, their journeys to remote parts of the world often driven expressly by professional choices and the determination to earn a living through writing. Mary Gaunt, Beatrice Grimshaw and G.B. Lancaster were popular, widely read novelists who also became respected authorities on the countries and regions about

---

81 Locke was not familiar with Rice's 1901 novel. Locke to Holt, 26 May 1916, Holt Archives.
82 Clarke, *Sumner Locke Elliott*, 19. Holt to A.E. Locke, 31 October 1916, Holt Archives. It was also recorded as a new book in libraries across the country: Harrisburg, PA; Bridgeport, CT; Wauseon, OH; Williston, ND.
83 Locke to Holt, 26 May 1916, Holt Archives.
84 Clarke, *Sumner Locke Elliott*, 46-47.
85 Peter Morton, "Australia's England, 1880-1950", in Peter Pierce, ed., *The Cambridge History of Australian Literature* (Cambridge: Cambridge University Press, 2009), 257, 261.
86 Simon Eliot, *Some Patterns and Trends in British Publishing 1880-1919*, Occasional Papers of the Bibliographical Society 8, 1994, London, 22-25.

which they wrote. As Angela Woollacott has argued, imperial, national and modernising impulses were interwoven as these independent women forged writing careers through the romance of travel and exotic locations: "For white women ... the empire proved a global stage upon which they could act out novel, modern desires and ambitions".[87] But their internationalism also extended beyond the empire, to the American market (if again often underwritten by the notion of a shared Anglo-Saxon world). The frontier romance provided a generic frame for much of their fiction, but the colonial or expatriate perspective, sharpened by that of an independent woman, worked against merely conventional stories. They were often critical of imperialism's local effects even while supporting the imperial mission at large, at least if it were left in the hands of the right kind of colonising men and women, usually Australians or other colonial types in preference to those sent out from imperial headquarters.

The interest in Gaunt's and Grimshaw's books in the American market was often managed via the trope of the author as the "first white woman" to have ventured into one or other remote and racially "other" location (because of her pseudonym, Lancaster was often assumed to be male). Unsurprisingly, these stories travelled well, from the London *Standard* to the *Arizona Republican*, for example: the American paper reported from its English contemporary that "the English novelist, Mary Gaunt", was the "first white woman to reach the far hinterland of west Africa alone and unaided by any member of her own race".[88]

Gaunt travelled briefly to London in the 1890s, then left Australia permanently in 1901 after the early death of her husband. From London she travelled alone to Africa, China and Jamaica, turning her journeys into both fiction and non-fiction. Later she settled in Europe. From 1910 to 1926, six of her books appeared in the United States, in addition to the reissued thriller, *The Mummy Moves*, noted in the previous chapter. Two were fiction, colonial adventure-romances set in Africa, *The Uncounted Cost* (Clode, 1910) and *The Forbidden Town* (Clode, 1926). The former, "told with rather more entanglement of plot and rather more vigor than is usual with feminine English novelists", had been banned from English libraries before its American publication, and the *New York Sun* described it as "a story of a pleasure loving woman, a man who ruins the career of his choice for her sake, a callous lover and his forsaken mistress, and Africa".[89] The other four books were travel and reportage and appeared from major publishers: *Alone in West Africa* (Scribner, 1912), *A Woman in China* (Lippincott, 1914), *A Broken Journey: Wanderings from the Hoang-Ho to the Island of Saghalien and the Upper Reaches of the Amur River* (Lippincott, 1919) and *Where the Twain Meet* (Dutton, 1922), about Jamaica.

---

87   Angela Woollacott, "Creating the White Colonial Woman: Mary Gaunt's Imperial Adventuring and Australian Cultural History", in *Cultural History in Australia*, ed. Hsu-Ming Teo and Richard White (Sydney: UNSW Press, 2003), 186. See also Robert Dixon, *Photography, Early Cinema and Colonial Modernity: Frank Hurley's Synchronised Lecture Entertainments* (London: Anthem Press, 2012), xxvi–xxix; Sydney Shep, "Books in Global Perspectives", in *The Cambridge Companion to the History of the Book*, ed. Leslie Howsam (Cambridge: Cambridge University Press, 2014), 53–67; Antoinette Burton and Isabel Hofmeyr, eds, *Ten Books that Shaped the British Empire: Creating an Imperial Commons* (Durham, NC: Duke University Press, 2014, 1–28.
88   *Republican* (Arizona), 21 September 1911. Reported from the *London Standard*.
89   Review of *The Uncounted Cost*, *New York Times*, 3 September 1919; "Censorship of Books", *Washington Herald*, 1 March 1910; "Recent Novels", *New York Sun*, 25 June 1910. See also Ian F. McLaren, *Mary Gaunt: A Cosmopolitan Australian: An Annotated Bibliography* (Melbourne, University of Melbourne Library, 1986), xvii.

4 Renegotiating the American Connection: Australian Fiction 1900–1930s

Gaunt was highly regarded in America as a serious, lively writer of works in this vein, full of description, first-hand experience, and forthright opinion.

Grimshaw travelled in the opposite direction, from Britain to the Pacific, as a journalist, in 1907.[90] From New Guinea she established a career as a contributor to magazines in Australia, Britain and America, and as a prolific novelist of Pacific romances, taking over from Becke and other male writers to become one of the bestselling authors of what one New York reviewer called "the geographical romance".[91] From 1908 to 1934, Grimshaw had at least fourteen novels and four non-fiction books published in the United States, about half her total output over this period. She featured regularly in the illustrated magazines and at least once in the *New York Times*.[92] Australian characters and connections appeared in many of her novels set in New Guinea and the islands. The appeal of her novels as registered in American reviews was the familiarity of their plots combined with the novelty of their settings: "Her books are to be placed with that little group of novels, the explorers among works of fiction, opening to us new lands and races, as well as telling the old, old story that is ever new … Don't read this book unless you have got some red blood in your veins" (*Guinea Gold*); "A South Sea tale with all the ingredients of high romance; ravishing scenery, treasure hunts by moonlight, cannibals, and a beautiful damsel who sets all masculine pulses humming" (*Conn of the Coral Seas*); "Stories of New Guinea are so rare that [*When the Red Gods Call*] has a novelty peculiarly its own. In its writing Miss Grimshaw has devised something out of the way in modern fiction".[93] Grimshaw retired to Australia in 1936.

"G.B. Lancaster" was the pseudonym of Edith Lyttleton. Born in Tasmania, Lancaster grew up in New Zealand from where she built a reputation in Australasia through the magazines and internationally through four novels published in London and New York. The American editions were all with Doubleday.[94] She departed for London in 1909, travelling across the Pacific to Canada then England. Articles written during her travels attracted the attention of publisher George Doran, and on Doran's suggestion she travelled for several months to the remote Canadian north-west in search of new material.[95] This was the first of several trips to Canada, and led to the writing of *The Law-Bringers*, the novel that established Lancaster's early reputation, published by Hodder & Stoughton in London and Doran in New York in 1913. Doran himself doubted "that there has been

---

90 See Hugh Laracy, *Watriama and Co: Further Pacific Island Portraits* (Canberra: ANU Press, 2013), Chapter 8, "Beatrice Grimshaw (1870–1953): Pride and Prejudice in Papua". Review of *When the Red Gods Call*, *New York Times*, 17 December 1911.
91 Review of *When the Red Gods Call*, *New York Times*, 17 December 1911.
92 Grimshaw is featured in advertisements for *Collier's*, the *Red Book*, *Hearst's International*, *Everybody's* and *McCall's* in the *New York Times* between January 1915 and November 1924. "Dark Mysteries of Papua", *New York Times*, 4 February 1923. Books included *Vaiti of the Islands* (A. Wessels, 1908), *Fiji and its Possibilities* (Doubleday, 1907; Dodd, Mead, 1917), *The New New Guinea* (Lippincott, 1911), *When the Red Gods Call* (Moffat, Yard, 1911), *Guinea Gold* (Moffat, Yard, 1912), *South Sea Sweetheart* (Macmillan, 1921), *Conn of the Coral Seas* (Macmillan, 1921), *The Wreck of the 'Redwing'* (Holt, 1927) and *Isles of Adventure* (Houghton Mifflin, 1931).
93 "Adventures in New Guinea", *New York Times*, 16 March 1913; advertisement, *New York Times*, 5 April 1913; advertisement citing *Boston Evening Transcript*, *New York Times*, 20 October 1911.
94 The books were *Sons o' Men* (1905); *A Spur to Smite* (London: Melrose, 1905) as *The Spur, or, The Bondage of Kin Severne* (1906); *The Tracks We Tread* (1907); *The Altar Stairs* (1908).
95 Terry Sturm, *An Unsettled Spirit: The Life & Frontier Fiction of Edith Lyttleton (G.B. Lancaster)* (Auckland: Auckland University Press, 2003), 94.

written or that there will be written a better book on the North West Mounted Police".[96] Lancaster was based in England until 1926, becoming a popular and well-paid magazine contributor before returning to New Zealand and further travels in Australasia, North America and Europe.

Like so many of her contemporaries, Lancaster worked within the conventions of adventure-romance fiction but often with a "dark undercurrent" of violence or tragedy in her stories and a determining interest in colonial characters settled in their environment rather than adventurist excursions into the frontier.[97] Reviews continually emphasised the "wild" settings and "masculine" character of her writing; like Becke, Dwyer, and a number of others she was hailed as "the new Kipling".[98] Although generally praised, American reviewers often struggled with her realist insistence on local description and vernacular: "One feels constantly that the author has a profound pity, almost a contempt, for all people who are not stockmen and miners and who do not live in New Zealand".[99] In 1908, Henry Larnier of Doubleday wrote to Lancaster with a very similar message:

> If you would write a novel or two, more of the sort that people are accustomed to buy in this country, it ought to be possible to secure a public here which would thereafter take anything good that you cared to put before them. But in the books so far, the people, the surroundings, the conditions and even the language, are all so foreign to any experiences or ideas which the average American has, that it is extremely difficult for him to establish that basis of human sympathy which a man has got to have for the characters in a novel in order to thoroughly enjoy it.[100]

This was serious business to an author attempting to earn a living by her pen. Terry Sturm suggests that *Jim of the Ranges*, Lancaster's first "Australian" novel, was her attempt to meet Larnier's suggestions, for it was also her "most deliberately 'American' novel", something like a western in an outback setting. Ironically, if that was the case, *Jim of the Ranges* never appeared in America, although Lancaster later sold the American motion picture rights for $1000.[101]

Lancaster shared with Gaunt and Grimshaw "the sense of high cultural calling which was part of the British imperial legacy throughout its overseas colonies".[102] Yet, as Sturm argues, in Lancaster's case expatriation confirmed her identity as a colonial rather than any sense of "coming home" to the imperial centre. This complex was mapped onto her sense of herself as an author. Determined to earn an independent living through writing, she was highly conscious of being divided between the demands of popular fiction and her own higher ambitions; a common enough dilemma but one intensified for colonial writers, Sturm insists, "by the fact that the requisite popular readership, and the mechanisms of publishing and distribution needed to reach it, were located *outside* the colonies themselves".[103] For our purposes what is most striking is Lancaster's

---

96 Sturm, *An Unsettled Spirit*, 140.
97 Sturm, *An Unsettled Spirit*, 59.
98 *Los Angeles Herald*, 23 July 1905.
99 "The Tracks We Tread", *San Francisco Call*, 8 December 1907.
100 Quoted in Sturm, *An Unsettled Spirit*, 80.
101 Sturm, *An Unsettled Spirit*, 85, 150.
102 Sturm, *An Unsettled Spirit*, 6.
103 Sturm, *An Unsettled Spirit*, 6.

4 Renegotiating the American Connection: Australian Fiction 1900–1930s

determination to conquer the American market, not only the British or imperial, an ambition that her colonial identity may well have encouraged. Very early in her career she engaged Paul Reynolds as her agent in New York, perhaps because her first encounter with the American market, in 1905, was having stories pirated by *Everybody's Magazine*. By 1908, she was represented by both Reynolds in New York and J.B. Pinker in London, and her correspondence with Pinker reveals her concern to master the commercial workings of the publishing industry, to retain control of her copyright, and to place her work in the United States as prominently and as profitably as possible.[104]

After her first two books – for which she had no contracts – she moved to Hodder & Stoughton in England while retaining Doubleday in America up until *The Law-Bringers* in 1913. Doran, as noted, had played a key role in the writing of this novel and Lancaster went with Doran, Hodder & Stoughton's partner, for her next two books as well, *Fool Divine* (1917) and *The Savignys* (1918). Lancaster was especially keen for *Fool Divine* to have the maximum opportunity in America as its subject was, as she put it, "essentially American".[105] It was a complex story of the discovery of the cause of Yellow Fever, set largely in Cuba and Brazil, and "thoroughly modern in temper".[106] Doran was impressed: "Certainly if personal interest and energy can compel its success, these you shall have".[107] It was widely reviewed, although emphasis fell on its picturesque and adventure elements rather than its modern political or ethical dimensions.

Lancaster remained focused on the magazine sector, especially on improving her success in the US market. In England, it would have taken sales of around 12,000 copies of a shilling reprint of one of her novels to match what she could earn at the height of her success from a single 8000-word story, and the more prestigious American magazines paid at much better rates.[108] She wrote to Pinker in November 1913: "I have told you before how disappointed I have been at having no American sales for so long … I do not want to lose my English market in any way, but America pays so much better that I naturally want to work up a position there if I can … I hope to be able to do more distinctive work, both for you and for America".[109] She tried various strategies: sending a story straight to *Harper's*, which they accepted immediately, and sending others to Reynolds, telling him she hoped he would be able to do better for her than he had been doing. Around 1921, she engaged a new American agent, Francis Arthur Jones.[110] Although she did appear in *Harper's*, *Scribner's*, *Everybody's*, *People's Magazine* and the *Women's Home Companion*, her American presence remained modest compared to her English success.

Lancaster was also very active in attempting to sell film rights in America. She engaged a Los Angeles-based film agent Edna Schley, who sold the rights to *Jim of the Ranges*. As *The Rider of the Law*, the film appeared in 1919 directed by John Ford, perhaps the first Hollywood film based on an Australian novel.[111] Earlier Lancaster had sold rights

---

104 Sturm, *An Unsettled Spirit*, 52. Correspondence between Lyttleton and Pinker, 13 April 1910 to 15 June 1926, James B. Pinker & Son Papers, 1893–1940, Berg Collection, New York Public Library, MSS Pinker (agency).
105 Lyttleton to Pinker, 5 September 1919, Pinker Papers.
106 Sturm, *An Unsettled Spirit*, 145.
107 Doran quoted in Sturm, *An Unsettled Spirit*, 140.
108 Sturm, *An Unsettled Spirit*, 149.
109 Lyttleton to Pinker, 26 November 1913, Pinker Papers.
110 Sturm, *An Unsettled Spirit*, 174.
111 Sturm, *An Unsettled Spirit*, 86.

to *The Law-Bringers* to Louis B. Mayer for £600.[112] Hodder & Stoughton brought out a new, abridged edition of the novel for the film's release, but attempts to persuade Doran to do the same were unsuccessful. *The Savignys*, released in 1918, marked the end of this first phase of Lancaster's career as a novelist. The generic frames had shifted significantly when she returned, in 1933, with *Pageant*, a large-scale historical novel of Tasmanian settlement published simultaneously in Sydney, London and New York. Its complicated journey across the three territories is discussed in Chapter 7.

Modern Girls: Ethel Turner and the Modern Girl Novel

Lancaster spent much of her writing career in Britain and North America, actively managing her professional interests in the United States as directly she could. It comes as more of a surprise to find Ethel Turner keenly pursuing her prospects and profits in the American marketplace from her Sydney home. The English firm of Ward, Lock & Bowden, her first publishers, had an office in New York as well as London and Melbourne, and could thus offer representation and distribution in the United States.[113] The firm published *Seven Little Australians* in London in 1894 and it was reviewed in the *New York Times* that year, while in 1897, as Ward, Lock & Co., they announced *The Little Larrikin* among their new books for America.[114] Like Lancaster, Turner was very deliberate about earning a living through her writing, and although her sales were high in Australia they remained disappointing elsewhere both to the author and her publisher. In particular, she felt that her potential in the American market had never been fulfilled, and she was almost certainly aware of the large market for contemporary children's books in the United States. She signed with A.P. Watt in 1897, upsetting Ward, Lock's Melbourne representative, but no doubt with the aim of improving her overseas sales. *Miss Bobbie* appeared from the New Amsterdam Book Co. in 1900, either through Watt's intervention or as an unauthorised edition, with the author advertised, perhaps inevitably, as "the British Louisa Alcott".[115]

In March 1904, Ward, Lock's London office wrote to Turner that they had an opportunity to place *Miss Bobbie* with an American publisher (there is no reference to the earlier US edition). Although the unnamed publisher "would probably make no payment for the rights" and wanted to make some minor alterations "so as to keep the reader from knowing that it was not an American story", Ward, Lock advised accepting the deal as "it would serve as a good introduction of your work in America".[116] This offer probably refers to an edition of *Miss Bobbie* published by A.L. Burt, a firm specialising in cheaply priced but well-produced clothbound reprints.[117] Next, in April 1904, Turner had a direct

---

112 Sturm, *An Unsettled Spirit*, 110 (p. 150, however, gives £500). Under the title *The Eternal Struggle*, the film was released in 1923. In 1921, Lancaster received $3500 for *The Altar Stairs* (150) and in 1926 two further films appeared based on Lancaster stories: *Bred in Old Kentucky* and *The Little Irish Girl* (181).
113 A.T. Yarwood, *From a Chair in the Sun: The Life of Ethel Turner* (Ringwood, Vic.: Viking, 1994), 86.
114 "Trouble in Australia", *New York Times*, 9 September 1894; "Books of the Spring", *New York Times*, 27 March 1897.
115 Advertisement, *New York Times*, 6 October 1900.
116 Ward, Lock (London) to Turner, 11 March 1904, Ethel Turner Papers, State Library of NSW MLMSS 667.
117 The edition is undated, but advertisements included at the back of the book suggest a date closer to 1904 than the 1900 listed in some catalogues.

4 Renegotiating the American Connection: Australian Fiction 1900–1930s

Figure 4.2 Ethel Turner, *Seven Little Australians*, Girls' Own Library (Philadelphia: David McKay, 1909?). Illustration by A.J. Johnson.

approach from the Penn Publishing Co., which specialised in children's and juvenile books, which she forwarded to William Steele, Ward, Lock's Melbourne manager. In the familiar way, he advised leaving all American dealings to the publisher's London office, "otherwise copyright complications may arise".[118] In September, George Lock wrote from London:

> for some time we have been trying hard to get two or three American Houses interested in your work, and … thought we were on the verge of success, but the terms offered were prohibitive. If as we hope you succeed in reaping an American harvest we should like you to remember that we have been easing the way by working up the interest over there.[119]

The publisher, in short, was nervous about losing a valuable property that might at any moment break through in the American market.

Turner's interest in American publication continued unabated. *In the Mist of the Mountains* was sent to Scribner in 1905 but politely rejected. Turner was disappointed precisely because, as she put it, she wanted to "get out of the Ward & Lock rut & into the American field" (Ward, Lock was right to be nervous).[120] She repeatedly urged her

---

118 Steele to Turner, 30 April 1904, Ethel Turner Papers. Some catalogues give a date of 1904 for a David McKay edition of *Seven Little Australians*, but inspection of the edition makes clear that the date is the copyright date of the English edition that McKay reprints.
119 Lock to Turner, 2 September 1904, Ethel Turner Papers.
120 Yarwood, *From a Chair*, 185, quoting a diary entry from 1905.

agents and publishers to try serialisation in American magazines, but without success. In July 1909, Ward, Lock again contacted her with an offer from America, a deal with David McKay to issue six of Turner's books, and this time a deal was done. *Seven Little Australians*, *The Family at Misrule*, *Three Little Maids* and *Little Mother Meg* were advertised for sale in December 1909 in David McKay's Girls' Own Library. *Miss Bobbie* and *That Girl* also appeared around this time (Fig. 4.2).[121] The last of these had been sold to David McKay earlier by Unwin, its original London publisher, who had written to Turner: "In regard to America, we quite failed to sell an edition though we offered the book in every direction. McKay's of Philadelphia, however, purchased a set of plates at a nominal price and your share of the small profits on this transaction were duly credited to you".[122] American editions, as we have seen, did not necessarily translate into significant earnings.

Nonetheless, on the back of the David McKay deal, "a very good House" (not identified) wanted to contract Turner for her next ten books at the rate of one a year. The offer is revealing of the copyright situation in the United States:

> You will remember we told you some time ago that we had disposed of a set of plates of half a dozen of your books to an American Publisher, thinking that his publication of the same might create for you a public in the States, where your books are not copyright. We are glad to say that the transaction has now borne fruit. After negotiations we have a proposal from a very good House who are desirous of issuing your work. They wish to enter into a contract to publish the next ten books you write i.e. one a year. Each must be a long story, and suitable for girls, they are willing to pay a Ten Per cent Royalty, which as things go is a very good royalty to get from the States, and will do their best to attain big sales. This, we think, they may be likely to accomplish.
>
> Of course the number of books proposed is a very big one, but their idea is that if they are to put a great deal of money down for advertising your work, they must stand to get it back on a long contract …
>
> Our friends will also make an arrangement that if by reason of any success they may attain with the new books, other publishers should be tempted to pirate the non-copyrighted ones, they would rush out cheap editions of the same so as to crowd the others out of the market, and pay you a royalty of Five Per Cent on any sales.[123]

Ward, Lock was interested in making a similar arrangement itself with a view to joint manufacturing, beginning with Turner's latest novel, *Fugitives from Fortune* (1910), which as it happened was an American story, an adult novel centred on an American millionaire seeking change to a simpler life.[124] However, Turner's response to what might have seemed her best chance yet to break into the American market was negative, not unreasonably given the proposal that terms be fixed for ten years: "As you know my great concern for years has been for the books to do better in England & America … The only hope of America you seem able to offer me is one that ties me for ten years, at same terms [sic]. I feel I *must* see whether this cannot be improved upon".[125]

---

121 The books are not dated. The David McKay edition of *Seven Little Australians* was advertised along with others in late 1909. McKay uses a uniform cover design for the series of Turner's books they publish in 1909-10, including for *Seven Little Australians*.
122 Unwin to Turner, 19 December 1911, Ethel Turner Papers.
123 Ward, Lock (London) to Turner, 15 July 1909, Ethel Turner Papers.
124 Yarwood, *From a Chair*, 192-93.
125 Turner to George Lock, 9 December 1909, Ethel Turner Papers. Yarwood, *From a Chair*, 196.

4 Renegotiating the American Connection: Australian Fiction 1900–1930s

What is remarkable across this history is less Turner's lack of success than her determination, over more than two decades, to break into the American market. She had recently signed with Hodder & Stoughton for another novel, *Fair Ines* (1910), precisely because they promised to "do their best for it in America - & without any binding clauses".[126] She wrote to Hodder & Stoughton on the same day as her rejection of Ward, Lock's proposal: "The American royalty (I trust that you will have an American edition) we must decide upon when I reach England".[127] She also changed literary agents, shifting briefly in 1910 to Curtis Brown & Massie.[128] But there were no American orders for *Fair Ines* and she abruptly cancelled the agreement, adding, perhaps ironically, "If I have been premature & the next mail or so brings news that you have retrieved the situation with some brilliant American or other serial openings then it will be an easy matter to renew the agreement".[129] In 1917, 1924 and again in 1926 she offered books to American publishers without success.[130]

Turner's stories were modernising in their own field. She insisted they were stories about children but not "children's books" in any narrow sense of that term.[131] Set largely in contemporary suburban Australia rather than a sentimentalised bush, they created a distinctive type of the Australian Girl, and, as Kerry White has shown, frequently adopted a dual plot, with a story about children framed by the concerns of its adult characters, a strategy "which allowed [Turner] to write about issues that were normally outside of children's fiction but kept her novels within that classification".[132] In particular, they focus on "the prospects of young women, wives and mothers". Although her novels struggled to make their way in the American children's market, an emerging interest in "modern girl" and young-women stories for more adult readers might well have been the attraction for American publishers of novels by Doris Egerton Jones, Lilian Turner, Ethel Gertrude Hart and Louise Mack. The first three wrote from Australia, while Mack spent a decade and a half in England and Europe, from 1901 to 1916, living by her pen. Despite extreme privations, she became "one of the most popular serial-writers in London, Queen of Romance with millions of readers".[133]

The novels of these women are diverse, but in them we begin to see a shift in the balance of power between older and newer forms of romance; between frontier or pioneering stories characteristically set in the past, and romances, sentimental or otherwise, set in the midst of modern living. Jones' *Time O'Day* (1915) was described as "a girl's own story of her romances, told with delicate intimacy and frankness … One of the very few portrayals of the real girl - the girl whom men think they understand, but don't".[134] Narrated in diary form, the book provided one-paragraph fillers on "love" for a number of American papers.[135] Lilian Turner's *Betty the Scribe* was published in 1907 by the Saalfield Publishing Co. of New York, one of America's largest publishers of children's and juvenile books. The novel's sixteen-year-old

---

126 Turner to George Lock, 9 December 1909, Ethel Turner Papers.
127 Turner to Hodder Williams, 9 Deember. 1909, Ethel Turner Papers.
128 Yarwood, *From a Chair*, 202.
129 Turner to Hughes Massie, 20 February 1911, Ethel Turner Papers. Yarwood, *From a Chair*, 210.
130 Yarwood, *From a Chair*, 196-97, 223, 251, 288.
131 Clare Bradford, "Ethel Turner (1872–1958)", in *Australian Literature, 1788–1914*, ed. Selina Samuels, Dictionary of Literary Biography, Vol. 230 (Detroit, MI: Gale Research, 2001), 398.
132 Kerry M. White, "The Real Australian Girl?: Some Post-Federation Writers for Girls", in *The Time to Write: Australian Women Writers 1890–1930*, ed. Kay Ferres (Ringwood, Vic.: Penguin, 1993), 77-78.
133 Nancy Phelan, *The Romantic Lives of Louise Mack* (St Lucia: University of Queensland Press, 1991), 148.
134 Advertisement, George W. Jacobs & Co., *Evening Public Ledger* (Philadelphia), 8 May 1915.
135 "Communion of the Spirit", *Tombstone Epitaph* (Tombstone, AZ), 2 May 1915; "Love as an Educator", *Madison Journal* (Tallulah, LA), 18 September 1915.

heroine is left to care for five young siblings but maintains her determination to be a writer, even if that interferes with her becoming a "true" woman. This was precisely the aspect the *New York Tribune* reviewer appreciated:

> *Betty the Scribe* ... is the story of an Australian girl who is as much of a failure in household management as is Miss Jackson's heroine, but her troubles arise not from vanity but from her unconquerable turn for authorship. All sorts of catastrophes occur ... while Betty in a frenzy of writing or reading, is lost to all going on about her. What can cure such a situation? Betty, at least, does not stop writing, as the feminine novelists of past generations would make her do.[136]

There was a writing girl, too, in Gertrude Hart's *The Dream Girl* (1913) "a mocking, chummy, practical typewriter girl", who becomes the "dream girl" of the title in a more sentimental resolution. Still, the *Times* adjudged it to be "more amusing and less sentimental than love idyls are wont to be" (unfortunately the novel was described as "a pretty little *Austrian* love idyl").[137] The *Sun* went further: "This is the age of feminine audacity, yet even militants may be taken aback at the attempt to improve on 'Marjorie Daw'".[138] Unusually, the novel seems to have gone straight from George Robertson in Melbourne to Doubleday without passing through London, one of the earliest novels to do so. Doubleday copyrighted and published it in a very attractive format. Finally, Louise Mack's *Theodora's Husband* (John Lane, 1910) was an "improbable melodramatic novel", an adult romance, and one definitely of the modern cast. Its love plot was entangled, as one reviewer put it, with "the radio-motors and the 'vertical lifting screws' of an 'ornithoptere'" (a kind of aircraft). Another reviewer linked it to a "wave of sensationalism" which had broken over recent fiction, and which was "as lurid as the most advanced of modernists could desire".[139]

The G.W. Dillingham Co. seems also to have had an interest in the lurid and modern, publishing Alfred Buchanan's *The Modern Heloise* in 1912 and the first edition of Dulcie Deamer's *The Suttee of Safa: A Hindoo Romance* in 1913. The firm did not hold back in their advertising. *The Modern Heloise* was "a tremendous love story: a fearless embodiment of the deep and impelling lure of sex, based on the burning and elusive query of modern life – is marriage an absolutely irrevocable step, and if so OUGHT it to be?"[140] In much the same register, *The Suttee of Safa* was proclaimed "a splendid and picturesque tale of the passion-scented, languorous East, wherein mother-love triumphs over the lure of sex".[141] Deamer later described her novel as "melodramatic, sugary, and immature" although in New York, she wrote, "it was considered 'hot stuff'".[142]

---

136 Review of *Betty the Scribe*, *New York Tribune*, 23 November 1907. See White, "The Real Australian Girl?", 79–81.
137 "Love in Letters", *New York Times*, 20 April 1913.
138 "Book Reviews and News", *New York Sun*, 5 April 1913. The reference is to a short story by Thomas Bailey Aldrich, "Marjorie Daw".
139 "Flying in Fiction", *New York Times*, 23 April 1910; "Theodora's Husband", *Times Dispatch* (Richmond, VA), 14 March 1910.
140 *The Modern Heloise* received a display advertisement all to itself: *New York Sun*, 11 January 1913.
141 Advertisement, G.W. Dillingham Co., *New York Tribune*, 12 April 1913.
142 Dulcie Deamer, *The Queen of Bohemia: The Autobiography of Dulcie Deamer: Being "The Golden Decade"*, ed. Peter Kirkpatrick (St Lucia: University of Queensland Press, 1998), 32.

4 Renegotiating the American Connection: Australian Fiction 1900–1930s

Deamer was in New York around this time, the first of three trips, and had met up with Dwyer, whom she knew as a "top-price author".[143] He introduced her to the editor of Hearst's *American Weekly*, a Sunday supplement distributed by papers throughout the country. With Dwyer's introductions and the help of her London agent, she had a "Conquest of Mexico" novel published as a magazine serial and three other novels serialised in Hearst newspapers.[144] These included her two later American books: *Revelation*, published by Boni & Liveright in 1922, a biblical drama "daring in its day ... not merely because of its ancient and exotic subject matter, but because of its frank eroticism";[145] and *The Devil's Saint*, a novel dealing with medieval witchcraft, from the otherwise unknown International Publishers in 1925. Although Horace Liveright had a reputation as a pirate, Boni & Liveright was among the most progressive of American publishing firms at this time, "taking chances with young, unknown, or controversial writers" including Theodore Dreiser, Ben Hecht, Sherwood Anderson, William Faulkner and Anita Loos, with *Gentlemen Prefer Blondes*.[146] For an author other than Deamer, a novel on Boni & Liveright's list may have been the beginning of a significant American career.

Pioneering Sex: Jean Devanny and Dale Collins

By the mid-1920s there was a definite market in the United States for "novels depicting the new moral codes of a rising generation", especially when those codes concerned young women, marriage and sexual relations. Bestsellers in the American market included *Gentlemen Prefer Blondes* in 1925, Ben Lindsey's *Companionate Marriage* in 1927, Viña Delmar's *Bad Girl* in 1928, "a temporary sensation because of its flat reportage of a casual romance ... and a fully described pregnancy", and from Britain, Michael Arlen's *The Green Hat* in 1924, which had a "nymphomaniac's tragic life" as its central subject.[147] New Zealand-born Jean Devanny and Australian-born Dale Collins were able to benefit from this new demand for modern fiction, each with a sequence of novels published in the United States between the wars.

The New York-based Macaulay Publishing Co. issued seven of Devanny's novels in the decade from 1926: *The Butcher Shop* (1926), *Dawn Beloved* (1928), *Unchastened Youth* (1930), *Bushman Burke* (1930), *All for Love* (1932), *Out of Such Fires* (1934) and *The Virtuous Courtesan* (1935).[148] We have no evidence as to why Devanny's novels attracted the firm's attention, but it is likely the publishers saw them, idealistically or opportunistically, within the frame of the "modern sex novel". Certainly, Macaulay's

---

143 Deamer, *Queen of Bohemia*, 36.
144 Peter Kirkpatrick, introduction to *The Queen of Bohemia*, viii; Dwyer, *Leg-Irons on Wings*, 9.
145 Kirkpatrick, notes to *The Queen of Bohemia*, 190.
146 Spoo, *Without Copyrights*, 108–9; Carmen R. Russell, "Boni and Liveright", in *American Literary Publishing Houses, 1638-1899*, ed. Dzwonkoski, 57–62; Tebbel, *Between Covers*, 242–43.
147 James D. Hart, *The Popular Book: A History of America's Literary Taste* (New York: Oxford University Press, 1950), 234.
148 *Unchastened Youth* was first published as *Riven* by Duckworth, London, in 1929; *All for Love* was published as *Poor Swine* by Duckworth in 1932. Carole Ferrier lists reissues by Macaulay of *Unchastened Youth* in 1931, *All for Love* in 1934 and *The Virtuous Courtesan* in 1936, but it has not been possible to confirm these. Carole Ferrier, *Jean Devanny: Romantic Revolutionary* (Melbourne: Melbourne University Press, 1999), 373–74.

Figure 4.3 Advertisement for *All for Love* by Jean Devanny (New York: Macaulay Publishing Co., 1932), from the *New York Times*, 29 January 1933.

publicity played up the appeal of "new" female sexuality in Devanny's works. For *Bushman Burke* (1926):

> She was pleasure-mad, cynical, and cunningly flirtatious. He came to hate her in her futile city life. Could he learn to love her in the wild bush country? The worldly woman whom he had abandoned to the city wastrels followed him into the rough and simple life of a lumber camp. There were the forces that could reveal a pure love hidden beneath wayward passion.[149]

And *All for Love*: "Though romance was stricken out of her by her uncontrollable fondness for men, yet she craved beauty. When men were attracted by her fine texture, she drifted on waves of desire into dramatic collisions of love" (Fig. 4.3).[150] In later novels,

---

149 Advertisement, *New York Times*, 10 August 1930.
150 Advertisement, *New York Times*, 29 January 1933.

4 Renegotiating the American Connection: Australian Fiction 1900–1930s

Macaulay published blurbs inside the books themselves. From *Out of Such Fires* (1934), and following the publisher's original setting:

> Out of such fires – tempestuous passion, and the stark realities of a pioneer land – Jean Devanny spins her most dramatic tale. It is the story of Helena Lavine, a sophisticated, worldly woman of fiery temperament and her impassioned love of a strong, elemental pioneer man with a primitive soul. Pagan sensuousness and stern religion come into searing conflict. Under Miss Devanny's ardent pen, against the background of Australia's primitive plains, one of the most amazing situations presented in recent fiction, comes throbbing to life.[151]

"Jean Devanny," the publishers claimed, "has become famous the world over for her frank and fearless stories of women in love."[152]

Devanny's English publisher, Gerald Duckworth & Co., had issued nine of her novels and one short story collection since *The Butcher Shop* in 1926, but *Out of Such Fires* and *The Virtuous Courtesan* were only published by Macaulay. Devanny recalled that Duckworth thought *Out of Such Fires* unsuitable for publication in England "on account of an anti-religious bias pervading its main theme".[153] Duckworth had published Galsworthy, Lawrence, the Sitwells, Dorothy Richardson and Virginia Woolf, among other contemporary authors, and although they also published Elinor Glyn their commitment to Devanny appears to have involved more than a merely cynical interest in the novels' sensational aspects, and to have been an interest, rather, in their modernity. Their early contracts with Devanny reserve for themselves the right to arrange publication in the United States, with royalties shared equally with the author (amended to 75 per cent in the author's favour for *Bushman Burke*) and 10 per cent of the net proceeds retained by the publisher as commission. These clauses indicate that it was Duckworth that made the initial arrangements with Macaulay for US publication. Macauley, however, printed and published their own copyrighted US editions, sold at the then standard fiction price of two dollars.[154]

Contracts survive for several of Devanny's American books. The agreement for *The Butcher Shop*, dated 24 February 1926, was between Duckworth and Macaulay.[155] It granted Macaulay the exclusive right to publish the book in both the United States and Canada, while Macaulay agreed to take out copyright in the United States (in the publisher's name). The terms were modest: there was an advance of £50, a flat 10 per

---

151 Front matter, *Out of Such Fires* (Macaulay, 1934).
152 Front matter, *All For Love* (Macaulay, 1932).
153 Jean Devanny, *Point of Departure: The Autobiography of Jean Devanny*, ed. Carole Ferrier (St Lucia: University of Queensland Press, 1986), 119.
154 *Dawn Beloved* appeared in the United States in 1928 before the Duckworth edition appeared the following year. The two editions of *The Butcher Shop* have similar pagination (Duckworth 313 pages; Macaulay 315 pages) as do the editions of *Bushman Burke* (320 pages each) but there are significant differences in settings for the remaining books.
155 Contracts from the Macaulay Publishers' Literary Contracts (Including Permissions and Correspondence), Ohio State University Library, SPEC.RARE.CMS.296, Box 1.

cent royalty for US sales, and a first option for Macaulay on Devanny's next two books. As Duckworth had rejected *Out of Such Fires* (perhaps under its original title, "Perverted People"), the agreement for this novel, dated 24 October 1933, was between the publishers and Devanny herself, via Curtis Brown's New York office. Terms had improved, with an advance of $250 and a standard sliding scale of royalties for US sales (10 per cent for the first 5000, 12½ per cent on the next 5000, and 15 per cent thereafter). The agreement for *The Virtuous Courtesan*, dated 8 January 1936, drops the advance to $150 – suggesting disappointing sales on earlier titles or perhaps just an estimation that this new title would sell less well – but otherwise the terms remain the same, with the publisher having first option on Devanny's next two novels. This was, however, the final title to appear from Macaulay. In November 1937, Macaulay wrote to Devanny to explain that, as sales had dropped, they were remaindering the bulk of the large stock of *The Virtuous Courtesan* they still held.

Macaulay published history, poetry and literary criticism, but their list was dominated by popular fiction – detective and spy novels, including a handful by Adelaide-based crime writer Arthur Gask, but many more in the field of risqué popular sex novels. At least sixteen Macaulay publications were banned entry to Australia, including Devanny's *The Butcher Shop* and *The Virtuous Courtesan*. Devanny was still living in New Zealand before 1929, and all her novels before *Out of Such Fires* in 1934 have New Zealand settings. But given her subsequent Australian career, *The Butcher Shop* could be claimed as the first "Australian" novel to be banned by Australian Customs.[156] It was also "banned in Boston" – the phrase itself became famous in the 1920s because of the moral crusade of Boston's Watch and Ward Society, which resulted in large numbers of books being banned in that city.[157] While they retained elements of romance, Devanny's books were uncompromising rather than glamorous in their exploration of women's autonomy and sexual relations inside and outside marriage, often linked to a socialist class consciousness. But as "frank and fearless stories of women in love" they could readily be incorporated alongside the popular sex novels in Macauley's list.

If Devanny's novels in this vein were a bonus to the publisher, they were often sport for reviewers. Devanny herself came to feel that *The Butcher Shop* was a "terribly confused and foolish book; its meagre merit sincerity, frankness and a certain power of phrasing".[158] The reviewers tended to agree. For the *Saturday Review of Literature*, it was only in the novel's concern for the sheep raising industry that it rose above mediocrity. When the "hitherto faithful Margaret" takes her husband's foreman as her lover, "the author totally destroys our early favourable impression by cutting loose with a vast deal of hysterical nonsense designed to persuade the reader that Margaret's infidelity is a perfectly justified and decent thing ... and that theoretically wives in their prime should have the privilege of an extra mate while living simultaneously with their wedded one".[159] The *New York Times* reviewer was crueller and funnier:

---

156 Nicole Moore, *The Censor's Library: Uncovering the Lost History of Australia's Banned Books* (St Lucia: University of Queensland Press, 2012), 91, 147.
157 "'Banned in Boston', The Watch and Ward Society's Crusade against Books, Burlesque, and the Social Evil". *Beacon Broadside: A Project of Beacon Press*. http://www.beaconbroadside.com/broadside/2010/09/banned-in-boston.html.
158 Devanny, *Point of Departure*, 94.
159 "The New Books", *Saturday Review of Literature*, 5 February 1927, 567.

4 Renegotiating the American Connection: Australian Fiction 1900–1930s

> The novel with the delicate title – while a story of very remarkable candor – is nevertheless not concerned with the slaughtering of cattle. The title is symbolical: it is even more – it is a forecast. The publisher offers the information that the publication of "The Butcher Shop" caused "turbulent controversy" in New Zealand, the scene of the novel. No details are added, however, and it is a sporting proposition to guess whether New Zealand womanhood or the moving background of sheep was the issue. Probably somebody protested in defense of the sheep. For in spite of reputations for sheepishness attributed to these poor animals, they never in their history could offer anything to compete with the behaviour of the characters of this "amazing" novel.[160]

Devanny did not fulfil the critics' expectations of either antipodean romance or working-life realism. Sales, however, must have been more promising than the reviews – perhaps the publishers knew that their potential book buyers were unlikely to be *Times* readers – for Macaulay continued to exercise their option on Devanny's new novels and to boldly publicise them in the face of puzzled or hostile notices.

The *New York World* found *Dawn Beloved* an improvement on *The Butcher Shop*: "The book, though gloomy and squalid enough, is more palatable than its predecessor, impressive in its realistic depiction of the mining community life, and very gravely occupied with the phenomena of sex".[161] The *Boston Transcript* was puzzled: "We are not sure whether Miss Devanny lacks a sense of moral values, or merely a sense of humor … The story is full of contradictions. It has some interesting ideas on the subject of matrimony, but pages and pages of some sort of quite unintelligible Socialism".[162] For the *Times*, *Bushman Burke* was simply "badly written" and their review of *Out of Such Fires* – under the interesting heading "Australian Moderns" – was equally negative. Macaulay's blurb again provided fodder for the reviewer's scorn. In likening the author to Ibsen, Dostoievsky and O'Neill, "the publishers were inviting adverse criticism" and the reviewer finds nothing to substantiate the claims made for the novel. The "marked individuality" also claimed might be valid, "but it is an individuality that is less personal than typical of a trend":

> You sense, behind the scenes and characters, a creed and a propaganda rather than an artist concerned with the depicting of life. The author's violently anti-religious bias is, in the book, taken for granted to be that of all cultured moderns and to be firmly grounded on science; but the writer's proselytism fails precisely because of the unscientific exaggeration of the attack.[163]

The Virtuous Courtesan was Devanny's last US title. Macaulay was wound up in 1941, but in any case the moment of the "modern sex novel" in the particular between-wars sense of that term had passed. The communist politics of Devanny's later fiction were unlikely to find a popular market in postwar America.

With a much less serious purpose than Devanny, if with more patient craft, Dale Collins wrote a series of modern sexual dramas or "sex adventure" novels that were

---

160 "Latest Works of Fiction", *New York Times*, 20 February 1927.
161 *New York World*, 17 March 1929.
162 *Boston Transcript*, 27 February 1929.
163 "Australian Moderns", *New York Times*, 22 April 1934.

successful on both sides of the Atlantic. He was well regarded by American reviewers as a sometimes brilliant writer of entertaining fiction that was at best more than mere entertainment. He received sustained attention in the book review pages of a kind he was unlikely to receive in Australia. Although now largely forgotten, for the best part of a decade from 1924 Collins was among the most successful Australian writers in America.

Like many of his compatriots, Collins had published stories and verse in the *Bulletin* and a first novel with the NSW Bookstall Co. His American career began in an unusual way when, in 1922, he accepted a position as chronicler on a motor yacht belonging to a Chicago millionaire that was in the middle of a round-the-world tour. Collins was a journalist with the Melbourne *Herald* when he joined the yacht in Brisbane for the second half of its journey, back to the United States. His chronicle, *Sea-Tracks of the Speejacks*, was published by Doubleday in 1923, and its success no doubt created interest, soon after, in his first novel, *Ordeal*, which used a similar setting, albeit with a plot involving nautical thrills and psychological suspense.[164] The *Bookman's* description of the novel as combining "sea adventure, sex adventure and shrewd psychology" captures the formula that Collins would deploy in his novels for the next dozen years.[165]

Ordeal was published in August 1924 by Knopf, and the imprint was an indication that Collins' novel was seen as something more than light reading. The reviews responded in kind. *Outlook* thought it "remarkable as a first novel" due to its "dramatic tenseness, psychological rather than nautical in its main interest".[166] The *New York Times* described it as "one of the most notable first novels which have appeared in some time"; indeed, one of those rare novels deserving higher praise than that printed by the publisher on its cover: "a novel which would certainly seem to mark the advent of a new writer who may not unreasonably be expected one day to enter the small company of the distinguished few whose work has real distinction and real significance."[167] It reminded William McFee in the *Saturday Review of Literature* of Conrad's *The Nigger of the Narcissus*.[168]

Collins settled in England in 1923, and although he travelled widely, his literary career was conducted primarily from London until his return to Melbourne in 1948.[169] Between 1924 and 1937, eleven of his fourteen novels were published in America by significant houses: two with Knopf (*Ordeal* in 1924 and *The Haven* in 1925), three with Boston's Little, Brown & Co. (*The Sentimentalists* in 1927, *Vanity Under the Sun* in 1928 and *Idolaters* in 1929) and three with Bobbs-Merrill (*Lost* and *Vulnerable* in 1933 and *The Mutiny of Madame Yes* in 1934) (Plate 6). Single titles appeared from Houghton Mifflin (*Rich and Strange*, 1931), Frederick A. Stokes (*The Love Watch*, 1937, under the pseudonym Michael Copeland) and the MGM Co. (*Race the Sun*, also 1937). Two were filmed in Hollywood – *Ordeal* as *The Ship from Shanghai* in 1929 and *The Sentimentalists* as *Sal of Singapore* in 1928 – while Alfred Hitchcock directed the British film adaptation of *Rich and Strange*,

---

164 Review of *Sea-Tracks of the Speejacks*, *New York Times*, 26 August 1923. A feature article by Collins, "Into Strange Lands with Dale Collins", occupied the front page of the book section in the *Boston Evening Transcript*, 24 January 1931.
165 "The Bookman's Guide to Fiction", *Bookman*, October 1924, 214.
166 *Outlook*, 10 September 1924, 68.
167 "Sea Thrills", *New York Times*, 3 August 1924.
168 *Saturday Review of Literature*, 2 August 1924, 3. For Alfred Knopf himself, *Ordeal* was "the most thrilling novel I have ever read". *New York Times*, 19 August 1924.
169 Stuart Sayers, "Collins, Cuthbert Quinlan Dale (1897–1956)", *Australian Dictionary of Biography*, http://adb.anu.edu.au/biography/collins-cuthbert-quinlan-dale-5735/text9707.

4 Renegotiating the American Connection: Australian Fiction 1900–1930s

released as *East of Shanghai* in 1931. Collins was also a prolific contributor to English and American magazines.

Favourable reviews kept appearing after *Ordeal*'s success, especially for *The Sentimentalists* and *Vanity Under the Sun*. For Miriam Colgate in the *Bookman*, reviewing *The Sentimentalists*, Collins' "feeling for words" meant that "to miss one of his books is a minor tragedy".[170] For the *Saturday Review*, the author had "a fresh and vigorous talent, a swing of perception, and a robustness of outlook that will not be denied".[171] The *New York Times* described *Vanity* as "an extraordinary and fascinating mixture of adventure and psychological analysis" and thought it "a notable advance in artistry on the part of its author".[172] The *San Francisco Chronicle* thought it "a novel in a thousand", while the *Philadelphia Inquirer* again drew a parallel with Conrad.[173] Collins' books were a kind of high-wire act, balanced between popular melodrama and modern literary fiction, and juggling conventional or thoroughly bizarre plots with a form of psychological and sexual realism – and over time reviewers began to doubt whether the balance was being maintained. The *Outlook* reviewer already thought *Vanity* a "distinct comedown" from *The Sentimentalists*: "Mr. Collins, the Australian, is already dangerously near the best-seller class".[174] With *Idolaters*, the *New York Times* thought Collins had revealed himself as "a writer who confuses violence with action, color with atmosphere and costume with character"; it was a disappointment for readers of *Vanity*, "who felt that they had found in Mr. Collins a good story-teller and a master of exotic detail".[175] Here the comparison with Conrad was not to Collins' advantage, for it was "the inevitable comparison of the ephemeral and the great in literature". Nonetheless, if the tendency of Collins' novels was towards "mere thrillerism", in H.M. Green's phrase, his new novels still intrigued reviewers and could receive top billing in the *New York Times* review pages.[176]

By 1930, Collins worked through Harold Ober, the New York-based literary agent, alongside John Farquarson in London. He had gained the commitment of three major publishers for successive titles. Sales records have not survived, but *Ordeal* appears to have sold well, and if sales on the subsequent titles were somewhat disappointing by comparison, faith among publishers in Collins' talent remained. Ober offered *Lost* to David L. Chambers at Bobbs-Merrill in September 1932, and they were keen to commit. Chambers wrote to Collins a month later: "May I tell you how delighted we are that we are to publish your novel, *Lost*. We have been your admirers since *Ordeal* made its appearance. *Lost* seems to us a most delightful story from first to last, and we look forward with deepest satisfaction to a long connection with you".[177] They dealt directly with the author and his agent rather than with Harrap, Collins' English publisher, and printed their own copyright editions. For *Lost*, Collins was paid a $500 advance against royalties and the publisher promised a big advertising campaign; but in depressed conditions in early 1933

---

170 Miriam Colgate, "Notes on New Novels", *Bookman*, November 1927, 333.
171 Amy Loveman, "A Virile Talent", *Saturday Review of Literature*, 10 September 1927, 102.
172 "A Man Like a Mastodon", *New York Times*, 18 September 1927.
173 Reviews quoted on the dustflap of Little, Brown's edition of *Idolaters*.
174 Harriet Hastings, "A Group of Novels", *Outlook*, 12 September 1928, 794.
175 "Melodrama in Java", *New York Times*, 18 August 1929.
176 H.M. Green, *A History of Australian Literature Pure and Applied. Vol. II 1923–1950*, rev. by Dorothy Green (Sydney: Angus & Robertson, 1985), 1222. The *New York Times*, 1 February 1931, gives *Rich and Strange* top billing.
177 Chambers to Collins, 23 November 1932, Bobbs-Merrill mss, Lilly Library, Indiana University.

the "experiment" did not bring "commensurate results". Chambers insisted to Ober: "I am quite crazy about his work but we haven't got a real start with *Lost*".[178]

The immediate problem was Collins' next novel, *Vulnerable: A Tale with Cards*, which had already arrived for consideration. Publishers were reluctant to publish two books from the same author in quick succession; further, the new novel was too short and one of three readers' reports was extremely negative ("makes me feel dreadfully sure that Mr Collins is going to get worse like an egg, instead of better like wine").[179] A second reader's report was positive, however, comparing the book to two recent bestselling novels with literary claims, Thornton Wilder's *The Bridge of San Luis Rey* and Vicki Baum's *Grand Hotel*, even though it was "not so profound in conception". Eventually Bobbs-Merrill decided to publish it as a "special" (not an option book as set out on the *Lost* contract), and taking their cue from a plot that turns on several games of cards they packaged it in a "novelty card box". Collins responded enthusiastically: "You haven't just printed it, you've *published* it." He also reported on a new book which he described as "sea with sex": "am making it fairly frank, for I feel the time is ripe for a sea story written in the modern vernacular rather than that of Marryat".[180]

It appears that *Vulnerable* sold only modestly, but Chambers was still keen to contract what became *The Mutiny of Madame Yes*, still believing in Collins' "great talent" and again offering a $500 advance. There were problems about the length – at 125,000 words it would normally have sold for $2.50, but as "light entertainment" it should be priced at two dollars.[181] The publishers themselves cut 14,000 words as Collins had left on a trip to Australia, and eventually the book was published at the lower price despite still having 320 pages. Bobbs-Merrill's publicity was as "modern" as Collins hoped the book itself would be: "Unwavering in its interest until it reaches its amazing and immoral climax, *The Mutiny of Madame Yes* is gay and grand entertainment".[182] The *New York Times* described the novel favourably as "A gay, outrageous yarn with a chuckle on almost every page", but sales were again disappointing – both *Vulnerable* and *Mutiny* showed a deficit – and the firm rejected Collins' next effort, *Race the Sun*.[183] This was virtually the end of Collins' American career as a serious novelist, and his two later American titles were one-offs. After his return to Australia, he focused on children's fiction, and three of his children's books appeared in America in 1949-50.[184]

Shockingly Alive and Scandalously Amusing: Norman Lindsay

Extending into the early 1930s, Devanny's and Collins' American appearances overlapped with a brief period of marked success for Norman Lindsay in what might

---

178 Chambers to Collins, 21 February 1933; 10 March 1933; Chambers to Ober, 24 March 1933, Bobbs-Merrill mss.
179 Readers' Reports, 28 March 1933 and 4 March 1933, Bobbs-Merrill mss.
180 Collins to Chambers, 22 August 1933, Bobbs-Merrill mss.
181 Chambers to Ober, 10 April 1934 and 24 May 1934, Bobbs-Merrill mss.
182 Bobbs-Merrill publicity, under the heading "What a woman!", Bobbs-Merrill mss.
183 "Another Sea Siren", *New York Times*, 2 September 1934. Royalty statements in Bobbs-Merrill mss (4 March 1935 and later note from 1936). Reader's report 7 August 1936.
184 *Robinson Care, Castaway* (Rinehart, 1949); *Bush Holiday* (Doubleday, 1949); *Shipmates Down Under* (Holiday House, 1950).

4 Renegotiating the American Connection: Australian Fiction 1900–1930s

be seen as a parallel subgenre, the modern sex comedy. Lindsay's American career is significant, not just because it is largely unknown in Australia, but because in America he was seen first and foremost as a modern novelist, indeed an author in the fullest sense of the term, uncomplicated by local nostalgia or nationalism, or by his controversial reputation as an artist and illustrator. Lindsay first appeared in the United States in 1931 with *Every Mother's Son*, published by Hearst's Cosmopolitan Book Corporation at the light entertainment price of two dollars. After having been rejected in Australia by Angus & Robertson, the novel had been published as *Redheap* by Faber in London in 1930. Fellow Australian novelist and journalist Brian Penton, then in London, had given the book to Curtis Brown, and most likely they sent it on to their New York office, which Lindsay later used as his American address. *Every Mother's Son* was a critical success. As Lindsay put it, "America has been very generous in its reception of my novel".[185] This generous reception, coming soon after the English edition had been banned by Australian Customs, persuaded Lindsay to sail for New York in July 1931.

Lindsay was impressed by the culture and enterprise of the younger American publishers:

> I have had proposals from Harpers, Scribners, John Day and Ray Long for the next novel, and have met and dined with representatives of these firms ... I had left *The Cautious Amorist* with [Ray] Everitt, who runs Curtis Brown's here, and he had handed it to Farrar and Rinehart. To my astonishment, Farrar made an immediate offer for the book, and also an offer for *An Evangelist* [*Pan in the Parlour*], which is in London and which he has not read. A very sporting offer and a pleasing compliment too. He offered exceptional terms, 1000 dollars down and 15 per cent on sales for *An Evangelist* and 500 dollars and 15 per cent for *The C.A.* On Everitt's advice I have accepted this contract. I like Farrar personally; he is one of the younger group, a very bright fellow, and with a lot of money behind him. As yet the specialization of publishing houses is not so defined here as in England, but I am inclined to believe that the young modern Yale-Harvard group will carry it ... They have the culture of the English university type without any of its maddening preciousness.[186]

Lindsay was also impressed by New York, describing it as "the third great experiment in a new earth", and he believed that the connections he was making would help establish a market there for Australian books.[187] When it appeared that the Australian government was to introduce a 35 per cent tariff on imported books, Lindsay contacted New York publishers trying to interest them in setting up a publishing house in Australia. All declined, largely because it would bring them into conflict with English publishers over copyright in what the latter still regarded as among their "traditional markets".[188]

In 1931, at the time of Lindsay's visit, Farrar & Rinehart, established in June 1929, had acquired the stock of the Cosmopolitan Book Corporation, including *Every Mother's Son*. In the following seven years, it published five Lindsay titles – all but one being first editions,

---

185 Norman Lindsay to Howard Hinton, July 1931, Norman Lindsay, *Letters of Norman Lindsay*, ed. R.G. Howarth and A.W. Barker (Sydney: Angus & Robertson, 1979), 305.
186 Lindsay to Godfrey Blunden, 17 October 1931, *Letters*, 308.
187 Lindsay to Blunden, 17 October 1931, *Letters*, 309. See also Norman Lindsay, "I Like New York", *Home* (Sydney), December 1931, 38-39.
188 Norman Lindsay, *My Mask: For What Little I Know of the Man Behind It, An Autobiography* (Sydney: Angus & Robertson, 1970), 239.

Figure 4.4 Advertisement for Norman Lindsay's *Mr. Gresham and Olympus* (New York: Farrar & Rinehart, 1932), from the *New York Times*, 28 February 1932.

appearing before the corresponding English releases. These were a novel completed in New York, *Mr. Gresham and Olympus* (1932); two earlier manuscripts Lindsay had taken with him, *The Cautious Amorist* (1932) and *Pan in the Parlour* (1933); a reissue of his celebrated children's book *The Magic Pudding* (1936); and a new novel, *Age of Consent* (1938). *The Cautious Amorist* was also serialised in *Cosmopolitan* magazine and reprinted by Grosset & Dunlap in 1932, and from this work onward the books carried Lindsay's own humorous, "frank" illustrations. He also made money through the magazines, receiving

4 Renegotiating the American Connection: Australian Fiction 1900–1930s

£300 for illustrating a story in *Cosmopolitan*, and writing articles for *Fortune* and the *Saturday Review*, "which paid at the same opulent rate".[189]

Lindsay's reputation in the United States was built on his first novel, although *The Cautious Amorist* was the greater sales success. For Burton Rascoe, celebrated literary editor of the *New York Herald Tribune*, *Every Mother's Son* was "a work of genius". For William Soskin in the *Evening Post*, Lindsay's "picture of adolescents in a small Australian town contains much brutality, much that is coarse, much that is full-blooded to a bursting degree".[190] For influential literary columnist Isabel Paterson, Lindsay's characters were "shockingly alive and scandalously amusing". The *Nation* compared Lindsay to Booth Tarkington, while for Rex Hunter, reviewing *Every Mother's Son* alongside G.B. Lancaster's *Pageant*, the two authors were "Attilas of the Antipodes [beating] at the gates of literary America".[191] Yet the reviews were mixed, not only because of the book's sexual interests but also, less predictably, because of its lack of distinctive Australianness. For *Outlook*, the writing was "spontaneous, hot, intense", but the book "teeters dangerously on the line which separates art from pornography".[192] The *New York Times* was uncomfortable with the novel's portrayal of young women: "If sentiment is gentleness, geniality, generosity, most certainly there is none in this Australian's novel. The young people are as hard as nails ... the girls merely throw themselves away".[193] More interesting are, first, the reviewers' expectations of what an Australian novel might be, and, second, their way of reading Lindsay's book as a modern novel.

The *Times* reviewer, for one, was puzzled by the lack of distinctive national traits: "it must be that the people of Australia, however modern the country may be, have traits of individuality which differentiate them, and to this commentator it seems a lapse on the part of Mr. Lindsay that he should not have been at more pains to make his characters more distinctly the product of their native culture". The *Saturday Review* felt much the same: "A fault that one discovers, not without irritation, is that though Mr. Lindsay is an Australian and though the scene of his book is laid in Australia, as one gathers from casual references, there is nothing essentially Australian about it and it might just as well be laid in Podunk, USA ... His mother's sons and daughters are just the same kind of semi-educated, carnal-minded, lecherous young people that realistic authors in America and England and France think that young people in small towns ought to be".[194]

Despite such reservations and the novel's modest sales, it made sufficient impact for John Farrar to contract future books on generous terms.[195] The firm offered a $500 advance for *The Cautious Amorist* and $1000 for *Mr. Gresham and Olympus*, which appeared in New York six months before the English edition with a bright colour jacket featuring one of Lindsay's

---

189 Lindsay, *My Mask*, 238.
190 Quotations from Rascoe, Paterson and *Nation* relating to *Every Mother's Son* used in publicity for *Mr. Gresham and Olympus*, *New York Times*, 28 February 1932; William Soskin, *New York Evening Post*, 18 September 1930, quoted in Joanna Mendelssohn, *Letters and Liars: Norman Lindsay and the Lindsay Family* (Sydney: Angus & Robertson, 1996), 212.
191 *Nation*, 15 October 1930, 421; Rex Hunter, *New York Sun*, 7 February 1933. Sturm, *An Unsettled Spirit*, 203.
192 "The Leisure Arts: Six Novels", *Outlook*, 1 October 1930, 187.
193 "Youth in Australia", *New York Times*, 28 September 1930.
194 "The New Books", *Saturday Review of Literature*, 29 November 1930, 398. See also Antony Clark, "Every Mother's Son", *Bookman*, 30 October 1930, 177.
195 A Royalty Statement from Farrar & Rinehart dated 1 March 1933 indicates that *Every Mother's Son* had an unearned balance against its advance of $224.26. Harry F. Chaplin Literary Papers, State Library of NSW MLMSS6473, Add-on 2225.

own illustrations (Fig. 4.4). But it was the former that "made the success", as Stanley Rinehart put it. *Mr. Gresham* earned only half its advance, but *The Cautious Amorist* sold more than 7500 copies in the second half of 1932, and around 1100 per week in the period leading up to Christmas.[196] It was Lindsay's most successful novel commercially in America, "a small dollar mine" as he later called it.[197] Farrar & Rinehart offered a $1000 advance on *Pan in the Parlour*, which had sold nearly 4000 copies by the end of 1933 and almost earned out its advance.[198] And in March 1933, they contracted for three new novels, offering an advance of $750 for each.[199] Lindsay was unable to deliver three new novels, but *The Age of Consent* appeared in 1938.

The relative compression of Lindsay's output in the United States – six books in eight years – meant that reviewers could identify an oeuvre, a distinctive style recurring over successive titles, something relatively rare, as we have seen, for Australian authors outside genre fiction. The *New York Times* compared *Mr. Gresham* with *Every Mother's Son*:

> [In *Mr Gresham*] Norman Lindsay created one of those freak books which, because of their freshness of language, the ironic detachment, the humor that touches absurdity, and the piercing wit, stand out as evidence of a new and original talent. Such brilliance usually dies out more quickly than soberer and heavier qualities. *Mr. Gresham and Olympus* is a wicked and amusing and often penetrating novel. It belongs on a high level; but it does not rise like its predecessor to outstanding distinction.[200]

The Cautious Amorist was received as "delectable entertainment quite unlike any of its numerous predecessors in island adventure"; a "social satire, ranging from sardonic irony to farce, carried through with a firm but delicate touch [and] rising to an impeccably worked out climax"; "a distinct product of this day and age, of the insouciant humor and dry wit that pepper the pages of *The New Yorker*".[201] While it would be "extremely shocking" to some readers, for others, including the latter reviewer, "it would make excellent fireside reading". Indeed, *The Cautious Amorist* kept on being successful in America right into the 1950s, reprinted by Grosset & Dunlap in 1940, by Grayson Publishers (New York) in 1946 and 1947, and as a paperback by Bantam from 1947 to 1955.[202] It was banned by Australian Customs in May 1933, following newspaper reports of reviews of the American edition.[203] Although it was only the second of Lindsay's books to be banned, the effect was that Lindsay established a much greater reputation as a novelist in the United States than in Australia where circulation of his books was limited.

---

196 Stanley Rinehart to Lindsay, 24 February 1933, Harry F. Chaplin Literary Papers, Add-on 2225.
197 Lindsay, *My Mask*, 238.
198 Farrar & Rinehart Royalty Statement dated 24 March 1934, Harry F. Chaplin Literary Papers, Add-on 2225.
199 Rinehart to Lindsay, 24 February 1933; C.R. Everitt to Lindsay, 14 March 1933, and Memorandum of Agreement (dated 14 March 1933), Harry F. Chaplin Literary Papers, Add-on 2225.
200 "Fresh and Breezy", *New York Times*, 28 February 1932.
201 First two quotations from "The New Books: Fiction", *Saturday Review of Literature*, 19 November 1932, 259; final quotation from "Back to Nature", *New York Times*, 13 November 1932.
202 Patricia Holt, "'It's Enough to Drive a Bloke Mad': Norman Lindsay's Art and Literature", *Bibliographical Society of Australia and New Zealand Bulletin*, 27, nos 1-2 (2003): 75. *Age of Consent* had Pocket Books editions in 1948 and 1960.
203 Holt, "Norman Lindsay", 76.

4 Renegotiating the American Connection: Australian Fiction 1900–1930s

Lindsay's later books could still attract high praise, as *Pan in the Parlour* did in the *New York Times* – where it was reviewed next to Dorothy Parker's *After Such Pleasure* – even though reviewers often looked back to *The Cautious Amorist* as the high point in Lindsay's career.[204] *The Magic Pudding* was also celebrated in a lengthy review in the *Times* accompanied by one of Lindsay's original illustrations.[205] While *Age of Consent* was one sex comedy too many for certain reviewers, Edith Walton in the *Times* could appreciate its "quiet wit and fancy" in the context of Lindsay's other books:

> If it lacks somewhat the zest of *The Cautious Amorist*, is not quite so clever nor so funny, *Age of Consent* is nevertheless a very inviting tidbit. Norman Lindsay, the author – who also serves as illustrator – is a writer with a curious brand of humor. It takes him a little while to get going, and it is not until his comedy is well under way that one realizes how amazing he is being. This was true, even, of his famous children's book, *The Magic Pudding*, and certainly it is true of his novels. So quietly does it start, in such an innocent and random fashion, that one is unprepared for the capers which *Age of Consent* cuts.[206]

Lindsay's drawings were especially praised; indeed they caught "the spirit of his characters almost better than his prose", and two drawings from the book were used to illustrate the review, adding to its prominence in the paper. Lindsay was taken seriously as a modern comic novelist in the New York book world.

Almost a decade later, Lindsay's final American title, *Cousin from Fiji*, was published by the prestigious Random House, where Bennet Cerf had had an interest in Lindsay since the earlier novels. *Cousin from Fiji* had first been published in Australia by Angus & Robertson in July 1945, and the firm pushed the book into the US market. Frances Pindyck of the Leland Hayward agency wrote to Cerf:

> Mr. Cousins [of A&R] tells me that you expressed great interest in Mr. Lindsay's work, so I am rushing the book to you. The Canadian market is still open, and should you decide to bring the book out in this country, you could have the Canadian rights too.
>
> The original title of the book was Virginity to Let, which was rather too strong for the Australian market; however, it might be considered for publication in this country.
>
> Angus & Robertson's first printing was 10,000 copies, on a per capita basis this is equal to a 200,000 run in the U.S., and having sold the first printing, they are going into a second printing immediately.[207]

Cerf liked the book, and a reader's report was also reasonably positive: "this might be considered Australia's entry for the whacky family saga ... it has the charm and nostalgic quality of remoteness in space and time ... It certainly has an authentic atmosphere quite unfamiliar to American readers". Pindyck urged Random House to take out *ad interim*

---

[204] "Australian Worldlings", *New York Times*, 29 October 1933.
[205] Ellen Lewis Buell, *New York Times*, 13 September 1936.
[206] Edith H. Walton, "Norman Lindsay's Novel and Other Recent Fiction", *New York Times*, 10 July 1938, 75.
[207] Pindyck to Cerf, 27 August 1945, Random House records 1925-1999, Rare Books and Manuscript Library, Columbia University, MS1048, Box 91.

copyright on the book, not least because she believed a film sale was likely. They did so in November, meaning the book had to be published by the following May.[208]

Lindsay welcomed the generous $1000 advance Random House offered and was delighted with Cerf's own commentary on the dustcover flap which recounted in humorous terms how he laughed himself sick over the book. Writing to Cerf, he emphasised how much he valued his year in America, "for some of the best talk I have ever had from a collective group of people. It is an important thing to this country, an easy exchange of nationalities with yours, for America, whether she likes it or not, must become the Fifth World Empire, and we in the Pacific are part of it".[209] Random House printed 7500 copies in January 1946 and a further 2500 in May; in June, Cerf wrote to Lindsay that sales were close to 7000, "not nearly as much as I had hoped for, but far from bad in this period of violent readjustment".[210] Cerf had hopes for a film deal, and was interested in anything new from Lindsay, especially if it was as "funny as *Fiji*". But although Lindsay wrote three further novels, they appeared only in Australia.

Conclusion

The first three decades of the twentieth century were a period of transition from the publishing habits and generic conventions of the nineteenth century to the industry structures and strategies of modern publishing. Although Australian authors were in certain ways better positioned to negotiate formal agreements in the United States, either directly or, more commonly, through their literary agents or British publishers, the fact that the majority of works still travelled via London meant that for most authors and most books the American market remained a title-by-title proposition. Only a small number of authors – Lancaster, Devanny, Collins – achieved an ongoing relationship with a single publisher over several years and multiple titles. A few, such as Dwyer and Sumner Locke, attacked the American market directly. Others maintained pressure on their agents or publishers to do more for them in America but success in the British market was not always a guarantee of interest from the other side. Authors could now have the advantage of separate, copyrighted American editions and standard royalty agreements, but for many the best offer was still a percentage of the payments made to their British publishers for plates or sheets from which American editions were manufactured. They often had little say in such arrangements, especially if writing from Australia, despite the evidence we have of so many authors' keen interest in making an impact in the American market. Magazine stories and articles remained a much more lucrative activity for those who could break into that domain, but it demanded a high level of productivity and a willing or unwilling submission to the demands of the popular fiction marketplace.

Australian settings and themes were still recognisable to reviewers and publishers in ways set down by the romance novels of the late nineteenth and early twentieth centuries, even as romance joined adventure in the category of "light fiction". But Australians also participated in the newer variations on and departures from these conventions represented by "modern girl" stories and "modern sex novels". In Ethel Turner's case, an equally

---

208 Reader's report by Belle Becker dated 4 September 1945, Random House records, Box 91.
209 Linday to Cerf, undated (November?) 1945, Random House records, Box 91.
210 Cerf to Lindsay, 20 June 20 1946. Random House records, Box 91.

4 Renegotiating the American Connection: Australian Fiction 1900–1930s

transnational development in the modern children's story promised international sales. As in the nineteenth century, women writers dominated. Although these works comprised only a very small percentage of the new fiction published in America in these years, the sheer number and range of names is still surprising. Many were published by the major American publishers, old and new. Bringing these stories to light alters our sense of Australian literature in these decades, which are typically seen as relatively barren years for literary production. Triangulating the local scene with the British and American markets, however, reveals a richer, more complex picture of writing across the three markets, a new density of books and book talk. What we cannot claim for this period is the recognition in America of *Australian literature* in any substantial sense of the term; but then again, the idea had yet to achieve any clear articulation in Australia itself.

Plate 1 Tasma's *A Sydney Sovereign* appeared in the most widely circulated fiction series of the 1880s and early 1890s, Munro's Seaside Library Pocket Editions (New York: George Munro, 1890).

Plate 2 "Never was scene of wilder desolation". Rosa Praed, *Fugitive Anne* (New York: R.F. Fenno & Co., 1904). Illustrations by Clare Angell.

Plate 3 "Romance in an entirely new form." Louis Becke's reputation in the United States was acknowledged by Lippincott's attractive uniform edition of his works. *By Reef and Palm and His Native Wife* (Philadelphia: J.B. Lippincott Co., 1900).

Plate 4 Satisfying the taste for orientalist tales. The original *japoniste* cover of Carlton Dawe's *Rose and Chrysanthemum* (Boston: Knight & Millet, 1900).

Plate 5 Australian authors could make a killing in the Egyptian mummy thriller market. Ambrose Pratt, *The Living Mummy* (New York: Frederick A. Stokes Co., 1910). Illustration by Louis D. Fancher.

Plate 6 "To miss one of his books is a minor tragedy." For a decade between the wars, Dale Collins was among the best-known Australian authors in the United States. Dale Collins, *Idolaters* (Boston: Little, Brown & Co., 1932).

Plate 7 "I'll try to behave." Maysie Greig gets front-page treatment in the *American Weekly*, the paper with the "greatest circulation in the world". "Kid Sisters Don't Count", *American Weekly*, 17 September 1933. Illustration by Charles D. Mitchell. Image courtesy of the Shadowlands Newspaper Archive.

Plate 8 Popular romance or artistic aspiration? The first edition dust-jacket of Christina Stead's *For Love Alone* (New York: Harcourt, Brace, 1944).

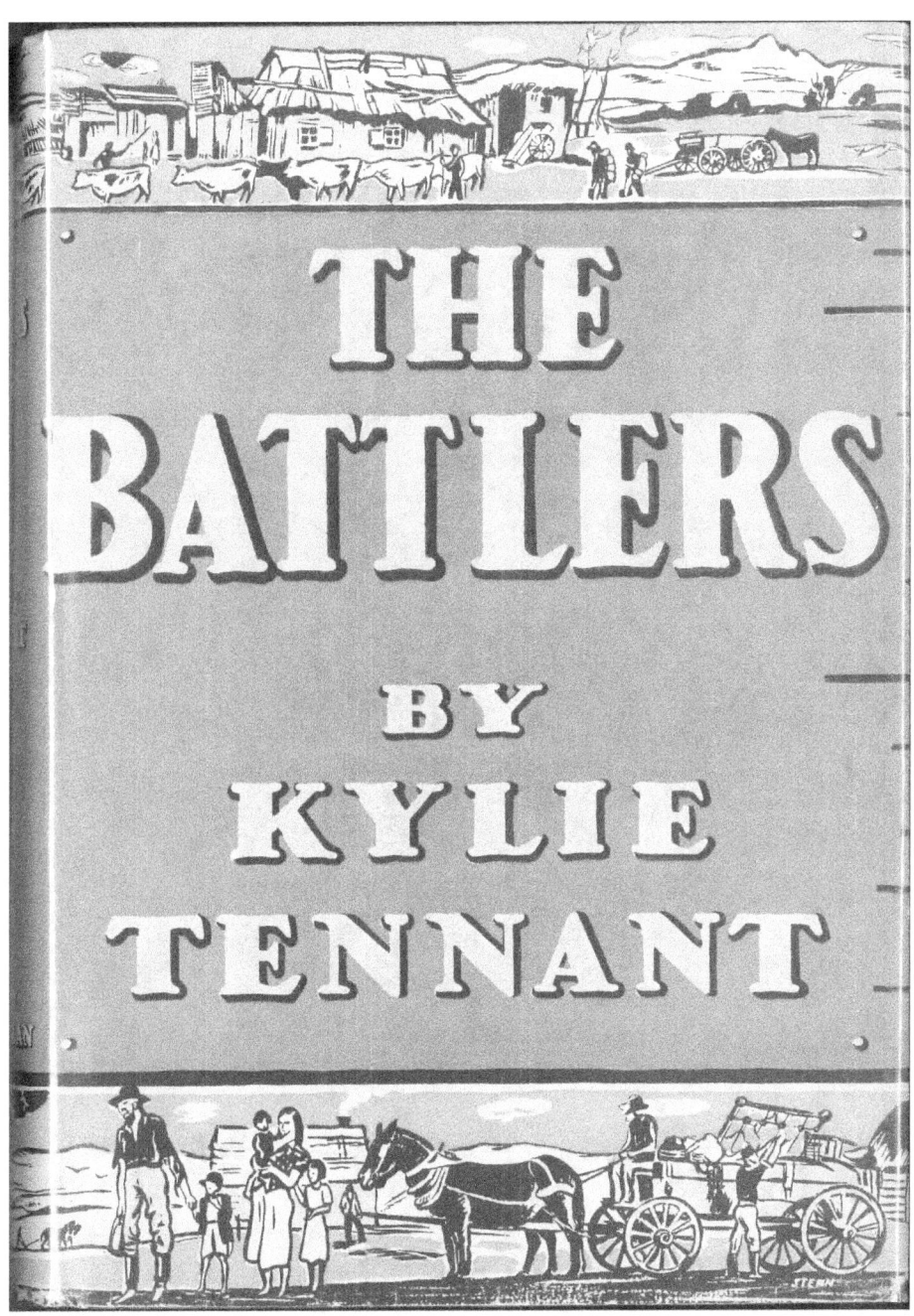

Plate 9 An "Australian *Grapes of Wrath*". Kylie Tennant's *The Battlers* (New York: Macmillan, 1941) packaged for American readers.

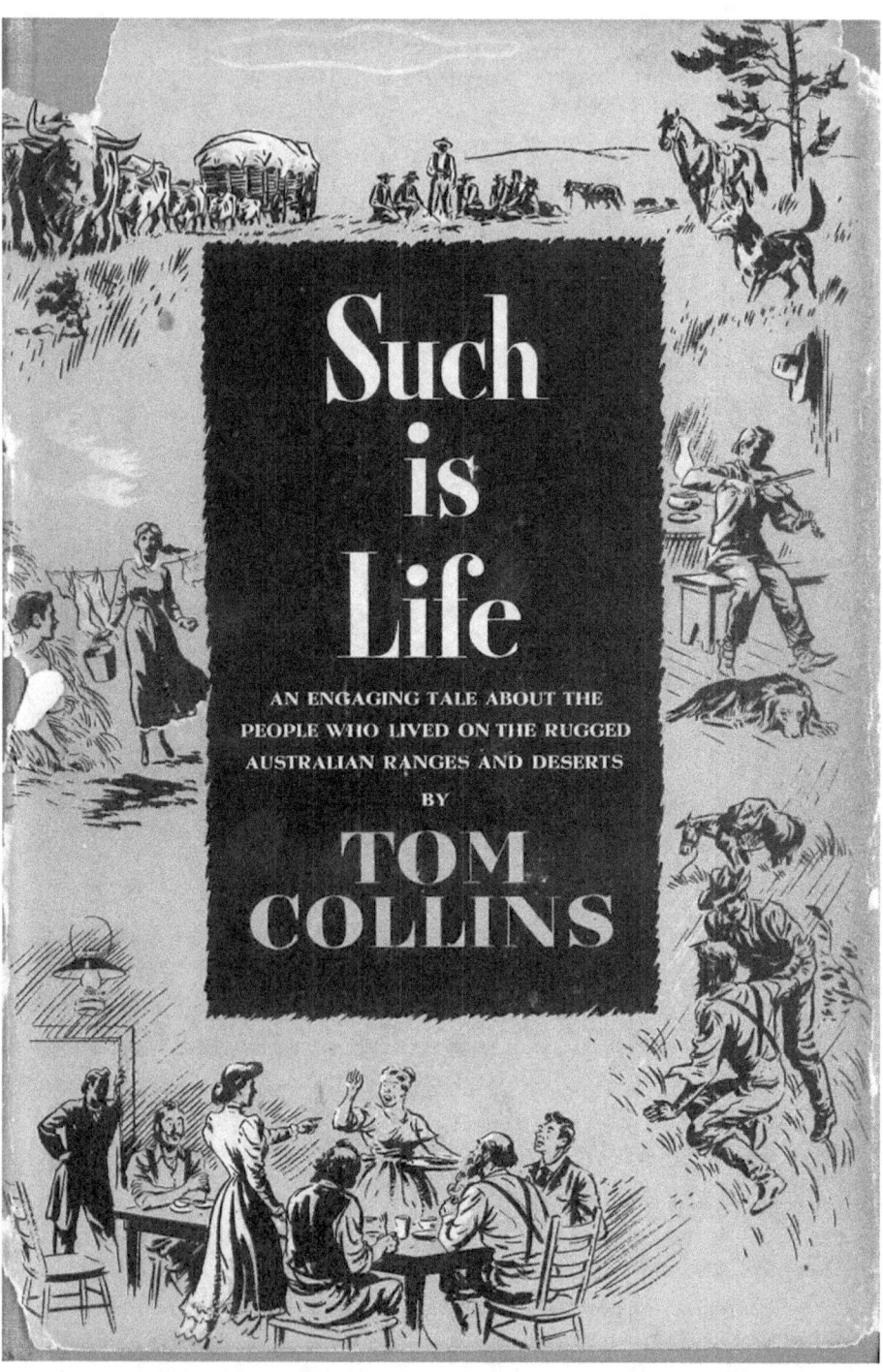

Plate 10 Marketing an Australian classic. Tom Collins [Joseph Furphy], *Such is Life* (Chicago: University of Chicago Press, 1948). Reproduced with permission of the University of Chicago Press.

5
Mystery and Romance: The Market for Light Fiction Between the Wars

On both sides of the Atlantic, the years between the two world wars witnessed the consolidation of the crime fiction genre, especially "golden age" murder mysteries and detection puzzles, and also the rise of women's romance fiction as a distinct market segment, in Britain in the late 1920s and in the United States across the following decade. Although both forms had much older precedents, together they helped constitute the booming field of " light fiction" in the interwar years. Understood as distinct from the cheapest forms of pulp, light fiction was identified as a discrete field within the mainstream of commercial fiction publishing. This new awareness can be seen in the fact that uses of the term "light fiction" in the *New York Times* increased from twenty-six in the 1910s to fifty-six in the 1920s and 141 in the 1930s, after which they tapered off again. Further, in January 1934, the *Times* began a special reviews section, "Fiction in Lighter Vein", where romance titles were reviewed by regulars such as Beatrice Sherman; and in the same period the *Saturday Review of Literature* launched "Over the Counter: the Saturday Review's Guide to Romance and Adventure", a weekly chart containing one-line reviews of romances, westerns and other popular genres. It matched the paper's similar guide to detective fiction, "The Criminal Record".

As we have already seen in the case of Fergus Hume, genre fiction allowed for spectacular careers in terms of numbers of titles published and reputation in the field. But for the small number like Agatha Christie or Arthur Upfield who would be remembered, many more were forgotten as soon as new titles stopped appearing. That was the nature of the field, a novel's success depending in many ways on its interchangeability with others of its type even when it introduced startling innovations to the conventional forms, such innovation in crime and mystery being almost a generic feature in itself. As LeRoy Lad Panek has argued, detective story writers between the wars "participated in a literary movement which was as conscious and definable as the well-known movements in regular literature. In fact, in many ways, it is difficult to fully appreciate golden age writers without seeing them as a group, simultaneously coherent and diverse, like the neo-classicists or the romantics".[1] Their self-consciousness about the genre in which they wrote and its place in the literary field was manifested in the first instance by their "revolt" against popular

---

1 LeRoy Lad Panek, *An Introduction to the Detective Story* (Bowling Green, OH: Bowling Green State University Popular Press, 1987), 122.

fiction; that is, their separation of detective fiction from the turn-of-the-century thrillers, the cheap, sensational murder mysteries aimed at a mass readership, or boys' adventure stories.[2]

Novels in the detective, mystery, spy and thriller genres were thoroughly transnational as saleable items in the marketplace and tradeable commodities between publishers. Although the trade worked across the Atlantic in both directions, the market for English crime and thrillers in America was especially vibrant, and this meant Australian authors could be part of the detective fiction "movement". A significant number at home and abroad were active participants in this transnational business, often recognised in England or America to a greater degree than they were in Australia with its much smaller market. Crime was published by the mainstream houses – Doubleday, Dodd, Mead and Simon & Schuster – and smaller operations such as The Dial Press, but typically its publishing economy was different from that for other fiction: more books, more often, and with forms of seriality built into publishing programs and successive titles (the sleuth or secret agent who reappears, a repeated motif in titles, or recurrent settings – London, the Riviera, the outback). Individual books in these popular genres were seldom mega-sellers but they could have good, regular sales as each new title appeared – 3000, 5000, 10,000 – and reprint, book club, serialisation and movie rights could earn even more.[3]

For American publishing, the years between the wars were a rich period for crime or mystery, with major publishers running special series: Doubleday's Crime Club, Dodd, Mead's Red Badge Detective and Red Badge Suspense series, Simon & Schuster's Inner Sanctum mysteries, Knopf's Borzoi Murder Mysteries and Dutton's Mystery of the Month. In 1946, it was estimated that around 300 new titles appeared annually, earning above $5 million.[4] Crime novels were regularly reviewed in the major papers – the *New York Times*, the *Saturday Review of Literature*, the *New York Herald Tribune*, the *New Yorker*, the *Washington Post* – and regular reviewers who were often syndicated across the nation brought real authority to the process.

America was slower to have dedicated romance publishers or imprints, but the rising phenomenon of modern romance novels, written predominantly by women and addressed primarily to women readers, was certainly recognised. Writing in the *Los Angeles Times* in July 1932, Lillian Ford noted the rise of romance "after a decade and more of realism, naturalism, experimentation", with Australian-born Alice Grant Rosman's "large following" among her examples.[5] While the romance-marriage plot and the recurrent device of an independent, passionate but morally upright young woman were scarcely new – variations had appeared in countless nineteenth-century romances – women's romance fiction emerged in the late twenties and thirties as a distinct genre and market sector. The novels were typically contemporary and familiar in setting (although orientalist scenarios never disappeared completely), the heroines were not too far removed from the reader's own social sphere, and the difficulties the heroines faced were those of "modern life". In

---

2   Panek, *Introduction*, 124.
3   In 1949, the Unicorn Mystery Book Club was paying $1000 as a guaranteed one-off payment, the Mystery Guild offered $2000, and the Detective Book Club $1500 (in 1950). Carol Hetherington, "In the Club: Australian Crime Fiction in the USA 1943–1954", *Australian Literary Studies*, 27, nos 3-4 (October–November 2012): 40.
4   Howard Haycraft, "The Burgeoning Whodunit", *New York Times*, 6 October 1946.
5   Lillian C. Ford, "True Love, Happy Ending: What Readers Now Want", *Los Angeles Times*, 24 July 1924.

5 Mystery and Romance: The Market for Light Fiction Between the Wars

Britain, Mills & Boon's focus on women's romance began in the late twenties, in part as a response to increased publishing costs in the postwar era and the profits to be earned from large sales of cheaper editions, an equation to which romance fiction was ideally suited.[6] Other publishers, such as Heinemann or Hodder & Stoughton, with its famous "Yellow Jackets" series launched in 1923, also invested in the expanding light fiction market and became important for Australian authors. Mills & Boon maintained a general list through the 1920s, but already by 1929 its bestselling authors were all writing romance. Over the course of the 1930s, it narrowed its focus onto "quality" romance novels and increased the number of new titles it published annually, with two to four new books fortnightly. Its growth in the 1930s was tied to the continued expansion of commercial circulating libraries in Britain; in 1934, W.H. Smith identified "romance authors" as a distinct category.[7] By the end of the decade, Mills & Boon's transformation into a specialist publisher of women's romance fiction was complete.

While there was no direct equivalent of Mills & Boon in the United States, romance novels were central to the category of light fiction. Rosman's American publisher deliberately released a new Rosman title each June, thereby pitching her novels explicitly as "summer reading", and reviewers responded accordingly, valuing the books for not pretending to be anything else. Romance was also a staple genre in the fiction magazines and women's magazines. The *Delineator*, for example, "paid a big price" for serialisation rights to Rosman's *Protecting Margot* and were willing to purchase her next serial story "at a figure 3,000 dollars higher".[8]

Australian authors made notable contributions to both the detective and romance sectors in the US market in the 1920s to 1940s period, and a small number continued well into the postwar years. The trajectories of their novels and their sometimes striking recognition in the US market is the subject of this chapter.

Fleeing the Country: Expatriate Crime Writers

Given the thousands of crime and mystery novels published across the English-speaking world in these decades, the Australian contribution was proportionally small, but by no means negligible. Writers such as Arthur J. Rees, Arthur Gask and Paul McGuire were recognised in the United States for a decade or more as successful, innovative practitioners of their art – and good sellers. For the Australian-born, expatriation remained a significant factor in overcoming the obstacles to being published in London and then in the United States. Rees, John G. Brandon, J.M. Walsh and Charles Rodda all became successful crime or thriller authors as expatriates between the wars, while Helen Simpson co-authored three murder mysteries with English novelist Clemence Dane, all published in America between 1928 and 1932.[9] Most expatriates became "English writers", at least as far as the market

---

6   Joseph McAleer, *Passion's Fortune: The Story of Mills & Boon* (Oxford: Oxford University Press, 1999), 42-47.
7   McAleer, *Passion's Fortune*, 59-73.
8   "Adelaide Author in America", *Southern Cross*, 9 March 1934.
9   Bruce Bennett and Anne Pender, *From a Distant Shore: Australian Writers in Britain 1820-2012* (Clayton, Vic.: Monash University Publishing, 2013), 36-40. Simpson's novels were *Enter Sir John* (Cosmopolitan Book Corp., 1928), *Author Unknown* (Cosmopolitan Book Corp., 1930), *Re-Enter Sir John* (Farrar & Rinehart, 1932).

was concerned. Others stayed at home but "expatriated" their fiction by eliminating or downplaying local references. By contrast, Arthur Gask began his career after moving from London to Adelaide in 1920 and set his novels locally even though they were written for the international marketplace. Arthur Upfield, another English migrant, was the most successful of all and most unusually his success was based at least in part on playing up the Australianness of his settings and of his central character, the part-Aboriginal, University of Queensland graduate, Detective Inspector Napoleon Bonaparte.

The most successful authors secured the support of a single publisher for successive titles, ideally a publisher with a dedicated crime list, often for more than a decade and typically at high levels of production, a novel a year or more. Rodda was at one stage producing three titles a year for Hodder & Stoughton, but he was also conscious that American publishers were generally reluctant to issue more than one title by an author in the publishing year – though in the crime field they would happily release one a year every year for extended periods.[10] A few authors, like Upfield, were able to deal with their American publishers directly, but for most Australian authors building a name and building sales meant a long-term relationship with one of the major English firms with a strong list in the area – Hodder & Stoughton, John Lane, Gollancz, Hutchinson, Heinemann – and then through their agents or agreements between publishers building a similar relationship with an American house. That did not mean the American firm would accept everything that had been published, even successfully, in the British market. Surviving correspondence – as in the case of Rodda below – indicates that the American publishers applied their own sense of what would work in the domestic market, for each individual book, for building an author's name, and for positioning the house itself.

Rees was the earliest among this group, with four titles appearing from the John Lane Co. in New York between 1916 and 1920 (John Lane was also their publisher in London). Rees worked as a journalist in Melbourne before leaving for England around 1910. Two of his early novels were co-authored with fellow Australian journalist John Reay Watson, *The Hampstead Mystery* (1916) and *The Mystery of the Downs* (1918), and the authors were highly praised on their American release. Either the jacket of *The Mystery of the Downs* or accompanying publicity appears to have created the impression among reviewers that the authors were former Scotland Yard detectives rather than former Australian journalists. But the novels themselves established the authors' credentials: "they have literary ability, as well as the skill to dig out the heart of a murder puzzle".[11] Rees next published two sole-authored novels with John Lane, *The Shrieking Pit* (1919), "a thriller of the first class", and *The Hand in the Dark* (1920), both of which were favourably reviewed and established Rees' reputation in America as an author in "the first rank of the writers of detective stories".[12]

Cleverly for an author with international ambitions, Rees' detective, who appeared subsequently in half a dozen novels, was half-American and half-English, "the famous

---

10 Laurence Pollinger (Curtis Brown London) to Alfred R. McIntyre (Little, Brown), 9 April 1934; Charles Rodda to McIntyre, 11 April 1934. Little, Brown & Co. Records, Houghton Library, Harvard University.
11 "Latest Works of Fiction", *New York Times*, 10 February 1918. Reviews in the *Los Angeles Times* (17 February 1918) and the *New York Times* (10 February 1918) both mention the ex-detectives detail.
12 *New York Times*, 18 May 1919; "Detective and Mystery Stories for Summer Reading", *New York Times*, 25 July 1920.

5 Mystery and Romance: The Market for Light Fiction Between the Wars

American detective" Grant Colwyn, who spoke like an Englishman.[13] The *New York Times* offered the fullest praise for American readers:

> Somebody ought to tell President Wilson about Mr. Rees's "The Hand in the Dark." Still, as he generally discovers for himself, perhaps by instinct, the best detective stories, it is unlikely that he will be long in finding this one … And if he read, as he probably did, Mr. Rees's previous novel, "The Shrieking Pit," it goes without saying that he will reach out for "The Hand in the Dark" as soon as he hears about it. For the author of these two novels has put himself by their means into the first rank of the writers of detective stories.[14]

In 1922, Dodd, Mead purchased John Lane's American operation and Rees became a Dodd, Mead author alongside G.K. Chesterton and Agatha Christie. Fourteen new, copyrighted titles and two reissues appeared from Dodd, Mead between 1922 and 1938 at an average of one a year until 1933. Rees was thus in the privileged position of having a single publisher for all his American titles, eighteen of his twenty novels in total, most published simultaneously with John Lane's English editions. At least six were also reprinted by Grosset & Dunlap between 1923 and 1930, with *The Mystery of the Downs* being reissued at least four times in 1928 alone.[15]

Rees' distinctive mark in the crowded mystery marketplace was fiction that mixed sensation, thriller and gothic elements with the tale of detection. As a review of *The Unquenchable Flame* (1926) put it: "Tall but exciting yarn concerned with 'cadaveric phenomena,' which are fully as creepy as they sound".[16] *Threshold of Fear* (1925) was described as a "super-thriller"; *Mystery at Peak House* (1933) was "strongly horrific, so-so deductive".[17] A couple of novels had more to do with romantic entanglements than crime, but Rees' primary reputation was as "a prolific and successful writer of mystery and crime stories" of the English kind.[18] *The Pavilion by the Lake* (1930) was "in the best tradition of English mystery stories … told in the quiet, unhurried, precise manner that distinguishes all Mr. Rees's stories".[19] A review of *Aldingham's Last Chance* (1933) began "Dear old England again", while Rees' final novel, *The Corpse that Traveled* (1938), was criticised for never rising above "British stolidity".[20] Although largely forgotten today, Rees was often praised for offering literary satisfaction as well as murder and mystery: for the *New York Times*, for example, *The Moon Rock* (1922), "besides being a well-handled mystery concerning a murder, is also a novel of some literary excellence".[21] By 1933, a reviewer in the *Los Angeles Times* could write that detective story readers would "sprint to the nearest bookshop or lending library" at the mere mention of Rees' name.[22] His Australian origins,

---

13 Arthur J. Rees, *The Shrieking Pit* (1918; Melbourne: Chimaera Publications, 2010), 8. Introduction to this edition by Sean Williams, iv.
14 "Detective and Mystery Stories for Summer Reading", *New York Times*, 25 July 1920.
15 Details of four printings from the Grosset & Dunlap 1928 edition.
16 "The Bookman's Guide to Fiction", *Bookman*, November 1926, 348.
17 Carty Ranck, *New York Herald Tribune*, 30 May 1926; "The Criminal Record", *Saturday Review of Literature*, 29 July 1933, 23: its one word summary was "Shuddery".
18 "The New Books", *Outlook*, 31 May 1922, 216.
19 William C. Weber, "Murder Will Out", *Saturday Review of Literature*, 11 October 1930, 232.
20 "The Bookman's Guide to Fiction", *Bookman*, March 1933, 305; "The Criminal Record", *Saturday Review of Literature*, 23 July 1938, 18. Its brief summary was "Slow motion".
21 *New York Times*, 7 May 1922.
22 "Three Thrillers", *Los Angeles Times*, 26 February 1933.

however, were invisible in the thoroughly English conventions within which he wrote, although he had earlier dedicated *The Shrieking Pit* to his sisters in Australia.

It is not clear when John Brandon left for London, but along with a fellow Australian expatriate in London, Coutts Armour, he became one of the many authors of the Sexton Blake mysteries. Brandon was extraordinarily prolific, with over sixty detective novels listed to his credit and many more children's titles, though even these are mainly detective stories.[23] In America, it was his adult detective mysteries and thrillers that appealed, with seven novels published, two by Brentano's and five by the high status Dial Press, between 1923 and 1935, in copyrighted editions. Brentano's advertised *The Big Heart* for at least four months from September to December 1923: a novel "for *everyone* to read, the novel that even the 'the hard-boiled professional book buyers' could not resist".[24] Brandon's characteristic feature was mixing comedy with mystery and suspense, inviting comparisons with P.G. Wodehouse. But he was also praised for his American characters and "New York argot", and for never confusing "British and Yankee slang", a test reviewers often applied to imported stories.[25] In *The Joy Ride* (1927), he repeated something like Rees' trick, making one of his detectives an American: "A modern 'Three Musketeers' with a Yale man in the rôle of d'Artagnan, this jolliest of mystery stories tells how the combined detective forces of London and New York were baffled by four youths, one girl and one bull-terrier".[26] The novel appeared with a striking modernist cover from The Dial Press, and had at least one reprinting.

Good reviews continued with *The Secret Brotherhood* (1928), "a thrilling mixture of detective work, Bolshevist fanatics' plots, high society life and daring blackmail",[27] and *The Silent House* (1928), based on Brandon's play of the same name which was performed in the United States in 1928 and 1929.[28] *Nighthawks!*, involving "two sinister Chinamen, several wily Greeks, a gigantic Hollander and two desperados from New York", was published by Brentano's in 1930.[29] But although his English career continued for another twenty years and another forty novels, many featuring "Inspector McCarthy of Scotland Yard", this release also marked the end of regular publication for Brandon in the United States. Only one more title appeared, after a gap of five years, *The One-Minute Murder*, an Inspector McCarthy mystery, released by The Dial Press in 1935. There is no clear evidence to suggest why his successful English career was no longer replicated in America - whether it was a question of changing tastes or changes in publishing networks - although his American connections might have been broken in the early thirties by changes in the industry. Brentano's folded as a publishing house in 1933, and in the same year founder Lincoln MacVeagh sold The Dial Press.[30]

---

23   AustLit lists 173 novels and novellas; 103 of these are tagged "children's fiction".
24   *New York Times*, 2 December 1923.
25   "Joy of Life", *New York Times*, 7 February 1926.
26   From the dust jacket front flap, *The Joy Ride* (New York: Lincoln MacVeagh The Dial Press, 1927).
27   "Detective Fiction", *Bookman*, December 1928, xliv.
28   *Springfield Republican*, 9 September 1928. Play: *New York Times*, 7 February 1928; *Washington Post*, 19 November 1928; *Los Angeles Times*, 20 March 1929. The play was co-authored with George Pickett.
29   Description of *Nighthawks!*, *Bookman*, March 1930, xxix.
30   Theodora Mills, "Brentano's", in *American Literary Publishing Houses, 1638–1899*, ed. Peter Dzwonkoski, Dictionary of Literary Biography, Vol. 49 (Detroit, MI: Gale Research, 1986), 66-67; Ernest Bevan Jr, "The Dial Press", in *American Literary Publishing Houses, 1900–1980*, ed. Peter Dzwonkoski, Dictionary of Literary Biography, Vol. 46 (Detroit, MI: Gale Research, 1986), 115-18.

5 Mystery and Romance: The Market for Light Fiction Between the Wars

A more revealing case perhaps, indicating both the opportunities and obstacles present in the American marketplace, is that of Charles Rodda. Rodda left Australia in 1919 for the United States, where, unusually, he became music critic for New York's *Musical America*. In New York he published a bushranger tale in one of the MacFadden magazines and other stories in *Munsey's* and *Brief Stories*, before relocating to England in 1925 or early 1926, at the beginning of his career as a novelist.[31] Rodda began writing detective novels under the name Gavin Holt, four of which appeared in America between 1930 and 1939, but each from a different publisher: *The Praying Monkey* (Dial Press, 1930), *Green Talons* (Bobbs-Merrill, 1931), *Death Takes the Stage* (Little, Brown, 1934) and *The Theme is Murder* (Simon & Schuster, 1939). In addition, in 1933, *Storm: An Epic Novel of the Sea* (Ronald Swain) appeared under his own name, while Putnam published *Invitation to Kill* by "Gardner Low" in 1937. Although often favourably received, none provided the breakthrough that would establish the Gavin Holt name despite the best efforts of author, agents and publishers. The lack of successive titles from the one publisher was a major disadvantage in a field where seriality was built into the book trade's expectations.

In a letter to the A.P. Watt agency in June 1927 after his first Gavin Holt novel had appeared from Hutchinson, Rodda explained that he intended to continue writing books under the pseudonym "in order to keep tales of the mystery and adventure type distinct from another type of novel that I wish to develop".[32] The habit is not an uncommon one in the genre fiction field – as we will see again with Maysie Greig – where names can function as "brands" for different generic products.[33] The consideration was no less important for the publisher attempting to establish a Gavin Holt "line" of thrillers. Bobbs-Merrill were keen not just to publish *Green Talons* in 1931 but to "establish the name of Gavin Holt as a writer of romances of international mystery and crime – the Oppenheim type".[34] They sought two further novels of the same kind, deciding against publishing *Storm* as a Gavin Holt novel because it was of a different type, then refusing it outright. The real difficulty was that they also found the next Gavin Holt novel – their option novel – disappointing: "It doesn't read at all like E. Phillips Oppenheim but it does read a good deal like Edgar Wallace ... It hasn't any great air of international crime, governments and famous men which marks *Green Talons* and which we think ought to mark the next Gavin Holt novel after it if we are to build this author".[35] Holt agreed that a new novel was preferable, but even though Hodder & Stoughton published each new book as it was finished across 1932 and 1933, the Bobbs-Merrill editors found them unsatisfactory: "Examination of the manuscript of *Red Eagle* ... has brought us great disappointment and some real distress

---

31 Correspondence between A.P. Watt and *Munsey's Magazine* (14 September 1925); Watt, the Paget Literary Agency (New York), and MacFadden Publications (June-December 1925); Watt, the Paget Agency and *Brief Stories* magazine (August 1926-February 1928): A.P. Watt Records 1888-1982, University of North Carolina. Rodda also wrote the book for an opera performed in Rochester, NY, in 1931: "Notes Here and Afield", *New York Times*, 3 May 1931. One earlier novel had appeared in Australia: *The Fortunes of Geoffrey Mayne* (Sydney: NSW Bookstall Co., 1919).
32 Rodda to W.P. Watt (A.P. Watt & Son), 25 June 1927, A.P. Watt Records.
33 John Frow, "Signature and Brand", *High-Pop: Making Culture into Popular Entertainment* (Malden, MA.: Blackwell, 2002), 56-74.
34 David L. Chambers (Bobbs-Merrill) to Ray Everitt (Curtis Brown New York), 1 May 1931. Bobbs-Merrill mss, Lilly Library, Indiana University, Curtis Brown Files.
35 Chambers to Everitt, 7 July 1931. Bobbs-Merrill mss.

because we have grown to like Mr. Rodda immensely and were keen to have another book in the vein of *Green Talons*".[36]

Despite the high degree to which generic tastes were shared, as the references to Oppenheim suggest, the British and American markets were distinct, and publishers read their own markets differently. The difficulties for Rodda were replayed after Little, Brown had agreed to publish *Death Takes the Stage* (a sequel to *Green Talons*) in early 1934.[37] Alfred McIntyre, president of Little, Brown, wrote to Laurence Pollinger, Rodda's London agent at Curtis Brown: "I hope very much that we are going to be able to build up a market for Holt here".[38] They decided against publishing the earlier novel *Dark Lady*, which Bobbs-Merrill had already rejected, and wrote "frankly" to Rodda that they preferred "novels with English and Continental scenes and characters".[39] They rejected *Trafalgar Square*, another Professor Bastion novel (in the line of *Green Talons* and *Death Takes the Stage*), again writing "frankly" that they did not feel it "a worthy successor": "We feel that the American reader would lose interest in the solution of the murders and that it would not add to your reputation here".[40] Despite the publisher's repeated desire to build a market for Gavin Holt in America, no new novels were accepted.

It was as thrillers rather than as pure detection that Holt's novels were welcomed, no doubt confirming the publishers' reading of the market. For *The Praying Monkey*, "There's murder, insurrection, jungles, a cave, a stone god, love and a last chapter explanation of the whole shooting match. All of which should provide predestined fans with thrills of the standard Latin-American brand"; for *Green Talons*, "As thrilling and entertaining as an Oppenheim tale of plots and counterplots that thrive on the Mediterranean"; and for *Death Takes the Stage*, "Master-criminals are always interesting and Continental color of this tale is lavishly laid on. Sleuthing a minor matter".[41] Curiously, *The Theme is Murder* was praised as "patterned after the best of the made-in-America variety" but also criticised as "soggily British".[42] *Invitation to Kill*, by contrast, was less thriller than sleuth, hence perhaps the change of pen-name for a title more modern in theme than the earlier books, a double mystery told by a writer and a psychiatrist. Published by Putnam, the book was copyrighted in the name of Henry Soskin, and a decade later, in 1947, Howell, Soskin & Co. would publish the next Gavin Holt novel to appear in the United States, *Send No Flowers*. At least one reviewer thought it "High-grade", but again there was no follow-up.[43] Rodda's final appearance in the American marketplace was as Eliot Reed, the pen-name he shared with the celebrated British crime writer Eric Ambler, with three novels published in Doubleday's Crime Club between 1950 and 1953.[44]

---

36 Chambers to Everitt, 20 January 1932. Bobbs-Merrill mss.
37 Laurence Pollinger (Curtis Brown London) to Alfred McIntyre (Little, Brown), 12 March 1934; McIntyre to Everitt, 24 March 1934. Little, Brown & Co. Records.
38 McIntyre to Pollinger, 24 March 1934. Little, Brown & Co. Records.
39 Jenkins to Pollinger, 10 April 1934. Little, Brown & Co. Records.
40 Jenkins to Rodda, 11 September 1934. Little, Brown & Co. Records.
41 *Boston Transcript*, 11 March 1931; *Bookman*, September 1931, vi; *Saturday Review of Literature*, 11 August 1934, 48.
42 *Time*, 8 January 1940, 60; *Saturday Review of Literature*, 16 December 1939, 18.
43 "The Criminal Record", *Saturday Review of Literature*, 24 May 1947, 32. One further Gavin Holt novel appeared in the United States, *Pattern of Guilt* in 1962, published by Walker, two years after its English release.
44 Hetherington, "In the Club", 32.

5 Mystery and Romance: The Market for Light Fiction Between the Wars

Murder in Adelaide

Adelaide-born Paul McGuire was another who travelled to England and began writing "English" detective fiction. His career is an extraordinary one as a poet and diplomat, a Catholic intellectual and activist, and a mystery and travel writer. McGuire spent several years in England around 1930, leading to a burst of novels published in London by Skeffington – two a year every year from 1931 to 1936 – but mostly written after his return to Australia. Other novels followed from Heinemann. He travelled widely in America, and had immediate success in the American marketplace with three of his first four novels being picked up by Brentano's and Coward-McCann, which acquired Brentano's publishing department in 1933.[45] *The Black Rose Murder* and *Three Dead Men* appeared in 1932 and *Death Tolls the Bell* in 1933. Doubleday followed with *Murder at High Noon* in 1935. Then, after McGuire's shift to Heinemann, two later novels were published by William Morrow, *A Funeral in Eden* in 1938 and *Enter Three Witches* in 1940. In between these, he published his lively, opinionated essay *Australia: Her Heritage, Her Future*, which the *Washington Post* reviewer thought had "all the earmarks of having been written for American, rather than for English readers".[46]

McGuire's novels were altogether in the golden age murder-mystery genre as the *Times*' introduction to *Death Tolls the Bell* suggests: "There are strange doings at Rympton Court, where Sir Appleby Frap is entertaining a house party".[47] Despite the perception of some detective tales as "soggily British", there was a real taste on the American side for the imagined "Englishness" of English mysteries, and an Australian could play the game. *Three Dead Men* was "the best Scotland Yard tale of the season", a "highly entertaining puzzle of the classic bulldog breed".[48] Possibly such reviews brought McGuire to Doubleday's attention, although there is no record as to why, as the largest publisher of crime, it released only one his novels. William Morrow, it appears, was prepared to invest heavily in him. *A Funeral in Eden*, a Morrow Mystery, was treated to an individualised publicity campaign, with a series of advertisements each telling part of the story from a different character's perspective.[49] Set on a tropical island, it was "the *South Wind* of detective stories" (the reference is to Norman Douglas' bestselling novel). Morrow quoted the *New Yorker*'s high praise: "Mr. McGuire has selected fastidiously every element needed in a superb mystery. *Recommended for the highest honors of the year*".[50]

McGuire could well have had a long-term relationship with Morrow, but his other intellectual interests intervened, and *Enter the Witches* – "another masterpiece of bafflement"[51] – was the last novel he wrote. In 1939, he toured the United States as the leader of Catholic Action, a "movement of the laity looking toward a Christian cooperative

---

45 Laura Masotti Humphrey, "Coward, McCann and Geoghegan", in *American Literary Publishing Houses, 1900–1980*, ed. Dzwonkoski, 98.
46 W.L. Schurz, "The Antipodean World", *Washington Post*, 24 September 1939. Frederick A. Stokes, the publisher, reported that 1836 copies had been sold to October 1940, probably a disappointing result given the reviews.
47 "New Mystery Stories", *New York Times*, 7 May 1933.
48 *New York Evening Post*, 3 September 1932; *New York Herald Tribune*, 25 September 1932.
49 The advertisements appeared in the *New York Times* (and probably elsewhere) across August 1938.
50 *New Yorker*, 20 August 1938, 63.
51 Isaac Anderson, "New Mystery Novels", *New York Times*, 25 February 1940. Anderson was a regular reviewer of crime and mystery across the period.

commonwealth".[52] Morrow nonetheless published McGuire's other works: a travelogue of Oceania in 1942, and in 1948 and 1949, two works on international relations. *Experiment in World Order* analysed the British Empire but "with a view to pointing up America's responsibilities in the postwar world".[53] McGuire was appointed Australia's first Ambassador to Italy in 1957.

Arthur Gask lived a quieter life as a dentist in Adelaide after migrating to Australia from London in 1920, but for a brief period in the 1930s he built a high reputation in the US mystery market.[54] From his first novel, he was picked up by Herbert Jenkins in London, and in the thirty years from 1923 the firm published thirty-four Gask titles – an average of more than one a year – often following serialisation in Australia. Many included as their detective Inspector Gilbert Larose of Scotland Yard, "a classic supersleuth".[55] In America, the Macaulay Co. issued six novels between 1931 and 1937, beginning with *The Lonely House*, which Herbert Jenkins had published two years earlier, and *Murder in the Night*, first published in England in 1923.[56] From that point on, titles appeared simultaneously or in the year following their London release: *Gentlemen of Crime* in 1933, *The Judgement of Larose* and *The Hidden Door* in 1935, and a little later, in 1937, *The Master Spy*, in which the retired Inspector Larose becomes a secret agent. Working through Curtis Brown New York, Gask received advances of $150 and half-share profits in second serial rights for *The Lonely House* and *Murder in the Night* in the United States, with Canada declared an open market. This level of advance was maintained for *The Hidden Door* in 1935, with cinema and dramatic rights added to second serial rights in the contract. These contracts suggest an ongoing commitment to the author. In 1936, Macaulay signed an agreement with Pioneer Publications, granting a three-year licence to Pioneer for $75 to reprint *Murder in the Night*.[57]

Macaulay promoted *The Lonely House* as an international bestseller – in England, Germany, Denmark – and they announced Gask himself as "the new sensation in mystery writers ... a new master of thrills".[58] Unusually, the novel's Australian origins were made visible: "An Australian thriller, and a good one".[59] *Murder in the Night*, again unusually, was set in Adelaide, a fact that struck *Outlook*'s reviewer: "Adelaide was in uproar – we mean the Australian city, not a lady of that name".[60] *The Judgment of Larose* was also judged favourably as "an absorbing, masterly example of detective fiction at its best, a mystery

---

52 "Catholic Action Head Here to Spread Move", *New York Times*, 5 January 1939.
53 *Westward the Course! The New World of Oceania* (reviewed by Grattan in the *Saturday Review of Literature*, 14 February 1942, 8); *Experiment in World Order* (reviewed by Grattan in *Nation*, 7 August 1948, 165); *There's Freedom for the Brave: An Approach to World Order*.
54 According to the *Australian Dictionary of Biography*, "while waiting for his patients, he began writing crime fiction": Michael J. Tolley, "Gask, Arthur Cecil (1869–1951)", *Australian Dictionary of Biography*, http://bit.ly/2JN3d4Z.
55 Advertisement, *New York Times*, 24 May 1931.
56 In England as *The Red Paste Murders*.
57 Contracts dated 31 July 1930, 23 March 1931, 27 March 1935 and 30 April 1936, in Macaulay Publishers' Literary Contracts (Including Permissions and Correspondence), Ohio State University Library, SPEC.RARE.CMS.296, Box 4. The 1935 contract specified an advance of £30, roughly equivalent to US$150 at this time.
58 Advertisement, *New York Times*, 24 May 1931. *The Hidden Door* was advertised under the heading "Mystery and Adventure", between a spy thriller and a western: *New York Times*, 28 July 1935.
59 *Outlook*, 27 May 1931, 121.
60 Walter R. Brooks, *Outlook and Independent*, 20 January 1932, 89.

5 Mystery and Romance: The Market for Light Fiction Between the Wars

novel whose merits are the equal of any thriller recently come to hand".[61] This, however, was the height of Gask's fame. The *New York Times* thought *Gentlemen of Crime* a "thin, stupid, repetitious tale"; *The Hidden Door* was "fair to middling"; *The Master Spy* had just enough thrills "to satisfy the average reader of spy stories".[62] Again, ongoing support in the British sphere did not translate directly to the US market, and the period of intense activity in the early to mid-thirties was not sustained. Falling sales, perhaps, matched the less enthusiastic reviews.

Another Adelaide author, A.E. Martin, began crime writing in middle age after a career as a journalist, circus and vaudeville promoter, travel agent and magazine publisher. His very first novel, *Sinners Never Die*, was picked up by Simon & Schuster for their Inner Sanctum mystery series. It appears Martin may have made a direct approach to Simon & Schuster, as the novel appeared in New York in 1944 before its serialisation in Australia, and Martin, unusually, had no English publisher. It was followed by *The Outsiders* in 1945 and *Death in the Limelight* the following year, both as Inner Sanctum mysteries (Fig. 5.1). Both were also reprinted by the Detective Book Club. Martin's novels were set in Australia, mostly in the world of circus, sideshows and vaudeville. As the *Saturday Review* summed up *The Outsiders*: "Murders in group of antipodean side-show freaks".[63] The novels were welcomed from the start. The often hard-to-please Isaac Anderson thought *Sinners Never Die* a "remarkable first novel" and asked for more; Simon & Schuster announced that the novel had been "unanimously selected as one of the ten best mysteries of 1944".[64] With *The Outsiders*, the *New Yorker* thought Martin was "shaping up into a first-rate mystery writer", and *Death in the Limelight* was even better, suggesting he was "almost ready to take his place beside his colleague from Down Under, Ngaio Marsh".[65] When crime writing expert Howard Haycraft reviewed the "evolution of the Whodunit" during the war, he included Martin in his list of "better newcomers" (alongside Upfield, "a promising beginner from Down Under").[66] Martin also published a number of stories in the celebrated *Ellery Queen's Mystery Magazine*, and in 1947 won one of its annual prizes for foreign writers alongside no lesser figure than Jorge Luis Borges.[67]

Less successful was his entry into Doubleday's Crime Club in 1952. *The Curious Crime* was poorly received on all sides and no more titles appeared with the Club. In 1954, however, one final title, *The Bridal Bed Murders*, appeared, again from Simon & Schuster, again a novel of "murder and conflict among the side show freaks of a traveling circus playing in a little Australian town", and again to good reviews.[68] While Martin's settings were never stereotypically Australian, they were usually noted as Australian and

---

61 E.C. Beckwith, "New Mystery Novels", *New York Times*, 3 March 1935.
62 *New York Times*, 20 August 1933; Isaac Anderson, "New Mystery Stories", 21 July 1935; Isaac Anderson, "New Mystery Stories", 31 October 1937.
63 "The Criminal Record", *Saturday Review of Literature*, 17 March 1945, 32.
64 Isaac Anderson, "The Crime Corner", *New York Times*, 17 September 1944; Simon & Schuster advertisement for *The Outsiders*, *New York Times*, 21 March 1945.
65 *New Yorker*, 31 March 1945, 84 and 23 February 1946, 91.
66 Howard Haycraft, "Evolution of the Whodunit in the Years of World War II", *New York Times*, 12 August 1945.
67 "Book Awards Listed", *New York Times*, 26 December 1947. The prize also involved publication in the Ellery Queen magazine and book publication by Little, Brown, but no record of the latter has been found. At least three stories appeared in *Ellery Queen's Mystery Magazine*: "The Flying Corpse", September 1947; "The Scarecrow Murders", April 1948; and "The Power of the Leaf", August 1948.
68 Advertisement, *New York Times*, 11 July 1954.

FREAKS, FAT AND BEARDED LADIES, giants, midgets and sword swallowers—all of us have seen them displayed on the platform at so much per look. A. E. Martin's* new novel shows how these bizarre "outsiders" live when the curtain is down—and what happens when murder strikes among them. Just Published.   Price $2.00

THE OUTSIDERS
by A. E. Martin

*Mr. Martin's first book, *Sinners Never Die*, was unanimously selected as one of the ten best mysteries of 1944

Figure 5.1 Advertisement for A.E. Martin's *The Outsiders* (New York: Simon & Schuster, 1945), from the *New York Times*, 8 April 1945.

their Australianness enjoyed. The new title suggests a renewal of Simon & Schuster's commitment to their author, and it was only Martin's death in 1955 that curtailed a longer publishing record and a stronger reputation in the United States.

Adelaide, the City of Churches, seems to have been unusually conducive to crime. Oxford-educated Scot J.I.M. Stewart held the position of Professor of English at the University of Adelaide between 1936 and 1945 before returning to the United Kingdom, but it was as crime writer Michael Innes that Stewart became internationally famous. He began writing his first detective novel on the voyage out to Australia. Between 1936 and

1946, twelve Michael Innes crime novels appeared from Gollancz in London, and from 1937 from Dodd, Mead in New York. Gollancz and Dodd, Mead would remain Innes' principal publishers right through to the 1980s, sharing almost fifty books. Fourteen were published by the end of the forties, all crime, all but two featuring Detective Inspector (later Sir) John Appleby, and most wearing the logo of Dodd, Mead's Red Badge Detective series. Stewart seems to have maintained a rather imperial attitude towards his provincial home.[69] Although there are Australian references in a number of his novels, the more typical setting is an Oxbridge-like college or the Scottish highlands. As *New York Times* crime reviewer Anthony Boucher put it, "the long-time Australian resident Michael Innes writes as an Englishman or, even more precisely, as a Scot".[70]

Innes was identified as a very particular kind of crime writer – erudite, witty and literary, "for those fastidious fans who exclude all but the works of Dorothy Sayers and R. Austin Freeman", at best "scintillating, shrewd and fearlessly and hilariously highbrow".[71] Of all the crime writers discussed here, he achieved the highest critical standing. On the appearance of his second novel, *Hamlet, Revenge!*, in 1937, Will Cuppy in the *New York Herald Tribune* pronounced it "the worthiest baffler in quite some time".[72] When *Lament for a Maker* appeared in 1938, Dodd, Mead quoted no less an authority than William Lyon Phelps, declaring Innes "The King of Mystery Writers". In 1946, the *Washington Post* selected him as the "Man of the Year in Murder".[73]

In Australia, however, J.I.M. Stewart is best remembered for his remarks at the beginning of his inaugural Commonwealth Literary Fund lecture on Australian literature in Adelaide in 1940: "I am most grateful to the Commonwealth Literary Fund for providing the funds to give this lecture on Australian literature, but unfortunately they have neglected to provide any literature – I will lecture therefore on *Kangaroo* by D.H. Lawrence".[74] But perhaps Australian literature had its revenge when it could. The entry in the *Oxford Companion to Australian Literature* reads "Stewart, John Innes Mackintosh, see 'Innes, Michael.'"[75]

Arthur Upfield and the Doubleday Crime Club

The most spectacular American success among the crime writers, however, was Arthur Upfield's career. Writing from Australia, with markedly Australian settings and an

---

69 Leigh Dale, *The English Men: Professing Literature in Australian Universities* (Canberra: Association for the Study of Australian Literature, 1997), 104.
70 Anthony Boucher, "Report on Criminals at Large", *New York Times*, 15 February 1953.
71 Paul Jordan-Smith, "I'll Be Judge You Be Jury", review of *Seven Suspects*, *Los Angeles Times*, 24 January 1937; Kay Irvin, "The New Mystery Stories", review of *The Daffodil Affair*, *New York Times*, 11 October 1942.
72 Quoted in Dodd, Mead publicity, *New York Times*, 3 October 1937.
73 Dorothy B. Hughes, "'46 Full of Mysteries – But Not All of It Good", *Washington Post*, 4 December 1946.
74 Quoted in Geoffrey Dutton, *Out in the Open: An Autobiography* (St Lucia: University of Queensland Press, 1994), 90. But see Philip Butterss, "Australian Literary Studies in the 1940s: The Commonwealth Literary Fund Lectures", *Australian Literary Studies* 30, no. 4 (November 2015): 115–17.
75 William H. Wilde, Joy Hooton, and Barry Andrews, eds, *The Oxford Companion to Australian Literature* (Melbourne: Oxford University Press, 1985), 654.

Aboriginal detective, Upfield published multiple titles with Doubleday over more than two decades, building a fan base in the United States and internationally that continues into the present.[76] Born in Gosport, England, Upfield arrived in Australia in 1911, aged twenty-one, and began writing journalism while working in the Australian outback. He turned to writing full time in 1931 and was able to live off his writing, not least off his American earnings. Upfield's success in the US market, however, was by no means immediate. In 1928, his agent in London, George Franklin, arranged to have his first published novel, *The House of Cain*, accepted by the Philadelphia-based publisher Dorrance.[77] Featuring a "serial wife-poisoning American millionaire" who hosts murderers on the run from the law in a remote South Australian homestead, the novel appeared in late 1929 following its publication by Hutchinson in London the previous year. It seems not to have sold well, even though the *Bookman* judged it "a veritable find for mystery and adventure lovers".[78] Almost a decade later, with Upfield's reputation established in Australia, his Sydney publisher Angus & Robertson attempted unsuccessfully to interest Dorrance in a second novel, *Wings Above the Diamantina*. In conveying the news to Upfield, Angus & Robertson quoted Dorrance's response: "it is something of greater Australian than American reading interest. His books are good, but we still have a quantity of *House of Cain*".[79] Upfield replied, "America wants either blood or sex and I am not at the present in the position to supply either".[80]

When *Murder Down Under* was published by Doubleday in 1943 it was as one of five books that Angus & Robertson's Walter G. Cousins forwarded to the firm's New York agent Leland Hayward. Cousins had been testing the American market for Upfield since the firm became his first publisher, with six titles released from 1936 to 1940.[81] Simon & Schuster had refused *The Bone is Pointed* in 1939, but Doubleday was responsive.[82] Travis Lindsey writes that the firm accepted three novels for immediate publication, took an option on the fourth, and rejected *The Bone is Pointed*, although it too would be published, in 1946.[83] The publishing record of five titles in 1943 to 1944 indicates perhaps that Doubleday accepted all five quite quickly and returned to *The Bone is Pointed* after their success. Their choice of title for *Murder Down Under* – released in Australia and England as *Mr Jelly's Business* – further suggests they saw from the beginning the opportunity for Upfield's distinctive "brand" in the crowded crime fiction marketplace. It appeared in January 1943, *Wings Above the Claypan* (the retitled *Wings Above the Diamantina*) in May and *The Mystery of Swordfish Reef* in November. These were followed by *Winds of Evil* in autumn 1944 and *No Footprints in the Bush* (originally *Bushranger of*

---

76 The sustained American interest in Upfield is well explained and exemplified in Kees de Hoog and Carol Hetherington, eds, *Investigating Arthur Upfield: A Centenary Collection of Critical Essays* (Newcastle-Upon-Tyne: Cambridge Scholars Publishing, 2012).
77 Travis B. Lindsey, "Arthur William Upfield: A Biography", PhD thesis, Murdoch University, 2005, 48.
78 "Notes on New Books", *Bookman*, January 1930, xxvi.
79 Lindsey, "Arthur William Upfield", 137. Angus & Robertson (A & R) to Upfield, 20 April 1937. Angus & Robertson Collection, Mitchell Library, State Library of NSW, MS3269, Box 82.
80 Lindsey, "Arthur William Upfield", 137. Upfield to A & R, 3 June 1937. A & R Collection.
81 *Wings Above the Diamantina* (1936), *Mr Jelly's Business* (1937), *Winds of Evil* (1937), *The Bone is Pointed* (1938), *The Mystery of Swordfish Reef* (1939) and *Bushranger of the Skies* (1940).
82 Hetherington, "In the Club", 41.
83 Lindsey, "Arthur William Upfield", 156. Upfield himself wrote that Doubleday accepted four and took an option on three others; later he mentions only four books. Doubleday, Doran & Co. existed from 1927 until 1946 when the firm became Doubleday & Co.

5 Mystery and Romance: The Market for Light Fiction Between the Wars

the Skies) in spring. All were published as part of the highly successful Doubleday Crime Club. Upfield's relationship with Doubleday would continue until 1965, with ten books in the 1940s alone and twenty-five in total. The United States became his primary market and readership. With *Death of a Swagman* in 1945, Doubleday caught up with Upfield's new novels and thence became his first publisher. They negotiated multiple reprints with the Unicorn Mystery Book Club and the Detective Book Club, and from May 1952 acted as Upfield's agent in the United States.[84]

The Doubleday Crime Club had been founded in 1928 – "the most important single event in the publication of hardcover mystery novels in the United States" – and by the 1940s it had achieved market dominance with "the largest mystery output under one imprint". As Carol Hetherington writes, "an aspiring writer could hardly do better than gain the support of this formidable marketing machine".[85] The Crime Club published four titles per month, forty-eight in a year. Upfield also developed a close relationship with Crime Club editor Isabelle Taylor, who edited sympathetically and in detail, with a "thorough knowledge of the craft of crime fiction".[86] A publishing relationship with the Club offered earnings far greater than were possible in the Australian or English markets. In six months alone, Upfield's first novel in the Club, *Murder Down Under*, earned around $1200 after taxes were deducted (based on regular sales of 6517 and Crime Club sales of 4291 copies).[87] The advance for *The Devil's Steps* (1946) was $600; Upfield claimed it sold 15,000 copies and a further 20,000 in the Unicorn reprint.[88] Whereas the average sales for the regular trade edition of a mystery novel were around 3000, Upfield put his own sales by the late 1940s at above 7000: "From 26,000 of [*Murder Down Under*] I came down to 7,000 for [*No Footprints in the Bush*] and since have crept up a little with and following *Death of a Swagman* [1945]".[89] The reprints Doubleday negotiated could also be lucrative: the Mystery Guild guaranteed $2000 to cover 40,000 copies, while Penguin, through the New American Library, offered $1000 for rights to reprint *Death of a Swagman*. Upfield later claimed this edition had sold 120,000 copies.[90]

Although many reviews contained reservations, the early novels made an impact and Upfield's distinctiveness within the generic field was emphasised. As the *New Yorker* put it reviewing *Murder Down Under*, "Most refreshing mystery to appear in a long time".[91] Sometimes the praise was as good as it gets: "a powerful thriller with unusual background, fine detection, honest to goodness horror and a climax you won't forget so soon, all adding up to Grade A entertainment in the gooseflesh field".[92] But the novels were by no means always a hit with the reviewers, including the authoritative regulars already referenced in this chapter such as Isaac Anderson in the *New York Times* and Will Cuppy in the

---

84 Hetherington, "In the Club", 39.
85 Hetherington, "In the Club", 37–38. The two quotations included by Hetherington are from Anthony Boucher, "Criminals at Large", *New York Times*, 5 April 1953, and Doubleday editor Isabelle Taylor, "Mystery Midwife: The Crime Editor's Job", in *The Art of the Mystery Story*, ed. Howard Haycraft (New York: Carroll & Graf, 1946), 292.
86 Hetherington, "Bony at Home and Abroad: The Arthur Upfield Phenomenon", *Journal of the Association for the Study of Australian Literature (JASAL)* 9 (2009): 6.
87 Hetherington, "In the Club", 39; Lindsey, "Arthur Upfield", 159.
88 Lindsey, "Arthur William Upfield", 173.
89 Upfield to A & R, 2 January 1948, A & R Collection, quoted in Lindsey, "Arthur William Upfield", 179.
90 Hetherington, "In the Club", 40; Lindsey, "Arthur William Upfield", 178.
91 *New Yorker*, 23 January 1943, 60.
92 Will Cuppy, review of *Winds of Evil*, *New York Herald Tribune*, 5 March 1944.

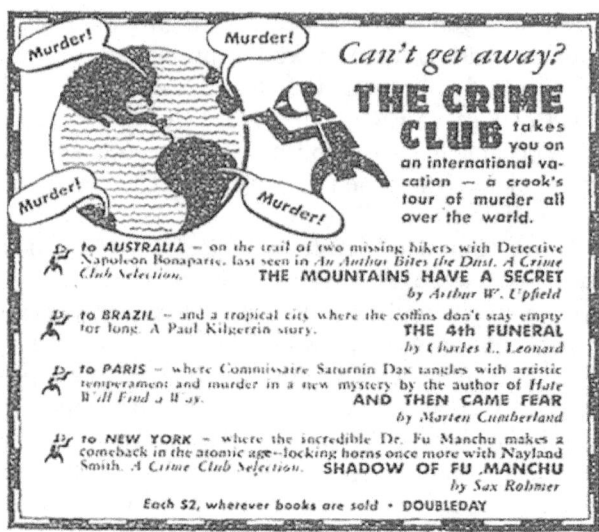

Figure 5.2 Arthur Upfield in the Doubleday Crime Club. *New York Times*, 22 August 1948.

Herald Tribune. Anderson, in particular, was impatient with Upfield's emphasis on the Australian "scenic background".[93] The good reviews were punctuated by judgements that the latest novel was "below par", "a disappointment", or "Grade-B Upfield".[94] But even these comments are clues to Upfield's overall success, testifying to the ways in which the cluster of novels published in the mid-forties had established an Upfield brand, identified powerfully with his detective "Bony", the part-Aboriginal Detective Inspector Napoleon Bonaparte, in a manner that was stronger than the weakness of any particular book. All the Doubleday titles were Bony novels. Like other Australian novelists, Upfield engaged a cuttings agency to forward American reviews and other notices, and in August 1944, with the earlier novels now out in the United States, he wrote to Angus & Robertson that "the lessons taught by the mass of reviews from the USA are being kept in mind" as he worked on his new novel, *Death of a Swagman*.[95]

Hetherington has argued there is little evidence to suggest American readers or reviewers were interested in Upfield's novels primarily because of their Australian dimensions – "genre not geography was their passport".[96] They were successful as crime fiction first and foremost and this depended in turn on the large-scale structures that comprised the American crime fiction industry, the "close-knit network of crime devotees, publishers, magazines and reviewers" with Doubleday and its Crime Club at its centre.[97] Doubleday's publicity had introduced Upfield as "Australia's Leading Mystery Story

---

93   Isaac Anderson, "Crime Corner", review of *Wings Above the Claypan*, *New York Times*, 16 May 1943.
94   Review of *Winds of Evil*, *New Yorker*, 4 March 1944, 84; review of *No Footprints*, *New Yorker*, 4 November 1944, 88; review of *The Mountains Have a Secret*, "The Criminal Record", *Saturday Review of Literature*, 18 September 1948, 39.
95   Upfield to A & R, 7 August 1944. A & R Collection. Lindsey, "Arthur William Upfield", 160.
96   Hetherington, "In the Club", 43.
97   Hetherington, "Bony", 5.

5 Mystery and Romance: The Market for Light Fiction Between the Wars

Writer", and reviewers followed their cue. For *Murder Down Under* they added "Particularly timely right now in view of Australia's sudden prominence", that is, due to the war. But otherwise it was the book's place in the Crime Club rather than its Australianness that was highlighted. As an advertisement for a later novel had it, the club offered "a crook's tour of murder all over the world" (Fig. 5.2).

The Australian settings and Aboriginal Australian detective in Upfield's novels worked generically in the way distinctive locations and detectives do in so much crime fiction, and there is evidence to suggest Upfield was ready to tone down Bony's mixed race characteristics under pressure from Doubleday: in a 1948 letter he wrote that "America has been harping at me to evade as much as possible Bony's mixed race" and that he had done so "rigidly" for *An Author Bites the Dust* in which Bony had to mix with "literary snobs".[98] At the same time, it would be a mistake to underestimate the extent to which the novels' Australian backgrounds were critical not just in defining the Upfield brand but in their own right as a point of narrative, even pedagogical attention. If there was no prior or deep interest in Australia among American readers, the interest Upfield's novels themselves created could "attach" his readers – and his publisher – to his novels over successive titles, sustaining their reception, as reviews suggest, even when the mystery and detection elements faltered: "Full of information about life in the bush, but the motivation is just too silly"; "A bit slow, but full of those Down Under details so agreeable to Upfield admirers".[99] As the final comment suggests, reviewers quite early had a sense of "Upfield admirers" and "Bonaparte fans", dedicated readers who would stay with the author or his detective even when individual novels were "below par".[100] Indeed, the "somewhat prima-donna-like person of Inspector Bonaparte [was] becoming one of detective fiction's more colourful characters".[101] Upfield is one of only a small number of authors in this study of whom we can say they genuinely had an American career and not merely a sequence of American editions. He was admitted to the Mystery Writers of America Inc., and in 1962 Doubleday presented him with a pair of gold cufflinks engraved with his initials and the logo of the Crime Club.[102] In the estimation of American scholar John G. Cawelti, "those five or six Upfields which fully develop the magical combination of Australian landscape, cultural conflict and the ambiguous relationship of law, loyalty, and justice are among the major achievements of the genre".[103]

Upfield was joined in the Doubleday Crime Club in the 1940s by a number of other authors with Australian connections. "Margot Neville" was the pen-name of Australian-born sisters Margot and Ann Neville Goyder. They spent an extended period in England between the wars, publishing light romantic comedies, three of which were

---

98 Upfield to Charles Lemon, 2 January 1948. Charles Lemon Collection, Battye Library, WA, MS 2138A. Lindsey, "Arthur William Upfield", 180.
99 Quotations in order: review of *Wings Above the Claypan*, *New Yorker*, 15 May 1943, 80; Elizabeth Bullock, review of *Wings Above the Claypan*, *Book Week*, 9 May 1943, 8; review of *Winds of Evil*, *Saturday Review of Literature*, 11 March 1944, 29; review of *The Widows of Broome*, *New Yorker*, 21 January 1950, 104; review of *The Bone is Pointed*, *New Yorker*, 25 January 1947, 88.
100 Review of *Death of a Swagman*, *New Yorker*, 20 October 1945, 115.
101 Review of *The Bachelors of Broken Hill*, *New York Herald Tribune*, 3 December 1950.
102 Carol Hetherington, "'In Their Different Ways, Classics': Arthur Upfield's Detective Fiction", in *Investigating Arthur Upfield*, ed. de Hoog and Hetherington, 211.
103 John G. Cawelti, "Murder in the Outback: Arthur W. Upfield", in *Investigating Arthur Upfield*, ed. de Hoog and Hetherington, 18.

released successfully in the United States to 1930 – "light fiction that is brazenly and audaciously light".[104] Returning to Australia before World War II, they began writing detective fiction. One novel – *Lena Hates Men*, the first Inspector Grogan story – appeared in the Mystery House imprint from Arcadia House publishers in 1943, before its appearance in England the following year (as *Murder in Rockwater*).[105] From 1944 to 1966, twenty-one titles appeared from Geoffrey Bles in London (all but seven with "Murder" in the title). Doubleday began publishing Margot Neville in 1949 with *Murder in a Blue Moon*, followed by *Murder of a Nymph* (1950), *Murder Before Marriage* (1951), *Diving Rod for Murder* (1952) and *Murder of the Well-Beloved* (1953).[106]

Although set in Sydney, the "Margot Neville" novels made little of Australia's distinctiveness or exotic potential. Reviewing *Murder in a Blue Moon*, Elizabeth Bullock wrote that "Except for the fact that you're told it's in Australia and that it's summer in January, you might think you were reading about something that happened at a waterfront estate at Oyster Bay or Greenwich".[107] Otherwise, Australia seemed at most an occasion for reviewers to have a bit of fun: "a blend of good Australian horse sense and fluttery femininity"; "Slippery people, these Australians".[108] *Murder of a Nymph* and *Murder Before Marriage* were well received – Bullock in the *New York Times* announced that with the former, "Margot Neville joins the ranks of solid writers in the mystery field".[109] The other novels struggled: "*Diving Rod for Murder* abandons the police novel for pure hysteria, with an absurd and unfair plot, tastelessly overwritten prose, and a new all-time high in Idiot Heroines".[110] Most striking perhaps is the contrast between the authors' American and English publication records – Geoffrey Bles published thirteen further titles following *Murder of the Beloved*.

In 1950, reviewing another Australian crime novel, *The Glass Spear* by Sidney Hobson Courtier, reviewer and novelist Anthony Boucher began: "With Arthur W. Upfield, A.E. Martin and Margot Neville in full production, Australia is becoming an important source of mystery novels. Many readers (including this enthusiastic reviewer) are fascinated by these novelistic glimpses of a civilization so much like our own, yet at times so colourfully different".[111] A few years later, Upfield and Martin were again singled out for praise, for giving mystery readers a glimpse of Australia, when Boucher reviewed two new Australian contributions, Charlotte Jay's *Beat Not the Bones* (Harper) and Bant Singer's *You're Wrong, Delaney* (Crown).[112] But leaving Michael Innes aside, Upfield was the only author from this period who sustained a reputation in America beyond the immediate postwar years.

---

104 *Safety First* (Houghton Mifflin, 1924), *Kiss Proof* (Robert M. McBride, 1929), *Giving the Bride Away* (Robert M. McBride, 1930). Quotation: J.L.G., review of *Giving the Bride Away*, *New York Evening Post*, 31 May 1930.

105 Reviewed (unfavourably) *New York Times*, 9 May 1943. The Mystery House imprint was launched by popular fiction publisher Arcadia in August 1940, William F. Deeck, "Mystery House", *Murder at 3 cents a Day: An Annotated Crime Fiction Bibliography of the Lending Library Publishers: 1936–1967*, http://bit.ly/2sZ2nIA.

106 *Murder of a Nymph* also appeared from Pocket Books in a twenty-five cent edition in 1951.

107 E.B., "Criminal at Large: Summer in January", *New York Times*, 29 May 1949.

108 Nancie Matthews, review of *Murder Before Marriage*, *New York Times*, 11 February 1951; review of *Divining Rod for Murder*, *Kirkus Reviews*, 1 December 1951, 689; review of *Murder of the Well-Beloved*, *Kirkus Reviews*, 1 September 1953, 599.

109 Elizabeth Bullock, "Criminals at Large: Murder Down Under", *New York Times*, 12 February 1950.

110 Anthony Boucher, "Criminals at Large", *New York Times*, 10 February 1952.

111 Anthony Boucher, "Done in Down Under", *New York Times*, 9 April 1950.

112 Anthony Boucher, "Report on Criminals at Large", *New York Times*, 15 February 1953.

5 Mystery and Romance: The Market for Light Fiction Between the Wars

Figure 5.3 "America's best loved novelist". Advertisement for Alice Grant Rosman's *The Sleeping Child* (New York: Minton, Balch, 1935), from the *New York Times*, 23 June 1935.

"America's Best Loved Novelist": Alice Grant Rosman

While Upfield's American career is remarkable, in some ways it is less spectacular than those of two Australian-born writers of romance fiction, Alice Grant Rosman and Maysie Greig. Rosman had fourteen of her seventeen novels published in the United States between 1928 and 1941 with an unusually sustained record of favourable reviews and bestselling success. Greig's record is truly extraordinary, even given that the rapid production of new books is characteristic of her field. More than 120 different titles were published in the United States under her own name or pseudonyms, the first in 1924, the last new title in 1966. Multiple reissues saw over 200 editions in total. Around sixty new Greig titles were published by Doubleday alone between 1933 and 1943, often five or six titles in a single year.

Although her output was much smaller, it was Rosman who in June 1935 could be claimed as "America's best loved novelist" (Fig. 5.3).[113] The claim was her publisher's, to

---

113 Putnam's, advertisement for Rosman's *The Sleeping Child*, *New York Times*, 23 June 1935.

be sure, but there is evidence to suggest that it was not mere hyperbole. Unlike many of the books and authors claimed as bestsellers, often in attempt to make them so, Rosman's novels achieved high sales for successive titles over more than a decade. She is an excellent example of what the American market could mean to an Anglo-Australian author over and above what the British and dominion market could offer.

Rosman was born in South Australia in 1882 and began writing for local and then national newspapers and magazines. She left for London in 1911 and published her first novels in 1915 and 1916. In 1927, in her mid-forties, she turned to fiction writing full time. As Rosman herself put it in an interview with an Australian newspaper, with her third novel, *The Window*, published in 1928, she "had the great fortune to come into contact with a new and enterprising publishing firm in New York named Minton and Balch".[114] The firm, she added, "seems determined to make my fortune for me as well as its own". It appears that she dealt directly with them, although by 1934 she had a New York agent.[115] Minton, Balch & Co. had been established in 1924. Although it became best known for non-fiction and illustrated children's books it also developed a small fiction list and Rosman was one of its most popular novelists.[116] When advertising her second novel in the US market, *Visitors to Hugo*, in July 1929, Minton, Balch announced that *The Window* had been the "best loved novel of 1928". The *New York Times* agreed, calling it "one of the most ingratiating of last year's novels". *The Window* was "in its 71st Thousand" of copies printed, and by December it was in its "14th large printing".[117] *Visitors to Hugo* itself was "A Best Selling Novel Ever Since Publication", with 25,000 copies sold three weeks in advance of its release, a sixth print run two weeks after publication, and an eighth a few months later. It was "Welcome in 50,000 Homes".[118]

Minton, Balch's enthusiastic advertising campaigns suggest their commitment to Rosman – to making her fortune and their own – and the author's gratitude to her publisher is indicated by the fact that she dedicated her 1931 novel, *The Sixth Journey*, to The Black Swan, the firm's colophon.[119] Rosman also toured America at the firm's invitation in 1933, for the release of *Protecting Margot*. From the beginning, as mentioned earlier, Minton, Balch chose the strategy of releasing a new Rosman novel as the highlight of their summer list in late June each year, and this in itself became newsworthy in the book news columns.[120] The publishers could boast that "Every year the new Rosman story captivates the country."[121]

In 1930, the firm merged with Putnam and by 1934 the two partners, Melville Minton and Earle H. Balch, gained financial control of the older firm. The Minton, Balch imprint was retained for certain books until 1938, including Rosman's novels. All of her fourteen

---

114 Quoted in Leslie Rees, "An Australian Novelist. Alice Rosman and Her Work", *West Australian*, 2 May 1931.
115 In an article in the *Southern Cross* (Adelaide), "Adelaide Author in America", 9 March 1934, Rosman talks of writing stories for the American magazines at the behest of her New York agent.
116 Edward J. Hall, "Minton, Balch and Company", *American Literary Publishing Houses, 1900–1980*. ed. Dzwonkoski, 237.
117 Minton, Balch advertisements, *New York Times*, 21 July 1929 and 8 December 1929; "Attractive People", *New York Times*, 16 June 1929.
118 Advertisements above plus *New York Times*, 23 June and 3 November 1929.
119 "Book Notes", *New York Times*, 26 June 1931.
120 "Gossip of the Book World", *Los Angeles Times*, 24 May 1931; "Book Notes", *New York Times*, 26 June 1936.
121 Minton, Balch advertisement for *Benefits Received*, *New York Times*, 26 June 1942.

5 Mystery and Romance: The Market for Light Fiction Between the Wars

books with the firm, released in copyrighted editions, were romances, except for *Jock the Scot* (1931), a dog story albeit with a romance plot, and Rosman's final US title, *Nine Lives* (1942), the story of a London cat during the Blitz. Only one, *Sixth Journey*, contained Australian characters, and the books were often praised in America for their portrayal of "the gentle loveliness and friendliness of England" and "the nicest sort of English family life".[122] Between 1928 and 1932, six of her novels appeared in London from Mills & Boon, just as the firm was consolidating its publishing into the field of women's romance fiction. For the remaining novels, Hodder & Stoughton was Rosman's English publisher.

The Australian newspaper article mentioned above gives US sales of over 70,000 for *The Window* and over 80,000 for *Visitors to Hugo* compared to English sales of between 30,000 and 40,000. These English sales were compared in turn to the average sales of "the vast majority of well-established authors of the better type", 2500 to 3000 copies.[123] With *The Young and Secret* (1930), an elegant photograph of the author accompanied reviews in the *New York Times*, and reviewers began to remark on Rosman's "constantly growing audience", her "large circle of readers".[124] *The Young and Secret* also appeared alongside Henry Handel Richardson's *The Way Home* in the *New York Sun*'s list of ten outstanding novels of 1930.[125] Rosman's "name on a novel [came] to stand for a very definite thing".[126]

Scribner's, Doubleday's and Brentano's bookshops all reported *The Sixth Journey* among their five or six bestselling titles in July–August 1931, while the 1932 offering, *Benefits Received*, appeared in bestsellers lists (when only three fiction titles were listed) in New York, Boston, Washington, Chicago and beyond, across July and August. *Protecting Margot* (1933), *Somebody Must* (1934), *The Sleeping Child* (1935), *Mother of the Bride* (1936), *Truth to Tell* (1937), *Unfamiliar Faces* (1938) and *William's Room* (1939) all appeared in the *New York Times* fiction bestseller list at least once. In August 1937, six weeks after its release, *Truth to Tell* was listed second, behind Kenneth Roberts' *Northwest Passage* but ahead of Virginia Woolf's *The Years*, John Steinbeck's *Of Mice and Men* and Margaret Mitchell's *Gone with the Wind* (more than a year after *its* initial publication).[127] *Protecting Margot* sold 25,000 copies in its first thirty-six days, and with the appearance of *Somebody Must*, Minton, Balch claimed sales of over 300,000 copies of Rosman's previous six novels with "well over a million" readers in America alone.[128] With this latter novel, the Book-of-the-Month Club also began to pay attention, including the title in its monthly recommendations: "Alice Grant Rosman wrote *Visitors to Hugo* and thousands read and loved it. And they have been reading and loving the Rosman work ever since."[129]

Rosman's novels appeared at a significant moment, before women's romance fiction had fully emerged as a distinct sector within American book publishing but when light

---

122 Review of *The Window*, Frances Bartlett, *Boston Transcript*, 21 July 1928; review of *William's Room*, Beatrice Sherman, *New York Times*, 18 June 1939.
123 Rees, "An Australian Novelist".
124 Fanny Butcher, *Chicago Tribune*, and *American News Trade Journal*, quoted in a bookshop advertisement, *New York Times*, 27 August 1933.
125 *New York Sun*, 5 May 1931, Henry Handel Richardson Papers, National Library of Australia, NLA MS 133, Press Cuttings Albums. The list was chosen by librarians.
126 Review of *The Sixth Journey*, "Fiction", *Saturday Review of Literature*, 27 June 1931, 931.
127 "Book Notes", *New York Times*, 11 July, 29 July, 12 August, 12 August 1931; "The Best-Selling Books", *New York Times*, 8 August 1937.
128 Putnam's advertisement, *New York Times*, 13 August 1933; Minton, Balch advertisement, *New York Times*, 24 June 1934.
129 *Book-of-the-Month Club* News, July 1934.

fiction – or "summer reading" – was increasingly visible as a distinct category. Importantly, it was still conceived within the bounds of general fiction and thus advertised and reviewed alongside literary fiction, not as part of a separate publishing economy as would later be the case. Rosman's novels were thus reviewed in the book pages of the major papers, and across her whole career they received a remarkably consistent level of praise and thoughtful criticism (as well as a bit of fun). Some reviewers happily assigned the novels to their rightful category: "a fluffy tale which should meet the clamor for hot-weather entertainment"; "the perfect present for a convalescent"; "a sprightly hammock tale, a book to be picked up at leisure and dropped at pleasure, one which can serve as a pacifier on a restless day. And it must be said in its favour, that it pretends no more".[130] But others were pushed further, towards defining the qualities that made the novels *more* than mere fluff.

> Miss Rosman's novels are, of their kind, as good as are being done today. They are not "sticky" or mushy. They have real sweetness and real sentiment to the exact degree which the modern reader will allow in his modern novels. They might be read aloud to any old-fashioned Sunday school class, and yet there is nothing goody-goody about them. In a word, they are superb fluff.[131]

Butcher and Margaret Wallace in the *New York Times* reviewed successive titles and delighted in trying to capture Rosman's distinctive qualities as a writer. For Wallace, reviewing *Mother of the Bride*:

> Alice Grant Rosman's growing popularity in this country is warranted by the fashion in which she sustains the level of her performance. Comparatively few writers of this kind of light and dexterous romance can be counted upon so confidently to produce an entertaining story without seeming at the same time to repeat a formula ... Her writing is so deceptively urbane and facile that one may fail to realize how wide a range of subject-matter she has really covered in half a dozen of her recent novels, or what a variety of moods she has contrived to explore.
>
> On the surface Miss Rosman's writing is nearly always light and tender and gracefully romantic. But just underneath the surface – and not too far underneath, at that – there is apt to be a touch of malice which gives bite to the whole thing.[132]

Or Gladys Graham reviewing *William's Room* for the *Saturday Review of Literature*:

> Ever since her "Visitors to Hugo" several years ago, Mrs. Rosman's novels have been doing much to fill the ever-present need for "light entertainment" in fiction that intelligent readers can enjoy. They maintain a delicate, difficult balance between the over-sophisticated, wise-cracking type, on the one hand, and the all too sweetly sentimental on the other.[133]

---

130 Fanny Butcher, review of *Somebody Must*, *Chicago Tribune*, 23 June 1934; review of *Mother of the Bride*, *Time*, 29 June 1936, 66; review of *The Window*, *Bookman*, September 1938, xviii.
131 Fanny Butcher, review of *Benefits Received*, *Chicago Daily Tribune*, 25 June 1932.
132 Margaret Wallace, "Miss Rosman's New Romance", *New York Times*, 28 June 1936.
133 Gladys Graham, review of *William's Room*, "Good Light Reading", *Saturday Review of Literature*, 24 June 1939, 14.

5 Mystery and Romance: The Market for Light Fiction Between the Wars

Despite such strong reviews for her last romance, no new books appeared after the war. Rosman was by then in her early sixties and perhaps felt that the world – or the romance market – had changed with the war, but we have no evidence as to why her writing or publishing ceased.[134]

"Ardent Love and Violent Heartaches": Maysie Greig

Maysie Greig's American publishing history offers a mini-history of popular fiction publishing in the United States across the twentieth century. Greig was born in Sydney in 1901 and began writing as a journalist with the Sydney *Sun* until leaving for England in 1920. She moved to New York in 1923 with her American first husband, then lived in Boston where her first two novels were issued by Small, Maynard & Co., a reputable literary and general publisher. *Peggy of Beacon Hill* appeared in 1924 and *The Luxury Husband* in 1927, the year the firm filed for bankruptcy. Both were first editions, both were filmed in Hollywood.[135] Later Greig lived in Greenwich Village, divorced, remarried, and divorced again, travelled widely, and lived in England. In 1935, she appeared on the front page of the *American Weekly*, a story magazine that boasted the "Greatest Circulation in the World", with her story "Kid Sisters Don't Count" (Plate 7).[136] In 1937, Greig met and married Australian-born journalist Max Murray in New York. The couple returned to England, then Australia in 1948, although they often travelled – staying at the Algonquin in New York City.

Greig's presence in New York no doubt helped her contract with the relatively new firm, The Dial Press, which had begun publishing in 1924 as a general fiction publisher rather than one specialising in genre fiction. It first reissued *The Luxury Husband* in 1928, then a series of new titles, mostly first editions, beginning with *Satin Straps* in 1929, then multiple titles each year to 1932, eight new novels in total. *Satin Straps* – "the adventures of a shop girl and model" – was reviewed in the *New York Times* as "melodramatic, improbable, and not a little cheap", and yet the reviewer could not help liking the book: the story "runs along quickly and amusingly" and all the heroine's wishes come true "in such an exciting fashion that it is fun to watch her".[137] This would become a familiar note in reviews of Greig's novels.

Founder Lincoln MacVeagh sold The Dial Press in 1933. In the same year, Greig's first title appeared from Doubleday. This was the "making" of Maysie Greig as an author in the American marketplace, with at least sixty novels following from Doubleday, including three under the pseudonym Jennifer Ames, between 1933 and 1943, often five or six titles in a single year. Many were set in New York or Hollywood; others made a virtue of their Englishness. In the earlier years, Doubleday also arranged cheaper hardcover reprints with Grosset & Dunlap, and later through their own subsidiaries, Sun Dial Press (twenty-one

---

134 Rosman lived until 1961. She suffered severe arthritis which might also have affected her capacities for writing. Suzanne Edgar, "Rosman, Alice Trevenen (1882–1961)", *Australian Dictionary of Biography*, http://bit.ly/2HNixcY.
135 Martha Rutledge, "Greig, Maysie Coucher (1901–1971)", *Australian Dictionary of Biography*, vol. 14, 1996, http://bit.ly/2JJp0aF. The title of this section comes from a review of *Odds on Love* by Maysie Greig, *New York Times*, 25 October 1936.
136 *American Weekly*, 17 September 1935.
137 "Shop Girl Adventures", *New York Times*, 9 June 1929.

titles from 1937 to 1941) and Blakiston-Triangle Books (eighteen titles, "thirty-nine-cent hardcover" reprints, from 1940 to 1946), and sometimes paperback sales as well.[138] Greig's *Doctor's Wife*, for example, was first published by Doubleday in 1937 then reprinted by the Sun Dial Press in 1938, by Blakiston in 1940 and under the Triangle Books imprint in 1942, and finally by Pocket Books – which used a kangaroo as its logo – in 1947 (a twenty-five cent paperback).

Bruce Bennett and Anne Pender describe Greig as "the most Americanised of Australian romance writers in the first half of the twentieth century". Certainly her American connections could provide copy for Doubleday's marketeers:

Presenting Maysie Greig:
She has led as exacting a life as any of her charming heroines –
She was known as the youngest reporter in Australia –
She has seen her novels filmed in Hollywood
She met her husband in America –
Now her serials and novels are in tremendous demand
If you haven't read them already get MEN ACT THAT WAY
What happens to a girl chauffeur in a fast North Shore set
And
A BAD GIRL LEAVES TOWN
Do bad girls make the best wives?[139]

At Doubleday, Greig became closely acquainted with editor-in-chief Harry E. Maule, until his departure for Random House in 1939. She later followed him there, and from 1945 to 1954 Random House became Greig's primary publisher, issuing nine new novels at the general trade publishing pace of one novel a year. Greig also published complete novels in the *Washington Post* in the early forties.[140]

From the early fifties, the linked imprints of Arcadia House, Bouregy & Curl and Avalon Books, together with paperback publishers Dell and Pocket Books, became the mainstays for Greig's books new and old.[141] Carlton House published two novels in the early 1940s by "Mary Douglas Warren", another of Greig's pseudonyms, while Arcadia House published eight Warren titles in the 1950s. The use of pseudonyms was a useful device for a prolific novelist like Greig, not only enabling more titles to be released into the market in a short space of time and more reprints from different publishers, but also allowing different kinds of novels to appear side by side without confusing the established

---

138 Doubleday purchased Triangle Books from Reynal & Hitchcock in 1939 and acquired Blakiston in 1944. Blakiston published reprints under the Triangle Books imprint from 1944, "budget books printed on cheap paper": Elizabeth Hoffman, "The Blakiston Company", *American Literary Publishing Houses, 1900–1980*, ed. Dzwonkoski, 49, 54; information on Triangle Books format from Timothy D. Murray, "Pocket Books", in the same volume, 294.

139 Quoted in Bennett and Pender, *From a Distant Shore*, 71–72, quoting from an unidentified dustjacket.

140 "So Very Innocent", 17 November 1940; "Heaven isn't Here", advertised for the forthcoming *Sunday Post*, 26 December 1940; "Honeymoon Alone", 9 February 1941; "Too Many Women", advertised 23 March 1941.

141 Bouregy & Curl was formed in January 1950. Samuel Curl owned Arcadia House. Bouregy & Curl published under the Avalon Books imprint. Martha A. Bartter, "Avalon Books", *American Literary Publishing Houses, 1900–1980*, ed. Dzwonkoski, 24. Arcadia House published new romances at $2.50.

5 Mystery and Romance: The Market for Light Fiction Between the Wars

brand, in this case the Maysie Greig romance. The Jennifer Ames novels usually had a mystery or detective element. Avalon published a series in the 1950s and 1960s.

As the more specialised genre fiction and dedicated paperback publishing houses moved into the "light fiction" market, the term itself began to disappear in favour of the generic terms "romance", "science fiction" and so on. Surviving correspondence between Maule, Greig and her American agents reveals something of the economics of publishing in this sector and the management of authorial branding. Early in 1948, with three novels already published through Random House, Maule reported variously to the author, her agent and in-house regarding Greig's prospects in the American market. Writing to Winifred Jones, Greig's New York agent to 1948, to explain the terms of the contract offered for *Yours Ever* (1948), he noted that the publisher made little from the standard editions of such books. They would need to sell over 10,000 copies to break even, whereas trade sales were likely to be around 3500 only. Where profits might be earned was in the reprint market. *Reluctant Millionaire* (1945) had been placed with Triangle and later with Dell, earning an additional $3000, but *Table for Two* (1946) had been rejected. *Candidate for Love* (1947) had been accepted by Dell "for a 25c edition which will just about bring us out even". The reprint royalties for Greig herself in April 1948 amounted to just over $1000 for the previous six months.[142] Despite the "inevitable loss" on the regular edition, Random House had decided to publish *Yours Ever* because they wanted to "go ahead with Maysie's work".[143] The regular edition had sold 2827 copies by the end of 1948, which Maule described as "only fair, if that good", a result he attributed to the way that "the 25c books have cut like hell into the market of the lending libraries"; ultimately, the success of the book would depend on whether they could sell a twenty-five cents edition – and Dell did accept it.[144] The rise of paperbacks would eventually kill off the cheap hardcover reprint market almost completely.

Greig herself was keen to (re)launch Jennifer Ames through Random House: "[*Shadow Across My Heart*] is a Jennifer Ames serial and novel and I want to keep it a Jennifer Ames as I believe it a very bad policy to mix the two styles".[145] The last Jennifer Ames in England had outsold the last Maysie Greig by a thousand, Greig reported from Jamaica (she also reported that she and her husband were enjoying going fishing daily with Les Hemingway, Ernest's brother). Maule, however, resisted, for he thought the amount of work needed "to establish Jennifer Ames in the American market" made it impossible, while the "combination mystery-adventure-romance" formula tended "to miss the American taste for book publication", perhaps because the demand was satisfied by the magazines.

For *Dark Carnival* (1950), Random House offered an advance of $600. Maule wrote to Greig's new agent, Toni F. Strassman, that given the "easy pitfalls of popular romance in the current market" they were gratified by the press and movie attention being given to the novel, which he attributed to "its triple threat formula of love, atmosphere and

---

142 Maule to Jones, 13 April 1948, Random House Records, 1925-1999, Rare Books & Manuscript Library, Columbia University, Box 239.
143 The royalties offered were "10% to 5,000 rather than 10% to 2,500, 12½% on the next 2,500, etc". Maule to Jones, 10 March 1948, Random House Records, Box 239. Other details from in-house correspondence, Maule to Mr Haas, 27 February 1948.
144 Maule to Greig and Max Murray, 30 December 1948. Random House Records, Box 239.
145 Greig to Maule, 10 March 1948; Maule to Greig, 17 March 1948, Random House Records, Box 239. The novel eventually appeared in the United States from Arcadia House, under the name Mary Douglas Warren in 1952.

suspense which has characterized the most successful of her previous titles". In June 1951, he estimated that Greig's total sales were approximately one million copies. For *Date with Danger* (1952), Greig agreed to "Americanise" the novel – "that is, make the two sisters Americans".[146] It was sold to the Unicorn Mystery Book Club and was reviewed as detective fiction.[147] Nonetheless, the publishing difficulties remained. While suggesting to Random House director Donald Klopfer that Greig's *This Fearful Paradise* was "fairly sure bread and butter" – it repeated "the formula of romance plus mystery [that] seems to work fairly well" – the uncertainty of the reprint market meant "some decision on Maysie Greig" would have to be made soon.[148] Dell had dropped her because of falling sales. Only one further title appeared from Random House, *Passport to Happiness* in 1954. Avalon, a dedicated genre fiction house, became Greig's primary publisher from that point on.

While there are no figures available for Greig's sales during her most prolific period with Doubleday, it would appear she was a very regular good seller rather than a bestseller like Alice Rosman. Similarly, while reviewers seemed to enjoy her novels, they never commanded the kind of attention Rosman's did. *Professional Lover* (1933) was a "simple, wholesome confection", *Ten Cent Love* (1934) was "Woolworth's".[149] Nonetheless, with so many novels appearing close together in the thirties and early forties it was inevitable that a distinctive Maysie Greig style would be observed: "Maysie Greig's speciality is feverish romance. In her stories lots of things happen, and at a rapid pace not too closely tied to plausibility"; "Maysie Greig is a sympathetic purveyor of romance to the working girl in fiction"; "Fantastic and far-fetched, these short and complicated annals of the working girl are fast-moving, feverish stuff".[150] Her prodigality itself was worthy of notice: "Miss Greig's innocuous novels of romantic young love now total over twenty issued in the last few years, the quality and quantity of that output easily ranking her one of England's – and America's – leading dispensers of popular sentimental fiction active in the trade today".[151]

Once or twice Greig's American characters are criticised as "very English in their speech and manners".[152] But otherwise her ability to please her fans and to untangle romantic tangles in an entertaining way was appreciated by those reviewers open to light fiction:

> [The heroine's] Hollywood adventures are varied, melodramatic and improbable anywhere except in Hollywood. The love interest, of which there is plenty, is exploited in Miss Greig's most torrid style, well suited for reading when the thermometer stands high. And the happy ending for the lovely redhead is wangled in rather an original way.[153]

---

146 Maule to Strassman, 6 March 1951; statement by Maule dated 26 June 1951; Maule to Greig, 11 June 1951. Random House Records, Box 310.
147 "The Criminal Record", *Saturday Review of Literature*, 3 May 1952, 47. The verdict was "Corny".
148 Maule to Klopfer, 3 July 1953. Random House Records, Box 310.
149 "Screen Sweetheart", *New York Times*, 14 January 1934; "Over the Counter", *Saturday Review of Literature*, 7 April 1934, 620.
150 *New York Times*, 26 May 1935, 20 October 1935, 7 June 1936.
151 "A Lonely Rich Girl", *New York Times*, 15 December 1935.
152 Charlotte Dean, "Fiction in Lighter Vein", review of *New Moon through a Window*, *New York Times*, 24 October 1937, and again, reviewing *Stopover in Paradise*, 27 February 1938.
153 B.S. [Beatrice Sherman], "Hollywood Redhead", review of *Girl on His Hands*, *New York Times*, 13 August 1939.

5 Mystery and Romance: The Market for Light Fiction Between the Wars

New hardcover trade titles were regularly reviewed, but the reviews dried up once Greig's involvement with Random House had ceased and her novels appeared in cheaper editions, and as the book pages became less likely to review romance fiction.

Max Murray, Greig's husband, also had his own short but successful publishing career in the United States as the author of light mysteries. Murray's main visibility in the American print market and greatest earnings were through the appearance of four of his novels in the *Saturday Evening Post*, which introduced him as "a brilliant new mystery writer" (and as Australian-born).[154] Murray told an Australian newspaper these earned £8000 each.[155] In the book market, crucially, he was picked up by Farrar, Straus & Co. (Farrar, Straus & Young after 1951) from his first novel, *The Voice of the Corpse* (1947). Murray's London representative, Innes Rose of the John Farquarson agency, had sent the book to the New York agent Sydney A. Sanders, formerly Raymond Chandler's agent, who placed it successfully. Five more titles followed, at the normal pace of one a year, all with the word "corpse" in the title.[156] After the firm rejected *Royal Bed for a Corpse* in 1954, Murray had this and two further titles published by the small New York firm of Ives Washburn. The last two, however, *A Corpse for Breakfast* and *Wait for a Corpse*, appeared posthumously in 1957.

Despite the strong support of Farrar, Straus' mystery editor Margaret Farrar and the firm's willingness to invest in successive titles, once again both publisher and author relied on the sale of subsidiary rights to make any real profit. Trade sales were around the three thousand mark or lower, and the books struggled to earn out their $1000 advances. After the third book the advances were reduced to $750. As Roger Straus wrote, "on all three mysteries we have not earned out our advance, although I quite realise that in mystery publishing we expect to 'get out' on subsidiary rights".[157] Fortunately, the books were attractive to the reprinters and the book clubs, with sales to Bantam, Dell, Lion Books, the Mercury Mystery series, the Detective Book Club and the Unicorn Mystery Book Club. Dell offered royalty guarantees of $3000 for *The Neat Little Corpse*, then $2500 for three subsequent titles. Royalties were one cent per copy to 150,000 then 1.5 cents thereafter. The novel was also sold to Hollywood, Paramount releasing it as *Jamaica Run* in April 1953.[158] *Good Luck to the Corpse*, probably in its first six months to December 1952, earned Murray $200 in addition to his $2500 advance on the basis of 230,000 copies printed. The Detective Book Club offered $1500 (split between author and publisher); it printed 60,000 copies of *The Doctor and the Corpse* producing a royalty of $2280 in November 1952.[159]

---

154 Advertisement, *New York Times*, 9 July 1947. The novels appearing in the *Post* were *The Voice of the Corpse* (1947), *The King and the Corpse* (1948), *The Neat Little Corpse* (1950, as "The Corpse in the Sea") and *Royal Bed for a Corpse* (1955, as "The Corpse on the Bed").
155 Wally Crouch, "He Makes a Fortune to the Tune of £20,000 a Year", *Mirror* (Perth, WA), 9 April 1955.
156 *The King and the Corpse* (1948), *The Queen and the Corpse* (1949), *The Neat Little Corpse* (1950), *The Right Honorable Corpse* (early 1951), *Good Luck to the Corpse* (late 1951) and *The Doctor and the Corpse* (1952).
157 Straus to Sydney Sanders, 13 July 1949, Farrar, Straus & Giroux Inc. Records 1885-1997, New York Public Library, Archives and Manuscripts Collection, Box 259 Max Murray.
158 Murray stated he earned £4500 from the movie deal. Crouch, "He Makes a Fortune".
159 Walter J. Black (Doubleday Crime Club) to Farrar, Straus & Young, 12 November 1952, Farrar, Straus & Giroux Records.

Murray's mystery novels were read as definitely at the lighter end of the crime fiction scale, with the emphasis on entertainment rather than the mystery as such. As the *New Yorker* put it: "The main purpose of this mystery [*The King and the Corpse*] is to divert rather than mystify. It's successful too". Unsurprisingly, his "suitably glossy manner" didn't please everyone; James Sandoe in the *Chicago Sun*: "The author's touch is appropriately light and his assembly skates along on a very high polish. I didn't care for it". But Isaac Anderson in the *New York Times* selected *The Voice of the Corpse* as one of the Outstanding Mysteries of 1947, while Murray made something of a fan of Anderson's successor, Anthony Boucher. *Good Luck to the Corpse* was "highly attractive", with "its articulate and amusing dialogue, its smooth, well-motivated characterization, its plausible romance". Summarising *The Doctor and the Corpse*, Boucher concluded: "Few light novelists can be as slickly readable as Mr. Murray; and his slickness this time has a surprising amount of backbone behind it".[160] The "vivid Australian setting" of *The Right Honorable Corpse* appears to have made it especially attractive to reviewers. In Kathleen Sproul's summary for the *Washington Post*: "Nice people logically knotted up in plot tentacles; diplomatic and Australian background fascinating; humor, narration, even love-interest high grade. Don't miss".[161] The romantic elements that emerged in Murray's novels and the mystery elements in some of Greig's suggest rather poignantly what a "working couple" they were, "such captains of industry" in Harry Maule's phrase, writing together whether in England, Jamaica, New York or Sydney.[162]

Sophistication, Sensation and Science

By contrast with the histories of successive titles – over five, ten or even fifty years – for a number of the genre authors described above, the history of Australian authors in the American marketplace is scattered with one-off successes. This is a common feature of fiction publishing everywhere – the promising first novel that is never matched again, the unexpected bestseller in a mid-list career – but it was magnified for Australian writers by the situation of Australian publishing, with its small domestic industry, its reliance on London, and the difficulties of direct dealings with US publishers or agents.

Almost certainly the earliest science fiction novel by an Australian author to have an American edition was Erle Cox's *Out of the Silence*, released by the small New York house of Rae D. Henkle in 1928. This is a remarkable story in which an Australian farmer, a vigneron, discovers, buried in his yard, an enormous sphere that houses in suspended animation a super-intelligent and beautiful woman from an ancient civilisation; her awakening by the farmer, who falls in love with her, threatens to "release forces that will probably purge and re-make the world by means of destruction and suffering."[163] Cox worked as a journalist and film critic in Melbourne, where his story had first been

---

160 Reviews quoted: *New Yorker*, 31 July 1948, 64; *New Yorker*, 25 June 1949, 87; *Chicago Sun*, 28 April 1950; Isaac Anderson, "Criminals at Large", *New York Times*, 7 December 1947; Anthony Boucher, "Criminals at Large", *New York Times*, 4 November 1951; Anthony Boucher, "Criminals at Large", *New York Times*, 9 November 1952.
161 Drexel Drake, *Chicago Sunday Tribune*, 6 May 1951; Kathleen Sproule, "The Coffin Corner", *Washington Post*, 24 June 1951.
162 Maule to Greig, 17 March 1948, Random House Records.
163 "'Out of the Silence' and Other New Fiction", *New York Times*, 7 October 1928.

5 Mystery and Romance: The Market for Light Fiction Between the Wars

serialised in 1919; it was then published in book form in Melbourne in 1925 and London in 1927. Nothing is known about how it then made its way to New York and to the Henkle company, which seems to have been primarily a publisher of non-fiction. *Out of the Silence* was featured in a full-page advertisement in the *Bookman*, complete with a sketch of the author, alongside works on agriculture, interior decoration, fascism, travel and what appear to be humorous or adventure stories ("A Henkle Book is a Book Worth Reading").[164] Reviewers linked Cox's novel both to earlier adventure-romances and to the new science fiction. The *Times* labelled it "a scientific fantasy". For the *Saturday Review* it recalled Rider Haggard and more than held its own:

> It is a 1928 version of a familiar product, and succeeds in getting about as far ahead of the earlier style as the new Ford is ahead of the good old "Model T." Mr. Cox has taken the notion of the discovery of a lost civilization, decked it out with all the paraphernalia of modern science and modern thinking, and made the result as fascinating and plausible as fairy stories were to us in our most impressionable youth. In short, "Out of the Silence" is great stuff – persuasive, exciting, ingenious. We wonder who could be so filled with sawdust as not to be carried away by its startling virtuosity.[165]

For the *Times* reviewer, the novel was "entitled to be listed among the striking books of the season ... based upon a startlingly original idea and developed with a degree of imagination, interest and thought that is rare in present-day fiction". The American interest in *Out of the Silence*, however, was a one-off detour in Cox's career as a newspaper film critic, although he did publish two later novels locally.

Another, even more spectacular, success was Mary Mitchell's *A Warning to Wantons: A Fantastic Romance*, published by Doubleday in early 1934. One of the few Australian writers not to have served an apprentice in journalism, Mitchell's family was Melbourne establishment. *A Warning to Wantons* was her first novel, "a combination of ultra-sophisticated worldliness and romantic melodrama in a Ruritanian setting". It was a Book Society choice in Britain and a great popular success; and as "a gay and entertaining romance with many an odd and surprising twist", this success was repeated in America.[166] Responding to early notices, Doubleday talked up the book's capacity to be talked about:

> Who started this?
> All this excitement about Mary Mitchell's A Warning to Wantons? Here we were – publishing the book in our own quiet way – when suddenly people began to call us up. "What are you doing about A Warning to Wantons?" they asked. "It's simply the most delightful thing we've read in ages." (Names on request – and some might surprise you!)
> In no time at all the book went through three big printings – became a "best-seller" – was widely talked about. Why? Well, perhaps because it records the fantastic adventures of a modern young beauty, and you'll find it a sheer delight in wit, charm and fun.[167]

---

164 *Bookman*, December 1928, xli.
165 "The New Books", *Saturday Review of Literature*, 1 December 1928, 440.
166 Summary above from E.M. Finlay, "Mitchell, Isabel Mary (1893–1973)", *Australian Dictionary of Biography*, http://bit.ly/2JHVDsv; "Another Female Casanova", *Los Angeles Times*, 1 April 1934.
167 Doubleday advertisement, *New York Times*, 25 March 1934.

The novel entered the *Times* bestseller lists in April (alongside the blockbuster *Anthony Adverse* and the Random House reissue of *Ulysses*).[168] The combination of fantasy, romance and wit attracted reviewers as well as ordinary readers. For the experienced Amy Loveman in the *Saturday Review*, it was "witty, sophisticated, frankly incredible, too long perhaps, but gay and amusing".[169] The *New York Times* found it a highly unlikely book to have come from Australia: "This wild, witty and frankly improbable story of amorous adventure seems an amazing book to have come out of Australia, which we are accustomed to associate with a very different kind of fiction".[170] The "different kind of fiction" was most likely the historical sagas and pioneering epics then prominent in the American market (the subject of Chapter 7). The *Boston Transcript* went even further: "*A Warning to Wantons* is that almost unbelievable miracle, a truly amusing, a truly first-rate French novel written by one of the Anglo-Saxon race."[171]

Perhaps *A Warning to Wantons* occupied a similar space in the fiction market to Dale Collins' sea and sex romances. But the "curious medley" the novel presented – its mix of fantasy and romance, melodrama and comedy of manners, its "primitive wooing [able] to please both Hollywood and the earthy literalists" – was a difficult act to repeat.[172] Mitchell's second novel published in London was the first of several detective novels written as Josephine Plain, but none was published in the United States. However, her third novel, *Pendulum Spring*, was picked up and released by Claude Kendall & Willoughby Sharp in late 1935. Kendall's reputation was as a provocateur and publisher of controversial works such as Octave Mirbeau's *Torture Garden* (1931), and perhaps he had been attracted by the risqué side of *A Warning to Wantons*.[173] *Pendulum Spring* was very different, a "serious and mordantly realistic" study of two sisters, but "too avowedly a close-up of a limited area to be long remembered".[174] It was the last of Mitchell's twenty-four novels to appear in the United States.

It is likely Kendall got something closer to what he wanted with Frank Walford's *Twisted Clay*, released in May 1934. It was another first novel, its author a journalist and newspaper editor. Published in London in 1933 by T. Werner Laurie, Kendall made arrangements with the Sydney A. Sanders agency for its publication. Described mildly as "a study of progressive insanity", *Twisted Clay* is a murder thriller about a lesbian serial killer.[175] Its "high-octane mix of sex, crime and morbid sensationalism includes an early abortion without regret, patricide, a love affair and euphemised sex between Jean [the central character] and a woman cousin, Jean's incarceration and escape to become a sex worker in Sydney, her rampage in various guises as a serial killer of men seeking sex in the streets, and then love and marriage to a drug-dealing gangster, when she is

---

168 *New York Times*, 23 April 1934.
169 Amy Loveman, "Quips and Cranks and Wanton Wiles", *Saturday Review of Literature*, 10 March 1934, 533 (front page).
170 "An Amusing Medley", *New York Times*, 4 March 1934.
171 W.E.H., *Boston Transcript*, 16 May 1934.
172 Phrases from Elizabeth Hart, *New York Herald Tribune*, 4 March 1934.
173 "The Controversies of Claude Kendall, Publisher", *The Passing Tramp*, http://thepassingtramp.blogspot.com.au.
174 Lucy Tompkins, "'Pendulum Swing' and Other Recent Works of Fiction", *New York Times*, 15 December 1935.
175 The book's cover can be viewed at http://bit.ly/2JMeN0ej.

5 Mystery and Romance: The Market for Light Fiction Between the Wars

transformed by the love of a 'real man'". There may have been a serious element, an interest in contemporary sexology, but Jean is "a wholly psychopathic, femme deviant written to thrill".[176] It has been claimed that the novel sold well, but no firm evidence exists and it appears the book was too hot for the newspapers to handle – no reviews have been traced.

Still in 1934, Velia Ercole's *Dark Windows* was much closer to both realism *and* romance. Published by Appleton, *Dark Windows* was Ercole's second novel. Her first, *No Escape*, had been a serious literary work which had been awarded the Sydney *Bulletin* prize in 1932. Appleton, however, chose to promote *Dark Windows* as "a rare and delightful romance", the "romance of an adolescent".[177] Reviewers noted how the book turned from realism to romance near its end, if not to a conventional resolution in marriage, as its heroine leaves a romantic entanglement in France and returns to Australia: "She has found herself; and she is going back to a country where you do not look at life through windows darkened by age-long custom".[178] Perhaps because of its mixed character, the book divided critics. It was awarded an extended review in the *New York Times* where it was praised as "an exquisite book", and for the *Herald Tribune* it was "a work of considerable power and clarity", its author "a novelist to be reckoned with". But for the *Saturday Review*, it was merely drab.[179] Ercole decided that English and American publishers did not favour Australian backgrounds.[180] Certainly, for an "ordinary" novel of contemporary life, an Australian setting could be an obstacle for American publishers. Whatever the cause, in the late 1930s Ercole transformed herself into the "English" romance writer Margaret Gregory. But despite the definite market in the United States for "charming" English romances, as Rosman and Greig had discovered, none of her nine Margaret Gregory novels appeared in America.

Finally, Leonard Mann's *A Murder in Sydney* was published by Doubleday in 1937. Mann was best known in Australia for his challenging First World War novel *Flesh in Armour* (1932), which had been awarded the Australian Literature Society's Gold Medal for outstanding book of the year.[181] He was not an author of "light fiction", and despite its title, *A Murder in Sydney* was not in the detective mystery genre – there is a murder, but no mystery puzzle in the plot. It was Mann's third novel, and the first to have been published in London, by Jonathan Cape, where it was a Book Club selection. It is not known whether the title appeared in Doubleday's Crime Club or as a separate publication, although it was sold at the Crime Club price of two dollars (the standard price for popular novels) and was noted by the *Saturday Review* in its weekly guide, "The Criminal Record". Here the plot was summed up in a way that makes the book sound more like a hard-boiled detective story than realist fiction: "Indignant daughter slays trollopy second bride-to-be of

---

176 Nicole Moore, *The Censor's Library: Uncovering the Lost History of Australia's Banned Books* (St Lucia: University of Queensland Press, 2012), 142–43.
177 Bennett and Pender, *From a Distant Shore*, 68. Appleton advertisement, *New York Times*, 7 September 1934. Ercole was born in New South Wales to an Italian father and an Irish-Breton mother, and this experience fed into her first two novels. She published many stories in Australian magazines before departing for England in the early thirties.
178 "Interlude in Brittany", *New York Times*, 9 September 1934.
179 "Interlude in Brittany"; *New York Herald Tribune*, 16 September 1934; see also *Boston Transcript*, 3 October 1934; *Saturday Review of Literature*, 8 December 1934, 356.
180 Bennett and Pender, *From a Distant Shore*, 68.
181 The novel was finally published in the United States in 2008. See Christina Spittel, "A Portable Monument? Leonard Mann's *Flesh in Armour* and Australia's Memory of the First World War", *Book History* 14 (2011): 187-220.

middle-aged parent, Australian 'tecs suspect both and murderess confesses".[182] The verdict was "well written", and the novel's larger ambitions, perhaps, were also noted: "Antipodean antipathies appear much like those of rest of world, likewise their artists, literati, and dissatisfied younger generation". Louise Maunsell Field in the *Times* saw the novel as "a study of character and environment rather than a detective story", and remarked how rare it was for Australian novels to have urban settings:

> Comparatively little fiction has as yet come out of Australia, and of that little, few novels have for their background life in any one of the large cities. Both the topography and the slang of Leonard Mann's arresting first novel are therefore strange to the average reader ... [But] the general air of the novel is not unlike that of a New York or Chicago story dealing with the early years of the depression. When Hughie Stair wonders why the world is such a generally loathsome place, "full of crawling maggots on a lump of cheesy earth," the reader recognizes a familiar sentiment.[183]

For Kerker Quinn in the *Herald Tribune*, *A Murder in Sydney* suffered from a kind of generic ambivalence, "at once too good and not good enough: detective stories are encumbered by so much characterization as this, while character studies cannot take so much for granted. One of these two stools should be set aside before Mr. Mann arranges the furniture for his next novel, which it is to be hoped will develop without these drawbacks his evident gift for looking into the dark corners of the heart".[184] Despite his next novel also being published by Cape, Mann had no further presence in the American market.

Conclusion

The transnational reach of the authors and books described in this chapter is again a dimension of Australia's literary history that remains largely unknown outside of a small number of studies devoted to these specific genres. Australian authors at home and abroad could benefit from the increasing investment in the light fiction market by mainstream American publishers between the wars – when "light fiction" was identified as a distinct market sector but still within the bounds of the general fiction market – and many actively sought to do so. As with the romance and adventure fiction of the late nineteenth century and the early crime and thriller fiction that followed, golden age detective novels and women's romance participated in a truly international Anglophone fiction industry and marketplace. Despite the close connections between the American and British book trades, however, and the shared tastes for mystery and romance on both sides of the Atlantic, this was never a single, homogenous marketplace, as publishers gauged their own industries and audiences separately. Only a handful of authors were equally successful in both markets. Many were unable fully to translate success in the British sphere into an American reputation. But a small number – Upfield and Rosman in particular – achieved their greatest recognition and earnings in the American market. Unsurprisingly, given the

---

182 "The Criminal Record", *Saturday Review of Literature*, 20 November 1937, 18.
183 Louise Maunsell Field, "An Australian Novel", *New York Times*, 28 November 1937.
184 Kerker Quinn, *New York Herald Tribune*, 21 November 1937.

5 Mystery and Romance: The Market for Light Fiction Between the Wars

generic nature of their success, they were seldom read in the context of Australian literature, even at a time when a series of major novels by Australian authors were being welcomed onto the lists of American publishers. The contemporary impact of these Australian novels is the subject of the following two chapters.

6
Becoming Articulate: Henry Handel Richardson and Katharine Susannah Prichard

"Publication of recent novels reveals literary talent of tiny continent."
—*Toledo Times*, 30 March 1930

From the late 1920s to the early 1940s, American reviewers were often compelled to remark on the increasing presence of Australian books and authors in the American marketplace. The publication in short succession of Henry Handel Richardson's *The Fortunes of Richard Mahony* trilogy (1929-30) and Katharine Susannah Prichard's *Working Bullocks* (1927) and *Coonardoo* (1930) appeared to announce Australia's literary coming of age: "Australia at last seems to have become articulate, when in so short a space of time it can produce such books as Henry Handel Richardson's *Ultima Thule*, Miss Prichard's own *Working Bullocks* and this fine story of white codes and primitive codes mixed and never fusing [*Coonardoo*]"; "Australia is taking her place as an important contributor to English letters ... It is no longer possible to ignore that country's claim to a definite attention".[1] By comparison to the authors discussed in the previous chapter, Richardson and Prichard together could draw attention, not just to individual books by Australian authors, but to works of literature about Australia and hence to the idea of Australian literature itself. As one US reviewer put it, *Ultima Thule* had "brought the Australian country into the deep consciousness of reading America" and *Coonardoo* promised to do the same.[2] Another concluded that "those who maintain that no literature comes out of Australia are beginning to revise their opinions as each new book is announced by Henry Handel Richardson, Katherine Susannah Pritchard [sic] and Dorothy Cottrel [sic]".[3]

As this last comment suggests, Prichard and Richardson provided a frame of reference for the reception of other Australian novels from writers as different as Dorothy Cottrell, M. Barnard Eldershaw, Norman Lindsay, Helen Simpson, G.B. Lancaster and Brian Penton. The following chapter will examine the broader phenomenon of Australian

---

1 Esther Forbes, "Coonardoo", *Bookman*, April-May 1930, 212; *Call* (Paterson, NJ), 22 March 1930. Quotations from reviews have been sourced largely from Richardson's and Prichard's press clippings scrapbooks held in the National Library of Australia: Henry Handel Richardson Papers, NLA MS 133, Press Cuttings Albums; Katharine Susannah Prichard Papers, NLA MSS 6201. Page numbers are not given and it has not been possible to locate all the originals.
2 Mae A. Conklin, "Books and Things", *Register* (New Haven, CT), 30 March 1930.
3 *Press* (Atlantic City, NJ), 10 May 1930.

historical and regional fiction in the United States between the wars. The present chapter traces the American careers of Richardson and Prichard, the two writers whose appearance together in the American marketplace in the years around 1930 made the biggest impact in terms of changing perceptions of Australian literature and of parallels between Australian and American settler histories.

Early Careers

Richardson, born in Australia in 1870, lived in Leipzig and Strasbourg before moving to London in 1903, where her first novel, *Maurice Guest*, appeared from Heinemann in 1908.[4] Prichard was born in Fiji in 1883 of Australian parents and grew up in Australia. She built a career as a journalist, first in Australia, then in London where she worked from 1912 to 1916 writing for a variety of newspapers and magazines. In 1915, her first novel *The Pioneers* was awarded £250 as winner of the Australasian section of Hodder & Stoughton's £1000 "All British" novel competition, guaranteeing its publication in London.[5] Both authors had a degree of early success with novels published in the United States before the 1920s, but these were isolated cases that could not be drawn into any sense of an oeuvre or understood in significant relation to a national literature. By the early to the middle thirties, however, they could be read as major novelists in their own right, especially in Richardson's case, and as representative of a new force in Australian literature.

Maurice Guest, set in Europe but with a young Australian woman as its central female character, was published, "very handsomely" in Richardson's own words, by Duffield & Co. in New York in January 1909.[6] It was followed in October 1910 by *The Getting of Wisdom*, Richardson's partly-autobiographical novel of an Australian girl's difficult "getting of wisdom" during her school years. Then in 1917, Henry Holt & Co. published *The Fortunes of Richard Mahony*, as the first volume of Richardson's trilogy was then known, advertised as "a romance of the Australian goldfields".[7] Prichard's *The Pioneers* was published by George H. Doran Co. in 1916 through the American firm's close ties to Hodder & Stoughton. The American edition followed the English in reproducing Frederick McCubbin's painting *The Pioneers* as a frontispiece.

In each case, the American investment in these titles was low-cost and low-risk. They were the product of deals between the London and New York publishers, with little

---

4   "Henry Handel Richardson" was the pseudonym of Ethel Florence Lindesay Robertson, née Richardson. See Michael Ackland, *Henry Handel Richardson: A Life* (Melbourne: Cambridge University Press, 2004).
5   Delys Bird, "Katharine Susannah Prichard (1883–1969)", *Australian Writers, 1915–1950*, ed. Selina Samuels, Dictionary of Literary Biography, Vol. 260 (Detroit, MI: Gale Research, 2002), 307-19. Richard Nile and David Walker, "The 'Paternoster Row Machine' and the Australian Book Trade, 1890–1945", in *A History of the Book in Australia 1891–1945. A National Culture in a Colonised Market*, ed. Martin Lyons and John Arnold (St Lucia: University of Queensland Press, 2001), 4-5.
6   Henry Handel Richardson, "Some Notes on My Books", *Virginia Quarterly Review* 16, no. 3 (Summer 1940), 338. This Duffield edition is sometimes recorded as 1908 (the date of the book's registration in Washington by Paul Reynolds described below); however, it is noted as "published to-day" in the *New York Times*, 20 January 1909.
7   "With Authors and Publishers", *New York Times*, 12 August 1917. Volume one of the trilogy was first published as *The Fortunes of Richard Mahony*, with *Australia Felix* planned as the overall title of the trilogy. These titles were later reversed.

intervention, if any, by the authors or their agents. All were printed from the English plates or manufactured from unbound sheets printed in England. They were therefore ineligible for copyright protection, although Duffield attempted to protect its editions in other ways. For *Maurice Guest*, the American literary agent Paul Reynolds was commissioned to register a token edition in Washington – only two copies were produced – one week before the English publication date, with the aim of establishing Heinemann's rights in the United States.[8] For *The Getting of Wisdom*, Duffield claimed copyright in a statement on the verso of the title page, despite the fact that the book was clearly printed from imported stereotypes.[9] For *Maurice Guest*, Duffield may have printed only 500 copies, suggesting they did not expect the sort of interest that would justify the cost of a separate American edition.[10] But while Richardson recalled that in America the novel "was greeted with ribaldry, or held up as a warning to parents not to send their sons and daughters abroad", Duffield advertised a second edition in April 1909, indicating better-than-expected sales.[11]

Doran's edition of *The Pioneers* was manufactured from imported sheets, with only 750 sets purchased initially, indicating their modest expectations. As it happens they were probably too conservative, for the book was well received. Certainly, in the British market, Hodder & Stoughton's records show that *The Pioneers* was a steady and profitable seller for more than twenty years. Sales exceeded 35,000 and the book was profitable for Hodder & Stoughton every year from 1916 to 1937 except when the large reprintings occurred.[12] For the American market, 750 copies was a very small number and provided little opportunity for the novel to have a lasting impact.[13]

A Little Group of People in New York

While the print runs for Richardson's novels were also limited, the seeds of her later reception were sown within the New York book world through the influence of *Maurice Guest*. Duffield reissued the novel in 1922, following Heinemann's edition of the same year with an introduction by English novelist Hugh Walpole.[14] Although by 1929 American

---

8   The verso of the title page of Reynolds' "edition" attributed copyright ownership to the English publisher. Reynolds appears to have used this strategy from time to time. A search in the Library of Congress catalogue uncovers a number of books that declare "P.R. Reynolds" as publisher on the title page with a copyright statement on the verso. The statement sometimes attributes copyright ownership to a publisher, but more frequently to the author.
9   Duffield bought sheets from the English publisher for one shilling and nine pence each: Clive Probyn and Bruce Steele, introduction to *The Getting of Wisdom*, by Henry Handel Richardson (St Lucia: University of Queensland Press, 2001), xlii, n. 44.
10 Clive Probyn and Bruce Steele, introduction to *Maurice Guest* by Henry Handel Richardson (St Lucia: University of Queensland Press, 1998), xli.
11 Richardson, "Some Notes", 388. The second edition was advertised in the *New York Sun*, 17 April 1909.
12 From the initial print run of 8000 copies at six shillings, over 7300 sales were made to 1920 (4815 of these in colonial editions). From 1917, cheap editions priced between one shilling and two shillings were printed: an initial 20,000, followed by 10,000 in 1918 and again in 1920, and a further 5000 in 1927. Hodder & Stoughton Authors' Ledgers, Vol. 36. London Metropolitan Archives. Prichard earned £47 in royalties on the six shilling edition but nothing on the cheaper editions.
13 It is not known whether additional copies were ordered following the novel's strong reviews, but nothing in the Hodder & Stoughton ledgers indicates further orders.
14 Probyn and Steele, introduction to *Maurice Guest*, xxxix–xl.

sales totalled only 3300, the book was still in print, and prominent critics such as Carl Van Vechten and Edna Kenton had kept the book alive with occasional appreciative articles.[15] In October 1917, in the progressive *Seven Arts* magazine, Kenton, "well-known both as an author and a feminist" as the editors put it, used Holt's publication of *The Fortunes of Richard Mahony* to bring all three of Richardson's published novels before the reading public (in this case, the small literary readership of a New York arts magazine). *Maurice Guest*, she asserted, "is one of the very great novels":

> In its finish, its brilliancy; in its insight, its poignant transmutation into words of emotion, aspiration, love, degradation, failure, hate; in its scope, its constructive energy, its power; in its extraordinary massing of selective detail that builds under and through and over two years of diverse lives, it stands as one of the most remarkable first novels ever written. It is conceived on a huge scale; its material the formless matter of life, its theme the eternal conflict between matter and spirit, body and soul, soul and soul. It is executed without sentimentality and without satire. Its integrity of artistic purpose would have availed nothing for accomplishment if it had not rested on an incredibly vivid, actual knowledge of life, if it had not been born of a vision into life that explains experience – a sensing of the shoreless waves that lie behind and beyond humanity and give it its only lasting beauty.[16]

Richard Mahony, Kenton believed, was scarcely a lesser achievement, and she drew attention to the role of Australia itself in the novel: "From the proem to the end Australia's personality shares honors with Richard Mahony's. Huge remainder of a huger continent, she lies stretched in the sun, in all her ugliness and beauty, taking her belated turn at man's brutal civilization of a new land; quiescent, but more powerful over the men tearing at her heart than they over her for decades to come". The devastated goldfields landscape "was the subtle revenge of the ancient, barbarian country on these lustful prisoners to the soil they ravished, working like dogged beasts in unquenchable hope of vast and sudden wealth".[17] In January 1918, she repeated her very high estimation in an extended essay in the *Bookman*.[18]

Despite this powerful response to the Australian landscape, Kenton describes Richardson as an "English woman". She had little biographical information available to her, but perhaps it was also difficult to conceive of an Australian novelist capable of such high literary achievement, not because of the condescension that might be felt in London but through a cognitive dissonance between such a place and such an accomplished expression of "European" art. *Richard Mahony* was unlikely to appeal to the "average reader" but it revealed, beneath the surface, "a master's unfaltering hand, shaping these shadow bodies of men out of the dust of unlovely flesh and common incident into foreseen, unswerving design". Richardson thought it the best notice the novel had received anywhere, and wrote

---

15 The figure of 3300 sales is given in Norton's advertisement for *Ultima Thule*, *New York Times*, 8 September 1929. An article in *Publishers Weekly*, 10 August 1929, gives 4000.
16 Edna Kenton, "By Henry Handel Richardson", *Seven Arts*, October 1917, 802. Description of Kenton quoted from the magazine. Kenton wrote to Richardson (HHR), who expressed her appreciation of Kenton's review in a letter to Carl Van Vechten, 5 November 1917: Clive Probyn et al., eds, *Henry Handel Richardson: The Letters, Vol. II 1917–1933* (Carlton, Vic.: Miegunyah Press, 2000), 355.
17 Kenton, "By Henry Handel Richardson", 804-5.
18 Edna Kenton, "'Maurice Guest' and 'Richard Mahoney' [sic]", *Bookman*, January 1918, 580-82.

back to Australia of "a little group of people in New York who seem to believe in my work, & have been saying very nice things about it".[19]

Carl Van Vechten, a reviewer of music, dance and books for the New York papers, was the other leading voice in this little company. He had been given a copy of *Maurice Guest* in 1911 by the English writer Robert Hichens and this led to an appreciative essay on the novel published in 1919 in his book of music criticism, *Interpreters and Interpretations*.[20] Van Vechten's request to Richardson herself for biographical information began a correspondence between the two writers that lasted until at least 1931.[21] On the republication of *Maurice Guest* in 1922, Van Vechten repeated his praise for the novel, this time in the *New York Tribune*, describing it as "one of the greatest English novels of the last fifty years, and one of the least known".[22] He had also encouraged leading American music critic James Huneker to read the book, and Huneker published his own appreciation in August 1919 in the *New York Times*: "It is sombre, powerful, imaginative … I haven't read any of the present-day novels that can hold a candle to *Maurice Guest* in the slow dissection of self-tormented souls".[23] Despite their high praise, both Van Vechten and Huneker felt the Americans in the novel were caricatures. Richardson wrote to Van Vechten apologetically that "caricature" had certainly not been her intention.[24]

Some reviews of the 1917 edition of *The Fortunes of Richard Mahony* had been half-hearted: "at the end one has the feeling of having travelled a long way without getting anywhere in particular"; "its faults and merits are so evenly balanced that it is not nearly so distinguished as if it were a little better or a little worse".[25] A note from the time of its re-release in 1930 suggested that in 1917 Americans had sought books about the war ahead of new fiction; therefore it was no surprise that "a quiet book that dealt with people who emigrated from England to Australia a half century ago" should escape public notice.[26] Yet Richardson felt that this novel, too, had had a better critical reception in America than in England: "in America he has *really* been a success, thanks to a group of very warm admirers who have sprung up to befriend me in New York". She mentioned Kenton's *Bookman* review in particular. Richardson was rather surprised that the book had done so well in the United States, as Holt had printed it without its final "End of Vol. I" tag, "so that people read it as a book for itself & no doubt wondered why it broke off so abruptly".[27]

The Pioneers, too, was widely and favourably reviewed: more than thirty American reviews are included in Prichard's scrapbooks, and again it appears there was greater sales interest than the publisher had anticipated as Doran announced in April 1916 that the book was in its third impression.[28] Although it could be received as a "bestseller" (the term here functioning as a generic description rather than an account of actual sales), praise

---

19   HHR to Mary Kernot, 27 January 1918, *Letters*, 9.
20   Carl Van Vechten, *Interpreters and Interpretations* (New York: Knopf, 1919), 342-53. The essay is dated 4 April 1917.
21   The last letter from HHR to Van Vechten is dated 2 May 1931. *Letters*, 269.
22   Carl Van Vechten, "Yesteryear Books", *New York Tribune*, 16 July 1922.
23   James Gibbon Huneker, "More Musical Fiction", *New York Times*, 17 August 1919.
24   HHR to Van Vechten, 5 November 1917, *Letters*, 6.
25   Reviews cited in Mary Ross, "An Author Who Could Wait", *New York Herald Tribune*, 26 January 1930; also Winnifred King Rugg, "Australia in Fiction", *Christian Science Monitor*, 18 March 1935, 9.
26   Arnold Mulder, "Adventures in the Library", *Daily News* (Ann Arbor, MI), 21 March 1930.
27   HHR to Mary Kernot, 5 October 1918. *Letters*, 13.
28   Doran advertisement, *Evening Ledger* (Philadelphia), 7 April 1916: "Third impression here, many more in London."

for the book in most quarters was strong, perhaps because of the way it worked within romance conventions but with a more confronting realism, and a passion that might break the bounds of romance. For the *Philadelphia Press*, the book was a "masterpiece", especially compared to many of its contemporaries:

> The story is an epic of Australia, nothing less, a noble outstanding mark in the sea of the ordinary and frivolous among novels that will long be remembered, perhaps reread many times, for its moving, powerful story and the vastness and grandeur of its setting.
> There is no unwholesome "eternal triangle" here, no piddling with domestic infelicity or misunderstanding, no toying with the soap bubble pictures of empty, useless lives. These are real men and women, these characters whose lives stand for greatness and achievement such as we read of but seldom in this modern day …
> We will await with interest other works by the same author, works that she needs must write now that her work has received recognition and won the interest of the reading world. That they will be strong and fine and able we well may believe, but that they will equal or even approach this masterpiece is almost beyond the most sanguine belief. It is the work of a life-time this book, and well worth the while.

Other reviewers agreed that *The Pioneers* was "high-class fiction", "remarkably well written", and of "huge quality"; it was a "big story – big in primitive feeling, big in the fearlessness of desperate men".[29] In a less enthusiastic notice, the *New York Tribune* asserted that it was "a competent piece of work, even though it clings of necessity to the tradition of Australian fiction, which is neither long nor complex".[30] The suggestion of familiarity with such a tradition is intriguing, although the reference here must be to settler romance fiction. The only dismissive voice was from the *Los Angeles Times*, which accused Prichard of being "unable to differentiate between worthy emotionalism and sheer hysteria of complications … She knows words, but is without skill in developing her story".[31]

Many reviewers drew parallels with American experience (and generic conventions), while some noted differences as well. For Galveston's *News*: "The pioneers of Australia have all that homely splendour of our own 49ers who crossed the plains by prairie schooner; and have besides the fascination of an alien land of wild men and strange animals, of great mountains and deserts, and the constant menace of escaped convicts."[32] Further north, a reviewer for the *Milwaukee Sentinel* proclaimed: "This is a 'Leatherstocking' tale from the Australian bush. It is a stirring adventure story in which are narrated the heart-breaking trials facing those indomitable colonists who crossed the southern continent in prairie schooners and founded a new nation in the lonesome spaces of the wilderness".[33] For others, the novel stood out against more conventional frontier stories. For the *Boston Advertiser*, the difference was its realism: "You feel that as you read it, with sad memories of the crudeness of many of our cowboy stories … the plot accumulates force in a way that

---

29 All quotations from a publicity leaflet printed in Australia, "Notes from American Reviews". Twenty different US reviews are cited. It appears that Prichard prepared the quotations herself, drawing on her press clippings. Quotations cited from: California *Bulletin*, *Boston Advertiser*, *New York Sun* and the *Bookseller* (New York).
30 "Views and Reviews of Current Fiction", *New York Tribune*, 29 January 1916.
31 "Books of Fiction", *Los Angeles Times*, 13 February 1916.
32 *News* (Galveston, TX), n.d.
33 *Sentinel* (Milwaukee, WI), n.d.

eliminates non-essentials and drives through to a definite, inevitable conclusion."[34] For the *New York Times*, the author was "no sentimentalist, and her book is very far indeed from the rose-coloured, spun-sugar fiction with which we are all so wearisomely familiar".[35] The *Bookman* responded, too, to the novel's incipient nationalism: "It is so good and so well told a story ... so instinct with the spirit out of which grew the Commonwealth of the island continent."[36]

Despite the favourable reviews, Prichard and Richardson largely disappeared from view after 1917 with the partial exception of the small, ongoing market for *Maurice Guest*. It was more than a decade before Prichard appeared again in the United States, with the publication of her novel *Working Bullocks* from the Viking Press in 1927.[37] Viking had only been in existence since 1925, making *Working Bullocks* a relatively early addition to its fiction list (certainly its first Australian novel). It was a modern, literary publishing house that in its own words aimed to have its name "a symbol of enterprise, adventure and exploration in the publishing field – to limit our enterprises to a few each session and to make those few represent the best – to cultivate home soil, yet seek foreign lands – to establish a trademark that will become the sign of good books and constructive publishing".[38] Published in London in 1926, *Working Bullocks* established a relationship between Prichard and Jonathan Cape, both the firm and the man himself, which would endure for the rest of Prichard's career, and it was through representations by Cape that Viking published the book, in an edition fully manufactured and copyrighted in the United States.[39] Publication by Viking was a major achievement and might well have promised a serious international reputation.

The period between *The Pioneers* and *Working Bullocks* saw a refocusing in Prichard's own career as she moved away from colonial romance towards her mature literary style and political commitment to communism. For Australian critics including Nettie Palmer and Miles Franklin, *Working Bullocks* announced Prichard as among the new "serious" authors around whom a modern Australian literature might be brought into view, indeed as the most important evidence yet that such a literature could be written (Richardson's expatriatism complicated her position in these accounts).[40] In the United States, the reviews would have confirmed Viking's decision to publish the work. In a lengthy article under the heading "Australian Realism", the *New York Times* acknowledged, somewhat uneasily, the novel's "post-romance" modernity. It also drew attention to similarities between the Australian and American experience as members of the colonising "Anglo-Saxon race", which it found depressing in a modern way rather than a cause for the usual celebration of pioneering.

---

34 *Advertiser* (Boston, MA), 29 January 1916.
35 "A Prize Novel", *New York Times*, 23 January 1916.
36 Florence Finch Kelly, "Some Novels of the Month", *Bookman*, March 1916, 82-83.
37 Prichard had only published two books in the intervening period: *Windlestraws* (1916) and the more substantial *Black Opal* (1921).
38 John Tebbel, *Between Covers: The Rise and Transformation of Book Publishing in America* (New York: Oxford University Press, 1987), 253.
39 Prichard to Norton, 17 August 1932, Prichard Papers, Series 10 Correspondence, Box 17, Folder 9.
40 Nettie Palmer, "Australian Literature" (1927), in *Nettie Palmer*, ed. Vivian Smith (St Lucia: University of Queensland Press, 1988), 334; Miles Franklin, *Laughter, Not for a Cage: Notes on Australian Writing* (Sydney: Angus & Robertson, 1956), 146.

It is rather significant of the obsessions that have overtaken current fiction that [Red Burke] should be propounded by Miss Katherine [sic] Susannah Prichard for our admiration and esteem in *Working Bullocks*, an impressive, realistic novel from Australia.

But those who open this latest offering with the hope of finding it suffused with the charm of an unfamiliar country are likely to be only partly repaid. Barring a few terminologies … the action of the story might very well pass in any of our Western States. As one reads on the conviction grows that the pioneering of the Anglo-Saxon race, in extending its activities over the greater part of the unclaimed and temperate zones of the earth, has evolved and standardized a society that is only remotely affected by its political loyalties. Even when all credit has been assigned it for its effectiveness, this society remains a bleak and arid affair, more crudely material in its perspective and less colored by idealism than any community since paganism …

In spite of a sort of fog of animalism that covers its psychology and which may in itself be in the nature of a protest, *Working Bullocks* is a startling and unusual novel, and all the more surprising as no previous work seems to stand to its author's credit.[41]

The review is a fascinating glimpse into the frameworks of expectation, both literary and national, within which Australian novels were received, and it confirms the low profile of Australian literature on the American horizon despite the number of individual titles released there. In the reviewer's own words, "Literature does not reach us in any appreciable bulk from the Antipodes." He or she was unaware of *The Pioneers*. Despite the good, forceful reviews of *Working Bullocks*, there was no follow-up with Viking.

The Amazing Story of Henry Handel Richardson

For Richardson, there was no American interest in *The Way Home*, the second volume of the Mahony trilogy, and Heinemann itself rejected the trilogy's final volume, *Ultima Thule*. Only a guarantee from Richardson's husband, John George Robertson, to cover publishing costs enabled a small print run of *Ultima Thule* to reach the London market in early 1929, but on the strength of laudatory reviews by Gerald Gould in the *Observer* and *Daily News*, Heinemann were persuaded to purchase the rights.[42] The first print run of 1000 copies sold out and the Heinemann edition was reprinted three times in as many months.[43] The sensation surrounding the English edition then caught the attention of Elling Aanestäd, associate editor at W.W. Norton & Co., who was visiting London. He secured rights to *Ultima Thule*, then to all of Richardson's works, Holt having relinquished its rights in *Richard Mahony* in 1925.[44]

---

41 "Australian Realism", *New York Times*, 24 April 1927.
42 Norton used Gould's praise in the *Observer* in its own publicity: "The book is a masterpiece, worthy to rank with the greatest and saddest masterpieces of the day." In the *Daily News*, Gould wrote: "I must record my belief that if our age has produced a masterpiece at all, this is a masterpiece." This assessment was subsequently used in Heinemann's advertisements. Ackland, *Henry Handel Richardson*, 228-31.
43 Ackland, *Henry Handel Richardson*, 230. A 1929 Heinemann edition records three new impressions in the first three months of that year after first publication in January.
44 HHR to Henry Holt & Co., 17 December 1923, *Letters*, 52.

Like Viking, W.W. Norton & Co. had only been established in 1925, and its early focus was on non-fiction rather than literary publishing. *Ultima Thule* was among the first novels it published, possibly the very first. Even more striking, its impact was such that William Norton sought to develop an "Australian list" – certainly the first evidence we have of such a notion in American publishing. As Carol Hetherington has shown, Norton himself had a "more than ordinary interest" in Australia.[45] Before entering publishing he had been in Australia for a year, in 1916 and 1917, and had enjoyed what he called "a never-to-be-forgotten experience". In October 1929, just after publishing *Ultima Thule* and while the firm was preparing its edition of Prichard's *Coonardoo*, he wrote to Nettie Palmer, perhaps on the recommendation of Richardson or that of American commentator C. Hartley Grattan, to explain the firm's interest in, as he put it, "publishing for Australia" and seeking Palmer's assistance "in the development of our Australian list".[46] In Palmer, then Australia's leading critic and reviewer, he was delighted to have "made a correspondent ... who is genuinely interested in having the literature of her country published in America".[47]

Ultima Thule was an unlikely choice to launch such a list. It was the third novel in a trilogy whose first two volumes were then unavailable in the marketplace; it had been initially rejected by its London publisher; its key story was of an "unmitigated tragedy" set in a remote time and place; and it was by a largely unknown foreign author whose sales record was not promising. As the publishers themselves put it with cunning understatement, it did not have "the unmistakable earmarks of a trade success".[48] But Norton must have been encouraged by the novel's English reception and was perhaps also aware of the enduring reputation of *Maurice Guest*. Possibly Grattan also recommended Richardson and the Mahony trilogy. Nettie Palmer had alerted him to the works, which he had missed in his earlier booklet *Australian Literature*, published in 1929 just before *Ultima Thule*'s breakthrough appearance.[49] He had nonetheless singled out *Maurice Guest* as "by far the greatest novel written by an Australian", but added "probably not one reader in ten associates its author ... with Australia".[50] Evidence suggests that William Norton both believed in the book itself and that his market sense told him he was onto a winner. He had the English reviews to quote, and then, even before it was published, it received the

---

45 Carol Hetherington, "Authors, Editors, Publishers: Katharine Susannah Prichard and W.W. Norton", *Australian Literary Studies* 22, no. 4 (2006): 420. Quotations here and in following sentences from letters by Norton to Nettie Palmer, 23 October and 30 December 1929. W.W. Norton & Co. Records, Rare Book and Manuscript Library, Columbia University, MS0938.

46 Palmer and HHR had begun correspondence sometime in 1927 (letter from HHR to Palmer, 15 December 1927, *Letters*, 73). See Ackland, *Henry Handel Richardson*, 235, and Brenda Niall, "Ettie and Nettie: When Nettie Palmer Visited Henry Handel Richardson", *Australian Book Review*, February 2013, 28–35.

47 Norton to Nettie Palmer, 30 December 1929. Norton Records.

48 From publicity for *Australia Felix*, where *Ultima Thule*'s "drawbacks" are used to boost Richardson's exceptional qualities. *Publishers Weekly*, 1 January 1930.

49 The essay "Australian Literature" appeared first in the *Bookman*, August 1928, 625–31, then slightly revised as a separate booklet, *Australian Literature* (Seattle: University of Washington Bookstore, 1929). Laurie Hergenhan, *No Casual Traveller: Hartley Grattan and Australia–US Connections* (St Lucia: University of Queensland Press, 1995), 39. Palmer herself had been unaware of Richardson's work when she published *Modern Australian Literature 1900–1923* (Melbourne: Lothian, 1924). Palmer's letter to Grattan (3 February 1929) is published in *Letters of Vance and Nettie Palmer 1915–1963*, ed. Vivian Smith (Canberra: National Library of Australia, 1977), 47–50.

50 Grattan, "Australian Literature", 627.

ultimate market boost when, "in the face of all the fall output of American publishers", the Book-of-the-Month Club chose it as its main selection for September 1929, guaranteeing a first printing of 80,000 copies.[51] As an observer in Dallas put it in a memorable phrase, "now it will automatically penetrate the living rooms of book-conscious America".[52]

The Book-of-the-Month Club was founded in 1926 by a New York advertising man, Harry Scherman, and it soon became the model for the many book clubs and readers' guilds that followed. It was an immediate success, with over 60,000 members within its first year, and more than 110,000 by 1929, the year *Ultima Thule* was offered to subscribers. Books were chosen by a Selecting Committee "comprised of five of America's most famous writers and critics": Henry Seidel Canby, Dorothy Canfield Fisher, Christopher Morley, Heywood Broun and William Allen White. Each month subscribers also received a copy of the substantial *Book-of-the-Month Club News*, which offered "a very careful description of the next chosen 'book-of-the-month,' *explaining exactly the type of book it is*, why the judges selected it, and something about the author".[53]

On a practical level, the club offered to solve some of the problems of book distribution across the vast United States by offering a mail-order subscription service. But with its emphasis on offering subscribers the best new book of the month as certified by its expert judges, its effects on the American book industry and book culture were much more profound than increased consumption alone. Because selection by the club meant guaranteed sales of eighty to one hundred thousand, books were often forwarded in typescript or proof copy, and the club's decisions could be used to determine print runs, editorial choices, or indeed whether a book would be published at all. Further, the club's own publicity meant exposure for a new book at a level few publishers could themselves provide. Book club sales, in turn, could generate higher bookstore sales. Selection by the Book-of-the-Month Club, in short, not only guaranteed a large print run, but subsequent commentary in newspapers and magazines that would activate New York's web of literary networks, ensuring that Henry Handel Richardson and *Ultima Thule* would become central topics in the book talk of critics, booksellers and discriminating readers.

In social terms, Joan Shelley Rubin and Janice Radway have analysed the Book-of-the-Month Club as a key institution in America's emerging "middlebrow" culture.[54] In a rapidly expanding book market, with the presence of high modernism on one side and a "mass market" on the other, the club's selections not only offered readers guidance on the best of the new books; with the aid of the *Book-of-the-Month Club News*, it also offered readers the opportunity "to become 'cultured' before anyone else could".[55] The target audience was the "average, intelligent reader", already "convinced of the value of culture" but struggling to keep up or to know just how to discern the best among the

---

51 Quotation from *Publishers Weekly*, 10 August 1929. A first print run of 80,000 is reported in the *New York Times*, 25 August 1929, and in many other papers (suggesting it came from the publisher). In an advertisement in the *Times* on 1 December 1929, Norton claimed "100,000 readers".
52 *News* (Dallas), 29 September 1929.
53 Joan Shelley Rubin, *The Making of Middlebrow Culture* (Chapel Hill: University of North Carolina Press, 1992), 95, 96, 101.
54 Rubin, *The Making of Middlebrow Culture*, 93-147; Janice Radway, *A Feeling for Books: The Book-of-the-Month, Literary Taste, and Middle-Class Desire* (Chapel Hill: University of North Carolina Press, 1997).
55 Rubin, *The Making of Middlebrow Culture*, 104, quoting R.L. Duffus, *Books: Their Place in a Democracy* (Boston: Houghton Mifflin, 1930), 93.

confusing multitude of new publications.⁵⁶ Hence, the club's famous advertising: "How often have outstanding books appeared, books widely discussed and widely recommended, books you were really anxious to read and fully intended to read when you 'got around to it,' but which nevertheless you *missed*! Why is it you disappoint yourself so frequently in this way?"⁵⁷ Hence, too, the quality of the books selected. Despite frequent attacks on the judging committee for "standardising" or "commercialising" literary values, the club's selections in the 1920s and 1930s were often works of literary stature, sometimes quite demanding or challenging, if within certain limits: "literary" but not "highbrow" works, and seldom modernist.⁵⁸ *Ultima Thule* thus belongs with other Club selections from English and European writers in the late 1920s, substantial works by Galsworthy, Wells and Shaw, Erich Maria Remarque's *All Quiet on the Western Front*, and Nobel Prize–winner Sigrid Undset's *Kristin Lavransdatter*. Still, one reviewer felt obliged to write, "*In spite of* its selection as Book-of-the-Month, 'Ultima Thule' is a serious and moving work of art".⁵⁹

Scherman himself contributed the report on *Ultima Thule* to the *Book-of-the-Month Club News*, and his appreciation of this challenging novel is in tune with its general critical reception in the United States.⁶⁰ He paid little attention to the novel's Australian setting, concentrating instead on the drama of Richard Mahony's mental disintegration balanced by the portrait of his wife Mary: "Rising out of the ruins of Mahony's life ... is humanity's answer to such personal disaster: the brave, beautiful, fighting loyalty of Mary, his wife". This difficult subject is approached "with a rare dispassionate tenderness ... an uncompromising but compassionate truthfulness". Scherman stressed the novel's challenging emotional power: "Read the book yourself, bring up all your critical standards, or, better, judge it simply by its profound and inescapable effect upon you, tough-minded as you may be". It embodies "true, not contrived, tragedy – tragedy in the best tradition of all literature – yes, in the tradition of Oedipus and Lear and Anna Karenina – arousing that ennobling pity ... which cleanses and does not depress, because there is both humility and understanding in it". These phrases are a vivid example of what Radway sees as the key mode of appreciation for the Book-of-the Month Club, what she calls "middlebrow personalism", a way of reading that emphasised affective connection and absorption rather than cognition or contemplation.⁶¹ Despite its examination of one man's descent into mental torpor, Scherman praises *Ultima Thule* for avoiding the lure of the fashionable psychological "problem novel". In the process he distinguishes Richardson's writing from other "modern fiction", from authors who "discover 'problems,' and insist upon worrying us about them": "Thank heavens, in this book there is no 'problem'. There is no smartness, no reliance upon literary tricks of any kind, but there is the sweep of action of a great drama".

On the back of such publicity, Norton launched its own promotional campaign, so effective that it seemed to a contemporary "impossible to pick up a book review or magazine without being confronted by a silhouette figure with stooped shoulders and bowed head, and a black shadow stretching out before him"; this was the image of Richard

---

56 Radway, *A Feeling for Books*, 296.
57 Rubin, *The Making of Middlebrow Culture*, 99.
58 Rubin, *The Making of Middlebrow Culture*, 144–46.
59 Henry Smith, "Stark Tragedy of Human Existence is Theme of Novel", *News* (Dallas), 29 September 1929. Emphasis added.
60 *Book-of-the-Month Club News*, August 1929, 1–3.
61 Radway, *A Feeling for Books*, 283–84.

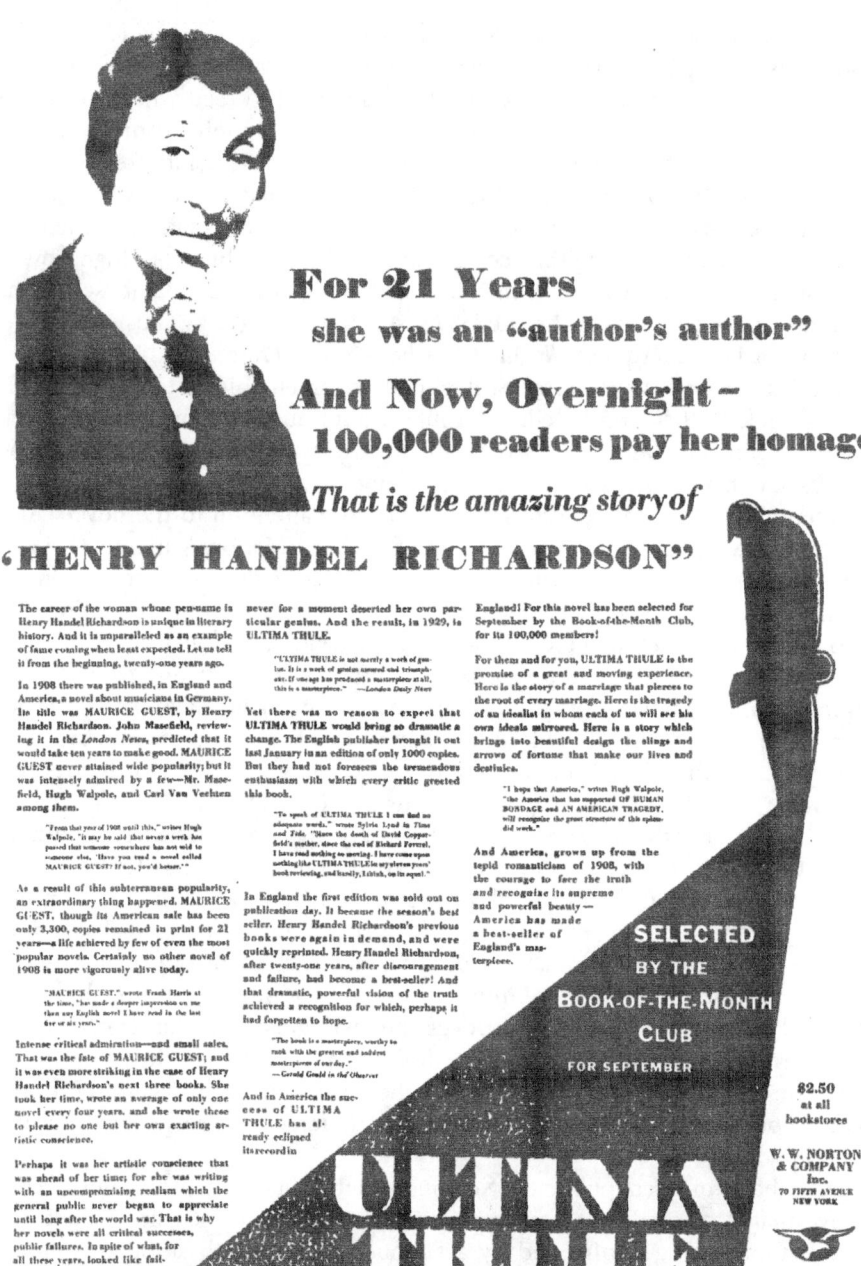

Figure 6.1 Advertisement for Henry Handel Richardson's *Ultima Thule* (New York: W.W. Norton & Co., 1929), from the *New York Times*, 8 September 1929.

Mahony used in Norton's advertisements and on the book's cover (Fig. 6.1). The article from the *Atlantic Bookshelf* from which this quotation is taken gives a fascinating industry insider's account of Norton's investment in the book and its promotion.[62] Aanestäd had sent one copy of the novel back to New York, hoping Norton would like it because he had already signed a contract committing the firm to publishing it. "Nobody in America had heard of the novel, and only a few had heard of the author. George Stevens of Norton's happened to be one of those who had: in fact, some years before he had been much impressed by a little-known novel of musical life called *Maurice Guest*." Norton then "called his advertising counsel to conference" and announced that *Ultima Thule* was "a BIG book!" Publishers and marketers worked together "to make the public realise, in spite of the novel's forbidding aspect, that *Ultima Thule* was supremely worth reading – and to make them buy the book".

An initial jacket design was scrapped because buyers disliked it, and a new design developed: "the jacket had to be simple and dignified, at the same time a design that would be quickly seen and remembered. It should carry some of the emotional quality of the story. And it must be a design that could be used in all the advertising, so that readers would at once recognize the book in bookstore windows, on circulating-library shelves, and on the tables of friends". Hence the memorable image of the silhouette figure with stooped shoulders.[63] Forty different colour combinations were prepared before one in bright yellow, orange and black was selected. The jacket carried Hugh Walpole's linking of *Ultima Thule* with two other challenging literary bestsellers: "I hope that America – the America that has supported *Of Human Bondage* and *An American Tragedy* – will recognise the great structure of this splendid work".[64]

Advertisements were made up in different sizes – full-page for the *New York Times Book Review*, a double-page spread for the *Atlantic Monthly*, fifty-line columns elsewhere. Stevens wrote the copy. On 8 September, the headline to the first advertisement announced: "For 21 Years / she was an 'author's author' / And Now, Overnight – / 100,000 readers pay her homage / *That is the amazing story of* / 'Henry Handel Richardson'". As William Howell Wells put it in his *Atlantic Bookshelf* article:

> The first page advertisement in the *Times Book Review* is well worth study … Most of it is in small type, some of it in six point, and it takes at least four minutes to read … Beside [the headline] appeared the photograph of a strangely Mephisthelean *woman*. The combination could not fail to arouse curiosity and lead to further reading of the advertisement. And whoever read it felt repaid. He learned not merely that the publisher thought this was a great novel, but the story of the author's difficult career and final recognition, a view of England's enthusiasm for the book, and a picture of what the novel was about: its theme, its leading characters, its emotional effect, and a suggestion of the story. No attempt was made to camouflage the fact that the story was a bitter tragedy … It made the readers of the advertising *able to talk about the book almost as though*

---

62 William Howell Wells, "Bringing Up a Book", *Atlantic Bookshelf*, December 1929. In Richardson's press clipping books.
63 The image was discussed by Norton and Richardson: HHR to Norton, 12 October 1929, *Letters*, 135.
64 Quotation used in Norton catalogue, spring 1929, in Richardson's press cuttings.

they had read it [thus stimulating] the most valuable of all sales factors – word-of-mouth advertising.⁶⁵

The advertisement was indeed both visually striking and information rich, its effect not unlike that of the *Book-of-the-Month Club News* lead articles (or indeed Random House's later advertisement for James Joyce's *Ulysses*).⁶⁶ It provided plenty of detail for readers, buyers and reviewers, describing the reputation of *Maurice Guest*, the author's long, unrewarded but principled travail, the difficulty of seeing the trilogy published, and then the unexpected success of the novel now before them. With its English reception and Book-of-the-Month Club selection, Norton could promote the book as a bestseller from the moment it was published:

> The career of the woman whose pen-name is Henry Handel Richardson is unique in literary history. And it is unparalleled as an example of fame coming when least expected. Let us tell it from the beginning …
>
> Perhaps it was her artistic conscience that was ahead of her time, for she was writing with an uncompromising realism which the general public never began to appreciate until long after the world war. That is why her novels were all critical successes, public failures. In spite of what, for all these years, looked like failure, Henry Handel Richardson never for a moment deserted her own particular genius …
>
> And in America the success of *Ultima Thule* has already eclipsed its record in England! For this novel has been selected for September by the Book-of-the-Month Club, for its 100,000 members!⁶⁷

Norton could even express a form of national pride in its selection, and a self-fulfilling prophecy: "America, grown up from the tepid romanticism of 1908, with the courage to face the truth and recognize its supreme and powerful beauty – America has made a best-seller of England's masterpiece".

Nowhere in the advertisement was the Australian setting or the author's origins mentioned. But Norton was not selling an Australian novel. It was selling a publishing sensation with a compelling rags-to-riches story (plus the added puzzle of the pseudonym). Two weeks after the initial advertisement, on 29 September, it produced a follow-up: "The critics of America / rise up and cheer – / *and* ULTIMA THULE *breaks all records!*"⁶⁸ When Norton discovered that the novel was especially popular with women, a new round of publicity gave greater emphasis to Mary's courage and less to Richard's defeat.⁶⁹ Norton himself wrote to Richardson about the strong response from American women writers, including Ellen Glasgow and Dorothy Canfield Fisher.⁷⁰ The advertisement of 29 September quoted a dozen different reviews, many of which made the highest claims for the novel's achievements: "belongs among those few really great books";

---

65 Wells, "Bringing Up a Book".
66 Trysh Travis, "Print and the Creation of Middlebrow Culture", in *Perspectives on American Book History: Artifacts and Commentary*, ed. Scott E. Casper, Joanne D. Chaison and Jeffrey D. Groves (Amherst: University of Massachusetts Press, 2002), 340–43.
67 Norton full-page advertisement, *New York Times*, 8 September 1929.
68 Norton full-page advertisement, *New York Times*, 29 September 1929.
69 Wells, "Bringing Up a Book".
70 Norton to HHR, 23 October 1929. Norton Records.

6 Becoming Articulate: Henry Handel Richardson and Katharine Susannah Prichard

"a novel of lasting quality"; "the sound, enduring stuff that makes great literature"; "a great novel in the best tradition"; and perhaps less noble, "makes the average good novel look like a relaxed oyster".[71] Then, like Scherman, the advertisement challenged the reader's human and critical capacities: "Read it yourself – for it is a great experience. Tragedy? Yes – but a superb tragedy of courage, and its final effect is inspiring and uplifting … a great experience sublimely enjoyed".

Of course, no amount of smart advertising would work unless the book itself could carry the serious claims made for it, but the success of the campaign can be gauged by the repetition of its narrative in countless reviews and news items across the country, and indeed its reuse by Norton and reviewers as subsequent titles appeared. This was the story that remained in New York's cultural memory – for a time at least. Norton sent over one hundred clippings to Richardson, and many more than that were collected and pasted into her scrapbooks, evidence of how widely the book was reviewed and how newsworthy both title and author had become. The novel was the subject of public lectures, reading group discussions, lists of recommended books, even social pages. The *New York World*'s social diarist recorded reading it: "a tragickall comedy of great poignancy, which I enjoyed beyond measure". And in the vernacular of the *Herald Tribune*: "They tell us that 'Ultima Thule,' by Henry Handel Richardson, is a swell book, and we're gonna read it next week at latest".[72] Newspaper headlines added their own unique twist: "Mad Man's Fate Makes Masterpiece"![73] Personality pieces followed, notably by Australian expatriate Alice Henry in the *Bookman* of December 1929 (Richardson resigned herself to its inaccuracies).[74] In March 1930, a newspaper columnist recalled that in the previous year, *Ultima Thule* "came upon the consciousness of a public quickened to realism and tragedy by the efforts of Dreiser, Sinclair Lewis and O'Neill" – an interesting contemporary American frame of reference for the novel. The *Women's Journal* announced "A book in the great tradition of English literature has come striding in among the moderns".[75] Sales of 2000 copies per week were reported a month after the book's release, and it figured on bestseller lists across the country – in Chicago, Milwaukee and Corry (PA), as well as in New York where it appeared alongside *All Quiet on the Western Front* and Ernest Hemingway's *Farewell to Arms*. The *Saturday Review* reported it as among the five "most discussed" novels of the week as reported

---

71 Quotations in order from Fanny Butcher, *Chicago Tribune*, 7 September 1929; "'Ultima Thule' a Novel of Lasting Quality", *New York Times*, 15 September 1929; "Recent Books", *New Yorker*, 14 September 1929; "Speaking of Books", *Outlook*, 11 September 1929, 278; Robert B. Macdougall, "Grim Power", *Saturday Review of Literature*, 14 September 1929, 130.
72 "The Conning Tower: The Diary of Our Own Samuel Pepys", *New York World*, 14 September 1929; *New York Herald Tribune*, 22 September 1929.
73 *Progress* (Greenville, PA), 18 September 1929.
74 HHR to Mary Kernot, 2 February 1930: "You will see I remain faithful to my principles of never correcting anything that is said abt me; & so for her, I shall remain 'Henrietta.' Well, well! – it's a better name than Ethel any day. Where she got her facts from goodness only knows". *Letters*, 158. She thanked Alice Henry politely (25 January 1930): "I am sure from the response it has already awakened in the American press that it will be of great service to my work in the States". *Letters*, 153. Another biographical piece, by Kathleen Ussher, was published in *Saturday Night* (Los Angeles), 23 November 1929.
75 E.H., "The Way Home Proves Climax to a Trilogy", *Times* (Buffalo, NY), 18 March 1930. Second quotation, from Richardson's clippings file, recorded as *Women's Journal*, October 1929; it has not been possible to identify the source definitively.

by bookstores from across the country.⁷⁶ In 1936, Norton claimed that *Ultima Thule* was "remembered by more than 200,000 readers as one of the great experiences of their lives".⁷⁷

The Furthermost Reach of Modern Storytelling

As the brief snippets used in Norton's advertising indicate, the range and level of praise accorded *Ultima Thule* in the American press was truly remarkable. In an age when reviews were often little more than brief notices of new books, the novel attracted long reviews in all the major New York papers; in magazines such as the *New Yorker*, the *New Republic*, the *Virginia Quarterly* and the *Saturday Review of Literature*; in major papers from Chicago, Boston, Washington, Philadelphia, and San Francisco; and in small-town newspapers across the United States. It was not just a good novel in the weekly parade of new fiction but a truly great novel, not just a book of the month but one of the great books of a generation, in "the best traditions of English prose fiction".⁷⁸

Few could resist the narrative that Norton and the Book-of-the-Month Club offered. But in the longer reviews especially, Richardson's novel brought out the best in reviewers, provoking eloquence, critical exactness, even philosophy. Thus William Soskin in the *New York Evening Post*:

> I began to think "Ultima Thule" an important book when I realized that I reacted to it as one does to large artistic accomplishment – in no simple and direct outburst of enthusiasm, but with the deliberate, highly complex, critical liking and love and aversion with which one reacts to the substance of existence itself. This story of the doctor Richard Mahony is, first of all, builded of the concrete, appallingly trivial and pathetically real facts of life …
>
> Richardson seems to have so much of the fundamental understanding and sympathy with all sorts and conditions of men that she can give generously and fully. "Ultima Thule" will impress you with its spaciousness, its warm detail, its easy relaxation. Yet it is not a sprawling book, for though its very style may vary radically, and though it may seem, at times, too much absorbed in apparently extraneous matters, there is a tightness and soundness of structure in it that makes one feel the inevitability of its tragedy in its very first few chapters.⁷⁹

And Joseph Henry Jackson in the *Argonaut*:

> This is Truth that Miss Richardson has set down; bitter and moving and utterly real. Stark as life itself, her narrative is yet imbued with the tenderness, the piercing beauty with which life seems unavoidably to inform its grimmest moments. Tremendous, epic

---

76 *Times* (Tampa, FL), 23 November 1929. Bestseller lists in Richardson's press clippings. *Saturday Review of Literature*, 16 October 1929, 269.
77 *All About Books* (New York), August 1936. Journal recorded as such in Richardson's papers; original not located.
78 "Fiction", *Bookman*, October 1929, 202.
79 "Books on Our Table", *New York Evening Post*, 3 September 1929.

in its comprehension of man and his destiny at once so small and so great, this is a novel in a thousand, the sort of living pulse-beat, clear and strong, which once or twice in a generation manifests itself to give the ordinary mortal an inkling of the nature of the steady Cosmic Stream.

It is difficult to say wherein Miss Richardson chiefly excels. Her story is as simple, as uninvolved and at the same time as majestic, as universal as the Greek tragedies. Her manner matches her theme; strong, direct, unvarnished, writing admirably suited to her matter. Her characterisation is superb; even the lesser figures of the book are clear, rounded, memorable. In a day of ephemeral, "tricky" writing, of cheap and easy effects, of specious journalistic fiction and meretricious mannerisms, Miss Richardson has produced an honest and beautiful piece of work, a novel which sets her down as one of the great writers of our time.[80]

Of course, not everyone agreed: "readers who like a bit of syrup in their fiction will be disappointed in this one".[81] Otherwise the praise was such that it drove one later reviewer to attack his fellow critics' enthusiasm, a sure sign of just how much favourable attention the novel had attracted: "Such a chorus of superlatives, such a clamor of adulation, had not been heard for a month at least. 'Ultima Thule' was compared to 'The Way of All Flesh,' 'The Return of the Native,' 'Of Human Bondage,' 'An American Tragedy.' Terrible, utter and ruthless were the least adjectives applied to it … Perhaps it is not necessary to demonstrate how unlike 'Ultima Thule' is to the sub-Rabelaisian 'Of Human Bondage' or to point out that it chiefly resembles 'An American Tragedy' in the detail that both heroes die in the end". Even so, the author concluded, "'Ultima Thule' is a very good book".[82]

Many reviewers made the contrast that Jackson, and Scherman before him, had made, distinguishing *Ultima Thule* from the masses of light fiction crowding the marketplace and from the "meretricious mannerisms" of fashionable modern novels: "There is nothing of sex in this unusual novel, nothing of the calamities of modern marriage, nothing to mark it as a novel of the jazz age".[83] The comparison enabled reviewers not just to air their prejudices but to align Richardson's novel with "a deep English tradition".[84] Another, more oriented to the modern, insisted that alongside *A Farewell to Arms* and *Kristin Lavransdatter*, *Ultima Thule* represented "the furthermost reach of modern story-telling".[85]

These claims were based quite legitimately on the novel's central human drama which touched the "universal" – "it is not essentially a book about the Antipodes" – and read this way considerations of the book's status as Australian were secondary, if mentioned at all.[86] As the *Atlantic Monthly* put it, "In a book so deep and sure as this it would seem irrelevant to talk of nationalities".[87] For American reviewers, *Ultima Thule* was more often an English novel than an "Australian tragedy", just as Richardson herself was as often an

---

80 "Books on the Table", *Argonaut* (New York), 14 September 1929.
81 *Star* (Minneapolis), 14 September 1929; the press cuttings scrapbook records that the same note appeared in sixteen other papers.
82 T.M. Hatfield, "Revival of a Novel of which 'Ultima Thule' is Sequel", *Baltimore Evening Sun*, 15 March 1930 (the occasion was a review of *Australia Felix*).
83 Neeta Belle Joiner, "Under the Reading Lamp", *Record* (Brooklyn, NY), 22 September 1929.
84 Henry Hazlitt, "An Australian Tragedy", *New York Sun*, 9 September 1929.
85 Florence Fisher Parry, "I Dare Say", *Press* (Pittsburgh), 4 November 1929.
86 Quotation from a Canadian review of the US edition: *Chronicle* (Halifax), 26 October 1929.
87 *Atlantic Monthly*, November 1929.

Englishwoman as an Australian author. This reflected the realities of the transatlantic book trade – the fact that Australian books travelled as British books – but again there could be a kind of cognitive dissonance. As the *Virginia Quarterly*'s critic wrote, thoughtfully, "It is a novel that must be discussed in the most catholic of critical terms – and yet its central character is abnormally an exception to the generality of us, and its locale is Australia, the continent that, to most of mankind, seems least a part of this goodly frame on which we read and have our being".[88]

Only two reviewers gave more than passing notice to the novel's Australian dimensions – Henry Hazlitt in the *New York Sun*, where he was literary editor, and Hartley Grattan in the *New Republic* – although *Plain Talk* described *Ultima Thule* as "one of the few truly great novels with an Australian background".[89] Hazlitt expanded on Richardson's vivid descriptions of the Australian bush, "the makeshift and slovenly towns ... the general absorption in the pursuit of wealth or of a bare living, to the exclusion of any cultural interests". But the parallels with American experience also struck him profoundly: "The picture is strikingly like that of our own Far West but a generation or two ago; indeed, in spite of our progress, the book constantly reminds us how deeply American culture in general is still influenced by the pioneer outlook".[90] Grattan's review was his first chance to promote Richardson following the publication of his *Australian Literature*, and he is the only reviewer to use the phrase "Australian literature" to situate the novel: "There is no novel in Australian literature that so cuttingly analyses the society of that country, for though it depicts conditions in the 1870s, in all essentials the same conditions obtain today". The comment manifests Grattan's understanding of Australian literature as an expression of its social context and national ethos, a powerful critical engine for him – he was almost alone among American readers in being able to make such connections authoritatively – but one that could also produce discomfort at negative portrayals of Australian experience. Because of Mahony's character, the book "presents the worst side of Australian life", and he recommends readers try Joseph Furphy's earlier *Such is Life* for the contrasting views of a "critical patriot".[91]

The Greatest Event in Modern Fiction

The success of *Ultima Thule* encouraged Norton to reissue Richardson's earlier novels in an extraordinary burst of publishing activity that saw the first volume of the trilogy, now bearing the title *Australia Felix*, released in January 1930, the second volume, *The Way Home*, in April, and *Maurice Guest* in August. *The Getting of Wisdom*, *The Fortunes of Richard Mahony* trilogy as a three-volume set, and then a one-volume edition of the trilogy, all appeared in 1931.[92] Norton reset all the books in order to

---

88 Walter L. Myers, "Make Beliefs", *Virginia Quarterly Review* 6, no. 1 (January 1930): 147.
89 *Plain Talk*, November 1929.
90 Hazlitt, "An Australian Tragedy".
91 C. Hartley Grattan, "Ultima Thule", *New Republic*, 23 October 1929, 278.
92 Norton first packaged the three separate volumes wrapped in cellophane at $7.50 (the standard price of the three novels sold separately at $2.50) in early 1931: noted in the *Courant* (Hartford, CT), 22 February 1931. The one-volume edition, released on 17 September 1931, retailed at $3.50, *New York Times*, 20 September 1931. Richardson Press Cuttings.

"make them worthy, in format, of the author's distinguished work".[93] Further rounds of publicity accompanied each new edition: "'ULTIMA THULE / was the best piece of fiction published in 1929' ... / And now – AUSTRALIA FELIX".[94] This time an outline of the continent was used for the cover and publicity, and in certain ways the "new" novel was promoted in more conventional terms as an adventure-romance or settler epic: "*Australia Felix* shows a new side of Henry Handel Richardson's realistic genius. Here is an exciting story of the Australian gold rush ... It is packed full of drama – 483 pages of it".

For *Maurice Guest*, the familiar theme was deployed: "*He waited twenty years for his audience ... Famous he is now – for his story is known, after twenty years, as one of the great novels of our time*".[95] This echoed the *New Yorker*'s opinion printed on the book's jacket, that *Maurice Guest* was "one of the few great novels of our time". Norton's new edition incorporated corrections that Richardson wanted, including the restoration of certain words that Heinemann had censored in their 1909 edition: "Coarse they certainly are," she wrote to Norton, "& coarse they are meant to be". She also accepted Stevens' corrections to the vernacular of her American characters.[96] Richardson was pleased with the design of all of Norton's books, particularly in comparison to her English editions: "I am delighted with the get-up of the book – it's a real pleasure to the eye, & very good to handle. I do love good print & paper, & all the little etceteras that make a book beautiful as well as practical; but so far they were not for me".[97] By December 1930, Norton reported that *Maurice Guest* was in its third printing.[98]

For *The Way Home*, Norton took a full page in the *Saturday Review of Literature* and a quarter page in the *New York Times* to announce "THE GREATEST EVENT IN MODERN FICTION" (Fig. 6.2).[99] This was the fact that with the appearance of *The Way Home* the complete Mahony trilogy was available for the first time in the American market. The familiar narrative of Richardson's twenty-year devotion to her art in obscurity was redeployed to promote the trilogy, but Australia – unusually – was also made a selling point: "Under the Southern Cross, twenty-odd years ago, Henry Handel Richardson planned her epic of the Australian pioneers. On a canvas as big as Australia itself, she projected the life of a man – a life in which every detail is momentous, every event profoundly stirring. And now, after twenty years, she has won the highest acclaim of the literary world". Quoting the *Saturday Review*, the advertisement announced: "We expect that discriminating readers will place it on a level with, if not higher than, Galsworthy's Forsyte Chronicles; nor are we unreasonable in suggesting that it may be considered the soundest accomplishment of English fiction in the twentieth century". Such comparison with Galsworthy and the *Forsyte Saga* was about the highest form of praise that could be offered in the book world of the time.

The publishers were still optimistic enough to make a virtue of the novels' unsaleability: "Every critic urges you to read Henry Handel Richardson's great trilogy; but

---

93   Norton to Nettie Palmer, 30 December 1929, Norton Records.
94   *Publishers Weekly*, 1 January 1930. The retail price was $2.50.
95   Norton advertisement, *New York Times*, 14 September 1930.
96   HHR to Norton, 10 May 1930 *Letters*, 179. See Clive Probyn and Bruce Steele, eds, *Maurice Guest*, by Henry Handel Richardson (St Lucia: University of Queensland Press, 1998), 792-97.
97   HHR to Norton, n.d. September 1929, *Letters*, 131.
98   Norton advertisement, *New York Times*, 7 December 1930.
99   *Saturday Review of Literature*, 12 April 1930.

*Completing

THE GREATEST EVENT IN MODERN FICTION

Under the Southern Cross, twenty-odd years ago, Henry Handel Richardson planned her epic of the Australian pioneers. On a canvas as big as Australia itself, she projected the life of a man—a life in which every detail is momentous, every event profoundly stirring. And now, after twenty years, she has won the highest acclaim of the literary world.

The appearance on April 10 of THE WAY HOME by Henry Handel Richardson completes the publication of her *magnum opus*—the trilogy of Mary and Richard Mahony. Exigencies of copyright made it impossible to publish here the three novels in the order of their composition. The publishers were obliged to issue ULTIMA THULE first, although it is the third part of the trilogy. Perhaps it was fortunate for the author, for ULTIMA THULE won her fame and 100,000 American readers. These readers have waited anxiously for the earlier two novels; and many others have postponed reading ULTIMA THULE until they had read AUSTRALIA FELIX and THE WAY HOME.

After the publication, in January, of AUSTRALIA FELIX, *The New York Times* wrote: "It is high tribute that, with only the English period of Richard's life withheld from us, we should await it with genuine impatience." *The New York Herald-Tribune* said, "After two volumes and 800 pages, I am eager for more!" Now you can read all three parts of this gigantic story in the order in which they were written.

The Trilogy of
HENRY HANDEL RICHARDSON

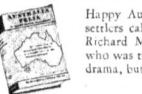

1 *AUSTRALIA FELIX*
Happy Australia! That was what the early settlers called the country. And here begins Richard Mahony's story—the story of one who was to find love, adventure, wealth, and drama, but never happiness.
Published January, 1930. $2.50

2 *THE WAY HOME*
"They change their skies, but not themselves, who go across the seas." This was what Richard was to learn when, having made his fortune, he tried to find again his old life in England. Just published. $2.50

3 *ULTIMA THULE*
Here, in the most memorable events of his life, the story of Richard Mahony is brought to its nobly tragic close. To its close also comes the most profoundly real and moving tragedy of our time. Published September, 1929. $2.50

"With the complete history of Richard Mahony before us, we can at last estimate its place in English fiction. We expect that discriminating readers will place it on a level with, if not higher than, Galsworthy's Forsyte Chronicles; nor are we unreasonable in suggesting that it may be considered the soundest accomplishment of English fiction in the twentieth century."
The Saturday Review of Literature

"Fifty years from now the works of Henry Handel Richardson will probably be read as classics of our day, and the figures of Richard and Mary Mahony will stand among great characters of fiction." *The Golden Book*

Every critic urges you to read Henry Handel Richardson's great trilogy; but her books are too real to become a literary fashion. You read them not to discuss the latest thing in fiction; you read them for one of the memorable experiences of your life.

At all bookstores

 W. W. NORTON & COMPANY, INC.
70 Fifth Avenue, New York
Books that Live

Figure 6.2 "Completing the greatest event in modern fiction": *Saturday Review of Literature*, 12 April 1930. Image courtesy of the Unz Review, www.unz.com.

her books are too real to become a literary fashion. You read them not to discuss the latest thing in fiction; you read them for one of the memorable experiences of your life". After the success of *Ultima Thule*, however, sales of the first and second volumes of the trilogy were disappointing. As Sinclair Lewis later suggested, perhaps "there were too many readers who supposed they already knew the whole story, and the trilogy met with one-tenth of the excitement it merited".[100] Nonetheless, Norton continued to promote Richardson's books to discriminating readers, advertising *The Getting of Wisdom* alongside Plato's *Dialogues* and books on physiology and psychoanalysis, as "Books For The Intelligent Minority ... for those to whom ideas are alive, to whom the pursuit of knowledge is an exciting adventure".[101]

As with *Maurice Guest*, the impetus for the reissue of *The Getting of Wisdom* came from the American side rather than from England. Again Richardson revised the novel, here "in the light of her later style as it had evolved during the writing of the trilogy".[102] Norton purchased sheets from Heinemann, releasing its edition in late 1931. Heinemann and Norton also worked together on the one-volume edition of the trilogy, published in England in November 1930 and in the United States in September 1931. In 1934, Norton published Richardson's stories, *The End of a Childhood*, and in 1936 it sold the rights to reprint *Maurice Guest* to Bennet Cerf and Donald Klopfer for the acclaimed Modern Library.[103] Cerf and Klopfer purchased plates for printing an edition of 5000 copies, published in late October 1936, alongside André Malraux's *Man's Fate* and William James' *The Varieties of Religious Experience*. Sales were poor, however, and the book was remaindered at the beginning of 1940. Still, the American edition of Richardson's new novel *The Young Cosima*, published in early 1939 – Richardson thought the production "most exquisite" – quickly sold out its first printing of 5000 and was well into a second printing of 2000 by mid-April.[104] By the end of the decade, Richardson had enjoyed a level of critical appreciation and, on at least one occasion, a level of sales success in the United States beyond any other living Australian author.[105]

An Australian Saga

With the appearance in rapid succession of *Australia Felix* and *The Way Home*, the whole Mahony trilogy was available and its Australian dimensions could not but impress themselves upon reviewers. The account of colonial society and the goldfields in *Australia Felix* attracted particular praise. While it could still be read conventionally as "a story

---

100 Sinclair Lewis, foreword to *The Fortunes of Richard Mahony*, by Henry Handel Richardson (New York: Readers Club, 1941), v; see also "Reprints, New Editions", *New York Herald Tribune*, 25 May 1941.
101 Norton advertisement, *New York Times*, 21 February, 1932.
102 Steele and Probyn, introduction to *The Getting of Wisdom*, liii-liv.
103 Correspondence between Norton and Bennet Cerf/Donald Klopfer (The Modern Library), 30 December 1935–39 October 1936. Random House Records, 1925-99. Rare Book and Manuscript Library, Columbia University, MS 1048 Box 101. Further information forwarded by Lise Jaillant.
104 Clive Probyn and Bruce Steele, introduction to *The Young Cosima*, by Henry Handel Richardson (Melbourne: Australian Scholarly Publishing, 2004), xx, xxxi.
105 In terms of sales, Alice Grant Rosman might exceed Richardson, and through their multiple editions some of the nineteenth-century novels may have sold larger numbers, but with little return to their authors as we have seen.

full of adventure and romance", most reviewers responded to its larger ambitions.[106] It showed "the whole scope of Australian society ... the whole panorama of the colony ... the fluidity of social and economic conditions in a young and booming land".[107] Henry Hazlitt reviewed both *Australia Felix* and *The Way Home* for the *Nation*, where he had become literary editor in 1930. He admired the great "richness and sweep" of the former, but found it most interesting as a revelation of the pioneer seen through the contrary eyes of Richard Mahony. Again it reminded him "how deeply the outlook of the pioneer still colors our own national life".[108] For John Chapman in the *Dallas Morning News*, "All Australians are the principal character, or rather something almost transcendental, like Man in Australia".[109] The trilogy was "pure Australian" and would do for Australia what writers of the American southwest had been attempting for their region. At the other end of the country and the day, Susan Wilbur in the *Chicago Evening Post* declared the trilogy "almost more the story of Australia itself than the story of two individuals".[110] In the *Atlantic Monthly*, the always interesting Mary Ross wrote that although its scene was "furthest removed" from the lives of its American readers, the trilogy was "far closer to American sympathies" than Russian and French novels, for in Australia, too, "a new country is on the make, scrambling diverse races and traditions, snubbing over-sensitivity, rewarding boldness".[111]

Louis Kronenberger, like Hazlitt a leading critic and close follower of Richardson's work, reviewed each new title for the *New York Times*. For *Australia Felix*, he emphasised the novel's focus on human character and its insistence that "character is fate", but he also stressed its achievement in providing "a permanent picture of Australia during the '50s and '60s, in the days which followed the gold rush", its "rawness and vulgarity".[112] Again, the parallels could not be resisted: "[This] materialistic wilderness having behind it just enough English tradition to be superior in 'gentility' to our own California of the same period, glares horribly on our eyes". His review of *The Way Home* was an opportunity to assess the whole trilogy as "a very remarkable work", bearing comparison with Maugham's *Of Human Bondage* and Thomas Mann's *Buddenbrooks*: it "stirs in us that deep response which we call the spiritual force of true literature".[113]

The publication of the trilogy was declared no less than "the most important event in the field of fiction in the American publishing seasons of 1929-30".[114] Although critics felt variously that the first and second volumes of the trilogy were less deeply tragic than the third, each had its own virtues, which some preferred. Its "consummate unity", one wrote, had "enabled the trilogy to survive the illogical order of its appearance".[115] Richardson's press clipping scrapbooks again show the novels being discussed by community reading

---

106 "Companion Book for Last Year's Hit is Published", *Times* (Buffalo, NY), 2 March 1930.
107 "Notes on Novels", *New Republic*, 5 March 1930, 80.
108 Henry Hazlitt, "The Pioneer Soul", *Nation*, 5 February 1930, 153.
109 John Chapman, "Significant Group of Novels Presents Epic of Australia", *Morning News* (Dallas, TX), 3 August 1930.
110 Susan Wilbur, "Australian Background", *Chicago Evening Post*, 6 June 1930.
111 Mary Ross, "The Bookshelf", *Atlantic Monthly*, June 1930, 22.
112 Louis Kronenberger, "In 'Australia Felix' the Prelude to Mrs. Richardson's 'Ultima Thule'", *New York Times*, 26 January 1930.
113 Louis Kronenberger, "Rounding Out the Richardson Trilogy", *New York Times*, 17 April 1930.
114 Marguerite S. Kerns, "'The Way Home' Reveals Henry Handel Richardson as Gifted Social Satirist", *Herald* (Grand Rapids, MI), 17 April 1930.
115 "Notes on Novels", *New Republic*, 9 July 1930, 214.

groups, selected for public lectures including one delivered at "California University" on the outstanding book of the year, recommended as reading for social workers and in a list of 100 books for Catholic readers, and featured in newspaper personality profiles and in magazines such as the *Catholic World* and *Good Housekeeping*.[116] The three volumes were very clearly among "the most discussed books of the day".[117]

Reviewers worked through their reactions to the trilogy's apparently Victorian or "old-fashioned" style, most finding that it was perfectly suited to the task; many praised its portrait of a marriage, managed without recourse to the stock-in-trade of the modern novelist, "no sex escapades, no adultery".[118] Evaluations remained high, especially for the trilogy considered as a whole: "one of the truly great novel series in contemporary English literature"; "one of the finest and soundest achievements in early twentieth century fiction"; "unquestionably one of the few securely outstanding works of fiction of our time".[119] Dorothy Canfield wrote an appreciative essay on the two "new" novels for the *Book-of-the-Month Club* News, concluding that they were "as good as novels can be, painting a portrait of two countries done not only with fearless honesty but with a deep if unobtrusive sympathy and understanding".[120]

Critical evaluations were further reinforced with the release of the one-volume edition (at over 1000 pages) in September 1931. For Margaret Wallace in the *New York Evening Post*, it was "a single work as important as, and perhaps more important than, any that has appeared in our generation".[121] She offered a considered, even prescient reflection on Richardson's critical standing in the longer term:

> It is too soon by half a century to form an estimate of the enduring worth of Henry Handel Richardson's trilogy. Her study of Richard Mahony is enormous in scope and almost surgical in its incisive accuracy. We are not asked to sympathise with him, nor are we asked to judge him; we may even suspect – although it seems almost impossible in a work as powerful as this one – that Henry Richardson herself neither sympathises nor judges. It is this intellectual detachment, and a consequent failure to enlist our deepest emotions, which may constitute for this book a claim to unique greatness. Or which, on the other hand, may ultimately bar it from immortality.[122]

Hazlitt and Grattan, again, gave more consideration to the novels' standing as Australian literature. For Hazlitt, the trilogy was "probably the most important single piece of literature ever to come out of Australia; it takes its place among the handful of fiction masterpieces in

---

116 Henry Neumann, "'Ultima Thule': A Tale of Courageous Duty", *Standard* (New York), 1 July 1930; "The Chronicles of the Fortunes of Richard Mahony", *Catholic World*, September 1930; Emily Newell Blair, "Books You Will Not Forget", *Good Housekeeping*, October 1930; "100 Books Selected by Catholic Clergy", *New York Times*, 28 February 1931.
117 *Sacramento Union*, 12 April 1930. The paper reports a meeting of student nurses discussing the books.
118 J.O. Myers, "One Man, One Woman – and the Paths They Took", *News* (St Paul, MN), 18 May 1930.
119 Arnold Mulder, "Adventures in the Library", *Daily News* (Ann Arbor, MI), 21 March 1930; "Important Work of Day's Fiction Now Completed", *Tribune* (Salt Lake City, UT), 1 June 1930; *Evening News* (Buffalo, NY), 3 May 1930.
120 Dorothy Canfield, "Australia Felix and the Way Home", *Book-of-the-Month Club News*, 1930, n.p.
121 Margaret Wallace, "Henry Richardson's Bid for Immortality", *Evening Post* (New York), 19 December 1931.
122 Wallace, "Henry Richardson's Bid for Immortality".

English that have so far appeared in this century".[123] Grattan similarly appraised it on both scales, as Australian and against the whole array of English-language fiction. He thought it "by far the most important piece of literature having its setting in Australia that has yet been produced". His wording was deliberate, however, for he added immediately:

> I do not consider it an Australian novel, for the very good reason that the central character is not an Australian and because so much of the action has to do with yearnings for England and with residence there. This novel stands in that tradition of Anglo-Australian literature of which Henry Kingsley's "Geoffrey Hamlyn" was the first example. It is the final flowering of that tradition, and anything that follows after it will have to be superlatively fine not to be dismissed with a shrug.[124]

This distinction was probably not of great import for Grattan's immediate readers. The trilogy was established as an "Australian saga" and one of the major works in English fiction of the period. Richardson herself was ambivalent about being "branded as the 'Australian authoress'", as she put it to Norton: "I have no desire to be marked for life as an 'Australian writer' (though of course I keep this private)".[125] But as one reviewer asserted, "In the public mind she is now indelibly associated with Australia".[126]

Richardson's Later Critical Reception

None of Richardson's other novels were as commercially successful as *Ultima Thule*. A later article suggests that *Australia Felix* sold less than 2000 copies and *The Way Home* less than 3000, although *Australia Felix* did appear in bestseller lists.[127] Although the publishing industry survived the Depression reasonably well, Richardson's sales might have been diminished by the economic conditions of the early 1930s, which possibly affected literary more than light fiction. Nonetheless, *Maurice Guest* in its new edition received a critical reception almost on a par with that of the Mahony trilogy. Despite its different setting and scope, many reviewers found in it precisely the qualities they had valued in the trilogy – its compassion but lack of sentimentality, its realism and "stern classical restraint of emotion", and its depth of characterisation, "modern in psychological acumen, modern in psychoanalytical appreciation".[128] For Mary Ross, again, in an odd but evocative image, it was "as alive and as impersonal as the view from a headland looking out to sea", with the "wide, clean sweep of authentic tragedy"; for Morton Zabel, it would "remind the reading public of the value of absolute aesthetic integrity".[129] Whether or not it was a deliberate

---

123 Hazlitt, "A Great Trilogy".
124 C. Hartley Grattan, "'Australia Felix': A Fine Unit in a Great Trilogy", *New York World*, 9 February 1930.
125 Richard quoted in Ackland, *Henry Handel Richardson*, 264-65.
126 Rex Hunter, "Twenty Years After", *New York Sun*, 5 September 1930.
127 Preliminary notice for the trilogy's appearance in the New York Readers Club, May 1941. *Australia Felix* was listed among bestsellers in two cuttings from the *Milwaukee Journal*, March 1930.
128 Harriet Sheldon, "An Earlier Novel Worthy Predecessor of 'Ultima Thule'", *Baltimore Sun*, 17 September 1930; *Washington Star*, 12 October 1930.
129 Mary Ross, "The Power of an Obsession", *New York Herald Tribune*, 16 November 1930; Morton Dauwen Zabel, "The Revival of 'Maurice Guest'", *Nation*, 8 October 1930, 380.

strategy by the publishers, releasing *Maurice Guest* after the trilogy enabled such qualities to be widely appreciated. While some again found the style dated, Richardson's best readers discovered the book's modernity. In the wonderful phrase of Marguerite Kerns, it was "a vindictively modern book":

> Miss Richardson's style, unpretentious, accurate, and occasionally acidulous, is exactly the same medium in her first published book that it is in her later work …
>
> Even more surprising is the boldness with which in 1908 she was attacking themes then almost unknown in the English novel. "Maurice Guest" is a study of love as a destroying force; its challenges are very much those raised by Aldous Huxley or those uttered more frivolously by Carl Van Vechten. That Miss Richardson is careful to present abnormality against a background of the normal proves her a better artist than either of these gentlemen, but does not alter the essential modernity of her theme.[130]

The Getting of Wisdom, though often seen as a "small" book in comparison to *Maurice Guest* and the trilogy, was nonetheless valued as "wholly realistic and wholly human", original in its field, and, indeed, "on the creative level of her greater novels". Richardson demonstrated again "those two great qualities of the born novelist: a love of truth and a gift of deep understanding … an integrity and a wisdom all too rare in current fiction".[131] Again, while one or two reviewers found it irretrievably old-fashioned – or simply foreign to American audiences – Richardson's modernity struck its best readers. Comparisons were made with Joyce, Colette and Katherine Mansfield.[132]

The End of a Childhood, the first new book Norton published, appeared in 1934 to a quieter, more mixed reception, unsurprisingly given the range of its contents; but as with *The Getting of Wisdom* reviewers still saw Richardson's strengths: "the easy mastery of the psychology of the mature and the immature, the ability to adjust the point of view to the person whose thoughts and understanding are being presented, the concreteness of imagery in the style, and the outstanding ability to strike a proper balance between psychological analysis as such and the environmental elements which have influenced or determined the psychology".[133] In Kronenberger's words, "'The End of a Childhood' is a minor book, but it bears the accent of a major author".[134] Reviewers were eager for the continuing story of Mary and Cuffy Mahony, and were not disappointed.

The Young Cosima, published in 1939 and Richardson's first new novel for a decade, divided reviewers more violently. It certainly had its supporters, proclaiming the novel "an artistic triumph" and, in one case, a "better book on a greater theme"

---

130 Marguerite S. Kerns, "Henry Handel Richardson's First Novel Notable for Mature Artistry, Originality", *Herald* (Grand Rapids, MI), 31 August 1930.
131 "A Revised Novel", *New York Times*, 24 January 1932; Rosamund Milner, "The Way of All Youth", *Courier Journal* (Louisville, KY), 14 February 1932.
132 For example, "To the Life", *Evening Sun* (Baltimore, MD), 6 February 1932; Hazel Hawthorne, "Mirror of Girlhood", *New Republic*, 3 February 1932, 329.
133 C. Hartley Grattan, "Australian Stories", *Saturday Review of Literature*, 17 November 1934, 289.
134 Louis Kronenberger, "New Tales by H.H. Richardson", *New York Times*, 18 November 1934. Other extended reviews appeared in the *New Yorker*, 17 November; and from Rex Hunter in the *New York Sun*, 10 November; C. Hartley Grattan, *Saturday Review of Literature*, 17 November; and Mary Ross, *New York Herald Tribune*, 18 November 1934.

than *Maurice Guest*.¹³⁵ Its highest praise was offered by its most qualified critic, the novelist and Mozart biographer Marcia Davenport, writing in the *Saturday Review of Literature*, and it was recommended as an alternate selection by the Book-of-the-Month Club.¹³⁶ Norton's publicity quoted Carl Van Vechten: "Who else but Henry Handel Richardson could bring to life the tortured love story of Cosima von Bülow and Richard Wagner? That she has succeeded brilliantly any reader of *Maurice Guest* can be sure".¹³⁷ Clifton Fadiman, by contrast, summed it up as "a carefully written failure" and a waste of Richardson's magnificent gifts. For John Erskine, her conscientious reporting had "tortured her style to a point where the book becomes extremely awkward". The dominant note in the major papers was disappointment: to Kronenberger it seemed "only a most competent and understanding 'study'"; for Zabel in the *Nation* it was a "comparatively slight display" of Richardson's great talents.¹³⁸

Richardson's final appearance in the American market in this period was in 1941 when the *The Fortunes of Richard Mahony* in one volume was reissued by the New York Readers Club. Launched in March 1941, the club's mission was "to save good books from oblivion" and its selections were made by a panel of influential authors and critics – Sinclair Lewis, Clifton Fadiman, Carl Van Doren and Alexander Woollcott.¹³⁹ Unlike other book clubs it did not offer bestsellers "but rather those fine books of yesterday which never reached best-seller status at all", giving readers "a second chance to savor literary delights familiar as yet to a handful of the discriminating only".¹⁴⁰ Richardson's reputation was still substantial enough in 1941 for the trilogy to appear as the club's third offering. An optimistic 75,000 copies were printed, a full-page advertisement was placed in the *New York Times*, and the book itself came with the imprimatur of an introduction by Sinclair Lewis.¹⁴¹ Lewis made the book available to a new generation of American readers through the familiar device of drawing parallels between the two nations' pioneering histories:

> Americans, most of them, are going to be a little astonished by the parallel of our own pioneering, and the harsher places of our land, with those of Australia. Here, in Mahony's Australia, are our own Californian and Alaskan and Coloradan gold-rushes. Here are our rich pioneers filling pine castles with every known piece of junk that will hold gilt, and their shanty villages that explode into cities, and their too "refined" families. Here are our own dust-bowl and Arizona deserts and ragged mountains. Here is our medley of British and Irish and Germans, loving the Old country yet, with a bitterness the citizenry Back Home do not comprehend, resenting their condescension.¹⁴²

---

135 "Musicians' Mingled Lives", *Chicago Tribune*, 18 March 1939; Georgiana S. Stevens, "Herr Wagner Played in Brass", *San Francisco Chronicle*, 2 April 1939.
136 Marcia Davenport, "H.H. Richardson's New Musical Novel", *Saturday Review of Literature*, 25 March 1939, 6; Amy Loveman, *Book-of-the-Month Club News*, April 1939.
137 Norton advertisement, *New York Times*, 7 April 1939.
138 Clifton Fadiman, *New Yorker*, 25 March 1939, 84; John Erskine, *New York Herald Tribune*, 2 April 1939; Louis Kronenberger, "Young Cosima and Her Two Men", *New York Times*, 2 April 1939; Morton Dauwen Zabel, "The Imperfect Wagnerites", *Nation*, 8 April 1939, 408.
139 *New York Times*, 11 May 1941.
140 "New Readers' Guild Revives Books Public Overlooked", *Los Angeles Times*, 10 August 1941.
141 *New York Times*, 11 May 1941, 15.
142 Lewis, foreword to *Fortunes of Richard Mahony*, vi–vii.

6 Becoming Articulate: Henry Handel Richardson and Katharine Susannah Prichard

An Australian List

When Norton published Katharine Prichard's *Coonardoo* in November 1930, the publisher made sure the fact was newsworthy, not least by connecting it to Richardson's current fame. *Publishers Weekly* printed a paragraph, no doubt provided by Norton itself, informing readers that *Coonardoo* was about to be released, that it had won the Sydney *Bulletin* prize for best Australian novel of the year, and that it came with an endorsement from the "author of 'Ultima Thule'" to the effect that Prichard stood "a very good chance of becoming *the* representative Australian writer".[143] Grattan had earlier advised Norton that Prichard was "the hope of the Australian novel".[144] Notices linking the two authors appeared in the *Saturday Review of Literature* and numerous newspapers, and on at least two occasions *Australia Felix* and *Coonardoo* were reviewed together.[145] Norton also used the inside back flap of its edition of *Coonardoo* to advertise the recent publication of Richardson's novel. As noted at the beginning of this chapter, the presence of Richardson and Prichard together compelled reviewers to reassess their understanding of Australia and its literature. "Australia is largely an unknown country to American readers," wrote one, "but 'Ultima Thule,' that literary sensation of last year, helped focus attention on that far-off land as a theme for fiction and now [with the publication of *Australia Felix* and *Coonardoo*] new evidence along that line comes to light"; indeed, *Coonardoo* was "even more distinctively Australian" than Richardson's novels.[146] The *Saturday Review of Literature* (under the vernacular heading "Coo-ee!") remarked that it was "predictable after the novels of Henry Handel Richardson had found recognition in America that other works of Australian origin" would be published. The force of *Coonardoo* was such that it presented "not only an Australian writer but the Australians".[147]

It is not clear why Prichard's relationship with Viking ceased rather than continuing alongside that with Jonathan Cape, but the fact underscores how publishing in the United States for Australian authors was even more than usual a title-by-title proposition.[148] Prichard had probably been brought to Norton's attention by Grattan, if not by Aanestäd in London, and adding Prichard to Richardson was the firm's first major step towards developing an Australian list. To Nettie Palmer, Norton wrote that *Coonardoo* "despite its obvious literary shortcomings, is to me a most beautiful and moving story". He also wondered whether Palmer might help in correcting Prichard's faults in sentence structure and style.[149] Norton sent a copy to Richardson, too, seeking her opinion. Richardson replied, using the phrase that Norton would pick up for its later publicity:

> I have now read the book, & think it undoubtedly the best thing Katherine [sic] Prichard has done so far. It is a very fresh, vivid & truthful picture of station life in far North West

---

143 *Publishers Weekly*, 1 November 1930.
144 Grattan to Norton, 25 January 1930. Copy in Prichard Papers, Box 19, Folder 7.
145 "Australian Novels", *Call* (Newark, NJ), 23 March 1930; "From Australia Come Two Distinctive Novels by Women", *Standard* (New Bedford, MA), 17 April 1930. In the latter, *Coonardoo* was seen as romantic rather than realistic but still strongly recommended.
146 "Australian Novels" (see above).
147 "Coo-ee!", *Saturday Review of Literature*, 8 March 1930, 798.
148 Prichard wrote that she had received no royalties account from Viking since the first payment. KSP to Norton, 17 August 1932.
149 Norton to Palmer, 23 October and 30 December 1930, Norton Records.

of Australia … If only she does not hurry too much in her production … she stands a very good chance, I think, of becoming *the* representative Australian writer …

As you say, K.P.'s style leaves much to be desired & as for her punctuation - I wonder who read the proofs, or if anyone read them at all.

I hope the book will do well in America. It deserves to.[150]

Like Richardson, Prichard valued Norton's commitment to book production. As Hetherington notes, Norton "displayed a care for Prichard's writing that seems both more personal and more meticulous than the treatment she received from Jonathan Cape".[151] A great deal of effort was put into the design and resetting of *Coonardoo*, as Norton thought Cape's edition "a tremendous handicap to any author's work [and] altogether the worst piece of printing I have ever seen".[152] The Norton wrapper and end papers featured an original two-colour design with white cockatoos flying over green farmland. The cockatoo design also featured in some of Norton's advertisements for the novel, which linked Prichard to Olive Schreiner and Louis Hémon: "What *The Story of an African Farm* did for South Africa - What *Maria Chapdelaine* did for French Canada - this dramatic novel does for the last frontier of tropic Nor'West Australia. Over the purple land the cockatoos whirl and scream, as they watch the tense movement of this powerful story … the story of a love that shatters the codes of white man and native alike" (See Fig. 6.3 for an alternative version).[153] Prichard wrote of her pleasure at the book's appearance, and imagined the cockatoos "screaming round the book as it drops into an American city."[154]

Norton replied in June 1930, his first letter directly to Prichard, noting that the book had had "splendid reviews throughout" and had been recommended by the American Library Association. Most of the letter, however, concerned his enthusiasm for Prichard's next novel, *Haxby's Circus*, published by Cape in 1930, which he had just finished "at the well known two or three AM":

It is a grand book and if only those additional chapters which you promise help us out on our point of criticism, I pledge you my word to back it to the limit … So, then, if you are able to dispatch these additional four chapters direct to us by early November - to arrive here in late December - we shall be all set for February publication; an event which you may be sure I am looking forward to in the effort to prove to you that you have a sympathetic publisher here in America.[155]

The additional chapters Norton mentioned refer to material that had been removed from Cape's edition, creating a structural weakness in the novel that Prichard herself had identified, partly in response to a reader's report by Grattan that Norton had forwarded to her. She reworked the material, which appeared in the American edition only, published

---

150 HHR to Norton, 30 January 1930. *Letters*, 155.
151 Hetherington, "Authors, Editors, Publishers", 420.
152 Norton to Palmer, 30 December 1929. Norton Records.
153 Norton advertisement in Prichard Papers, Series 10 Correspondence, Box 17, Folder 9. All KSP correspondence from this source unless otherwise indicated.
154 KSP to Norton, 20 May 1930. Norton explained in his reply (see next note) that he had hoped the colour scheme "had been happier" but it was about the sixth different combination that had been tried. He was delighted with the binding, however, "both color and cloth".
155 Norton to KSP, 27 June 1930.

Figure 6.3 Advertisement for Katharine Susannah Prichard's *Coonardoo* (New York: W.W. Norton & Co., 1930) alongside Richardson's *Australia Felix*, from the *New York Times*, 16 March 1930.

as *Fay's Circus* in 1931, making for a much stronger novel. Prichard wrote how "absolutely delighted" she was with the American version: "Would rather use it myself than the English".[156] Despite Prichard's comments, only the Cape edition has ever been reprinted in Australia.

Norton may have been worried about sales, for he appears to have suggested selling *Fay's Circus* at a lower price than *Coonardoo*.[157] Its first American review, in the *New York Times*, was also disappointing, "the only thoroughly mean review of my work I've ever seen", Prichard remarked. She wrote to Norton: "The first cheque for 'Fay's' was a little ray of sunshine; but this reverse, the only American review I've had so far, will overcast your plans, I'm afraid. I'm more distressed on your account than my own really - though it matters so much for the book to go well". In September 1932, Norton reflected on the limited sales success of the two novels: "I have a feeling that if we had only made *Coonardoo* a little easier for Americans to read we could have done much better with it. As to *Fay's Circus* ... there is this strange prejudice in the USA against circus novels ... Donald Adams, the editor of the *NY Times Book Review* ... said 'My God, not a circus novel after *Coonardoo*!' because he, our most important critic, was really genuinely impressed with both *Working Bullocks* and *Coonardoo*".[158]

Despite the presence of Richardson's and other Australian novels in the marketplace, *Coonardoo* was largely reviewed in isolation. In his lengthy *New York Times* review, John Carter made no mention of *Australia Felix*, despite both books being published in early 1930 and by the same publisher.[159] He invoked a framework similar to that the publishers had used, comparing Prichard with other "distinguished women writing of the inarticulate dark-skinned races of the world in their tragic contacts with the whites": writers such as Julia Peterkin, who wrote about African Americans in the Carolinas, and Sarah Gertrude Millin, who wrote of black South Africans. This made good sense for contemporary American readers, however discomfiting it might be for Australian readers then and now. *Coonardoo*, Carter wrote, would introduce Americans to an idiom "as distinctive and compelling as the wigwams, moccasins and papooses of North America or the Afro-American locutions of Uncle Remus", even if the "aboriginal lingo" was "apt to strike the American ear as absurd". He thought the novel lacked "dramatic interest" and a coherent structure. Predictably perhaps, he praised its representation of landscape, above all, and less predictably its portrayal of "the strange aboriginal tribes dying of civilization as though it were a deadly disease, as perhaps it is". Nonetheless, he concluded, *Coonardoo* "stands as a forceful piece of social documentation and bids fair to do for Australia what *Uncle Tom's Cabin* did for America and Mrs. Millin is doing for South Africa - to make the white race face the facts of its treatment and study of the black descendants of the aborigines, through an authentic piece of national literature which raises a parochial problem to the level of the universal".[160]

Reviews of *Fay's Circus* often did make a link to *Coonardoo*, if only to note that the Australian setting was less important in the new novel. The *New York Times* review of *Fay's*

---

156 KSP to Norton, 4 June 1931. See Hetherington, "Authors, Editors, Publishers", 421-27.
157 Prichard writes: "I like the idea of a lower price for the book. The more accessible books are the better". *Coonardoo* sold at $2.50, *Fay's Circus* at $2.00. KSP to Norton, 4 June 1931.
158 Norton to KSP, 27 September 1932.
159 A *New York Times* "Books and Authors" column of 22 December 1929 notes *Australia Felix* as forthcoming in January and *Coonardoo* in late February 1930.
160 John Carter, "In the Back Country of Australia", *New York Times*, 16 March 1930.

Circus that upset Prichard in fact had praised its "authentic, unsentimentalized picture of circus life", but the reviewer found the novel dull and long-winded, lacking convincing characters and "imaginative lift": "There is no magic in her writing, no exuberance".[161] There were several more positive notices praising the book's "color and drama, pathos, and comedy, and best of all [its] unquestionable stamp of authenticity"; it was a "strong story with great literary merit".[162] These were in much less prestigious publications, however, with next to no influence on readers, critics and booksellers of the kind that the New York papers could have. The *New York Sun* at least was welcoming, making *Fay's Circus* its "Book of the Day".[163] The framework of comparison this time was provided by other recent "travelling entertainment" novels: Edna Ferber's *Showboat* (1926) and J.B. Priestley's equally bestselling *The Good Companions* (1929). Indeed, these were the kind of comparisons that could underwrite a successful international career.

The End of the Line

The fact of having had two consecutive novels published by one of America's emerging literary houses, accompanied by a string of favourable reviews, could well have augured a strong future for Prichard in the American market, but in comparison to Richardson her later dealings in the United States present a somewhat sad, drawn-out finale. Her collection of stories, *Kiss on the Lips*, appeared from Cape in 1932, but Norton did not believe short stories were viable in the American market. He was keen, though, to see a copy of *Intimate Strangers* in order to start working on "any necessary Americanizations", suggesting he was committed to publishing the new novel.[164] However, there would be a gap of almost five years before the novel was finally ready for publication, a period of intense political activity and personal tragedy for Prichard, and this appears to have broken the close relationship between author and publisher. Whether Norton rejected the novel or whether it was never sent is unknown.

Prichard's next novel, *Moon of Desire* (1941), was something of a detour, written expressly, as she put it, "with a view to film sales", partly in response to the presence of American troops in Australia, partly because of her own financial needs.[165] It appears not to have been offered to Norton. Prichard signed a contract instead with New York's Greenberg: Publisher in November 1941, but learnt more than a year later, in January 1943, that months earlier the firm had decided not to publish any more fiction and so were not proceeding. Letters from Curtis Brown New York sent to Prichard in May 1942 informing her of this decision had not arrived, and Prichard had been waiting for her author's copies of the published book unaware that the publisher had reneged on the deal.[166] The novel sold well for Cape, but it was never published in the United States. Prichard did receive a share of the $200 American advance, which, according to the common pattern, amounted

---

161 "Circus Life", *New York Times*, 12 April 1931.
162 "Fay's Circus", *Patriot Ledger* (Quincy, MA); "Scanning New Books", *Daily Argus-Leader* (Sioux Falls, SD), n.d.
163 Henry Wolcott Boynton, "The Book of the Day: Fate Spins the Life of a Young Girl Under the Big Tent in Australia", *New York Sun*, 19 May 1931.
164 KSP to Norton, 4 November 1931; Norton to KSP, 27 September 1932.
165 KSP to Alan Collins (Curtis Brown New York), 4 April 1942.
166 Correspondence between KSP and Naomi Burton and Collins, 4 April 1942 to 19 January 1943.

to £37 5s 9d by the time it arrived in Australia minus 10 per cent agent's commission, 27.5 per cent US alien tax, and three dollars for *ad interim* copyright registration.[167] Curtis Brown had, in the meantime, tried three other publishers without success and also failed to interest the film studios, despite Prichard's urgings.

William Norton's death in November 1945 came only six months after Prichard had made contact with him again after a long silence. He had replied warmly, affirming that *Coonardoo* remained one of his favourite books and apologising that it was impossible because of wartime restrictions to reprint either of her Norton titles. He was therefore returning the copyrights to her; but he assured Prichard he would ask Cape for an advance copy of her new novel, "which we will most certainly want to give careful consideration for publication here in the USA".[168] The new novel was *The Roaring Nineties*, the first book in a projected goldfields trilogy. Australian historical trilogies, of course, had done well for Norton and large-scale historical fiction had been a dominant form in the US market over the previous decade, including the Australian examples discussed in Chapter 7. Nothing came of Norton's interest, however, and Curtis Brown's New York office decided against taking on the novel as they were, in Jonathan Cape's words, "not sufficiently assured of its attractions for American publishers".[169] Cape, by contrast, on the strength of *The Roaring Nineties*, offered a new and favourable contract for three additional novels.[170] Both Cape and Spencer Curtis Brown in London repeatedly expressed their confidence in the book's chances in the United States. Curtis Brown wrote of his surprise at the unfavourable American reaction, but added, "I am perfectly certain that the book will be sold there and will be successful. I have spoken about it to several American publishers who have been over here and all of them have been keenly interested".[171] He gave it to a representative from Harpers, and had Scribner, Doubleday and Macmillan in his sights.[172]

The New York branch's lack of interest in the book and their failure with *Moon of Desire* led Prichard, like other Australians before her, to change her American agent, from Curtis Brown to Leland Hayward in New York. Ellen Newald from Leland Hayward's Foreign Department was also confident of the new novel's chances in the American market: "Three of us in the office have read the book with very keen interest and pleasure and we are not at all discouraged by the list of rejections, but do agree with you that there should be an American publisher who will want to put your work on his list".[173] She sent *The Roaring Nineties* to Farrar, Straus, then to Random House, with no success. The completion of *Golden Miles*, the second book in the trilogy, sparked another round of optimism and disappointment. In April 1947, Cape wrote: "I have had two enquiries from the United States about your work, following on the success, as they understand it to be, of *The Roaring Nineties*. These two firms, Harper and Scribner, both turned down *The Roaring Nineties* when I offered it to them, but they seem to be nibbling round again". Macmillan in the United States had also been keen but declined, doubtful they could sell enough copies.[174]

---

167 KSP to Collins, 22 June 1942.
168 Norton to KSP, 11 July 1945.
169 Cape to KSP, 25 March 1946.
170 Cape to KSP, 25 March 1946.
171 Spenser Curtis Brown (London) to KSP, 26 April 1946.
172 Spenser Curtis Brown to KSP, 21 May 1946.
173 Ellen Newald to KSP, 9 October 1946.
174 Cape to KSP, 30 April and 19 September 1947.

6 Becoming Articulate: Henry Handel Richardson and Katharine Susannah Prichard

Prichard's American agents were especially hopeful because of a further article on Australian literature by Grattan in the *New York Times* Book Review in June 1947, which described Prichard as "unquestionably the most important fiction writer" in Australia, and *The Roaring Nineties* as "unquestionably the most important Australian novel of recent years".[175] Newald offered *Golden Miles* to Harper, Scribner and Appleton-Century, but pointed out there might be difficulties given that the earlier volume had not been published in the United States.[176] By the middle of 1947, Prichard had lost hope: "if American publishers don't like 'Roaring', I am not at all sanguine about their attitude towards 'Golden Miles.' The American political atmosphere, just now, does not seem to favour books which express sympathy for the working people".[177] The books' politics might well have influenced their reception among American publishers – as they did some reviews in England and Australia – but there is no direct evidence that this was the case. Either way, Prichard's American career had stalled. In 1947, "The Grey Horse", a story first published in 1924, appeared in an American anthology, *A World of Great Stories*.[178] But apart from an invitation in 1949 from editor Charles Humbolt for her to submit sections of the goldfields novels to the radical magazine *Masses & Mainstream*, Prichard's American career had effectively come to an end in 1931 with the appearance of *Fay's Circus*.[179] Unlike Richardson's novels, none of Prichard's works was included by Norton in their 1962 classics series.

Forgotten Masterpieces

Over the period from late 1929 to 1932, Richardson had five novels plus the omnibus edition of her trilogy in the American marketplace simultaneously, extraordinary for any writer but especially for a demanding literary novelist. She had had a stable of leading critics such as Henry Hazlitt, Louis Kronenberger, Hartley Grattan and Mary Ross promoting her work through intelligent, enthusiastic reviews. Her stature as one of the major English-language novelists of the era was established. The award of the Australian Literature Society's Gold Medal to *Ultima Thule* was widely reported, and in 1935 when Nettie Palmer wrote a piece on the contemporary development of Australian literature for the *Christian Science Monitor*, Richardson's portrait filled the cover.[180] She had become the face of Australian literature in American print culture, and her success drew attention to other Australian authors whose novels were then appearing in the United States. In 1940, the *Virginia Quarterly Review* published Richardson's own account of her career.[181] While Prichard's reputation could not be sustained because of the lack of regular new titles, Richardson's was supported by Norton's release of *The End of a Childhood* and reaffirmed with the Modern Library edition of *Maurice Guest*; it was still present for the reception of *The Young Cosima* and could be revived in 1941 for

---

175 C. Hartley Grattan, "Readers and Writers Down Under", *New York Times*, 22 June 1947.
176 Newald to KSP, 23 June 1947 and 6 April 1948.
177 KSP to Newald, 1 July 1947.
178 As "The Gray Horse", in *A World of Great Stories*, ed. Hiram Collins Hadyn and John Cournos (New York: Crown, 1947).
179 Charles Humboldt to KSP, 10 February 1949.
180 Nettie Palmer, "Australia Writes of Herself", *Christian Science Monitor*, 28 August 1935, 10.
181 Richardson, "Some Notes". Reprinted in *Southerly* 23, no.1 (March 1963): 8-19.

the New York Readers Club. A play based on the trilogy was performed in 1938, and in 1945 MGM paid £18,000 (or US$55,000) for film rights in *The Fortunes of Richard Mahony*, with Greer Garson and Gregory Peck earmarked for the lead roles. The film was never made, but MGM did adapt *Maurice Guest* under the title *Rhapsody*, released in 1954, directed by Charles Vidor and starring Elizabeth Taylor.

Such was her standing in literary circles that in the mid-1940s American literary agent Armitage Watkins began an ultimately fruitless search for "another Henry Handel Richardson" among Australian writers.[182] Yet even selection by the Readers Club in 1941 implied that Richardson's major work was unknown to the general reading public. Packaged as a "forgotten masterpiece", Richardson seems to have been forgotten again almost immediately except for a few committed readers who remembered *Maurice Guest* or the trilogy. In July 1946, when American academic Bruce Sutherland contributed a long article on her to the *New York Herald Tribune*'s Weekly Book Review, he was not only summing up Richardson's career but also introducing her anew to American readers.[183] And when her unfinished autobiographical sketch, *Myself When Young*, appeared posthumously in 1948, Orville Prescott could tell *New York Times* readers, "Few persons today, save those who take a semi-professional interest in literature, remember much about Henry Handel Richardson, the brilliant Australian writer who died two years ago last March at the age of 77".[184] Her books went out of print until 1962 when Norton reissued the Mahony trilogy in separate volumes, and *The Getting of Wisdom* as a children's book.

What is surprising is not that Richardson should fade from the American marketplace as a bestselling author but that her presence in the United States as a major English-language novelist should evaporate so completely. No doubt the causes were multiple. Richardson's reluctance to promote herself made it difficult for publishers to sustain the interest necessary to repeat the commercial success of *Ultima Thule*. Her slow rate of composition and especially the gap of ten years between *Ultima Thule* and *The Young Cosima* would not have helped, and as Richardson herself remarked, her novels did not have "the power to gain immediate sympathy" from a wide range of readers.[185] Norton's death in 1945 meant that Richardson lost a committed publisher in the American trade. For some, she remained a reference point for Australian literature, or for historical or musical novels, well into the 1940s, but apart from enthusiasts such as Grattan or Sutherland there were no substantial critical institutions outside the periodical press to sustain an interest in Australian literature. Nor was she drawn into higher critical discussions about the course of English fiction or the modern novel. Despite the modernity that some critics discerned in her writing, Richardson suffered the fate of other celebrated Edwardian and Georgian novelists in so far as her books fell just on the wrong side of

---

182 From a typescript by Australian-born, US-resident journalist and critic Alwyn Lee, "Australian Books Boom in the US … Maybe: American Publishers Still Seek Another H.H. Richardson", in A. Watkins Inc. papers, Watkins Loomis Records 1883-2007, Rare Book and Manuscript Library, Columbia University, Box 4, "Australia" file.
183 Bruce Sutherland, "The Career of Henry Handel Richardson: Analyst of Character, Proponent of Tragedy, Her Novels Live", *New York Herald Tribune*, 21 July 1946. Sutherland developed a lifelong interest in Australian literature and is credited with teaching the first separate course in Australian literature in the United States, in 1942. See Chapter 9 and Laurie Hergenhan, "A Literary Visit to the USA: A Memoir", *Antipodes* 26 (June 2012): 77.
184 Orville Prescott, *New York Times*, 26 July 1948, 15.
185 Richardson, "Some Notes on My Books", 338.

6 Becoming Articulate: Henry Handel Richardson and Katharine Susannah Prichard

modernism (so she disappeared as well from the record of *English* fiction). As Morton Zabel, one of her critical admirers, put it, "they play no part in the experiments or artistic advances of the modern novel".[186] But it is difficult not to conclude that Richardson's "Australianness" also played a role in making her reputation less secure, less "locatable", when critical accounts were drawn up in later decades. Her fame could not be transferred to a new generation of critics emerging in the United States postwar.

Richardson's greatest immediate impact, reinforced by Prichard's appearance in the early thirties, was to create both a market and a sense of critical anticipation for a certain genre of Australian novels – historical sagas, regional epics, "big books", no longer in the style of nineteenth-century romances but more realistic, more challenging, more modern in their approach. This larger appreciation of Australian literature is the subject of the following chapter.

---

[186] Morton Dauwen Zabel, "The Revival of 'Maurice Guest'". Zabel was the editor of *Literary Opinion in America: Essays Illustrating the Status, Methods, and Problems of Criticism in the United States since the War* (New York: Harper, 1937).

7
"Australia is very American": Australian Historical Fiction in America 1920s–1940s

The previous chapter revealed how, in the early 1930s, Norton's publication of Henry Handel Richardson's *Ultima Thule* and the *Fortunes of Richard Mahony* trilogy brought Australia and its literature "deep into the consciousness of reading America".[1] The impact of Richardson's novels was strengthened by the appearance of Katharine Susannah Prichard's *Coonardoo* in 1930 from the same publisher. Richardson's and Prichard's novels were in fact part of a longer sequence of ambitious Australian works published in the United States from the late 1920s to the mid 1940s. In contrast to the decline in the number of Australian novels published in America across the first three decades of the twentieth century, at the very end of the 1920s we begin to see a cluster of substantial novels appearing together – and being brought together by reviewers. Fiction publishing in general in the United States grew rapidly from a low point in 1919 to a peak in 1929; the number of titles dipped slightly through the Depression years but high levels continued until the early forties.[2] Against this background, the pattern of publication and increased receptivity for Australian novels was sustained until the mid-forties, but with little continuity into the postwar years when many writers had, in effect, to begin again in establishing the viability of Australian work in the American marketplace. There is, then, a relatively discrete historical trajectory across the two decades from the late twenties, emerging from almost nothing and collapsing in the later forties as both cultural and industrial circumstances change.

Among the substantial novels published in this period are Martin Boyd's family saga *The Madeleine Heritage* (1928), Dorothy Cottrell's *The Singing Gold* (1929) and *Tharlane* (1930), M. Barnard Eldershaw's *A House is Built* (1929) and *Green Memory* (1931), Helen Simpson's *Boomerang* (1932) and *The Woman on the Beast* (1933), and G.B. Lancaster's *Pageant* (1933).[3] The cumulative impact of this sequence of novels – and what enabled them to be perceived *as* a sequence – was their convergence around a number of key genres: the family or regional saga, the pioneering "epic", and the epochal historical novel.

---

1 Mae A. Conklin, "Books and Things", *Register* (New Haven, CT), 30 March 1930.
2 John Tebbel, *A History of Book Publishing in the United States, Vol. III: The Golden Age Between Two Wars, 1920–1940* (New York: Bowker, 1978), 682-84.
3 Some of Jean Devanny's novels might also be brought into this field, especially *Bushman Burke* (1930) and *Out of Such Fires* (1934).

The works are typically large scale, often in the classic saga form of the trilogy or the long novel divided internally into three books, as were *The Madeleine Heritage* and *A House is Built*. Some veer towards historical romance, others towards irony; some are conventional, others more experimental in technique. What draws them together is not simply that their stories are set in Australia but that they all in their different ways tell a larger story, the story of the "making of Australia". The effect is such that even short books could be reviewed as "big books": *Coonardoo*, for example, as an epic of frontier settlement and a compressed family saga; or Frank Dalby Davison's story of a cow, *Man-Shy*, published in 1934 in the United States as *Red Heifer* and with the addition of an epic subtitle, *A Story of Men and Cattle*: "It is a 'little' story and yet a 'big' story – it has a quality of greatness".[4] Publisher Thomas Coward of Coward-McCann thought Davison's book a "minor classic" and convinced Carl Van Doren to take it for the Literary Guild.[5] It was also recommended in the *Book-of-the-Month Club* News and chosen by the *New York Times* as one of the Books of the Times for 1934, alongside Pamela L. Travers' *Mary Poppins*, the first book by an Australian-born author to sell more than a million copies in the United States.[6]

The sequence continued in the second half of the decade and into the war years. Brian Penton's challenging novel *Landtakers* appeared in 1935, the first book in a projected trilogy and bearing the telling subtitle *The Story of an Epoch*. Winifred Birkett's *Earth's Quality* was sold to Dodd, Mead by Angus & Robertson and published in America in 1936. It was received as a romance, but one with larger ambitions as a family saga.[7] Eric Lowe's *Salute to Freedom*, the third volume of a trilogy, was published in 1938, while Patrick White's first novel, *Happy Valley*, appeared from the Viking Press in 1940, modernist in style but still related to the novel of place or region.[8] Other significant works include Eleanor Dark's *The Timeless Land* (1941) and *The Little Company* (1945); Ernestine Hill's travelogue *Australian Frontier* (1942) and her historical novel *My Love Must Wait* (1944); Xavier Herbert's *Capricornia* (1943); and late in this history, Martin Boyd's family saga *Lucinda Brayford* (1948). Twenty years and a number of minor novels had passed between

---

4   Arthur Rush, "Men and Cattle", *Saturday Review of Literature*, 15 December 1934, 372. *New York Herald Tribune*, 18 November 1934: "Here there is the elemental urge of 'The Call of the Wild' without that book's heavy wholesomeness, the real tenderness of 'Bambi' but no cuteness, the powerful excitement of 'Smoky' and no heroics".
5   Thomas Coward to Frank Dalby Davison, 31 July 1935. Frank Dalby Davison Papers, National Library of Australia, MS1945/1/92-93. Coward arranged for Kermit Roosevelt, author, explorer and son of Theodore, to write an introduction to their edition, and later published Davison's *Children of the Dark People* (1937) and *Dusty: An Australian Dingo* (1946).
6   Alice Payne Hackett and James Henry Burke, *Eighty Years of Best Sellers 1895–1975* (New York: Bowker, 1977), 47. Travers was born in Queensland in 1906 and established a youthful reputation as a poet and journalist before leaving for England in 1924. Her Australian origins were not visible to US reviewers.
7   Although largely forgotten, the novel was awarded the Australian Literature Society Gold Medal in 1935. Lucy Tompkins in the *New York Times* worried away at its generic identity: it had "a whiff of the atmosphere (nothing else) of Galsworthy". It was predictable "light fiction" and yet its multigenerational family story meant it was also something more. A new "semi-dignified name", she suggested half-seriously, should be invented for such works: "Blood Will Tell", *New York Times*, 26 July 1936.
8   *Salute to Freedom* was the third volume chronologically in the planned trilogy but the first written. The subsequent volumes were *Beyond the Nineteen Counties* (1948) and *O Willing Hearts* (1951). Neither was published in the United States.

7 "Australia is very American": Australian Historical Fiction in America 1920s–1940s

The Madeleine Heritage and *Lucinda Brayford*, but these two family sagas were Boyd's most successful novels in the American market.

Some earlier novels of historical interest were also released: in 1929 the newly discovered convict novel *The Adventures of Ralph Rashleigh* was published with an introduction by the noted critic Joseph Wood Krutch,[9] and in 1933 Louis Stone's 1911 novel *Jonah* appeared under the new title *Larrikin* and with a Glossary of Australian Slang compiled by C. Hartley Grattan.[10] In the field of history itself, W.K. Hancock's major work *Australia* was released by Scribner in 1931; in 1939, Frederick A. Stokes published Paul McGuire's essay *Australia: Her Heritage, Her Future*, reviewed by Grattan in the *New York Times*; and Grattan's own *Introducing Australia* was published by John Day in New York in 1942.[11] *Introducing Australia* includes an extended section on literature, foregrounding Richardson and Prichard as the most significant among twentieth-century novelists.[12] Although it was still a minor thread in the overall fabric of American book culture, there was a new kind of textual density for Australia and its literature, Australian novels especially.

Grattan remained a key figure across the 1930s and 1940s. Following the publication of his extended essay, "Australian Literature", in 1928, Grattan became a dedicated reviewer of the new Australian novels as they appeared and an important advocate among publishers and editors. In addition to his reviewing, he regularly published survey articles in major venues such as the *New York Times*, the *New Republic* and *Nation*, updating American readers and providing an historical and social perspective on Australian literature. In 1934, for example, he wrote an overview essay for the *New York Times*; accompanied by a large portrait of Henry Handel Richardson, its subtitle captured the contemporary sense of a resurgent Australian literature: "Not Since the Nineties Has Australia Known Such a Vigorous Revival of Publishing Activity".[13] (Nettie Palmer's article on Australian literature for the *Christian Science Monitor* in 1935 bore an even more expressive subtitle: "Book Production Has Taken a Sudden Spurt on that Continent, with Literature about Both the Historical and Contemporary Scenes Winning Respectful Attention in the World".)[14] Grattan's emphasis on the novels as profound expressions – at best – of the society, the land and the nation's history was a good fit for the kinds of novels described above, which largely shared these assumptions, although he did not shy away from criticising those he thought inadequate to the task.

An important critical work, Marjorie Barnard and Flora Eldershaw's *Essays in Australian Fiction*, was also distributed in the United States in 1938. The first modern study of Australian fiction, the book begins with Richardson and Prichard, then offers chapters

---

9 The full US title was *Adventures of an Outlaw: The Memoirs of Ralph Rashleigh, a Penal Exile in Australia, 1825–1844*, published in New York by Jonathan Cape & Harrison Smith. Grattan reviewed *Ralph Rashleigh*, as "by far the most exciting book of adventure that I have read in years": *New York Sun*, quoted in publisher's advertisement, *New York Times*, 8 September 1929.
10 *Jonah* had been republished by the Endeavour Press in Sydney in 1933 and it is likely that Norman Lindsay's American connections led to its release there, by Ray Long and Richard R. Smith.
11 Paul McGuire: *Australia, Her Heritage, Her Future* (New York: Frederick A. Stokes, 1939), published in London as *Australian Journey* (Heinemann, 1939). C. Hartley Grattan, "Opinions on Australia that Have a Fighting Edge", *New York Times*, 3 September 1939.
12 C. Hartley Grattan, *Introducing Australia* (1942; rev. ed. New York: John Day, 1947), 156-58.
13 C. Hartley Grattan, "Literature in the Antipodes", *New York Times*, 7 January 1934.
14 Nettie Palmer, "Australia Writes of Herself", *Christian Science Monitor*, 28 August 1935, 10.

on Davison, Vance Palmer, Leonard Mann, Boyd, Dark and Christina Stead. Although its impact appears to have been limited, for one reviewer at least it signalled Australia's literary coming of age, a study of "eight writers who have helped their country out of 'the dark days' of a few years back. Colonial and even empire boundaries have already been crossed by Henry Handel Richardson and Katherine [sic] Prichard. A new book by Christina Stead is international news. Dawn is at hand in Australia".[15]

The Fact of Historical Fiction

If Boyd's two family sagas provide a chronological frame for the works listed above, a more significant framing in terms of genre and reception is suggested by the two novels near the beginning and the end of the sequence selected by the Book-of-the-Month Club: Richardson's *Ultima Thule* in August 1929 and Dark's *The Timeless Land* in October 1941. The Book-of-the-Month Club had become the most important arbiter of contemporary fiction in mainstream book culture, defining middle-class realism and the "best of the new books", and distributing its selections widely across the country.[16] *Ultima Thule* and *The Timeless Land* were both volumes within large-scale historical trilogies (still to be completed in Dark's case). Both were serious, demanding literary novels but accessible, realist, and driven by story and character. To recall the comment used in relation to *Ultima Thule*, Book-of-the-Month Club selection meant they would "automatically penetrate the living rooms of book-conscious America".[17] For both authors, it also meant the highest sales and earnings of their careers.

Other titles were brought to the attention of book-conscious America as alternate selections, meaning they were briefly presented to subscribers in the *Book-of-the-Month Club News*. Novels receiving this privilege included *A House is Built, Coonardoo, Australia Felix, The Way Home, The Fortunes of Richard Mahoney, The Getting of Wisdom, Pageant, The Woman on the Beast, Red Heifer, Landtakers, Under Capricorn, Promenade, Capricornia, My Love Must Wait* and *The Little Company*, and among non-fiction works, McGuire's *Australia* and Grattan's *Introducing Australia*. Other novels were selected by the Literary Guild, the other major American book club, including *Pageant, Red Heifer* and *Lucinda Brayford*, guaranteeing sales of at least 30,000 copies. The Guild had been established in 1926 by Samuel Craig and Harold Guinzberg, founder of the Viking Press, as a competitor to the Book-of-the-Month Club and on a similar model. Its expert panel included Carl Van Doren, Zona Gale, Elinor Wylie and Joseph Wood Krutch. These venues were powerful in drawing critics' attention beyond the individual author or novel to an accumulating sense of Australian literature as an entity, as a national literature. When Penton's *Landtakers* was promoted in the *Book-of-the-Month Club News* in July 1935, that was the context: "In the last few years a number of books about Australia, led by the

---

15 A.C., "Belles Lettres", *Saturday Review of Literature*, 6 August 1938, 6. The book was published by Melbourne University Press in association with Oxford University Press, and probably distributed in the United States by the latter. Barnard and Eldershaw co-authored as M. Barnard Eldershaw.
16 The term "middle-class realism" is derived from Gordon Hutner's *What America Read: Taste, Class and the Novel 1920–1960* (Chapel Hill: University of North Carolina Press, 2009). For the Book-of-the-Month Club, see Chapter 6.
17 Henry Smith, "Stark Tragedy of Human Existence is Theme of Novel", *News* (Dallas, TX), 29 September 1929.

7 "Australia is very American": Australian Historical Fiction in America 1920s–1940s

memorable novels of Henry Handel Richardson, have brought Antipodean life sharply within the consciousness of lively-minded readers in other parts of the world. This is the latest important one in that procession".[18] Similarly, for William Soskin, reviewing the book for the *New York American*, Penton's name could be added "to the roster of accomplished writers emerging in the continent of Australia".[19]

As a rule, the books were widely noticed in the leading New York newspapers and magazines, in other major cities and towns, and indeed in small-town and regional papers across the country. Newspaper literary supplements and "book news" pages had begun to proliferate in the 1920s.[20] As a consequence, some of the key American bookmen and bookwomen of the period came to review the new Australian novels as they appeared – Dorothy Canfield Fisher, Carl Van Doren, Clifton Fadiman, Henry Seidel Canby, Louis Kronenberger, William Soskin, Joseph Henry Jackson, Henry Hazlitt, Lilian Rogers, Mary Ross, Orville Prescott and Jane Spence Southron – many now forgotten like the bulk of the books they reviewed but the major figures in the busy book world of the interwar years. Hazlitt was literary editor of the *New York Sun* and then, from 1930, of *Nation*; Canby was founding editor of the *Saturday Review of Literature* and, with Canfield Fisher, a key member of the Book-of-the-Month Club Selection Committee; as editors and reviewers, Van Doren and Fadiman were key figures in the New York book world. Together with Grattan, they came to form something of an informed constituency for Australian fiction, although given the crowded book marketplace and the weekly cycle of most book reviewing, this could never achieve enduring form. Nonetheless, with the memory of Richardson's books still alive, even critics less attuned than Grattan to developments in Australian literature could begin to remark, for example, that "Australia itself, that unique and formidable terrain, is the real theme of many Australian novels". Richardson's works appeared "representative of the spirit of much less well-known Australian fiction" in which "the 'real story' is the land itself".[21]

The Book-of-the-Month Club had described Richardson's trilogy as "an Australian saga", and this is the key term for the Australian novels' reception in this period. *A House is Built* was welcomed as a "saga of three generations", *Pageant* as "a family saga of Tasmania".[22] The intergenerational historical saga was of high standing internationally in the 1920s and 1930s as suggested by the award of the 1928 Nobel Prize to Swedish author Sigrid Unset, between Knut Hamsun in 1920 and John Galsworthy in 1932. Undset's historical trilogy *Kristin Lavransdatter* was a Book-of-the-Month Club selection and an utterly familiar reference point on both sides of the Atlantic. As one newspaper put it in 1931: "There has been a noticeable tendency among outstanding novelists of the past ten years to create families of several generations"; examples included Richardson,

---

18 Gladys Graham Bates, "Landtakers", *Book-of-the-Month Club News*, July 1935, n.p.
19 William Soskin, "Reading and Writing: A New Novelist from Way Down Under", *New York American*, 28 June 1935. Henry Handel Richardson Papers, National Library of Australia, NLA MS 133, Press Cuttings Albums. Soskin cites Richardson, Lancaster and Norman Lindsay.
20 See Karen Leick, "Popular Modernism: Little Magazines and the American Daily Press", *PMLA* 123 (January 2008): 126–27.
21 *Record* (Philadelphia), review of *The Fortunes of Richard Mahony*, 1 October 1942. Richardson press cuttings.
22 Lillian Rogers, "Australia is Very American: Prize Novel, 'A House is Built', Recalls Our Own Frontiers", *New York Evening Post*, 21 December 1929; Dorothea Brande, "Four Novels", *Bookman*, February 1933, 190.

Galsworthy and Hugh Walpole.[23] But while the taste for such works was shared across national borders, there were distinct histories behind the American, British and Australian investments in the form.

In Australia, the interwar years saw major reassessments of the colonial legacy in which earlier frontier romance conventions were displaced in a series of large-scale novels, often exploring the destructive aspects of colonisation even where a progressive history of nation-building was redeemed from an unlikely past. Writing in the early 1960s, from a point in time when Patrick White's achievement had already reconfigured Australian literary history, Harry Heseltine noted that the major novelists of the 1920s and 1930s "fashioned for the first time what can be described as a formal tradition of the Australian novel. The forms that they shaped were basically three – the saga, the picaresque, and the documentary".[24] Heseltine writes in fact to celebrate this achievement even though these were "forms passed over elsewhere", their dominance a "sign of a backward provincialism in Australian writing of this period".[25] Governed as it is by a sense of evolving literary modernism, however, his periodisation misrepresents the contemporaneity of the saga form in these years. In late 1929, for example, Marjorie Barnard had herself reflected on the "amazing popularity of the period novel at the present time", second only to detective fiction.[26] Barnard in effect draws a distinction between the popular historical romance and its serious literary counterpart. The period novel had "a manifestation for every taste, educated or otherwise, ponderous or whimsical". It ranged from "the titanic fabric of *Jew Süss* to the fantastic gossamer of Arnoux's *Abishag*; from Sabatini's plume and rapier romance to learned and meticulous reconstructions like Atherton's *Immortal Marriage*".[27] She recognised it as on one level romantic, even anti-modern, "a recoil from an overdose of reality and a reaction from the problem play and the triangle novel", but it was also "the product of certain tendencies in the psychological and social life of Europe at work upon literature".

Interestingly, Barnard sees the historical novel as "a European not an American development":

> *Babbitt* not the *Jew Süss* remains the super-novel of America. The Americans are not sated with looking at themselves ... They do not want to escape from their present, though they like patting their past on the back with the delicate hand of a Hergesheimer or a Willa Cather ... Her eyes are on the future. Europe, not so hopeful, looks back and, now that democracy seems to be failing her, broods on her colourful and autocratic past as a time full of lessons for her.

---

23 *Enterprise* (South San Francisco), 13 October 1931. Richardson press clippings.
24 Harry Heseltine, "Australian Fiction since 1920", in *The Literature of Australia*, ed. Geoffrey Dutton (Harmondsworth, UK: Penguin, 1964), 184.
25 Heseltine, "Australian Fiction", 186.
26 M. Barnard Eldershaw, "The Period Novel: An Infinity of Problems", *Sydney Morning Herald*, 23 November 1929, and "The Reader and the Writer", *Sydney Morning Herald*, 30 November 1929. Barnard was sole author.
27 The references are to Lion Feuchtwanger's *Jew Süss* (1925), Alexandre Arnoux's *Abishag* (1925), Rafael Sabatini, bestselling author of pirate romances, and American Gertrude Atherton's *The Immortal Marriage* (1927).

7 "Australia is very American": Australian Historical Fiction in America 1920s–1940s

But American *readers* had made *Jew Süss* a bestseller in 1925, and as Gordon Hutner demonstrates, American historical fiction was an increasing presence in both publisher and bestseller lists across the 1920s and 1930s through authors such as Booth Tarkington, O.E Rølvaag and Willa Cather.[28] Indeed, by January 1941, Ralph Thompson in his *New York Times* "Books of the Times" column could remark: "The historical novel, which started out as a literary trend, is now an established historical fact. On American themes alone there must have been at least fifty new titles last year, or, roughly, one every Monday morning".[29] The comment suggests both the possibilities and difficulties for Australian fiction in such a crowded market. In the same column, Thompson noted White's *Happy Valley* as the most promising first novel of the previous year.

American historical novels, Hutner argues, were frequently "overlaid with a region's story too, as if to suggest that the development of a locale is central to a family's tale of rise and decline".[30] Indeed, the enormous success of Margaret Mitchell's *Gone With the Wind* (1936) can be explained by the way it combined the three dominant modes, "historical fiction, regionalism and the family saga", all at once.[31] For Hutner, the key to such novels "was their explanations of how the past becomes the present, how our circumstances have been forged for us through the sins of the fathers, the failures of the sons, the determination of the mothers, and the exertions of the daughters". Through their story of generations, they "spoke to an America trying to make sense of its destiny".[32] The Australian novels could appeal to American readers in similar terms, although fewer of their stories had the restorative appeal Hutner sees in the American examples. Some, like Penton's and Herbert's, were decidedly anti-romantic.

Interestingly, D.H. Lawrence's co-authored Australian novel, *The Boy in the Bush* (1924), had also been received as a version of the pioneering epic – at least by the *New York Times* – overlaid of course with Lawrence's own concerns "with environment, with God and with one's self":

> The experiences with which the novel is concerned are the familiar ones of pioneer life on the frontiers of civilization ... [Jack Grant] listens to the tales of pioneers, the men and women who arrived in Australia in the early years of the last century. We follow him through his gradual adaptation to the primitive environment of the farmers and ranchers and woodsmen of the interior, through his adventures in the sparsely settled bush where all contact with civilization is lost ... Mr. Lawrence has not only re-created an epoch; he has populated a continent.[33]

Despite such framing – and references to the "mysterious beckoning spell of the bush" – there are no later commentaries that connect the new Australian works back to Lawrence's example. Lawrence's own authorial presence consumed whatever interpretive fuel this earlier book might have provided.

---

28 Hutner, *What America Read*, 162-74.
29 Ralph Thompson, "Books of the Times", *New York Times*, 1 January 1941.
30 Hutner, *What America Read*, 86.
31 Hutner, *What America Read*, 172.
32 Hutner, *What America Read*, 85.
33 Lloyd Morris, "Mr. Lawrence on the Frontiers of Civilization", *New York Times*, 26 October 1924.

In Britain, the contemporary force of the saga was due to the highly regarded Edwardian novelists, Arnold Bennett and John Galsworthy above all. Although they would soon fall on the wrong side of modernism, these authors were major figures in contemporary estimation, in the United States no less than in Britain; Galsworthy dedicated the third novel in *The Forsyte Saga* to Charles Scribner. If it is difficult for us now to re-enter this literary chronotope, Virginia Woolf's famous essay "Mr Bennett and Mrs Brown" might stand as negative testimony to the prestige of these authors in the 1920s and 1930s.[34] Woolf sought to draw a line between old and new, but for many ordinary readers Galsworthy and Bennett themselves represented a clear line between "old" romance and " modern" realism. The family saga was a way of taking seriously both determining social forces and the psychological conflicts shaping character. The perspective was largely secular and materialist, hence their impact as modern, and while the saga was a form of historical fiction, the ethical questions posed were distinctly contemporary. At the same time, their realism could be held against *other* forms of contemporary fiction: light fiction, on one side, and, on the other, as Barnard's account of the period novel suggests, the modern "problem" novel. For the *Boston Evening Transcript*, Barnard Eldershaw's *Green Memory* was a "brilliant book" precisely because it was "affiliated with no modern school, but possesses the timeless virtues of skill, understanding and human sympathy".[35]

The historical family saga, then, was not merely residual or provincial as Heseltine implied but a modern phenomenon even as it was reassuring in its realism and deep investment in human character, historical time and social realities. Here we can see the middlebrow register in which the Australian novels – serious, substantial novels but seldom modernist in style or theme – were assimilable into an American market already disposed towards historical, regional and family sagas.

Martin Boyd and the Family Chronicle Novel

The Madeleine Heritage was the second of Martin Boyd's novels to be published in America, but the first with a substantial Australian dimension and "his first real success as a novelist".[36] Boyd had been actively pursued by the Indianapolis-based Bobbs-Merrill Co. since *Brangane*, his first novel, had appeared from Constable in July 1926 under the pseudonym Martin Mills. In August 1926, Bobbs-Merrill wrote to Constable enquiring whether rights in the book were still free, and in a tortuous chain of correspondence Constable forwarded the letter to Boyd's London agent, J.B. Pinker, who sent a copy of the book to New York agents Brandt & Brandt for forwarding, in turn, to Bobbs-Merrill.[37] In November, Bobbs-Merrill's president David L. Chambers replied, insisting that the firm was "awfully interested in it".[38] Retitled *The Aristocrat*,

---

34   Virginia Woolf, "Mr Bennett and Mrs Brown", in *Virginia Woolf: Selected Essays*, ed. David Bradshaw (Oxford: Oxford University Press, 2008), 32–36.
35   M.M., review of *Green Memory*, by M. Barnard Eldershaw, *Boston Evening Transcript* 7 October 1931.
36   Brenda Niall, *Martin Boyd: A Life* (Carlton, Vic.: Melbourne University Press, 1988), 113.
37   Correspondence in Papers of Martin Boyd, National Library of Australia, NLA MS6812 Series 2, Box 3 Folder 17. This archive also includes photocopies of correspondence from the Curtis Brown Ltd Records, Columbia University, and the Bobbs-Merrill mss, Lilly Library Manuscript Collection, Indiana University. All subsequent correspondence from this source unless otherwise indicated.
38   Chambers to Bernice Baumgarton (Brandt & Brandt), 6 November 1926.

7 "Australia is very American": Australian Historical Fiction in America 1920s–1940s

the book appeared in the United States in early 1927, copyrighted and in a new setting. The copyright record indicates "revision and new material", allowing its registration beyond the date limits set in the Act. It was received quietly. For the *New York Times*, unlike Galsworthy or Aldous Huxley its author had failed to make his "social climbers" and "bores" interesting as characters.[39] The book thus became "a somewhat monotonous moral tract before the last page comes gratefully to hand". Yet even with such a damning report, the reviewer concluded that the author's style would serve him well if he found a suitable subject, "for it is direct, not a little ruthless, and clear".

Certainly, Bobbs-Merrill wanted Boyd's next novel. Chambers wrote to Pinker's New York office, which was now handling Boyd directly, that both the length and title of the new work awoke his eager expectations: "This author can write!"[40] They received the manuscript of "Great-Great-Grandmother Madeleine" in September 1927, and rather than wait for authorial changes or corrected proofs from London, the novel went to the printers before English publication was finalised. Both publishers decided the original title should be changed but their publishing schedules meant that two different titles appeared. The American edition, *The Madeleine Heritage*, appeared first and included sensitive passages relating to family history that were deleted from Constable's later edition entitled *The Montforts*.[41] It was as *The Montforts* that the novel was awarded the first Australian Literature Society Gold Medal in 1928, the year before Richardson's *Ultima Thule*.

The Madeleine Heritage was Boyd's first extended exploration of the themes of his major works in the family saga mode. In the present context it can also be seen as the first modern historical novel of Australia released in the American market. American reviews, on balance, were strongly favourable: "Delightful, realistic, vivacious. Delicious irony. Quite unusual talent".[42] Chambers sent copies of the reviews to Pinker with the comment that "they recognise the quality of the author as a fiction writer, though they point out what seem to the critics defects in the making of this particular novel. We have been made to feel ourselves both among the trade and the public that the multiplicity of characters may make it difficult to sell the book, but at the same time we are more than ever convinced of Mr. Mills' brilliant future".[43]

The *Boston Evening Transcript* found that the "canvas is far too large for the author to handle successfully". Yet there was "a great deal to praise": "Mr. Mills has a remarkable sense of character and at the same time a feeling for harmony between character and environment". The novel prompted this reviewer and others to think about the nature of Australian settlement, and in this case to praise the novel's Australianness:

To many persons the predominant success of the novel lies in its picturing of the Australian scene. However loyal Australians may be to their own section of the world they have a habit in their writings of stressing rather insistently the fact that they are English. One feels at times that their books are something in the order of real estate

---

39 "A Social Climber", *New York Times*, 29 May 1927.
40 Chambers to J. Ralph Pinker (New York), 11 August 1927.
41 Niall, *Martin Boyd*, 114.
42 Bobbs-Merrill advertising, *New York Times* 29 April 1928; phrases drawn from review by Alice Beal Parsons, "Madeleine and the Montforts", *New York Herald Tribune*, 11 March 1928.
43 Chambers to Pinker, 14 March 1928.

prospectuses. They are designed to assure the Englishman that he will be very, very much at home in Australia, and they place far too little stress on the characteristics of the country which distinguish it from other lands. In this book there is none of that tendency exhibited. The author is delighted to unfold the colony. The first Montforts who go to Australia know their share of homesickness, but they have no doubts about the fact that they are prosperous and successful as they could not have been at home in England. They are good colonials. And Australia becomes their own land, pulling them back whenever they wander away from it. In fact in the ending they return not only to Australia but to the land. Mr. Mills gets the feeling of Australia and for Australia into his story as we can recall no other author doing.[44]

"Few new authors," the review concludes, "promise more goldenly than this Mr. Martin Mills". Similarly, Alice Beal Parsons in the *Herald Tribune* praised the book as "realistic and encyclopedic", and again suggested some familiarity with Australian novels in drawing attention to its more complex representation of being Australian:

I have never before read any novel that gave me a real perception of the Australian social scene. Whether or not Mr. Mills is the first to do this, he does it very vivaciously and livingly. Most young Australians are obsessed by England and parade in their books all of its mannerisms of thought and morals and social behaviour that they have been able to absorb. Mr. Mills' characters feel the same continual pull of England on their imagination but sooner or later they all go back to their more abundant and free Australia.[45]

For the *New York Times* the novel's historical sense was compelling: "The scheme of the book enables the author to depict the development of Melbourne, and the change in social life, from its dominance by people who, like the Montforts, had some degree of taste and culture, to the reign of the vulgar new-rich. *The Madeleine Heritage* is a thoughtful, carefully worked out study of the development and decay of a family, projected against the background of a new country and a passing epoch."[46] The novel even inspired the *Saturday Review* to announce the arrival of the modern historical saga: "The three volume novel is dead, long live the three volume novel!"[47]

The third title in this early phase of Boyd's American publications, *Dearest Idol*, was published under another pseudonym, Walter Beckett. It was a contemporary novel, advertised by the publishers as "A subtle story of a Beloved Youth, adored by women and taught to consider himself the center of their world".[48] The book had been rejected by Constable, but Bobbs-Merrill liked it and were puzzled by Constable's decision. Nonetheless, they decided at the last minute that it would not add to the reputation that *The Madeleine Heritage* had begun to build for Martin Mills and therefore to publish it under a pseudonym as "strongly urged by our salesmen as important for best results".[49] The

---

44 D.L.M., "Madeleine Heritage: Hereditary in the Midst of the Australian Scene", *Boston Evening Transcript*, 21 April 1928.
45 Parsons, "Madeleine and the Montforts".
46 "Four Generations", *New York Times*, 11 March 1928.
47 "The New Books", *Saturday Review of Literature*, 12 May 1928, 869.
48 Bobbs-Merrill advertisement, *New York Times*, 17 May 1929.
49 Cable from Bobbs-Merrill to Pinker (New York), 3 January 1929. Niall, *Martin Boyd*, 115-6.

book intrigued reviewers with its "excellent bits of analysis" but like the *Saturday Review*'s critic many asked, "Why isn't this a better book?"[50]

Bobbs-Merrill had an option on Boyd's next novel, called "Bitter Sauces", and Pinker urged the publisher to consider submitting it to both the Literary Guild and the Book-of-the-Month Club. It is not known why the book remained unpublished, but it was also rejected by Farrar & Rinehart and possibly Harcourt, Brace. Nor is it clear why Boyd's relationship with Bobbs-Merrill ceased, although by July 1930, sales of his early books had dried up.[51] There followed a gap of some five years before Dent in London released the first of six new Boyd titles in 1934. Of these, the first edition of *The Lemon Farm* was published in America in 1936 by Norton, who had also been pursuing Boyd for its list as a writer "I very much believe in" (though not as an Australian writer). Although the book had "a good press", it was, in Norton's own words, an "ill-fated venture".[52] Naomi Burton of Curtis Brown New York also sold *The Picnic* to Putnam in early 1937.[53] Both were "English" novels published under Boyd's own name, so reviewers had no means or motive for considering any Australian connections; and both were one-off titles. Neither publisher exercised its options on subsequent novels, Norton rejecting one as an inferior work, the other because of its treatment of homosexuality.[54]

Another decade would pass before Boyd's mature "Australian" novels appeared in America, beginning with *Lucinda Brayford* in 1948. Rejected by Dent, Boyd thought because it "ridiculed savagely the Establishment", it was published in London by the small Cresset Press in 1946 before being picked up by Dutton for American release. The book may have been offered to American publishers by Curtis Brown who were now Boyd's agents, or perhaps Dutton learnt of its favourable reception in London.[55] Dutton offered a generous advance of $1000 compared to Cresset's £100, and an attractive royalty scale.[56] The contract also gave the publishers first option on Boyd's next two full-length works. *Lucinda Brayford* appeared in America in February 1948 and its sales success was guaranteed when it became the March selection of the Literary Guild, with an introduction by Carl Van Doren. Selection by the Literary Guild meant sales of at least thirty thousand, although as a consequence of its selection Dutton renegotiated Boyd's royalties down to a flat 10 per cent to 30,000 copies so it could make an "advertising appropriation": in effect,

---

50 "The New Books", *Saturday Review of Literature*, 20 April 1929, 934.
51 Bobbs-Merrill to Pinker (London), 13 July 1931; Pinker (London) to Pinker (NY), 2 October 1929.
52 Correspondence between Dent, Curtis Brown and Norton regarding *The Lemon Farm*; quoted letter, Norton to Curtis Brown New York rejecting Boyd's "Colour and Skin", 29 March 1938. The *New York Times* review of *The Lemon Farm* was mixed, finding the novel "not nearly so good as the usual flowery quotations from English critics would lead one to expect"; and yet "it has a certain frail charm". Again something better is predicted if the author can find a "sturdier theme".
53 Contract details in Papers of Martin Boyd, Series 1–2, Box 2, Folder 12. Putnam offered an advance of $250 and royalties at 10 per cent to 3500 copies, 12½ per cent to 6000 and 15 per cent thereafter. Naomi Burton to J.M. Dent, 13 April 1937, J.M. Dent Collection, University of North Carolina, Curtis Brown Folder: series 1.2, no. 1883.
54 Earlier Norton had shared his anxieties about the homosexual theme in Boyd's "Shepherd of Admetus" (his first option) with Alan Collins of Curtis Brown New York and Richard Church of Dent (7 April and 26 May 1936).
55 Niall, *Martin Boyd*, 137.
56 Dutton offered 10 per cent to 3500 copies sold, 12½ per cent to 6000, 15 per cent thereafter (contract dated 2 April 1947); Cresset offered 15 per cent to 5000, 20 per cent thereafter. Summary of Boyd's contracts prepared for Curtis Brown, Papers of Martin Boyd.

it was claiming "$10,000 as initial appropriation to cover the sale of 36,666 copies of the book".[57] Dutton went on to publish *Bridget Malwyn* in October 1949 and *The Cardboard Crown* in April 1953.[58]

Boyd later reported that *Lucinda Brayford* had sold half a million copies in the United States, and while this figure cannot be confirmed the book seems to have done well; well enough for Dutton to offer an increased advance of $1500 for each of the next two works.[59] In the most influential papers – the *New York Times*, the *Saturday Review of Literature* and the *New York Herald Tribune* – it was seen as a substantial achievement and compared, almost inevitably, with Galsworthy. As with other historical or family sagas, it was seen as part of a contemporary movement back to earlier novel-writing traditions in the face of literary fashion. For Horace Reynolds in the *Times*, the novel sat "in the objective, well articulated, Victorian tradition, to which many novelists are returning today in reaction against those who have broken with it".[60] For Soskin in the *Saturday Review*:

> The family hearthstone seems a mighty cozy place these days not only to sentimental escapists. Honest realists, too, who look upon the ruins of so many large, liberal movements, modern causes and schools of thought, have fled to the shelter of their familiar homesteads ... It is not surprising, therefore, that fat family novels which burgeon with generations of clannish love, births, deaths, fortunes made and lost, codes of honor recognized or violated, are finding ready response from a large audience.[61]

Both critics praised the novel in modest terms that seemed to match the novel's own. For Reynolds, it was "a good story throughout", and he notes perceptively that Boyd "writes out of an almost mystical sense of the continuity of the life stream". For Soskin, the novel had "a sturdy texture, a life-like opacity that seems to contain all [its] ingredients in natural proportion". Boyd's "mellow way with family *mores*" was so insidious, he added, "the innocent reader hardly realizes he has ... absorbed a number of highly immoral relationships, illegitimate births, and other such daring matters!"

In *Commonweal*, the Galsworthy comparison was paramount: "So far as the story-telling goes, Mr. Boyd stands up well with Mr. Galsworthy; he has a far keener sense of satire but his preoccupation with sex narrows his outlook and his characters like his writing lack a certain distinction. 'Lucinda,' however, comprises enough action for four Galsworthy novels". By contrast, for the trendsetting *New Yorker*, the novel offered only "stock characters, antique plot, and pedestrian style" and for the *Catholic World* it was "abysmally boring".[62] Either way, the primary frame for the novel's reception was that of the family saga, identified now, in 1948, primarily as an English or European genre. Unlike for *The Madeleine Heritage*, this time there was very little consideration of the novel as an Australian novel. The "Richardson effect" had dissipated, and there was no reference back

---

57 Summary of Boyd's contracts prepared for Curtis Brown, Papers of Martin Boyd.
58 *Bridget Malwyn* was the US title – and original title – of *Such Pleasure* (Cresset 1949).
59 Summary of contracts in Boyd papers, plus Boyd to Peter Grose (Curtis Brown Australia), 31 December 1971.
60 Horace Reynolds, "Written in the Victorian Tradition", *New York Times*, 22 February 1948.
61 William Soskin, "From Sheep Station to Mayfair", *Saturday Review of Literature*, 13 March 1948, 30.
62 *Commonweal*, 28 May 1948; *New Yorker*, 28 February 1948, 86; *Catholic World*, June 1948, 286.

7 "Australia is very American": Australian Historical Fiction in America 1920s–1940s

to Boyd's earlier work. When *Bridget Malwyn* appeared the following year, Boyd could be described as "the veteran British novelist".[63]

Dutton's second option novel was *The Cardboard Crown*, the first novel in the Langton tetralogy, Boyd's next family saga, released in early 1953. It had the advantage of being reviewed by Bruce Sutherland in the *New York Times*; that is, by a critic who came to the novel with an understanding of Australian literature as a field or tradition. Sutherland was able to highlight the theme of loyalties divided between "two countries and two cultural traditions" and to bring into perspective Boyd's career "as a master of the art of the family chronicle novel".[64] Dutton, however, appears to have had no further interest in Boyd, while Boyd himself changed agents, from Curtis Brown to A.D. Peters, in mid-1954. The following Langton novels appeared from the small New York publisher Reynal & Co., *A Difficult Young Man* in 1956 and *Outbreak of Love* in 1957. In February 1957, Eugene Reynal wrote to John Murray in London that "Boyd's sales have gone way, way off in this country from his first and only success *Lucinda Brayford*. I do like the way he writes and I do believe he has a future here but the present is mighty slim pickings".[65]

Although in general Boyd was better appreciated in England, he could still call forth enthusiastic notices in American review pages. James Stern described *A Difficult Young Man* as "a wise, amusing, gloriously quotable book – the kind of book that makes one want to go out and buy everything the author has written".[66] Interestingly, the *Times* invited Australian academic Brian Elliott, then living in the United States, to review *Outbreak of Love*, and Elliott was able to place the novel in a sequence extending back to *Lucinda Brayford*. Unusually in the American context, he stressed the Australianness of both author and work. If Boyd's manners were English, his "thoughts" were Australian and his recent novels showed "an increasing preoccupation with Australia as a setting".[67] But there was no follow-up of the kind that might have consolidated Boyd's reputation. The final Langton novel, *When Blackbirds Sing*, did not appear in England until 1962, and while Boyd later remembered it being released separately in America no reviews have been located.[68]

---

63 Horace Reynolds, "Luck of the Irish", *New York Times*, 23 October 1949.
64 Bruce Sutherland, "Gentry Down-Under", *New York Times*, 9 August 1953.
65 Eugene Reynal to John Murray 19 February 1957. Papers of Martin Boyd.
66 James Stern, "Eccentric Victorians", *New York Times*, 15 April 1956. Stern was Irish but lived in the United States in the 1940s and 1950s. His reviews of Patrick White's novels were crucial in establishing White's reputation in America. See Chapter 8 and David Marr, *Patrick White: A Life* (1991; Sydney: Vintage, 1992), 254, 303–5.
67 Brian Elliott, "Wit Was a Weapon", *New York Times*, 26 May 1957.
68 Boyd to Grose (Curtis Brown Australia), 4 December 1971. *When Blackbirds Sing* was published in London by Abelard-Schuman, and the Library of Congress gives London and New York as place of publication. *Much Else in Italy* was published by Macmillan in London and by its American offshoot, St Martin's Press, in New York (1958). *Nuns in Jeopardy*, first published by Dent in 1940, was re-released in 1975 by Harcourt Brace Jovanovich (A Helen and Kurt Wolff Book) following representation by Curtis Brown Australia. There was also interest from St Martin's in 1977 in publishing the Langton books in one volume but costs proved prohibitive, partly because the Landsdowne Press in Australia had not used the same typeface for all four novels so they would have to be reset.

Australian Epics: Dorothy Cottrell and M. Barnard Eldershaw

Boyd wrote from England, then Europe. Dorothy Cottrell, by contrast, began her career as a novelist from the remote Ularunda station in western Queensland. From there, unusually, she sold her first novel, *The Singing Gold*, directly to her American publisher, Houghton Mifflin, and it is one of the few cases before the 1970s where the American edition precedes the English. This is not the place to recount Cottrell's extraordinary life – wheelchair-bound after contracting childhood poliomyelitis, she married secretly, "eloped" to Dunk Island off the Queensland coast, and worked as a black-and-white artist in Sydney before returning to Ularanda – but she followed her novel to America, in October 1928, in part to avoid the "iniquitous taxation" on her American earnings. She lived in the United States for the rest of her life except for two years in the 1950s back in Queensland.[69]

Cottrell first sent the manuscript of *The Singing Gold* to the high-circulation *Ladies' Home Journal* which paid her $5000 in April 1927 for serial rights in the United States and Canada – an extraordinary way for an isolated Australian writer to break into publishing.[70] She also sent the novel of her own accord to Houghton Mifflin and to Martin Secker in London, although Hodder & Stoughton was ultimately its English publisher.[71] Houghton Mifflin would almost certainly have been aware of the serial's success in the *Ladies' Home Journal*, and they matched Secker's terms: no advance but a standard royalty rate.[72] Cottrell wrote that she thought the terms generous for a first book, although in fact the original offer had only been improved at her insistence. Indeed, she proved herself an astute custodian of her literary property despite being a beginner. She granted Houghton Mifflin only volume rights and only in America, later modified on Cottrell's advice to include Canada as well; and she herself deleted clauses extending the copyright territories and granting translation, abridgement, broadcast and second serial rights to the publisher. Ira Rich Kent at Houghton Mifflin responded generously nonetheless to the "beastly expensive" exchange of cables by which their negotiations had been conducted, even sending Cottrell a copy of *The Truth About Publishing*, presumably Stanley Unwin's book of that title. Kent's wife – the author Louise Andrews Kent – also wrote to Cottrell, expressing her appreciation of the novel.[73] *The Singing Gold* appeared in the United States in January 1929.

A female-centred celebration of land and rural life, *The Singing Gold* sold almost 25,000 copies in British and colonial markets and we might guess at even larger numbers in the American market.[74] As Nettie Palmer wrote memorably for her Australian readers:

---

69 For two recent appreciations of Cottrell's novels, see the essays by Chris Lee and by Robin Trotter and Belinda McKay in *By the Book: A Literary History of Queensland*, ed. Patrick Buckridge and Belinda McKay (St Lucia: University of Queensland Press, 2007).
70 Dorothy Cottrell to Geo. Robertson, 10 May 1927, Angus & Robertson (A & R) Publishing Files, 1927, State Library of New South Wales MLMSS 314, Vol. 19, 547–59.
71 In a letter to A & R, 27 June 1927, complaining of press reports that the book had been rejected by several Australian houses before being submitted to America, she writes of having sent it directly to both the journal and Houghton Mifflin. A & R Publishing Files.
72 Royalties of 10 per cent to 5000 copies, 15 per cent to 15,000 and 20 per cent thereafter. Dorothy Cottrell to Ira Rich Kent (Houghton & Mifflin). 30 October 1927. Houghton Mifflin Co. Records, Houghton Library, Harvard University.
73 Cottrell to Kent, 30 October 1927, Houghton Mifflin Records.
74 Hodder & Stoughton's figures show that almost the entire print run of 23,500 copies including 6600 of the colonial edition was sold between 1928 and 1937. Hodder & Stoughton Authors' Ledgers, London Metropolitan Archives.

7 "Australia is very American": Australian Historical Fiction in America 1920s–1940s

"Dorothy Cottrell has been greatly praised, and will be praised again: she has thus been given the freedom of the popular book world".[75] The novel's success was despite – and of course because of – its sentimentality, although Cottrell's narrative skills were always noted. In the *New York Times*, under the heading "Romance in Australia":

> Miss Cottrell is one of those writers with an effortless style, a true sense for narrative, and a refreshing sense of humor. The sentimentalism she allows herself in this novel seems all the more deplorable because it is all so shrewd. She rings all its changes with a knowing dexterity. She makes those who value sentiment for its own true sake writhe. And she makes *The Singing Gold* hardly bearable because of it …
>
> Miss Cottrell makes it all an appealing story, romantic and perhaps implausible as can be, but one's quarrel is not with its idyllic quality. One is always in luck to find a writer with charm. Miss Cottrell has it … But the sentimentality is another matter.[76]

For the most part, the reviews were more positive, and at least one commentator linked her explicitly with Richardson and Prichard.[77] Certainly the book did well enough for Houghton Mifflin to exercise their option on Cottrell's second novel, published as *Earth Battle* in England and *Tharlane* in America in June 1930. Indeed, they added a $4000 advance. *Tharlane* was a more complex story of outback struggle and ultimate defeat, and for reviewers it approached the epic scale: "a magnificent novel of the Australian Plain"; "the epic of a wild land and an unconquerable race".[78] At least two reviewers recalled Richardson's trilogy when noting the book, one affirming that "literature out of Australia takes on a new interest", the other that Cottrell's novel was "of Australians, not of Englishmen visiting them".[79] It had also been serialised in the *Ladies' Home Journal*, as were five other stories between May 1931 and April 1932, but this phase of her career, as a writer of epic Australian novels, was over.[80]

In both the Australian and American case, the field of the intergenerational family saga was significantly claimed by women authors, as if the crisis-filled decades of the early twentieth century had produced a new, deeper sense of female lives "coming into history". Alongside *Coonardoo* and *Ultima Thule*, Barnard Eldershaw's *A House is Built* was recognised by American reviewers as the most substantial work of Australian fiction before American readers in this period. The *Book-of-the-Month Club News* asked, "Is Australian fiction all at once immensely better than we thought? Or are we only now beginning

---

75   Nettie Palmer, "Australian Books of 1930", *All About Books*, 5 December 1930, 309.
76   "Romance in Australia", *New York Times*, 3 February 1929, 63.
77   See the quotation in the opening paragraph of Chapter 6 above: "those who maintain that no literature comes out of Australia are beginning to revise their opinions as each new book is announced by Henry Handel Richardson, Katherine Susannah Pritchard and Dorothy Cottrel [sic]". *Press* (Atlantic City, NJ), 10 May 1930.
78   Both quotations from Houghton Mifflin publicity, *New York Times*, 8 June and 20 July 1930.
79   *Tribune* (Salt Lake City, UT), 27 April 1930; Antony Clark, "A Novel of Australians, Not of Englishmen Visiting Them", *Boston Herald*, 17 May 1930. Both in Richardson's press clippings.
80   Cottrell had further stories published in *Liberty*, *Cosmopolitan* and the *Saturday Evening Post*, and Houghton Mifflin published her children's book, *Winks*, in 1932. The New York firm J. Messner published another, *Wilderness Orphan*, in 1940. A & R's 1936 Australian edition was the basis for Ken G. Hall's film, *Orphan of the Wilderness* (1936). A final novel, *The Silent Reefs*, was published by Morrow in 1953 after having been serialised in the *Saturday Evening Post*. It was later filmed in Hollywood as *The Secret of the Purple Reef* (Witney, 1960).

to know it? On the heels of the superb *Ultima Thule*, comes another novel of the first order, *A House is Built*".[81] The notice defined exactly the Book-of-the-Month Club's sense of what would appeal to a "lover of good fiction": "unfailing narrative interest, portraits both delicately and vigorously true, the sense of the passage of time fully conveyed, a new background, a strong and lovable hero surrounded by touching and life-like women". Some American papers noted that it had shared the 1928 Sydney *Bulletin* novel prize with Prichard's novel.

No documentation survives to indicate how *A House is Built* came to the attention of Harcourt, Brace, but the American edition is a wholly new setting not merely a reprint of Harrap's English edition. The success of *Ultima Thule* would have come too late to influence the decision to invest in a new edition, so it is likely that the main factor was the novel's reception in England, above all Arnold Bennett's verdict that it represented "a major phenomenon of modern fiction".[82] He also identified its key generic features: "Its quality is epical. Time marches through it in the grand manner".

These were exactly the qualities to which a serious American publisher and serious reviewers in 1929 might be attuned. For the *New York Times*, echoing Bennett: "The story marches ahead, almost relentless in its unfolding, with one purpose and one end in view". Again, its substantial qualities were seen against those of other modern fiction:

> There is much quiet humor in the book, and a great deal of insight that needs no heavy sexy passages to make itself understood ... Although they speak in the stilted dialogue of the Victorian era, and the emotions, particularly of the women, are never allowed free expression, they live passionately within themselves, and the reader is allowed to glimpse the undercurrent, not through long Freudian discussions, but through the ordinary, every-day events of ordinary life. This is real art and in this the Misses Barnard and Eldershaw have succeeded where many present writers fail. Life is never, for the Hyde family, a clinic.[83]

In the same issue, the *Times* reviewed an "epic of a New England family" and a Canadian frontier novel. The *Nation*'s review drew comparison with Galsworthy and Thomas Mann who had also been used to gauge Richardson's achievement, and although it found the novel wanting in the "unity of a family with its time or place", the quality that lent greatness to their works, its restraint, poignancy and realism were valued. Grattan reviewed it as a work of "high excellence" for the *New Republic*, and found precisely the qualities the *Nation* had missed: "There is a perfect correlation between the rise of the house and the growth of the country ... Intertwined with the story of the business is an excellent account of social life in Australia for the years covered, with the result that we have a picture of unusual merit of the bourgeois English colonial spirit in action".[84]

Somewhat differently, Lillian Rogers in the *New York Evening Post* drew attention to the American parallels in this "saga of three generations":

---

81   *Book-of-the-Month Club News*, October 1929, n.p.
82   Arnold Bennett, *Evening Standard*, 4 July 1929, in *Arnold Bennett: The "Evening Standard" Years: Books and Persons 1926–1931*, ed. Andrew Mylett (London: Chatto & Windus, 1974), 283-84.
83   "Family Fortunes", *New York Times*, 17 November 1929.
84   *Nation*, 4 December 1929, 700; C.H.G. [Grattan], *New Republic*, 8 January 1930, 205.

7 "Australia is very American": Australian Historical Fiction in America 1920s–1940s

The background of the story is almost the thing. The reason why Australians who come to America feel that they are merely visiting relatives and are not travelling in foreign places becomes apparent from this book. The growth of the town, the various stages of social development through which the Hyde family passes, the fluctuations of values as the rush for gold begins and then diminishes, all duplicates the experience of our own moving frontiers. On the other hand, the background of English tradition and custom reflects the early settlers of our Atlantic seaboard who took the same traditions westward with them later on. Yet in this story there is the Australian bush and the inversion of the seasons to make the piquant difference.[85]

Rogers' review was entitled "Australia Is Very American".

In England, *A House is Built* was reprinted six times in two months and remained in print for almost fifty years.[86] Although only one American edition was published, the book was successful enough to encourage Harcourt, Brace to maintain its relationship with Harrap and take on Barnard Eldershaw's next novel, *Green Memory*, another historical family story. This time it appears the cheaper option of importing sheets or plates was deployed and copyright left to chance.[87] Still, when it appeared in 1931 the book was again taken seriously by serious reviewers. The *Nation* thought it "spotty and formless" but judged that "some of the spots are brilliant". The *New York Times* praised the novel's characterisation and its account of Sydney, and again drew local comparisons: "Sydney … reminds one a little of some of our American cities in the Middle West … [T]he best families of *Green Memory* stamped out and suppressed all that was indigenous to Australian soil and surrounded themselves with what was accepted by the upper middle class in England in Queen Victoria's day".[88]

Grattan was always the most welcoming but also the sternest critic of Australian fiction, seeking something essentially and distinctively Australian but not finding it in *Green Memory*:

When "A House Is Built" appeared it seemed as though the two young women who call themselves M. Barnard Eldershaw were destined to give a series of brilliant fictional reconstructions of early Australian life. The astonishing skill with which they handled the story of the rise and fall of a great commercial family in Sydney before, during and after the gold rush was a heartening portent. But optimism has been somewhat dashed by their new novel, "Green Memory," which starts out well enough and then narrows down the interest to a psychological analysis of a group of women and children. In "A House Is Built" the focus was on the men and they led us naturally and inevitably into the fascinating social and economic world and offered us something that was not generally available. The story of the new book might have taken place anywhere in the

---

85 Rogers, "Australia is Very American", *New York Evening Post*, 21 December 1929.
86 Details from AusLit (www.austlit.edu.au) and Maryanne Dever, "Marjorie Barnard (1897–1987) and Flora Eldershaw (1897–1956) (M. Barnard Eldershaw)", *Australian Writers, 1915–1950*. ed. Selina Samuels, Dictionary of Literary Biography, Vol. 260 (Detroit, MI: Gale Research, 2002), 3-13.
87 It would appear that *Green Memory* circulated less widely. Indeed, American critic Louise Rorabacher wrote that no American edition appeared: *Marjorie Barnard and M. Barnard Eldershaw* (New York: Twayne, 1973), 41.
88 *Nation*, 6 January 1932, 26; "Victorian Australia", *New York Times*, 27 September 1931.

English-speaking world and accordingly required a greater brilliance than the authors possess to make it interesting.[89]

Green Memory was the last of Barnard Eldershaw's work to appear in America, and the last in the genre they wrote together. The authors' most ambitious work, the futuristic historical novel *Tomorrow and Tomorrow*, missed its historical moment, its Australian publication delayed until 1947 by wartime censorship. There were no English or American editions until the novel in its original form was released by Virago and The Dial Press in the 1980s.

Colonising, Civilising, Realising: Helen Simpson, G.B. Lancaster, Eric Lowe

The generic power of the historical saga in this period wrought dramatic changes in the careers of Helen Simpson and G.B. Lancaster. For both, turning to Australia as subject in the mid-1930s meant turning to the historical novel in saga form. Before the appearance of her major Australian historical saga *Boomerang* in 1932, Helen Simpson had published three murder mysteries, as noted in Chapter 5, and a period novel, *Desires and Devices*, published by Doubleday, Doran in 1930. Barnard's description of the contemporary literary field as dominated by detective fiction and period novels pretty well captures Simpson's oeuvre. Recognising the currency of the period novel and its generic reach, the *Saturday Review* saw *Desires and Devices* as attempting to "reconcile realism and romance", an attempt it adjudged to be "conscientious but not wholly a success for it would seem that the period novel must become truly historical in its characters as well as in its setting to interest today".[90] Between 1925 and 1940, twelve of Simpson's thirteen novels appeared in the American market, fifteen books in total in fifteen years.[91] She first published with Knopf, the distinguished literary publisher, then from 1929 to 1935 with the more commercially oriented Doubleday, Doran, which brought out her two Australian epics, *Boomerang* and *The Woman on the Beast*. Simpson had left Australia in 1914 aged sixteen but returned a number of times in the twenties and thirties, and although she was thoroughly integrated into English literary networks Australia emerged as setting and theme in her most significant historical novels.

Boomerang was certainly an historical saga, 500 pages extending from 1789 to the First World War, and a significant departure from Simpson's earlier novels, although they prepared the way for its reception. By the time *Boomerang* appeared, Simpson had established a reputation in the American market as an accomplished writer of intelligent, entertaining fiction. *Outlook*'s reviewer wrote: "We always look forward eagerly to anything of Helen Simpson's. Her fine, sensitive prose seems still untroubled by the swirl and splash of the swift modern literary currents in which so many of our authors flounder about ungracefully".[92] For the *New York Times*, Simpson's "very long and very ambitious novel" fell just short of being "exceptionally noteworthy", for the main Australian story

---

89 C. Hartley Grattan, "Recent Australian Books", *New York Herald Tribune*, 15 May 1932.
90 "The New Books", *Saturday Review of Literature*, 3 May 1930, 1015.
91 Simpson also published a collection of short stories, *The Baseless Fabric* (1925), "eleven tales turning upon the supernatural and filled with dark romanticism": "Supernatural Tales", *New York Times*, 14 February 1926.
92 Review of *Boomerang*, *Outlook* (April 1932), 230.

7 "Australia is very American": Australian Historical Fiction in America 1920s–1940s

was anti-climactic. Nonetheless, the novel provided "a detailed account of present-day Australia, its political and religious conflicts, as seen by a native-born Australian returning to the country".[93]

The even more extravagant *The Woman on the Beast* – which ranges from sixteenth-century Indo-China to Australia in 1999 – was also well received. The *Saturday Review* was sufficiently aware of Simpson's career to perceive the book as "a synthesis of all that Miss Helen Simpson has hitherto written", including the historical romance of her earlier *Devices and Desires*: "She has written *The Woman on the Beast* with a delicate combination of the ironic, the imaginative, the supernatural, and the romantic, with each element deftly applied to produce a fascinating pseudo-historical trilogy of a missionary, a revolutionary, and a humanitarian".[94] Confirming Barnard's earlier reading of the literary field, the reviewer used the book to define a "neo-romanticism common to that group of eminent Englishwomen, Helen Butts, Clemence Dane, Rose Macauly, and Helen Simpson". The same question struck the *New York Times* reviewer, who described the novel as "of, but by no means altogether in, the romantic tradition". It was at once "romantic and cynical, vivid, dramatic and picturesque, challenging and always interesting, the product of a fertile and well-nourished imagination".[95]

It was a few years before Simpson turned again to an Australian historical story, in *Under Capricorn*, set in 1830s New South Wales. Heinemann published the novel in London in 1937. The American edition, sharing the same pagination, was published by Macmillan in January 1938 and reprinted by Grosset & Dunlap later that same year. For the first time in the American book pages, Simpson was identified clearly as "a fourth-generation Australian".[96] *Under Capricorn* was reviewed as "a graphic romance in a strange setting".[97] Reviewers again recalled Richardson's Australian trilogy. The *New York Herald Tribune* thought that although the novel was not perfect, "You may put it on the shelf with a greater work, Henry Handel Richardson's magnificent trilogy … without prejudice".[98] Jane Spence Southron, in an extended review in the *New York Times*, praised its comedy above all, noting that "Australia [gets] lighter treatment than is usually accorded it in fiction" (perhaps she also had *Ultima Thule* in mind). "It is shot through with clean, tender laughter," she concludes, "and it makes you feel that Australia is a country to know more of."[99] Simpson's last novel, *Maid No More*, was published in the United States by Reynal & Hitchcock in 1940. It had no Australian content.

G.B. Lancaster's turn to the family saga was if anything even more striking, for there was a gap of fifteen years between her previous novel, *The Savignys*, and her major Australian novel, *Pageant*, published in 1933. There was an even longer break between

---

93 "Several Generations", *New York Times*, 20 March 1932.
94 J. Connop Thirlwall, *Saturday Review of Literature*, 2 December 1933, 305.
95 "A Satire on Fanatics", *New York Times*, 12 November 1933. Doubleday published only one more of Simpson's books, another period novel, *Saraband for Dead Lovers*, in 1935.
96 William Rose Benét, "Drama Down Under", *Saturday Review of Literature*, 15 January 1938, 7. A biographical feature was printed in the same issue, 19.
97 Benét, "Drama Down Under". "The hot and crowded streets of the new and difficult colony swarm with strange life … [The] book has atmosphere and verve, and fully acquaints one with the drama of early Sydney".
98 *New York Herald Tribune*, 30 January 1938.
99 Jane Spence Southron, "Comedy in Australia", *New York Times*, 30 January 1938.

the earlier colonial romances and her uptake of the "saga-novel", the term the American *Bookman* found to describe *Pageant*.[100] During this period Lancaster had travelled to all the dominions and begun planning a series of large-scale novels on the colonial experience in Australia, New Zealand and Canada. She was fully conscious of the genre into which she was writing: "the family novel – the book which starts its story many years ago, and works down gradually to the present day, bringing in perhaps three generations of one family in the process".[101] If her earlier work had been compared to Kipling or Stevenson, the appropriate point of reference now was inevitably Galsworthy's *Forsyte Saga*, but Richardson and Lancaster could also be linked. *Pageant* was headlined as "A full-blooded family saga from Australia".[102] It was in three parts as the saga form seemed to demand: "Colonising", "Civilising" and "Realising".

Pageant was a success in Britain, Australia and the United States – *especially* in the United States where the Century Company's edition sold over 15,000 copies in addition to the 30,000 copies taken by the Literary Guild as their February choice.[103] It was also recommended as a Book-of-the-Month Club alternate selection. The novel remained in the American bestseller lists for five months, and Century's publicity celebrated "the quarter million readers who thrilled to *Pageant*".[104] Introducing the book for Literary Guild subscribers, Carl Van Doren drew attention to its distinctiveness for American readers:

> [*Pageant*] is a frontier novel with a difference. The settled colonists are menaced, not by Indians as in American Western fiction, but by the despised and sullen convicts whom the British Empire has dumped upon the island with imperial unconcern for how they shall be made into citizens of the growing state. The antagonism is therefore not racial, as in the familiar novel, but social. The privileged are ranged against the unprivileged, with the result that the people in the story live always on the precipice of collapse or near the crater of insurrection.[105]

Century advertised *Pageant* as "probably the finest novel that [had] appeared under its imprint in twenty years".[106]

Despite Lancaster's earlier successes, in many ways she was starting again as a novelist in a new sector of the marketplace. Dorothea Brande in the *Bookman* could not help exclaiming: "The publishers assure us, astonishingly, that not only has Miss Lancaster published six of her eight novels in this country, but that three of them have been filmed".[107] Her astonishment was caused by the strengths of this new novel by an

---

100 Dorothea Brande, "Four Novels", *Bookman*, February 1933, 201.
101 Terry Sturm, *An Unsettled Spirit: The Life and Frontier Fiction of Edith Lyttleton (G.B. Lancaster)* (Auckland: Auckland University Press, 2003), 195.
102 William Soskin, "Reading and Writing", *New York Post*, 6 February 1933.
103 Sturm, *An Unsettled Spirit*, 195.
104 Sturm, *An Unsettled Spirit*, 236. Lancaster reported to Stanley Unwin that six American booksellers listed *Pageant* among the bestsellers, 2 March 1933, Records of George Allen & Unwin Ltd, Special Collections, University of Reading. All subsequent correspondence and contract information from this source unless otherwise indicated.
105 Van Doren quoted in Sturm, *An Unsettled Spirit*, 199.
106 Sturm, *An Unsettled Spirit*, 203.
107 Brande, "Four Novels", 191.

7 "Australia is very American": Australian Historical Fiction in America 1920s–1940s

"unknown" author: "a family saga of Tasmania, rich in its material, too rich in its writing". With his greater knowledge of Australia, Grattan was one of the few in a position to understand the novel's historical complexity as a "swan song for the aristocracy, or what the Australians call the squattocracy", but most reviewers were moved to take on its historical ambition as something more than period romance.[108]

For Gladys Graham Bates in the *Book-of-the-Month Club News*, *Pageant*'s tale of three generations had "the ampleness of many-charactered tales": "The life of the colony, politically and socially, is woven cleanly into the story ... Mr. Lancaster [sic] keeps the reader conscious throughout of the conditions that beset these colonizers and of the state of affairs in England as well as in Tasmania".[109] For Jonathan Daniels in the *Saturday Review of Literature*, the interest of this "beautifully detailed book" was less its historical romance than its "magnificent pageant" of the English colonisers, building "a new world in fixed reflection of an old one".[110] He valued the book's irony that Lancaster herself thought most reviewers missed: "The parade goes on: colonists and convicts, ladies and gentlemen, officers in her Majesty's army, bush rangers and sheep herders and harlots and dealers in tallow and hides. The parade will go on after the book is ended. It began with a race reshaping itself. It continues in a growing commonwealth". Southron, again, reviewed *Pageant* for the *New York Times*. If most Americans would think Tasmania "a most unlikely subject for a considerable epic", she wrote, the novel succeeded through its historical fidelity in proving otherwise. As the pageant unfolds, the country itself "remains invariable": "all through the book you sense 'the strange cleansing fragrance of the bush' to a degree almost physical."[111]

Lancaster was unused to the rejections that came when J.B. Pinker began to offer *Pageant* to publishers in the first half of 1930. The novel languished in manuscript for more than two years until her New York agent, Francis Arthur Jones, finally secured a contract with Century. Although Lancaster was at first delighted to be associated with such a prestigious publisher, she later came to think the contract "by far the worst" she had ever had: "I only signed it under what I thought to be a promise that the next would be so infinitely better that I would not regret it."[112]

Lancaster's international dealings reveal very clearly the difficulties for an Australasian author, not only in being published across three territories, but in earning an income from that publication. Anglophone publishing markets were divided by mutual consent into separate spheres: for British publishers, as we have seen, this meant the "traditional markets" of Britain, her colonies and dominions; for the United States, it meant the Americas and the Philippines. Canada was often disputed, claimed by both parties and sometimes declared an open market in order to break a deadlock. This gentleman's agreement would be formalised among British publishers in 1947 as the Traditional Markets Agreement. It made *Australian* publishing a difficult proposition, as British publishers were unlikely to take on any title if the rights to the lucrative Australian market had already been assigned; and without a British publisher, the chance for a book to be sold

---

108 C.H. Grattan, *Nation*, 15 February 1933, 181. Grattan wrote: "*Pageant* interests me far more in its sociological implications than as a work of fiction aesthetically considered".
109 Gladys Graham Bates, *Book-of-the-Month Club News*, February 1933, n.p.
110 Jonathan Daniels, "The House of Comyns", *Saturday Review of Literature*, 11 February 1933, 424.
111 Jane Spence Southron, "A Rich Canvas of Life in the Tasmanian Bush", *New York Times*, 12 February 1933.
112 Edith Lyttleton to Stanley Unwin, 16 June 1933.

on to an American publisher was extremely small. As Innes Rose of the John Farquharson agency explained to Eleanor Dark: "While it is of course a good thing to try and publish in Australia if you have been unsuccessful in finding a publisher in either London or New York, prior publication there would make it impossible to find a publisher in either of these two cities".[113]

But in this period of expansion for Australian fiction there were attempts to break the pattern. Angus & Robertson took the successful sale of British and American rights in Davison's *Man-Shy* as a model, and tried repeatedly over the next decade to arrange publication in the United States for its own more successful books and others from authors associated with the firm. It helped arrange US publication for at least eighteen Australian books during the war and immediately afterwards.[114] More aggressively nationalist, editor and critic P.R. Stephensen established the Endeavour Press in Sydney at the end of 1932, committed to publishing Australian titles locally and in "repatriating" rights for others already published overseas. Stephensen organised the American publication of Louis Stone's *Jonah* after reissuing the novel in 1933, published the first edition of Penton's *Landtakers*, and with Lancaster's support secured the Australian rights to *Pageant*.

The key clause of Lancaster's contract with Century was the very first, that giving the firm *world* rights.[115] This would prove more of an issue than the disappointing terms offered: a modest advance of $250 and a sliding royalty scale that moved from 10 to 15 per cent only after the sale of 10,000 copies. It meant that Lancaster was unable to make any separate deal with a British or Australian publisher. It was Century who sold the English publication rights to Allen & Unwin, and as Stanley Unwin wrote to Lancaster: "We actually paid the Century Company for the British and Colonial rights double what they paid you for the world rights, and as the Century Company claim half of what we pay them it means in effect that they did not have to pay any advance at all".[116] Century later explained that they had treated *Pageant* as a first novel and had not anticipated its success. They promised they would expect only American rights in future books and offer higher royalties for them.[117]

A combination of contractual arrangements and taxation laws across the different territories meant that *Pageant*'s bestseller status did not translate into riches. Lancaster's American royalties were subject to a non-resident alien income tax of 8 per cent, a constant difficulty for Australian authors publishing in the United States, and her royalties on English sales faced a 25 per cent tax because under the terms of the contract they were remitted to Century and thus also attracted the US tax. Her earnings were boosted by income from the Literary Guild, which paid $6000 for their 30,000 copies, of which Lancaster received half (again minus tax). But, as Terry Sturm has shown, for every £100

---

113 Innes Rose to Eleanor Dark, 25 October 1933, cited in Barbara Brooks and Judith Clark, *Eleanor Dark: A Writer's Life* (Sydney: Pan Macmillan, 1998), 127. And see Jason Ensor, *Angus & Robertson and the British Trade in Australian Books, 1930–1970: The Getting of Bookselling Wisdom* (London: Anthem Press, 2012), 11-15.
114 See Ensor, *Angus & Robertson*, 38. Henry Lamond's *Kilgour's Mare* (Morrow/Armed Services Edition, 1943) can be added to the list. The list includes titles not published originally by Angus & Robertson such as Hill's *Australian Frontier* (*The Great Australian Loneliness*) and Lamond's *Dingo* (*White Ears the Outlaw*).
115 Contract dated 29 July 1932.
116 Unwin to Lyttleton, 27 July 1933.
117 Sturm, *An Unsettled Spirit*, 205-6.

7 "Australia is very American": Australian Historical Fiction in America 1920s–1940s

Pageant earned in Great Britain, Lancaster received little more than £30, and that was before she paid her actual income tax in New Zealand.[118]

Further complications arose when in January 1933, Lancaster (via Alice Grant Rosman, who was acting on her behalf) received an attractive offer from the Sydney Bulletin Co. for an Australasian edition.[119] As the Endeavour Press, under Stephensen's direction, it offered a royalty of 10 per cent rising to 15 per cent after 5000 copies sold, against an advance of £50.[120] Lancaster was keen to have the book published in Australia, but Australasian rights had already been sold to Allen & Unwin. She had corresponded with Stanley Unwin about the Century contract – he had confirmed it was bad – and although initially resistant to ceding Australasian rights he ultimately persuaded Century to allow him to negotiate a separate agreement with the Endeavour Press.[121] Lancaster was keen for such an outcome: "I hope that you have come to some arrangement about P. with the Bulletin. As it would be – I understand – the first book to be published in this way it would be likely to have a good chance".[122] The Endeavour edition also sold well, 6000 copies in its first nine months, and Lancaster followed Richardson and Boyd in winning the Australian Literature Society Gold Medal. Yet the contractual and taxation tangles remained. With taxation in Australia and America, with royalties divided between Allen & Unwin and Century, and with her agent's commission, Lancaster received less than £16, equivalent to a 1.5 per cent royalty.[123] Later she managed to have her English royalties paid to Century's London office, thus avoiding the US alien tax, and with Unwin's support she persuaded Century to forgo its share of her Australian royalties.

Lancaster's struggles continued with her next book, the Yukon story *The World is Yours*, which had become hot property after the success of *Pageant*. The Society of Authors advised her that she was indeed bound by her earlier contract with Century, but she was able to negotiate a new contract "almost wholly on her own terms" with the newly formed Appleton-Century Co.: American and Canadian rights only, a flat-rate royalty of 15 per cent, and an advance of $1000. The Endeavour Press again published in Australia. Appleton-Century made *The World is Yours* their "Premier novel for the Spring season" of 1934. In the 1933 merger that formed Appleton-Century, Lancaster's main contact at Century, vice-president Curtice Hitchcock, left to form Reynal & Hitchcock with Eugene Reynal and the new firm made an attractive offer for *The World is Yours*. Although Lancaster felt bound to Appleton-Century for that novel, Reynal & Hitchcock subsequently became the American publishers for her big New Zealand and Canadian historical romances: *Promenade* (1938) and *Grand Parade* (1943). *Promenade* became the feature novel in Reynal & Hitchcock's spring list for 1938 and sold well over 12,000 copies

---

118 Sturm, *An Unsettled Spirit*, 206-7, 211.
119 Typescript of telegram dated "January 1933".
120 The Bulletin Co. cabled George Allen & Unwin, January 1933: "Can we have Australasian rights Lancaster's novel". The Endeavour Press was a new publishing venture launched by the Bulletin Co. on Stephensen's urging. Craig Munro, *Wild Man of Letters: the Story of P.R. Stephensen* (Carlton, Vic.: Melbourne University Press, 1984), 117.
121 Unwin to Lyttleton, 27 July 1933 and preceding correspondence over June-July.
122 Lyttleton to Unwin, 29 January 1933. In the letter she quotes a Sydney "literary friend": "If we could help break up this Australian situation that is so dreadful for Aus. Authors you would be a pioneer in the cause of literature both in NZ and the Commonwealth". Alice Grant Rosman assisted in the negotiations.
123 Sturm, *An Unsettled Spirit*, 208.

in its first two months. Almost inevitably, it was described in the *Book-of-the-Month Club News* as "New Zealand's *Gone with the Wind*".[124]

Lancaster herself was fascinated by the differences between British and American publishing houses: "She thought that the British system offered better contracts to authors, with substantially higher royalty levels and larger advances; but she also admired the marketing and promotional skills of the American syndicates, which produced substantially larger print runs and sales".[125] She also thought English readers less interested than American readers in Australia and the other dominions. As she wrote to Unwin soon after *Pageant*'s appearance: "I heard from America that six booksellers list P. among the best sellers. I don't know how it is going here, but England is not interested in her Dominions very much, I'm afraid. She is too long past the colonization stage to view it with the same sympathy that America does".[126]

A rather different, if equally ambitious historical novel, Eric Lowe's *Salute to Freedom*, was also published by Reynal & Hitchcock in late 1938, around the time of Lancaster's *Promenade*. *Salute to Freedom* was "big in scope as well as in size", extending from the beginning of the twentieth century to the Spanish Civil War where the central character dies fighting for the republican cause.[127] Intellectually, it extends from the decline of the pastoral aristocracy to the rise of international communism. The book was highly praised in the *New York Times*, the *Herald Tribune*, the *Saturday Review*, and by Grattan in the *New Republic*, for whom it ranked "well up toward the top of any list of recent Australian novels".[128] The fullest appreciation came from Southron, as it often did, and her response suggests that her experience of reviewing several Australian novels in this period had forced her to reflect on the country itself:

> Here is one long novel at least that is not too long. From beginning to end it is full of the meat of thought. Written by an Australian about present-day Australia it throws a steady, brilliant light on the mentality of a young nation that counts enormously, and will count increasingly, in British imperial policy; and that also, as the book implicitly reveals, will have a big future part to play in world politics. Australia, in the past, may sometimes have seemed not unlike a "dark horse" with unpredictable running possibilities; but, in this large-scale contemporary picture of her people, we see a nation wholly conscious of her destiny, standing on her own feet and thinking for herself. This, we are made to realize, is not only a young nation but a nation uniquely affected by a unique environment.[129]

---

124 Sturm, *An Unsettled Spirit*, 215, 220, 236. Henry Seidel Canby, "Promenade", *Book-of-the-Month Club News*, May 1938, n.p.
125 Sturm, *An Unsettled Spirit*, 216.
126 Lancaster to Unwin 2 March 1933. *Pageant* was reissued by Triangle Books, New York, in 1942.
127 Quotation from James Gray, "Searcher for Truth", *Saturday Review of Literature*, 11 February 1939, 7. As well as its three main parts it had a final Coda. None of the other volumes in the trilogy were published in America.
128 Grattan, *New Republic*, 1 March 1939, 108.
129 Jane Spence Southron, "A Novel of Modern Australia", *New York Times*, 12 February 1939. *Time* was not impressed: "Reading fat, second-rate novels nowadays is like watching the wake of a ship: they stir up a lot of suds, produce a certain hypnotic effect, and a few hundred yards back, leave no trace at all. *Salute to Freedom* churns thus for 615 pages". 13 February 1939, 71.

7 "Australia is very American": Australian Historical Fiction in America 1920s–1940s

Reynal & Hitchcock also published Lowe's *Framed in Hardwood* (1940), but it disappointed those who had welcomed *Salute to Freedom*. Grattan concluded that Lowe had "the knowledge to do a fine and powerful novel of the squattocracy", and despite the new novel's failure, "readers interested in the subject should carefully attend to his books for they contain the elements which must be worked".[130]

Epics of Violence: *Landtakers* and *Capricornia*

Neither Brian Penton's *Landtakers* nor Xavier Herbert's *Capricornia* is a family saga, but both have something of the genre's epic and epochal scale even as the heroic pioneering romance is savagely undone. Again, both had to make their way into the American market after having first been published in Australia. *Landtakers* was influenced by Penton's reading of *The Fortunes of Richard Mahony* and conceived as the first volume of a trilogy.[131] It was first published in Sydney by Stephensen's Endeavour Press in mid-1934. They sold it to Cassell in London who published in May 1935, one of the small number of cases where a British publisher purchased British Empire rights excluding Australasia.[132] The Endeavour Press also sold US and Canadian rights to Farrar & Rinehart, Norman Lindsay's publisher, and possibly on his recommendation. Farrar & Rinehart's contract was scarcely generous – a £25 advance and a flat 10 per cent royalty rate – and there is no evidence as to how well the book sold.[133] Unsurprisingly, though, it made a strong impact on reviewers, who placed it in the lineage of recent regional sagas:

> The people of Australia have in this powerful story of their forebears what Norwegians have in Hamsun's "Growth of the Soil" and Americans in Rølvaag's "Giants in the Earth." It is a more terrible tale than either. The sweep of its style is as elemental and vast as the lonely bush it describes. The story of an epoch, its first chapters are so brutal that the mind shudders at the realism of this writer who can sustain them in their savage deeds, their crude life, their hatred between men, their cruelty, and their despair. It grows in interest and in grip, its characters harsh and enormous as the forces that shaped them.[134]

By contrast, Tony Clarke in the communist *New Masses* criticised Penton for not showing that it was the machinations of English merchants that made Australia "such a hell-hole",

---

130 Grattan, "Australian Squatters", *New York Times*, 11 February 1940. J.G. [James Gray], *Saturday Review of Literature*, 17 February 1940, 21.
131 There are references in Australian newspapers to the second volume, *Inheritors*, appearing in the United States (Adelaide *Advertiser*, 26 September 1936; Gavin Casey in the *West Australian*, 15 December 1938) but no evidence of an American edition has been located. The third volume has never been published. See Patrick Buckridge, *The Scandalous Penton: A Biography of Brian Penton* (St Lucia: University of Queensland Press, 1994), 173, 198.
132 Munro, *Wild Man of Letters*, 127-34. The terms of the agreement between the Endeavour Press and Cassells (30 October 1935) were a £50 advance on account of royalties; 10 per cent to 2000 copies sold; 15 per cent to 5000; 20 per cent to 15,000; 25 per cent thereafter (and 3d per copy for a colonial edition).
133 Contract dated 13 November 1934, signed for Farrar & Rinehart by Stanley Rinehart. A.P. Watt Records 1880-1982, University of North Carolina, Collection no. 11036, Box 346: 12.
134 *Boston Transcript*, 15 June 1935.

Figure 7.1 C. Hartley Grattan's review of Brian Penton's *Landtakers* (New York: Farrar & Rinehart, 1935), featuring jacket design by James Reid. *New York Times*, 16 June 1935.

not the land or the "essential coarseness of the people": "Novel of the soil, though it is, there is no touch of poetry such as pervades the work of Hamsun".[135]

Under the heading "Violence Down Under", Alvah Bessie in the *Saturday Review* recalled *Pageant*, contrasting that "long romantic novel" with the brutal realism of Penton's work, which he found utterly convincing: "The novel is frank melodrama from cover to cover, but so profoundly has Mr. Penton observed his materials and so expertly has he made use of them, that the reader moves from horror to violence, through rare moments of peace, with the utmost confidence in his author's integrity and his authority to speak

---

135 Tony Clarke, "Ossification", *New Masses*, 23 July 1935, 27.

7 "Australia is very American": Australian Historical Fiction in America 1920s–1940s

for an epoch long since ended". The work had "the hallmarks of a novelist of major stature".[136] Grattan reviewed *Landtakers* at length for the *New York Times* and in the *New Republic*, which referenced Richardson with its heading "Australia Infelix" (Fig. 7.1). He saw *Landtakers* in relation to other Australian works – *For the Term of His Natural Life*, *Ralph Rashleigh*, *Geoffry Hamlyn*, the Brent of Bin Bin novels, and *Red Heifer* – and its impact on him is clear. But his response was uneasy. Penton had written "a coarse, brutal and powerful novel that reveals cold intellectual force and honesty of purpose, even while it betrays ... that the author entirely lacks that sense of awe and pity which alone would give adequate dignity and meaning to the terrible story he has to tell ... Only truthfulness prevents the performance from degenerating into a Gothic chamber of horrors". If superior as a revelation of how convict "slavery" had built up and poisoned Australian life, it was inferior to many other Australian novels "of social interest".[137]

Herbert's *Capricornia* was first published in Australia in 1938 but not released in the United States until five years later, by Appleton-Century, in spring 1943. In October of that year the firm announced that *Capricornia* had spent twenty-six weeks on the bestseller lists.[138] The novel's complicated publishing history has been recounted elsewhere, but it depended again upon Stephensen, first with the Endeavour Press and then his next venture, the Publicist Publishing Co., which issued *Capricornia* in January 1938.[139] Its success attracted Angus & Robertson, which had rejected an earlier version of the novel and the firm released an Australian edition in 1938, negotiated an English edition, and continued to reprint it throughout the 1940s. *Capricornia* soon became one of Grattan's touchstones. Since its first appearance while he was visiting Australia, he had tried to interest American publishers, lending his personal copy to Alfred Knopf. Knopf's readers, however, "condemned the book because of many dull stretches ... lack of sound narrative and ... a tendency to labor the question of racial relations".[140] Kinsey & Co. rejected it because of the Australian background.[141] Angus & Robertson continued pushing through Leland Hayward, and eventually Herbert signed with Appleton-Century in January 1943.

Appleton-Century's offer was a modest advance of $350, but a reasonably generous royalty scale that moved upwards from 10 to 12.5 per cent at 3000 copies sold and to 15 per cent after 6000. Although the book had been published in Australia and Britain five years earlier, the firm copyrighted it in the United States, setting and printing its own edition. The addition of a new foreword, again by Carl Van Doren, who must by this time have been building a small library of Australian novels, allowed copyright to be registered.[142]

---

136 Alvah C. Bessie, "Violence Down Under", *Saturday Review of Literature*, 15 June 1935, 7.
137 Grattan, "A Novel of Fiery Australians", *New York Times*, 16 June 1935; "Australia Infelix", *New Republic*, 31 July 1935, 342.
138 Appleton-Century letter to booksellers, 13 October 1943, Papers of Sadie and Xavier Herbert, Fryer Library, University of Queensland. All subsequent correspondence and contract and royalties information from this source unless otherwise indicated.
139 Frances De Groen, *Xavier Herbert: A Biography* (St Lucia: University of Queensland Press, 1998), 90-99; Munro, *Wild Man of Letters*, 136-47 and 177-85; Laurie Clancy, *Xavier Herbert* (New York: Twayne, 1981), 36-39.
140 Knopf to Grattan, 25 November 1941, quoted in Laurie Hergenhan, *No Casual Traveller: Hartley Grattan and Australia–US Connections* (St Lucia: University of Queensland Press, 1995), 192.
141 De Groen, *Xavier Herbert*, 301, note 29.
142 The contract (dated 8 January 1943) required the author to "covenant" that the book had not previously been published, but it is unlikely that Appleton-Century was unaware of the previous editions.

The publisher's confidence in the book was rewarded when it sold over 26,000 copies in its first three months.[143]

Their advertising was bold – "From out of the bush where the Tropic of Capricorn crosses Australia, comes this stupendous novel of white man, native woman and half-caste" – and they had plenty of enthusiastic phrases from reviewers with which to make a noise: "Far and away, the best novel of the year"; "Lusty, forceful, exciting"; "Boils with action ... fresh ... exotic"; "Hot with passion ... rowdy and witty" (Fig. 7.2).[144] Although focused on the immediate past rather than a long historical span (except in its opening pages), *Capricornia* was received in terms of the generic frames of its predecessors, as a "panoramic novel", a "picaresque adventure tale, a family saga, a work of social criticism", and for the *Book-of-the-Month Club News* a "saga of elemental living".[145] Its distinctiveness within the genre was also remarked. For *Book Week*, it had "a newness and originality ... which is as different from American and English writing as the kangaroo is different from our familiar animals". For the picky Clifton Fadiman in the *New Yorker*, Herbert's voice was "vigorous, reckless, and impolite. It will be heard". And while Herbert had "only a rudimentary sense of plot, very little sense of selection, and no notion of when he has finished making his point", *Capricornia* was still one of the most powerful novels he had read in several years: "The impression one gets from this book is of a new country, tormented by flood and drought, but miraculously vigorous and healthy."[146]

The country perhaps looked less vigorous and healthy to those struck by the novel's revelation of race relations and miscegenation. Some drew comparison with Richard Wright's *Native Son*. Van Doren placed the novel for his American readers by comparison with Lancaster's historical romance and as *late* in the history of frontier and historical fiction:

> For more than a century the English-speaking peoples have been writing and reading novels about their frontier, in the United States, Canada, South Africa, Australia. Though most such novels have been simple melodrama, some have been romantic or sentimental or humorous or realistic, varying with general literary fashions but through all these variations continuing to celebrate the hardships and heroisms of men and women who have gone from settled regions to build up new societies in this or that wilderness, however abundant, however hostile.
>
> As the earlier frontiers have retreated into history the frontier novels dealing with them have become historical romances ... This same restoration of a past appears in recent novels like G.B. Lancaster's *Pageant* ... History has power over them, unavoidably touching their characters and actions with the lingering colors of a vanished world.[147]

---

143 By 1947, the American edition had earned Herbert $14,000. Royalty statement from Leland Hayward forwarded to Angus & Robertson, 8 November 1943. In the six months to 30 June 1944, the novel still sold over 900 copies in the United States. See also De Groen, *Xavier Herbert*, 168.
144 Appleton-Century advertisement, *New York Times* 9 May 1943. Sources quoted: *Albany Times-Union*; *Boston Herald*; *New York Times* (Orville Prescott); *Herald Tribune*.
145 *Library Journal*, 1 April 1943, 406; *Newsweek*, quoted in the 1969 Award Books paperback edition; Charles David Abbott, "Capricornia", *Book-of-the-Month Club News*, May 1943, 15.
146 *Book Week*, 25 April 1943, 1; Clifton Fadiman, *New Yorker*, 1 May 1943, 72.
147 Carl Van Doren, foreword to *Capricornia: A Novel*, by Xavier Herbert (New York: Appleton-Century, 1943), v.

7 "Australia is very American": Australian Historical Fiction in America 1920s–1940s

Figure 7.2 Advertisement for Xavier Herbert's *Capricornia* (New York: Appleton-Century, 1943). *New York Times*, 9 May 1943.

Capricornia, by contrast, was "emphatically a book of these times", its background "the Australian town most often mentioned in the papers" (Darwin, the fictional Port Zodiac, only recently bombed by the Japanese).[148] Further, where the American frontier novels had been "remarkably sexless", Herbert had made miscegenation his central theme.

Unusually, *Capricornia* was also reviewed in the international affairs journal *Current History*, no doubt because of the Pacific war and the presence of American troops in Australia. *Capricornia* was important "in what might be called, and not facetiously, a study in black and white – and yellow".[149] For Maxwell Geismar in the *New York Times*, Australia had been "largely a terra incognito in fiction as well as in fact", with only Richardson and Prichard as exceptions. Even so, Richardson resembled a European visitor alongside Herbert, "as native as a 'crazy bob' typhoon, which he resembles in other ways also".[150] Showing a remarkable fluency in Australian slang, Geismar described *Capricornia* as "based squarely on an indigenous tradition of graziers and cattle droving, of swagmen and booze artists and 'Binghis,' as well as governmental heads and Oxford boys in the bush". Mixed "with the often highly civilized tribal habits of the Australians Blacks", this muddle had created the curious democracy of "Australia Felix". It was as a Marxist, perhaps, that Geismar drew attention above all to the story of race. *Capricornia* should interest American readers, "because, with all its strange compounds of the tropics and the East, the Australian frontier is still close to our own, and because the novel bears down hard on an issue as crucial to us as it is to Australia. The problem of the black race has preoccupied our own writers in America from Tocqueville to Richard Wright, but seldom has it been presented with such remarkable honesty". That the conditions described still existed was "both startling and humiliating to a white man".

Despite many qualifications about Herbert's craft, the only extended negative notice was in the *Saturday Review of Literature*, where Ellis Roberts concluded that the novel's violence "achieves in the end only incredulity".[151] More interesting are his remarks on Australian novels generally (and the evidence this provides of the reviewer's awareness of the field):

> Nearly all novels about Australia suffer from the thesis bug. It is true of one of the earliest and still one of the best, Marcus Clark's "For the Term of His Natural Life"; it was true of that fine book "The Timeless Land," and it is extremely, sometimes wearisomely true of Mr. Herbert's "Capricornia." It is as if … Australians cannot yet rid themselves of the painful stigma of their ancestry. Only the late Helen Simpson was completely free from the self-defensive attitude adopted by most serious Australian novelists.

Grattan, meanwhile, had written to Appleton-Century congratulating them on introducing *Capricornia* to American readers, and reviewed it for the *New Republic*. Despite his enthusiasm, he once again expressed a certain ambivalence, for like *Landtakers* it was a powerful but partial representation of Australian society: "'Capricornia' is without

---

148 The *Book-of-the-Month Club News* described "Port Darwin" as "the North Australian city now so spectacularly and continuously in the news".
149 Jasper R. Lewis, "Books in Review: Light on Darkest Australia", *Current History* 4 (August 1943): 406. *Capricornia* was reviewed alongside Griffith Taylor's *Australia* (Dutton, 1943).
150 Maxwell Geismar, "Nomads and Adventurers on the Australian Frontier", *New York Times*, 25 April 1943.
151 R. Ellis Roberts, "Back of Port Darwin", *Saturday Review of Literature*, 1 May 1943, 10.

7 "Australia is very American": Australian Historical Fiction in America 1920s–1940s

doubt an important Australian novel. But, as some American reviewers have suspected, it deals not with the central facts of Australian life, not even with a typical frontier region, but with a peculiarly recalcitrant area ... I do not intend to deprecate its power *qua* novel, though I do think the reviewing boys and girls a bit extravagant in their praise. It is, however, a staggering piece of work".[152]

Despite the impact of *Capricornia* on reviewers and book buyers, Herbert was to join the long list of Australian authors unable to turn early success into a sustained presence in the American marketplace. Appleton-Century (from 1948, Appleton-Century-Crofts) was certainly keen to take up its option, writing to Herbert regularly at least to 1953 enquiring as to the progress of his new novel.[153] Finally, in early 1956, Herbert forwarded the manuscript of "Of Mars, the Moon, and Destiny" (later published in Australia as *Soldiers' Women*) but the firm rejected it because of its length and didacticism. They invited Herbert to resubmit a shorter, revised version, but in mid-May he replied ending his relationship with the firm.[154] Herbert also wrote to MCA Management, which had absorbed Leland Hayward, asking them to represent the book, sight unseen and with a stipulation that he would not cut or rewrite. They politely suggested he might do better elsewhere.[155]

A new phase began in early 1959 when Herbert sent Mavis McIntosh, then Angus & Robertson's US agent, a copy of his humorous novel *Seven Emus*. She thought it delightful but unlikely to appeal to a "large enough segment of the American novel buying public to persuade most publishers it is a 'must book'". She was encouraging nonetheless, recalling *Capricornia*'s success. In May, having read *Seven Emus* and another manuscript, she wrote again to Herbert declining the chance to represent him and noting the difficulties of length and style his books would present any agent.[156] Herbert next tried Angus & Robertson's new American representative, Paul Reynolds, who offered *Seven Emus* and *Soldiers' Women* to various publishers. Reynolds' Malcolm Reiss reported the familiar issues with *Soldiers' Women* – "too rambling and too loquacious" – while for *Seven Emus* the problem was "the Australian background": "most of the houses felt the material was somewhat Australian for this market ... The Australian background ... is against you, since so many novels that are published in the US are almost as topical as non-fiction". And again: "As for the quality of your writing, there is no question about that, it is excellent. The Australian scene and point of view, however, tend to make the novels difficult to market".[157] While generalisations are dangerous across an entire industry, there is supporting evidence to suggest that the "Australian scene and point of view" were indeed more likely to be an obstacle than an advantage in the postwar decades, certainly more than they had been in the 1930s and the war years. In these novels at least, and at this point in time, Herbert's Australianness could not be read through a generic frame that would engage American readers or, in Hutner's terms, be brought into the conversations America was having with itself.[158]

---

152 C.H. Grattan, *New Republic*, 24 May 1943, 708.
153 Archibald G. Ogden (Appleton-Century-Crofts) to Herbert, 6 January 1953 ("this is my annual reminder").
154 Patricia Schartle (Executive Editor, Appleton-Century-Crofts) to Herbert, 13 April 1956; Herbert's reply, 15 May 1956.
155 Phyllis Jackson (Literary Department, MCA Management) to Herbert, 8 May 1956.
156 Mavis McIntosh to Herbert, 10 March and 1 May 1959. McIntosh was also letting go of her arrangement with A & R.
157 Malcolm Reiss (Paul R. Reynolds & Son) to Herbert, 2 November and 20 December 1960.
158 Hutner, *What America Read*, 45.

Despite his earlier break with Appleton-Century, in late 1960 Herbert wrote to the firm offering the revised *Soldiers' Women*, as it was about to be published by Angus & Robertson. Editor-in-Chief Ted Purdy answered Herbert's concern about its Australianness: "The Australianness of *Capricornia* did not interfere with its reaching a great many readers and having excellent reviews, and I do not see why *Soldiers' Women* would be handicapped even if it is even more of a Down Under novel".[159] Appleton-Century held the manuscript for five months as it did the rounds of the editorial and sales staff, but again the answer was, very regretfully, no. It was still "enormously long", and although in general it was "an impressive and frightening piece of work" they could see no real public for it in America.[160]

At the end of 1963, Herbert tried Appleton-Century again, with his autobiographical work *Disturbing Element*, and again, it declined. Purdy wrote to Herbert, "I'm afraid there is no answer, really, to the old complaint about your work being so 'Australian.' I don't see what else it could be, and that quality gave *Capricornia* its particular flavour, but in the case of an autobiography it is perhaps more of a handicap than in fiction".[161] He passed the book on to Harper & Row who sent it to William Morrow, who sent it in turn to Farrar, Straus & Giroux. All declined. Perhaps the only good news came when the Universal Publishing and Distributing Corporation of New York signed an agreement with Appleton-Century to publish an Award Books paperback edition of *Capricornia*. First released in December 1969 and reprinted in August 1976, the book was made to look every inch an epic cowboy romance with a dramatic cover image and blurb to match: "What every frontier story should be – tough, sprawling, rampant with physical action".[162]

American Success Is Success: Eleanor Dark

As we have seen, the presence of the Australian historical saga in the American marketplace can be framed by the two most successful novels of the period, the Book-of-the-Month Club selections *Ultima Thule* and *The Timeless Land*. There were later successes, including *Capricornia* and *Lucinda Brayford*, and Ernestine Hill's two books published in this period. *Australian Frontier* was the American title of Hill's remote outback travelogue *The Great Australian Loneliness*, first published by Jarrold in London in 1937 but picked up by Doubleday, Doran in 1942 and published alongside a US Council on Books in Wartime edition, meaning thousands of copies were distributed to US troops in the Pacific. Hill felt it "a grand thing to be known in America, especially through Doubledays".[163] Grattan reviewed the book sceptically for the *New York Times*, praising Hill's journalism when she was merely reporting but challenging her notion of the outback as the "real" Australia and her "dogmatizing" about future development in the remote regions: "Mrs. Hill's frontier will always be

---

159 Theodore (Ted) Purdy to Herbert, 4 January 1961.
160 Purdy to Reiss, 2 May 1961.
161 Purdy to Herbert, 21 May 1964.
162 Quotation from *Time* printed on the front cover.
163 Quoted in Anna Johnston, "American Servicemen Find Ernestine Hill in their Kitbags", in *Telling Stories: Australian Life and Literature, 1935–2012*, ed. Tanya Dalziell and Paul Genoni (Clayton, Vic.: Monash University Publishing, 2013), 89.

7 "Australia is very American": Australian Historical Fiction in America 1920s–1940s

the Australian frontier".[164] Doubleday followed up in 1944 with Hill's historical novel *My Love Must Wait*, first published by Angus & Robertson in 1941. It was given a paragraph in the *Book-of-the-Month Club News* and praised in the *New York Times* as a well-written, informative "historical romance". Grattan appeared in the *Saturday Review*. He found the book lacking precisely *as* an historical novel, "in these days when the genre is flourishing". His benchmark was *The Timeless Land*: "Compare the two books ... and you will, I think, come up with the conclusion that success is granted to the novelist who sees life through a complex temperament".[165]

The Timeless Land was in fact the fourth of Dark's novels to appear in the United States, but the first historical novel and her first major success. Encouraged by the response to *Return to Coolami* in London, William Collins sent a proof copy to Macmillan New York who published the novel (with a $250 advance) in mid-1936.[166] The book was seen as a more commercial novel than Dark's previous work, something of a romance despite the modernist complexities of its multiple narrative perspectives, "weaving the memories and nostalgias of the past over immediate moods and dangerous speculations".[167] The New Zealand-born journalist and regular book reviewer for the *New York Sun*, Rex Hunter, described Dark's technique positively, but through a comparison with Richardson identified her as little more than an author of light fiction:

> Miss Dark is no Henry Handel Richardson; it is unlikely that she will ever set the Thames, the Murray or the Hudson on Fire. But she can be relied on to turn out a series of nice, safe, comfortable novels on the eternal sex theme for the porch and hammock trade. Feminine patrons of drug store circulating libraries will swoop joyously upon "Return to Coolami" and have a splendid time snuffling over the sorrows of Susan. They will like the book all the better because there is hardly an original idea in it.[168]

This was an idiosyncratic assessment. Elsewhere, *Return to Coolami* was widely and favourably reviewed – even as "one of the exceptional answers to the prayers of publishers and reviewers" – despite many sharing Alfred Kazin's sense that it was a fine achievement despite the obstacles the author had created for herself with her technique.[169] Springfield's *Evening Union* declared that it would be "high treason against American readers if Macmillan allows her future writings to escape them now that they have discovered her".[170] It was less successful commercially than critically, however, selling fewer than 2000 copies, but perhaps on the strength of the good reviews Macmillan agreed to take Dark's

---

164 C. Hartley Grattan, "'Outback' Australia: The Country and the People", *New York Times*, 18 October 1942.
165 C. Hartley Grattan, "The Story of Matthew Flinders", *Saturday Review of Literature*, 19 February 1944, 20.
166 Brooks and Clark, *Eleanor Dark*, 145.
167 A.C., "Fiction", *Saturday Review of Literature*, 20 June 1936, 19.
168 Rex Hunter, "Sorrows of Susan", *New York Sun*, 13 June 1936. Dark's press clipping files, Papers of Eleanor Dark, National Library of Australia, NLA MS 4998.
169 C.E.S., "Books of the Moment", *Evening Union* (Springfield, MA), 11 June 1936. Dark press clippings. Alfred Kazin, "Australian Journey", *New York Times*, 14 June 1946.
170 C.E.S., "Books of the Moment".

next work, *Sun Across the Sky* (1937). Reviews this time were half-hearted and the novel struggled to earn out its $250 advance.[171]

Despite this setback, Macmillan was still willing to gamble on *Waterway* (1938), Dark's third novel in as many years, which did do better, selling over 2000 copies and being highly praised in the key literary papers. Most reviews were accompanied by a photograph of the novelist. In a prominent, wholly positive review, the *New York Times* highlighted its "literary excellence" if in thoroughly middlebrow terms, as "neither too light nor too heavy [and] in the best novel tradition".[172] The *Saturday Review* was more questioning and more intellectually engaged. The reviewer, journalist and historian George Dangerfield, provides a nicely ironic sense of Australia's image in New York: "It is surprising – it shouldn't be, but it is – to think that there are suburbs in the Antipodes, which the imagination ignorantly fills with only the larger forms of life". The harbourside Sydney suburb Dark presents seems always about to "throw off its domesticity and return to something more primitive": "It won't, of course and alas, but the threat is there". Dangerfield's conclusion would have been gratifying: "as you read it, it does seem as if an infinitesimal part of the map of the world had suddenly shivered and come alive".[173]

Despite the novels' uneven sales, Dark progressively built a reputation as a writer of "emotional power and psychological acuteness", encouraging Macmillan to persevere with successive titles.[174] Orin Borsten, reviewing *Waterway* for the *Atlanta Journal*, identified something of even greater significance, and his awareness of Dark's literary nationalism is striking:

> It is paradoxical that Eleanor Dark, one of the most vigorous nationalists in that brave band which has espoused the cause of Australian literature, should break as solidly with tradition as she has in her new novel. Here the wild, savage strength of the bush gives way to a land drenched by gentle sunlight, a land that boldly turns from its past to face its today and its tomorrow. There is excellent reasoning in Miss Dark's excursion into new directions. It establishes Australia as something more than an odd little continent and points the way to the achievement of a cultural uniformity by its writers and artists … In Eleanor Dark, Australian literature has found one of its most brilliant spokesmen, one whose role in its cultural destiny may be as significant as was Lady Gregory's in Ireland's own renaissance. No other writer has succeeded so well in depicting the tragedy of a land whose inhabitants constantly cry "exile" and whose discipline must therefore be fierce and violent.

It is unclear what informed this unusually perceptive view of Dark and Australian literature except for the cluster of novels from her contemporaries discussed in this chapter. Perhaps Borsten had read Richardson and Penton.

---

171 There was a favourable review in the *Saturday Review of Literature*: C.H.M., "Fiction", 4 December 1937, 50, 54.
172 Percy Hutchison, "A Dramatic Novel of Australia: Eleanor Dark's 'Waterway' is the Story of a Climactic Twenty-four Hours in the Lives of a Group in Sydney", *New York Times*, 7 August 1938.
173 George Dangerfield, "Twenty-four Hours in the Antipodes", *Saturday Review of Literature*, 13 August 1938, 6. Dangerfield had been editor of *Vanity Fair* (1933-35) and was the author of *The Strange Death of Liberal England* (1935).
174 Review of *Waterway*, *New Republic*, 17 August 1938, 56.

7 "Australia is very American": Australian Historical Fiction in America 1920s–1940s

Throughout the late 1930s, Dark drew on criticism of her earlier novels in planning the work that would make her famous in America. William Collins suggested to Dark that she needed to rethink her penchant for writing "one-day action books".[175] Dark in turn had been discussing with Collins the "idea of a semi-historical novel about Australian life" since at least November 1937, starting with "a blackfellow, and the idea of Australia".[176] Perhaps considering her publisher's advice, she wrote that such a book might have a wider appeal because "there seems to be rather a fashion for semi-historical stuff at present". She was also a fan of *Gone with the Wind*.[177] The resulting novel was completed by mid-1940 and two copies of the manuscript were sent to Curtis Brown London, one being forwarded to the New York office at the end of August. All this work paid off for author and publisher when it was announced that *The Timeless Land* would be the Book-of-the-Month Club's main choice for October 1941. Referring to the war in Europe, Collins admitted that he was "particularly glad because it should all help to bring the two countries, Australia and the States, together, the more they know about each other, especially in these times".[178]

The announcement that *The Timeless Land* was a Club selection influenced advance sales, resulting in a second large printing by Macmillan in September exclusive of the Book-of-the-Month Club edition. Congratulating Dark, Marjorie Barnard wrote, "American success is success, & should be profitable".[179] Barnard's prediction quickly came to pass. In London, Collins sold more than 5000 home and colonial copies and the subsequent Australian issue also sold an additional 5000, but neither came close to American sales. By November 1941, Macmillan had sold almost 10,000 copies independent of Book-of-the-Month Club sales. By the end of April 1942, the Book-of-the-Month Club had distributed more than 100,000 copies, earning Dark approximately $25,000. Sales remained in the thousands for several years.[180]

This was an exceptionally good run for an Australian novel in New York, but still not enough to guarantee future American releases. Despite her success with *The Timeless Land*, Dark had trouble selling the subsequent volumes of her trilogy. Macmillan rejected *Storm of Time* in November 1948 after Dark's "disgusted" literary agent, Naomi Burton, knocked back the publisher's proposed contract.[181] The novel was subsequently accepted by McGraw-Hill's Whittlesey House, which offset 6000 copies of the English edition. *Storm of Time* paid its way with modest sales, and again it was favourably reviewed: "It is an historical novel (in the richest meaning of the term) which is alive with people and events".[182] By 30 June 1950, McGraw-Hill had sold 5794 copies, enough for Dark to

---

175 William Collins to Dark, 5 November 1937, Eleanor Dark Papers, State Library of New South Wales, ML MSS 4545 Box 26. All subsequent correspondence referenced from this source unless otherwise indicated. Brooks and Clark, *Eleanor Dark*, 205.
176 Dark to Collins, 5 and 26 November 1937.
177 Brooks and Clark, *Eleanor Dark*, 193.
178 Collins to Dark, 1 October 1941.
179 Barnard to Dark, 18 August 1941, in *As Good as a Yarn with You: Letters between Miles Franklin, Katharine Susannah Prichard, Jean Devanny, Marjorie Barnard, Flora Eldershaw and Eleanor Dark*, ed. Carole Ferrier (Cambridge: Cambridge University Press, 1992), 68; Brooks and Clark, *Eleanor Dark*, 248. Barnard continued "not that I know much about that". Papers of Eleanor Dark, National Library of Australia, NLA MS 4998/1.
180 In 1947, Macmillan reported that few copies were moving out of Macmillan's warehouse and the novel was out of print by the early 1950s.
181 Naomi Burton (Curtis Brown New York) to Dark, 17 November 1948.
182 V.P. Hass, "Storm of Time", *Saturday Review of Literature*, 25 February 1950, 19.

earn out her $1000 advance with a further $500 in royalties. However, Whittlesey House's Lois Cole then rejected *No Barrier*, the third volume in the trilogy, telling Curtis Brown: "She is writing so exclusively for her Australian market and is so eager to give a rounded picture that she has almost forgotten the need of a novel to give the reader a good story ... Perhaps when she is through with it, however, she will return to lighter novels and realize the potential she showed in the first one or two".[183] Similar responses came from other publishers to which Curtis Brown sent the book, such as those from Harper's reader: "It is for us a job to respect for its authority rather than a story to live with".[184]

It was anything but a "lighter novel", however, that would bring Dark a new round of critical appreciation. Dark's devotion to her trilogy was broken by the composition of *The Little Company*, a novel closer in technique to her early work but with the expansiveness of a historical novel. Although focused on the crisis-ridden present, with Australia facing the threat of Japanese invasion, the novel expands internally as the main characters reflect back on their own family history and its parallels to the history of nation and empire.[185] In late 1942, responding to Dark's suggestion of an American edition of her earlier *Prelude to Christopher*, Macmillan's James Putnam advised caution and stressed instead the need for a new work to appear as a follow-up to *The Timeless Land*: "It seems to me that as a native Australian, with a cosmopolitan point of view, you might make a very interesting book about the life there which would, if necessary, be a very personal product and not necessarily a comprehensive survey of Australian geography and resources".[186] Putnam had a book of non-fiction in mind, but by November the following year Dark had completed a rough draft of *The Little Company*, a novel that explores the psychology and politics of a family of Sydney writers and intellectuals in this tumultuous wartime world.

After reading a final draft six months later, Putnam was interested "to see how the problems of Australian intellectuals seem to parallel those of similar individuals over here".[187] American reviewers agreed. In a fascinating notice for the *Chicago Daily News*, Howard Baer added that the style would also be familiar to American readers:

> Mrs. Dark's effort shares kindredness of expression with the American rather than the British writer. Her work finds better comparison with the vigor of the dramatist, Lillian Hellman, than with the novelist, Virginia Woolf. She has less the predisposition to the beautifully descriptive and introspective than to the vigorous exposition, through colloquy, of her – and her characters' – philosophic idea.[188]

As a novel about novelists, full of serious talk on literature, history, and economics, *The Little Company* was never likely to appeal to a wide audience; it was widely reviewed and taken seriously, but the reviews were mixed. As the *New York Times* summed it up:

---

183   Allan Collins (Curtis Brown New York) to Dark, 6 November 1952.
184   Allan Collins to Dark, 3 February 1954.
185   David Carter, *Always Almost Modern: Australian Print Cultures and Modernity* (North Melbourne, Vic.: Australian Scholarly Publishing, 2013), 181-83.
186   Putnam to Dark, 20 November 1942, Dark Papers, ML MSS 4545, Box 22; Brooks and Clark, *Eleanor Dark*, 293.
187   Putnam to Dark, 30 June 1944.
188   Howard Baer, "World's Search for Faith Theme of Australian Novel", *Daily News* (Chicago), 13 June 1945. The book was widely reviewed, with almost ninety reviews in Dark's press clippings.

7 "Australia is very American": Australian Historical Fiction in America 1920s–1940s

Above and beyond the flood of cerebration, the author gives us a sense of Australia's freedom and space; glimpses of beauty; interesting British-flavored reactions to current events. She has made an honest effort to analyse the predicament of the creative instinct trapped into immobility by circumstances. To a great extent she is successful in arousing our sympathy for her case, but not her characters; a tribute to her intelligence, rather than to her novel.[189]

The Little Company nonetheless returned the publisher's investment, selling around 6500 copies and earning Dark close to $700 on top of her $1000 advance. Canby's notice in the *Book-of-the-Month Club* News was addressed to serious readers interested in the international comparison: "For those who wish to see how the psychological conflicts of these difficult decades react in other lands and cultures this novel is to be recommended. It is grim, but highly descriptive and sincere".[190]

The Timeless Land in Its Time

Despite the respect accorded her earlier novels and *The Little Company*, Dark's American reputation rested on the success of *The Timeless Land*. But why did this novel have such an appeal to American critics and readers? The endorsement of the Book-of-the-Month Club and the resulting discussion in newspapers and magazines obviously made it a novel that readers of "good books" might desire to have on their bookshelves (Fig. 7.3). The process can be seen most significantly in the advertisements, reviews and commentary published in the *New York Times*. As was their custom, the Book-of-the-Month Club placed a full-page advertisement in the paper including an extract from Dorothy Canfield's report on the novel, while the extended report was sent to its more than four hundred thousand members. This preceded Katherine Woods' featured review in the *Times* by more than two weeks. Macmillan's publicity also quoted Canfield: "Who can read it without that lift of the heart that comes at contact with greatness!"[191] And in December, *The Timeless Land* was recommended among the *Times'* "Books for Christmas". Close to a million readers might thus have become aware of the novel through Canfield's report and its sentiments filtered through the many reviews and recommendations that subsequently appeared across the country.

But the effects were also generic. *The Timeless Land* represents the culmination of the sequence described in this chapter in bringing together as it did historical, intergenerational and nation-building themes, and in its power of invoking parallels with the American colonial experience, at once familiar and unfamiliar. As the heading to Milton Rugoff's review in the *Herald Tribune* put it: "This Big Novel is a Rich Reconstruction of an Historical Saga Strangely Kin to Our Own".[192] Its scope and style were such that it could receive an uplift both from the general esteem at this point in time of the historical novel "in the richest meaning of the term" and from the accumulated weight of

---

189 Jane Martin, "Other Recent Fiction: The Little Company", *New York Times*, 20 May 1945.
190 *Book-of-the-Month Club News*, May 1945, 11.
191 *New York Times*, 16 October and 7 December 1941.
192 Rugoff, "The Birth of a Nation – Down in Australia: This Big Novel is a Rich Reconstruction of an Historical Saga Strangely Kin to Our Own", *New York Herald Tribune*, 5 October 1941.

Figure 7.3 Eleanor Dark's *The Timeless Land* (New York: Macmillan, 1941) as a Book-of-the-Month Club selection. *Book-of-the-Month Club News*, September 1941.

7 "Australia is very American": Australian Historical Fiction in America 1920s–1940s

the distinctive Australian examples that had made an impact in the American marketplace. In the high middlebrow terms of the Book-of-the-Month Club, serious but accessible historical fiction could be associated with "greatness", as Canfield Fisher put it, and with universal qualities. *The Timeless Land* offered "our first profound, satisfying, emotionally moving interpretation in fiction of what the arrival of white settlers in a natural world really meant".[193] For Woods, "the stuff of epic drama is given a living expression that is nobly worthy of its subject. 'The Timeless Land' is a novel of towering stature, beautifully molded, soundly and broadly based, penetrating and challenging in its contribution to knowledge".[194] She thought Dark had "reached the high level of the historical novel at its best", assessing the novel in relation to its genre rather than as a representative of Australia literature. For the *Saturday Review*, *The Timeless Land* was "a novel of stern beauty and profound reality which unquestionably ranked among the best books of the year".[195]

Other commentators compared the novel more narrowly with Australian fiction. In the *Christian Science Monitor*, Dark was praised for finding "new things to say about Australia": "She avoids all the over-reiterated detail of the Australian scene and introduces masses of fresh and interesting material in a mature style that breaks entirely with the old romantic frontier medium of the Adam Lindsay Gordon order that has governed so much of Australian literature hitherto".[196] Ralph Thompson recommended the novel for the "average American" with little knowledge of Australian history, and contrasted it with Lancaster's *Pageant*: it had "little or no melodrama or embroidered G.B. Lancaster romance". Similarly for Rugoff, Dark had avoided the "besetting sins of historical fiction" – "gaudy romance" and "attractive adventuresomeness" – but thankfully, also, she was no "furious realist".[197]

For many, the historical saga encouraged, even compelled parallels to be drawn between the American and Australian histories of settler colonialism. This was an easy mode of familiarisation from reviewer to reader, but the strongest novels, like *The Timeless Land*, could produce a much stronger effect, a sense of *unexpected* familiarity, almost a shock of recognition. This combination of strangeness and familiarity could interpellate American readers in new ways, making the Australian novels suddenly more readable, more engaging, more *original* than the merely exotic or provincial stories they might otherwise have become. As the earlier review of *A House is Built* had put it, "Australia is very American"; or the later review of *The Timeless Land* quoted above, "an Historical Saga Strangely Kin to Our Own". In Canfield Fisher's words: "There is a unique, compelling quality about our very first experience of something different from what we have known before. When this 'first taste' of something quite different is in the higher, richer field of literature or the graphic arts, a comment on it requires exclamation points of surprise as well as pleasure".[198] Both the kinship and the strangeness of discovering it were recurrent notes:

---

193 Dorothy Canfield, "Eleanor Dark Writes Moving, Emotional Novel of Australia", *Bookman*, 28 September 1941.
194 Katherine Woods, "Eleanor Dark's Novel of Australia's Settlement", *New York Times*, 5 October 1941.
195 Klaus Lambrecht, "It Happened in Australia", *Saturday Review of Literature*, 4 October 1941, 5.
196 H.J.S., *Christian Science Monitor*, 17 January 1942, 10.
197 Ralph Thompson, "Books of the Times", *New York Times*, 8 October 1941.
198 Canfield, "Eleanor Dark".

Many Americans, vaguely educated to think our colonial beginnings a unique act of history, know scarcely the first thing of the parallel saga of the great continent, almost as large as the USA, "down under." It happens to be a very remarkable story, even a terrible one, with such aspects as the part played by convicts and adventurers, neglect by the mother country, demoralization of the natives, and pioneering fortitude even more clearly defined than in our own history.[199]

But despite the repeated discovery of parallels between Australian and American history, and despite the Pacific war, there is surprisingly little evidence of any sustained interest in Australia or its literature beyond this moment. Indeed, that interest, at least from publishers, seems to fade just when we might have expected it to burgeon.

In the United States and in Australia itself, the saga-novel had largely run its course by the later forties; and while we have emphasised the impressive sequence of Australian novels published in America from the late 1920s to the mid-1940s, these books represented only a tiny fraction of the novels appearing annually in America and landing weekly on reviewers' desks. Only a very small circle of readers could apprehend them *as* a sequence and hence as Australian literature. The degree to which this did occur is significant, but it could scarcely be maintained once this particular generic sequence was played out. Further, there was a progressive changing of the guard in the New York newspapers and periodicals such that Australian books and authors lost their small constituency among reviewers of the previous generation.

For "ordinary" fiction in the postwar decades, an Australian setting was more likely to be an obstacle than an advantage in the American market. As Kylie Tennant's American agent reported to her in 1946, "Perhaps in the near future apathy towards the Australian scene, which few books have been able to hurdle, may be destroyed".[200] This was an extraordinary claim in many ways given the serious reception accorded Australian novels over the previous two decades, but it reflects the present-mindedness of publishers focused on the marketplace of the day. Both histories are true: a remarkably sustained and intensified interest in Australian fiction over almost two decades, alongside a general apathy, or better, the absence of compelling commercial or cultural arguments for maintaining Australian books before American readers.

---

199 Rugoff, "The Birth of a Nation".
200 Naomi Burton (Curtis Brown New York) to Tennant, 26 February 1946, Kylie Tennant Papers, National Library of Australia, MS10043, Box 1, Folder 11.

8
"Australian moderns": Christina Stead and Patrick White in New York

> "I am *at home* in good old, bad old NY."
> —Christina Stead 1979[1]

Widely regarded as the two most important Australian writers of the twentieth century, certainly of its middle decades, the literary careers of Christina Stead and Patrick White were fundamentally shaped by the authors' American experience and more particularly by their contacts with New York publishing. Both were networked into the New York book world in ways that are rare among our examples although they recall W.W. Norton's support for Henry Handel Richardson; and, like Richardson, both for a time became part of contemporary American book talk on the state of the modern novel. Major figures in the New York book world including Clifton Fadiman, Max Schuster and Stanley Burnshaw were closely engaged in Stead's career, while Ben W. Huebsch of the Viking Press and then his successor Marshall Best were White's primary contacts in the publishing world, and much more than that in Huebsch's case. Some key reviews in the American papers, such as those by James Stern in the *New York Times*, were critical for White's sense that the "right readers" could be found for his challenging novels. For both authors, America was more than just a supplementary market. Stead, on the ground in New York and absorbed in its cultural politics and intellectual networks, came close to being read as an "American writer". White, by contrast, maintained his New York connections largely from a distance. Triangulated between English, American and Australian literary cultures, their writing had multiple homes but also a sense of homelessness, of not belonging easily to any single place or time. If this gave their fiction an unusual power, it also made it difficult for them to be assimilated into an evolving American or international modern tradition. In Pascale Casanova's words, "to be decreed 'modern' is one of the most difficult forms of recognition for writers outside the centre".[2]

---

1   Stead to Stanley Burnshaw, 12 September 1979, in Christina Stead, *Talking into the Typewriter: Selected Letters 1973–1983*, ed. R.G. Geering (Sydney: Angus & Robertson, 1992), 295.
2   Pascale Casanova, "Literature as a World", *New Left Review* 31 (January–February 2005): 75. For Stead and White see Simon During, *Exit Capitalism: Literary Culture, Theory, and Post-Secular Modernity* (London: Routledge, 2010), 57–94, and *Patrick White* (Melbourne: Oxford University Press, 1996); Paul Giles, *Antipodean America: Australasia and the Constitution of US Literature* (New York: Oxford University Press, 2013), 345–64.

Stead lived in the United States for a year from July 1935 and then for the best part of a decade between July 1937 and the end of 1946. All her books were published in America, and from *House of All Nations* (1938) to *The Puzzle-Headed Girl* (1967), America was the first place of publication. She wrote a trilogy of New York novels and set *The Man Who Loved Children* (1940) in America despite its sources in her own Australian childhood. Even in *The Salzburg Tales* (1934) at the very beginning of her career as a published writer, and in later works set elsewhere, America is a recurring theme, New York especially, as one site of the cosmopolitan trade in talk, money, art and sex that would fascinate Stead across so many of her books. Stead's career is inconceivable without the United States as an imaginative and intellectual provocation, a social and moral environment, and a publishing home. More than a place of residence, America was present to Stead through her almost forty-year relationship with William Blake (Wilhelm Blech), German-Jewish American stock trader, Marxist, political economist and author; their involvement with left-wing literary circles in New York; and Stead's own immersion in America's literary past. Stead's biographers have covered much of the detail of her and Blake's New York years, and recent critics have examined Stead's attitudes to America and engagements with American communism.[3] The focus in the present chapter is on Stead's publishing history and critical reception in the United States over this critical, formative decade.

Although never resident in the United States for an extended period, the most significant publishing relationship for Patrick White across the first three decades of his career was with his American publisher, the Viking Press, and above all his relationship with Ben Huebsch, senior editor and partner at Viking. Huebsch was a major figure in American publishing, one of the earliest publishers of modernist works and someone wholly sympathetic to White's sense of himself as a serious writer. While White's first novel, *Happy Valley*, appeared first in London, in 1939, his next seven novels, from *The Living and the Dead* in 1941 to *The Vivisector* in 1970, were released first by Viking. Little attention had been given to White's American career before David Marr's 1991 biography, and subsequently only Simon During's short book on White has shown much interest in the question. But as During argues, "White's reputation was originally built in America, and was then transferred, more or less simultaneously, to Australia and the UK".[4] There was no simultaneous transfer, for the American and British markets operated too independently for that to occur; but the claim does express the significance of America in building and sustaining White's career through to the late 1960s.

---

3   Stead was born in Sydney in 1902, moved to London in 1928, then worked in London and Paris before moving to the United States. Biographical information drawn from Hazel Rowley, *Christina Stead: A Biography* (Melbourne: Minerva, 1994), Chris Williams, *Christina Stead: A Life of Letters* (Melbourne: McPhee Gribble, 1989), and published and unpublished correspondence (references below). Articles on Stead's attitudes towards America and communism include Michael Ackland, "'A Skyrocket Waiting to Be Let Off', but to Where? Christina Stead's First Impressions of the United States and Her Postwar Literary Rehabilitation" and Fiona Morrison, "The 'American Dilemma': Christina Stead's Cold War Anatomy", in *Reading across the Pacific: Australia–United States Intellectual Histories*, ed. Robert Dixon and Nicholas Birns (Sydney: Sydney University Press, 2010), 225–39, 241–53; Ackland, "Christina Stead and the Politics of Covert Statement", *Mosaic* 43 (March 2010): 127–42. Further references below.

4   During, *Patrick White*, 6; David Marr, *Patrick White: A Life* (1991; Sydney: Vintage 1992). White was born in London in 1912 to an Australian family, was educated in England, and lived in Cambridge and London in the 1930s.

8 "Australian moderns": Christina Stead and Patrick White in New York

This chapter traces Stead's American career in the 1930s and 1940s and the early stages of White's career to the immediate postwar period. These were critical decades for both writers, in Stead's case covering her New York years and in White's case the years of his expatriation in London and his first American travels, before his return to Australia after the war. With Stead and White, expatriation takes on a very different quality from what we have seen across all our previous examples. Through their investments in international modernism, and international communism for Stead, they loosened the imperial bonds that governed most other expatriations.[5] But in neither case was this a simple replacement of the national or imperial by the cosmopolitan for there was also a form of displacement involved in their transnational careers.

Stead moved from London to Paris then the United States and Europe, while White's early American experience helped break the mould of colonial expatriation, an effect completed by his war experience in the Middle East and North Africa. There is an extremely complex dynamic between cosmopolitanism and a kind of homelessness for both writers. At points in their writing careers, both claimed the United States, and (Jewish) New York in particular, as a spiritual home; both could use America against the British world, including Australia; and yet both could also claim an ineradicable Australianness. Stead's life was defined by a form of "nomadism"; indeed, her time in New York was the longest she spent in any one place after leaving Australia. White returned to Australia after the war but to a kind of writing-in-exile at home; his closest literary connections were still with Huebsch in New York.

In literary terms, too, both writers were cosmopolitan but also displaced, a combination that might help explain their shared feeling of affiliation with New York's Jewish writers and publishers. While international modernism helped launch their careers and both were celebrated as major writers, they were never quite assimilated into either the American or British narrative of the progress of the modern novel. Stead has been described as "un-Australian, un-English, un-American" (though we might also remove the negatives).[6] In During's terms, she wrote "either without a particular national audience in mind or for an American readership to which she had no deep personal connection".[7] We could almost say the same for White, at least for his early career. Both belonged to the generation who "came to literary maturity after the first wave of modernism",[8] the generation of Faulkner, Nabokov, Hemingway and Steinbeck, but again their relation to modernism was angular, never quite part of an evolving tradition, "after" modernism but in some ways also anachronistic. The point for the present analysis is the central role American publishing and American reviewing played in making and sustaining these unusual writing careers.

---

5   Richardson, J.F. Dwyer and Maysie Greig present comparable but very different instances, Richardson through her strong European links, Dwyer and Greig via their American connections.
6   Lorna Sage quoted by Louise Yelin, *From the Margins of Empire: Christina Stead, Doris Lessing, Nadine Gordimer* (New York: Cornell University Press, 1998), 3.
7   During, *Exit Capitalism*, 77.
8   During, *Exit Capitalism*, 63.

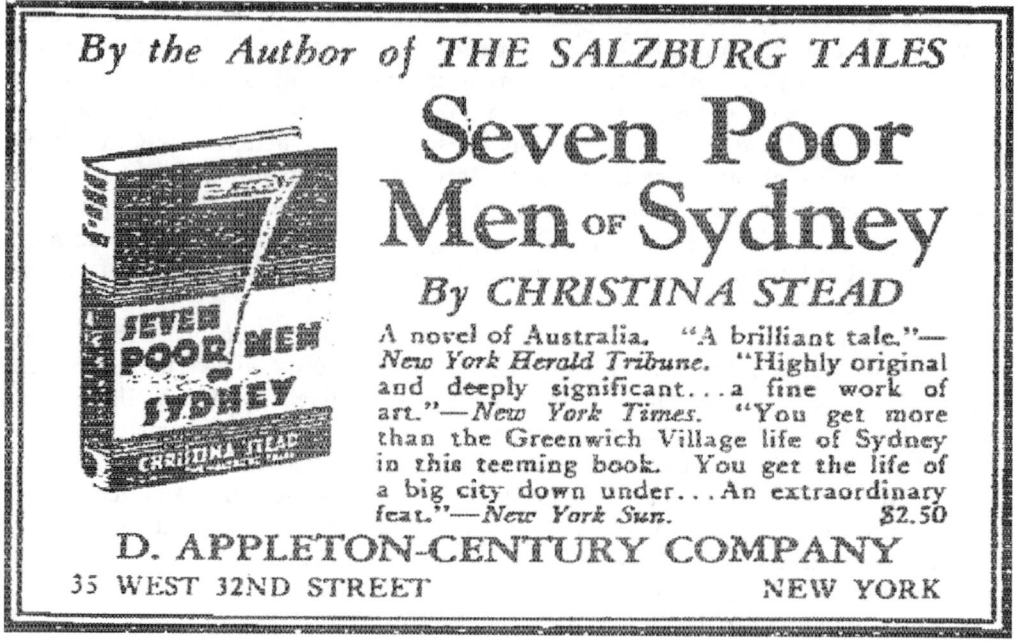

Figure 8.1 Christina Stead's *Seven Poor Men of Sydney* (New York: D. Appleton-Century Co., 1935), advertised in the *New York Times*, 24 March 1935.

Australian Moderns

Stead's first three books appeared initially in London from the young English publisher Peter Davies, who arranged with Appleton-Century for their publication in America.[9] (Fig. 8.1) *The Salzburg Tales* appeared first, in September 1934, followed by *Seven Poor Men of Sydney* in March 1935 and *The Beauties and Furies* in April 1936.[10] Stead and Blake were in New York when *The Beauties and Furies* appeared, and they were welcomed at Appleton-Century's offices: "The manager, John L.B. Williams, wanted Stead to see reporters and give interviews, write an article on her first impressions of America and produce more of her highly successful short stories".[11] Three novels from Appleton-Century in a little over eighteenth months was a remarkable introduction to the American market, and together with some positive reviews in important places it meant that in a very short space of time Stead was inserted into the New York book world as an author to be noticed, as part of the talk about new books and modern literature.

While Davies had accepted *Seven Poor Men* in early 1931, he wanted Stead to revise the manuscript and sought another novel to publish first, "to attract readers to the new

---

9   D. Appleton & Co. merged with The Century Co. in March 1933 to form the D. Appleton-Century Co., David Dzwonkoski, "Appleton-Century-Crofts", in *American Literary Publishing Houses, 1900–1980*, ed. Peter Dzwonkoski, Dictionary of Literary Biography, Vol. 46 (Detroit, MI: Gale Research, 1986), 8.

10 Rowley gives the publication date of *Seven Poor Men* as December 1934 (161) but the US edition is dated 1935 and the first advertisement appeared in the *New York Times* on 3 March 1935.

11 Rowley, *Christina Stead*, 183.

author with a less unconventional book".[12] A new novel was announced then abandoned, and in its place Stead embarked on the extraordinary tapestry of interwoven stories, "comic, tragic, fantastic, occult, and ghostly", that would be published as *The Salzburg Tales*.[13] Davies agreed to go ahead with the book, although it was scarcely less unconventional, and Appleton-Century followed, resetting and copyrighting their own edition.

The reviews of *The Salzburg Tales* were mixed or uncertain rather than "overwhelmingly positive" as has recently been claimed, setting a pattern for the reception of almost all Stead's works in the American market.[14] This is altogether unsurprising given the demands her style and the sheer scale of the books made on readers; and the reviewers by and large were struggling with exactly the same features of Stead's works that would challenge and excite later scholars. Although her books summoned various comparisons, particularly with European novels, they were strange objects even for the accomplished, urbane reviewers of the weekly and monthly book papers, belonging neither to the historical sagas or well-made realist novels that crossed their desks every week, nor to the modernist works that were increasingly present in the mainstream market.[15] While not manifesting the bleakness or astringency of some of Stead's later books, the earlier novels were still challenging both to conventional and modernist tastes. While strongly character-based, they did not attempt psychological realism. As During has said of *Seven Poor Men of Sydney*, Stead's language (which is often the characters' own talk) "threatens to exceed and break down both individuality and typification through a non-mimetic prose lyricism".[16] There is little space for readers to identify sympathetically with the characters, yet at the same time "one of Stead's most characteristic notes was a smothering intimacy with her characters", an intensity of emotion that co-exists in an uncanny, disconcerting way with an anti-sentimental, naturalistic perspective.[17] Stead's fictional world could thus be at once phantasmagorical and pitilessly materialist.

By the 1930s, Stead was also "a committed, if heretical, Stalinist".[18] While never constrained by Communist Party dictates as to literary style, she was deeply engaged with Marxian theory, and as During and Michael Ackland have argued, her communism was central to her novels in their larger conception and ideational structure rather than in overtly agitational or sentimental realism. They offer a sustained critique of bourgeois capitalism but no space of liberal morality to which readers might retreat. In During's summary, "Marxist theory," for Stead, "tells the truth about society under capitalism but it offers no ethical or epistemological aids for everyday and private life. [It] leaves private

---

12 Rowley, *Christina Stead*, 137.
13 Rowley, *Christina Stead*, 144-45; quotation from Drake De Kay, "Another Decameron", *New York Times*, 21 October 1934.
14 The quoted phrase is from Michael Ackland, "Whatever Happened to Coppelius? Antecedents and Design in Christina Stead's *The Salzburg Tales*", *Journal of the Association for the Study of Australian LIterature (JASAL)* 2 (2003): 53. Ackland is drawing on Rowley's biography, which states more circumspectly that the reviews were "almost all positive" (156).
15 See Karen Leick, "Popular Modernism: Little Magazines and the American Daily Press", *PMLA* 123 (January 2008): 125-39. Catherine Turner, *Marketing Modernism Between the Two World Wars* (Amherst: University of Massachusetts Press, 2003).
16 During, *Exit Capitalism*, 66.
17 During, *Exit Capitalism*, 70.
18 During, *Exit Capitalism*, 57.

intensities – especially sexual/romantic passion – disconnected from legitimate moral or social frameworks".[19]

Although it could be appreciated simply as an entertaining collection of fantastic stories, *The Salzburg Tales* was still demanding in its odd mix of social density and expressionist unreality. Nonetheless, it appears to have sold well, registering itself on bestseller lists alongside Hervey Allen's *Anthony Adverse*, James Hilton's *Good-bye, Mr. Chips* and Lloyd Douglas' blockbuster *The Magnificent Obsession*.[20] Most reviews carefully weighed the rare imagination of the tales against their artificiality and mannered style, although the *Saturday Review* could see only "a highly artificial performance that shows little more originality than the original idea ... of writing a new 'Decameron'". The reviewer invoked Isak Dinesen's *Seven Gothic Tales*; Stead's book by comparison was a "collection of inconsequentialities" producing only "mild ennui". The *North American Review* made the same comparison but this time by way of acclaiming *The Salzburg Tales*: "Miss Stead also has the true Gothic touch, seems to know everything and to have been everywhere, and writes with real magic. There hasn't been a better piece of imaginative fiction around this year than her volume, a three-star recommendation".[21]

In the middle were mixed reviews, among others those by Beatrice Bettinger in the *New Republic* and Drake de Kay (a name almost worthy of Stead's invention) in the *New York Times*:

> Miss Stead's style is extremely mannered. She relishes mockery, fantasy and tenuous philosophical implications. On the other hand, she evidently disdains the old-fashioned rules of story-telling ... These tales are as varied in their quality as in their theme; many of them insubstantial stuff, though undeniably clever.[22]

More surprising than these divided views is the widespread praise *The Salzburg Tales* received in the New York dailies: "Some of the most brilliantly sophisticated entertainment I have come across" (*New York Evening Post*); "A *tour de force* supreme" (*New York Herald Tribune*). Appleton-Century quoted both remarks in their advertisements for the book, alongside the most important review of all – the most important for Stead's early career in America – from Clifton Fadiman in the *New Yorker*.[23] Aged just thirty, Fadiman was already an influential figure in the New York book scene, first as a reader for Simon & Schuster and then as principal book critic for the *New Yorker* (1933-1943). He became a judge for the New York Readers Club in 1941 and for the Book-of-the-Month Club in 1944. Stead and Blake met him in New York in early spring 1936. They "got on extremely well", and Fadiman introduced them to publisher Max Schuster.[24]

---

19 During, *Exit Capitalism*, 83.
20 *New York Times*, 22 October 1934.
21 A.C.B., *Saturday Review of Literature*, 15 December 1934, 375; Herschel Brickell, "The Literary Landscape", *North American Review* 238 (December 1934): 576.
22 B.E.B, *New Republic*, 17 October 1934, 284; de Kay, "Another Decameron".
23 "Four Unusual Books", *New York Times*, 28 October 1934. Before the local reviews appeared the firm also quoted British novelist Susan Ertz, another Appleton-Century author: "Beautiful, erudite and almost incredibly accomplished ... Is the author woman or wizard?": *New York Times*, 16 September 1934.
24 Rowley, *Christina Stead*, 203. On Fadiman, see Joan Shelley Rubin, *The Making of Middlebrow Culture* (Chapel Hill: University of North Carolina Press, 1992), 144-45, 320-27.

8 "Australian moderns": Christina Stead and Patrick White in New York

Fadiman reviewed Stead's first three books, and despite the flaws he noted in each, by the time *The Beauties and Furies* appeared he could describe Stead as "a simon-pure genius showing not a trace of mere workaday talent", indeed "the most extraordinary woman novelist produced by the English-speaking race since Virginia Woolf".[25] This praise would accompany Stead for the rest of her career, continually cited by publishers and reviewers (sometimes by the latter in order to disagree). Fadiman's enthusiasm for *The Salzburg Tales* produced a lengthy and exuberant lead review, in which he described Australia incidentally – or rather by way of contrast with Stead's writing – as "the most unromantic of continents".[26] Enjoying himself, he wrote that the "ordinarily sober face" of the *New Yorker* books department was "in a lather"; he himself was "slightly balmy" about the book. But his account of the tales was acute in defining how "the wild grotesquerie of [their] plots is cunningly counterbalanced by the gleaming, witty precision of their style". Fadiman also drew comparison with Dinesen, but saw Stead's tales as "more compressed and truly gothic … Gnomelike mockery alternates with a luxuriance of chills and fevers". Stead, he concluded, might be an "artificer" rather than an artist, but she "gets away" with her passion for the improbable "partly because of the precise beauty of her style … and partly because a faint ring of mockery sounds behind the heaviest and most shadowy of her gothic portals". She had "wit, fancy, variety, light-brushwork satire, and almost offensive polish"; her portraits were "shrewdly cosmopolitan". This was perceptive, sophisticated criticism, evocatively and precisely expressed, answering the book's own sophisticated artifice.

It is not surprising perhaps that after such enthusiasm Fadiman found *Seven Poor Men of Sydney* "a bit of a disappointment".[27] The book's Australian settings were likely to be less familiar, more disorienting, strangely, than those of a highly literary, gothic Salzburg. The novel did not come off as realism or as character study; nonetheless, "in her descriptions, in her marvellous wild dialogues, in interpolated stories, in quite fantastic excursions, [Stead's] flashing talents reveal themselves". Fadiman was unsure whether Stead *was* a novelist ("this book doesn't demonstrate the fact one way or the other") but he was happy to claim she could "do things with the English language few of her contemporaries have even thought of". She was already "one of the few young British writers of fiction worth keeping an eye on". "British" and "Australian" were still interchangeable terms.

It is misleading to suggest that by contrast with *The Salzburg Tales*, *Seven Poor Men* was met with "an avalanche of negative criticism".[28] Alongside Fadiman's qualified praise, once again there were enthusiastic, intelligent reviews in important places – the *New Republic* and the *Times* – and quotable quotes from the New York newspapers which were put back into circulation in Appleton-Century's publicity: "A strange, half-mad, brilliant tale" (*New York Herald Tribune*); "You get more than the Greenwich Village life of Sydney in this teeming book. You get the life of a big city down under … An extraordinary feat" (*New York Sun*).[29] Kenneth White in the *New Republic* paid due respect to the novel's literary credentials, citing Fyodor Dostoevsky, Jakob Wassermann and James Joyce: "There is a

---

25 "Books", *New Yorker*, 25 April 1936, 69.
26 "Books", *New Yorker*, 29 September 1934, 59-60.
27 Clifton Fadiman, "Books", *New Yorker*, 2 March 1935, 62-63.
28 Rowley, *Christina Stead*, 161.
29 "Weekly News of Books", *New York Times*, 17 March 1935. Authors cited are Lewis Gannett and James Gray. Another familiar name, William Soskin, was cited, from the *New York American*: "Distinctly worth your while".

debt to the Joyce of 'Dubliners' and Stephen Dedalus: the debt is paid in full with the quickness of the reality perceived and the splendid writing".

> The novel, in a way, with the symbolic reference that its every simple and very real act has, possesses a curious dream quality, the dream quality of a modern, frantic world. Yet scenes like that of Michael's farewell, in all their loose, sprawling, immediate drama, have a smashing reality that you have only to look out your window to see. "Seven Poor Men of Sydney" is not a simple novel; it moves tortuously and deviously, it is depressing, it is tragic and actual. The writing alone would make the book deserve all the attention it can get.[30]

Even more important for a New York reputation, Jane Spence Southron, the astute, open-minded reviewer for the *Times*, acknowledged more explicitly even than White the book's modernity. Her review was entitled "Australian Moderns", and her point was to show this was not an oxymoron: "There is in the reader's mind an undercurrent of amazement that Australia, so far removed in space from Europe and America, should be so intimately bound to both not only in its necessarily connected material problems but in those of a spiritual nature".

> [Stead's novel] is highly original both in conception and treatment, and in its subject it is deeply significant of the mental and spiritual unrest of the age. [The characters] are recognizably present-day internationals …
>
> Miss Stead's art is in the integrity of its framework closely akin to sculpture. Reading her book is like watching the sculptor at work. You sense an austere purpose; you see the figures coming gradually into being; their meanings are unveiled to you in completeness only when the group is finished. Over and above we have the movement and liveliness for which words – or musical sounds – are the finest mediums.[31]

The characters are "talkers" and their talk is full of "religion, communism, socialism and sex". Despite the work being a "deadly indictment" of poverty, Southron concludes that Stead's "love for her country, nowhere explicit, is implied in every word".

There *were* negative reviews of course, unsurprising given the novel's unusual features: in the Sunday *Herald Tribune* ("she is far too willing to sacrifice the growth or consistency of her characters for the sake of a curious anecdote or a felicitous aphorism or a bit of descriptive pyrotechnics"); in the *American Mercury* ("A fine bitter prose-hymn to Australia suffers from opium-dream confusion"); and, not least, from C. Hartley Grattan in the *Saturday Review*.[32] Grattan wrestled with the novel, wanting, we might suspect, to celebrate another major Australian work, but finally being defeated by it. He finds its "brilliant, febrile, rebellious" characters somewhat like their New York intellectual contemporaries yet without their scope for action. Grattan's preferences were realist and nationalist in the Australian case, so Stead would always be a difficult proposition for him:

---

30   K.W. [Kenneth White], "Books in Brief", *New Republic*, 17 April 1935, 293-94.
31   Jane Spence Southron, "Australian Moderns", *New York Times*, 10 March 1935.
32   Elizabeth Hart, *New York Herald Tribune*, 3 March 1935; Frances C. Lamont Robbins, "The New Fiction", *American Mercury*, May 1935, xiii; C.H.G. [Grattan], *Saturday Review of Literature*, 23 March 1935, 573.

8 "Australian moderns": Christina Stead and Patrick White in New York

"The un-Australian, semi-Lindsay-ish culture of all is a curious amalgam of mysticism, folk-lore, pseudo-Freudianism, fantasy, irony, and plain bitterness, the whole topped off by a curiously un-Leninistic communism" (such lists can never be entirely wrong for Stead). *Seven Poor Men* showed an "astonishing violence of imagination that can only be explained by saying that the book was written by Christina Stead!" He could not see it contributing to the Australian literature he was himself committed to, although much of his characterisation of the book does capture its unusual qualities. Grattan met Stead in the 1940s, but there is no evidence they knew each other closely or even that she was aware of his role as an advocate for Australian literature in the United States.[33]

If there was an avalanche of negative criticism it was provoked rather by *The Beauties and Furies*. Sometimes it was as if Stead's own style invited rhetorical extravagance in her reviewers. The *Herald Tribune* pronounced it "pretentious, heavy-footed literary clap-trap" marked by an "ostentatiously putrescent flavour and verbal showiness".[34] James Gray, writing in the *St Paul Dispatch*, was one of the few critics to refer to Stead's nationality and to link her to her then very prominent fellow Australian, Henry Handel Richardson. The comparison was not to Stead's advantage:

> There must be some special reason for writing a book so pretentious and elaborate and altogether absurd. I think in Miss Stead's case it may be the fact that she comes from Australia. She has wished to demonstrate, once for all, that people from Australia can belong to the great world of hyper-sophisticates just as much as anyone else.
>
> One is quite willing to admit that point after reading "The Beauties and Furies." But the question inevitably rises: Can they also be human beings?[35]

It is at this point that Gray conjures Richardson. While Richardson's novels "deal to a great extent with Australians in Australia ... no more utterly human and appealing work has been done in our time". Another reviewer, however, linked Richardson and Stead as equals, finding Stead's writing "reminiscent of that other feminine genius of Australia" and linking them both *as* Australians, if in a dubious manner: "there is a force and imagination in both writers, something gripping but appalling about the atmosphere which they both create which must have something to do with the air of Australia".[36]

As a backhanded testimony to Fadiman's influence, Gray signed off his review by declaring that "Stead just happens to be a novelist who is 90 per cent too fancy for my taste. Mr. Fadiman may have all my copies of her works". More disturbing than slick dismissals like Gray's, no doubt, was the extended review in *Nation* by novelist Dorothy Van Doren, wife of critic and Columbia professor Mark Van Doren, and thus someone extremely well connected in New York literary circles. Van Doren begins with Fadiman's high praise of Stead before launching on her own "dissenting opinion". She was neither the first nor last reviewer to find a Stead novel to be "literally hundreds of pages of gaseous conversation pretending to wit and erudition":

---

33 Laurie Hergenhan, *No Casual Traveller: Hartley Grattan and Australia–US Connections* (St Lucia: University of Queensland Press, 1995), 187.
34 *New York Herald Tribune*, 26 April 1936.
35 James Gray, *Dispatch* (St Paul, MN), 6 May 1936. Papers of Henry Handel Richardson, Press Cuttings, National Library of Australia, NLA MSS 195.
36 *Capital Times* (Madison, WI), 24 May 1936. Richardson Press Cuttings.

Not her garrulous pretentiousness, not the lush commonplaceness of her images counts most heavily against Miss Stead. These merely make her tiresome. But her book has another more serious defect … It is without virtue, seriousness, morality, if you like. These talkers are lost souls, with no anchor, no port to put into, no course by which to steer. They pay allegiance to no idea, no person, no tradition. Nor is there, as in the case of Proust or Aldous Huxley, a seeming awareness of their futility in a world that is also lost. They are little over-dressed marionettes whirling around in a meaningless sea of words.[37]

Hazel Rowley recounts that Blake came across a copy of this review in his office in Antwerp where they were living after leaving New York at the end of May 1936. Van Doren's account of Stead's characters as lost souls in a lost world was not without point, but the charge that her novel was without seriousness or morality kept Stead awake with anxiety about her next novel, the almost-completed *House of All Nations*.[38]

Against such disturbing criticism, Stead had probably seen the more favourable reviews that appeared before the couple had left New York. The *Times* and *Saturday Review* critics were bemused but still impressed. Harold Strauss, in the *Times*, felt "forced to praise in Miss Stead's work everything that we would ridicule as stilted, overambitious and pretentious in a less gifted writer": "She is in love with words; but unlike so many of her fellow-suitors, she has wooed and won. Her ardour has made of her a master phrase-maker. She now dwells by choice in a luxuriant, orchidaceous jungle, and to read her is to wander awesomely among the rare, steaming flora of an equatorial fancy … She is no novelist, but that does not seem to matter".[39] Stead's fancy and erudition suggested "a Joyce writing in straight English". Less happily, for the *Saturday Review*, "everything ends up nowhere" and "the characters blow out like candles". And yet even here, and typically, the reviewer, almost against his or her own better judgement, cannot but praise: "for a modernized picture of Paris-as-you-would-have-it; for sophistication, if polysyllabic incomprehensibilities and unexcited chatter about adultery be sophistication; for weird dreams within dreams; and, so help me, for some trick of style that keeps you merrily on to the end, 'The Beauties and Furies' is to be recommended".[40]

Fadiman's lengthy review appeared in the *New Yorker* in April, praising Stead's "streaming imagination … tireless wit [and] intellectual virtuosity". In once again making the comparison with Joyce, he insisted on Stead's originality. Her "mercurial mind careers in a universe of its own, glittering with red planets and cold-blue infernos. To follow it you will have to hold on tight and trust to luck. It is not everyone's excursion, but on the other hand no other agency on earth is offering a trip anything like it".[41] *Time* magazine was also enthusiastic, and precisely for the demands Stead made on her readers: "Readers who know where they are with the *Saturday Evening Post* will get little or nothing out of *The Beauties and Furies*. Its trolls and hobgoblins may show less timid readers a thing or two not visible except by moonlight".[42]

---

37 Dorothy Van Doren, "Dissenting Opinion", *Nation*, 10 June 1936, 751-52.
38 Rowley, *Christina Stead*, 219.
39 Harold Strauss, "Phantoms of Wit", *New York Times*, 3 May 1936. As well as being a regular reviewer, Strauss was an editor at publisher Covici-Friede and from 1938 an editor-in-chief at Knopf.
40 S.N., "The New Books: Fiction", *Saturday Review of Literature*, 9 May 1936, 18.
41 "Books", *New Yorker*, 25 April 1936, 70.
42 Clifton Fadiman, "Books", *New Yorker*, 25 April 1936, 69-70; *Time*, 27 April 1936, 86.

8 "Australian moderns": Christina Stead and Patrick White in New York

In sum, the critical reception of Stead's first three novels was not so much "lukewarm" as decidedly hot and cold, divided between extremes of praise and bafflement even in the one review, sometimes strongly positive even when the reviewer struggled with the fact that the book in question broke all the normal rules.[43] In less than two years, in fact, Stead had had a substantial series of favourable, considered notices in the main New York book papers and magazines, and although still early in her career, she was visible in the New York book world in a way comparable only with Richardson among earlier Australian writers.

Alongside Fadiman's, perhaps the most significant review of *The Beauties and Furies* was Stanley Burnshaw's in the communist *New Masses*.[44] Although obviously more limited in its reach than the *New Yorker*, in the Popular Front era of the 1930s *New Masses* was read widely beyond its immediate left-wing circle. Like all reviewers, Burnshaw noted the extraordinary language of the novel, but drew this into the problems for interpretation it poses, especially for a politically oriented reading. Stead, he writes in a memorable phrase, is "a fugitive from ready interpretation": "Miss Stead constructs around each character an elaborate wall of words with patterns so arresting that the reader may forget to consider the configurations at once: the picture of a business world in action, the 'sombre, nuggety little passion' of the runaway *petite bourgeoise* ... [It is] a study of types fringing the revolutionary movement – a ruthless hounding of these types till they are cornered and expose themselves". Burnshaw is aware the novel *needs* interpretation, for all readers but in a special sense for its *New Masses* readership, and he offers it without compromising the work's complexities. When Stead received the review, she replied that she found it "the most satisfactory of all because it has the best view of the anatomy" – her anatomy of the "types fringing the revolutionary movement".[45] It is in this same letter that Stead writes, from Antwerp, that "The whole spirit of New York is opposed to the creative mind".

For Stead herself, of course, the opposite would prove true. New York would become her publishing home, and the place where she produced or located her major, mid-career works. Stead and Blake were well connected in New York's overlapping literary, radical political and Jewish circles and became more so when they returned to live in the city in mid-1937. In 1935, they had met Burnshaw and two other radical Jewish figures who would become lifelong friends, Harry Bloom and the celebrated proletarian novelist Mike Gold.[46] Despite Stead's own reservations about the party line on literature, radical New York was a congenial environment, even as she kept her own writing a largely private affair.

Stead also wrote occasional reviews for the *New Masses* in the thirties, and although she disliked reviewing, the *New Masses* articles are critical sites for understanding her views on the possibilities and responsibilities for politically engaged novelists.[47] She defended André Malraux for his "extremely austere sense of duty towards his fellow man and towards his art", not a casual statement in the context of calls for a revolutionary proletarian literature. At the Third American Writers' Congress, organised in June 1939 by the League of American Writers, she shared the platform with Louis Aragon, Richard Wright, Sylvia Townsend Warner and Dashiell Hammett. Stead spoke on "the many-charactered novel", like her own

---

43   During, *Exit Capitalism*, 77.
44   J.G. Conant [Stanley Burnshaw], "The Revolutionary Fringe", *New Masses*, 4 August 1936, 25-26.
45   Stead to Burnshaw, 2 October 1938, in Christina Stead, *A Web of Friendship: Selected Letters (1928-1973)*, ed. R.G. Geering (Sydney: Angus & Robertson, 1992), 65.
46   Rowley, *Christina Stead*, 192-95.
47   Rowley, *Christina Stead*, 287; Ackland, "Christina Stead", 131-32.

House of All Nations, "as essential to [the] metropolis as the many-windowed wall".[48] Further, her name was kept circulating in the New York book world: Fadiman repeated his praise of *The Salzburg Tales* in his 1941 collection *Reading I've Liked*; Stead was included in an anthology of "marvellous" stories published in New York in 1944; from 1943 to 1946 she taught writing workshops at New York University; and in 1945, Stead and Blake together edited *Modern Women in Love* for Burnshaw's Dryden Press, a remarkable collection of international stories covering "the enigmas, perversities and 'byways' of desire", including an excerpt from Richardson's *Maurice Guest*.[49] The anthology was successful enough to be reissued in 1947 by the Doubleday subsidiary, the Garden City Publishing Co.

An Absolutely Unique Experience in Modern Literature

Appleton-Century did not merely distribute Stead's novels or reprint from Peter Davies' sheets. They reset and copyrighted each book, and published them in a uniform format with jackets featuring modernist designs in striking black, silver and red, with a matching label on the cloth cover. These investments suggest a longer-term commitment to Stead as an Appleton-Century author. But Stead and Blake came to believe the firm was run by "financial rather than literary men" and to suspect its in-house politics, which Stead characterised as "liberal-conservative" and "more or less strictly Gentile".[50] Relations would not have been improved when the publishers, according to Rowley, suggested to Stead she should "aim more for the female market and include some sex in her next novel".[51] A new opportunity arose through Clifton Fadiman's and Max Schuster's ongoing enthusiasm for *The Salzburg Tales*.

In Stead's own words, "Appleton-Century ... had no sales ideas, very jogtrot; so Kip Fadiman took me up and put me in S & S".[52] As Rowley recounts the episode, Schuster "offered Stead a contract for her next three books. She felt honoured and excited. Rumour had it that Simon & Schuster never put out a book which sold less than 10,000 copies".[53] Appleton-Century in response offered Stead "unusually high rates to renew her contract with them. Simon & Schuster then matched the Appleton offer: $500. Stead did not hesitate".[54] As will be evident from examples cited in earlier chapters, $500 was a good advance but not unusually high, good for a "difficult" writer if not for a popular or established author. While they mostly "avoided modernism", Simon & Schuster certainly was one of the most dynamic

---

48 Christina Stead, "Uses of the Many-Charactered Novel", in *Christina Stead: Selected Fiction and Nonfiction*, ed. R.G. Geering and Anita Kristina Segerberg (St Lucia: University of Queensland Press, 1994), 196-99; Rowley, *Christina Stead*, 195-98, 254-55, 308.
49 Christina Stead and William Blake, eds, *Modern Women in Love: Sixty Twentieth-Century Masterpieces of Fiction* (1945), published with an introduction by influential critic Louis Untermeyer (quoted phrase from Untermeyer's introduction). See Giles, *Antipodean America*, 361. On Stead's writing workshops, see Alison Burns and R.A. Goodrich, "Christina Stead, Georges Polti, and Analytical Novel Writing", *Antipodes* 29, no. 2 (December 2015): 415-28.
50 Rowley, *Christina Stead*, 183.
51 Rowley, *Christina Stead*, 203.
52 Stead to Cyrilly Abels, 27 July 1965, letters of Christina Stead to Cyrilly Abels and Joan Daves, 1964-82, National Library of Australia, MSS Acc 10.038.
53 Rowley, *Christina Stead*, 205.
54 Rowley suggests the $500 was an advance for the next three books (211). But if so it would almost certainly have been a partial advance: $500 per book would be more in the average range.

of the new publishing firms launched in the mid to late twenties alongside Viking, Norton and Random House, and it is not hard to imagine Stead fascinated and impressed by Max Schuster himself.[55] Ironically perhaps, the firm's dynamism was due to its market sense, the partners' "extraordinary skill … at aligning the book industry with consumer culture".[56] They were, after all, the publishers of Dale Carnegie's *How to Win Friends and Influence People* in 1936, still being advertised alongside Stead's *House of All Nations* at the end of 1938.[57] They had by far the biggest advertising budget among trade publishers, five to ten times that of their competitors.[58] But Schuster also had a cultural mission as a publisher, to broaden access to good literature by providing "better and better books for more and more people, at lower and lower prices". These commercial and cultural goals came together in the firm's famous "From the Inner Sanctum" column, an "unpredictable, amusing, and delightfully well written" column of book news composed by Schuster and published regularly in the *Times* and the *Saturday Review*. Although their early fiction was not especially profitable, Simon & Schuster had always included literary titles on its lists and was expanding its literary publishing at this time.[59]

Stead's account of the firm is as good as any, and suggests the energy she could generate for herself from that of New York City: "The boys I am now with are the wows of the publishing game, young, brilliant, millionaires of their own making, organised speedsters; and every member of the firm is himself a writer, or publishes books on something, if it's only photography. Most publishers are businessmen with an itch to write but these boys are 'de woiks'".[60] Stead understood their orientation to the marketplace, but like other modernist writers also understood about getting one's name about: "It is no good throwing up my hands in despair because they are simply moneymakers: they are also very anxious to help you make money and get your name about in other fields (it all helps their game) and so, one way or another, short stories or articles and so forth, they will help us out".[61] It was not all plain sailing. Fadiman, now a Simon & Schuster editor, had visited Stead in London in October 1936 and urged major revisions to the manuscript of *House of All Nations*. His editorial notes were detailed and encouraging but he also wanted cuts: "You overwhelm the reader … Condense".[62] Stead agreed to some reduction, but resented Fadiman's suggestions. Later, in December 1937, he disappointed Stead again with criticisms of some unfinished manuscripts: "His criticisms, 'confused', 'too intellectual', 'too romantic', 'faded like Ibsen', 'unnatural', 'nineteenth century', 'too elliptical, too oblique', 'true but uninteresting', (all under the guise of compliment, strange as it seems) made me decide to go in for selling hats".[63]

---

55 Catherine Turner, *Marketing Modernism*, 33.
56 Rubin, *The Making of Middlebrow Culture*, 245. See also John Tebbel, *A History of Book Publishing in the United States, Vol. III: The Golden Age Between Two Wars, 1920–1940* (New York: Bowker, 1978), 554-55; Jane I. Thesing, "Simon and Schuster", in *American Literary Publishing Houses, 1900–1980*, ed. Dzwonkoski, 340-44.
57 Simon & Schuster advertisement, *New York Times*, 11 December 1938.
58 Rubin, *The Making of Middlebrow Culture*, 246. Following sentence: Rubin quoting Schuster, 247; further details, 252-53.
59 Thesing, "Simon and Schuster", 343.
60 Stead to Gilbert Stead, 7 November 1937, quoted in Stead, *A Web of Friendship*, 73.
61 Quoted in Rowley, *Christina Stead*, 243.
62 Rowley, *Christina Stead*, 233.
63 Stead to Stanley and Madeleine Burnshaw, 17 December 1937, Papers of Christina Stead, National Library of Australia, NLA MS 4967; Rowley, *Christina Stead*, 242.

If we assume that Stead's summary is accurate, the criticisms suggest Fadiman was looking for something modern but not "too modernist", and this might support During's suggestion that he successfully pressured Stead to move away from modernism towards the middlebrow.[64] During sees *House of All Nations* as making less demands on its readers than her earlier works, turning towards "a quasi-Balzacian social realism", although this hardly captures the sheer talkativeness of Stead's narrative, its unplottedness, or the oddly "depthless" characters During himself notes. And while Stead's next novel, *The Man Who Loved Children*, turns to the family and to more realistic, if extreme, characterisation, there seems to be much more motivating that shift intellectually and autobiographically than can be explained by pressure from a publisher or editor. Again, as During himself notes, Stead's retreat from formal experimentation was shared with a great deal of serious fiction from the late 1930s on.[65] Simon & Schuster certainly tried to market *The Man Who Loved Children* as a middlebrow novel, but few reviewers responded accordingly.

House of All Nations was the fourth of Stead's books to appear in the United States, but the first with New York as its place of origin.[66] Set in Paris "in the uneasy hiatus between the Wall Street Crash and the rise of Nazi Germany", this large-scale, "many-charactered" novel dramatises the logic and fraudulence of high-level banking through an extraordinary range of personalities, shifting scenes, and self-justifying or self-deceiving talk.[67] Despite Stead's later dissatisfaction, Simon & Schuster promoted the novel generously. When the American edition appeared on 8 June 1938, it was the sole topic of that week's Inner Sanctum column, which introduced it as "the first detailed fictional study, since the days of Balzac, of money and what it does to human beings".[68] The column gave a lively sense of the novel's world, populated by "millionaires of all nations, playboys, pool operators, middle-class blackmailers and down-at-heel cheats":

> *House of All Nations* is complex and exhaustive, full of satirical scenes, some delicately ironic, some grotesque. Its humor is Hogarthian. To the alert reader, willing to follow the winding path of the story and able to pursue the mental flights of its chief characters, it offers an absolutely unique experience in modern literature.

They got Stead's portrait onto the front cover of the *Saturday Review* and inside the *New York Times*, and they advertised the novel serially in solo advertisements, a Simon & Schuster innovation, rather than the catalogue-style grouping of titles common from other publishers. Each advertisement featured a quotation from the book on the theme of money – "Of course there's a different law for the rich and the poor; otherwise, who would go into business?" Stead's novel sometimes appeared alongside Blake's first novel, *The World is Mine*, which outsold Stead's. Still, *House of All Nations* sold well, appearing as a bestseller in San Francisco's bookstores, for example, in late July.[69]

Despite Simon & Schuster's reputation for market savvy, they underestimated the novel's saleability, although they had the wit to turn their miscalculation into a selling

---

64 During, *Exit Capitalism*, 74.
65 During, *Exit Capitalism*, 70.
66 Reversing the common pattern, the English edition was printed from sheets sent on to Peter Davies.
67 Giles, *Antipodean America*, 348.
68 The column appeared in the *New York Times* on 8 June and the *Saturday Review* on 11 June 1938.
69 For example, *New York Times*, 18 and 25 July 1938.

point. As early as 20 June they announced in the *Times* that the book had sold 1693 copies in its first week and was now out of stock:

> Candidly, this immediate demand has caught us flat-footed. An immediate print order was rushed through Wednesday, to be increased the following day. It is impossible to print, bind and deliver books before next Friday at the earliest. If you hurry to your bookstore, though, you may be able to get a copy of the 1st edition.[70]

Thus the advertisements that continued to appear across July and August were for the second printing rather than the first. Nonetheless, Stead was bitterly disappointed by what she saw as the publisher's lack of investment in the book. She wrote to the Burnshaws in July 1938: "I don't believe they're going to do much on my book, but they will probably struggle into a third edition by Christmas; what more can you ask, when they really regard me as a dud, dragged in by Kip [Fadiman]? Now they want 'another Salzburg Tales,' they suddenly realise I'm alive."[71] And to Florence James in December:

> The publishers … thought it was just another "lady's" maundering novel and only printed 3000. The superb reception it had here took them by surprise and their first action was to write to me asking me to reduce my royalty because they were losing money, and making a vague threat – otherwise they wouldn't reprint … They refuse to reprint more than 6000 and now have dropped it. I thought of breaking contract – but who is better?[72]

House of All Nations was in fact the most widely and overall the most favourably reviewed of Stead's novels to date. Even so, the critics were again divided even in their own minds, and this time there were negative reviews in important places such as the *Nation*, where poet and critic Louise Bogan concluded extraordinarily that the novel belonged on the "padded shelves" of the circulating libraries alongside Ouida and gothic romance.[73]

More seriously, in a substantial review in the *New Republic*, John Chamberlain proclaimed the book "a virtuoso performance, a prodigious *tour de force*, an epic exercise of sheer writing will" and yet concluded that it was "one of the dullest novels which it has ever been my misfortune to read": "We see the iridescent scum on the pond; we do not see the fish gasping for oxygen in the blackness below … Miss Stead has merely given the froth on the surface".[74] There were similar estimates by Ralph Thompson in his "Books of the Times" column and again in the *Yale Review*: "I have more respect for 'House of All Nations' than enthusiasm. The talent and versatility behind the book are obvious, likewise the imagination, nervous energy and specialized knowledge. But something is lacking, an essential quality. I don't know how to define it exactly, but it bears some relation to the idea of literary form".[75]

While Bogan's critique may simply have been maddening, these respectful reviews were potentially more subtly demoralising. But again there were enough favourable

---

70 *New York Times*, 20 June 1938, 13.
71 Stead to Stanley and Madeleine Burnshaw, 13 July 1938, Stead Papers, NLA MS 4967.
72 Stead to Florence James, 12 December 1938. Rowley, *Christina Stead*, 246–47.
73 Louse Bogan, "Padded Shelves", *Nation*, 18 June 1938, 703-4.
74 John Chamberlain, "International Bucket Shop", *New Republic*, 6 July 1938, 255–56.
75 Ralph Thompson, "Books of the Times", *New York Times*, 9 June 1938, and *Yale Review* 29 (Autumn 1938): viii. He argued that the novel "could and should have made its point in half the space", but left open whether this was "Miss Stead's fault, or her publishers".

comments in influential places to counteract the negative: in *Time* magazine, and from Fadiman again in the *New Yorker*, from Harold Strauss in the *New York Times*, Elliot Paul in the *Saturday Review*, and a young Alfred Kazin in the *Herald Tribune*.[76] *Time* introduced Stead as "a critics' favorite [and] a popular failure", but reckoned the new novel "one of the most savage satires on 'the principle of money' since Balzac". Strauss resumed the struggle he had begun with *The Beauties and Furies*, citing his own earlier review. The new novel was "a provoking jumble of brilliance and blatherskite, the like of which has seldom appeared between boards":

> While it brings within the horizons of literature material never before mastered by a novelist, while it seethes and froths with a pyrotechnic imagination and spews forth characters and situations by the gross, it is perverse in technique, contemptuous of intelligibility, and loaded down with a vast amount of documentary material and endless pedantic reproduction of the exact speech of inarticulate boors ...
>
> And yet, difficult and formless as the novel is, one cannot simply dismiss it as inchoate. For, when one has worked through it, one is rewarded, I know not how, by a marvellous glimpse of the methods and jungle morality of finance capitalism. We seem somehow to have been taken for a moment to a high eminence from which we can perceive the whole of humanity with its conflicts and greeds and money lusts seething below us.

Even in its criticism, as in the first paragraph quoted, the review is fully alert to Stead's exceptional qualities. For Kazin, astutely, "What you feel throughout is that Miss Stead is much bigger than her novel, that she will need a stream of novels to shelter her fully, for no one novel can hold her at this point".

Although Fadiman reviewed the novel only briefly in the *New Yorker*, perhaps because of his links to its publisher, he pronounced it "full of rich comedy, crowded with Balzacian characters, and, despite certain flaws and a tendency to congested detail ... a work of extraordinary talent. Dogmatically recommended to those who do not require their summer novel reading to be lighter-than-air".[77] But again it was in the *New Masses* that the novel received the political reading it warranted. The key point was that Stead, in the spirit of *The Communist Manifesto*, understood that bankers were in a certain way Marxists, their banks "founded on the Marxist principle of the decay of capitalism". The reviewer, Edwin Berry Burgum, stressed the book's objectivity, thus claiming it for the new radical literature in terms that Stead would have appreciated as "significant evidence of the trend in contemporary fiction away from spiritual autobiography and toward an objective account of the social forces that work through the conflict of human wills".[78] Such reviews – even those where reviewers struggled before admitting Stead's overwhelming strength – tied her writing more and more closely into America's or New York's book culture.

---

76 Alfred Kazin, *New York Herald Tribune*, 12 June 1938.
77 Clifton Fadiman, "Briefly Noted", *New Yorker*, 11 June 1938, 59. Simon & Schuster's publicity quotes Fadiman as saying: "The most important novel about money and what it does to human beings that has been written since Balzac". *New York Times*, 11 December 1938.
78 Edwin Berry Burgum, "The House that Jack Built", *New Masses*, 21 June 1938, 23-24.

8 "Australian moderns": Christina Stead and Patrick White in New York

Stead's "First American Novel"

Stead's next novel, *The Man Who Loved Children*, was ready for the publisher by mid-1940. While it has subsequently become her most celebrated novel, in the American book market at the time it was less prominent than *House of All Nations* and *The Salzburg Tales*, which remained key points of reference for reviewers. *The Man Who Loved Children* entailed a shift of focus for Stead, to her own "atrociously wretched" childhood and her intensely ambivalent relationship with her father.[79] Rowley asserts that it was Simon & Schuster who insisted Stead transfer the setting of the novel from Australia to America to make the book more marketable in the United States.[80] They announced it as "her first novel about American people".[81] But while this explanation is certainly plausible, Rowley provides no supporting evidence and Stead never gave this explanation herself. The more important point is that even if the suggestion was the publisher's, Stead's *made* it her own, not only embarking on extensive research into American locations, folklore and vernacular, but also shifting the time frame two decades forward to the 1930s, and embedding the story of the Pollit family into a rich fabric of American political, social and literary history. Although it was her most autobiographical novel to date (and in that sense her most Australian) it was also her most "American" novel until her New York trilogy in the late forties.

The Americanisation of the novel involved much more than background or dialect. As Rowley points out, the changes meant the novel could focus more on the America Stead knew, and there were useful parallels between New Deal programs and the state socialism of the New South Wales Labor government earlier in the century.[82] Ackland goes much further, arguing persuasively that the transpositions were driven by a very deliberate engagement with US history and politics as represented in the novel's "political geography", that is, its mapping of political trajectories through the characters' family histories, and above all its extended critique of the progressive inheritance present in Roosevelt's New Deal: "In this microcosm of 1930s American society, wealth and the will-to-power, the twin drivers of modern capitalism, remain all-powerful."[83] The novel offers a covert Marxist critique of Browderism, named after Communist Party leader Earl Browder, who argued for accommodation to the reformist programs of the New Deal. It is in this deeper, political sense that *The Man Who Loved Children* was Stead's "first American novel".[84]

The book appeared on 11 October 1940 "with very little fanfare", in Rowley's words.[85] But this comment appears to reflect Stead's own disappointment with its impact as much as the reality of Simon & Schuster's marketing. A generous advertisement featuring quotations from the *New Yorker*, the *Herald Tribune* and the *New York Times* appeared in

---

79 Stead to Thistle Harris, 7 July 1939, Stead, *A Web of Friendship*, 90.
80 Rowley, *Christina Stead*, 261. We could find no evidence for this in the Simon & Schuster archives at Columbia University
81 In the brief "About the Author" note printed at the beginning of the book.
82 Rowley, *Christina Stead*, 261.
83 Michael Ackland, "'Socialists of a New Socialism'?: Christina Stead's Critique of 1930s America in *The Man Who Loved Children*", *ELH* 78 (2011): 390 and 401. See also Ackland's "Christina Stead", 127-42 and Yelin, *From the Margins of Empire*, 26-31.
84 Charles Poore, "Books of the Times", *New York Times*, 18 October 1940.
85 Rowley, *Christina Stead*, 270. The English edition appeared the following year, from Peter Davies.

the latter on 21 October (Fig. 8.2). The publishers marketed the book, perhaps nervously, as a kind of middlebrow novel about ordinary families:

> *You will recognize your own family in this novel*
> This novel is the story of an American family. It is an astonishingly revealing study of the relationships we all have with our nearest kin. It is full of the fascinating detail, the daily drama, the laughter, the happiness and the tragedy that human beings create in their seemingly casual associations with each other.

Three further advertisements followed with similar catchphrases: "A novel that every father and mother of growing children should read"; and, slightly more challenging, "Do you believe unhappy marriage is better for children than divorce?"[86]

The Man Who Loved Children would never sit easily within the genre of the middle-class social novel. Nonetheless, only a small number of Simon & Schuster's books received as much publicity as Stead's demanding novel. For the three months October to December 1940, the only title that did receive more was the wholly market-driven *Treasury of the World's Great Letters*. Possibly the later advertisements reflect the fact that early sales had been disappointing. Rowley notes that *The Man* sold slowly at $2.75, but when the price was reduced to $1.75 around 5000 copies sold quite quickly.[87] Stead wrote later that the "real reason" Simon & Schuster, in her words, "torpedoed *TMWLC*" was her refusal to agree to the reduction of her royalties on *House of All Nations* from the contracted 15 per cent to 8 per cent. There was further fallout: "Clifton Fadiman was behind the move also. It finished him with me".[88]

Whatever the truth, Stead believed the firm had little interest in promoting her novel, and it does seem clear they did not see the potential for marketing it as a "modern classic", despite the line of reviews comparing Stead to Joyce or Woolf: "S & S are disgusted with the book and are doing nothing for it. I should have called it *How to Have Children and Generate People ... I am quitting them*".[89] It was a good joke about the firm's big money-maker and how they had advertised her own novel, but she was serious about breaking her contract.

Stead may well have been disappointed by the reception of her "best book to date",[90] not because it was ignored or savaged, with one important exception, but because the favourable judgements were almost always qualified and in all too familiar terms. The novel was powerful, astounding, "an unforgettable experience" – but flawed, over-long, lacking discipline, the whole "not as great as its parts": "Every page of it and every person in it is an experience, but they do not add up to a mounting triumph".[91] And again: "It is a good deal easier to be certain about Christina Stead than about the 527 pages of novel actually before us".[92] Rather strangely, the dust jacket copy advertised the fact that the novel had been cut from a million words to its final count, as good as inviting reviewers to comment on its length.

---

86 The first phrase appeared on 12 and 24 November 1940, the second on 17 November. The Inner Sanctum column was not being published at this time, only its crime fiction cousin, *The Gory Gazette*.
87 Stead quoted in Rowley, *Christina Stead*, 270.
88 Stead to Abels, 19 May 1965 and 27 March 1972, NLA MSAcc 10.038; Stead to Burnshaw, 18 May 1965, Stead, *A Web of Friendship*, 239.
89 Stead to Isidor Schneider, 7 November 1940, quoted in Rowley, *Christina Stead*, 270.
90 Stead to Thistle Harris, 6 April 1942, quoted in Rowley, *Christina Stead*, 270.
91 Quoted phrases from *New York Herald Tribune*, 13 October 1940, and N[athan]. L. Rothman, "Enter 'Pollitry'", *Saturday Review of Literature*, 16 November 1940, 12.
92 Rothman, "Enter 'Pollitry'".

8 "Australian moderns": Christina Stead and Patrick White in New York

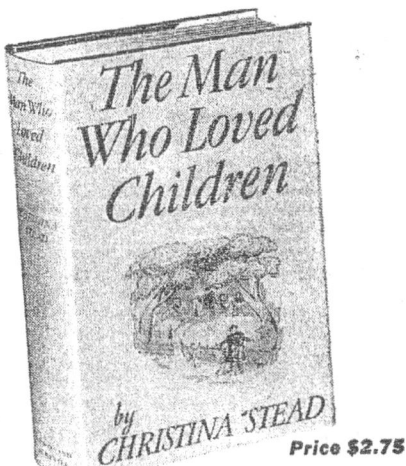

Figure 8.2 Advertisement for *The Man Who Loved Children* (New York: Simon & Schuster, 1940), *New York Times*, 21 October 1940.

And yet it is only partly true that reviewers were "unable to assimilate the novel to the standards of the literary culture they inhabit[ed]".[93] Reviewed in the *New York Times* on the same day as *For Whom the Bell Tolls*, the reviewer noted that as with Stead's earlier novels *The Man Who Loved Children*'s weaknesses were "somehow inseparable from the best in the book, which is one of the criteria of a good novel".[94] There were phrases throughout the reviews that caught something of Stead's distinctive qualities. In "Books of the Times", Charles Poore invoked Stead's "allergy to sentiment": "When Miss Stead really begins to go to work on the fissures of human character there are few living novelists who can match her". In *Nation*, Louis Salomon, who had reviewed Patrick White's *Happy Valley* the previous month, anticipated Randall Jarrell's introduction to the 1965 reissue:

> Miss Stead's portrayal of Sam Pollitt is as razor-edged and pitiless as a dissecting knife: she exposes him, front view, side view, top, bottom, and cross-section, rips him apart to display the squashy, fungoid soul that underlies his bumptious exuberance …
>
> Most terrible of all is the growing realization of Louisa … that her father, with a perverted possessiveness, is winding himself about her and strangling her like a slimy snake, and that only by murdering both her parents can she hope to win a normal life for herself and the other children.[95]

For N.L. Rothman in the *Saturday Review*, "you are in direct contact with a mind pulsing like a muscle, powerful, effortless, fierce, fecund, original, as rare as any mind at work today". He thought "Pollitry" deserved to become a word in its own right, as "Babbitry" had "in a simpler realm".[96]

The outstanding exception was Mary McCarthy in the *New Republic*. McCarthy was not yet a famous novelist but she already had a reputation as a critic. More to the point, she was closely associated with *Partisan Review* and its attack on the Soviet communism supported by Stead and Blake. It is not clear whether McCarthy knew Stead's politics, but as Louise Yelin suggests her "vehemence prefigures her rather more famous attack … on Lillian Hellman".[97] McCarthy also seems to be reacting against the high claims made for Stead by critics such as Fadiman and Rebecca West, which were quoted yet again on the book's jacket.[98] She found *The Man Who Loved Children* a "peculiar, breathless, overwritten, incoherent novel … like an hysterical tirade":

> That this has an effect on the reader is undeniable; whether this is a literary effect is another question …
>
> With its callousness, its imperfect reception (in the radio sense) of the real world, its blunt, bludgeoning manner, its outsize measurements and its enormous energy potential, this novel is a sort of mechanical monstrosity, like Electro at the World's fair.

---

93 Louise Yelin, "Fifty Years of Reading: A Reception Study of *The Man Who Loved Children*", *Contemporary Literature* 31, no. 4 (Winter 1990): 473.
94 M.H., "Christina Stead's Fantastic Gallery", *New York Times*, 20 October 1940.
95 Louis B. Salomon, "Scalpel, Please", *Nation*, 26 October 1940, 399.
96 Rothman, "Enter 'Pollitry'".
97 Louise Yelin, "Fifty Years of Reading", 474.
98 The oft-repeated Rebecca West quotation described Stead as "one of the few people really original we have produced since the war".

8 "Australian moderns": Christina Stead and Patrick White in New York

But it is the sort of monstrosity that is highly esteemed today when our culture (or its leaders) is feeling itself soft and puny.[99]

Stead might have agreed with the final sentiment. More devastating, perhaps, was McCarthy's attack on the novel's "feeble" grasp of American reality: Sam Pollitt's tastes and references were twenty to thirty years out of date, she asserted, and much of the slang British rather than American. There was a "dislocation in time" and a "dislocation in geography". Similar criticisms had been made by earlier reviewers, including Fadiman, who remarked that "the key throughout is just detectably false".[100] While more recent scholars have learnt to value such dislocation, in Paul Giles' terms as "engendering a dialectical style whose strength involves the way it comes at recognizable worlds from unfamiliar angles", for American reviewers at the time, as Yelin points out, there was a pervasive sense of Stead as "not-American" but no easy resolution either in reading her as a British or Australian writer.[101] The comparisons offered were largely with European authors, Balzac, Strindberg, Joyce, Emily Bronte and Woolf, although the *New York Times* reviewer went for Melville's *Moby-Dick*, one of the novel's own many references to American literature.[102] In the novel, Stead also alludes to the still bestselling *Gone with the Wind* – the "saga of upland Georgia gentility" being read as distraction by Henny Pollitt – thereby inscribing herself, by contrast, "in the ranks of serious writers and novelistic realists".[103]

As Rowley suggests, Fadiman's review, while announcing Stead's genius in the strongest terms, was also disappointing. He described the novel memorably as "'Little Women' rewritten by a demon", but he was "less impressed with *The Man Who Loved Children* than with *House of All Nations* – and he had been less impressed with *that* novel than with *The Salzburg Tales*".[104] Nonetheless, his memorably phrased opening and closing paragraphs would surely have made an impact in New York's book world:

Eventually, Christina Stead will impose herself upon the literature of the English-speaking countries. I say "impose herself" because her qualities are not apt to win her an immediate, warm acceptance. She may have to fight as long and as hard as did Joyce before gaining the suffrage of the majority ... Her books are long, perhaps too long. They do not develop one out of the other but are massively solitary. Her humor is savage, her learning hard to cope with, her fancies too furious ... Nevertheless, I predict that the sheer originality, weight, and conscientiousness of her talent will sooner or later win her a place among the acknowledged leaders of her generation.[105]

---

99 Mary McCarthy, "Framing Father", *New Republic*, 13 January 1941, 61.
100 In the *Herald Tribune* (13 October 1940) the "essential qualities" of the cities where the action occurs seemed lacking; in the *New York Times* "Books of the Times" column (Charles Poore, 18 October 1940), the novel appears to have "some undivulged roots in, say, Australia"; Rothman in the *Saturday Review* (see above) thought few American readers would recognise the characters but in part because the characters were "timeless and placeless"; Fadiman, "Christina Stead Continues", *New Yorker*, 19 October 1940, 86.
101 Giles, *Antipodean America*, 351; Yelin, "Fifty Years of Reading", 475.
102 Yelin, "Fifty Years of Reading", 475.
103 Yelin, "Fifty Years of Reading", 477.
104 Rowley, *Christina Stead*, 271.
105 Fadiman, "Christina Stead Continues".

As Yelin notes, one way of accommodating or acclaiming Stead's fiction was through the trope of "savage genius".[106] By contrast, the *New Masses*, less bound to the weekly cycles of New York book reviewing, was more attuned to Stead's own understanding of social rather than psychological dynamics. For Isidor Schneider, who would also become a long-term friend, the "solid realistic base" on which Stead's "sustained and fascinating stylization" rests "is an understanding of a social truth, the plasticity of the human 'soul'; and of what mutilated images are pressed out of it in the decomposing molds and under the crooked stampings of a class society".[107] The core of the novel is "the tragedy of the bourgeois family – or rather the family in bourgeois society". Stead would surely have been delighted by Schneider's assessment that the work was "in a sense ... a novelization of Engels' *Origin of the Family*"; its distinction was that it succeeded in this "without prejudice either to the integrity of the ideas or to the embodying art". As such, *The Man Who Loved Children* assumed "immediate stature among social novels". This was a judgement reaffirmed the following year, when Ruth McKenny, another *New Masses* friend, placed Stead alongside Steinbeck, Hemingway, Dreiser and Dos Passos in a list of major *American* writers.[108]

Sexual Documents

Stead's determination to break her three-book deal with Simon & Schuster was no doubt reinforced when in early 1942 Pascal Covici from Viking began to woo her for her next book. Covici had been partner in another of the new, adventurous houses launched in the 1920s, Covici-Friede.[109] When that firm collapsed a decade later, Covici went to Viking, taking with him his biggest success, John Steinbeck. As the leading literary publisher in New York, Viking would have been a natural home for Stead's unconventional fiction as it was for Patrick White's, but Covici was no Ben Huebsch, at least not for Stead. Still, the early signs were very positive. Covici-Friede had been interested in Stead since *The Salzburg Tales*, and still in June 1942 Donald Friede was urging Bennet Cerf at Random House to include the book in the Modern Library.[110] Stead met Covici in May 1942 and was impressed, at least by his publishing credentials: "although not personally attractive he is a publisher, he has heard of the existence of letters, and he has read most books: which is a considerable change, thank you, from our late friends."[111] Stead and Blake could

---

106 Yelin, "Fifty Years of Reading", 479.
107 Isidor Schneider, "In the Bosom of the Bourgeois Family", *New Masses*, 12 November 1940, 19-20.
108 Quoted in an advertisement for *The Cross and the Arrow*, *New York Times*, 1 November 1941. McKenny is the model for Emily Wilkes in Stead's *I'm Dying Laughing*. See Rowley, *Christina Stead*, 361-64; Williams, *Christina Stead*, 152-57.
109 Friede left the firm before its collapse in 1938 and went to Hollywood to head the story department for Myron Selznick, a major Hollywood agent: John Tebbel, *Between Covers: The Rise and Transformation of Book Publishing in America* (New York: Oxford University Press, 1987), 252. Friede and Selznick were involved in discussions with Bill Blake over a film based on *For Love Alone*. See letters between Stead and Blake 18-27 June 1942 in *Dearest Munx: The Letters of Christina Stead and William J. Blake*, ed. Margaret Harris (Carlton, Vic.: Miegunyah, 2005), 239-82. All subsequent correspondence from this volume unless otherwise indicated.
110 Blake to Stead, 19 June 1942, 243.
111 Stead to Blake, 15 May 1942, 96. It is not clear from the letters whether this was their first meeting. A letter from 12 May (92) indicates that they were already corresponding about Viking taking the new novel for its autumn list.

contrast Viking to Simon & Schuster as Simon & Schuster had earlier been compared to Appleton-Century. In Blake's words: "Viking battling for a literary production is different from Simon & Schuster – the people who are in bookshops here and know the trade, tell me that the Viking imprint ranks first among the belles-lettres hounds."[112]

Covici planned to include Stead's new novel in the firm's autumn list. Its title, *For Love Alone*, suggested by Viking editor Marshall Best, was settled at the end of May.[113] Blake was in Hollywood looking for script-writing work and trying to interest agents in film rights for their books, convinced that their agent in New York, Mavis McIntosh, could not get results. Stead had engaged McIntosh in 1939 for contract negotiations with Simon & Schuster over *The Man Who Loved Children*.[114] The McIntosh & Otis agency had Steinbeck on their list, while their film agent, Anne Laurie Williams, was famous for having sold both *The Grapes of Wrath* and *Gone with the Wind* to Hollywood.[115] These were not necessarily the best credentials in the couple's eyes! As Blake wrote to Stead: "If Covici does not at first understand [the new novel] I would not be downcast for remember he thinks Steinbeck is not merely a good writer but of classic stature."[116] Stead was in New York, working intensely to deliver the first part of the new novel to Covici before she too left for Hollywood.[117] She sent off a few chapters in late May, and the whole of parts one and two in mid-June, and was keen to get the $675 due to her as her share of Viking's $750 advance.[118] She wanted to discuss future books with Covici, too, with a further advance in mind, although if Viking showed no interest she thought she might still have a "hedge" in Max Schuster for a book of "American Tales".[119] Covici was most interested in Stead's plan for a novel about "New York and 'the revolutionary' as a type" which he promised to publish one year after *For Love Alone*.[120]

Covici was enthusiastic about what he had read of *For Love Alone*, and thought it the "most commercial" of Stead's books.[121] The problem was he had read only the first twenty-five pages and thought the manuscript as delivered was the whole novel and exactly the right length: "without reading the story he is insistent that it is long enough now and cannot take more".[122] When Stead informed him there would be at least ten more chapters, Covici insisted she try to reduce it and Stead resigned herself to the task:

> I am afraid his assurance that it would be a work of literature was mere come-on ... But love of literature as such even in men supposed to love it (Covici's reputation is based on it) is miserably low ... My heart gives a jump when I remember that Steinbeck is his ideal and I wonder if he is going to tell me to take out all that makes the writing *me*.[123]

---

112 Blake to Stead, 1 June 1942, 158.
113 Stead to Blake, 29 May 1942, 148.
114 Stead to Burnshaw, 27 August 1963, Stead Papers, NLA MS 8645.
115 It appears Stead was especially keen to free herself from Williams for film rights (Stead to Blake, 22 June 1942, 258). http://mcintoshandotis.com/history/.
116 Blake to Stead, 30 May 1942, 155.
117 For Stead's time in Hollywood, see Rowley, *Christina Stead*, 303-6.
118 Stead to Blake, 25 May and 15 June 1942, 125, 222.
119 Stead to Blake, 15 June 1942, 221.
120 Stead to Blake, 26 June 1942, 278-79.
121 Stead to Blake, 19 June 1942, 241.
122 Stead to Blake, 24 June 1942, quoted in Rowley, *Christina Stead*, 298.
123 Stead to Blake, 16 June 1942, 223.

Stead sought assurances that Viking would publish her novel, and began work on "a short end to the book" to please Covici. (Critics often note that the final part of the book seems thinner than the rest, although Stead's unconventional ending, beyond the marriage plot, is also one of the book's most original aspects.) Despite everything, she still thought Covici might be a good publisher for her.[124]

At the end of August, Stead wrote to Burnshaw that she was "quarrelling badly with Viking's [sic]", especially over the American character based on Blake, which they thought "unreal", "not an American":

> They are dithered with the success of that brainless pamphlet of monosyllables – Mr Steinbeck's *Moon is Down* and went so far as to recommend me to imitate the genius. My agent has lost her head also (she "sold" – as they put it – Gone with the Wind and Steinbeck) and literature is not a nightmare that troubles her sleep; instead of trying to put my point of view, she writes me letters telling me how right the publishers are and advising me how to write ... Covici intimated that apparently they wanted to make a best-seller out of my book, two-thirds apparently strike them as suitable for that but not the last third in which, alas, appeared the "cardboard American" (Bill Blake) ... This is the kind of nonsense I have to stand every time a book is a best-seller. May the word perish.[125]

Stead's return to Steinbeck's reputation was much more than professional rivalry. If *Gone with the Wind* was one symptom of America's cultural bankruptcy, Steinbeck's sentimental realism, taken as serious literature, was another – worse, for Stead, because its claims to realism were in a sense in competition with her own. Both had been Book-of-the-Month Club selections.[126]

It is not clear exactly when Viking rejected *For Love Alone* outright – in late 1942 or early 1943 – but by this time Stead and Blake had changed literary agents, dumping McIntosh for Helen Strauss of the renowned William Morris Agency. Strauss not only sold *For Love Alone* to Harcourt, Brace & Co., but arranged a three-book contract for Stead. While not quite the literary publisher that Viking represented, Alfred Harcourt had established the firm in 1919 expressly to publish "books dealing with the new ideas with which the world was seething" – serious books but marketed to a broad readership he believed was interested in those new ideas. Harcourt himself was "neither radical nor cultivated"; rather, he prized his marketing skills, and judged that there was a market for more challenging writers.[127] The firm published Sinclair Lewis, E.M. Forster and Virginia Woolf in the 1920s, and Gertrude Stein and Dos Passos in the 1930s. Stead could feel at home in such a list, even with the firm's strong interest in American writers. She dealt with editor John Woodburn, who not long before had joined the company from Doubleday, Doran, bringing Eudora Welty with him.[128]

---

124 Stead to Blake, 22 June 1942, 259.
125 Stead to Burnshaw, 31 August 1942, Stead, *A Web of Friendship*, 100.
126 Steinbeck with *The Grapes of Wrath*.
127 Turner, *Marketing Modernism*, 112-17.
128 "Eudora Welty *A Curtain of Green*", in George Parker Anderson, *American Modernism, 1914–1945*, Research Guide to American Literature Vol. 6 (New York: Bruccoli, Clark & Laymen, 2010), 233.

8 "Australian moderns": Christina Stead and Patrick White in New York

For Love Alone appeared in October 1944 in a wartime edition produced "in full compliance with government regulations".[129] It was printed on thin paper, but was otherwise a solidly produced hardcover, and Harcourt, Brace announced its appearance with a large advertisement in the *New York Times*, alongside Katherine Anne Porter's *The Leaning Tower* and, ironically perhaps given Stead's antipathy to *Gone with the Wind*, a deep-south historical saga by Henrietta Buckmaster.[130] It reprinted the familiar quotations from West and Fadiman regarding Stead's originality. Rowley suggests that the book's jacket illustration of a bare-breasted girl leaning out of her window on a starry night gave the impression it was a popular romance. But while "suggestive of the drugstore rental shelf" for one reviewer, it would have been extremely unlikely for a romance novel to feature a bare-breasted woman on its cover.[131] Such an image was more likely to be found on a literary novel, and the design was "arty" rather than titillating (see Plate 8). Still, it might have encouraged the *Library Journal*'s verdict: "five hundred morbid pages of lust and abnormality".[132] Whether despite or because of such reactions, the novel sold quite well, around 13,000 Stead later reported.[133]

Most reviewers took the novel seriously as what Diane Trilling called a "sexual document".[134] For Ruth Page in the *Times*: "It would be easy to be flippant about this book and miss its gravity, or be gross and miss its pathos". Her comparison was D.H. Lawrence's "early and best fiction". As others before her, Page registered the force of Stead's writing in a memorable phrase: it "will not endure indifference and one does not come away unscathed". Marjorie Farber in the *New Republic* worked judiciously at defining the book's sexual politics: "if in the end [Stead] seems to evade the mysteries of human relations in having recourse to an Eternal Mystery of Man (something 'we can get along neither with nor without'), even this is an interesting change from tradition". The *New Yorker* was brief, and less impressed. If the book had less of the faults of her earlier works it also lacked "the wit that glittered through 'The Beauties and Furies'". Although unsigned, this reference back suggests Fadiman again as reviewer.[135]

The reviews support Rowley's claim that *For Love Alone* was better understood by women than men. Trilling's review in *Nation* was perhaps the most understanding, but also in some ways the most curious. Trilling read the book in the light of a current

---

129 Rowley's phrase "a cheap wartime edition" (314) might easily give the wrong impression. The quotation comes from the verso of the book's title page. Again Peter Davies' British edition appeared later, in 1945.
130 It was listed among other novels in the publisher's advertisements through to the end of the year.
131 First quotation from review cited in Rowley, *Christina Stead*, 314. Rowley gives the publication date as 6 October but Harcourt's advertisement announcing the novel appeared in the *New York Times* on 22 October, the day after the first review, in the *New Yorker*.
132 Quoted in Rowley, *Christina Stead*, 315.
133 Stead to Abels, 4 October 1966, NLA MS Acc 10.038.
134 Diana Trilling, "Women in Love", *Nation*, 28 October 1944, 535-56. Other quotations in this paragraph from: Ruth Page, "The Search for Love", *New York Times*, 29 October 1944; Marjorie Farber, "Amor, Amor, Amor", *New Republic*, 13 November 1944, 632; "Briefly Noted: Fiction", *New Yorker*, 21 October 1944, 94. There were also strong endorsements from McKenny ("the only true book about love I know"), the *Herald Tribune* (the author "dares to tell what she knows of the human heart") and the *Weekly Book Review* ("subtle, lilting prose", "pitiless clarity of vision"): Williams, *Christina Stead*, 163.
135 Rowley suggests otherwise, but Fadiman had used the earlier novel as the occasion for his highest praise of Stead's genius.

flood of unsatisfactory novels of female love: "Substituting intensity for understanding and confusion for dramatic conflict, they produce instead of good novels, disturbing case histories." What makes Stead's novel stand out is "the baldness with which it states the resolution of its sexual problem": "I know no novel, including the novels of Jane Austen, which reveals as frankly as 'For Love Alone' the frantic need young women have for a husband and the brutal hypocrisy with which society surrounds their efforts to find one". (She adds in passing that Sydney's suburbs "feel like a World's Fair after the fair is over".) Trilling presents all the challenges and rewards of Stead's novel, its "flashes of real wit and downright intelligence", but concludes ambiguously: "It is a misfortune of our culture that a talent like Miss Stead's should be at the service of so much ardent confusion".[136]

Stead would attack this ardent confusion again in *Letty Fox: Her Luck*, which she had begun in early 1941 before *For Love Alone*. Although very different in emotional register, the two novels are linked as sexual documents, if perhaps as "thesis and antithesis" as Angela Carter suggests, *For Love Alone* promising love and self-fulfilment, *Letty Fox* revealing a "society that treats sex and love as commodities" and marriage as inescapably a bad deal.[137] *Letty Fox* picked up something, too, of the novel set in New York's radical circles Stead had proposed to Covici. Letty joins the communist movement when young and continues to call on its theory to explain her life even as she exploits her sexuality to make the best deal she can. Set largely in New York between the wars, Stead was confident enough to tell the story in Letty's own voice:

> I reckoned I knew enough about life to write a real book of a girl's life. Men don't like to think that we are just as they are. But we are much as they are; and therefore I have omitted the more wretched details of that close connection, that profound, wordless struggle that must go on in the relation between the sexes ... I have written everyday facts which, doubtless, have happened in the life of almost every New York middle-class girl who has gone out from high school or college to make a living in the city.[138]

In a brief preface, Stead wrote that "the language and opinions are those of a type of middle-class New York office worker". If *Letty Fox* was Stead's "first *truly* American novel", it was perhaps even more profoundly her first truly New York novel, the first in her New York trilogy.[139]

In autumn 1941, Stead had submitted an early draft of the book to Angus Cameron, a friend, politically radical and soon to be editor-in-chief at Little, Brown & Co.[140] Cameron wanted major revisions and the project lapsed, although soon after he supported Stead's

---

136 A later review in the *Virginia Quarterly Review* (Winter 1945, 131–32) linked Stead to Aldous Huxley and American novelist Jean Stafford as "real novelists". Still, Stead's novel was "profuse and wasteful of character and situation" and seemed to mistake its theme as representative when it was merely individual.
137 Rowley, *Christina Stead*, 278-79. Rowley quotes Angela Carter on the two novels as thesis and antithesis, from "Unhappy Families", *London Review of Books* 4, no. 17 (September 1982): 11-13.
138 Christina Stead, *Letty Fox: Her Luck* (Sydney: Angus & Robertson, 1974), 11-12.
139 Rowley, *Christina Stead*, 323 (emphasis added); the phrase "New York trilogy" is from Jennifer Gribble, *Christina Stead* (Melbourne: Oxford University Press, 1994), 76.
140 Founded in Boston, the firm opened a New York office in the mid-1920s (http://www.littlebrown.com/175.html). Cameron joined in 1938 and was made editor-in-chief in 1943.

8 "Australian moderns": Christina Stead and Patrick White in New York

unsuccessful application for a Guggenheim Fellowship and organised Fadiman among other prominent figures as referees.[141] By the time Stead returned to *Letty Fox*, it was as the second in her three-book contract with Harcourt, Brace. She delivered the completed book in August 1945 and it was published at the beginning of October the following year. Rowley writes that "Harcourt, Brace once again presented the novel like a cheap romance, with a soft cameo drawing of two pretty girls on the jacket", but again this is misleading.[142] Although the jacket was not elaborate or expensively produced – simple type in black and red and a pastel sketch reproduced in red on matt yellow paper – it was "tasteful": the sketch featuring the head of one young woman was neither salacious nor sentimental. The book was 517 pages at $3.50, way out of the market for cheap romances.

Letty Fox was advertised in the *Times* in early December and accompanied with the usual upbeat quotations: "A tingling, fluid, intense chronicle of a girl on her own" (*Washington Post*); "Miss Stead proves once more that she is one of the greatest novelists of our day".[143] It would be Stead's bestselling book in the United States, shifting well over 12,000 copies, perhaps more than 20,000, although again she had to endure bad management from her publishers.[144] The book had sold out of the New York bookstores by early November and a second run of 5000 copies had been delayed, meaning "nearly three weeks without a copy to sell in the whole town". Still, in mid-December she received $2500 in royalties, suggesting sales of well over 7000 in two months. Stead reported in November that the publishers had ordered a third edition.[145]

There were reviewers shocked and scandalised, as Stead anticipated. For the *Sun*, it was "a quagmire of promiscuity and misinformation about New York". For the *Times* (in a generally thoughtful review), all was "distorted, turgid, and overblown ... with sex rampant and passion unbridled"; Letty was not "an ordinary girl" at all, but "a very special type, no more representative of her sex than any of the other poor creatures in the book".[146] The *New Yorker*'s disenchantment with Stead was almost complete:

> A seedy and fairly ingenuous satire on husband-hunting and sexual promiscuity among middle-class radicals and others in New York during the thirties and early forties. In her nearly interminable exploration of this unkempt subject, Miss Stead, who is an Australian and something of a newcomer to America, is unfortunately handicapped by a rather shaky grip on the local idiom and mores, and the subject appears to have sapped her of the originality and the wit with which she enlivened such earlier novels as "The Beauties

---

141 Rowley, *Christina Stead*, 282: "Stead's proposal was to collect legends and contemporary lore from diverse regions in the United States, and to base a cycle of stories upon them".
142 Rowley, *Christina Stead*, 331.
143 Advertisement, *New York Times*, 1 December 1946. The first quotation is labelled *New York Post* but the phrase comes from Martha MacGregor's *Washington Post* review (27 October) – the original sentence ends "a girl on her own in Greenwich Village"; the review may have been reprinted. The second is by Harrison Smith, who also reviewed the novel at length for the *Saturday Review* (see below).
144 Rowley gives "well over 12,000". She notes that Stead later reckoned 21,000 copies sold, but thinks this an exaggeration: *Christina Stead*, 333 and n. 152, 600.
145 Stead to Blake, 21 November, 25 November and 15 December 1946, Harris, *Dearest Munx*, 361, 363, 399.
146 Review from the *Sun* quoted in Williams, *Christina Stead*, 168-69; Mary McGrory, "Letty Gets Her Men", *New York Times*, 6 October 1946.

and Furies" and "House of all Nations." An almost completely disappointing performance by a writer who has shown in the past that her talent is of a very high order.[147]

Strongest support came from Martha Macgregor in the *Washington Post* and Harrison Smith in the *Saturday Review*. Macgregor authored the line used in Harcourt, Brace's publicity quoted above. She "got" Letty; that is, she got the novel's point and perspective. Letty is "noisy, greedy, unscrupulous, likable but not lovable, pretty and always on the make ... Only two sins exist for [her]: feminine timidity and spinsterhood ... The men in Letty's life are a necessary, delectable evil".[148] Smith asserted Letty's representativeness: "they are amongst us by the tens of thousands, the Letty Foxes". His was a full-page review and took the book seriously as a social document: "Why have we had to wait until today for a novel sufficiently comprehensive in outline, background, and knowledge to reveal in the cold light of reason the disintegration of family life in American cities over the last twenty years and the debauchery of young girls that has resulted from this phenomenon". No less important for Stead, he praised as miraculous her ability "to capture so accurately the American scene and the nuances of American speech". Perhaps the only sour note was Smith's opinion that *For Love Alone* was such an inferior novel it did not deserve to sit on the same shelf as *Letty Fox*.

New Masses reviewer Barbara Giles also got Letty and the novel's social arguments, its "chilling drama of greed and frustration".[149] Giles' review is not as simply doctrinaire as Stead's biographers imply, although it does suggest the hardening of categories in the communist literary world postwar. For all its chilling drama, the novel's portrayal of society for Giles was radically incomplete, for it lacked any perspective outside Letty's own; her yardstick for comparison was *The Man Who Loved Children*, "one of the greatest [novels] of the last decade". Giles' orthodoxy emerged in her conclusion that the novel's portrayal of the revolutionary movement was lacking; "without the contrast of one genuine Communist", it distorted the picture "beyond even the broadest limits of caricature".

Both *Letty Fox* and *House of All Nations* – but not *The Man Who Loved Children* – were selected for notice in the *Book-of-the-Month Club* News. This reception provides a good sense of how Stead might have been entertained in mainstream literary culture. Both works were at the limits of the Club's appreciation of novels that did not meet the conventions of well-made realism, but as we have seen, it was not unusual for more challenging works to be brought to members' notice. Dorothy Canfield admitted the challenges and took on the task of sharing with readers what – nevertheless – made the books compelling. *House of All Nations* was "one of those books which cannot be fitted into any standard critical band-box. A reviewer would be quite within his rights in objecting to its length, the confusion of its innumerable episodes, its lack of plot-development, of a hero, or a heroine ... indeed the almost total absence of characters with whom we can sympathize".[150] It lacked, in other words, the very things praised in most Club selections. And yet: "it has a quality of its own and some readers at least will enjoy it as much as I did".

---

147 "Briefly Noted: Fiction", *New Yorker*, 5 October 1946, 123-24.
148 Martha Macgregor, "Greenwich Village Rat Race to the Altar Makes a Fine Novel", *Washington Post*, 27 October 1946; Harrison Smith, "Love is Where You Find It", *Saturday Review of Literature*, 12 October 1946, 40-41. Similarly in the *San Francisco Chronicle*: "It's a worldly, ribald magnificent tale, this story of Letty Fox": Williams, *Christina Stead*, 168.
149 Barbara Giles, "Destination: Nowhere", *New Masses*, 10 December 1946, 23.
150 Dorothy Canfield, "House of All Nations", *Book-of-the-Month Club News*, June 1938, n.p.

8 "Australian moderns": Christina Stead and Patrick White in New York

Within the alien characters "one begins to recognise and identify one after another of the types ... even the Frenchiest"; "Nowhere is it cut-and-dried, nowhere 'just another novel.' Above all, you cannot read it through without emerging with a clearer understanding of the recent period of get-rich-quick hysteria".

For *Letty Fox* we have readers' reports as well as Canfield's brief notice in the Club *News*. Both readers replied in the negative when asked if there were "anything in the book which might incline the judges to consider it for selection" (that is, as the one book of the month); yet both thought it worthy of mention in the *News*.[151] Bernadine Scherman thought this novel about "a New York City girl making a career of men" read like a case history and the characters would "sink back into unreality" once the book was finished. And yet it was "a remarkable feat of the imagination to have conceived this sprawling menagerie of a family and to have been able to follow it in all its details of living for so many years". Even more "amazing" was "that an Australian would choose to do this New York background". While Letty was not especially a New Yorker, this was because she and her whole family were "originals". Gladys Bates began with an exclamation, "What a crew!", but struggled with Stead's language: "The English here, as in other books by this author is handled strangely often giving the impressions [sic] of being in translation". Again this is a quality later critics have learnt to read positively, its intimacy with New York life playing against its sense of "deterritorilization", its critical distance from American dreams.[152]

Canfield's notice in the *News* had once again to negotiate the book's unusual qualities (as literature and as life), which she did by highlighting her own experience as an ordinary American reader:

> For an ordinary person immersed in ordinary, stable American life, especially an elderly person as I am, it is an exploration into the quite unknown to read this story. It is about a chic, pretty, clever, good-for-nothing New York girl, without personal morals or everyday business honesty, quite heartless, so far as I could make out, but not inhuman for all of that. I never encountered such a person in all my life – how could I? – and yet the author skilfully makes her sound very real to me.[153]

Perhaps unaware of Stead's long residence in New York, Canfield also notes how odd it was that an Australian author should choose to write about this "very special kind of New York life and people".

Pale Shadows

The remaining two books in Stead's New York trilogy clearly belong with the earlier American novels although they were not published until 1948 and 1952 respectively. Their relative lack of success signals a hiatus in Stead's career that continued until the 1965 reissue of *The Man Who Loved Children*. By the time *A Little Tea, a Little Chat* appeared in August 1948, Stead was living in Europe. Having failed to find any new prospects of

---

151 Reports dated 26 and 27 March 1946. Book-of-the-Month Club Records, 1939–67, Library of Congress.
152 Giles, *Antipodean America*, 353-55; During, *Exit Capitalism*, 71-72.
153 Dorothy Canfield, "Letty Fox", *Book-of-the-Month Club News*, October 1946, 12-13.

earning an income in the United States and fearing increased Cold War interference in their lives, Blake left New York in November 1946 and Stead followed in December. For the next six years, they moved constantly between different European cities before settling in England in 1953. But Stead's dependence on New York publishing increased, if anything, as their financial and political position and Stead's literary standing came under increasing pressure. Peter Davies had continued to publish her books in London following their American release, but they parted ways in 1947.[154] Stead thought a London agent and a new publisher might serve her better, but neither *A Little Tea, a Little Chat* nor *The People with the Dogs* were published in England until the 1980s.[155]

Stead had begun *A Little Tea, a Little Chat* in New York after *Letty Fox*'s appearance in autumn 1946 and finished the manuscript by the end of 1947. In the words of the Publisher's Note attached to the book, it was an extraordinary "portrait of a modern libertine, Wall Street variety, living on the shady fringe of the financial world"; or as the *New York Times* put it, "a mean, lecherous, depraved member of a choice group of crooks, blackmailers, pimps and prostitutes that frequent certain fashionable cafes in mid-Manhattan".[156] But the reviews on the whole were miserable, even if Harcourt, Brace managed to find two bright quotations for its publicity: "Abounds in intrigue and excitement" (*Boston Herald*); "Swift and Goya could not have done it any better" (*San Francisco Chronicle*).[157] The common refrain was that Stead gave no moral perspective from which to view or escape her "distasteful characters": they come "distastefully alive", but by "ruthlessly eliminating any suggestion of decency or honor in her money-crazed and lecherous characters [she] deprives herself of all possibilities for moral contrasts and dramatic conflicts".[158] For Ernest Jones in the *Nation*, the novel differed from a nightmare "only in lacking the meaning which any respectable nightmare should have". For John Farrelly in the *New Republic*: "There can be no response to a mere welter of corruption which touches nothing more sensitive than a dead nerve or a fat purse". Blake's view was that the novel had been reviewed with fear: "None dared say it was not true: they suggested rather that such truth was too pervasive to be 'artistic'".[159] None of the reviewers' critiques is inaccurate, but neither are they far from describing the novel's unsettling power.

The People with the Dogs fared little better. Despite being an affectionate portrait of New Yorkers, more comic than satiric, it was still propelled by talk rather than plot or structure. The three-book deal with Harcourt, Brace had already been fulfilled, and in May 1949 editor Robert Giroux informed Stead they were rejecting the new book. In Stead's summary: "It is below my standard and will not do my reputation any good".[160] However, her agent, Helen Strauss, thought it better than *A Little Tea, a Little Chat* and remained

---

154 Rowley, *Christina Stead*, 399.
155 She first engaged David Higham of Pearn, Pollinger and Higham, one of the most successful London agencies, but soon decided he was ineffectual. In 1964, as negotiations over the republication of *The Man Who Loved Children* began, she signed with Laurence Pollinger, who had parted ways with Higham in 1958. Harris, *Dearest Munx*, 419-20; http://www.pollingerltd.com/history/.
156 The character was based on Blake's long-time business associate Robert Knittel, "Unpleasant Little Group", *New York Times*, 22 August 1948.
157 Harcourt, Brace advertisement, *New York Times*, 31 October 1948.
158 *Time*, 13 September 1948, 113. Following quotations: Ernest Jones, "Some Recent Novels", *Nation*, 25 September 1948, 353; John Farrelly, *New Republic*, 25 September 1948, 25.
159 Blake to Florence James, 28 October 1948, cited in Rowley, *Christina Stead*, 354.
160 Stead to Blake, 4 May 1949, 448.

8 "Australian moderns": Christina Stead and Patrick White in New York

confident she could place it, although other publishers also declined.[161] Eventually the novel was accepted by Angus Cameron, Stead's old friend at Little, Brown, and contracted in May 1950 with an advance of $1500, half of what she had received for *A Little Tea, a Little Chat* three years earlier. Cameron was cautious about royalties too on discovering that the manuscript was over 250,000 words, for at that "fabulous length" he would have to sell 22,000 copies at $3.50 to break even. Still, he wrote to Strauss about how happy the firm was to have Stead on their list and with an option on her next two books, echoing an earlier remark of Fadiman's: "I can assure you this is true and I believe, just as surely as anything is true, that some day Christina Stead will hit with a big sale and where quality is as high as hers, it might be with any book including this one, although I have my doubts about that".[162] With revisions and the complex process of sending proofs between the United States and Stead's shifting addresses, it was more than eighteen months before the novel finally appeared, in January 1952. It wore a brightly illustrated jacket showing New York tenement buildings. Cameron had promised that the book would be "published and published properly", although by the time it appeared Cameron himself had been forced out of his position at Little, Brown over his plan to publish a novel by communist Howard Fast.

The People with the Dogs would not be the "big sale"; it had sold under 3000 copies to the end of March 1952.[163] Most reviewers found the characters simply not interesting enough to warrant Stead's attention: "half bored and half tired" (*New Yorker*); "the limpest, talkingest bunch of people to appear in recent fiction" (*New York Times*). At best, the kind of old New York family Stead presented "deserve to be noticed before they go" (*Time*) and Stead wrote with "a grace … these crazy people hardly deserve" (*Commonweal*). At worst, it was "a terribly tired novel" (*New Republic*). John Barkham in the *Times* looked back to *House of All Nations*, remarking that her "three books since then have been pale shadows of that abundant work" (he had missed one book altogether). He did at least compliment Stead's sense of the "sights and sounds" of New York: "The author's ear for our talk, her perception of our ways, all bespeak memories warm with affection".[164]

Little, Brown pursued various possibilities for publishing in magazines, book club listings or cheap reprints, but none was successful. In October 1952, the firm wrote to Strauss expressing its lack of enthusiasm about Stead's next project, "Mrs Trollope and Madame Blaise" (an early version of *The Little Hotel*):

> The first 93 pages of Christina Stead's new novel leave no sign of success in this office. Maybe the rest of it will show why the book will find a market but it would seem best to advise her now to drop this project or to change to a more direct style. She has created good characters and enough situations but she has left it up to the reader to discover the story. Why does she want to do this? Her last book never found a market because of the obscure story development and it seems certain that this one will do no better.[165]

---

161 Stead to Blake, 4 May 1949, 448, quoted in Rowley, *Christina Stead*, 354.
162 Cameron to Strauss, 20 April 1950, Final royalty scale was 10 per cent to 5000; 12.5 per cent to 10,000; 15 per cent after that. Little, Brown & Co. Records, Houghton Library, Harvard University, Box 83.
163 Jane Lawson (assistant editor, Little, Brown) to Stead, 10 April 1952, Little, Brown & Co. Records.
164 *New Yorker*, 26 January 1952, 98; John Barkham, "Sights and Sounds", *New York Times*, 13 January 1952; *Time*, 28 January 1952, 100; John A. Lynch, *Commonweal*, 22 February 1952, 502.
165 Little, Brown to Strauss, 6 October 1952, Little, Brown & Co. Records, Box 98.

Nothing more appeared from Little, Brown, and no new titles at all for the next fifteen years, until Holt, Rinehart & Winston published *Dark Places of the Heart* in 1966. Such obscurity was a dramatic change of fortune for an author who had had nine books published in the United States – ten if we include the anthology *Modern Women in Love* – in the eighteen years from 1934. Stead left the United States at the end of 1946 "as a mature writer with an international reputation", her books "praised by major reviewers in major journals".[166] But her New York trilogy had dissipated rather than consolidated her reputation in the United States, and although she remained in close contact with American friends, by the early fifties she was isolated and dislocated from the New York book world. Stanley Burnshaw was perhaps to her career what Ben Huebsch would be for Patrick White's, mounting a "campaign", as Stead called it, on her behalf, organising the reissue of *The Man Who Loved Children* and other works, and publishing new books to 1975, but this was late in Stead's career in contrast to the support White received from his very first novel.

Patrick White Can Write

Although his sales would rise and fall, Patrick White's relationship with the Viking Press was sustained to the very end of his career, beyond the death of Ben Huebsch in August 1964. In David Marr's words, the five novels White wrote after the two men met in 1940 "were, in some ways, written *for* Huebsch".[167] Through his own company, Huebsch had been the first in the United States to publish Joyce and Lawrence, the two most influential writers in White's early career, plus contemporary European authors and American moderns such as Sherwood Anderson. Huebsch's taste for modern writing went together with a commitment to publishing values he identified with older firms such as Scribner, an "unwillingness to commercialise culture and [a] commitment to protecting works of art from impersonal market exchange".[168] Of course, Huebsch brought his publications to market; indeed, he played a key role in bringing modernist writing from the avant-garde margins into the commercial mainstream. But he advertised modestly, addressing only the small circle of readers he felt had the taste and training to appreciate the works he put before them. Huebsch's modern readers were "lovers of – connoisseurs of – literature".[169]

Huebsch's approach might limit sales, but his reputation as a publisher committed to serious modern books was itself a valuable asset and made his company "an attractive acquisition for the partners in Viking".[170] In August 1925, B.W. Huebsch Inc. had merged with the newly formed Viking Press. Huebsch brought enormous cultural standing to the new firm, both personally and through his prestigious list. He became acquisitions editor at Viking, "working face-to-face with authors" and leaving the business side to his partners. Viking built on Huebsch's reputation, establishing itself as a quality literary publisher oriented to the modern. It added Steinbeck, Graham Greene and Joyce's *Finnegan's Wake* to its list, and Katharine Prichard's *Working Bullocks*, as we have seen.

---

166 Rowley, *Christina Stead*, 339.
167 Marr, *Patrick White*, 438.
168 Turner, *Marketing Modernism*, 49.
169 Turner, *Marketing Modernism*, 61-62.
170 Turner, *Marketing Modernism*, 77.

8 "Australian moderns": Christina Stead and Patrick White in New York

By 1940, in White's own words, Viking was "practically the best publisher in New York" and he did not dare aspire to it.[171] In London, White's first novel *Happy Valley* had been rejected by at least eight publishers before Geoffrey Grigson, the editor of *New Verse* and a reader for Harrap, persuaded this "most unlikely publisher" to accept it. Published in January 1939, the book drew high praise from prestigious reviewers including Greene, Herbert Read, Elizabeth Bowen, Stephen Spender and V.S. Pritchett, despite some feeling that the author, in Prichett's words, had "not yet got *Ulysses* out of his system".[172] Harrap ordered a second printing after the first run of 2000 copies had sold out. On the strength of this success but perhaps also to escape it, White sailed to New York, arriving in April 1939 "with a couple of copies of *Happy Valley* in his bag and a smart new studio photo for the American dust jacket".[173] Despite the efforts of Curtis Brown's New York office, which initiated a close twenty-year association for White with literary agent Naomi Burton, American publishers showed no interest in the novel. Burton, like White's London agent Juliet O'Hea, demonstrated the role that agents could play not merely as financial brokers but "caretakers of the artistic temperament".[174] White left New York to travel south and west across America then returned to New York, to rejection slips from Harcourt, Brace and Farrar & Rinehart. Marr recounts what happened next. White used the letters of introduction he had brought with him from London, one of which was to the poet Jean Starr Untermeyer, whose first book had been published by Huebsch. She read the novel then passed it on to Huebsch. He was enthusiastic, and early in 1940 accepted it for the Viking Press.[175] Viking's edition appeared in New York in June 1940.

Huebsch was a gift to the young author. In White's own words, "he became as much a part of my writing as those other necessaries, paper and ink".[176] They met probably after White's return to New York in March 1940, and although they saw each other only a few times in later years, the relationship was more than merely professional. Huebsch's attitudes towards literature and the marketplace gave White the support and freedom both would have agreed were necessary to a serious writer:

> Huebsch left White free to express himself in his own style, although the publisher would haggle at times over his grammar. Huebsch was not deterred by length. The manuscripts of authors like White were not to be cut. He put no pressure on authors to be commercial, and was happy for the Viking Press to carry unprofitable writers in whom he had faith.[177]

As White later remarked to his English publisher: "Ben Huebsch used to say: reviews don't matter; in the long run a book will reach the people for whom it's intended".[178]

---

171 White quoted in Marr, *Patrick White*, 187.
172 Marr, *Patrick White*, 177-78.
173 Marr, *Patrick White*, 182.
174 Linda Marie Fritschner, "Literary Agents and Literary Traditions: The Role of the Philistine", in *Paying the Piper: Causes and Consequences of Art Patronage*, ed. Judith Huggins Balfe (Urbana: University of Illinois Press, 1993), 61.
175 Marr, *Patrick White*, 187, 197. White sailed for England in September 1939 but returned to New York in March 1940.
176 White quoted in Marr, *Patrick White*, 198.
177 Marr, *Patrick White*, 198.
178 White to Tom Maschler (Jonathan Cape), 16 August 1970, cited in Marr, *Patrick White*, 198.

Huebsch's early faith in White was rewarded by enthusiastic reviews. For regular *New York Times* columnist Ralph Thompson, *Happy Valley* was "one of the surprises of the season", "one of the finds of the year". He distinguished it precisely from those books where "style" meant "those who can't be read, like James Joyce" or "Art with an upper-class A". White, too, "uses the inner monologue and leaves out punctuation here and there, but he knows what to do with words – and with people".[179] *Happy Valley* was "tart and unusual".[180] For Louis Salomon in *Nation*, the novel manifested "an unusually mature and objective perception of the springs of personality, a startling insight into the mechanism of the mind".[181] Like Stead, White was compared to Woolf, for his stream of consciousness technique. "Given a more significant story", Salomon concluded, White "may turn out a novel of foremost distinction." In the *New York Times*, Jane Spence Southron nailed the author's purpose, "that of getting behind the façade of mental and spiritual impenetrability which hides people from each other and, often, from themselves"; a purpose, she added, "achieved with a success which gives the writer immediate and far from negligible footing among today's introspectively dramatic novelists". She too drew attention to White's "free-lance stream-of-consciousness technique", deployed "in skeletal, sometimes almost in vestigial, prose"; but this was "only one of the weapons with which he attacks the citadel of personality".[182] Despite being a frequent reviewer of Australian novels by this time, Southron did not draw any comparisons with other Australian work. One reviewer, in the *Herald Tribune*, described White as the most outstanding Australian writer to appear since Christina Stead, but nothing more was made of the comparison.[183]

Reading such reviews, Huebsch might well have felt that *Happy Valley* had found the readers for whom it was intended. White's relationship with "Mr Huebsch" and "the Viking", as he called them, was reinforced when the firm quickly accepted his second novel and Harrap rejected it, initiating a pattern that would mark White's career until signing with Jonathan Cape in late 1969: "immediate acceptance of White's work in New York and a struggle to find a publisher in London".[184] White had begun *The Living and the Dead* on Cape Cod in 1939, finding release in America while writing 1930s London out of his system. He typed the third and final draft in New York on his return the following year, and it was released in February 1941. Back in London, the manuscript was rejected by Faber, Chatto, Jonathan Cape and Heinemann, before Hebert Read accepted it for George Routledge & Sons. As Viking had not Americanised White's spelling – they never would – Routledge could set from the American edition, and it published the book in July.[185]

Viking released *The Living and the Dead* in a jacket by modernist designer Edward McKnight Kauffer, and when White's copy finally reached him on war service in Egypt he was delighted by the book's presentation. Like Prichard and Richardson before him, White came to value the superior design and production of American books (although this changed along with his other views on America and American publishing in the 1970s). The reviews this time were more mixed, often (as with Stead) within themselves.

---

179 Ralph Thompson, "Books of the Times", *New York Times*, 22 May 1940.
180 Ralph Thompson, "Books of the Times", *New York Times*, 1 July 1940. In his column of 1 January 1941, Thompson recalled *Happy Valley* as the previous year's most promising first novel.
181 Louis B. Salomon, "Newcomer from Australia", *Nation*, 7 September 1940, 198.
182 Jane Spence Southron, "A Novel of Life in New South Wales", *New York Times*, 26 May 1940.
183 John Scott Mahon, "Australian Ranch Town", *New York Herald Tribune*, 2 June 1940.
184 Marr, *Patrick White*, 201.
185 Marr, *Patrick White*, 202-8.

8 "Australian moderns": Christina Stead and Patrick White in New York

For Iris Barry in the *Herald Tribune*, "the background is always clear, the details precise: it is only the main figures that seem to lack definition as they peer out, suffering small indescribable horrors, each in his or her own private hell" (a rather good definition of the novel's characterisation). Similarly, in the *Saturday Review*: "Mr. White is no Joyce in scope or mastery, but he must be seriously recognised as working in the tradition of 'Ulysses,' and working, furthermore, with a literary vitality quite his own". Despite the author's virtuosity, however, his principal characters ultimately "seem more dead than living".[186]

But *The Living and the Dead* also found its right readers. For *Time* magazine, it was "an uncommonly searching and sordid study"; "scene after scene is worked out with exactness and subtlety which no second-string novelist can scent, far less nail to paper".[187] For Salomon, reviewing his second White novel, the author's serious talent was confirmed. Drawing comparisons again with Woolf and Joyce, he concluded:

> There is no sentimentality in Patrick White's work, no blurred outlines to pamper the lazy mind or the namby-pamby heart. He aims at a discriminating audience, at the "living" rather than at the "dead," and for this audience he puts on a brilliant and masterful performance. He is a bold and original, and penetrating observer, who probes too deeply for comfort. Let the comfort-lovers beware.[188]

Southron again provided a perceptive and prominent review, noting of the book's bitterness: "it hurts".[189] Both the *Saturday Review* and the *New York Times* notices carried the photographic portrait of White he had taken with him to America. Again praising White's technique, Southron thought the new novel better "on its constructional and verbal sides" despite its occasional excess of realism. "Patrick White can write. And he has bedrock strength. Perhaps his present devotion to the cult of ultra-realism is only a milestone on the road to greater things." Realism was still at issue as the shapes of the contemporary novel emerged in the wake of high modernism. Indeed, White's own style was in transition, away from the qualities Southron read as ultra-realism and the modernist styles of the interwar years, towards a more universalist symbolic language that exceeds both psychology and social context.

Spinster Aunt from Down Under

White returned to Australia to live in 1948, but despite a gap of seven years between books, his critical reputation and sales success in America were boosted with each new novel: *The Aunt's Story* in January 1948 and *The Tree of Man* in August 1955. Having sent off the manuscript of *The Aunt's Story* in January 1947, White wrote to Huebsch: "Needless to say, I hope you like it! … I am still unable to judge from the angle of a publisher or a public". He added modestly that if Huebsch did not like the book could he please return it to Curtis

---

186 Iris Barry, *New York Herald Tribune*, 9 February 1941; R.L. Nathan, "White …", *Saturday Review of Literature*, 15 February 1941, 11.
187 "Sex for Three", *Time*, 10 February 1941, 74.
188 Louis B. Salomon, "As Though to Breathe Were Life", *Nation*, 8 March 1941, 276.
189 Jane Spence Southron, "'The Living and the Dead' and Other Works of Fiction: Patrick White's Novel of Despairing Moderns", *New York Times*, 9 February 1941.

Brown. In May he received Huebsch's cabled congratulations followed by a characteristic letter: "Those of us who have read your manuscript are keenly appreciative of its quality. The book will surely add to your reputation among the discerning". Sales were unlikely to be large, he added, but Huebsch assured White "our risk will be justified by books to come".[190]

There were difficulties with the production this time around. Viking was unconvinced by the title and preferred "Theo's Story". White insisted that "The Aunt's Story" had been the book's title from the beginning, and so it stayed. More seriously, he had been unable to check proofs until it was too late to forward corrections. The worst of the errors White identified was that Viking had a "fiord" instead of a "ford" in an Australian paddock: "The other mistakes may quite well earn me the reputation for intellectual bogusness, but that is not so hard to bear as ignorance of one's own country". Viking tipped an errata slip into the first printing which sold 6000 copies in a few weeks, enabling a second, corrected edition.[191] In Britain and Australia, by contrast, the novel sold poorly, confirming White's sense that it was America that best understood him.

The second and third parts of *The Aunt's Story* break the limits even of "ultra" realism, and the novel was bound to divide the critics. It tested those like Orville Prescott, Ralph Thompson's successor, who wanted good middlebrow fiction: "Theodora Goodman is so nice a person one wants to know what happened to her".[192] The novel's "oblique and opaque use of words" was "sometimes emotionally suggestive but more often intellectually bewildering". Still, the novel was able to command the full "Books of the Times" column. Prescott announced that White's previous two novels had not been published in the United States – this despite their earlier favourable reviews in the *Times* itself – indicating again the difficulties of sustaining a career from a distance. Diane Trilling *supposed* the novel should be "catalogued as art" but found it "pretty dull going, and totally unconvincing to boot". Even so, she insisted it could "not be dismissed as merely pretentious and 'literary'". It had some "striking visual moments" and the last scene she thought "superb".[193]

Like Richardson and Stead before him, the force of White's writing, acknowledged even by sceptical reviewers, meant he could occasionally be brought into conversations about the current state of the novel and of American literature itself. In an extended review in the *New Republic*, John Woodburn, Stead's one-time editor, promoted White's writing as a tonic for the American novel. White's earlier novels had been "properly and respectfully hailed by a few discerning critics" but "ignored by an extremely huge number of American readers".

> When I first encountered this man's work, in 1941, it seemed to me that here was an author whose influence could be seriously destructive to our American cult of mediocrity. Patrick White was even then writing with extreme sensibility, thoughtfulness, perception and taste – ingredients alien to the mainstream of contemporary American letters … White has now brazenly extended his discordant propaganda, as it were, by the publication of an extraordinarily good novel … and he stands exposed as the fine

---

190 Huebsch quoted in Marr, *Patrick White*, 244, 250.
191 Marr, *Patrick White*, 254.
192 Orville Prescott, "Books of the Times", *New York Times*, 7 January 1948.
193 Diane Trilling, "Fiction in Review", *Nation*, 21 February 1948, 219.

8 "Australian moderns": Christina Stead and Patrick White in New York

writer he is. I feel it my agreeable duty to urge that Patrick White's book be thoroughly investigated by all adult Americans able to read …

And so I am quite serious when I say that Patrick White is a man to be watched. There are others like him: a few, who, undismayed by our indifference, persist in flaunting their integrity in the face of The Best Seller, The Selection and The Sale to Hollywood.[194]

In fact, what is most striking is the widespread praise that this challenging novel received. In the *New Yorker*: "It depends for its distinguished success upon the two things that every novelist must depend upon – an understanding of human beings and a knowledge of how to write. Mr. White's prose is as much a delight as the story he tells with it". In the *Library Journal*: "Patrick White dissects and analyses character and emotion with perception … He is a philosopher and writer of exceptional ability and this book will be an important addition to current lists". In the *Saturday Review*: "an acrid, astringent novel". (An excerpt from the novel also appeared in the paper's "Literary Sampler" in December 1947.) And in the *Herald Tribune*: "A contemporary exercise in the picturesque style, this exceedingly brilliant and likable novel is written with an almost miraculous liveliness. Its character-drawing is at once incisive and profound … The oddly unusual and delicious book ripples with gaiety and a razor-edged love of life. It is as bright and as poignant as the sound of a brass band".[195] We don't know whether White ever read that final sentence, but the comments suggest that for some critics at least *The Aunt's Story* could be brought back into the middlebrow fold as a well-written character study.

Viking featured the novel in the middle of a half-page advertisement in the *Times*, with quotations from the *Herald Tribune* (excluding the brass band) and from Alfred Kazin: "a very real expression of imagination and intelligence and subtly moving in a way it is not easy to express".[196] White thought that the American reviews "that mattered were as good as any I have seen of anybody's book. Even so," he added, "very few people seem to have read it".[197] *The Aunt's Story* also gave White his first review by James Stern, an Anglo-Irish writer then resident in New England, whose reviews for the *New York Times* came to be highly regarded.[198] Despite its heart-sinking title – "Spinster Aunt from Down Under" – Stern's review was more than just favourable. It proceeded as if White's place was naturally among the important modern novelists: Woolf, George Moore, Ronald Firbank, Frank Norris, Henry James and Flaubert. The novel was "a brilliant, original and highly intelligent piece of work … gay and witty – as well as tragic, sometimes profound". Stern's review of *The Tree of Man*, which was featured on the front page of the Book Review in August 1955, would go to even greater heights. In a phrase that reappeared in Viking publicity, he declared the novel "a timeless work of art from which no essential element of life has been

---

194 John Woodburn, "Fiction Parade", *New Republic*, 16 February 1948, 27-28.
195 Hamilton Basso, *New Yorker*, 10 January 1948, 80; E.H. Kennedy, *Library Journal*, 1 December 1947, 1686; Walter Havinghurst, "Homeless World", *Saturday Review of Literature*, 3 January 1948, 11; "The Literary Sampler: Theodora's Baby", *Saturday Review of Literature*, 6 December 1947, 77-78; Iris Barry, *New York Herald Tribune*, 4 January 1948.
196 Viking advertisement, *New York Times*, 25 January 1948.
197 White to Jean Scott Rogers, 26 September 1948, in *Patrick White: Letters*, ed. David Marr (Milsons Point, NSW: Random House, 1994), 73.
198 James Stern, "Spinster Aunt From Down Under", *New York Times*, 11 January 1948. Marr, *Patrick White*, 304: "Stern's high reputation as a critic in the 1950s was underpinned by a small body of short stories which earned him, in Auden's judgement, a place of permanent importance in fiction".

omitted".[199] White had achieved the "artist's greatest ambition [and] rarest achievement", to reveal the life of the soul "in such a way that by the time the last page is reached all questions have been answered, while all the glory and mystery of the world remains … The novel grows a little the way nature grows". In his ability to "lay bare the conscious, romantic yet private daydreams, the unlived life", Stern declared, White "towers over most other living novelists". Although the groundwork had been laid, Stern's review more than any other established White's reputation in New York and in North America.[200]

The Aunt's Story appeared in the United States just as White was sailing to Australia in early 1948. Following his wartime experiences in the Middle East, North Africa and Greece, London seemed dominated by the dead rather than the living, and despite the fact that his public and his publishers were in London and New York, by 1946 he had determined to return to Australia. The deserts of North Africa had made him feel he had to revisit Australia and to live there or in the United States rather than Europe.[201] He returned first in October 1946 – realising "how Australian I have been all the time underneath" – and completed *The Aunt's Story* in Sydney.[202] He returned to London in 1947 to organise his permanent return and the immigration to Australia of his partner Manoly Lascaris before arriving for good in February 1948, where the American reviews of *The Aunt's Story* awaited him. The novel began in Australia and almost returned there – the central character Theodora Goodman abandons her journey in New Mexico. With *The Tree of Man*, however, White's fiction would return wholly to an Australian story, in one sense *the* Australian story of "settlers in the wilderness". White's interests are in the spiritual mysteries in the lives of his central characters rather than the narrative of pioneering, but there was enough in the novel for his American readers to connect it with the earlier frontier epics, if only to signal its difference as a serious work of art. (And at least one Australian critic could link it to *Gone with the Wind*.)[203] In many ways it signalled a new beginning for White's American reputation, more available to mainstream appreciation as a major twentieth-century novelist treating of the "universal" even as he reinvested in Australia.

In America, *The Tree of Man* quickly became White's greatest critical and commercial success (Fig. 8.3). Ten thousand copies were sold in the first fortnight, a little disappointing perhaps given the high critical praise, but more than White had ever enjoyed before and enough to indicate that the book should continue selling.[204] Sales eventually came in at around 16,000 copies, making *The Tree of Man* something of a bestseller in its class. Huebsch would later write that White had gathered a band of admirers with his earlier novels, but it was only with *The Tree of Man* that he "ceased to be caviare to the general and became the delectable fare of large numbers".[205]

Once more, the contrast with Britain was striking. *The Tree of Man* was rejected by Routledge and perhaps as many as twenty publishers in all. White wrote to Huebsch that he felt he no longer had "much to say to the English", and he considered publishing the novel first in Australia. Both Huebsch and Juliet O'Hea, his longstanding agent at

---

199 James Stern, "The Quiet People of the Homestead", *New York Times*, 14 August 1955.
200 Marr, *Patrick White*, 305.
201 Marr, *Patrick White*, 211. Following biographical details, 242-55.
202 White to Pepe Mamblas, 26 January 1947, cited in Marr, *Patrick White*, 245.
203 Cecil Hadgraft, *Australian Literature: A Critical Account to 1955* (London: Heinemann, 1960), 242.
204 Marr, *Patrick White*, 306.
205 *Book-of-the-Month Club News*, August 1957, on the appearance of *Voss*.

8 "Australian moderns": Christina Stead and Patrick White in New York

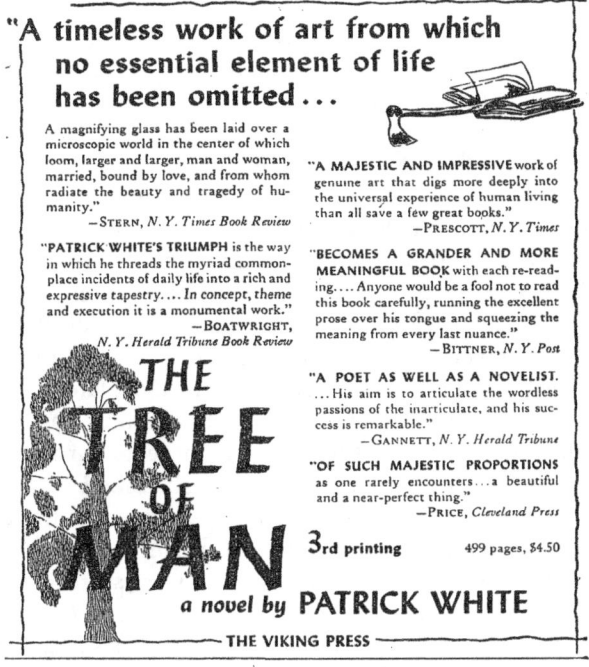

Figure 8.3 Advertisement for Patrick White's *The Tree of Man* (New York: The Viking Press, 1955), *New York Times*, 31 August 1955.

Curtis Brown London, strongly advised against doing so for it would almost certainly ruin his chances of publication or distribution elsewhere in the British sphere.[206] It was Huebsch's intervention that finally saw the novel go to Eyre & Spottiswoode. In Australia, the Melbourne *Age* reviewer, interestingly, thought White had little in common with other Australian novelists and more with Americans such as Truman Capote and Carson McCullers. The *Sydney Morning Herald* printed academic and poet A.D. Hope's infamous description of White's prose as "pretentious and illiterate verbal sludge".[207] White told fellow-novelist Kylie Tennant, "If it hadn't been for the Americans I would have felt like putting my head in a gas oven".[208]

Postwar Reputations

There were always reviewers on hand to praise Stead and White as major writers who should be better known. Indeed, postwar, both developed reputations as among the great forgotten or unread novelists, even as their virtues came to be seen in some respects as

---

206 White to Huebsch, 15 February 1955, Marr, *Letters*, 98; Marr, *Patrick White*, 301-2.
207 Geoffrey Hutton, "A Poet at Loose on Cow Cockies", *Age*, 12 May 1956; A.D. Hope, "The Bunyip Stages a Comeback", *Sydney Morning Herald*, 16 June 1956.
208 Quoted in Marr, *Patrick White*, 311.

"old-fashioned". The reference was to their deep investment still – unfashionably – in the full powers of the novel. White's novels were "elegant, superbly intelligent, full of authority and more or less premodern in the English mode", and the one time Stead and White were compared it was for "an architectural quality, a solid structure like an old-fashioned apartment building".[209]

Stead's postwar reputation was kickstarted by the 1965 reissue of *The Man Who Loved Children*. This was timely in the context of changes in the New York book world, as a new generation of literary intellectuals joined the bookmen and women of earlier decades; they were more comfortable with modernism, which they took as an inheritance rather than an intrusion. Stead's advocate at Holt, Rinehart & Winston, her old friend Stanley Burnshaw, shared this perspective.[210] In a manner that again recalls Richardson's American fortunes, Stead's achievements were recalled from time to time by influential true believers: in essays by Randall Jarrell and Elizabeth Hardwick in 1955, Hardwick again in 1962, and Jarrell again in his celebrated introduction to the novel which also appeared in the *Atlantic Monthly*.[211] Each of the essays – and the supporting comments Burnshaw organised for *The Man Who Loved Children*'s jacket, from Hardwick, Robert Lowell, and other prominent writers and critics – worked to "re-register" the novel's status, not merely as a book of the season, but as "one of the enduring masterpieces of fiction".[212] Some like Hardwick could bring Stead's whole oeuvre into visibility, in ways that were scarcely possible in Australia at that point in time. She drew together *The Salzburg Tales*, *House of All Nations*, *For Love Alone* and *Letty Fox* as works of "unusual power". Stead's standing as a major literary novelist was reasserted but always against a background of neglect.

Two new books followed quickly from Holt, Rinehart & Winston, *Dark Places of the Heart* in 1966 and *The Puzzle-Headed Girl* in 1967, alongside a paperback reprint of *The Man Who Loved Children* from Avon in 1966. Holt reissued *House of All Nations* in 1972 with an Avon paperback in 1974. Other reprints followed, but only two new novels appeared in Stead's lifetime: *The Little Hotel* from Holt in 1975 and *Miss Herbert* from Random House in 1976. There were always positive reviews – often recalling the earlier novels – and Stead could still command the "Books of the Times" column; but even though *The Little Hotel* sold well enough to go into a third printing none of the later works made much of an impression.[213] Stead's name was kept before the reading public, however, in reviews of other novels (often about dysfunctional families) or in feature articles about great neglected books; and in a rare acknowledgement of her standing,

---

209 Catherine Peters, "Miss Herbert (The Suburban Wife)", *Washington Post*, 11 July 1976. By contrast, when *For Love Alone* and *Letty Fox* were released as HBJ/Harvest paperbacks in 1979 they could be read as "precursors of contemporary styles": "Paperbacks: New and Noteworthy", *New York Times*, 20 May 1979.
210 During, *Exit Capitalism*, 75.
211 Elizabeth Hardwick, "The Novels of Christina Stead", *New Republic*, 1 August 1955, 17-19, and "The Neglected Novels of Christina Stead", in *A View of My Own: Essays in Literature and Society* (New York: Farrar, Straus & Cudahy, 1962), 41-48. Randall Jarrell, "Speaking of Books", *New York Times*, 24 July 1955; "The Man Who Loved Children", *Atlantic Monthly* 215 (1965): 166-71; "An Unread Book", introduction to *The Man Who Loved Children* (New York: Holt, Rinehart & Winston, 1965).
212 The phrase is from J. Donald Adams, editor of the *New York Times* from 1925 to 1943, and used in Holt, Rinehart & Winston's publicity for the 1965 edition. It is quoted in a negative review of the novel's 1976 reissue: Evan Connell, "Less than Meets the Eye", *Harper's Magazine*, 1 July 1976, 75.
213 Christopher Lehmann-Haupt, "Books of the Times: People In and Out of Control", review of *The Little Hotel*, by Christina Stead, *New York Times*, 16 June 1973.

8 "Australian moderns": Christina Stead and Patrick White in New York

Random House published a *Christina Stead Reader* in 1978, initiated and compiled in the United States.[214] Stead had achieved a minor place in the modern fiction canon, one that was reinforced through the emerging category of women's literature, as in Joan Lidoff's 1982 monograph *Christina Stead*.[215] But it was always as if she must be rediscovered. There was prescience in Fadiman's remark that each of Stead's novels was "massively solitary", an effect reinforced by the discontinuities in her own career after leaving America.

Something similar can be said about White's later American career, despite a more regular output of new titles and the Nobel Prize in 1973. *The Tree of Man* was the peak of White's recognition, even though *Voss* was the Book-of-the-Month Club's selection for August 1957, the first Australian novel in that position since Eleanor Dark's *The Timeless Land*.[216] Trade sales were disappointing, and many reviewers rated the novel less successful than its predecessor. By contrast, *Voss* was White's first real success in Britain, beginning a lengthy process in which White's editorial and publishing loyalties were reoriented away from New York and towards London. His relationship with Huebsch was perhaps at its strongest with *Riders in the Chariot* (1961), with its deep investment in Jewish character and mysticism. But after Huebsch's death and Marshall Best's retirement, White felt, perhaps with some reason, that Viking had progressively lost interest in him, despite assurances that he was still "one of their top authors".[217] As White's American sales slumped, so did the terms Viking could offer, and his sense that his true readers were to be found in the United States swung dramatically to its opposite. By contrast, with *The Vivisector* (1970) he had a new and enthusiastic publisher in London in Jonathan Cape, and for *The Eye of the Storm* (1973) White insisted that he be published first in England: "the Americans aren't really interested: even the 'good' reviews are awful and the sales are miserable; nor do I feel the Viking particularly wants me except as a duty to Huebsch … But I don't want to offend Viking and have them drop me; I mightn't find another publisher in the States, and one still wants to be published there for the small flock of faithful".[218] Reviews had always been mixed and they remained so, but as each new lot arrived White was confirmed in his disenchanted view that "beyond a few cosmopolitans and Jews", Americans couldn't read him and were no longer interested in serious literature.[219]

---

214 *The Man Who Loved Children* was nominated by Denis Donoghue as one of the books that may be considered among "the hundred or so most important books of Western literature": "Immortal Nominations", *New York Times*, 3 June 1979; and following his Nobel Prize, Saul Bellow suggested Stead as a worthy winner: Herbert Mittgang, "Saul Bellow Taking his Laureateship Lightly", *New York Times*, 14 November 1976. Jean Read, ed., *A Christina Stead Reader* (New York: Random House, 1978).
215 Joan Lidoff, *Christina Stead* (New York: Frederick Ungar, 1982).
216 Roger Osborne, "Patrick White and the American Middlebrow", in *Telling Stories: Australian Life and Literature, 1935–2012*, ed. Tanya Dalziell and Paul Genoni (Clayton, Vic.: Monash University Publishing, 2013), 188–94.
217 Alan Collins (Curtis Brown New York) to White, 21 April 1964, Curtis Brown Ltd Records, Rare Book and Manuscript Library, Columbia University, MS0314.
218 White to Juliet O'Hea (Curtis Brown London), 9 December 1972, John Cushman Associate Records, Columbia University, Rare Book and Manuscript Library, Box 82.
219 Quoted in letter from O'Hea to John Cushman (John Cushman Associates, New York), 13 August 1970; White to Cushman, 22 August 1970, Cushman Records, Box 82.

White remained, or rather *became*, a relatively unknown writer, although, like Stead, he too could command the "Books of the Times" column.[220] The *New Republic*'s review of *The Eye of the Storm*, soon after the Nobel Prize, was memorably entitled "Patrick *Who*? From *Where*?", although its point was that White should be better known among American readers.[221] Despite ten books released in the United States since 1940, it was as if the Nobel Committee had discovered this unknown author and plucked him from obscurity. Sales bounced back with *The Eye of the Storm*, and following the Nobel award Viking reissued all six of White's novels following *The Aunt's Story* in hardcover and licensed paperbacks to Avon. *The Eye of the Storm* made the *New York Times* bestseller lists. But by this stage White's primary publisher was Jonathan Cape in London, supported by Penguin paperbacks. White had become an *Australian* writer, too, in a way that Stead had not, writing for (or against) Australian readers first and foremost. In America, his reputation became that of a great "unread writer", something repeated with every new book. As a late review put it, inaccurately but tellingly in its opening claim, "White was virtually unread in the United States before the 1973 [Nobel Prize] citation put his name in the papers, and even now American readers of his work are rare. This neglect should stop; a strong case could be made for White as the finest and most profound novelist anywhere in the world now working in English".[222]

---

[220] Christopher Lehmann-Haupt, "Books of the Times: The Heart of Darkness", review of *A Fringe of Leaves*, by Patrick White, *New York Times*, 18 January 1977.
[221] Peter Wolfe, "Patrick *Who*? From *Where*?", *New Republic*, 5-12 January 1974, 17-18.
[222] Bob Halliday, "The Intricate Artistry of Patrick White", review of *Memoirs of Many in One*, by Patrick White, *Washington Post*, 16 November 1986.

9
Bestsellers, Modest Sellers and Commercial Failures: The Postwar Years

> "The Yank literary market is absolutely the best in the whole blinkin' world."
> —Henry Lamond, 1945[1]

Previous chapters have demonstrated the presence of Australian novels in American print culture from the small-scale, low-key importation of British sheets for rebinding and local distribution, to the large-scale manufacture of copyrighted American editions, extended by book club circulation or reprints, sometimes with sales of hundreds of thousands of copies. Over time, Australian authors contributed to a wide variety of markets: nineteenth-century romance and pioneering narratives; a genre system that sought tales of detection, sensation, and romantic love; and more serious fare in the form of historical sagas that were taken as a sign of the emergence of a distinct and distinguished national literature. With writers such as Henry Handel Richardson, Eleanor Dark, Christina Stead and Patrick White, certain Australian novels could occasionally find a more prominent and recognisable place in the conversations of New York's book culture.

The 1940s promised to be the decade when this emergence would be consolidated, especially when the Second World War turned American eyes sharply towards the Pacific region. When Japanese bombs fell on Pearl Harbor on 7 December 1941, repercussions were felt across all aspects of American society, including publishing. The war in Europe had already affected the publishing industry with paper shortages and rising production costs, and this was compounded by immediate American engagement in the conflict. As a strategic base, Australia became a part of American life as never before, a military base where Americans served their country abroad. Publishers, literary agents and government agencies all noted this rise in American awareness of Australia and the Pacific, and the 1940s saw the most significant attempts to date to strengthen connections between the Australian and American book trades through visits by American publishers and editors to Australia, the establishment of a US-oriented literary agency in Sydney, and the intervention of Australian government offices promoting Australian books. But despite these initiatives, a significant increase in American editions of Australian novels did not

---

1   Henry Lamond to family, ca. 1945, Henry George Lamond Papers 1905-68, John Oxley Library, State Library of Queensland, OM73-49.

follow, either during the war or in the immediate postwar years. The number of American editions of Australian novels fell after 1939 in line with the general decrease in production due to wartime restrictions, rose sharply in 1946, but then fell again until another rise in 1950.[2]

The marketplace for new fiction remained a very competitive one, dominated by a relatively small but highly influential group of reviewers, critics and editors in New York who held sway over the book culture of American newspapers and magazines.[3] Australian novels, as we have seen, had an impact in these circles across the 1930s and into the early years of the war, producing a small but enthusiastic constituency of interested readers. But in larger terms Australian literature remained on the periphery of the professional or intellectual concerns of such groups and institutions. It could not attract or sustain the attention necessary to consolidate the advances of the 1930s and establish a stable field for the appreciation of Australian literature. A few Australian books and authors were welcomed as major contributions to English fiction or the modern novel; others as worthy books of the month or season; others as good commercial prospects. But even with the impact of the Pacific war in the United States, only rarely did the "Australianness" of Australian books provide a selling point.

Making Spaces for Australian Books

The low status of Australian novels in America in the postwar years is apparent in the recollections of one of the more famous New York literary agents. At 5pm on Sunday 4 October 1950, Paul R. Reynolds landed at Sydney International Airport, beginning a visit to Australia that had been organised and financed by his friend, the Australian newspaper proprietor Frank Packer. Answering the questions of a waiting reporter from Packer's *Daily Telegraph* and posing for the paper's photographer, Reynolds declared, "I want to meet any Australian writer who wants to meet me". Next morning, after waking in his well-appointed room at the Australia Hotel, he was alarmed to see the *Daily Telegraph* announcing that he would be glad to read any manuscript submitted to him. Downstairs, at least fifteen Australian authors were waiting for Reynolds' appearance, each holding well-thumbed manuscripts that had already been rejected by Australian publishers. This scenario was repeated for several days, forcing Reynolds to arrange shipment of a large pile of manuscripts to New York where he could consider them away from the authorial frenzy his visit had created. Almost 200 manuscripts were delivered to Reynolds' New York office. Only three were deemed suitable for submission to an American publisher, and only one proved successful in this competitive process, Charles Shaw's otherwise unknown *Heaven Knows, Mr. Allison* (1952). The novel told the story of a US Marine and a young

---

2   The number of new titles averages eighteen in the years 1935-38, but falls to twelve in 1939-45; in 1946 it rises to twenty new titles and in 1950 to twenty-one; 1949 is anomalous with only five new titles appearing. Adding reprints to the totals produces a similar pattern despite the "distortion" of large numbers in certain years from Maysie Greig and Arthur Upfield: an average of twenty-four in the years 1935 to 1938; seventeen between 1939 and 1945; and totals of thirty-one in 1946 and twenty-four in 1950. The 1950s numbers remain at or above this level.
3   See Roger Osborne, "New York City Limits", in *Reading Across the Pacific: Australia–United States Intellectual Histories*, ed Robert Dixon and Nicholas Birns (Sydney: Sydney University Press, 2010), 299–308.

9 Bestsellers, Modest Sellers and Commercial Failures: The Postwar Years

nun stranded on a Pacific island behind Japanese lines. Reviewed respectfully, a cheap reprint from the Popular Library appeared in December 1953 and a film adaptation in 1957, directed by no lesser figure than John Huston.[4]

In his biography, from which the Australian incident is taken, Reynolds offers a dim view of Australian writing at this time:

> Australia has produced quite a number of important writers such as Alan Moorehead, Jon Cleary, Nevil Shute, and above all the brilliant outstanding genius, Morris West. This is a recent occurrence. Thirty years ago Australia was an insignificant country with almost no writers who were published in America.[5]

Writing these words in the early 1970s, Reynolds implies that the early 1940s was a barren period for Australian writers. But as we have seen, and as we show further in this chapter, Australian novels could, on occasion, reach a prominent position in American print culture. Reynolds' focus is clearly on mainstream commercial fiction (and non-fiction in Moorehead's case), and this was perhaps the most difficult sector for writers from a "distant" literary culture like Australia's in that it lacked the distinguishing characteristics that might, in their different ways, draw both literary fiction and genre fiction to a publisher's or critic's attention.

The relatively small number of Australian novels appearing in the United States made it difficult for Australian writers and their novels to maintain a profile in the weekly or monthly book talk of American newspapers and magazines. From 1940 to 1950, around 140 Australian novels were published as genuine first American editions and just over 200 titles when reprints are added. Of these, Doubleday published more than thirty, mainly Maysie Greig romances and Arthur Upfield's Bony detective series. Few other publishers came close to double figures. Macmillan published two novels by Dark and four by Kylie Tennant; Harcourt, Brace three by Stead; Viking three by Patrick White; and Little, Brown three by James Alridge. Other publishers less devoted to a single Australian author included Dodd, Mead (six titles, including several each by Eric Baume and George Johnston), E.P. Dutton (six), William Morrow (five), Simon & Schuster (four), Scribner (four), and Houghton Mifflin (three). For most Australian authors, a short sequence of two or three American editions was the best that could be expected. Nevertheless, some of those mentioned maintained strong working relationships with influential publishers and publishing institutions, occupying relatively stable positions in the competitive and dynamic networks of American print culture.

As an indication of hopes on the Australian side for an increased Australian presence in the American marketplace, a number of US literary agents were surveyed for the 1946 publication *Australian Writers and Artists' Market, Including New Zealand: A Practical Selling Guide for the Freelance*. Some, like Jacques Chambrun, provided candid responses: "May we suggest ... that, because of the difficulty and time lost in sending material from Australia to USA and back, we be sent only MSS.

---

4   Published in 1952 by Crown Publishers; the film adaptation bears the same title. John C. Neff, "Each Helped the Other", *New York Times*, 11 January 1953; "Books Published Today", *New York Times*, 14 December 1953.
5   Paul Reynolds, *The Middle Man: The Adventures of a Literary Agent* (New York: Morrow, 1972), 142.

of outstanding qualities likely to interest our audience here".⁶ Reynolds stressed that "a very considerable amount of material suitable for Australian publication proves useless in USA".⁷ Yet there were agents and publishers who remained willing to take a punt on Australian books during the war and the early postwar years.

The most obvious impact of the war was the opportunity for authors writing fiction or non-fiction *about* the war, writers such as Aldridge, Johnston, Jon Cleary and Osmar E. White. With a focus on the Pacific theatre, their work attracted the interest of American publishers and, with the exception of White, helped establish relationships that would eventually lead to longer-term publishing success in other genres. Johnston saw his journalistic reports from the Mediterranean and New Guinea published in book form by Angus & Robertson in Sydney, Gollancz in London, and various publishers in New York. The books' titles as released for American readers indicate their topical content: *Grey Gladiator: H.M.A.S. Sydney with the British Mediterranean Fleet* (Houghton Mifflin, 1942), *Toughest Fighting in the World* (Duell, Sloan and Pearce, 1942) and *Pacific Partner* (World Book Co., 1944). Johnston's career as a novelist in the United States began with a crime novel, *Death Takes Small Bites*, published in Dodd, Mead's Red Badge Detective series in 1948. Eleven more novels followed through to *My Brother Jack* in 1965, the last to appear, including three from Bobbs-Merrill and six from Morrow.⁸ Aldridge's long American career began with two war novels, *Signed with Their Honour* (1942), which had first appeared in *Collier's Magazine*, and *The Sea Eagle* (1944). Their publisher, Little, Brown, would go on to publish twelve of Aldridge's nineteen American novel titles through to 1979. Osmar White's memoir of his experience in New Guinea, *Green Armour*, was published in 1945 by Angus & Robertson, and in the same year Allen & Unwin and W.W. Norton shared sheets of the London printing for simultaneous editions in London and New York.⁹

One of the most successful careers to emerge from this period was Jon Cleary's. While still on active service in New Guinea in 1943, Cleary sent a bundle of stories to Reynolds in New York following the advice of R.G. Campbell, editor of the Melbourne-based *Australian Journal*. Reynold's initial success in placing them in US magazines was limited, although he sold several to *Cosmopolitan* for $400 each; but he persisted with Cleary, offering patient and detailed advice on writing for the American market: "From an American point of view [the stories] seem to us pretty much sketches … I wish you'd try some stories laid in Australia or in the Pacific and don't hesitate to use Australian characters. It would probably be a mistake for you to try to use American characters".¹⁰ The breakthrough came with *You Can't See Round Corners*, Cleary's novel about an Australian

---

6   *Australian Writers and Artists' Market (Including New Zealand): A Practical Selling Guide for the Freelance* (Melbourne: Australian School of Journalism Pty Ltd and Art Training Institute Pty Ltd, 1946), 24.
7   *Australian Writers and Artists' Market*, 31.
8   Bobbs-Merrill published *High Valley* (1950), *The Big Chariot* (1953) and *The Sea and the Stone* (1955), all co-authored with Charmian Clift; Morrow published Johnston's sole-authored novels from 1961 to 1965, including two detective novels under the pseudonym Shane Martin. Doubleday published a third Shane Martin, *Mourner's Voyage*, in its Crime Club in 1962. *The Far Road* (Morrow, 1964) returned to Johnston's experience as a war correspondent.
9   Alan Moorehead's US publishing also began with war books: *Mediterranean Front* (Whittlesey House, 1942) and *Eclipse* (Coward, McCann & Geoghegan, 1945).
10 Reynolds to Cleary, 26 November 1944, Paul Reynolds Collection, Columbia University, Box 34, "Jon Cleary".

9 Bestsellers, Modest Sellers and Commercial Failures: The Postwar Years

deserter embroiled in gambling, robbery and accidental death, which had won second prize in the *Sydney Morning Herald* Literary Competition in 1946. Even so, Reynolds' initial reaction was cautious (and already, by 1946, it appears the war had lost its market interest, at least in fiction):

> With regard to the sales possibilities of this novel, it has become harder and harder in this country to sell anything pertaining to the war. This isn't a war novel but the draft and the army and deserting and whether your leading character should go back into the army is basically a war theme rather than a peace-time theme.
>
> If you got an idea for a novel around attractive, reasonably sympathetic characters or at least a novel in which the two or three main characters were sympathetic, I think you might have a chance for making quite a success in this country. I realise that you are an Australian and should think of Australia first but the number of books that an Australian publisher can sell is inevitably limited by the population of your country. I don't suppose there is any chance of your coming to this country, is there? I don't want you to write stories laid in this country or about Americans. *We are interested in Australia and Australians*, in fact I think you have more chance writing about Australia because, from our point of view, there are so few good Australian writers, but I think if you came to this country you could get a better impression of what fiction laid in Australia can go successfully over here and what cannot.[11]

Nonetheless, with a revised version to hand by late 1946, Reynolds was able to sell the novel to Scribner for a $750 advance. Scribner published what was the first edition in autumn 1947 – slightly retitled *You Can't See Around Corners* for American readers – a full year before Angus & Robertson's Australian edition (Fig. 9.1). They followed up with *The Sundowners* in March 1952, another commercial success, with four subsequent US editions.[12] As an internal office memo at Scribner put it, the publishers hoped *The Sundowners* "may very well break through the apathy towards Australian books (and in fact it isn't strongly 'Australian')".[13] The last comment is surprising given the novel's vernacular title and setting in the Australian bush, but the contrast perhaps was with the Australian historical sagas of the previous decade.

You Can't See Around Corners was advertised as "An Australian Prize-Winning Novel", and praised for its "hard, underplayed prose – reminiscent of Hemingway at times, plus a distinctive down-under flavour of its own".[14] *The Sundowners* was advertised alongside James Jones' bestselling *From Here to Eternity*. It certainly did break through whatever apathy there was towards Australian books, even as its Australian setting struck reviewers forcefully. The comparison with *The Grapes of Wrath* was perhaps inevitable:

> No matter what critical yardstick is employed, "The Sundowners" – Jon Cleary's second novel to reach us from down under – is a thoroughly satisfying job. Like so many

---

11   Reynolds to Cleary, 24 August 1945, Paul Reynolds Collection.
12   Reprinted in paperback by Pocket Books (1953) and Fawcett (1981). Scribner reprinted the trade edition in 1965 and 1984.
13   Burroughs Mitchell to Whitney Darrow et al., 21 May 1951, Archives of Charles Scribner's Sons, Princeton University Library Manuscripts Division, Author Files III, Box 13, Folder 1.
14   Scribner's advertisement, *New York Times*, 5 October 1947; James MacBride, "Backwash of Battle", *New York Times*, 5 October 1947.

Figure 9.1 Advertisement for Jon Cleary's *You Can't See Around Corners* (New York: Charles Scribner's Sons, 1947), *New York Times*, 5 October 1947.

Australian novels by and about Australians, the man-against-nature theme is dominant ... Yet Mr. Cleary never permits his magnificent (and, at times, terrifying) scenery to dwarf his cast. "The Sundowners" is a novel about people, first, last and always. Australia, in all its moods, is both the hero and villain of the piece. But the Carmodys, following another dusty road to yet another sunset, are as deeply human as the Joads, and just as engrossing.

... [The] reader begins to understand the strange power of Australia to set a pattern on men's lives – and to relish it almost as much as Paddy himself as the novel ends.[15]

Cleary's short stories also became popular, bringing him a considerable income from the weekly *Saturday Evening Post* as he worked on longer fiction. These early successes were hard-won, but they underwrote Cleary's long-term career: more than forty novels over seven decades, almost all from Morrow. Most significant to his success was Reynolds' devotion to establishing and consolidating his career. Cleary accepted his agent's advice to take up residence in New York to better engage with the American marketplace and wrote *The Sundowners* on Long Island during 1951. Reynolds remained Cleary's agent for most

---

15 Scribner's advertisement, *New York Times*, 30 March 1952; William Du Bois, "Paddy Was a Nomad", *New York Times*, 9 March 1952.

9 Bestsellers, Modest Sellers and Commercial Failures: The Postwar Years

of his decades-long career, one of the longest associations between an American agent and an Australian author.

A secondary impact of the war came from the publishing initiatives aimed at boosting the production of books to provide reading material for American troops stationed overseas. One of these initiatives was the US Council on Books in Wartime, the precursor of the Armed Services Editions, which produced hundreds of thousands of books for distribution overseas.[16] Only three Australian titles made it into this list: Ernestine Hill's *Australian Frontier* (1942), and less predictably two of Henry Lamond's animal stories, *Kilgour's Mare* (1943) and *Dingo: The Story of an Outlaw* (1945), released in America by Morrow at the same time. Morrow followed with Lamond's *Brindle Royalist: A Story of the Australian Plain*, a first edition, in 1946.[17] Their being noticed at all might have been the result of promotion by Australia's Department of Information, which around this time engaged the advertising company J. Walter Thompson to promote Australian books in New York, but the war also prompted local firms to seek American publication for their more successful books.

Robertson & Mullens dealt through the New York literary agent Brandt & Brandt, securing Doubleday, Doran as publisher for *Australian Frontier*, while Angus & Robertson worked directly with the Leland Heyward agency. In a statement to a 1946 Tariff Board inquiry, Angus & Robertson's Walter G. Cousins described the situation for the firm: "whereas up to 1939, it was almost impossible for us to interest an American publisher in obtaining the rights of an Australian book for sale in America, the American interest in Australia has now so increased that they are keen to consider many of our manuscripts".[18] Over the previous three or four years the firm had been able to arrange for American publication of at least eighteen Australian books. Hill, Lamond, Johnston, Osmar White, Xavier Herbert and Margaret Trist were among those to benefit, although the only long-lasting success was Arthur Upfield. Cousins lists six Upfield titles, and before the end of the 1940s, ten Bony novels had appeared in the United States, earning Upfield more money with six months' sales than he had earned in a year in his position with the Australian military.[19] Indeed, Upfield was soon in a position to deal directly with

---

16   Carol Ann Wilkinson, "Armed Services Editions", *American Literary Publishing Houses, 1900–1980*, ed. Peter Dzwonkoski, Dictionary of Literary Biography, Vol. 46 (Detroit, MI: Gale Research, 1986), 16. John B. Hench, *Books as Weapons: Propaganda, Publishing, and the Battle for Global Markets in the Era of World War II* (Ithaca, NY: Cornell University Press, 2010).

17   Ernestine Hill Papers, University of Queensland Fryer Library, UQFL18, Box 28, Folder 11. See Anna Johnston, "American Servicemen Find Ernestine Hill in their Kitbags", in *Telling Stories: Australian Life and Literature, 1935–2012*, ed. Tanya Dalziell and Paul Genoni (Clayton, Vic.: Monash University Publishing, 2013), 84-90. Lamond's works, like Hill's travelogue, had first appeared in the 1930s: *Kilgour's Mare* from Angus & Robertson in 1937 as *Amathea: The Story of a Horse*, and *Dingo* as *White Ears the Outlaw* in the *Australasian* (April-June 1934). Angus & Robertson's edition of the latter did not appear until 1949, making Morrow's the first edition. Two further Lamond novels appeared in the USA: *Kangaroo* (John Day 1953) and *Towser, Sheep Dog* (Dutton 1956).

18   W.G. Cousins in "Tariff Board Inquiry into the Publishing Industry in Australia", *Ideas: Booksellers, Stationers, Fancy Goods Journal of Australia and New Zealand* (January-February 1946): 35. Tariff Board Australia, *Tariff Board's Report on Publishing Industry* (Canberra: Commonwealth Government Printer, 1946), 14. Jason Ensor, *Angus & Robertson and the British Trade in Australian Books, 1930–1970: The Getting of Bookselling Wisdom* (London: Anthem Press, 2012), 38.

19   Travis Lindsey, "Arthur William Upfield: A Biography" (PhD thesis, Murdoch University, 2005), 158-59.

Doubleday, and Angus & Robertson could not repeat its success. Its other great hope was Australia's bestselling author Ion Idriess, but despite Angus & Robertson forwarding a dozen of his earlier books to Bobbs-Merrill, no further works were accepted as a follow-up to *Dog of the Desert*, a war story about a battalion dog, which the American firm released in 1945. Despite some references in readers' reports to the heightened profile of Australia and the Pacific in America, Idriess' other works were declined as out of date or limited in appeal "to an Australian audience and the extremely small percentage of Americans interested in Australia".[20] Despite Cousins' anticipation, direct engagement with the American market became less of a priority for the firm after the war.

No publisher since W.W. Norton with Richardson at the helm had attempted to establish an Australian list. Nonetheless, Richardson's impact and that of her contemporaries was almost certainly behind the decision by representatives from the American Book Publishers' Bureau to travel to Australia in 1945 to investigate the prospects of the Australian market for writers and readers. The visit, however, was designed more to expand the market for American books than to search for Australian products for the American market. Even so, Scribner's Whitney Darrow, for one, believed that "the war and the presence of American troops in Australia has generated a desire in America to get to know each other better ... One of the best ways of achieving this was by a more intimate study of the literature of each other's country".[21] In the same year, accepting Melbourne University's invitation, Henry Seidel Canby, celebrated Book-of-the-Month Club judge and editor of the *Saturday Review of Literature*, also visited Australia. Canby later wrote in *A New Land Speaking*, a thirty-page essay published by Melbourne University Press, that Joseph Furphy's *Such is Life* was "one of the most remarkable of frontier books in English", prefiguring the University of Chicago Press American edition of that book by almost three years.[22] High-profile visits such as these confirm that Australia had attracted the interest of the American publishing elite, but such interest was no guarantee of ready acceptance of individual writers or works.

The distance between the two markets is demonstrated by the first attempt by an American firm to set up a literary agency in Australia. By the 1940s, long-lived agencies like Paul Reynolds, Curtis Brown and A.P. Watt had been joined by competitors such as Harold Ober, Brandt & Brandt, McIntosh & Otis and Jacques Chambrun, all of whom represented a variety of Australian writers in the book and magazine market. The A. Watkins Agency Inc. was more proactive than most in working with Australian writers, setting up an office in Sydney in 1946, the first of its type. Founded in 1907 by Ann Watkins, Armitage Watkins, her son, joined the business in 1945. He had worked for the educational publishers Charles E. Merrill & Co. during the 1930s and was an intelligence officer during the Second World War before joining the Office of War Information as a publishing consultant. He was soon elevated to Assistant Chief of the Publication Division and ended his career with the military as a Liaison Officer in the Overseas Branch dealing with foreign correspondents in Washington and New York.[23] Watkins developed a strong

---

20 *Dog of the Desert* was published as *Horrie the Wog Dog* by Angus & Robertson in 1945. Quotation from a reader's report on *Lasseter's Last Ride*. Most of the books had first appeared in the 1930s. Bobbs-Merrill mss, Lilly Library, Indiana University, Box 90.
21 "USA Book Publishers' Visit", *Telegraph* (Brisbane), 1 June 1945.
22 Henry Seidel Canby, *A New Land Speaking: An Essay on the Importance of a National Literature* (Melbourne: Melbourne University Press, 1946), 14.
23 "Armitage Watkins, 83; Was a Literary Agent", *New York Times*, 22 December 1989.

9 Bestsellers, Modest Sellers and Commercial Failures: The Postwar Years

interest in Australia and made a concerted effort to find Australian writers suitable for the American magazine and book markets. To achieve this, he engaged Noëlle Brennan and Dorothy Cubis, who had worked together in government departments and at the Australian Broadcasting Commission, as representatives in Sydney. On 1 October 1946, the Noëlle Brennan literary agency opened for business in Rushcutters Bay, hoping to gather a list of Australian writers who might fulfil Watkins' wish "to further the activities of Australian writers, bringing about closer understanding between the two countries".[24] His hope was to discover "another Henry Handel Richardson".[25]

This enterprise appears to have been a complete failure, with few, if any, of the hundreds of submissions meeting Watkins' criteria for American publication. A letter to Watkins from Scribner indicates that the disappointment was widespread: "This sounds as though they had been sending you the same kind of manuscripts as we have been getting from there which we hoped would have been weeded out at the other end".[26] These included novels and short stories by E.M. England, Lyndall Hadow, V.J.A. O'Connor and Mary Pinney, none of whom achieved any success beyond Australia and only modest success within. Indeed, the enterprise seemed to attract only those writers who had failed to build significant publishing relationships in Australia and Britain.

Less than twelve months later, Watkins was signalling the demise of the venture, writing to Brennan that "the quality is so wide of the mark, in almost every case, that were the stories submitted to us by local residents of the United States we would quickly decline them".[27] Rejections were reported all round with an assessment that Australian writers were out of date. American readers were "becoming too sophisticated" for fiction like E.M. England's contrived romance *Strange Sequence*, and publishers were not willing to take a chance on anything that looked likely to sell less than 8000 copies. To support his position, Watkins enclosed a draft of an article by the Australian expatriate journalist Alwyn Lee who reported that the New York agency was embarrassed to be in "possession of some hundred Australian novels and some three hundred Australian short stories".[28] Instead of another Richardson, Watkins found only "literary fashions of thought and style which disappeared [in America] a generation ago".

Watkins' "Australian experiment", the first concerted American attempt to source Australian writing directly from Australia, came to nought and the Noëlle Brennan literary agency appears to have folded due to the New Yorker's growing disappointment. The limited success of previous initiatives and the agency's collapse reveal the differences between the two markets – the relative paucity of the Australian magazine market for

---

24   Brennan to Watkins, 26 February 1947, A. Watkins Inc. Papers, Watkins Loomis Records 1883–2007, Rare Book and Manuscript Library, Columbia University, MS 1309, Box 4, "Australia" file. All subsequent references to the Watkins experiment are drawn from this source. It appears that the initiative had the support of the US Consulate in Sydney: the Watkins papers contain a letter from Charles H. Peters, Managing Director of Robertson & Mullens, to the Consulate's Robert Burlingame (6 December 1946), thanking him for information about the agency and promising to contact him in order to help place some of its books in America. Peters mentions the firm having used Brandt & Brandt "with some measure of success but that has not been recently" – perhaps not since *Australian Frontier* in 1943.
25   Alwyn Lee, "Australian Books Boom in the US ... Maybe: American Publishers Still Seek Another H.H. Richardson", in A. Watkins Inc. papers.
26   Charles Scribner's Sons to Watkins, 7 February 1947.
27   Watkins to Brennan, 6 June 1947.
28   "Australian Books Boom in the US".

example and the absence of a strongly competitive publishing industry – and hence the difficulties of selling Australian literature to American publishers in ways that were commercially viable, whether through quality or quantity. With the rare exceptions of writers such as Upfield, Cleary or Patrick White, who dealt directly with their American publishers, success in the United States still largely depended on a push from London.

C. Hartley Grattan and the Promotion of Australian Books

As we have seen in earlier chapters, Hartley Grattan's knowledge of Australia and its potential interest to Americans made him the strongest American supporter of Australian literature in the middle decades of the twentieth century. As a reviewer, journalist, historian and commentator on foreign affairs, Grattan corresponded regularly with a long list of publishers, agents, editors and others in the publishing industry and provided private and public support for Australian writers seeking American publication. His summaries of the state of Australian literature for the *New York Times* – such as "Literature in the Antipodes" (1934), "The Literary Scene in Australia" (1937) and "Readers and Writers Down Under" (1947) – and his wide reviewing of Australian books provide rare examples of an American reader attempting to engage, not just with individual books, but with Australian literature as a field and as a social phenomenon. Following his 1947 *Times* essay, the Australian short story writer Gavin Casey, in his role as director of the Australian News and Information Bureau in New York, wrote to Grattan relating "the rather amazing results" that the piece had produced, with a flurry of interest from publishers, magazine editors and film companies.[29] And for those American readers with a more serious interest in Australian history, culture and society, Grattan's *Introducing Australia* provided the best, most up-to-date account available. First published by John Day in 1942, the book went through eight impressions during the war and a revised and expanded edition was published in 1947, the same year the University of California Press published the volume *Australia*, a collection of essays from prominent Australians compiled and introduced by Grattan. With such an extensive list of publications about Australian literature, he was frequently called on to offer advice about Australian writers and publishing prospects.

Grattan was particularly active in the 1940s. His correspondence exhibits his determination not just to promote Australian writing but to have it published, with letters to and from firms such as Norton, Appleton, Bobbs-Merrill and Morrow; but the success of his advocacy was sporadic. Inspired by the achievements of Viking's Portable Library series, Grattan proposed a "Portable Australian Literature", but Viking's Pascal Covici was reluctant. "Offhand, I wouldn't think that a Portable of Australian literature would have enough of a sale to justify its publication. Maybe it is because I know only two or three Australian writers and then, of course, I am alarmed also at the copyright situation".[30] A genuine interest in Australia and Australian writing could be found in the 1940s, but commitment to an individual publishing project was much more difficult to secure.

Despite such frustrations, Grattan took every opportunity to contribute to other initiatives as they arose, not least a special display of Australian books organised by the

---

29 Gavin Casey (via Acting Director Lloyd Clarke) to Grattan, 15 July 1947, C. Hartley Grattan Papers, Harry Ransom Research Center, University of Texas, Austin.
30 Pascal Covici to Grattan, 19 August 1946, Grattan Papers.

9 Bestsellers, Modest Sellers and Commercial Failures: The Postwar Years

Australian Government Trade Commission in New York's Rockefeller Center during the last months of 1948. In the optimistic words of the Commission's press release: "American interest in Australia has led to an increasing public demand throughout the USA for Australian books. These are now established as an important trade item". Casey enlisted Grattan to write a comment about the display, a mixed bag that included copies of the American editions of Dark's *The Timeless Land*, Cleary's *You Can't See Around Corners*, Furphy's *Such is Life*, Tennant's *The Battlers*, Patrick White's *The Aunt's Story*, Norman Lindsay's *Age of Consent*, John Ewers' *Written in Sand* and Joan Colebrook's *The Northerner*. Recruiting his American readers to the cause, Grattan declared: "It is surprising indeed how many [Americans] recall with pleasure that they have read a novel or two by H.H. Richardson, Eleanor Dark, Patrick White, Xavier Herbert, Christina Stead, Robert Close, Katharine Prichard, Barnard Eldershaw, Brian Penton, Leonard Mann, Dalby Davison – all of whom have had books published in America in recent years. Readers of detective stories have had a whole string of books by Arthur Upfield". He concluded, "it cannot be long before it is generally recognized that the Australian writers are working a rich vein of human experience" and, more pointedly, that "no overseas people are so well prepared as the Americans to savour their quality to the full".[31]

At the same time, Grattan was forced to accept that most Australian writers would still only be recognised by American publishers if they had first been taken up in the British market, continuing what had been the state of play for almost a hundred years. In 1943 he wrote to author Dal Stivens, who was keen to find an American publisher: "Australian writers have long thought that London was a bottleneck as far as 'dinkum' Australian books are concerned and have looked to New York with hope. Now that New York is opening up, it seems that only what gets through the London barricade can get here".[32] In certain ways this was an unduly pessimistic account, for as we've shown there were important exceptions to this rule, books that made their way directly to American publishers or agents, and authors who achieved a level of success in the United States they never managed in the British sphere. Grattan's viewpoint is a product of his own sense of what were the "dinkum" Australian books, those that *should* be published in the United States, those that contributed to the establishment of a truly national literature. But there was still a good deal of truth in the statement.

Modest Success in the Mid-List: Kylie Tennant

Beginning with her novel of the Australian backblocks, *The Battlers*, Tennant forged a strong relationship with Macmillan's New York office that produced four American editions during the 1940s, a testament to her status as a modest, yet profitable seller. Finding a place in the market for fiction that rode the wave of John Steinbeck's success with *The Grapes of Wrath* – and anticipating the reception of Cleary's *The Sundowners* – Tennant probably had more readers in New York than in Australia, demonstrating that fiction with distinctive Australian settings and characters could still find a place in the

---

31 Press Release, Office of the Australian Government Trade Commissioner, 17 November 1948. Grattan Papers.
32 Laurie Hergenhan, *No Casual Traveller: Hartley Grattan and Australia–US Connections* (St Lucia: University of Queensland Press, 1995), 191.

American market if it was "legible" within that market. *The Battlers* was promoted and read as "a sort of *Grapes of Wrath* of Australia".[33] Her novels invoked literary comparisons from reviewers, but they also had to find a place in the mainstream commercial fiction market where relatively few authors or books from elsewhere were bestsellers.

When Tennant sat down to write *The Battlers*, her third novel, in her Dulwich Hill home in Sydney's inner western suburbs, she had already won one of Australia's major literary prizes and she was contracted to London publisher Gollancz for her next novel. In the spring of 1938 she had spent several months on the track with the unemployed and itinerant workers of rural New South Wales, collecting data that would inform the social realism of her new book. The novel was finished by January 1940 and typescripts were prepared for transmission to prospective publishers.[34] With an option on Tennant's next novel after publishing *Foveaux* in 1939, Gollancz acknowledged receipt of the first typescript and accepted *The Battlers* on 25 June 1940. No contract for *The Battlers* is extant, but a Gollancz statement shows that Tennant agreed to a 10 per cent royalty on the first 2000 copies, rising to 15 per cent beyond that. A small but significant fee on the statement was that for copyright in the United States of America, revealing that the novel was being considered for publication in New York.[35]

Curtis Brown had tested the American market with *Fouveaux*, a novel of Australia's urban working poor, sending the book to at least twelve publishers, but all exercised caution and passed on what they judged to be an interesting but commercially unviable book, for some in part because of its Australian content. Bobbs-Merrill expressed the most interest: "There is too much irrelevant material, but complained that there was "too much irrelevant material, too much abrupt switching from one group of characters to another, [making] the book too much of a publishing risk".[36] Others expressed similar reservations. Harper admitted, "we aren't sufficiently sure of its sales possibilities in this country"; for Houghton Mifflin, "its remote scene will make it seem unimportant to the general reading public here"; and for Putnam, "We think readers would have to have a really considerable knowledge of and interest in Australian life to be interested in it".[37]

Despite this setback, Curtis Brown were enthusiastic about *The Battlers'* chances in the United States. On the back of brisk sales in London from the outset, Curtis Brown Snr wrote to Tennant and forecast a bright future: "I can't quite see *The Battlers* adding to your riches with film or second-serial rights; but I *can* foresee another book from you that will achieve both serial and film rights".[38] More to the point, he added a handwritten addendum to the typed letter insisting on the book's potential in the US market: "I am sending a copy of this letter to our New York Office. We *must* find an American publisher for this book". The New York office worked fast, but had little good news to report when writing to Tennant a week later. The novel had been rejected by four publishers and an

---

33 *Book-of-the-Month Club News*, October 1941, 18.
34 Details here and below sourced from the Kylie Tennant Papers, National Library of Australia, MS10043.
35 Tennant was paid an agreed £40 advance on the novel's publication on 9 January 1941. By 25 March, 2561 copies had been sold in London and 457 copies had been sent overseas, most to Australia. Royalties were halved by the usual subtractions, leaving Tennant with £45 11s 10d.
36 Constance B. Sheldon (Curtis Brown New York) to Tennant, 5 January 1940. Tennant Papers, Box 5, Folder 35. All subsequent correspondence from this source unless otherwise indicated.
37 Sheldon to Tennant, 5 January 1940.
38 Curtis Brown Snr to Tennant, 21 January 1941.

9 Bestsellers, Modest Sellers and Commercial Failures: The Postwar Years

extract from Lippincott's response revealed their reasons: "The weakness of the thing as I see it is that it is a picaresque narrative without any plotting beyond the sequence of adventures through which the characters go".[39] Lippincott acknowledged that it was "an eminently publishable book" but did not think "it would do much in the way of sales". Curtis Brown persisted until it found a publisher willing to take the risk.

Macmillan had published several of Dark's books by this time and had already accepted *The Timeless Land* when *The Battlers* (Plate 9) arrived for their consideration. However, there is no evidence to suggest that Dark's success influenced the decision to take on *The Battlers* or that the two novels were accepted to provide an Australian focus or list; indeed, there is no mention of the other novel in either Dark's or Tennant's extant business correspondence. They were not advertised together and the selection of *The Timeless Land* by the Book-of-the-Month Club gave Dark a much greater profile. Nonetheless, Tennant was granted a $250 advance on 25 July 1941, again losing almost $100 of this to taxes, commissions and miscellaneous fees. Macmillan might not have expected *The Battlers* to sell many copies and, based on a later contract, probably offered a 10 per cent royalty on the first 5000 sold. It is not known how many copies it printed, but a modest sale of 1126 had been achieved by 30 April 1942. Sales quickly dropped off and only 477 copies were sold in the following twelve months, but after her advance had been earned out Tennant earned additional royalties of close to $160 in the two years after publication. Combined with a largely positive reception, this record helped establish Tennant's standing as a reliable mid-list writer.

Copies of *The Battlers* were sent to reviewers across the United States, attracting a generally warm reception, often along the lines of the review in Indiana's *South Bend Tribune*: "'The Battlers' is a many-sided story. For insight into certain phases of life in Australia it is invaluable. As a study of humanity, irrespective of race, it is impressive. Whether it is approached for information or diversion it will be found worth reading".[40] The *Kansas City Star* remarked tht "'The Battlers' seems to confirm ... that of all other people, the Australians are most akin to Americans". Many reviewers followed Macmillan's promotional material that presented *The Battlers* as an Australian *Grapes of Wrath* or, in the publisher's words, as "The 'Oakies' Down-Under" (Fig. 9.2).[41] Steinbeck's novel had been made into an award-winning film in 1940 providing a major reference point. The *Saturday Review* announced "The 'Oakies' of Australia", while for Milton Merlin in the *LA Times*, Tennant had the "Steinbeck touch".[42] While reviewers acknowledged the similarities they also noted differences, sometimes in Tennant's favour. For Boston's *Morning Globe*: "Steinbeck is a master of scorn and fury. Tennant is a good writer with a story to tell". For the *Washington Post*, Tennant's novel was "not weighed down with a lot of self-conscious sociological preaching and false sentimentality (yes, I mean you, John Steinbeck)".[43]

---

39 Naomi Burton (Curtis Brown New York) to Tennant, 28 January 1941.
40 The Tennant Papers include several scrapbooks that contain cuttings sent from various clipping agencies in England and the United States. In many cases, dates are obscured. All reviews are taken from this source unless otherwise indicated.
41 Macmillan advertisement, *New York Times*, 31 August 1941.
42 Klaus Lambrecht, "The 'Oakies' of Australia", *Saturday Review of Literature*, 9 August 1941, 7; Milton Merlin, "Australian Nomads Form Vivid Parade", *Los Angeles Times*, 17 August 1941: *The Battlers* added "a new and original chapter in the history of peoples on the move, a chapter with moments of gayety and beauty as well as gravity and mishap".
43 John T. Appleby, *Washington Post*, 10 August 1941.

Figure 9.2 Kylie Tennant's *The Battlers* (New York: Macmillan, 1941) advertised in the *New York Times*, 31 August 1941.

9 Bestsellers, Modest Sellers and Commercial Failures: The Postwar Years

Tennant's story-telling was thus widely praised with only a few baulking at the novel's potential obscurity to American readers. Again an Australian novel commanded a whole "Books of the Times" column, where Ralph Thompson, thoroughly enjoying himself, suggested the need for a glossary: "the richness of Australian slang is something to make even the editors of *Variety* jealous".[44] He summoned the *Grapes of Wrath* comparison but qualified it, for while the Joads of Oklahoma were forced to become migrants, for Tennant's cast of battlers "it is a way of life; they love it and wouldn't stay put if they were nailed down". While as a story Thompson thought the novel "conventional enough and none too remarkable", he also declared it "almost solid with local color and amusing detail, and the atmosphere is the genuine atmosphere of back country New South Wales". Beatrice Murphy of Washington DC's *Afro American* suggested that in Dick Tyrell's relationship with brown-skinned Mary Burns, "We are once more reminded that the so-called 'race-problem' is not exclusively an American problem".

Christina Stead reviewed *The Battlers* for *New Masses*, and in praising the book she rejected the easy comparison with Steinbeck (perhaps unsurprisingly given her judgement of his fiction) and drew a more demanding link to Gorky. Tennant's battlers "are not the suddenly unlanded farmers of *The Grapes of Wrath*, but Gorky's wanderers, the perpetually expelled and disinherited, who must walk till times change". Stead's review offered a powerful, evocative account of the battlers, their social circumstances, and the history that had made them:

> *The Battlers* is a story of the dispossessed of eastern Australia ... They know Australia better than any others; and they feel they are the true people of the land, they are its heart. So did Gorky's wanderers feel ...
>
> The drama is great that lies behind the great canvas of this book. These people are the victims of an antique system which took over a vast continent with the simplehearted notion of sending chain gangs there to work in peonage for a few high caste land owners. That has changed because the exploitation of the land has become more efficient. But it is still woefully out of date. Australia is a kind of czarist Siberia in the South Pacific ...
>
> Mrs. Tennant has painted the picture as clear and moving as one of Steinlen's great cartoons ... [The novel's] splendid double-meant title is symbolic of the book.[45]

The only review to match Stead's sense of the novel's social dimensions was Jane Spence Southron's in the *New York Times*: "It is the story of an unregimentable breed facing the unemployment of pre-war and early war days in its own way; accepting government aid, as a right, on its own terms ... Battlers is the author's term: significant of a definite quality, a definite attitude to life, a definite determination". *The Battlers*, she concluded, is "a book whose outstanding feature is the sort of strength that compels admiration".[46]

Tennant's subsequent novels all paid their way in New York. Macmillan followed *The Battlers* with *Ride on Stranger* and *Time Enough Later* in 1943, and *Lost Haven* in 1946, the final two titles appearing in New York before London. Sales and royalty statements from Macmillan and Curtis Brown show that all earned out their advances and continued to

---

44 Ralph Thompson, "Books of the Times", *New York Times*, 11 August 1941.
45 Christina Stead, "Wandering Workers", *New Masses*, 30 September 1941, 25-26.
46 Jane Spence Southron, "Unbeatable Breed", *New York Times*, 10 August 1941. Southron also saw the battlers' qualities as a "preview" of those shown in Australia's war effort.

produce royalties throughout the 1940s. Sales numbers suggest that Macmillan produced small but standard print runs of around three thousand copies. *Lost Haven*, informed by Tennant's time living in a fishing village and working as a boat repairer, achieved sales of 1612 copies by 29 July 1946, not enough to clear Tennant's $325 advance, but by the end of the next royalties period an additional 1197 copies had been sold, producing earnings of $313.[47] Tennant's sales never came close to 10,000, but Macmillan accepted such levels as "satisfactory".[48] Macmillan's Harold S. Latham wrote to Tennant to report on the progress of *Time Enough Later*:

> You will be interested to know that *Time Enough Later*, which was published on February 10th, is off to a nice start. We have sent out approximately 1400 copies so far, including both outright sales and consignment copies, the latter subject to return if not sold. Of course this is not a big sale, but few novels these days are enjoying big sales, and we are hopeful that *Time Enough Later* will build slowly but surely to a satisfactory total.[49]

With her style and content, Tennant was seen as a strong contender to expand interest in Australia and so to increase the opportunities for Australian books. The hope that Tennant's work might overcome the "apathy towards the Australian scene" in America, related in Chapter 7, came in a letter to the author from Curtis Brown's Naomi Burton in February 1946. Burton was quoting a report from the American magazine *News of Books*: "there is another [novel] coming, *Lost Haven* by the Australian author, Kylie Tennant, a lady who can write in anyone's league. Perhaps in the near future apathy towards the Australian scene, which few books have been able to hurdle, may be destroyed".[50] This undercurrent of apathy towards Australian books among American publishers and readers – echoing the Scribner office memo about Cleary's *The Sundowners* quoted earlier – suggests the difficulty facing Australian writers, especially for those who did not fit easily within a particular field or genre such as the historical novel, popular romance or crime.

Grattan reviewed *Ride on Stranger* for the *New York Times* and used the opportunity to sum up Tennant's oeuvre to that point: of her five novels, two were memorable, especially *The Battlers*; one was "definitely phony" (*Foveaux*); and two were "clever but light" (*Time Enough Later* and now *Ride on Stranger*).[51] Grattan had a good deal of respect for Tennant's humour, intelligence and story-telling capacities, and the new novel could show American readers that Sydney had elements of Greenwich Village, but she had "more important work to do" than *Ride on Stranger* had achieved. With the exception of *The Battlers*, Tennant did not quite meet Grattan's demanding criteria for the national literature. Without such demands, other reviewers could simply enjoy Tennant's novels – the "flow of fun and spurts of wit", the "vigorous prose [and] cutting dialogue", and not least her Australian settings.[52] She was known and enjoyed enough to command another "Books of the Times" column, on *Time Enough Later*, accompanied by the author's portrait, while Irene Elwood in the *LA*

---

47 Macmillan Statement, "Lost Haven", 29 July 1946. Tennant Papers.
48 Curtis Brown to Tennant, 26 March 1943.
49 Harold S. Latham (Macmillan, New York) to Tennant, 26 March 1943, Tennant Papers, Box 1, Folder 11.
50 Burton to Tennant, 26 February 1946, Tennant Papers, Box 1, Folder 11.
51 C. Hartley Grattan, "Bohemia Down Under", *New York Times*, 12 September 1943.
52 Charlotte Dean, "Vacation from Bohemia", *New York Times*, 14 February 1943; John Chamberlain, "Books of the Times", *New York Times*, 9 February 1943.

9 Bestsellers, Modest Sellers and Commercial Failures: The Postwar Years

Times was able to summon the *type* of "a novel by Kylie Tennant" as if her readers would know and value the reference.[53]

Stead also reviewed Tennant once more, in a review of three "Tales from Down Under" in the *New York Times*: Tennant's *Lost Haven*, Norman Lindsay's *Cousin from Fiji* and Margaret Trist's *Sun on the Hills*, all recently published in the United States.[54] While acknowledging their entertaining qualities, Stead dismissed Lindsay's and Trist's books as "easy-reading" summer novels. *Cousin from Fiji* was contrasted to Lindsay's major achievements as an artist; Trist was "a good writer of the popular magazine variety". Tennant had more to offer, even in this "small story". What Stead finds in Tennant's writing is "the power of the author", even if that power was not yet fully realised:

> She has the poet's soul and spleen. She is not soured, she likes humanity; but she has the relation to humanity of other poets; a cloud, a man, a suffering, a fit of temper, a murder, can be equal in her feelings. This makes her rather cold to her characters, even when she has the warmest feeling for them.
>
> ... The real talent often tries to submerge itself in anonymity and poverty to get that solitude its growth requires ... The artist ... has to wait for complete expression, until he can love something; and we must perhaps wait till Kylie Tennant has found a love, no doubt as impersonal and austere as her unvicious misanthropy.

The final phrases might well have been applied to Stead herself. In concluding her review, Stead noted the similarities in "the picture of Australian life" offered by all three books, a picture of an easygoing, egalitarian society that is, she argues, both "true and false". Most acutely, she suspected that this particular batch of titles indicated the predilections of American publishers more than the present state of Australian writing: "One wonders if the publishers have not had a hand in this odd selection of material, for certainly other books are written by other Australians about other types of my countrymen."

Perhaps the artist in Tennant never did achieve complete expression, certainly not for the American marketplace. Following *Lost Haven*, two later novels and Tennant's historical work, *Australia: Her Story*, were released by the St Martin's Press, which had been established in New York in 1952 by the UK Macmillan & Co. to distribute its books that did not have an American publisher.[55] This suggests that Macmillan New York stopped pursuing Tennant's new books. Nonetheless, like Dark, Tennant maintained a profile in America that supported the publication of a sequence of novels, four in five years. Even if her entertaining social realism failed to capture the attention of as many American readers as Dark's historical fiction, she achieved regular, reliable sales and good reviews, and received a modest return for her work. Reviewing *Time Enough Later* in the *New York Times*, Charlotte Dean wrote appreciatively that "Miss Tennant, from Australia, will have all of us wanting to go there to live if she keeps on writing books like this one about it".[56]

---

53   Chamberlain, "Books of the Times". His theme was the new phenomenon of female authors hunting down poor specimens of "the male animal"; Irene Elwood, "Revival of Buried Scandal Arouses Decadent Village", *Los Angeles Times*, 31 March 1946.
54   Christina Stead, "Tales from Down Under", *New York Times*, 7 April 1946.
55   *The Joyful Condemned* (an abridged version of *Time Enough Later*) and *Australia: Her Story* in 1953; *The Honey Flow* in 1956; and a book of short stories, *Ma Jones and the Little White Cannibals*, in 1967.
56   Dean, "Vacation from Bohemia".

Tennant's career suggests that there were possibilities in postwar America for Australian authors with mid-range or mid-list careers, even if for overseas authors this was the most difficult position of all in which to thrive.

Postwar Careers

As we have seen, several attempts to establish a place for Australian books in American print culture occurred in the later forties. American publishers' representatives visited Australia in 1945, Armitage Watkins set up his Sydney agency in 1946, and the Australian Trade Commission mounted a display of books in New York in 1948. Otherwise American publishers went about their business as they had always done, book by book. Mainstream publishing consolidated after the war, with a clearer demarcation of genre fiction, not only from literary fiction but also from the mainstream of "good commercial fiction", in the words of long-time Book-of-the-Month Club president and Viking editor Al Silverman.[57] A small number of Australian novels and novelists entered this mainstream in the late 1940s. With the support of Angus & Robertson and American literary agent Frances Pindyck of Leland Hayward, Margaret Trist was able to place her first novel, *Now that We're Laughing*, with Harper, released in 1946 as *Sun on the Hills*. It sold around 3500 copies, possibly 4000, and as Elizabeth Lawrence from Harper put it: "While the sale was not sensational, it was highly respectable for an unknown novelist and considering of the fact that it treated of the war period". Her guess was that "the bulk of the reorders came from the Book-of-the-Month Club which gave it a very nice mention in their monthly Bulletin".[58] Lawrence had sent proofs of the novel to Christina Stead, but Stead's reply was uncompromising: "I am quite ashamed of this book, because I know so much better exists (and even take the books that have been published here, from Australian writers still living in Australia not to mention Richardson)".[59] Harper, however, was keen to publish a follow-up novel and Lawrence offered Trist detailed advice on revisions, but it finally rejected "Daddy" as a weaker novel – "we are extremely doubtful of its sales chances in the present rather precarious market". Lawrence encouraged Trist to write the novel of "larger range" she was sure Trist was capable of, but a later story proposal was also rejected. After a substantial gap, Harper also decided they could not publish "The Walls Whisper" despite their readers being enchanted by it. They forwarded the manuscript to agent Mavis McIntosh; perhaps this was an early version of *Morning in Queensland*, released by Lippincott in 1958 (its first edition).

Eric Baume found success with *Yankee Woman* (the American title of *Sydney Duck*), released by Dodd, Mead in 1945, a sensational story of Australian gangs in San Francisco during the mid-nineteenth century that he would later call his "second worst novel".[60] Dodd, Mead followed with *I'll Always Be with You* (1946), *Ponty Galler* (1947) and *Devil Lord's Daughter* (1948). Baume's biographer admits the literary quality of these works

---

57 Al Silverman, *The Time of Their Lives: The Golden Age of Great American Book Publishers, Their Editors and Authors* (New York: Truman Tally-St Martin's, 2008), 12.
58 Lawrence to Trist, 23 July 1946, Harper and Brothers Publishing Archive. Subsequent references: Lawrence to Trist 19 May 1947, 19 August 1949, 2 May 1957.
59 Stead to Lawrence, 5 October 1945, Harper and Brothers Publishing Archive, Harry Ransom Center, University of Texas, Austin.
60 Arthur Manning, *Larger than Life: The Story of Eric Baume* (Sydney: Reed, 1967), 106.

9 Bestsellers, Modest Sellers and Commercial Failures: The Postwar Years

was low, but attributes his success to the circumstances of the war as they appeared "at a time when the supply of books was reasonably short in the United States and completely inadequate for the demands of the book-hungry servicemen and civilians in England".[61] In 1947, Robert S. Close, still in the midst of legal action in Melbourne concerning his "obscene" first novel *Love Me Sailor*, had *The Dupe: A Story of the Sea* published by the quality Vanguard Press. As the publisher's advertisement enticingly put it: "A new Australian writer magnificently conjures up the sea and all its torments in this tale of sadism and terror".[62] *Love Me Sailor* itself was published by Frederick Fell in New York in October 1950, then in paperback by the Popular Library in 1952.[63] Two further titles appeared: *Eliza Callaghan*, a novel of convict Tasmania, released first by paperback genre publishers Ace as *Penal Colony* in 1957, then under its original title by Doubleday in 1958; and *With Hooves of Brass*, also from Doubleday, in 1961. Grattan reviewed *Eliza Callaghan*, on Australia Day as it happened, as "a realistic historical story, replete with sex, booze, violence and malevolence".[64] That was the good news, for Grattan suggested such themes were justifiable given the novel's historical setting. What he found "annoying" was the "romantic improbability" of convict Eliza marrying the historical figure of John Batman, founder of Melbourne, which destroyed the novel's otherwise convincing realism. "American readers should be warned", Grattan advised, that Close had little or no evidence for his plot. But this time, it appears, Grattan's historical knowledge of Australia was wanting. Close responded to the review with a letter to the *New York Times* detailing his historical evidence and attacking Grattan's review as "a preposterous piece of writing wherein presumption postures as knowledge, and impertinence struts to screen ignorance".[65]

Ruth Park began her American career with *The Harp in the South*, from Houghton Mifflin, in 1948, two years after it had won the *Sydney Morning Herald* Literary Competition ahead of Cleary's *You Can't See Round Corners*.[66] Two more novels appeared from Houghton Mifflin, *Poor Man's Orange* (as *12½ Plymouth Street*) in 1951 and *The Witch's Thorn* in 1952, then a series of titles from other publishers in later decades, six adult novels in total. It was Grattan who reviewed *12½ Plymouth Street* for the *Times*, and again he was able to place the single novel in a larger context, recalling *The Harp in the South* and comparing Park's new novel with Louis Stone's *Jonah* and Tennant's *Foveaux* as "Australian studies of slum life".[67] Rarely, he felt, had anybody "written of the lower depths

---

61 Manning, *Larger than Life*, 106.
62 Vanguard Press advertisement, *New York Times*, 7 December 1947.
63 The *New York Times* "Books and Authors" column (30 September 1950) announced the book's impending release with suggestive understatement: "The novel deals with the ill-fated voyage of a sailing ship from Chile to San Francisco with a cargo of nitrates, a crew of twenty-four men, and a woman".
64 "Batman's Bride", *New York Times*, 26 January 1958.
65 "Letters to the Editor: Eliza Callaghan", *New York Times*, 23 March 1958. Close wrote from Cannes, France, following his departure from Australia in 1950.
66 Park had been offered a job on the *San Francisco Examiner* but the war stopped her travel plans: Ruth Park, *Fishing in the Styx* (Ringwood, Vic.: Penguin, 1994), 16. The American careers of Park and her husband D'Arcy Niland are recorded in the Ruth Park and D'Arcy Niland Papers held at the Mitchell Library, State Library of New South Wales. Restricted until 2020, these papers will provide important evidence for future studies of this period.
67 C. Hartley Grattan, "The Lower Depths", *New York Times*, 28 January 1951.

of any society with such humane sympathy", although "dour critics" might find that Park's novels lacked the power that more art might have given them.

The apathy towards Australia and its books that had been reported to Tennant and Cleary could be overcome as these examples suggest, often by the enthusiasm of an individual publisher, editor or agent; and sometimes still the Australian setting was the hook that grabbed the individual's attention. One such case was Joan Colebrook's *The Northerners*; or perhaps this is rather a case of what might have been, for the protracted process of editing and revising Colebrook's sprawling manuscript was overseen by the great American editor Maxwell Perkins.

Colebrook was born in North Queensland, growing up in the rural environment she would eventually draw on for her best-known novel. She studied at the University of Queensland in Brisbane, and attempted to make a living as a freelance writer in the 1930s, publishing poetry and fiction in northern newspapers and southern magazines. She married Mulford Colebrook, an American diplomat, and moved with him to London before eventually settling in the United States. Her first novel, *All That Seemed Final*, was published by Houghton Mifflin in 1941. Set in wartime Europe, *Kirkus Review* labelled it "a woman's book, tight keyed, effective, a little inconclusive – and very readable".[68] But disappointing sales prompted Houghton Mifflin to pass on Colebrook's second novel, an unwieldy manuscript that required significant editorial work.

Scribner were prepared to offer a contract, however, and assigned the book to Perkins who had played such a prominent editorial role in the work of Hemingway, Fitzgerald and, most famously, Thomas Wolfe. Another Wolfean task seemed at hand. Perkins worked with Colebrook to reduce the bulk of "Kiss Your Father", but failed to reach a length suitable for publication. All at Scribner saw promise in the novel: an anonymous reader's report directed attention to the region covered, explaining that "from the publicity point of view the proximity to New Guinea & the islands might have some value", while Perkins reassured Colebrook that "Americans know about pioneers from their own tradition, and they will quickly catch on to the general ways of life and to the newness of the troubles of a little while before".[69] In May 1945, he pointed to the contemporary interest in Australia that made the work distinctly marketable:

[E]verybody – well, Henry Canby of the BOMC, for instance, and others – is on the lookout for an Australian novel. Some of them went on a junket down there during the war, and went over the whole publishing situation. As a result of this, two prize-winning serials from an Australian paper came to us. And we accepted the second, which was the better, but neither amounted to anything to speak of, nor did they reflect Australian life. One might as well have been in the London slums, and the other in the United States. You are writing a real novel about Australia that does give you the quality of the country, and the people, so don't take too long about it. Let us get it out before the edge is taken off that special interest.[70]

---

68 *Kirkus Review*, 21 October 1941, https://bit.ly/2MlF8Az.
69 Reader's report for "Kiss Your Father", undated, Charles Scribner Records. Perkins to Colebrook, 29 May 1945, Charles Scribner Records, Princeton University, Author Files II, Box 9, Folder 7.
70 Perkins to Colebrook, 6 February 1947, Charles Scribner Records.

9 Bestsellers, Modest Sellers and Commercial Failures: The Postwar Years

Perkins' easy dismissal of Cleary's *You Can't See Around Corners* and Park's *The Harp in the South* suggest that he saw a significant difference in the form and content of Colebrook's bulky manuscript. But time was of the essence to take advantage of the "special interest" in Australia.

Even Perkins' experience honing Wolfe's manuscripts was put to the test by Colebrook's. He was committed to the task but did not live to see the book published, dying in May 1947. Burroughs Mitchell took over the editing and insisted that Colebrook shorten the novel. But a combination of Colebrook's resistance and loyalty to Perkins meant the book was published, in 1948, before it was completed to the satisfaction of Scribner's editors. Advance sales of 1000 copies suggested that Perkins' faith in Colebrook might have been justified, but few copies were sold beyond that. By the end of the 1940s, the edge had been taken off the special interest in Australia that Perkins had detected among his peers and reviewers were more likely to note the novel's sexual content.[71]

An Australian Classic in Chicago: Furphy's *Such is Life*

In his 1947 survey of Australian literature for the *New York Times*, Grattan announced his pick of the most notable Australian novels from the period 1939 to 1946.[72] Interesting as much for the novels he leaves out as for those he includes, Grattan offers Langley's *The Pea Pickers*, Tennant's *The Battlers*, Dark's *The Timeless Land* and *The Little Company*, Lindsay's *The Cousin from Fiji*, Leonard Mann's *The Go-Getter* and Trist's *Now That We're Laughing* (he used the Australian titles). He also notes Richardson's passing and nominates Katharine Susannah Prichard her natural successor as "the most important fiction writer of Australia". The notable absences from Grattan's summary are Patrick White and Christina Stead, both of whom had established reputations in the United States by 1947, and, perhaps less surprisingly, Arthur Upfield, despite his burst of success at this time. He would list them in his blurb the following year for the Australian Trade Commission's display of books.

As noted above, the display included White's *The Aunt's Story*, alongside American editions of *The Battlers*, *The Timeless Land*, Lindsay's *Age of Consent* (published in paperback in 1948), Colebrook's *The Northerner* and Cleary's *You Can't See Around Corners* – books selected as official representatives of Australia's recent literary output, but also, given the Commission's brief, as examples of tradeable commodities. In addition to these recently published novels, the Commission's display also included the American edition of Joseph Furphy's *Such is Life*, a novel first published in Sydney in 1903 by the Bulletin Newspaper Co. Published by the University of Chicago Press in 1948, this was the first American edition of a culturally sanctioned Australian "classic" from the past, an expression, perhaps, of an emerging sense in America of Australian literature as a distinct and distinguished national literature. Publishing a literary classic was a different proposition from taking on a new novel by an unknown author from overseas, but given

---

71 "A protracted two generation story of personal lives, particular national issues, with phases which may prove a hurdle to conservative public library standards", *Kirkus Review*, 25 October 1948, https://bit.ly/2sS9x1n; "The assumptions of Freud lie behind the behaviour of her people, and I have not seen anywhere such clinical detail of the feminine side of love-making", Bradford Smith, *Saturday Review of Literature*, 18 December 1948, 18. In June 1950, 1719 copies of *The Northerners* were remaindered. Colebrook subsequently submitted two additional novels, but Scribner rejected both and returned the copyright of *The Northerners* to the author in August 1961.

72 C. Hartley Grattan, "Readers and Writers Down Under", *New York Times*, 22 June 1947.

the novel's provenance the risks were much the same. As it turned out, the book failed to capture the attention either of the general reading public or of a specialist audience that might have been attuned to the intentions of the Press, and the Press suffered a significant loss on its investment. If *The Timeless Land* was a bestseller and *The Battlers* a modest success, *Such is Life* proved to be a complete commercial failure.

Furphy had only recently been canonised in a significant way in Australia. The centenary of his birth was marked by *Meanjin* in 1943, and together with Jonathan Cape in London, Angus & Robertson had published a new edition of *Such is Life* in 1944. A special issue of *Southerly* was published in the same year, as was the first book-length study of Furphy's life and work, Miles Franklin and Kate Baker's *Joseph Furphy: The Legend of the Man and His Book*. These celebrations and vigorous debates raised awareness of the novel and had a positive effect on sales in Australia: almost three thousand copies of the new edition were sold in 1944 and a further five thousand the following year before sales returned to pre-celebration lows. Much more than a simple publishing event, the re-emergence of Furphy and *Such is Life* in the 1940s animated Australia's literary culture and began to attract international attention.

The production of the American edition would take a familiar course via Grattan's advocacy, but without the initial support of a figure unknown to Australian literary history the project would probably have never begun. Grattan had published an article on *Such is Life* in the *Australian Quarterly* in 1937, but it was Howard Daniel, a Sydney University graduate, who initiated interest in the novel as a publishing project. Daniel worked for some time in Washington for the Australian Purchasing Commission before beginning a long career with the United Nations Economic Commission. He is best known in Australia as an art collector, but his position as a University of Chicago Press author brought him into contact with the Press's editor, John Scoon:

> In discussing some of his current publications with him I discovered that he had just started a series of "classics" from lesser known countries about whose literature even educated Americans were ignorant. I became particularly interested in his Brazilian "Classic"; this was the extraordinary work of da Cunha: "Rebellion in the Backlands". After reading this work I suggested to Scoon that he might consider an Australian classic which was completely dissimilar in subject matter to da Cunha's work but which had certain things in common with it. I lent him my Jonathan Cape edition. He read this immediately, was very enthusiastic, said he would bring out an American edition, and asked me to write a foreword. With an excess of modesty I told him that my friend C. Hartley Grattan, an American with a great deal of knowledge of Australia, would be a more appropriate person to prepare an introduction.[73]

Scoon began investigating Daniel's proposition during 1944. On 22 July, Grattan sent a long reply to a request from Scoon for advice on the project, urging the editor not to consider Vance Palmer's abridged version of the novel which had been published in 1937 and suggesting that a small sale of 3000 copies was all that could be expected. While warning that *Such is Life* "is not an easy book to read [being] neither novel nor autobiography nor essay", Grattan advised Scoon that "if the book is read and digested more will be learned about the outlook of the Australian common man than from any other single source".[74] He also advised that readers

---

73 Howard Daniel, "The Genesis of the American Edition of 'Such is Life'", *Biblionews* 5, no. 12 (1952): 42.

would be assisted by a substantial introduction written to "'place' the book for American readers and to supply the necessary personal and general background information". Beyond its obvious historical interest, *Such is Life* expressed "a set of values, which are alive in Australia" and which "bear constant reassertion for the good of the community". In Grattan's words, if the Press accepted the book "the cult of slick writing will not be advanced"; but a relatively small group of discerning readers would receive unrivalled intellectual benefit and historical understanding.

Scoon also recruited E.K. Brown, a University of Chicago English Professor, to provide an assessment, but almost two years passed before the Press proceeded any further. At this time, the esteemed Scottish literary historian David Daiches was asked to provide reader's reports on both *Such is Life* and *Rigby's Romance*.[75] Daiches had been at the university from 1937 to 1943, and was still in the United States.[76] While the Press was probably as much concerned with the prestige of the project as with profit, it still sought reassurance regarding its commercial viability and from someone further removed from the Australian scene than Grattan. Scoon planned to produce a trilogy of books, comprising *Such is Life*, *Rigby's Romance* and a specially commissioned biography of Furphy. For this, Daiches provided a very positive report, recommending publication because of the similarity of the frontier traditions that had been "so far unexpressed in fiction" by either Australian or American writers.[77] Looking to Sterne's *Tristram Shandy* for comparison, Daiches accepted the book's lack of plot, but suggested that the author "leans on his personality rather too deliberately"; this was acceptable in the older example, he reasoned, "but in a book which is essentially the saga of a new country the author should put the atmosphere of that country and its society before that which derives from his own idiosyncrasies". Nevertheless, Daiches conceded that it was this personality that "gives life" to the book and suggested that "a trilogy would be a remarkable chapter in Australian life and letters". With Daiches' belief that *Such is Life* "might well have an excellent sale", publication was approved on 10 May 1946.[78]

Scoon had suggested Vance Palmer and Grattan as possible biographers to Daiches. Daiches admitted that he had only heard of the latter, but believed Grattan would "do a first rate job".[79] From Grattan, Scoon received the advice that the possibility of a trilogy would rest on the success or failure of *Such is Life*. Grattan nominated himself as a suitable biographer, but suggested a biographical introduction would be more suitable than a separate volume because of the lack of primary evidence. In the published biographical sketch, Grattan described *Such is Life* as "by general acknowledgement an Australian classic, one may as well say *the* Australian classic", and provided his American readers with substantial textual, biographical and historical information to help them place the novel in Australian and American print culture. He warned readers to pay close attention to the plotless complexity of the diary entries that Furphy used as a narrative device, for a careful reader would bear witness to a "primary document … of

---

74 Grattan to Scoon, 22 July 1944, Chicago University Press Records, University of Chicago Library, Box 117, Folders 1–2. Unless otherwise stated, all evidence about the production of the American edition of *Such is Life* comes from these folders.
75 Scoon to Daiches, 9 January 1946.
76 During the war he worked for the British Information Service, then the British embassy in Washington, before taking up a position at Cornell University. David Purdie, "David Daiches: A Life", http://www.iash.ed.ac.uk/Daiches.
77 David Daiches, reader's report, 19 March 1946.
78 Publication Committee meeting, 10 May 1946.
79 Daiches to Scoon, 25 March 1946.

Australian social attitudes" that "still animate the Australian masses to some degree".[80] The digressions of narrator Tom Collins and the conversations between his companion bullock drivers illustrate the conflict in nineteenth-century Australian society between wealthy property owners and these "men of no property" who struggle to feed and water their bullock teams. An "undercurrent of fear that the country will be conquered by the plutocracy" pervades the book, but Grattan urged readers not to see *Such is Life* as a "crude proletarian novel". Like many others, he made the comparison with Melville's fiction, which also "carried a freight of philosophy hardly less important than the story", assuring readers they would experience an Australian classic whose significance reached beyond antipodean shores.

Grattan also took the opportunity to offer readers a primer on Australian history and the literary culture of the 1890s from which Furphy and his novel emerged. Furphy's letter to the *Bulletin* in which he introduced his novel with the memorable phrase "temper, democratic; bias, offensively Australian" is quoted in full before Grattan's brief history of Furphy's life as farmer, bullock driver, foundry worker and auto-didact, emphasising the literary achievement of this ordinary worker, "a plain-looking man, long and lean of face and body, slow-walking as became a bushman". Through the efforts of Furphy's supporters, Grattan argued, "*Such is Life* continued to fascinate the discriminating and more and more obviously to demonstrate that it had the qualities that make for classic permanence."[81]

The American edition was offset from Angus & Robertson's 1944 edition and 4000 copies at a retail price of four dollars were ordered for delivery by 1 August 1948. The novel was published in the United States and Canada on 20 September (Plate 10). Perhaps in order to overcome the Press's relatively low profile, as a university press, in mainstream bookstores and the usual distribution networks for fiction, review copies had been sent out to a wide variety of professional readers with a paragraph that provided a hint of how the publisher wanted the book to be read across a variety of potential audiences. Hilda Flaitz from the Press's advertising department anticipated *Such is Life* would "have a good sized audience": "Readers interested in historical Westerns, in 19th century literature, in foreign countries and customs, in sociology, in political science (socialism is the core of the book), and readers who simply like an entertaining story, should enjoy this frontier classic".[82] To Kenneth B. Murdock of Harvard University, the author of *Literature and Theology in Colonial New England*, she wrote: "I thought you might wish to compare this Australian book with the tongue-in-cheek, semi-autobiographical work of such writers as Mark Twain and Artemus Ward".[83]

If recipients did not receive such a personal note, they were prompted by dust-jacket blurbs from Canby and excerpts from Daiches' reader's report. For Canby, *Such is Life* was "one of the ... major books in English dealing with pioneering and the Frontier. We have nothing quite like it in American literature".[84] For Daiches: "*Such is Life* is something the U.S. ought to have produced in the nineteenth century and didn't - something that no country except Australia seems to have produced during that period in its development - a

---

80 C. Hartley Grattan, "About Tom Collins", afterword to *Such is Life: Being Certain Extracts from the Diary of Tom Collins*, by Joseph Furphy (Chicago: Chicago University Press, 1948), 376, 380.
81 Grattan, "About Tom Collins", 390, 394.
82 Flaitz to E.K. Brown, 5 August 1948.
83 Flaitz to Murdock, 6 August 1948.
84 Canby's blurb was taken from *A New Land Speaking* (see above).

real frontier (or immediately post-frontier) novel". The jacket promised "An Engaging Tale About The People Who Lived On The Rugged Australian Ranges and Deserts". Over the flap, readers were promised a more familiar experience: "They were frontier people, much like those colorful, adventurous, and heroic figures who travelled the plains of our own country at the opening of the West". This address to the familiar was repeated when the first advertisements appeared featuring an extract from the *New York Herald*: "If you relish 'Life on the Mississippi,' *Such is Life* is your book."[85] The Press's main advertisement featured *Such is Life* below Ralph Chaplin's *Wobbly*, "the rough-and-tumble story of an American radical", and beside Leslie Thompson's *The Politics of Equality: New Zealand's Adventures in Democracy*. As the Press was not known for its fiction list, *Such is Life* was delivered to the book market as a semi-fictional account of frontier life and early socialism in Australia.

The Press therefore cast its net very widely for readers, hoping to attract critical notice in important places and so have the novel pay its way. Over 200 complimentary copies had been sent out by 12 August 1948 and the first reviews appeared in early September.[86] Like Margaret Hubbard in the *New York Herald*, the reviewer for *America* suggested a kinship with *Life on the Mississippi*, a "mark of authenticity", but also added Thomas Carlyle's *Sartor Resartus* because of the book's "powerful lines on voluntary and involuntary poverty". In the *Chicago Illustrated Sun and Times*, Felke Felkema predicted that *Such is Life* would challenge *Capricornia* as the representative text of Australian literature, comparing it with Melville's *Moby-Dick* and Charles Doughty's *Arabia Deserta*. *Such is Life* was reviewed alongside Colebrook's *The Northerner* in the *Dallas Morning News*, the reviewer preferring the former because "Tom Collins could be human without taking his characters all the way to the bedroom". Other reviews noted the difficulty of Furphy's style. McCready Huston told readers of the *Philadelphia Inquirer* that *Such is Life* was a good example of the "amateur novel of the frontier"; it was "strictly an Australian classic, without the universality of language and statement that would be necessary for its full comprehension outside that country". This might well have been the majority view. The only review to show any empathy for the novel's egalitarian themes was that in New York's *Daily Worker*: "this sprawling, pioneersman's work is so imbued with a hatred for privilege, a fervor for egalitarian socialism … and a great gift for sardonic observation that making its acquaintance is very much worth while".

These relatively positive reviews failed to generate the sales predicted by Grattan and Daiches and so the idea of *Such is Life* as an Australian classic registered with very few American readers. Only 442 copies were sold in 1948–49, thirty-seven copies in 1949–50 and just one in 1950–51. In 1951, a special sale of *Such is Life* was organised at the discount price of $1.50, but few copies were sold until an unnamed customer proposed to bulk-buy 3300 copies at a price of fifteen cents each. The American edition of *Such is Life* earned just $1472.11 amounting to a loss of almost $2000 when the Press closed the account in May 1952.[87] In 1966, the Press's Maurice English declared, "We really did very badly by *Such is Life*" and rejected calls from Grattan for a reprinting.[88] Royalties from the American edition were to be shared by Angus & Robertson and Jonathan Cape, owners of the Australian and empire rights respectively, but concerns about poor sales had been

---

85 *New York Times*, 31 October 1948.
86 All reviews noted in this chapter are sourced from the University of Chicago Press records, delivered by the Romeike press clipping company.
87 Ethel Pieske (University of Chicago Press) to Jonathan Cape, 28 May 1952.
88 English (University of Chicago Press) to Grattan, 24 August 1966. Grattan Papers.

flagged before publication and both publishers were asked to forgo royalties on the first 4000 copies.[89] Furphy's novel had missed its moment by a decade or more, for its reception may have been very different had it appeared alongside novels such as *Australia Felix*, *Landtakers* or *The Timeless Land*.

Professing Australian Literature

As American troops returned home from the Pacific theatre during the second half of the 1940s, the position of Australian literature in American print culture, small as it was, had been consolidated by the series of important publications that had followed Richardson's critical and commercial success; or, perhaps more realistically, there was something like an "archive" that could be drawn upon to invoke the history and characteristics of Australia and its literature. When in 1951 the *Christian Science Monitor* launched a new feature called "Exploring our World", a series of reading lists about other countries, Australia was the first nation featured. A dozen books were recommended: Grattan's *Introducing Australia* and the edited volume *Australia*, Hill's *Australian Frontier*, Richardson's *Myself When Young*, Dark's *The Timeless Land* and *Storm of Time*, Herbert's *Capricornia*, Park's *Harp in the South*, Martin Boyd's *Lucinda Brayford*; two books by American authors, Margaret Macpherson's *I Heard the Anzacs Singing* (1942) and Kay Stevens' *Walkabout Down Under* (1944); and Furphy's *Such is Life*, the "recently rediscovered pioneer folk classic".[90] The period also saw the establishment of one of the first university courses devoted to Australian studies through the engagement of Bruce Sutherland, an English professor at Pennsylvania State University, who was to become the first American Professor of Australian Writing in 1950. The establishment of a program in Australian studies at Penn State marks an understated moment in the historical presence of Australian literature in America, at least in the academic world. Sutherland's teaching and his growing collection of Australian books became a touchstone for the organised study of Australian literature in the United States. But this small and isolated group interest had little effect on mainstream publishing cycles. To access Australian writing, Sutherland and his students would face the same barriers that American readers had experienced for years.

From the early 1920s, Penn State employed several professors who had an interest in the literature of the British dominions, and in 1938, soon after he arrived at the university, Sutherland was encouraged to develop a course in the area. In addition to Australia, Sutherland's proposal included the literatures of India, Jamaica, Canada and New Zealand. It was approved in late 1941, just months before the attack on Pearl Harbor. The course was "very popular from the first time it was taught, especially among the servicemen. The war in the Pacific had turned our attention to Australia as never before. Americans were eager to learn about the culture through its literature".[91] In Sutherland's words, "Good American

---

89 Internal memo, Rollin D. Hemens to Howard Moore, 2 November 1946. W.T. Couch (Chicago University Press) to Jonathan Cape, 24 September 1947; Kate Baker to Grattan, 20 October 1947. University of Chicago Press Records, Box 117, University of Chicago Library.
90 Doris Peel, "Exploring Our World", *Christian Science Monitor*, 12 April 1951, 11. Henry Handel Richardson Papers, National Library of Australia, NLA MS 133, Press Cuttings Albums.
91 Nancy Tischler and Nan Albinski, "Bruce Sutherland and Images of Australia", in *Australia in the World: Perceptions and Possibilities*, ed. Don Grant and Graham Seal (Perth: Black Swan Press, 1993), 161; and Nancy Tischler, "Bruce Sutherland and Images of Australia", *Antipodes* 7, no. 2 (1993): 135-38.

9 Bestsellers, Modest Sellers and Commercial Failures: The Postwar Years

novels and good Australian novels ... illuminate American and Australian life [and] help us to understand how we and our neighbours tick".[92] In the summer of 1942, Sutherland offered the first American university course devoted exclusively to the study of Australian literature.

The procurement of Australian books, however, presented a barrier to teaching and research. In 1942, the Penn State University library held just four "Australian" titles: Fergus Hume's *The Mystery of a Hansom Cab*, E.W. Hornung's *Stingaree*, the *Life of John Boyle O'Reilly Together with his Complete Poems and Speeches* and Richardson's *The Fortunes of Richard Mahony*. Sutherland tackled this problem by building one of the most significant collections devoted to Australian studies in the United States.[93] He also became an advocate for Australian literature, publishing articles in both American and Australian journals, such as "Australian Books and American Readers", published in the American *Library Quarterly* in 1945. Here he provided a general introduction to the history of Australian literature, recommending a wide range of contemporary writers including Richardson, Prichard, Mann, Upfield, Stead, Tennant and Dark. While admitting that the books of these authors were difficult to procure, he suggested that "enough Australian books have been published in the United States to serve as an introduction to the literature ... A clearer understanding of a people who were close to us before, and who are being brought even closer by the war, is well worth the effort required by the reading of a few books".[94]

When Sutherland made his first visit to Australia in 1950, he found himself an accidental advocate for Australian literature in the country of its origin, arguing for the establishment of university courses and better conditions for the export of Australian books into the United States. But even as the seeds of Australian studies as an academic discipline in the United States were being sown, the small but influential constituency for Australian literature that had been established across the 1930s and early 1940s among prominent reviewers and critics in the New York newspapers and magazines had begun to dissipate.[95] The most successful careers postwar, such as Jon Cleary's, did not depend upon the idea of "Australian literature" to make their way in the marketplace. For the next few decades, Australian literature would continue to be rediscovered by American readers one book at a time – and as if for the first time.

---

92 Tischler and Albinski, "Bruce Sutherland", 161.
93 Bruce Sutherland, *Australiana in the Pennsylvania State University Libraries* (Philadelphia: Pennsylvania State University Libraries, 1969).
94 Bruce Sutherland, "Australian Books and American Readers", *Library Quarterly* 15, no. 3 (1945): 230.
95 Other early academic commentators on Australian literature in the United States included A. Grove Day at the University of Hawaii, author of *Australian Fiction: The First Hundred Years* (University of Hawaii occasional paper, 1951) and of single-author studies of Louis Becke (1967), Robert Fitzgerald (1974) and Eleanor Dark (1976); Herbert C. Jaffa, New York University, author of a book on Kenneth Slessor (1977); Louise E. Rorabacher, author of books on Marjorie Barnard and Flora Eldershaw (1973) and Frank Dalby Davison (1979); and Joseph Jones, University of Texas, Austin, author of *Radical Cousins: Nineteenth Century American and Australian Writers* (1976).

Epilogue: Completing the Triangle?

Across the century or so covered by this book, Australian novels were a consistent presence in the American marketplace even while their numbers in any particular year or publishing season were never large. Most of the novelists who would become defining, canonical figures in the articulation of an Australian literary tradition over the course of the twentieth century were published in the United States, their standing as serious authors and in certain cases as major contributors to English fiction acknowledged by American publishers, reviewers and critics (not least in their roles as book club judges). Many Australian authors also participated in and profited from the burgeoning markets on both sides of the Atlantic for light fiction or genre fiction, sometimes with careers as good-selling novelists over several decades, their books reviewed widely and favourably in the weekly book pages. Less predictably, our research has revealed a dense undergrowth of writers with more modest reputations or less obvious claims on Australian literature who were published and found different kinds of success in America. A large and diverse range of authors, as we have shown, had a small number of titles published by mainstream houses, reviewed at least briefly in the major book papers, and sometimes noticed in the bookstores – a sequence of modest successes or perhaps more commonly one big success followed by a series of "disappointments". If they made no lasting impression in the American marketplace and contributed little, if anything, to American readers' sense of Australian literature, they might nonetheless have made a small return on the publisher's investment and some additional earnings for the author. In short, these works inhabited the mainstream commercial world of books, so often characterised by the short life span of individual titles and reputations, and the small number of genuinely bestselling books. Nonetheless, it is with these ordinary mid-range titles no less than the major literary works or popular bestsellers that we see literary transnationalism in operation – a function of publishers' interests and investments as much as a specifically textual or authorial capacity, manifested in new editions as much as in new texts.

The display of Australian books mounted by the Australian News and Information Bureau at the Rockefeller Center in New York in 1948 can be seen in retrospect as marking the end of an epoch, not the beginning of a new era as its sponsors and supporters like Grattan no doubt wished it to be. New initiatives such as the Noëlle Brennan literary agency came to nothing. More broadly, the "traditional markets agreement" between American and British publishers continued to limit the development of any deeper institutional relations between American and Australian publishers, agents and authors.[1] In the postwar American book world there was a new focus on "modern fiction", often led by America's own emerging writers and connected back to the now canonised figures from the twenties and thirties, a development that made it more difficult for new authors from elsewhere to make a mark in the literary field. Stead and White, as we have seen, could sometimes be drawn into discussions of the modern novel; Martin Boyd's late novels were published in the United States, but with little impact following the success of *Lucinda Brayford*, which had been reviewed – favourably – as an old-fashioned novel; others struggled in the late forties and early fifties to sustain careers. Arthur Upfield and Maysie Greig remained the most successful of those who began publishing in America before the war, with around twenty-five and sixty new titles respectively published in the United States between 1945 and 1970.

As described above, a group of new authors including James Aldridge, George Johnston and Jon Cleary built careers beginning in the war years in what became an expanding, increasingly identifiable sector of the book marketplace, that of "good commercial fiction", in Silverman's phrase. They were joined after the war by writers such as Ruth Park, Darcy Niland, Barbara Jefferis, recent immigrant to Australia Nevil Shute, and, above all, the bestselling Morris West.[2] West's story has many parallels to Cleary's, beginning with the Paul Reynolds agency and secured through successive titles from William Morrow, the dominant publisher in the field. West's first major success, *The Devil's Advocate* in 1959, was dedicated to Reynolds. Established in the field of good commercial fiction, the two authors occupied an important sector of the international fiction market, one we know well as consumers but struggle with as literary scholars; a middle register of well-written, readable, marketable fiction (to use the industry's own terms) that was particularly strong in the American marketplace from the 1940s to the 1970s, defining what Al Silverman sees as a "golden age" for American publishing.[3] West and Cleary sustained English and American careers largely from an Australian base, though with extended periods in the United States; their international careers were launched from America; and both were soon in a position to negotiate separate contracts with English and American houses. Reversing the usual equation, their Australian careers were a by-product of their international success, and they have been correspondingly difficult to place in relation to Australian literature.

Shute's career was also based on successive titles from William Morrow, which had released eleven of his novels before the American edition of *A Town Like Alice* was published, as *The Legacy*, in 1950, around the time he settled in Australia. Morrow

---

1   The informal agreement between US and British publishers that divided the world into two publishing spheres was formalised in 1947 as the Traditional Markets Agreement. It remained in place until 1976, but even after that date many of the practices it sustained continued to be followed. Mary Nell Bryant, "English Language Publication and the British Traditional Market Agreement", *Library Quarterly* 49 (October 1979): 371-98.
2   Shute visited Australia in 1948-49, then settled in Victoria from 1950 (AustLit, www.austlit.edu.au) or 1951 (New American Library, "Editorial Dopesheet" [sic], 6 June 1958, New American Library Archive, Fales Library and Special Collections, New York University, MSS 070, Box 66).
3   Al Silverman, *The Time of Their Lives: The Golden Age of Great American Book Publishers, Their Editors and Authors* (New York: Truman Tally-St Martin's, 2008). Neither West nor Cleary was identified primarily with genre fiction in the manner of Upfield and Greig, in Cleary's case despite twenty crime/detective novels featuring Sydney detective Scobie Malone, beginning with *The High Commissioner* in 1966; but these titles were always interspersed with others in a range of genres.

published nine further novels to 1961, mostly one a year, and all with multiple paperback reissues. A number had Australian themes and settings, including *The Far Country* (1952), *Beyond the Black Stump* (1956), and of course, the most successful of all, *On the Beach* in 1957.[4] Cleary, West and Shute contributed to a steadily growing number of "good commercial" Australian novels appearing in the United States across the 1950s and 1960s.[5]

The present study establishes the significance of the US publishing industry, the American print market and the transatlantic book trade for Australian writers across the full range of fictional kinds through to the mid-twentieth century. While many authors throughout this period took their primary bearings from their Australian or British contexts – and while American editions were as often driven by publishers' interests on both sides of the Atlantic as by those of the authors themselves – many Australian writers were keenly interested in being published in America and maximising their opportunities for financial or reputational gain when such publication occurred. There is a rich archive of publishers', agents' and authors' correspondence testifying to these interests and to what we might call the contemporaneity of Australian writers' relations to the international fiction market. Although Australian works were only ever a small percentage of the new (and old) fiction titles being released in the United States each week, the numbers are much greater and the range of names more diverse than Australian literary history has recognised.

And although they were seldom free from the limitations of Australia's subordinate position within the world literary system, our study shows that Australian writers, whether at home or abroad, were never wholly contained within local, national or imperial structures. Publishers, agents and the authors themselves created networks of exchange – transnational and transnodal – that pushed books beyond these borders into new markets, and the American market was potentially the most lucrative and culturally rewarding of all. Australia's distance and lack of institutional weight or cultural prestige meant that the typical problems of achieving publication and sustaining success in the commercial book world were often doubled for its writers – given which, the density of business transacted and the degree of success are both considerable. Nonetheless, the triangle of publishing relations remained largely a two-sided affair across the period examined, the trade in rights and professional networks still largely routed through London. It was only with the collapse of the Traditional Markets Agreement in the late 1970s that the third side of the triangle – the axis of direct negotiations between Australian authors, publishers and agents and the American book trade – could be fully activated and strategically deployed. This change helped produce another "mini-boom" in American editions of Australian novels in the 1980s and an increased recognition of Australian literature. If that, too, was short-lived, over the longer term it helped normalise separate US, UK and Australian contracts for mainstream fiction in a truly international rights market.

---

4   *On the Beach* was also the first of Shute's novels published in paperback by Signet/New American Library (NAL), a major additional source of earnings. Victor Weybright, founder and chairman of NAL, wrote to Thayer Hobson at Morrow, "Not since *1984* has there been such a book!": 27 May 1957, NAL Archive, Box 66.
5   Around 275 different editions in the 1950s and over 500 in the 1960s. The numbers in the 1960s are boosted by more than 100 titles from pulp novelist Carter Brown, published under the Signet imprint/NAL. Another Australian author, Richard Wilkes-Hunter, under various pseudonyms, contributed more than seventy, also as Signet editions.

Works Cited

The present study refers necessarily to a very large number of books published in the United States and an even larger number of book reviews and brief notices in newspapers and periodicals. In general, individual editions, book reviews and brief newspaper articles have not been listed here. Details can be found in the main text and notes. Much of the biographical and bibliographical information presented in the book is discoverable in AustLit (http://www.austlit.edu.au), which we have supplemented by archival and library searches both physical and online. American newspapers and magazines were sourced from library holdings and through important online databases: Chronicling America: Historical American Newspapers (Library of Congress); The Making of America (Cornell University Library); UNZ.org - Periodicals, Books, and Authors (www.unz.org/Pub/); and the commercial databases, EBCSO's Book Review Digest Retrospective: 1903-1982 and ProQuest's Historical Newspapers. We should also mention the wonderful resource offered by press clipping files or scrapbooks held in the papers of certain writers, including Henry Handel Richardson, Katharine Susannah Prichard and Eleanor Dark, and in the records of literary agents such as Curtis Brown.

Ackland, Michael. "'A Skyrocket Waiting to Be Left Off', But to Where? Christina Stead's First Impressions of the United States and Her Postwar Literary Rehabiliation". In Dixon and Birns, *Reading Across the Pacific*, 225–39.
———. "Christina Stead and the Politics of Covert Statement". *Mosaic* 43, no. 1 (2010): 127–42.
———. *Henry Handel Richardson: A Life*. Melbourne: Cambridge University Press, 2004.
———. "Marcus Clarke (1846–1881)". In Samuels, *Australian Literature, 1788–1914*, 81–93.
———. "'Socialists of a New Socialism'? Christina Stead's Critique of 1930s America in *The Man Who Loved Children*". *English Literary History* 78, no. 2 (2011): 387–408.
———. "Whatever Happened to Coppelius? Antecedents and Design in Christina Stead's *The Salzburg Tales*". *Journal of the Association for the Study of Australian Literature (JASAL)* 2 (2003): 53–66.
Ahern, Susan K. "The G.W. Dillingham Company". In Dzwonkoski, *American Literary Publishing Houses, 1638–1899*, 124–25.
Alexander, Alison. *A Mortal Flame: Marie Bjelke Petersen, Australian Romance Writer, 1874–1969*. Hobart: Blubber Head Press, 1994.
"America at the Jubilee". *New York Times*, 24 June 1897.
Anderson, George Parker. *American Modernism, 1914–1945*. Research Guide to American Literature Vol. 6. New York: Bruccoli, Clark & Laymen, 2010.

Ardis, Ann L., and Patrick Collier. Introduction to *Transatlantic Print Culture, 1880–1940 Emerging Media, Emerging Modernisms*, edited by Ann L. Ardis and Patrick Collier, 1–12. Basingstoke, UK: Palgrave Macmillan, 2008.

Ashley, Mike. *The Age of the Storytellers: British Popular Fiction Magazines, 1880–1950*. London; New Castle, DE: British Library & Oak Knoll Press, 2006.

Attenborough, John. *Living Memory: Hodder & Stoughton Publishers, 1868–1975*. London: Hodder & Stoughton, 1975.

Australian Writers and Artists Market (Including New Zealand): A Practical Guide for the Freelance. Melbourne: Australian School of Journalism Pty Ltd and Art Training Institute Pty Ltd, 1946.

"Back in Black: The Little Sisters". *Girl Detective*. www.girl-detective.net/little.html.

Baldick, Chris. *The Oxford English Literary History, Volume 10 1910–1940: The Modern Movement*. Oxford: Oxford University Press, 2004.

"Banned in Boston: The Watch and Ward Society's Crusade against Books, Burlesque, and the Social Evil". *Beacon Broadside: A Project of Beacon Press*. http://www.beaconbroadside.com/broadside/2010/09/banned-in-boston.html.

Barnard Eldershaw, M. "The Period Novel: An Infinity of Problems". *Sydney Morning Herald*, 23 November 1929.

———. "The Period Novel: The Reader and the Writer". *Sydney Morning Herald*, 30 November 1929.

Bassett, Troy J., and Christina M. Walter. "Booksellers and Bestsellers: British Book Sales as Documented by *The Bookman*, 1891–1906". *Book History* 4 (2001): 205–36.

Becke, Louis. "The Strangest, Wildest, and Saddest Story". In *Moby-Dick*, by Herman Melville, edited by Hershel Parker and Harrison Hayford, 636–37. Norton Critical Editions. 2nd ed. New York: Norton, 2002.

Belich, James. *Replenishing the Earth: The Settler Revolution and the Rise of the Anglo-World, 1783–1939*. Oxford: Oxford University Press, 2009.

Bennett, Bruce, and Ann Pender. *From a Distant Shore: Australian Writers in Britain 1820–2012*. Clayton, Vic.: Monash University Publishing, 2013.

Bevan Jr, Ernest. "The Dial Press". In Dzwonkoski, *American Literary Publishing Houses, 1900–1980*, 115–18.

Bird, Delys. "Katharine Susannah Prichard (1883–1969)". In *Australian Writers, 1915–1950*, edited by Selina Samuels, 307–19. Dictionary of Literary Biography Vol. 260. Detroit, MI: Gale Research, 2002.

Birns, Nicholas. "Trollope and the Antipodes". In *The Cambridge Companion to Anthony Trollope*, edited by Carolyn Dever and Lisa Niles, 181–95. Cambridge: Cambridge University Press, 2010.

Bloom, Clive. *Bestsellers: Popular Fiction Since 1900*. New York: Palgrave, 2002.

Bode, Katherine. *Reading by Numbers: Recalibrating the Literary Field*. London: Anthem Press, 2012.

"Boothby, Guy Newell (1867–1905)". In *Australian Dictionary of Biography*, Vol. 7, 1979. http://adb.anu.edu.au/biography/boothby-guy-newell-5293/text8931.

Boyd, J. Hayden, and William S. Lofquist. "New Interests in Old Issues: Antiprotection and the End of the Manufacturing Clause of the US Copyright Law". *Publishing Research Quarterly* 7, no. 4 (Winter 1991–1992): 21–39.

Bradford, Clare. "Ethel Turner (1872–1958)". In Samuels, *Australian Literature, 1788–1914*, 393–400.

Bradstock, Margaret. "Mary Gaunt (1861–1942)". In Samuels, *Australian Literature, 1788–1914*, 143–51.

Bradstock, Margaret, and Louise Wakeling. *Rattling the Orthodoxies: A Life of Ada Cambridge*. Ringwood, Vic.: Penguin, 1991.

Brisbane, Katharine, ed. *Entertaining Australia: An Illustrated History*. Sydney: Currency Press, 1991.

Brooks, Barbara, and Judith Clark. *Eleanor Dark: A Writer's Life*. Sydney: Pan Macmillan, 1998.

Bryant, Mary Nell. "English Language Publication and the British Traditional Market Agreement". *Library Quarterly* 49, no. 4 (1979): 371–98.

Buckridge, Patrick. *The Scandalous Penton: A Biography of Brian Penton*. St Lucia: University of Queensland Press, 1994.

Works Cited

Burns, Alison, and R.A. Goodrich. "Christina Stead, Georges Polti, and Analytical Novel Writing". *Antipodes* 29, no. 2 (December 2015): 415–28.
Burton, Antoinette, and Isabel Hofmeyr. "The Spine of Empire? Books and the Making of an Imperial Commons". In *Ten Books That Shaped the British Empire: Creating an Imperial Commons*, edited by Antoinette Burton and Isabel Hofmeyr, 1–28. Durham, NC: Duke University Press, 2014.
Butterss, Philip. "Australian Literary Studies in the 1940s: The Commonwealth LIterary Fund Lectures", *Australian Literary Studies* 30, no. 4 (November 2015): 115–27.
Campbell, Rosemary. "Catherine Martin (ca1847–1937)". In Samuels, *Australian Literature, 1788–1914*, 254–61.
Canby, Henry Seidel. *A New Land Speaking: An Essay on the Importance of a National Literature*. Melbourne: Melbourne University Press, 1946.
Carter, Angela. "Unhappy Families". *London Review of Books* 4, no. 17 (16 September 1982): 11–13.
Carter, David. *Always Almost Modern: Australian Print Cultures and Modernity*. North Melbourne, Vic.: Australian Scholarly Publishing, 2013.
———. "Transpacific or Transatlantic Traffic? Australian Books and American Publishers". In Dixon and Birns, *Reading Across the Pacific*, 339–59.
Casanova, Pascale. "Literature as World". *New Left Review* 31 (2005): 71–90.
———. *The World Republic of Letters*. Translated by M.B. DeBevoise. Cambridge, MA: Harvard University Press, 2004.
Caterson, Simon. "Fergus Hume's Startling Story". Introduction to *The Mystery of A Hansom Cab*, by Fergus Hume, vii–xviii. Melbourne: Text Publishing, 1999.
———. "The Gilded Cage". Introduction to *Madame Midas*, by Fergus Hume, v–xiv. Melbourne: Text Publishing, 1999.
Cawelti, John G. "Murder in the Outback". *New Republic*, 30 July 1977.
———. "Murder in the Outback: Arthur W. Upfield". In *Investigating Arthur Upfield: A Centenary Collection of Critical Essays*, edited by Kees de Hoog and Carol Hetherington, 14–18. Newcastle-upon-Tyne, UK: Cambridge Scholars Publishing, 2012.
Chambers, Ross. *Story and Situation: Narrative Seduction and the Power of Fiction*. Minneapolis: University of Minnesota Press, 1984.
Clancy, Laurie. *Xavier Herbert*. New York: Twayne, 1981.
Clarke, Patricia. "Rosa Praed (Mrs Campbell Praed) (1851–1935)". In Samuels, *Australian Literature, 1788–1914*, 301–12.
———. *Rosa! Rosa!: A Life of Rosa Praed, Novelist and Spiritualist*. Melbourne: Melbourne University Press, 1999.
———. *Tasma: The Life of Jessie Couvreur*. St Leonards, NSW: Allen & Unwin, 1994.
Clarke, Sharon. *Sumner Locke Elliott: Writing Life*. St Leonards, NSW: Allen & Unwin, 1996.
"Constance & Gwenyth Little". *Mystery Books from the Golden Age of Detective Fiction: Rue Morgue Press*. http://archive.is/YTKh4.
Cornwall, Edward E. "Are the Americans an Anglo-Saxon People?" *New York Times*, 14 January 1900.
Cox, J. Randolph. *The Dime Novel Companion: A Source Book*. Westport, CT: Greenwood, 2000.
Dale, Leigh. *The English Men: Professing Literature in Australian Universities*. ASAL Literary Studies. Canberra: Assoc. for the Study of Australian Literature, 1997.
Daly, Nicholas. "Railway Novels: Sensation Fiction and the Modernisation of the Senses". *English Literary History* 66, no. 2 (Summer 1999): 461–87.
Damrosch, David. "Literary Study in an Elliptical Age". In *Comparative Literature in the Age of Multiculturalism*, edited by Charles Bernheimer, 122–33. Baltimore, MD: Johns Hopkins University Press, 1995.
Daniel, Howard. "The Genesis of the American Edition of *Such is Life*". *Biblionews* 5, no. 12 (1952): 42.
De Serville, Paul. *Rolf Boldrewood: A Life*. Carlton, Vic.: Miegunyah Press, 2000.
Deamer, Dulcie. *The Queen of Bohemia: The Autobiography of Dulcie Deamer: Being "The Golden Decade"*. Edited by Peter Kirkpatrick. St Lucia: University of Queensland Press, 1998.

Deeck, William F. "Mystery House (1940–1948)". *Murder at 3 Cents a Day: An Annotated Crime Fiction Bibliography of the Lending Library Publishers: 1936–1967*. http://www.lendinglibmystery.com/MHouse/Covers.

de Groen, Frances. *Xavier Herbert: A Biography*. St Lucia: University of Queensland Press, 1998.

de Hoog, Kees, and Carol Hetherington, eds. *Investigating Arthur Upfield: A Centenary Collection of Critical Essays*. Newcastle-upon-Tyne, UK: Cambridge Scholars Publishing, 2012.

Depasquale, Paul. *Guy Boothby: His Life and Work*. Seacombe Gardens, SA: Pioneer Books, 1982.

DeSpain, Jessica. *Nineteenth-Century Transatlantic Reprinting and the Embodied Book*. Farnham, UK: Ashgate, 2014.

Devanny, Jean. *Point of Departure: The Autobiography of Jean Devanny*. Edited by Carole Ferrier. St Lucia: University of Queensland Press, 1986.

Dever, Maryanne. "Marjorie Barnard (1897–1987) and Flora Eldershaw (1897–1956) (M. Barnard Eldershaw)". In *Australian Writers, 1915–1950*, edited by Selina Samuels, 3–13. Dictionary of Literary Biography Vol. 260. Detroit, MI: Gale Research, 2002.

Dixon, Robert. "Australian Literature, Scale and the Problem of the World". In *Text, Translation, Transnationalism: World Literature in 21st Century Australia*, edited by Peter Morgan, 173–95. North Melbourne, Vic.: Australian Scholarly Publishing, 2016.

———. "Scenes of Reading: Is Australian Literature a World Literature?" In *Republics of Letters: Literary Communities in Australia*, edited by Robert Dixon and Peter Kirkpatrick, 71–83. Sydney: Sydney University Press, 2012.

———. *Photography, Early Cinema and Colonial Modernity: Frank Hurley's Synchronized Lecture Entertainments*. London: Anthem Press, 2012.

———. Introduction to *The Mystery of a Hansom Cab*, by Fergus Hume. Sydney: Sydney University Press, 2010.

———. *Writing the Colonial Adventure: Race, Gender, and Nation in Anglo-Australian Popular Fiction, 1875–1914*. Cambridge: Cambridge University Press, 1995.

Dixon, Robert, and Nicholas Birns, eds. *Reading across the Pacific: Australia-United States Intellectual Histories*. Sydney: Sydney University Press, 2010.

Docker, John. *The Nervous Nineties: Australian Cultural Life in the 1890s*. Melbourne: Oxford University Press, 1991.

During, Simon. *Exit Capitalism: Literary Culture, Theory, and Post-Secular Modernity*. London: Routledge, 2010.

———. *Patrick White*. Melbourne: Oxford University Press, 1996.

Dutton, Geoffrey. *Out in the Open: An Autobiography*. St Lucia: University of Queensland Press, 1994.

Dwyer, James Francis. *Leg-Irons on Wings*. Melbourne: Georgian House, 1949.

Dzwonkoski, David. "Appleton-Century-Crofts". In Dzwonkoski, *American Literary Publishing Houses, 1900–1980*, 8-12.

Dzwonkoski, Peter, ed. *American Literary Publishing Houses, 1638–1899*. Dictionary of Literary Biography Vol. 49. Detroit, MI: Gale Research, 1986.

———, ed. *American Literary Publishing Houses, 1900–1980. Trade and Paperback*. Dictionary of Literary Biography Vol. 46. Detroit, MI: Gale Research, 1986.

———. "John W. Lovell Company". In Dzwonkoski, *American Literary Publishing Houses, 1638–1899*, 283–86.

Edgar, Suzanne. "Rosman, Alice Trevenen (1882–1961)". In *Australian Dictionary of Biography*, Vol. 11, 1988. http://adb.anu.edu.au/biography/rosman-alice-trevenen-8269/text14485.

Eggert, Paul. *Biography of a Book: Henry Lawson's "While the Billy Boils"*. Philadelphia; Sydney: Pennsylvania State University Press; Sydney University Press, 2013.

———. "Australian Classics and the Price of Books: The Puzzle of the 1890s". *Journal of the Association for the Study of Australian Literature (JASAL)* 2008: 130–57.

———. *Securing the Past: Conservation in Art, Architecture and Literature*. Cambridge: Cambridge University Press, 2009.

Works Cited

Eggert, Paul, and Elizabeth Webby. Introduction to *Robbery Under Arms: A Story of Life and Adventure in the Bush and in the Goldfields of Australia*, by Rolf Boldrewood, xxiii–lxxxix. Academy Editions of Australian Literature. St Lucia: University of Queensland Press, 2006.

Eliot, Simon. *Some Patterns and Trends in British Publishing, 1800–1919*. Occasional Papers of the Bibliographical Society 8. London: Bibliographical Society, 1994.

Ensor, Jason D. *Angus & Robertson and the British Trade in Australian Books, 1930–1970: The Getting of Bookselling Wisdom*. London: Anthem Press, 2012.

Fadiman, Clifton. *Reading I've Liked: A Personal Selection Drawn from Two Decades of Reading and Reviewing with an Informal Prologue and Various Commentaries*. New York: Simon & Schuster, 1941.

Feather, John. *A History of British Publishing*. 2nd ed. London: Routledge, 2006.

Ferrier, Carole, ed. *As Good as a Yarn with You: Letters between Miles Franklin, Katharine Susannah Prichard, Jean Devanny, Marjorie Barnard, Flora Eldershaw, and Eleanor Dark*. Cambridge: Cambridge University Press, 1992.

———. *Jean Devanny: Romantic Revolutionary*. Carlton, Vic.: Melbourne University Press, 1999.

Finlay, E.M. "Mitchell, Isabel Mary (1893–1973)". In *Australian Dictionary of Biography*, Vol. 10, 1986. http://adb.anu.edu.au/biography/mitchell-isabel-mary-7605/text13285.

FitzHenry, W.E. "Some 'Bulletin' Books and Their Authors". In *The Books of the Bulletin 1880–1952: An Annotated Bibliography*, edited by George Mackaness and Walter W. Stone, 1–36. Sydney: Angus & Robertson, 1955.

Foxton, Rosemary. "'Another Fresh Australian Tale': The American Publication of Catherine Martin's *The Silent Sea*". *Australian Literary Studies* 15, no. 4 (1992): 351–54.

———. Introduction to *The Silent Sea*, by Catherine Martin, xv–xli. Colonial Texts Series. Sydney: UNSW Press, 1995.

Franklin, Miles. *Laughter, Not for a Cage: Notes on Australian Writing*. Sydney: Angus & Robertson, 1956.

Franks, Rachel. "Catching a Cab". www.sl.nsw.gov.au/stories/catching-cab.

Fritschner, Linda Marie. "Literary Agents and Literary Traditions: The Role of the Philistine". In *Paying the Piper: Causes and Consequences of Art Patronage*, edited by Judith Huggins Balfe, 54–72. Urbana: University of Illinois Press, 1993.

Frow, John. "Signature and Brand". In *High-Pop: Making Culture into Popular Entertainment*, edited by Jim Collins, 56–74. Malden, MA: Wiley-Blackwell, 2002.

Gelder, Ken. "Guy Boothby, Fergus Hume and Arthur Upfield: Colonial Popular Fiction Acquisitions in the Special Collections". *University of Melbourne Library Journal* 10, no. 2 (December 2005): 2–6.

Gelder, Ken, and Rachael Weaver. *The Colonial Journals and the Emergence of Australian Literary Culture*. Crawley, WA: UWA Publishing, 2014.

Giles, Paul. *Antipodean America: Australasia and the Constitution of US Literature*. New York: Oxford University Press, 2013.

———. *Transatlantic Insurrections: British Culture and the Formation of American Literature, 1730–1860*. Philadelphia: University of Pennsylvania Press, 2001.

———. *Transnationalism in Practice: Essays on American Studies, Literature and Religion*. Edinburgh: Edinburgh University Press, 2010.

Gillies, Mary Ann. "A.P. Watt, Literary Agent". *Publishing Research Quarterly* 9, no. 1 (1993): 20–33.

Glazener, Nancy. *Literature in the Making: A History of US Literary Culture in the Long Nineteenth Century*. Oxford Studies in American Literary History. New York: Oxford University Press, 2016.

Glover, David. "Publishing, History, Genre". In *The Cambridge Companion to Popular Fiction*, edited by David Glover and Scott McCracken, 15–32. Cambridge: Cambridge University Press, 2012.

———. "The Thriller". In *The Cambridge Companion to Crime Fiction*, edited by Martin Priestman, 135–53. Cambridge: Cambridge University Press, 2003.

Grattan, C. Hartley. "About Tom Collins". Afterword to *Such is Life*, by Joseph Furphy, 375–94. Chicago: Chicago University Press, 1948.

———, ed. *Australia*. Berkeley, CA: University of California Press, 1947.
———. "Australian Literature". *Bookman* 67, no. 6 (1928): 625–31.
———. *Australian Literature*. University of Washington Chapbooks. Seattle, WA: University of Washington Book Store, 1929.
———. *Introducing Australia*. 1942. Rev. ed. New York: John Day, 1947.
———. "Literature in the Antipodes". *New York Times*, 7 January 1934.
———. "Readers and Writers Down Under". *New York Times*, 22 June 1947.
———. "The Literary Scene in Australia". *New York Times*, 15 August 1937.
———. "The Literary Scene in Australia". *New York Times*, 14 January 1940.
———. "The Literary Scene in Australia". *New York Times*, 11 August 1940.
Green, H.M. *A History of Australian Literature, Pure and Applied: Volume II, 1923–1950*. 1961. Revised by Dorothy Green. Sydney: Angus & Robertson, 1985.
Green, Richard Lancelyn. Introduction to *Raffles: The Amateur Cracksman*, by E.W. Hornung, xvii–xlvii. Harmondsworth: Penguin Classics, 2003.
Gribble, Jennifer. *Christina Stead*. Melbourne: Oxford University Press, 1994.
Griffiths, Andrew. *The New Journalism, the New Imperialism, and the Fiction of Empire, 1870–1900*. Basingstoke, UK: Palgrave Macmillan, 2015.
Gross, Robert A. "Building a National Literature: The United States 1800–1890". In *A Companion to the History of the Book*, edited by Simon Eliot and Jonathan Rose, 315–28. Malden, MA: Blackwell, 2007.
———. *Louis Becke*. New York: Twayne, 1966.
Groves, Jeffrey D. "Courtesy of the Trade". In *A History of the Book in America, Volume 3: The Industrial Book, 1840–1880*, edited by Scott E. Casper, Jeffrey D. Groves, Stephen W. Nissenbaum, and Michael Winship, 139–48. Chapel Hill: University of North Carolina Press, 2007.
Gwynn, S.L. "McCarthy, Justin (1830–1912)". Rev. by Alan O'Day. *Oxford Dictionary of National Biography*, 2004. http://www.oxforddnb.com/index/101034681/Justin-McCarthy.
Hackett, Alice Payne, and James Henry Burke. *Eighty Years of Best Sellers, 1895–1975*. New York: Bowker, 1977.
Hadgraft, Cecil. *Australian Literature: A Critical Account to 1955*. London: Heinemann, 1960.
Hammond, Mary. *Reading, Publishing and the Formation of Literary Taste in England, 1880–1914*. Aldershot, UK: Ashgate, 2006.
Hardwick, Elizabeth. *A View of My Own: Essays in Literature and Society*. New York: Farrar, Straus & Cudahy, 1962.
———. "The Novels of Christina Stead". *New Republic*, 1 August 1955, 17–19.
Harris, Margaret, ed. *Dearest Munx: The Letters of Christina Stead and William J. Blake*. Carlton, Vic.: Miegunyah Press, 2005.
Hart, James D. *The Popular Book: A History of America's Literary Taste*. New York: Oxford University Press, 1950.
Haycraft, Howard. "Evolution of the Whodunit in the Years of World War II". *New York Times*, 12 August 1945.
———. "The Burgeoning Whodunit". *New York Times*, 6 October 1946.
Haydn, Hiram Collins, and John Cournos. *A World of Great Stories*. New York: Crown Publishers, 1947.
Hench, John B. *Books as Weapons: Propaganda, Publishing, and the Battle for Global Markets in the Era of World War II*. Ithaca, NY: Cornell University Press, 2010.
Hergenhan, Laurie. "A Literary Visit to the USA: A Memoir". *Antipodes* 26, no. 1 (June 2012): 74–78.
———. *No Casual Traveller: Hartley Grattan and Australia–US Connections*. St Lucia: University of Queensland Press, 1995.
Heseltine, Harry. "Australian Fiction since 1920". In *The Literature of Australia*, edited by Geoffrey Dutton, 181–223. Harmondsworth: Penguin, 1964.
Hetherington, Carol. "Authors, Editors, Publishers: Katharine Susannah Prichard and W.W. Norton". *Australian Literary Studies* 22, no. 4 (2006): 417–31.

Works Cited

———. "Bony at Home and Abroad: The Arthur Upfield Phenomenon". *Journal of the Association for the Study of Australian Literature (JASAL)* 9 (2009): 1–12.

———. "In the Club: Australian Crime Fiction in the USA 1943-1954". *Australian Literary Studies* 27, no. 3-4 (November 2012): 31–45.

———. "'In Their Different Ways, Classics': Arthur Upfield's Detective Fiction". In *Investigating Arthur Upfield: A Centenary Collection of Critical Essays*, edited by Kees de Hoog and Carol Hetherington, 210–21. Newcastle-upon-Tyne, UK: Cambridge Scholars Publishing, 2012.

Holt, Patricia. "'It's Enough to Drive a Bloke Mad': Norman Lindsay's Art and Literature". *Bibliographical Society of Australia and New Zealand Bulletin* 27, no. 1-2 (2003): 62–81.

Horsford, Howard C. "Harper and Brothers". In Dzwonkoski *American Literary Publishing Houses, 1638–1899*, 192–98.

Hume, Fergus. Preface to *The Mystery of a Hansom Cab*, vii–ix. London: Jarrold & Sons, 1896.

Humphery, Laura-Masotti. "Coward, McCann and Geoghegan". In Dzwonkoski, *American Literary Publishing Houses, 1900–1980*, 96–99.

Hutner, Gordon. *What America Read: Taste, Class, and the Novel, 1920–1960*. Chapel Hill: University of North Carolina Press, 2009.

Irvine, Ian. Introduction to *A Bid for Fortune or Dr Nikola's Vendetta*, by Guy Boothby, ii–iv. Mt Waverley, Vic.: Chimaera Publications, 2010.

Jaillant, Lise. *Modernism, Middlebrow and the Literary Canon: The Modern Library Series, 1917–1955*. London: Pickering & Chatto, 2014.

James, Elizabeth. "Letters from America: The Bretts and the Macmillan Company of New York". In *Macmillan: A Publishing Tradition*, edited by Elizabeth James, 170–91. Basingstoke, UK: Palgrave, 2002.

Jarrell, Randall. "An Unread Book". Introduction to *The Man Who Loved Children*, by Christina Stead, v–xli. New York: Holt, Rinehart & Winston, 1965.

———. "Speaking of Books". *New York Times*, 24 July 1955.

———. "The Man Who Loved Children". *Atlantic Monthly* 215 (1965): 166–71.

Johnston, Anna. "American Servicemen Find Ernestine Hill in Their Kitbags". In *Telling Stories: Australian Life and Literature, 1935–2012*, edited by Paul Genoni and Tanya Dalziel, 84–90. Clayton, Vic.: Monash University Publishing, 2013.

Jolly, Roslyn. "Piracy, Slavery, and the Imagination of Empire in Stevenson's Pacific Fiction". *Victorian Literature and Culture* 35, no. 1 (March 2007): 157–73.

Jones, Joseph Jay. *Radical Cousins: Nineteenth Century American & Australian Writers*. St Lucia: University of Queensland Press, 1976.

Joseph, Michael. *This Writing Business*. London: Faber & Faber, 1931.

Kato, Megumi. *Narrating the Other: Australian Literary Perceptions of Japan*. Clayton, Vic.: Monash University Press, 2008.

Keating, Peter. *The Haunted Study: A Social History of the English Novel, 1875–1914*. London: Fontana, 1991.

Kenton, Edna. "By Henry Handel Richardson". *Seven Arts*, October 1917, 802–5.

———. "'Maurice Guest' and 'Richard Mahoney'". *Bookman*, January 1918, 580–82.

Kirkpatrick, Peter. Introduction to Deamer, *The Queen of Bohemia*, vii–xi.

Knight, Stephen. *Continent of Mystery: A Thematic History of Australian Crime Fiction*. Carlton, Vic.: Melbourne University Press, 1997.

———. *Crime Fiction, 1800–2000: Detection, Death, Diversity*. Basingstoke, UK: Palgrave MacMillan, 2004.

Lake, Marilyn and Henry Reynolds. *Drawing the Global Colour Line: White Men's Countries and the International Challenge of Racial Equality*. Carlton, Vic.: Melbourne University Press, 2008.

Laracy, Hugh. *Watriama and Co.: Further Pacific Island Portraits*. Canberra: ANU Press, 2013.

Lee, Chris. "'From Progress into Stand-Still Days': Literature, History and the Darling Downs". In *By the Book: A Literary History of Queensland*, edited by Patrick Buckridge and Belinda McKay, 111-39. St Lucia: University of Queensland Press, 2007.

Leick, Karen. "Popular Modernism: Little Magazines and the American Daily Press". *PMLA* 123, no. 1 (January 2008): 125-39.

Lewis, Sinclair. Foreword to *The Fortunes of Richard Mahony*, by Henry Handel Richardson, v-vii. New York: New York Readers Club, 1941.

Lidoff, Joan. *Christina Stead*. New York: Frederick Ungar, 1982.

Lindsay, Norman. "I Like New York". *Home* 12, no. 12 (December 1931): 38-39.

———. *Letters of Norman Lindsay*. Edited by R.G. Howarth and A.W. Barker. Sydney: Angus & Robertson, 1979.

———. *My Mask; for What Little I Know of the Man behind It: An Autobiography*. Sydney: Angus & Robertson, 1970.

Lindsey, Travis B. "Arthur William Upfield: A Biography". PhD, Murdoch University, 2005.

Lyons, Martyn, and Lucy Taksa. *Australian Readers Remember: An Oral History of Reading 1890-1930*. Melbourne: Oxford University Press, 1992.

Madison, Charles A. *Book Publishing in America*. New York: McGraw-Hill, 1966.

Manning, Arthur. *Larger Than Life: The Story of Eric Baume*. Sydney: Reed, 1967.

Marcus, Laura. "Oedipus Express: Trains, Trauma and Detective Fiction". *New Formations* 41 (2000): 173-88.

Marr, David. *Patrick White: A Life*. Sydney: Vintage, 1992.

———, ed. *Patrick White: Letters*. Milsons Point, NSW: Random House, 1994.

Martin, Susan K., and Kylie Mirmohamadi. *Sensational Melbourne: Reading, Sensation Fiction and "Lady Audley's Secret" in the Victorian Metropolis*. North Melbourne, Vic.: Australian Scholarly Publishing, 2011.

Matthews, Brander. "Cheap Books and Good Books". 1891. In Dzwonkoski, *American Literary Publishing Houses, 1638-1899*, 580-86.

McAleer, Joseph. *Passion's Fortune: The Story of Mills & Boon*. Oxford: Oxford University Press, 1999.

McCleery, Alistair. "The Book in the Long Twentieth Century". In *The Cambridge Companion to the History of the Book*, edited by Leslie Howsam, 162-80. Cambridge: Cambridge University Press, 2014.

McDonald, Peter D. *British Literary Culture and Publishing Practice, 1880-1914*. Cambridge: Cambridge University Press, 1997.

McGill, Meredith L. *American Literature and the Culture of Reprinting, 1834-1853*. Philadelphia: University of Pennsylvania Press, 2003.

McGuire, Paul. *Australia, Her Heritage, Her Future*. New York: Frederick A. Stokes, 1939.

McLaren, Ian. *C.J. Dennis: A Comprehensive Bibliography*. Adelaide: Libraries Board of South Australia, 1979.

Mellick, J.S.D., Patrick Morgan, and Paul Eggert. Introduction to *The Recollections of Geoffry Hamlyn*, by Henry Kingsley, xix-lxx. Academy Editions of Australian Literature. St Lucia: University of Queensland Press, 1996.

Mendelssohn, Joanna. *Letters & Liars: Norman Lindsay and the Lindsay Family*. Sydney: Angus & Robertson, 1996.

Miller, E. Morris. *Australian Literature From Its Beginnings to 1935: A Descriptive and Bibliographical Survey of Books by Australian Authors in Poetry, Drama, Fiction, Criticism and Anthology with Subsidiary Entries to 1938*. 1940. Facsimile ed. Vol. 2. Sydney: Sydney University Press, 1973.

Mills, Carol. *The New South Wales Bookstall Company as a Publisher*. Cook, ACT: Mulini Press, 1991.

Mills, Theodora. "Brentano's". In Dzwonkoski, *American Literary Publishing Houses, 1638-1899*, 66-67.

Moore, Nicole. *The Censor's Library: Uncovering the Lost History of Australia's Banned Books*. St Lucia: University of Queensland Press, 2012.

Works Cited

Morrison, Elizabeth. Introduction to *A Black Sheep: Some Episodes in This Life*, by Ada Cambridge, xi–lxvii. Carlton, Vic.: Australian Scholarly Editions Centre, 2004.

Morrison, Fiona. "The 'American Dilemma': Christina Stead's Cold War Anatomy". In Dixon and Birns, *Reading Across the Pacific*, 241–53.

Morton, Peter. "Australia's England, 1880–1950". In *The Cambridge History of Australian Literature*, edited by Peter Pierce, 255–81. Cambridge: Cambridge University Press, 2009.

———. *Lusting for London: Australian Expatriate Writers at the Hub of Empire, 1870–1950*. New York: Palgrave Macmillan, 2011.

Mott, Frank Luther. *A History of American Magazines, Volume IV: 1885–1905*. Cambridge, MA: Belknap, 1957.

Munro, Craig. *Wild Man of Letters: The Story of P.R. Stephensen*. Carlton, Vic.: Melbourne University Press, 1984.

Mylett, Andrew, ed. *Arnold Bennett, The "Evening Standard" Years: Books and Persons, 1926–1931*. London: Chatto & Windus, 1974.

Newark Free Public Library, *A Thousand of the Best Novels*. Newark, NJ: Newark Free Public Library, 1904.

Niall, Brenda. "Ettie and Nettie: When Nettie Palmer Visited Henry Handel Richardson". *Australian Book Review*, February 2013, 28–35.

———. *Martin Boyd: A Life*. Carlton, Vic.: Melbourne University Press, 1989.

Nile, Richard, and David Walker. "Marketing the Literary Imagination: Production of Australian Literature, 1915–1965". In *The Penguin New Literary History of Australia*, edited by Laurie Hergenhan, 284–302. Ringwood, Vic.: Penguin, 1988.

———. "The "Paternoster Row Machine" and the Australian Book Trade, 1890–1945". In *A History of the Book in Australia, 1891–1945: A National Culture in a Colonised Market*, edited by Martyn Lyons and John Arnold, 3–18. St Lucia: University of Queensland Press, 2001.

Nowell-Smith, Simon. *International Copyright Law and the Publisher in the Reign of Queen Victoria*. Oxford: The Clarendon Press, 1968.

Ohmann, Richard. "Diverging Paths: Books and Magazines in the Transition to Corporate Capitalism". In *A History of the Book in America, Volume 4: Print in Motion: The Expansion of Publishing and Reading in the United States, 1880–1940*, edited by Carl F. Kaestle and Janice A. Radway, 102–15. Chapel Hill: University of North Carolina Press, 2009.

———. *Selling Culture: Magazines, Markets, and Class at the Turn of the Century*. London: Verso, 1996.

Osborne, Roger. "Australian Literature in a World of Books: A Transnational History of Kylie Tennant's *The Battlers*". In *Resourceful Reading: The New Empiricism, eResearch and Australian Literary Culture*, edited by Katherine Bode and Robert Dixon, 105–18. Sydney: Sydney University Press, 2008.

———. "New York City Limits: Australian Novels and American Print Culture". In Dixon and Birns, *Reading Across the Pacific*, 299–308.

———. "Patrick White and the American Middlebrow". In *Telling Stories: Australian Life and Literature, 1935–2012*, edited by Paul Genoni and Tanya Dalziel, 188–94. Clayton, Vic.: Monash University Publishing, 2013.

"Oversea Writers Capture England". *Salt Lake Tribune*, 16 July 1911.

Palmer, Nettie. "Australia Writes of Herself". *Christian Science Monitor*, 28 August 1935, 10.

———. "Australian Books of 1930". *All About Books*, 5 December 1930, 307–10.

———. "Australian Literature". (1927) In *Nettie Palmer*, edited by Vivian Smith, 332–36. St Lucia: University of Queensland Press, 1988.

———. *Modern Australian Literature 1900–1923*. Melbourne: Lothian, 1924.

Panek, LeRoy Lad. *An Introduction to the Detective Story*. Bowling Green, OH: Bowling Green State University Popular Press, 1987.

Park, Ruth. *Fishing in the Styx*. Ringwood, Vic.: Penguin, 1994.

Peel, Doris. "Exploring Our World". *Christian Science Monitor*, 12 April 1951, 11.

Phelan, Nancy. *The Romantic Lives of Louise Mack*. St Lucia: University of Queensland Press, 1991.

Pittard, Christopher. "From Sensation to the Strand". In *A Companion to Crime Fiction*, edited by Charles J. Rzepka and Lee Horsley, 105–16. Chichester, UK: Wiley-Blackwell, 2010.

Probyn, Clive, and Bruce Steele. Introduction to *Maurice Guest*, by Henry Handel Richardson, xxv–lxxi. Academy Editions of Australian Literature. St Lucia: University of Queensland Press, 1998.

———. Introduction to *The Getting of Wisdom*, by Henry Handel Richardson. Academy Editions of Australian Literature. St Lucia: University of Queensland Press, 2001.

———. Introduction to *The Young Cosima*, by Henry Handel Richardson, i–xl. Melbourne: Australian Scholarly Publishing, 2004.

Probyn, Clive T., Bruce Steele, Rachel Solomon, and Patrick O'Neill, eds. *Henry Handel Richardson: The Letters. Volume II: 1917–1933*. Carlton, Vic.: Miegunyah Press, 2000.

Purdie, David. "David Daiches: A Life". *The University of Edinburgh: IASH*. http://www.iash.ed.ac.uk/Daiches.

Putnam, George Haven. "Analysis of the Provisions of the Copyright Law of 1891". 1891. In Dzwonkoski, *American Literary Publishing Houses, 1638–1899*, 570–72.

Radway, Janice A. *A Feeling for Books: The Book-of-the-Month Club, Literary Taste, and Middle-Class Desire*. Chapel Hill: University of North Carolina Press, 1997.

Read, Jean B., ed. *A Christina Stead Reader*. New York: Random House, 1978.

Rees, Arthur J. *The Shrieking Pit*. 1918. Mt Waverley, Vic.: Chimaera Publications, 2010.

Reynolds, Paul. *The Middle Man: The Adventures of a Literary Agent*. New York: Morrow, 1972.

Richardson, Henry Handel. "Some Notes on My Books". *Virginia Quarterly Review* 16, no. 3 (Summer 1940): 334–47. Reprinted *Southerly* 23, no. 1 (March 1963): 8–19.

Rorabacher, Louise. *Marjorie Barnard and M. Barnard Eldershaw*. New York: Twayne, 1973.

Rowley, Hazel. *Christina Stead: A Biography*. Port Melbourne, Vic.: Heinemann, 1993.

Rubin, Joan Shelley. *The Making of Middlebrow Culture*. Chapel Hill: University of North Carolina Press, 1992.

Russell, Carmen R. "Boni and Liveright". In Dzwonkoski, *American Literary Publishing Houses, 1900–1980*, 57–62.

Rutledge, Martha. "Greig, Maysie Coucher (1901–1971)". In *Australian Dictionary of Biography*, Vol. 14, 1996. http://adb.anu.edu.au/biography/greig-maysie-coucher-10364/text18357.

Samuels, Selina, ed. *Australian Literature, 1788–1914*. Dictionary of Literary Biography Vol. 230. Detroit, MI: Gale Research, 2001.

Sayers, Stuart. "Collins, Cuthbert Quinlan Dale (1897–1956)". In *Australian Dictionary of Biography*, Vol. 8, 1981. http://adb.anu.edu.au/biography/collins-cuthbert-quinlan-dale-5735/text9707.

Schaffer, Kay. *In the Wake of First Contact: The Eliza Fraser Stories*. Cambridge: Cambridge University Press, 1998.

Seed, David. "Spy Fiction". In *The Cambridge Companion to Crime Fiction*, edited by Martin Priestman, 115–34. Cambridge: Cambridge University Press, 2003.

Seville, Catherine. *The Internationalisation of Copyright Law: Books, Buccaneers and the Black Flag in the Nineteenth Century*. Cambridge: Cambridge University Press, 2006.

Shep, Sydney. "Books in Global Perspectives". In *The Cambridge Companion to the History of the Book*, edited by Leslie Howsam, 53–67. Cambridge: Cambridge University Press, 2014.

Silverman, Al. *The Time of Their Lives: The Golden Age of Great American Book Publishers, Their Editors, and Authors*. New York: Truman Talley Books, 2008.

Smith, Erin A. "Pulp Sensations". In *The Cambridge Companion to Popular Fiction*, edited by David Glover and Scott McCracken, 141–58. Cambridge: Cambridge University Press, 2012.

Smith, Vivian. *Letters of Vance and Nettie Palmer 1915–1963*. Canberra: National Library of Australia, 1977.

Spoo, Robert. *Without Copyrights: Piracy, Publishing, and the Public Domain*. Oxford: Oxford University Press, 2013.

Works Cited

Stead, Christina. *A Web of Friendship: Selected Letters, 1928–1973*. Edited by R.G. Geering. Sydney: Angus & Robertson, 1992.

———. *Letty Fox: Her Luck*. 1946. Sydney: Angus & Robertson, 1974.

———. *Talking into the Typewriter: Selected Letters, 1973–1983*. Edited by R.G. Geering. Sydney: Angus & Robertson, 1992.

———. "Uses of the Many-Charactered Novel". In *Christina Stead: Selected Fiction and Nonfiction*, edited by R.G. Geering and Anita Kristina Segerberg, 196–99. St Lucia: University of Queensland Press, 1994.

———. "Wandering Workers". *New Masses*, 30 September 1941, 25–26.

Stead, Christina, and William Blake, eds. *Modern Women in Love: Sixty Twentieth-Century Masterpieces of Fiction*. New York: Dryden Press, 1945.

Stuart, Lurline. Introduction to *His Natural Life*, by Marcus Clark, xix–lx. Academy Editions of Australian Literature. St Lucia: University of Queensland Press, 2001.

Sturm, Terry. *An Unsettled Spirit: The Life and Frontier Fiction of Edith Lyttelton (G.B. Lancaster)*. Auckland: Auckland University Press, 2003.

Sussex, Lucy. *Blockbuster! Fergus Hume and The Mystery of a Hansom Cab*. Melbourne: Text Publishing, 2015.

Sutherland, Bruce. "Australian Books and American Readers". *Library Quarterly* 15, no. 3 (1945): 224–30.

———. *Australiana in the Pennsylvania State University Libraries*. Philadelphia: Pennsylvania State University Libraries, 1969.

———. "The Career of Henry Handel Richardson: Analyst of Character, Proponent of Tragedy, Her Novels Live". *New York Herald Tribune*, 21 July 1946.

Sutherland, John. *Bestsellers: A Very Short Introduction*. Oxford: Oxford University Press, 2007.

———. Introduction to *A Bid for Fortune or Dr Nikola's Vendetta*, by Guy Boothby, ix–xx. Oxford: Oxford University Press, 1996.

Tariff Board Australia. *Tariff Board's Report on Publishing Industry*. Canberra: Commonwealth Government Printer, 1946.

"Tariff Board Inquiry into the Publishing Industry in Australia". *Ideas: Booksellers, Stationers, Fancy Goods Journal of Australia and New Zealand* (January 1946): 22–86.

Taylor, Isabelle. "Mystery Midwife: The Crime Editor's Job". In *The Art of the Mystery Story*, edited by Howard Haycraft, 292–97. New York: Carroll & Graf, 1946.

Tebbel, John. *A History of Book Publishing in the United States. Volume II: The Expansion of an Industry, 1865–1919*. New York: Bowker, 1975.

———. *A History of Book Publishing in the United States. Volume III: The Golden Age between Two Wars, 1920–1940*. New York: Bowker, 1978.

———. *Between Covers: The Rise and Transformation of Book Publishing in America*. New York: Oxford University Press, 1987.

Tennant, Kylie. "Letter to Tom Collins: The Case for Critics". *Meanjin* 1, no. 10 (Spring 1942): 13–14.

"The Manufacturing Clause: Copyright Protection to the Foreign Author". *Columbia Law Review* 50, no. 5 (1950): 686–99.

"The Unpossessed: A Novel of the Thirties". *New York Review of Books: NYRB Classics*. https://www.nyrb.com/collections/classics/products/the-unpossessed?variant=1094932697.

Thesing, Jane I. "Simon and Schuster". In Dzwonkoski, *American Literary Publishing Houses, 1900–1980*, 340–44.

Tiffin, Chris. "'By Mrs Campbell Praed': Author and Text". *Bibliographical Society of Australia and New Zealand Bulletin* 22, no. 2 (1998): 67–80.

———. "'Our Literary Connexion': Rosa Praed and George Bentley". *Australian Literary Studies* 27, no. 3–4 (2012): 107–23.

———. *Rosa Praed (Mrs Campbell Praed), 1851–1935: A Bibliography*. St Lucia: Victorian Fiction Research Unit, University of Queensland, 1989.

Tischler, Nancy. "Bruce Sutherland and Images of Australia". *Antipodes* 7, no. 2 (December 1993): 135–38.

Tischler, Nancy, and Nan Albinski. "Bruce Sutherland and Images of Australia". In *Australia in the World: Perceptions and Possibilities*, edited by Don Grant and Graham Seal, 159–66. Perth: Black Swan Press, 1993.

Tolley, Michael J. "Gask, Arthur Cecil (1869–1951)". In *Australian Dictionary of Biography*, Vol. 14, 1996. http://adb.anu.edu.au/biography/gask-arthur-cecil-10283/text18191.

Travis, Trysh. "Print and the Creation of Middlebrow Culture". In *Perspectives on American Book History: Artifacts and Commentary*, edited by Scott E. Casper, Joanne D. Chaison, and Jeffrey D. Groves, 339–66. Amherst: University of Massachusetts Press, 2002.

Trotter, Robin, and Belinda McKay. "'Where the Pelican Builds': Writing in the West". In *By the Book: A Literary History of Queensland*, edited by Patrick Buckridge and Belinda McKay, 185–209. St Lucia: University of Queensland Press, 2007.

Turner, Catherine. *Marketing Modernism Between the Two World Wars*. Amherst: University of Massachusetts Press, 2003.

"Twisted Clay: Frank Walford". *Salt*. https://www.saltpublishing.com/products/twisted-clay-9781844717163.

Tylutki, George E. "D. Appleton and Company". In Dzwonkoski, *American Literary Publishing Houses, 1638–1899*, 23–27.

Untermeyer, Louis. "Introduction". In *Modern Women in Love: Sixty Twentieth-Century Masterpieces of Fiction*, edited by Christina Stead and William Blake, i–xviii. New York: Dryden Press, 1945.

Unwin, Stanley. *The Truth About Publishing*. London: George Allen & Unwin, 1926.

Van Doren, Carl. Foreword to *Capricornia: A Novel*, by Xavier Herbert, i–xiv. New York: Appleton-Century, 1943.

Van Vechten, Carl. *Interpreters and Interpretations*. New York: Knopf, 1919.

———. *Literary Digest International Book Review* 1, no. 6 (May 1923): 7.

Vucetic, Srdjan. *The Anglosphere: A Genealogy of a Racialized Identity in International Relations*. Stanford, CA: Stanford University Press, 2011.

Wadsworth, Sarah. *In the Company of Books: Literature and Its "Classes" in Nineteenth-Century America*. Amherst: University of Massachusetts Press, 2006.

Walker, David. *Anxious Nation: Australia and the Rise of Asia 1850–1939*. St Lucia: University of Queensland Press, 1999.

Waller, Philip. *Writers, Readers, and Reputations: Literary Life in Britain 1870–1918*. Oxford: Oxford University Press, 2008.

Waugh, Arthur. *One Man's Road: Being a Picture of Life in a Passing Generation*. London: Chapman & Hall, 1935.

Webby, Elizabeth. "The Novel Newspaper and Its Role in the Transmission of American Fiction to Australia". In Dixon and Birns, *Reading Across the Pacific*, 167–76.

Wells, William Howell. "Bringing Up a Book". *Atlantic Bookshelf*, December 1929.

West III, James L.W. *American Authors and the Literary Marketplace since 1900*. Philadelphia: University of Pennsylvania Press, 1988.

———. "The Chace Act and Anglo-American Literary Relations". *Studies in Bibliography* 45 (1992): 303–11.

White, Kerry M. "The Real Australian Girl?: Some Post-Federation Writers for Girls". In *The Time to Write: Australian Women Writers, 1890–1930*, edited by Kay Ferres, 73–87. Ringwood, Vic.: Penguin, 1993.

Wilde, W.H., Joy W. Hooton, and Barry Andrews, eds. *The Oxford Companion to Australian Literature*. Melbourne: Oxford University Press, 1985.

Wilkinson, Carol Ann. "Armed Services Editions". In Dzwonkoski, *American Literary Publishing Houses, 1900–1980*, 16.

Williams, Chris. *Christina Stead: A Life of Letters*. Melbourne: McPhee Gribble, 1989.

Works Cited

Williams, Sean. Introduction to *The Shrieking Pit*, by Arthur J. Rees, ii–iv. Mt Waverley, Vic.: Chimaera Publications, 2010.

Williams, Vernon Mrs. "Australian Women Novelists, Part I". *Corroboree* 1, no. 10 (1922): 6–8.

Winship, Michael. "The International Trade in Books". In *A History of the Book in America, Volume 3: The Industrial Book, 1840–1880*, edited by Scott E. Casper, Jeffrey D. Groves, Stephen W. Nissenbaum, and Michael Winship, 148–57. Chapel Hill: University of North Carolina Press, 2007.

———. "The Rise of a National Book Trade System in the United States". In *A History of the Book in America, Volume 4: Print in Motion: The Expansion of Publishing and Reading in the United States, 1880–1940*, edited by Carl F. Kaestle and Janice A. Radway, 56–77. Chapel Hill: University of North Carolina Press, 2009.

———. "The Transatlantic Book Trade and Anglo-American Literary Culture in the Nineteenth Century". In *Reciprocal Influences: Literary Production, Distribution, and Consumption in America*, edited by Steven Fink and Susan S. Williams, 98–122. Columbus, OH: Ohio State University Press, 1999.

Woolf, Virginia. "Mr Bennett and Mrs Brown". In *Virginia Woolf: Selected Essays*, edited by David Bradshaw, 32–36. Oxford: Oxford University Press, 2008.

Woollacott, Angela. "Creating the White Colonial Woman: Mary Gaunt's Imperial Adventuring and Australian Cultural History". In *Cultural History in Australia*, edited by Hsu-Ming Teo and Richard White, 186–200. Sydney: UNSW Press, 2003.

Yarwood, A. T. *From a Chair in the Sun: The Life of Ethel Turner*. Ringwood, Vic.: Viking, 1994.

Yelin, Louise. "Fifty Years of Reading: A Reception Study of *The Man Who Loved Children*". *Contemporary Literature* 31, no. 4 (1990): 472–98.

———. *From the Margins of Empire: Christina Stead, Doris Lessing, Nadine Gordimer*. Ithaca, NY: Cornell University Press, 1998.

Zabel, Morton Dauwen, ed. *Literary Opinion in America: Essays Illustrating the Status, Methods, and Problems of Criticism in the United States since the War*. New York: Harper, 1937.

Zinkhan, Elaine. "Ada Cambridge, 'A.C.' Later Mrs George Frederick Cross 1844–1926." In *The Cambridge Bibliography of English Literature: Volume 4, 1800–1900*, edited by Joanne Shattock, 1480–86. Cambridge: Cambridge University Press, 2000.

———. "Early British Publication of *While the Billy Boils*: The A.P. Watt Connection". *Bibliographical Society of Australia and New Zealand* 21, no. 3 (1997): 165–82

———. "Ada Cambridge: *A Marked Man*, the *Manchester Weekly Times Supplement*, and Late-Nineteenth Century Fiction Publication". *Bibliographical Society of Australia and New Zealand Bulletin* 17, no. 4 (1993): 155–79.

Index

A. Watkins Agency Inc. 320; *see also* Watkins, Armitage
Ackland, Michael 275, 287
A.L. Burt Company 31, 33, 130
Alfred A. Knopf, Inc. 140, 257
Allen & Unwin/George Allen & Unwin/Stanley Unwin 68, 252, 254, 316
American characters (in Australian novels) 164, 166, 186, 186, 213, 291, 294
American setting 124, 272
Ames, Jennifer *see* Greig, Maysie
Anderson, Isaac 171, 175, 188
Anglo-Saxonism 19–21, 49, 99, 126, 201, 202
Angus & Robertson 72, 116, 143, 147, 174, 252, 257, 316–320, 334
Appleton-Century Company *see* D. Appleton & Company: Appleton-Century Company; *see also* Town and Country Library (Appleton)
Arcadia House 178, 184
Archibald, J.F. 69, 71
Art in Advertising Association 61
Arthur Westbrook Company, The 94, 101
Australian Literature Society 191, 227, 232, 239, 253
Australian News and Information Bureau 322, 341
Australian settings 25, 26, 41, 46, 55–60, 79, 103, 119, 170, 171, 177, 188, 192, 232, 258, 261, 277
Authors Syndicate 61
Avalon Books 184
Avon Books 310

Banfield, E.J. 116
Bantam Books 146, 187
Barnard, Marjorie 233, 236, 265; *see also* Eldershaw, M. Barnard

Baume, Eric 315, 330
Becke, Louis 51, 67–81, 115; *see also* Jeffery, Walter James
 By Reef and Palm 69, 74, 76
Bennett, Arnold 238, 246
Bennett, Bruce 184
Bentley, George 37, 53, 61
bestsellers 86–91, 113, 135, 179, 324
 bestseller lists 181, 190
Bjelke-Petersen, Marie 116, 120
Blake, William (Wilhelm Blech) 272, 276, 281, 292–294
Blakiston Company, The 184; *see also* Triangle Books
Bloom, Clive 84
Bobbs-Merrill Company, The 117, 140–142, 167, 238–241, 316, 320, 322, 324
Boldrewood, Rolf 37, 41–48
 Crooked Stick, The 43, 48
 Robbery Under Arms 41, 45
Boni & Liveright 115, 135
Book-of-the-Month Club 118, 181, 204–208, 220, 234, 235, 241, 250, 265, 267, 269, 276, 294, 311, 325, 330
 Book-of-the-Month Club News 181, 204–205, 208, 217, 217, 232, 232, 234, 245, 245, 251–263, 267, 298, 299
Books of the Times *(New York Times)* 232, 237, 285, 290, 306, 310
Boothby, Guy 84, 86, 98–104, 109, 115
 A Bid for Fortune 98, 102
 Race of Life, The 101, 103
Boucher, Anthony 178, 188
Bouregy & Curl 184
Boyd, Martin 231, 238–243

Lucinda Brayford 241–243
Madeleine Heritage, The 118, 231, 238–240
Brandon, John G. 163, 166
Brandt & Brandt Literary Agents 238, 319–321
Brentano's 66, 166, 169, 181
Brett, George P. 44
Bridges, Roy 117–121
British publishing industry 18, 64, 112–114, 251
Brown, Curtis 34, 138, 143, 266
Browne, Thomas Alexander *see* Boldrewood, Rolf
Bulletin 67, 69, 140, 336
  Bulletin prize 191, 221, 246
Bulletin Company 253
Burnshaw Stanley 271, 281, 302, 310
Burton, Naomi 241, 265, 303, 328
bushrangers 16–19, 27, 88, 105, 118
B.W. Huebsch (company) 115, 302; *see also* Huebsch, Ben W.

Cable, Boyd (Ernest Andrew Ewart) 117, 125
Cambridge, Ada 15, 32–37, 47
  A Marked Man 32, 35
  Materfamilias 33, 36
  Three Miss Kings, The 32
Cameron, Angus 296, 301
Canada 33, 127, 147, 222, 244–258, 338
Canby, Henry Seidel 204, 235, 320
Canfield, Dorothy (Dorothy Canfield Fisher) 204, 208, 217, 235, 267
Cape, Jonathan 201, 222, 226; *see also* Jonathan Cape (company)
Carlton House 184
Casanova, Pascale 7, 10, 271
Cassell & Company (UK) 65, 255
Cassell Publishing (USA) 26
Caterson, Simon 91
Cawelti, John G. 177
Century Company 250, 252–253
Cerf, Bennet 147, 215, 292; *see also* Modern Library
Chace Act *see* US International Copyright Act of 1891
Chambers, Ross 5
Charles Scribner's Sons *see* Scribner
Chatto & Windus 61, 66
Clark Russell, William 21
Clarke, Marcus 25–28
  His Natural Life 25
Cleary, Jon 316–318
  You Can't See Around Corners 316–317, 323, 331–333

Clode, Edward J. 109
Close, Robert S. 331
Cobb, Chester
  Mr. Moffat 118
Colebrook, Joan 323, 332
Colles, William Morris 62, 74
Collins, Dale 117, 139–142, 190
Collins, Tom *see* Furphy, Joseph
Collins, William 265; *see also* William Collins, Sons & Company
colonialism 3–7, 17–21, 20, 45, 47, 68, 87, 98–99, 110, 115, 126–129, 269
communism 254, 255, 272, 273, 275, 278, 287, 290, 298
Conan Doyle, Arthur 40, 67, 89, 98
Conrad, Joseph 67–69, 71, 80, 141
Constable & Company 238, 240
contracts 62, 63, 72, 133, 170, 257, 288
convicts (as a theme in fiction) 16–27, 25, 70, 105, 118, 250, 331
copyright 22–35, 28, 43, 52, 61–66, 69–74, 111–124, 132, 197; *see also* US International Copyright Act of 1891
Corelli, Marie 57, 98, 99, 121
Cosmopolitan Book Corporation 143, 143
Cottrell, Dorothy 244–245
  The Singing Gold 244
Cousins, Walter G. 174, 319
Covici, Pascal 292, 322
Coward-McCann Publishing Company 169, 232
Cox, Erle
  Out of the Silence 188
crime novels *see* detective fiction
Curtis Brown (& Massie) 133, 143, 170, 225, 241–243, 324, 327

D. Appleton & Company 30–37, 40, 48, 52–68, 102, 115, 120
  Appleton-Century Company 227, 253–262, 274, 282, 293
Daiches, David 335, 336
Dalby Davison, Frank
  Red Heifer 13, 232
Damrosch, David 9
Daniel, Howard 334
Dark, Eleanor 263–269
  Little Company, The 232, 266, 267, 333
  Timeless Land, The 262, 265–265, 323
Daskein, Mrs (Quin, Tarella) 116, 119
David McKay Company, The 132
Davies, Peter *see* Peter Davies (Ltd)

Index

Davis, Porter & Company 18
Dawe, Carlton 87, 104–107
Dawson, A.J. 26, 116
Deamer, Dulcie 134
Dell Publishing Company 184–187
Dennis, C.J. 116
Dent, J.M *see* J.M. Dent & Company
DeSpain, Jessica 20
Detective Book Club 171, 175, 187
detective fiction 68, 84, 92–101, 109, 161–178, 185–192
Devanny, Jean 135–139
  Butcher Shop, The 137
  Out of Such Fires 137–139
Dial Press, The 166, 183
Dillingham, G.W. *see* G.W. Dillingham Company
dime novels 26, 83
Dixon, Robert 10, 68, 99
Dodd, Mead & Company 24, 70, 115, 116, 165, 173, 315
Donnelly, Lloyd & Company 26, 30
Donohue & Henneberry 26, 94
Doran, George H. 127, 129; *see also* George H. Doran Company
Doubleday 113–129, 134, 169, 174–191, 248, 262, 315, 319
  Crime Club 162, 171–177, 191
Doubleday, Doran & Company *see* Doubleday
Doubleday, Page & Company *see* Doubleday
Dryden Press 282
Duckworth, Gerald *see* Gerald Duckworth & Company
Duffield & Company 196, 197
During, Simon 272
Dutton, E.P. *see* E.P. Dutton & Company
Dwyer, James Francis 121–124, 135
  Bust of Lincoln, The 122
  White Waterfall, The 122

E.P. Dutton & Company 26, 117, 162, 241–243
Eggert, Paul 12
Eldershaw, M. Barnard 245–248
  A House is Built 231, 235, 245
empire *see* colonialism
Endeavour Press 252–257
Ercole, Velia
  Dark Windows 191
expatriation 15, 86–94
Eyre & Spottiswoode 309

F.M. Buckles & Company 103

Faber & Faber 143, 304
Fadiman, Clifton 220, 235, 258, 271, 276, 277, 279, 280, 282, 283, 286, 288, 290, 291, 295, 297, 301, 311
Farjeon, Benjamin 19
Farrar & Rinehart 143–146, 241, 255
Farrar, Straus & Company 187
Farrar, Straus & Giroux 262
Farrar, Straus & Young 187
Fenno, R.F. *see* R.F. Fenno & Company
fiction libraries 52–54
film rights and adaptations 129, 140, 183, 187, 245, 307, 315
Foxton, Rosemary 49
Franklin Square Library (Harper) 30, 37–39
Frederick A. Stokes Company 90, 108
Frederick Warne & Company 96
Furphy, Joseph 21, 334
  Such is Life 333–338

G.W. Dillingham Company 84, 95–96, 109, 115, 134
Galsworthy, John 137, 205, 213, 235, 238, 250
Gask, Arthur 164, 170
Gaunt, Mary 125
genre 83–110, 161–163, 181–183, 234
George Allen & Unwin *see* Allen & Unwin/George Allen & Unwin/Stanley Unwin
George G. Harrap & Company 247, 303
George H. Doran Company 66, 115–118, 127–130, 196, 199
George Routledge & Sons *see* Routledge
Gerald Duckworth & Company 137
Gerstaecker, Friedrich 18
Giles, Paul 8, 19, 291
gold-mining (as a theme in fiction) 18, 105, 118
Gollancz 164, 173, 316, 324
Gould, Nat 87, 89, 90
G.P. Putnam's Sons 23, 26, 52, 64, 66, 79, 115, 117, 167, 168, 180, 266, 324
Grattan, C. Hartley 227, 322–323, 328, 331–338
Greenberg: Publisher 225
Greig, Maysie 179, 183–188
Grimshaw, Beatrice 116, 125–128
Grosset & Dunlap 31, 144, 146, 165
Grove Day, A. 71
Gunn, Mrs Æneas (Jeannie Gunn) 116, 119
  We of the Never-Never 116, 119

Haggard, H. Rider 21, 65
Hammond, Mary 92

Harcourt, Brace & Company 115, 241–247, 294–300
Hardwick, Elizabeth 310
Harper & Brothers 16, 19, 23, 25–31, 37–39, 52–54, 121, 226, 330
Harper & Row 262
Harrap, George *see* George G. Harrap & Company
Hart, Ethel Gertrude 116, 133
Haycraft, Howard 171
Hayward, Leland 147, 174, 226, 257
Hazlitt, Henry 212, 216, 227, 235
Heinemann, William 34, 44; *see also* William Heinemann Limited
Hemingway, Ernest 185, 209, 273, 292, 317, 332
Henkle, Rae D. *see* Rae D. Henkle Company
Henry Holt & Company 124–125, 196
Herbert S. Stone & Company 102
Herbert, Xavier 257–262, 319, 323
  Capricornia 257, 338
Hergenhan, Laurie 1
Heseltine, Harry 236, 238
Hetherington, Carol 175, 176, 203, 222
Hill, Ernestine 232, 319
historical fiction 234–254
Hodder & Stoughton 113, 119–129, 163, 164, 196, 197
Hollywood *see* film rights and adaptations
Holt, Gavin *see* Rodda, Charles
Holt, Rinehart & Winston 302, 310
Hornung, E.W. 84, 87, 88, 115
Houghton Mifflin Company 29, 244–245, 324, 331
Howitt, William 18
Huebsch, Ben W. 271, 272, 302–311; *see also* B.W. Huebsch (company)
Hume, Fergus 83–98, 109
  Mystery of a Hansom Cab, The 87, 93–97
Hutchinson & Company 33, 107, 120, 174
Hutner, Gordon 237

Idriess, Ion 320
imperialism *see* colonialism
Innes, Michael 172
International Copyright Act of 1891 *see* US International Copyright Act of 1891
Ivers, M.J. *see* M.J. Ivers & Company

J.B. Lippincott & Company *see* Lippincott, J.B
J.M. Dent & Company 241, 243
J.S. Ogilvie Publishing Company 94
Jarrell, Randall 290, 310

Jeffery, Walter James 69, 72, 77; *see also* Becke, Louis
John Farquarson agency 187
John Lane Company, The 64, 107, 116, 164–165
Johnston, George 315, 342
Jonathan Cape (company) 191, 201, 221–226, 233, 304, 311, 334, 337
Jones, Doris Egerton 116, 133
Joyce, James 208, 219, 277, 280, 288, 291, 302, 302, 304, 305

Kazin, Alfred 263, 286, 307
Kendall, Claude 190
Kenton, Edna 198
Kingsley, Henry 15, 22–25
  Hillyars and the Burtons, The 23
  Ravenshoe 23
  Recollections of Geoffry Hamlyn, The 15, 22, 23
Kipling, Rudyard 67, 67, 75, 80, 98, 128, 250
Klopfer, Donald 186, 215
Knopf, Alfred A. *see* Alfred A. Knopf, Inc.
Kronenberger, Louis 216, 219, 220, 227, 235

Laird & Lee, Inc. 18, 26
Lamond, Henry 313, 319
Lancaster, G.B. 125–130, 249–254
  Pageant 249–254
Lane, John *see* John Lane Company, The
Lawrence, D.H. 118, 137, 173, 237, 295, 302
Lawson, Henry 21
Lewis, Sinclair 209, 215, 220, 294
Lidoff, Joan 311
light fiction 81, 85, 161, 163, 178, 181–186, 191, 192, 263
Lindsay, Norman 142–148
  Cautious Amorist, The 143–147
  Cousin from Fiji 147
  Every Mother's Son 143, 143–146
Lindsey, Travis 174
Lippincott, J.B 26, 54, 68–77, 81, 325
literary agents 6–8, 19, 34–35, 44, 47, 61–62, 64, 72, 86, 108, 114, 129, 133, 148, 185–188, 226–228, 261, 303, 320–323, 330
Literary Guild 232, 241, 250, 252
Little, Brown & Company 140, 168, 296, 301, 316
Locke, Sumner 124–125
Long, John (publisher) 89, 96
Longmans, Green & Company 24, 69
Lovell, Coryell & Company 33, 39
Lovell, Frank F. 30, 38, 53

Index

Lovell, John W. (& Company) 19, 24, 29, 32, 38, 52, 94
Low, Gardner *see* Rodda, Charles
Lowe, Eric 232, 254
Lyttleton, Edith *see* Lancaster, G.B.

M.J. Ivers & Company 32, 94
Macaulay Publishing Company, The 135–139
Mack, Louise 115, 133, 134
Macmillan & Company (London) 22, 23, 41–44, 243, 329
Macmillan Company, The (New York) 43–45, 102, 116, 263–267, 323, 325, 327
Macmillan, Frederick 23, 43
magazines 8, 35, 47, 70, 85–91, 97, 107, 108, 113, 121–132, 148, 171, 320–322
Mann, Leonard
   A Murder in Sydney 191
Manning, Frederic 117, 125
   Her Privates We 117
Marr, David 272, 302
Martin, A.E. 171
Martin, Catherine 37, 38, 48
   The Silent Sea 37
Matthews, Brander 30
Maule, Harry E. 184, 185
MCA Management Ltd 261
McCann & Geoghegan *see* Coward-McCann Publishing Company
McCarthy, Justin *see* Praed, Rosa (Mrs Campbell Praed): in collaboration with Justin McCarthy
McCarthy, Mary 290
McGraw-Hill 265
McGuire, Paul 169
McIntosh, Mavis 261, 293, 330
McIntosh & Otis 293, 320
McKay, David *see* David McKay Company, The
McLaren, Jack 117
Melville, Herman 25, 79, 291, 336, 337
Meredith, Louisa Anne 18
middlebrow fiction 204–205, 238, 264, 269, 284, 288, 306–307
Mills & Boon 85, 118, 163, 181
Mills, Martin *see* Boyd, Martin
Minton, Balch & Company 118, 180–181
Mitchell, Margaret
   Gone With the Wind 181, 237, 291–295
Mitchell, Mary
   A Warning to Wantons: A Fantastic Romance 189
modern girl stories 130–135
Modern Library 215, 292

modern sex novel 135
modernism 5, 204, 229, 232, 236, 238, 263, 272–275, 278, 282–284, 302, 305, 310
modernity 3–6, 25, 59, 80–81, 85, 87, 92, 103, 126, 133–137, 141, 143, 201, 201, 211, 217, 219, 228, 238
Morrow, William *see* William Morrow Company
Munro, George 19, 24, 30–32, 38, 52, 94
   Seaside Library *see* fiction libraries
Munro, Norman L. 30
Murray, John 243
Murray, Max 183–188
mystery fiction *see* detective fiction
Mystery Guild 175

Neville, Margot (Margot and Ann Neville Goyder) 177
New American Library 175
New Amsterdam Book Company 63, 69, 73, 130
new imperial history 3, 87, 99, 126
New Masses 281, 286, 292, 298, 327
New York literary scene 271–310, 314
New York Readers Club 220, 276
New Zealand 19, 91, 127, 139, 253
Nile, Richard 3
Nisbet, Hume 26, 48, 54
Nobel Prize for Literature 205, 235, 311–312
Norton, William (W.W.) 203, 207, 210, 213, 218, 222–226, 228, 241, 271; *see* W.W. Norton & Company
Noëlle Brennan literary agency 321–321, 341
NSW Bookstall Company 105, 124, 140

Oppenheim, E. Phillips 167
O'Reilly, John Boyle 18, 53
   Moondyne: A Story from the Underworld 18
orientalist tales 105

Palmer, Nettie 201, 203, 221, 227, 233, 244
paperback publishing 27, 184–185
Park, Ruth 331
   The Harp in the South 331
Pender, Anne 184
Penguin Books 175, 312
penny and sixpenny paperbacks *see* dime novels
Penton, Brian 234, 255
   Landtakers 234, 257
Perkins, Maxwell 332
Peter Davies (Ltd) 117, 274, 282, 300
Pinker, J.B. 74, 108, 129, 238–241
pioneering 80, 201, 216, 220

pirate publishing 19
Pittard, Christopher 93
Pocket Books 184, 184
Praed, Rosa (Mrs Campbell Praed) 15, 27, 51–68, 81
   in collaboration with Justin McCarthy 52, 66
   Insane Root, The 59, 63
   Mrs Tregaskiss 54–57
   Nyria 63–65
   Outlaw and Lawmaker 53, 55
Pratt, Ambrose 104, 107–109
   Franks, Duellist 107
Prichard, Katharine Susannah 111, 195–196, 199–203, 221–227
   Coonardoo 195, 221–224, 231
   Fay's Circus 224–225, 227
   Pioneers, The 196, 199–202
   Roaring Nineties 226–227
   Working Bullocks 201
Publicist Publishing Company 257
Putnam, George Haven 113
Putnam, James 266

R.F. Fenno & Company 63, 105, 108
Radway, Janice 204, 205
Rae D. Henkle Company 188
Rand McNally & Company 37, 53, 94
Random House 147–148, 292, 310
realism 68, 76, 81, 106, 200, 201, 275, 284, 294, 305, 331
Reed, Eliot *see* Rodda, Charles
Rees, Arthur J. 163–166
reprint publishing 19, 22, 28–33, 95, 175, 183
Reynal & Company 243
Reynal & Hitchcock 253–255
Reynolds, Paul R. Jnr 314–318
Reynolds, Paul Revere 66, 70, 129, 261
Richard Bentley & Sons 25, 37, 52
Richardson, Henry Handel 111, 118, 195–221, 227–229, 231–235, 245, 249, 279
   Fortunes of Richard Mahony, The (trilogy) 5, 195, 212
   Maurice Guest 196–199, 203, 213, 218
   Ultima Thule 195, 202–221
Roberts Brothers 105
Roberts, Morley 27
Robertson (née Richardson), Ethel Florence *see* Richardson, Henry Handel
Rodda, Charles 163, 167–168
Rogers, Lilian 235, 246

romance 19–27, 36–49, 55–60, 67–71, 76–81, 84, 97–108, 162
   antipodean romance 8, 48, 55, 89, 102
   geographical romance 125
   women's romance fiction 161–163, 179–186, 189–191
Rosman, Alice Grant 162, 179–183
Ross, Mary 216, 218, 227, 235
Routledge 89–90, 304
Rowcroft, Charles 16–17
   Bush Ranger of Van Diemen's Land, The 16
Rowley, Hazel 280, 282, 287, 288, 291, 295, 297
royalties *see* contracts
Rubin, Joan Shelley 204

sagas *see* historical fiction
Sanders, Sydney A. 187, 190
Scherman, Harry 204
Schuster, Max 271, 276, 282, 293; *see also* Simon & Schuster
science fiction 188
Scribner 24–24, 88, 115, 226, 302, 317, 320, 332
Seaside Library *see* Munro, George: Seaside Library
sensation fiction 84, 91–94, 107–109
serialisation 27, 42, 71, 122, 132, 135, 170
sex (theme in fiction) 135–142, 145
Shaw, Charles 314
   Heaven Knows, Mr. Allison 314
Shute, Nevil 315, 342
Silverman, Al 330, 342
Simon & Schuster 162, 171–172, 276, 282–288, 292
Simpson, Helen 248–249
Skinner, M.L. (Mollie)
Small, Maynard & Company 66, 183
socialism 278, 287, 336
Society of Authors 62, 86, 253
Soskin, William 145, 210, 235
South Sea tales 67–70, 80, 127
Southron, Jane Spence 235, 249, 278, 304, 327
Spoo, Robert 114
spy fiction 100, 107
Stead, Christina 271–312
   For Love Alone 292–296, 298, 310
   House of All Nations 282–285, 298
   Letty Fox 296–300
   Man Who Loved Children, The 287–293, 299, 310
   relationship with William Blake 272
   Salzburg Tales, The 274–277, 282
   Seven Poor Men of Sydney 274–279

Index

Stern, James 243, 271, 307
Stevenson, Robert Louis 59, 68, 74, 80, 250
Stewart, J.I.M. *see* Innes, Michael
Stokes, Frederick A. *see* Frederick A. Stokes Company
Stone, Herbert S. *see* Herbert S. Stone & Company
Strauss, Helen 294, 300
Street & Smith 86, 94
Stuart, Lurline 25
Sturm, Terry 128, 252
Sutherland, Bruce 228, 243, 338
Sutherland, John 99
Sydney A. Sanders agency *see* Sanders, Sydney A.
Sydney Morning Herald Literary Competition 317, 331

T. Fisher Unwin 63–65, 71–74; *see also* Allen & Unwin/George Allen & Unwin/Stanley Unwin
T. Werner Laurie 74, 190
Tasma, Jessie Couvreur 38–40, 47
Taylor, Isabelle 175
Tebbel, John 21, 84
Tennant 315, 323–329, 332
  Battlers, The 323–328
thriller 100–101, 107, 162–171
Ticknor & Fields 18, 22–25
Tiffin, Chris 62
Town and Country Library (Appleton) 32, 39, 48, 54, 61, 98, 102; *see also* fiction libraries
trade courtesy 16, 22
Traditional Markets Agreement 251
traditional markets 6, 143, 251
transatlantic book trade 2, 5, 7, 19–23, 21, 27, 41–47, 54, 86, 107, 112–113, 212, 343
transnationality 2–3, 9–12, 16, 83, 98, 149, 162, 192, 273, 343
traveller's tales 16–19
Triangle Books 184; *see also* Blakiston Company, The
Trilling, Diane 295, 306
Trist, Margaret
Trollope, Anthony 19–20
Turner, Ethel 130–133
Turner, Lilian 115, 133
Twain, Mark 20, 25, 69, 336

Unicorn Mystery Book Club 175, 186, 187
United States Book Company 39, 53, 59
University of Chicago Press 320, 333, 337
Unwin, Stanley 113, 252; *see also* T. Fisher Unwin
Unwin, Thomas Fisher *see* T. Fisher Unwin

Upfield, Arthur 164, 173–178
US Council on Books in Wartime (Armed Services Editions) 262, 319
US International Copyright Act of 1891 12, 20, 43, 44, 61, 86, 111, 114
US publishing industry 18, 23, 60, 62, 71–72, 101, 195, 313

Van Doren, Carl 220, 232, 234, 241, 250, 257
Van Vechten, Carl 198, 199, 219, 220
Viking Press 118, 201–203, 221, 232, 234, 271, 272, 292–294, 302–307, 312

W.W. Norton & Company 118, 202, 212–215, 221, 241, 316
Wadsworth, Sarah 31
Walford, Frank 190
  Twisted Clay 190
Walker, David 3
Waller, Philip 90
Ward, Lock & Bowden/Ward, Lock & Company 24, 94–101, 104, 107, 130–133
Warne, Frederick *see* Frederick Warne & Company
Warren, Mary Douglas *see* Greig, Maysie
Watch and Ward Society 138
Watkins, Armitage 228, 320–321, 330
Watt, A.P. 34–35, 44, 72–74, 119, 130, 167
West III, James L.W. 65, 112, 115
West, Morris
  Devil's Advocate, The
Westbrook, Arthur *see* Arthur Westbrook Company, The
White, F.V. 54, 95
White, Kerry 133
White, Patrick 271–273, 302–312
  Aunt's Story, The 305–308
  Eye of the Storm, The 311
  Happy Valley 232, 237, 272, 290, 303–304
  Tree of Man 307–308
Whittlesey House 265; *see also* McGraw-Hill
William Collins, Sons & Company 263, 265
William Heinemann Limited 113, 163, 169, 196–197, 202, 215; *see also* Heinemann, William
William Morrow Company 169, 262, 315–319
Winship, Michael 16
Woolf, Virginia 137, 181, 238, 266, 277, 288, 291, 294, 304, 305, 307
World War I 84, 191

World War II 313, 320; *see also* World War II: war in the Pacific
war in the Pacific 260, 270, 314, 338

Yelin, Louise 290

Zabel, Morton 218

www.ingramcontent.com/pod-product-compliance
Lightning Source LLC
Chambersburg PA
CBHW081823230426
43668CB00017B/2360